ATLANTIC OCEAN

Loch
Olabhat

Ceíde Fields

Hadrian's
Wall

Leman and Ower

Kunda

Rothwell

Uppsala

Tollund

York
Star Carr
Flag Fen

Aamosen
Svaerdborg

Gallehus

Wroxeter
Avebury Easton Down
Butser Hill
Somerset Levels
Brixham Cave
Kent's Cavern
Danebury
Maiden Castle
Cranborne Chase

Thorpe
Hoxne
Haddenham
Sutton Hoo
Clacton
Nonsuch
Swancombe
Winchester
Stonehenge
Abbeville

Meer II

Neanderthal

Koln Lindenthal

Carnac

Somme R.

St. Acheul

Speyer

Dolní Věstonice

Mezhirich

Grand Pressigny

Solutré

La Téne

Wasserburg

Hallstatt

La Quina
Lascaux
Cassegros
Altamira

Combe Grenal

Abri Pataud
Dordogne R.

Mitterburg
Similaun

Opovo

BLACK
SEA

Douro R.

Hvar

Torralba/Ambrona

Grotte De
Chauvet

Terra Amata

Herculaneum
Pompeii

Samothrace

THESSALY

Troy

MITANNI

MEDITERRANEAN SEA

Sounion
Laurion

Aphrodisias

Hacilar

Corinth
Olympia

Athens

Siphnos
Phylakopi

Mycenae

Santorini

Epidauros

Knossos

Ice limit at height of Wüm Glaciation

Archaeological Sites in Europe

W9-DID-422

In the Beginning

Artist's reconstruction of *Australopithecus afarensis* walking on soft volcanic ash at Laetoli, Tanzania, c. 3.6 million years ago.

ELEVENTH EDITION

In the Beginning

An Introduction to Archaeology

Brian M. Fagan

University of California, Santa Barbara

Christopher R. DeCorse

Syracuse University

PEARSON

Prentice
Hall

Upper Saddle River, New Jersey 07458

Library of Congress Cataloging-in-Publication Data

FAGAN, BRIAN M.
    In the beginning : an introduction to archaeology / Brian M. Fagan, Christopher R.
DeCorse.—11th ed.
        p. cm.
    Includes bibliographical references and index.
    ISBN 0–13–032906–1
    1. Archaeology—Methodology.   2. Archaeology—History.   I. DeCorse, Christopher R.   II.
Title.

CC75.F34 2005
930.1—dc22   2003068921

Editorial Director: Leah Jewell
AVP/Publisher: Nancy Roberts
Editorial Assistant: Lee Peterson
Senior Marketing Manager: Marissa Feliberty
Production Editor: Joan Stone
Manufacturing Buyer: Ben Smith
Cover Art Director: Jayne Conte
Cover Design: Bruce Kenselaar
Director, Image Resource Center: Melinda Reo
Manager, Rights and Permissions: Zina Arabia
Manager, Visual Research: Beth Brenzel
Manager, Cover Visual Research & Permissions: Karen Sanatar
Image Permission Coordinator: Debbie Hewitson
Photo Researcher: Francelle Carapetyan
Composition: Interactive Composition Corporation
Printer/Binder: Courier Companies, Inc.
Cover Printer: Phoenix Color Corp.
Typeface: 11/12 Adobe Garamond
Cover Photo: Pete Turner/Getty Images Inc.—Image Bank. Tunnel view of the Great Wall of China.

Acknowledgments for photographs from other sources and reproduced,
with permission, in this textbook appear on page 560.

Pearson Education LTD.
Pearson Education Singapore, Pte. Ltd
Pearson Education, Canada, Ltd
Pearson Education-Japan
Pearson Education Australia PTY, Limited

Pearson Education North Asia Ltd
Pearson Educación de Mexico, S.A. de C.V.
Pearson Education Malaysia, Pte. Ltd
Pearson Education, Upper Saddle River, NJ

10 9 8 7 6 5 4 3 2 1
ISBN 0-13-032906-1

*The whole earth is the sepulcher of famous men; and their story is not graven
only on stone over their native earth, but lives far away, without visible
symbol, woven into the stuff of other men's lives. For you now
it remains to rival what they have done.*

—Thucydides, *The Funeral Oration of Pericles*

BRIEF CONTENTS

CONTENTS

PART II

A Short History of Archaeology:
Sixth Century B.C. through A.D. 2000
31

Chapter 2
The Beginnings of Scientific Archaeology:
Sixth Century B.C. to the 1950s   32

Chapter 3
Science, Ecology, and the Many-Voiced Past:
From the 1950s to Today   55

PART III

Basic Processes and Principles
76

Chapter 4
Matrix and Preservation   77

Chapter 5
Doing Archaeological Research   98

Chapter 6
Culture, Data, and Context   112

Chapter 7
How Old Is It?   133

PART IV

Recovering Archaeological Data
166

Chapter 8
Finding and Assessing Archaeological Sites   167

Chapter 9
Archaeological Excavation   201

PART V

Analyzing the Past: Artifacts and Technology 236

**Chapter 10
Classifying Artifacts   237**

PART VI

Environments, Lifeways, People, and the Intangible
289

Chapter 13
Subsistence and Diet   319

PART VII

Cultural Resource Management
479

Chapter 18
Managing the Past and Public Archaeology   480

PART VIII

Careers and Resources
509

Many people think of archaeology as a romantic subject, a glamorous pastime spent with pyramids, mysterious inscriptions, and buried treasure. This stereotype originated in the nineteenth century, when both archaeologists and the ancient civilizations they uncovered became legendary. Today, more than 150 years of archaeological investigations have turned archaeology into a meticulous discipline. But the excitement is still there, in the many diverse and highly detailed reconstructions of life in the past that come from scientific inquiry. Archaeologists have reconstructed the lifeways of the earliest humans, documented some of the earliest art in the world, outlined the processes of plant domestication, and even examined the garbage produced in modern urban America. In this book we describe how archaeologists make and study such finds to illuminate the human past.

In the Beginning introduces the history and methods of archaeology and its significance today. We discuss archaeological concepts and procedures and show how archaeologists describe cultures as part of time and space to interpret the prehistoric past. One objective in this book is to provide a comprehensive summary of the field for people who have little or no experience with it. A second objective is to alert you to a major crisis facing archaeology in our time. All archaeological sites are finite records of the past; once destroyed, they can never be replaced. But treasure hunting by individuals and a huge increase in the construction of buildings, roads, dams, and the like have destroyed thousands of archaeological sites all over the world. Without access to intact sites, we cannot possibly complete a picture of the human past. The crisis of site destruction is, in its way, as important as the ecological crisis we face. *In the Beginning* is meant to alert you to the need for living responsibly with your cultural heritage.

Archaeology has become a sophisticated "high-tech" discipline in recent years, and there are many more professional archaeologists working in the field than even a decade ago. The result has been not only a knowledge explosion but also the development of ever more sophisticated and fine-grained methods for studying the past. We cannot examine even a small fraction of these elaborate, often expensive, and invariably fascinating methods within the compass of this book. Nor do we delve deeply into the powerful statistical methods and computerized approaches that are commonplace in archaeology today. This book focuses on the basic principles of our discipline, on the fundamental tenets that are equally important whether one uses a trowel, a laser recording system, or a complicated computer graphics program in pursuit of the past.

The chapters close with summaries highlighting the major themes and concepts. Whenever practicable, drawings and photographs illustrate the subjects the text describes. We use specialized terminology as little as possible and define every new term when it first appears. In addition, a Glossary at the back of the book provides definitions of the words used in the book as well as of some words you may encounter in other reading.

We hope that you will pursue the topics that interest you in more advanced and specialized archaeology courses or in the many excellent books and articles listed in the Bibliography at the back of the book and in the Guide to Further Reading at the end of each chapter.

We have written this book from predominantly English-language sources for two main reasons. First, our reading in the vast archaeological literature has been necessarily selective and mostly in English. Second, for most of you, English is your native tongue. Although linguistic abilities and time have thus biased this volume toward the achievements and writings of English-speaking archaeologists, archaeology is indeed a global activity, conducted with great energy and intelligence by every nation and in every corner of the world.

May you enjoy the world of the past as much as we have! Good luck with your adventures in archaeology—and please be a careful steward of the past for future generations.

Brian Fagan   *Christopher DeCorse*

A Note on Dates

The following conventions are used:

- Dates before 10,000 years ago are expressed in years before present (B.P.). By scientific convention, "present" starts at A.D. 1950.
- Dates after 10,000 years ago are expressed in years before Christ (B.C.) or anno domini (A.D.).
- Another common convention, B.C.E./C.E. (Before Common Era/Common Era), is not employed in this book.

All radiocarbon dates and potassium-argon dates are statistical estimates and should be understood to have a plus-or-minus factor that is omitted from this book in the interests of brevity. Where possible, radiocarbon dates have been calibrated with tree-ring chronologies to add a substantial element of accuracy (see Chapter 7). For calibration of radiocarbon dates, see Stuiver and others (1998).

When I (BMF)[1] started writing the first edition of *In the Beginning*, back in 1968, I had no idea that it would still be in print more than thirty years later and that I would one day be revising it for the tenth time! *In the Beginning* has become an integral part of my life, and I have been humbled to hear it referred to as a "venerable classic." "Classic" is flattering; perhaps "venerable" is a reflection of my advancing years. . . .

This after 1998

For this eleventh, and for future, editions, I am delighted to welcome a valued colleague and friend as co-author, Christopher DeCorse of Syracuse University. Chris is a historical archaeologist with a broad practical experience in both teaching and field research. Like myself, he is an Africanist, which means that we share many common perspectives on archaeology. He has also worked in cultural resource management in North America, adding another dimension to his extensive background.

After three decades, any book like this is the work of far more than one person. Many instructors and students have written to me (BMF), or button-holed me at a meeting, to make suggestions or to offer criticism or even reprints of their own work. We are deeply grateful for their constant input and for both their critical and kind words. *In the Beginning* is truly a product of both authors and readers.

The eleventh edition of *In the Beginning* appears at a time when archaeology is in the midst of a major revolution, in large part driven by circumstances beyond archaeologists' control. Until very recently, archaeology was a purely academic discipline, little concerned with such issues as the destruction of sites, cultural heritage and conservation of the past, or global tourism. Archaeologists thought of themselves as objective scientists, studying the past for the benefit of all humankind. Now archaeology is rapidly becoming a profession, with a large population of archaeologists in government positions and working for private companies. The academic sector shrinks, while the professional one grows.

As a group, we archaeologists are increasingly concerned with the management and conservation of the rapidly vanishing archaeological record. Our daily activities encompass strategies to combat looting, measures to mitigate the destruction and potential ravages caused by thousands of tourists' feet at places like Egypt's pyramids, and, above all, finding ways to preserve our cultural heritage and to ensure the long-term survival of the archaeological record. This dramatic shift from the academic to the applied is not a mirage the size of a person's hand dimly visible on a theoretical horizon. It is a vast, numbing, and fast-moving reality that offers us extraordinary challenges in training the professional archaeologists of the twenty-first century.

The debate about the training of future professionals has only just begun, but it is a debate that concerns, for the most part, advanced undergraduate and graduate

---

[1] When there are first-person references in the text, we have inserted our initials after them (i.e., BMF or CRDC).

training. There is still a need for a sound basic grounding in archaeological methods and theoretical approaches, for courses and texts that introduce a beginning student to the fascination and intricacy of modern-day archaeology. This book is a predominantly academic introduction to archaeology, with a deliberately international flavor. We discuss stewardship, archaeological ethics, cultural resource management, and the vanishing archaeological record—all important aspects of archaeology. But our main focus is on the basic intellectual and practical principles that underpin archaeology everywhere, whether a painstaking excavation of an early hominid camp in Africa, or a once-thriving Mesopotamian city, or a Native American town, or a weeklong contract to investigate an urban lot in the heart of New York City.

Basic principles change little over the years: the importance of context, of time and space, of meticulous excavation methods and precise recording, the basics of artifact classification, zooarchaeology, and so on. But important trends have surfaced in recent years, some a direct result of the dominant role of cultural resource management in today's archaeology. They include:

- An increasing emphasis on field survey and high-technology methods for locating, surveying, and mapping sites.
- A major stress on "nonintrusive" archaeology, nondestructive ways of recording sites and their features.
- A remarkable proliferation of highly specialized, often high-technology methods, some of which have become subspecialties in their own right. Archaeology today is far more specialized than even a generation ago.
- A realization that there are many ways of thinking about the past, of which the archaeological perspective is one.
- A long, and often passionate, debate not only about the morality of archaeology and about the ways in which we practice North American archaeology but also about the relationships between archaeologists everywhere and indigenous peoples. This debate includes the important issue of burials and skeletal material,
- A new generation of archaeological theory that emphasizes the archaeology of people rather than more general processes of culture change. This new emphasis is reflected in research into gender, ethnicity, and inequality, and also in the slow acceptance of "cognitive archaeology," sometimes called the "archaeology of mind," as a major theoretical trend.

We are at a fascinating point in archaeological method and theory, with archaeologists divided into a minority engaged in intensive theoretical debate and the remainder continuing to carry out empirical research, albeit in more sophisticated ways that have been commonplace for generations. Archaeologists are engaged in intense debates about the future of the discipline and about its role in the contemporary world, debates stimulated in part by the divisive and fractious times in which we live. What is happening in archaeology has already happened in many other sciences and is still taking hold in much of biology: the development of distinctive and scientific methods and theories that not only enrich our understanding of the past but also add to our understanding of ourselves. Inevitably, these developments have led to ever more intense specialization in ever more high-tech methods and increasingly esoteric research. This high degree of specialized research and the overspecialized archaeologists who accompany it are not necessarily a positive development.

Please encourage your students to think of archaeology as one enterprise, not as dozens of unrelated activities. Above all, encourage them to look at the broad picture as well as at the local one, for the greatest advances in archaeology, as in other sciences, have come not from slavish specialization but from inspirations born of broad vision. This is why this book unashamedly draws on examples from many parts of the world. It is myopic to teach archaeology from a narrow, say, British or North American, perspective, when our discipline encompasses so much more fascinating research into the brilliant diversity of our forebears.

Changes in the Eleventh Edition

This eleventh edition of *In the Beginning* reflects not only our biases but also the teaching experience of hundreds of instructors over the years whose comments have been invaluable. Almost all of them have urged that we retain the basic format and global coverage of earlier editions. Despite attempts to telescope some chapters into others, the existing organization, honed as it has been over eleven editions, seems to work well for most users. We have, however, moved more archaeological theory to the front of the book, on the argument that this important topic should be discussed early on as background to later, more specific material. We still retain coverage of the nature of the archaeological record and other basic principles close to the front of the book so that they are covered before the chapters on recovering archaeological data.

A successful innovation in the tenth edition, unique in any method and theory text, is retained for this one: an introduction entitled What Happened in Prehistory?, designed to give the beginning reader a brief summary of world prehistory as a reference point for the examples that appear in the main text. There are many substantial changes in this edition. Ethics and stewardship, as well as cultural resource management, receive more extended coverage in Chapter 1. We have moved the discussion of archaeological theory into Chapter 3, which has been extensively rewritten. Relative and chronometric chronology form a single Chapter 7. Chapter 8, Finding and Assessing Archaeological Sites, has been revised to reflect the burgeoning concern with archaeological survey and ancient landscapes, with new examples. We have retained a popular new chapter from the previous edition, Chapter 12, Ancient Environments, which reflects the remarkable advances in paleoclimatology in recent years, especially in the study of short-term climatic shifts, such as the well-known El Niños. Chapter 15, Settlement Archaeology, has been rewritten in response to an increasing interest in ancient landscapes. Chapter 16, Interactions: People of the Past, and Chapter 17, Archaeology of the Intangible, cover such current topics as gender, ethnicity, and the study of ancient religion. Part VII is devoted to cultural resource management as a stand-alone topic, a feature of this book since 1981. This sole chapter, 18, which has been substantially updated and expanded, deals with some of the most pressing issues that face modern archaeologists. Part VIII, Careers and Resources, consists of Chapter 19, Becoming an Archaeologist, another innovation in the tenth edition, which proved extremely popular with readers. This chapter contains some frank and hard-hitting advice about archaeology as a career. The text is followed by a Glossary and a Bibliography.

It would have been easy to make this book a mere catalog of method and theory and to stretch it to a thousand pages, but, as the great archaeologist Sir Mortimer Wheeler once said (1954), "Dry archaeology is the driest dust that blows." We have done everything we can to make this book an interesting read, keeping jargon to a minimum. In the interest of brevity, we have had to cover some topics, such as population carrying capacity and sampling, in almost indecent haste. We have also omitted discussion of the more exotic experimental methodologies that now crowd the pages of archaeological literature and more advanced textbooks. Although valuable, many of them are not strictly relevant to the basic goals of archaeology outlined in these pages. We leave it to you to fill in details on topics that you think are inadequately covered here.

We urge you, however, to give full coverage to the growing crisis of the archaeological record. This subject demands full factual and moral coverage in all introductory courses, where many students arrive with the notion of finding buried treasure or collecting beautiful artifacts. Every course in archaeology must place responsibility for preserving the past emphatically in public, as well as professional, hands. It is for this reason that this book ends with a stark statement of basic archaeological ethics for everyone.

In the Beginning surveys the broad spectrum of archaeological method and theory. With the very first edition, it was decided not to espouse any one theory of archaeology and to provide global coverage of archaeology, to give each instructor a basis for amplifying the text with his or her own viewpoint and theoretical persuasion. This decision has been endorsed by many users and by my new co-author. A reviewer said some editions ago: "This is the fun with this book." Long may it continue to be so.

A Note on the World Wide Web

The World Wide Web is becoming an important medium of communication for archaeologists, as it is for everyone else. This is a confusing universe for those unfamiliar with the Web, especially since so much is changing all the time. However, the major Websites are here to stay and offer links to other important locations. Everything operates with Universal Resources Locators (URLs), some of which we list here.

The Virtual Library for archaeology worldwide is ArchNet: **http://www.archnet @asu.edu.** This is both geographically and subject-matter based, covering everything from the archaeology of Australia to method and theory and site tours. There are also listings of academic departments, museums, and other archaeological organizations, even of journals. ArchNet is an extraordinary resource; it does not claim to be comprehensive, but it covers a huge range of topics. The European equivalent is ARGE, the Archaeological Resource Guide for Europe: **http://www.bham.ac.uk/ARGE.** It also lists areas and subjects, and it is multilingual. Both ArchNet and ARGE have links to virtually any kind of archaeology you are looking for. Many departments of anthropology and archaeology and dozens of excavations and sites have Websites that you can access through ArchNet. For example, for information on archaeology in southwestern Asia and the eastern Mediterranean, go to **http://www.argonet.co.uk/ education/diggings.**

Internet Archaeology is an international Web-based periodical for professionals, complete with a discussion list: **http://intarch.ac.uk/.** And you can contact the authors at **brian@brianfagan.com** or **CRDecors@maxwell.syr.edu** if you have a question.

Ancillary Materials

The ancillary materials that accompany this textbook have been carefully created to enhance the topics being discussed.

Instructor's Manual with Tests.   For each chapter in the text, this manual provides a detailed outline, list of objectives, discussion questions, classroom activities, and additional resources. The test bank includes multiple choice, true-false, and essay questions for each chapter.

Companion Website.   In tandem with the text, students and professors can now take full advantage of the World Wide Web to enrich their study of archaeology. The Fagan Website correlates the text with related material available on the Internet. Features of the Website include chapter objectives and study questions, as well as links to interesting material and information from other sites on the Web that can reinforce and enhance the content of each chapter. Address: **http://www.prenhall.com/fagan.**

Research Navigator™.   Research Navigator™ is the easiest way for students to start a research assignment or research paper. Complete with extensive help on the research process and three exclusive databases of credible and reliable source material, including EBSCO's *ContentSelect™* Academic Journal Database, *The New York Times* Search-by-Subject Archive, and *Best of the Web* Link Library, Research Navigator™ helps students quickly and efficiently make the most of their research time.

Prentice Hall Guide to Evaluating Online Resources, Anthropology.   This guide encourages students to be critical consumers of online resources. References related specifically to the discipline of anthropology are included. Included with the guide is an access code for Research Navigator™. This guide is free when packaged with *In the Beginning: An Introduction to Archaeology, 11/E.*

Acknowledgments

As always, this edition is the result of input and advice from many people, both professional archaeologists and students. We have even received correspondence from Australia, Slovakia, and Japan and are gratified to learn that *In the Beginning* has been translated for use in Indonesia. The comments of our correspondents are always challenging and provocative, and we only hope that our efforts to navigate between conflicting viewpoints and priorities meet with their approval.

The following kindly reviewed the book for this edition: Elliot Abrams, Ohio University; Katina Lillios, Ripon College; Randall H. McGuire, Binghamton University; and Tamra L. Walter, Texas Tech University.

Finally, many thanks to Nancy Roberts, our editor at Prentice Hall, who has adopted *In the Beginning* as her own and mothered it (if such a thing is possible with a textbook). The production staff, a team headed by Joan Stone, worked miracles with our arabesques. Thank you one and all.

Brian Fagan   *Christopher DeCorse*

Brian Fagan is one of the leading archaeological writers and an internationally recognized authority on world prehistory. He studied archaeology and anthropology at Pembroke College, Cambridge University, and then spent seven years in sub-Saharan Africa working in museums and in monuments conservation and excavating early farming sites in Zambia and East Africa. He was one of the pioneers of multidisciplinary African history in the 1960s. From 1967 to 2003, he was professor of anthropology at the University of California, Santa Barbara, where he specialized in lecturing and writing about archaeology to wide audiences. He is now Emeritus Professor of Anthropology.

Brian Fagan has written six best-selling textbooks (all published by Prentice Hall): *Ancient Lives: An Introduction to Archaeology and Prehistory; In the Beginning; Archaeology: A Brief Introduction; World Prehistory; Ancient Civilizations* (with Chris Scarre); and this volume—which are used around the world. His general books include *The Rape of the Nile,* a classic history of Egyptology; *The Adventure of Archaeology; Time Detectives; Ancient North America; The Little Ice Age; Before California: An Archaeologist Looks at Our Earliest Inhabitants;* and *The Long Summer.* He was also General Editor of the *Oxford Companion to Archaeology.* In addition, he has published several scholarly monographs on African archaeology and numerous specialized articles in national and international journals. An expert on multimedia teaching, he has received the Society for American Archaeology's first Public Education Award for his indefatigable efforts on behalf of archaeology and education.

Brian Fagan's other interests include bicycling, sailing, kayaking, and good food. He is married and lives in Santa Barbara with his wife and daughter, four cats (who supervise his writing), and last but not least, a minimum of four rabbits.

Christopher R. DeCorse received his bachelor of arts and master's degrees in anthropology and archaeology at the University of New Hampshire and the University of California, Los Angeles, completing his doctorate in archaeology at UCLA. His theoretical interests include the interpretation of ethnicity, culture change, and variability in the archaeological record. Dr. DeCorse has excavated a variety of prehistoric and historic period sites in the United States, the Caribbean, and Africa, but his primary area of research has been in the archaeology, ethnohistory, and ethnography of Sierra Leone and Ghana. His most recent research has focused on culture contact and change at the African settlement of Elmina, Ghana, the site of the first European trading post in sub-Saharan Africa. He is currently collaborating on several projects that are examining connections between Africa and the Americas.

Christopher DeCorse has taught archaeology and general anthropology in a variety of undergraduate and graduate programs, including the University of Ghana, Legon; Indiana University, Pennsylvania; and Syracuse University, New York, where he is currently an associate professor in the Department of Anthropology. He is particularly interested in the interpretation and presentation of anthropology for undergraduates and the general public. In addition to *In the Beginning,* he has authored *The Record of the Past: An Introduction to Archaeology and Physical Anthropology,* and co-authored *Anthropology: A Global Perspective,* a four-field anthropology text, and *Worldviews in Human Expression,* an introduction to the humanities from an anthropological perspective. He serves on the advisory or editorial boards of *Annual Editions* in physical anthropology and archaeology, *International Journal of Historical Archaeology, Journal of African Archaeology,* and *Beads: Journal of the Society of Bead Researchers.* He has participated on a number of committees and panels, including work as a consultant on human evolution and agricultural origins for the National Center for History in the Schools.

Christopher DeCorse has received several academic honors and awards, including Fulbright and Smithsonian fellowships and the Maxwell School of Citizenship and Public Affairs Daniel Patrick Moynihan Award for outstanding teaching, research, and service. He has published more than forty articles, reviews, and research notes in a variety of publications, including *The African Archaeological Review, Journal of African Archaeology, Historical New Hampshire, Historical Archaeology,* and *Slavery and Abolition.* Books dealing with his work in West Africa include *An Archaeology of Elmina: Africans and Europeans on the Gold Coast* and an edited volume *West Africa during the Atlantic Slave Trade: Archaeological Perspectives.*

In the Beginning describes the basic methods and theoretical approaches of scientific archaeology. In so doing, we use numerous examples from the entire 2.5-million-year time span of the human past. Although the historical sites described in these pages are probably familiar to most readers, there is value in providing a short summary of human prehistory as a framework for the method and theory chapters that follow. This is, at best, a cursory story. Readers are referred to the books listed at the end of this introduction for more information. (For an outline chronology, see the Chronological Table.)

Human Origins and Early Prehistory

In 1871, Charles Darwin, the Victorian biologist who is the father of modern evolutionary theory, hypothesized that humanity originated in Africa. He based his argument on the great diversity of ape forms south of the Sahara Desert and on the close anatomical relationships between humans and such living primates as the chimpanzee. A century and a quarter later, we know that Darwin was correct and that humanity did indeed evolve in tropical Africa.

Staggering advances in multidisciplinary research have changed our perceptions of human origins dramatically since 1959, when Louis and Mary Leakey announced the discovery of a robustly built hominid at Olduvai Gorge in Tanzania, East Africa. At the time, the entire span of the human past was thought to encompass a mere quarter of a million years. Soon, the hominid-bearing levels at Olduvai were potassium-dated to over 1.75 million years ago. Today, we know that the first toolmaking humans appeared in East Africa at least 2.5 million years ago, while earlier hominid ancestors flourished on the savanna woodlands of the region as early as 4 million years before the present. A recent discovery in Chad, Central Africa, may take hominid evolution back as far as 7 million years ago.

The critical behavioral changes that separated humans from nonhuman primates developed over several million years; among them were a shift to bipedal (two-footed) posture, significant increases in brain size and communication skills, and the appearance of hands capable of making and manipulating simple tools. These changes took place during a period of gradual global cooling, which culminated in the dramatic climatic shifts of the last Ice Age. By 3 million years ago, a wide variety of hominid species inhabited tropical Africa, among them the direct ancestors of the first human beings. The very first human-manufactured artifacts came into use about 2.6 million years ago; they were little more than sharp-edged flakes knocked from lava cobbles and used for butchering animals and other tasks. We know little of the behavior of these earliest humans, although laboratory studies of broken animal bones strongly suggest that they scavenged much of their meat from predator kills. At the same time, they relied heavily on wild plant foods, as have most hunter-gatherers ever since.

	Old World	The Americas
A.D. 1500	European Age of Discovery	Spanish Conquest of Aztecs and the Inca
	Renaissance	Columbus
	Medieval Times	Aztecs
		Toltecs
		Mississippian and the Anasazi
A.D. 1	Han civilization in China	Maya civilization
	Roman Empire	Moche state
	Unification of China (221 B.C.)	Moundbuilder cultures
	Mycenaean civilization	(North America)
	Minoan civilization	Chavin
	Shang civilization (China)	Olmec
	Harappan civilization	Village farmers
3000 B.C.	Ancient Egyptian and Sumerian civilization (metallurgy and writing)	Maize agriculture?
5000 B.C.	Euxine Lake disaster	
10,000 B.P.	Origins of food production	Paleo-Indian and Archaic cultures
20,000	Great diversity of increasingly complex forager societies First European art tradition First settlement of Australia Modern humans in Europe	First settlement of the Americas?
50,000	European Neanderthals Modern humans in southwestern Asia	
100,000	First modern humans in Africa	
250,000 B.P.	Archaic *Homo sapiens*	
	Fire domesticated *Homo erectus* radiates out of Africa	
1–9 million B.P.		
2.5 million B.P.	*Homo habilis* and other hominids First toolmaking	

The earliest hominids flourished and evolved in sub-Saharan Africa. At the time, the rest of the world was still uninhabited. Around 2 million years ago, more advanced humans with larger brains and more humanlike limbs evolved out of earlier hominid populations. About this time, too, humans tamed fire, which became a potent tool for adapting to much cooler environments. This was the moment at which humanity foraged its way across the Sahara Desert and into Asia and then Europe, adapting to a wide variety of tropical and temperate environments. This radiation of archaic humans, grouped generically under the label *Homo erectus,* may have taken place about 1.9 million years ago or somewhat later, as part of a general movement of many mammal forms out of Africa into other parts of the world.

Three-quarters of a million years ago, the human population of the Old World was probably no more than a few tens of thousands of people, living in small family bands in temperate and tropical environments. By this time, the world had entered a seesaw-like pattern of alternating glacial and interglacial periods, oscillating between cooler and warmer conditions in such a way that global climate has been in a state of transition for 75 percent of the past 750,000 years. Our archaic ancestors adapted successfully to these dramatic long- and shorter-term shifts with brilliant opportunism. By 400,000 years ago, European hunters at Schoningen, Germany, were using long wooden spears to pursue large and formidable game, while a simple and highly effective stone technology based on choppers and axes evolved slowly into much more sophisticated and specialized tool kits.

The Origins and Spread of Modern Humans

Between 750,000 and 200,000 years ago, human biological and cultural evolution continued at a slow pace, as *Homo erectus* evolved gradually into more modern forms, toward ourselves, *Homo sapiens sapiens.* Most famous among these early *Homo sapiens* forms are the Neanderthals of Europe and central and southwestern Asia, who appeared over 200,000 years ago and adapted successfully to the extreme temperatures of the late Ice Age.

A vast anatomical and cultural chasm separates *Homo sapiens sapiens* from its more archaic *Homo sapiens* predecessors. We are the "wise people," capable of fluent speech and intelligent reasoning, brilliant innovators with the ability to adapt successfully to every extreme environment on Earth. Great controversy surrounds our origins, with scientists divided into two broad camps. One school of thought believes that modern humans evolved separately in different parts of the world more or less simultaneously. However, most experts, including molecular biologists, think that our direct ancestors evolved out of more archaic human populations in tropical Africa between 150,000 and 200,000 years ago. They base their argument on a scatter of human fossil finds south of the Sahara Desert and on mitochondrial DNA, inherited through the female line, which places our ultimate roots in Africa. A find of three modern human fossils in Ethiopia dating to about 150,000 years ago provides dramatic support for this theory.

Fully modern humans appeared in Africa well before 100,000 years ago, then foraged their way across the Sahara Desert during a period of increased rainfall that turned much of the desert into semiarid grasslands. By about 90,000 years ago, anatomically modern people were living in southwestern Asia alongside more archaic Neanderthal populations. Soon afterward, modern humans may also have moved into southern, then southeastern Asia. We do not know. But some 40,000 years passed before modern humans spread northward and westward into the colder environments of late–Ice Age Europe and Eurasia. But this time, our ancestors had developed much more sophisticated tool kits based on blade technology, which, like the modern-day Swiss Army knife, formed a basis for many more specialized artifacts such as knives, spear points, and chisel-like tools that could be used to cut and shape bone and antler. This was also the critical period when humanity acquired the fully developed cognitive abilities characteristic of people like ourselves. In a cognitive sense, we became "modern" somewhere between 100,000 and 45,000 years ago.

Between 40,000 and 15,000 years ago, modern humans settled in every corner of the world. As the Cro-Magnons, they replaced European and Eurasian Neanderthal populations, developing an elaborate tool kit that enabled them to adapt to a highly changeable, often intensely cold environment. These are the people who produced the magnificent cave paintings and engravings of western Europe. By 40,000 years ago, perhaps earlier, small hunter-gatherer populations had crossed open water to New Guinea and Australia. Ten thousand years later, they had settled on the Solomon Islands and other relatively close southwestern Pacific Islands. The settlement of the offshore Pacific Islands did not take place until the development of root agriculture and outrigger canoes took settlers to the offshore islands of Melanesia and Polynesia nearly 30,000 years later.

The First Settlement of the Americas

By 20,000 years ago, human beings had penetrated far into northern latitudes, onto the frigid steppe-tundra of central Asia, to Siberia's Lake Baikal, and perhaps into extreme northeastern Siberia. But the Americas were still virgin continents, joined to Siberia by a low-lying land bridge during the late Ice Age, when sea levels were about 300 feet (91 m) lower than today.

The first settlement of the Americas remains one of the great mysteries of archaeology. Everyone agrees that the ultimate ancestry of the Native Americans lies in northeast Asia and perhaps China, but there is little agreement on when or how the first settlers arrived in the New World. There are a few unsubstantiated claims for settlement before 20,000 years ago, perhaps even as early as 40,000 years before the present. Unfortunately, none of the sites purported to document such early settlement stands up to close scientific scrutiny. Nor is there evidence for human occupation of the inhospitable reaches of extreme northeastern Siberia before some 15,000 to 18,000 years ago. Most archaeologists believe that the first settlers arrived either by crossing the land bridge or perhaps in skin boats along the frigid coastline during the very late Ice Age or immediately thereafter, perhaps as early as 15,000 years ago.

The earliest well-documented human settlement in Alaska dates to just before 10,000 B.C., but there are also sites of that age, and even slightly earlier, much farther south. No one knows, either, how the first human settlers moved from Alaska into the heart of the Americas. Perhaps they traveled southward along the coastline along now-submerged shores, or overland, as the great ice sheets that once mantled northern North

America retreated at the end of the Ice Age. We do know, however, that hunter-gatherer populations were scattered throughout the Americas by 10,500 B.C., well adapted to every kind of environment from open plains to tropical rain forest. From these early populations developed the great diversity of later Native American societies that were the direct ancestors of the much more elaborate indigenous societies of later times.

The Origins of Food Production

Since 15,000 years ago, the endless cycle of global climate change has moved into another warming mode. The great ice sheets that had covered northern Europe and North America receded rapidly. World sea levels rose closer to modern levels. Global warming brought major shifts in rainfall patterns and vegetation. Birch and oak forests replaced open plains in Europe. The Sahara again supported dry grassland. Birch forests populated much of Canada. Hundreds of animal species large and small became extinct in the face of global warming, among them the long-haired arctic elephant (the mammoth) and the mastodon. Human societies everywhere adapted to radically different environments, many of them turning to intensive exploitation of small game, fish and sea mammals, and plant foods of every kind.

Many groups settled at the boundaries of several ecological zones or by estuaries, lakes, or seacoasts, where they could exploit diverse food resources and stay in one place for much of the year. In these resource-rich areas, local populations rose considerably and the landscape filled up, to the point at which each group had its own territory and there was sometimes competition for valuable food supplies. By about 10,000 years ago, demographers believe, the Old World was close to the limits of its ability to support growing human forager populations, even in favorable environments.

Post–Ice Age global warming did not proceed steadily but in stops and starts. The mechanisms that drive long- or short-term climatic change are still a mystery, but they are closely connected to changes in the complex interactions between the atmosphere and the ocean, including the circulation of warm water from the tropics to northern latitudes and the downwelling of salt to the ocean floor in the North Atlantic.

Whatever the causes of the change, the past 15,000 years have been marked by dramatic millennium- and centuries-long climatic shifts, among them the famous "Little Ice Age" that caused famines in Europe between A.D. 1400 and 1850. But the most dramatic of these shifts occurred between 11,000 and 10,000 B.C., when the world suddenly returned to near-glacial conditions during the so-called Younger Dryas event (named after a polar shrub).

Early Food Production in the Old World

The Younger Dryas saw advancing glaciers in northern Europe and North America, while bringing severe drought to southwestern Asia. This drought had catastrophic effects on the sedentary forager populations clustered in favorable environments such as the Euphrates and Jordan river valleys and elsewhere between Turkey and southern Iraq. Within a few generations, many of these societies turned to the cultivation of

8 BC

wild cereal grasses as a way of supplementing wild plant foods. Only a few generations passed before wild wheat and barley became domesticated crops, and agriculture replaced plant foraging as a staple of human existence. At about the same time, some groups also domesticated wild goats and sheep, pigs, and, later, cattle. By 8000 B.C., farming societies were widespread throughout southwestern Asia. Agriculture also began in Egypt's Nile Valley at about the same time, but the exact date remains unknown.

The new economies were brilliantly successful and spread rapidly through the eastern Mediterranean world and around the shores of the Euxine Lake (now the Black Sea), which was then a freshwater lake separated from the Mediterranean Sea by a huge natural earthen bank that crossed what is now the Bosporus between Turkey and Bulgaria. Farmers lived in Greece and southeastern Europe by 6000 B.C. Some five centuries later, the rising Mediterranean burst through the Bosporus and flooded the Euxine Lake in a natural disaster that unfolded over a few weeks, causing the new Black Sea to become brackish and rise hundreds of feet, displacing the many agricultural societies on its shores. The flooding of the Black Sea must have caused massive disruption and population movements away from the inundated areas, accelerating the spread of farming peoples northwestward into temperate Europe, where agriculture was well established by 5000 to 4500 B.C.

Food production did not develop in one region alone. Rice cultivation had developed in southern China along the Yangze River by at least 6500 B.C. and probably earlier, and cereal agriculture in the north by 6000 B.C. As in southwestern Asia, the new economies were a logical response to growing population densities and unpredictable climatic shifts. In southwestern Asia, southern Asia, and China, food production provided the economic foundation for the world's earliest preindustrial civilizations.

Early Farmers in the Americas

When Europeans arrived in the Americas in the fifteenth century A.D., they marveled at the expertise of native populations with cereal and root crops. The native Andeans domesticated hundreds of potato forms, while maize (corn) was the staff of life for millions of farmers between tropical South America and Canada's St. Lawrence Valley in northeastern North America.

Despite intensive research, we still know little of the origins of food production in the Americas. Thanks to AMS (accelerator mass spectrometry) radiocarbon dating, and generations of botanical research, we know that maize was domesticated from a wild grass named teosinte somewhere in south-central Mexico, at least as early as 3000 B.C., and probably earlier. Maize, as well as other crops such as beans, spread rapidly in various strains—into lowland and highland South America by at least 1000 B.C., and into the southwestern United States by 1500 B.C. The first domestication of the potato took place in the highland Andes at least as early as 2500 B.C., along with other staples, such as quinoa.

Maize agriculture spread widely among North American forager societies that had been preadapted to food production by millennia of intensive hunting and gathering, often in densely populated environments such as the river valleys and lakes of the midwestern and southeastern areas. Some of these people were already cultivating native plants such as goosefoot and squashes many centuries before maize and bean agriculture became established among them.

As in the Old World, the new economies spread rapidly from their points of origin. By the time Europeans arrived, in the fifteenth century A.D., Native Americans were exploiting hundreds of domesticated plants in every environment where agriculture was feasible. In many areas, such as the highland Andes, growing populations tested the limits of maize and other crops by planting them at ever higher altitudes and by breeding cold- and drought-resistant strains. It is no coincidence that many Native American crops are now staples of the modern global economy. At the same time, Native Americans domesticated few animals other than the alpaca, dog, llama, and turkey, for they lacked the potentially domesticable animals that abounded in the Old World.

Only two thousand years or so after the domestication of plants, Native American societies in Mesoamerica and the Andean region developed much more complex societies, and soon thereafter, the first indigenous New World civilizations.

The First Civilizations

Five thousand years after farming began in southwestern Asia, the first literate, urban civilizations developed almost simultaneously in southern Mesopotamia and along the Nile River. Their roots lay among increasingly complex farming societies that had become interdependent and centralized. Numerous innovations accompanied the emergence of the first civilizations—intensified agriculture, often relying on irrigation, metallurgy, the sailing ship, and writing among them.

The origins of state-organized societies constitute one of the most hotly debated issues in archaeology, for we still lack a definitive explanation of how civilization began. The most plausible scenario combines fast-rising population densities and increased competition for economic and political power, with environmental changes that included a stabilization of global sea levels at modern levels. The complex economic, political, and social changes to civilization have been likened to a game of ancient Monopoly that pitted chief against chief in fast-moving diplomatic and economic games where the strongest and most decisive leaders survived.

You can see the process along the Nile River, where increasingly large and more powerful riverside states competed over many centuries. Eventually, powerful rulers in Upper (southern) Egypt conquered the states of the fertile delta region in the north and created a unified kingdom in about 3100 B.C. under a pharaoh (king) named Menes. Over the next few centuries, his successors created a powerful religious ideology and royal culture that turned the pharaoh into a divine ruler with supreme powers on the earth. Egypt's conservative, yet surprisingly flexible, civilization endured for nearly three thousand years as a preindustrial society that created the pyramids and nurtured some of the greatest rulers in history.

The route to civilization in Mesopotamia involved similar complex processes of environmental, political, and social change in a lowland environment where powerful cities became a patchwork of small city-states that competed over water rights, trade routes, and land. The Sumerian civilization, made up of competing city-states such as Eridu, Ur, and Uruk, was rarely unified into a large entity until the third millennium B.C., when the rulers of Ur patched together a civilization that unified, at least nominally, a mosaic of smaller states from the Mediterranean coast to the Persian Gulf. Successive civilizations rose from the disintegration of Sumerian society after 2500 B.C., when Akkadians based in Babylon to the north created a new empire in southern Mesopotamia, followed in turn by the Assyrians of the first millennium B.C.

By this time, the civilizations of the eastern Mediterranean world were linked by increasingly close economic ties, to the point that some scholars have written of this as the first "world economic system," perhaps a somewhat grandiose term for a vast region between India and mainland Greece linked by land and ocean trade routes that handled goods and commodities of every kind. By 2600 B.C., Sumerian monarchs boasted of ships from distant Meluhha that docked at their ports. Meluhha was probably the Indus Valley in what is now northwestern Pakistan, where the indigenous Harappan civilization developed before 2000 B.C. The Harappan was a loosely connected riverine civilization with numerous large towns and several large cities, among them Harappa and Mohenjodaro. Harappa traded regularly with Mesopotamia on such a scale that it had its own script and systems of weights and measures. Harappan civilization declined about 1700 B.C. A few centuries later, the center of gravity of early Indian civilization moved eastward into the Ganges River valley, where the great Mauryan civilization flourished in the first millennium B.C.

The Greek mainland and Aegean islands nurtured their own distinctive civilizations, which developed from many centuries of long-distance trade in olive oil, wine, timber, and other commodities. Crete's Minoan civilization prospered from far-flung trade routes that linked the Aegean with the eastern Mediterranean and the Nile Valley. Egyptian inscriptions and paintings show Minoan traders at the pharaoh's court as early as 1600 B.C., and the famous Uluburun shipwreck off the southern Turkish coast in 1310 B.C. chronicles the astounding wealth of foreign trade at the time. After 1450 B.C., the Mycenaeans ruled both the Greek mainland and Crete, strengthening their ties with the powerful Hittite civilization in what is now Turkey, the Assyrians in Mesopotamia, and the Egyptians. This prosperous, highly competitive world collapsed in political turmoil about 1200 B.C. for reasons that are still little understood. The first millennium B.C. saw the rise and fall of the Persian empire and of Alexander the Great's vast domains, the glories of classical Greece, and then, finally, the rise of the Roman Empire, which dominated the western world from before the time of Christ until the Dark Ages.

As Egyptian and Mesopotamian civilizations appeared in the west, more complex societies developed in northern and southern China. By 2500 B.C., these Lungshan cultures enjoyed highly centralized, elaborate social organization and were developing into highly competitive and much larger political units. By about 2000 B.C., Chinese history enters an era of legend with a basis in fact, with the competing Xia, Shang, and Zhou dynasties of the Huang Ho (Yellow). Between 1766 and 1100 B.C., the Shang civilization dominated the north, to be succeeded by the Zhou dynasty, which in turn gave way to a historical jigsaw puzzle of warring states that were finally unified by the ruthless and despotic Emperor Shihuangdi in 221 B.C. The emperor is famous for his lavish and still unexcavated royal tomb, guarded by a regiment of spectacular terra-cotta soldiers.

By the time of Christ, Greek sea captains had discovered the secrets of the monsoon winds of the Indian Ocean, which allowed a sailing vessel to sail to India and back with favorable winds. Within a few centuries, the Roman world was linked to India and, indirectly, to the Han empire in distant China. The Mediterranean and Asian worlds became interconnected with economic and diplomatic ties that endured until Portuguese explorer Vasco da Gama sailed around Africa's Cape of Good Hope and directly to India along the monsoon route in A.D. 1497. His voyage took place as the European Age of Discovery brought Columbus to the Indies and other explorers to the Pacific and southeastern Asia.

Early American Civilizations

The indigenous civilizations of the Americas developed a brilliant complexity, with many resemblances in general characteristics and organization to preindustrial states in the Old World.

Mesoamerican Civilization

When Spanish conquistador Hernán Cortés and his motley band of followers gazed down on the glittering Aztec capital, Tenochtitlán, in the heart of the Valley of Mexico in 1519, they were astounded by the gleaming temples and palaces that could be seen from miles away. They marveled at the vast market, larger than that in Constantinople, attended by as many as 20,000 people a day. More than 250,000 Aztecs lived in or around Tenochtitlán, which was, at the time, one of the largest cities in the world. Within two years, the Aztec capital was a pile of smoking ruins after months of bitter fighting. Soon, the dazzling Aztec civilization was just a memory.

The Aztec empire developed out of more than 2,500 years of Mesoamerican civilization. The architecture of the Aztec capital, cosmology, religious beliefs, and their institutions of kingship had deep roots in earlier, much-revered, civilizations.

Mesoamerican civilization developed from ancient village roots, but the religious beliefs and institutions of the Olmec people of the Veracruz lowlands were of paramount importance after 1500 B.C. The Olmec developed their religious ideology and distinctive art style from farmers' beliefs, which involved both shamanism and a profound belief in the power of the fierce jaguar. By 1200 B.C., their religious beliefs and the art style that accompanied them were widespread throughout lowland and highland Mesoamerica. Massive, brooding figures of Olmec rulers (see Figure 17.7) give an impression of immense shamanistic power, of individuals who traveled freely between the material and spiritual worlds; travel between those two realms is always a feature of Mesoamerican civilization. The Olmec had still little-known equivalents in other parts of the lowlands and highlands, but their influence on later Mesoamerican civilizations was enormous.

As the Olmec flourished, Maya civilization developed out of village cultures in the Yucatán lowlands. Some small ceremonial centers were flourishing by 1500 B.C. A thousand years later, the first large Preclassic Maya cities rose in the southern Yucatán, among them Nakbé and El Mirador, places where kingship became a formal institution and Maya lords became powerful rulers who presided over ever-changing city-states. By A.D. 100, the Classic Maya civilization was well under way, as a jigsaw puzzle of city-states large and small competed ferociously for political power, trade monopolies, and prestige. The Maya developed their own indigenous script, whose decipherment was one of the great scientific triumphs of the twentieth century. This decipherment has allowed us to reconstruct not only the complex Maya calendar but also many details of their political history and cosmology.

Classic Maya civilization flourished in the southern lowlands until the ninth century. The four largest city-states—Calakmul, Copán, Palenque, and Tikal—were all ruled by long-lived dynasties of authoritative lords. Meanwhile, the great city of Teotihuacán rose to prominence in the highlands. This was a city of more than 120,000 people and a trading and religious center of enormous power. From 200 B.C. to A.D. 750, Teotihuacán was the dominant presence on the highlands, ruled by increasingly militaristic rulers who traded with the city of Monte Albán in the Valley of Oaxaca and with the Maya, who were strongly influenced by the city's militaristic beliefs. In about A.D. 750, Teotihuacán abruptly collapsed, leaving a political vacuum in the highlands. In the eighth century, Maya civilization collapsed in the southern highlands, probably as a result of stress brought about by drought, environmental degradation, and internal social disorder. The dense urban populations scattered, but Maya civilization endured and flourished in the northern Yucatán until the arrival of the Spanish in 1517.

In the highlands, several centuries passed before the Toltec civilization emerged as a new, dominant force in the Valley of Mexico, only to implode in A.D. 1200, probably as a result of fierce external and internal rivalries. The Aztecs arrived in the valley soon afterward as obscure nomads entering a political environment of vicious competition between well-established city-states. With brilliant diplomatic and military skill, the Aztecs became mercenaries, then conquerors. By 1425, they were masters of the Valley of Mexico and were in the midst of expanding their empire, which extended from the Gulf of Mexico to the Pacific Ocean and from Guatemala to northern Mexico, when the Spaniards gazed on Tenochtitlán in 1519. The Aztecs held their domains together by force and harsh tribute assessments. Inevitably, many vassal cities joined the newcomers as a way of overthrowing the hated Aztec masters, only to suffer a different form of bondage after the Spanish Conquest.

Andean Civilization

Andean civilization also developed from ancient village roots. It was to encompass the vast Inca empire, overthrown by Spaniard Francisco Pizarro in the early 1530s. At the time, as many as 6 million people lived under Inca rule, part of Tawantinsuyu, "the Land of the Four Quarters," which extended from Chile and Bolivia in the south to Ecuador in the north and encompassed the Andes highlands, some Amazonian rain forest, and the arid Pacific coast.

The origins of Andean civilization may be associated with the intensive exploitation of anchovies and other coastal fish that flourished in the cold Humboldt Current, which flows close to the arid Pacific shoreline. This bounty, when combined with intensive agriculture in irrigated coastal river valleys, provided ample food surpluses for complex societies centered on increasingly elaborate ceremonial centers. By 900 B.C., a distinctive Andean religious ideology had appeared at Chavín de Huantar in the foothills and spread widely through the entire region along trade routes that linked highlands and lowlands.

The first millennium A.D. saw the development of two poles of Andean civilization. The first, centered on Peru's north coast, consisted of river valley societies that traded cotton, textiles, and marine products such as fishmeal with the highlands. The Moche state, which flourished for much of the early and mid-first millennium A.D., enjoyed great wealth, as its leaders organized elaborate intervalley canals and irrigation systems. North coast civilization was volatile and vulnerable to drought and catastrophic El Niño floods. By 1100, the Chimu state dominated the region, only to be overthrown by Inca conquerors in the fourteenth century.

The southern pole of Andean civilization was centered around the shores of Lake Titicaca and was dominated by a ceremonial site at Pukara, and especially the city of Tiwanaku, which reached the height of its powers in the first millennium A.D. before collapsing in the face of intense drought about A.D. 1000. The highland plains around Lake Titicaca were conquered early by the Inca, who began aggressive campaigns of conquest to expand their domains after 1438. The Inca empire was at its maximum extent when Spanish conquistadors brought smallpox and destruction to the Andean world in the 1530s.

The conquest of the Aztec and Inca empires was part of the final chapter of prehistory, which saw Western civilization expand to every corner of the world and the creation of the first truly global economy. But the great diversity of humankind in the modern world serves to remind us of our common roots in the remote past, a past reconstructed in large part by archaeology, the only scientific discipline that studies and explains human cultural evolution over long periods of time.

GUIDE TO FURTHER READING

Three widely read college texts provide more specifics on human prehistory and are available in most academic libraries:

FAGAN, BRIAN. 2004. *People of the Earth: An Introduction to World Prehistory,* 11th ed. Upper Saddle River, NJ: Prentice Hall.

PRICE, DOUGLAS, and GARY FEINMAN. 2004. *Images of the Past,* 4th ed. New York: McGraw-Hill.

WENKE, ROBERT. 1994. *Patterns in Prehistory,* 2d ed. New York: Oxford University Press.

PART I

Background to Archaeology

Of all ruins, possibly the most moving are those of long-deserted cities, fallen century by century into deeper decay, their forsaken streets grown over by forest and shrubs, their decadent buildings quarried and plundered down the years, gaping ruinous, the haunt of lizards and owls; . . . the marble and gold of palaces, the laurel and jasmine of gardens, are now brambles and lagoons; the house built for Caesar is now dwelt in by lizards.

Rose Macaulay, *The Pleasure of Ruins*

Why study archaeology? What is the importance of this popular and apparently romantic subject? We begin by looking at the place of archaeology in the twenty-first-century world. Unfortunately, the discipline faces a crisis brought about by rapid destruction of important sites by industrial development and treasure hunting. Furthermore, all kinds of pseudo-archaeologies purporting to tell the truth about lost worlds, ancient astronauts, and sunken continents undermine archaeology's credibility with a wider audience. The reality of archaeology is much less romantic but just as fascinating. We define archaeology by placing it within its broad context as part of anthropology and history.

CHAPTER 1

Introducing Archaeology

Archaeologist Howard Carter peers through the doors of one of pharaoh Tutankhamun's golden shrines, undisturbed for more than 3,000 years. (Photography by Egyptian Expedition, The Metropolitan Museum of Art.)

"All was mystery, dark, impenetrable mystery, and every circumstance increased it. In Egypt, the colossal skeletons of gigantic temples stand in unwatered sands in all the nakedness of desolation; but here an immense forest shrouds the ruins . . . Giving an intensity and almost wildness to the interest . . . " (Stephens, 1841). American traveler John Lloyd Stephens wrote those words as he explored the overgrown ruins of the great Maya city at Copán in Honduras in the mid-nineteenth century. He called Copán the "Mecca or Jerusalem of an unknown people" and made the exploration of the past high adventure. It is still a fascinating adventure.

Archaeology is the stuff dreams are made of—buried treasure, gold-laden pharaohs, the romance of long-lost civilizations. Many people believe archaeologists are romantic heroes, like the film world's Indiana Jones. Cartoonists depict them as elderly, eccentric scholars in sun helmets digging up inscribed tablets in the shadow of Egyptian temples. They are thought to be typical absentminded professors, so deeply absorbed in the details of ancient life that they care little for the pressures and frustrations of modern life. Archaeology is believed to open doors to a world of romance and excitement, to discoveries like the spectacular tomb of the Egyptian pharaoh Tutankhamun, opened by English archaeologists Howard Carter and Lord Carnarvon in 1922 (see the Discovery box).

The first archaeologists were, indeed, adventurers. The Maya civilization of Mexico and Guatemala was first described by American travel writer John Lloyd Stephens, who traveled in the forests of the Yucatán with artist Frederick Catherwood in 1839 (Figure 1.1). Stephens tried to buy the Copán ruins for fifty dollars so he could mount an exhibit to sell a travel book. The deal fell through because there was no way to ship his finds to New York.

Some early archaeologists dug for profit, others out of intellectual curiosity. None was more single-minded than Heinrich Schliemann, a German businessman

Figure 1.1   The nineteenth-century archaeologist as adventurer. A lithograph of the Castillo at Chichén Itzá, Mexico, by artist Frederick Catherwood, who accompanied John Lloyd Stephens.

(Traill, 1995). In his early forties he gave up business, married a young Greek woman, and set out to find Homer's legendary city of Troy in 1871. His hectic search ended at the mound of Hissarlik in northwestern Turkey, already identified as Troy by the local American consul, Frank Calvert. Schliemann recruited 150 men and moved 325,000 cubic yards of soil in his early seasons, but he proved the Homeric legends had some basis in reality. His archaeological methods were brutal; he destroyed almost as much as he discovered.

Archaeology has come a long way since the days when one could find a lost civilization in a month. In this chapter we define archaeology and explore its role in the modern world. We also discuss archaeology's relationship to other academic disciplines, its goals, and the ethics of studying the past.

Why Study Archaeology?

Few archaeologists are fortunate enough to discover a royal burial or a forgotten civilization. Most excavate for a lifetime, finding nothing more spectacular than some fine pottery or delicately made stone tools. Archaeologists spend their lives investigating the surviving and abandoned remains of ancient societies. It is not gold or fine objects that interest them, though, but the information that comes from digging up finds and properly recording them. The archaeologist today is as interested in why people lived the way they did as in the objects they made and the buildings they erected.

Discovery

Tutankhamun's Tomb, Egypt, 1922

The small party of archaeologists and onlookers stood in front of the doorway that bore the seals of the long-dead pharaoh. They had waited six long years, from 1917 to 1922, for this moment. Silently, Howard Carter pried a hole through the ancient plaster. Hot air rushed out of the small cavity and massaged his face. Carter shone a flashlight through the hole and peered into the sepulcher. Gold objects swam in front of his eyes, and he was struck dumb with amazement.

Lord Carnarvon fidgeted impatiently behind him, as Carter remained silent.

"What do you see," he asked, hoarse with excitement.

"Wonderful things," whispered Carter as he stepped back from the doorway (Carter and others, 1923–1933:63).

They soon broke down the door. In a daze of amazement, Carter and Carnarvon wandered through the antechamber of the pharaoh Tutankhamun's tomb. They fingered golden funerary beads, admired beautifully inlaid wooden chests, and examined the pharaoh's chariots stacked against the wall. Gold was everywhere—on wooden statues, inlaid on thrones and boxes, in jewelry, even on children's stools (Reeves, 1990). Soon Tutankhamun was known as the golden pharaoh, and archaeology as the domain of buried treasure and royal sepulchers (Figure 1.2).

As for Carter and Carnarvon, they immediately installed an iron door to the tomb and placed a 24-hour guard at the entrance while they planned the clearance of the sepulcher. But late that night they returned on their own, chiseled a small hole in the sealed

Figure 1.2 The golden mask and sarcophagus of Egyptian king Tutankhamun. (Photograph by the Egyptian Expedition, The Metropolitan Museum of Art.)

burial chamber, and slipped through to check that the pharaoh lay undisturbed in his sarcophagus.

It took Howard Carter eight years to clear Tutankhamun's tomb, one of the greatest archaeological discoveries ever made.

Figure 1.3   Englishman Austen Henry Layard floated his Assyrian finds from ancient Nineveh down the Tigris River on wooden rafts supported by inflated goatskins. When the raft reached the Persian Gulf, the skins were deflated and packed upstream on donkeys, and the wood was sold. The Assyrians themselves had used similar river vessels.

On the face of it, the study of archaeology, however fascinating, seems a luxury we can ill afford in a world beset by economic uncertainties and widespread poverty and famine. But to regard archaeology in such a way would be to treat the entire cultural heritage of humanity as irrelevant and unnecessary to the quality of our lives; in reality, it is integral, as we shall see (Layton, 1994; Trigger, 1984).

Archaeology Is Fascinating

The great public fascination with archaeology began with the classic archaeological discoveries of the nineteenth century (Figure 1.3), with the finding of the biblical Assyrians of Mesopotamia and ancient Troy. Today, archaeology is as much a part of popular culture as football or the automobile. Thousands of people read archaeology books for entertainment, join archaeological societies, and flock to popular lectures on the past. Discoveries such as the spectacular Sipán burials in Peru (Figure 1.4) (Alva and Donnan, 1993) and the Stone Age rock paintings of Grotte de Chauvet in France make front-page headlines around the world (see the Discovery box).

Armchair archaeology is one thing, to experience the past firsthand is another. The monuments of antiquity cast an irresistible spell. The jetliner and the package tour have made archaeological tourism big business. Fifty years ago only the wealthy and privileged could take a tour up the Nile, visit Classical Greek temples, and explore Maya civilization. Now package tours can take you to Egypt, to the Parthenon (see Figure 1.9), and to Teotihuacán, Mexico (Figure 15.12). The immense Pyramids of Giza in Egypt (Figure 16.5), the ruins at Tikal in Guatemala (Figure 15.2) bathed in

Figure 1.4 A mannequin wears replicas of the ceremonial regalia of a Moche warrior priest, similar to those found in a royal tomb from A.D. 400 at Sipán, Peru. The lords of Sipán were one of the greatest archaeological discoveries of the twentieth century.

the full moon's light—as sights alone, these overwhelm the senses. To sit in the great amphitheater at Epidauros, Greece, and to hear Euripides' stanzas recited in the perfect acoustics of the highest seats is a deeply moving experience. Tutankhamun's golden sarcophagus (Figure 1.2) or a giant Olmec head with snarling face (Figure 17.7) lifts us to a realm where achievement endures and perceptions seem of a higher order. There are moments when the remote past reaches out to us, comforting, encouraging, offering precedent for human existence. We marvel at the achievements of the ancients, at their awesome legacy to all humankind.

Archaeology and the Remote Past

Every society on earth has some form of origin myth: folklore that is the official, sanctioned account of how the earth and humankind came into being. Western society is no exception. "And God said, 'Let us make man in our image, after our likeness: and let them have dominion over the fish of the sea, and over the fowl of the air, and over the cattle, and over all the earth, and over every creeping thing that creepeth on the earth.'" Thus reads the first chapter of Genesis in the biblical Old Testament, a majestic

Discovery

Grotte de Chauvet, France, 1994

On December 18, 1994, three speleologists with an interest in archaeology, Eliette Brunel Deschamps, Jean-Marie Chauvet, and Christian Hillaire, crawled into a small opening in the Cirque de Estre gorge of the Ardèche in southeastern France. The entrance was a mere 31 inches (80 cm) high and 12 inches (30 cm) wide, but it led to a narrow vestibule with a sloping floor. The three explorers felt a draft flowing from a blocked duct. They pulled out the boulders that blocked it and saw a vast chamber 9 feet (3 m) below them. After returning with a rope ladder, they descended into a network of chambers adorned with superb calcite columns. Calcified cave bear bones and teeth lay on the floor, and they noticed shallow depressions where the beasts had hibernated. Suddenly, Deschamps cried out in surprise. Her lamp shone on two lines of red ocher, then a small mammoth figure.

The group then penetrated into the main chamber and came upon more paintings: hand imprints—both positives and negatives—and figures of mammoths and cave lions, one with a circle of dots emerging from its muzzle (Figure 1.5). As they gazed at the paintings, the three explorers were "seized by a strange feeling. Everything was so beautiful, so fresh, almost too much so. Time was abolished, as if the tens of thousands of years that separated us from the producers of these paintings no longer existed" (Chauvet and others, 1996:42). Like the excavators of the tomb of the Egyptian pharaoh Tutankhamun three quarters of a century before, they felt like intruders: "The artists' souls and spirits surrounded us. We thought we could feel their presence" (p. 42).

Grotte de Chauvet had lain undisturbed since the late Ice Age. Hearths on the floor looked as if they had been extinguished the day before. Flaming torches had been rubbed against the wall to remove the charcoal so they would flare anew. A little farther on in the chamber lay a slab that had fallen from the ceiling. A bear skull had been set on top of

account of the Creation that was accepted as the authorized version of human origins for centuries.

Origin myths, such as that of Genesis, developed in response to humanity's deep-seated curiosity about its origins. They also reflect each society's perspective on human existence. For many peoples, existence is defined by their close relationship to the natural world and by the endless cycles of passing seasons. Such definitions assume that human existence is unchanging, that both past and future generations will share the same existence as those alive today. In contrast, Western civilization has a linear view of human existence, depicting it as unfolding in all parts of the world over an enormously long period of time.

For more than two thousand years, Westerners have speculated about their ancestry and tried to develop theoretical models to explain their origins. Some of these models are purely philosophical; others are based on archaeological data. Archaeology is fascinating because it enables us to test theoretical models of changing societies: why some people have flourished, others have vanished without a trace, and still others have sunk into obscurity (Trigger, 1984).

Figure 1.5 Cave painting of lions from Grotte de Chauvet, France.

it, and the remains of a small fire lay behind it. More than thirty calcite-covered and intentionally placed bear skulls surrounded the slab. In an end chamber, the three explorers came across another 30-foot (10-m) frieze of black figures dominated by lionesses or lions without manes, rhinoceroses, bison, and mammoths. Far to the right they discerned a human figure with a bison head. They wrote that it "seemed to us a sorcerer supervising this immense frieze" (p. 58).

Chauvet was a priceless archive of Cro-Magnon painting preserved in its original context, artifacts and bones still in the exact places where they had been dropped between 31,000 and 26,000 years ago.

Archaeology is unique among the sciences in its ability to study changes in human societies over long periods of time. It provides a way of studying the collective cultural heritage of humankind. Why are we biologically and culturally diverse? In what ways are we similar or different? When did the great diversity of humanity come into being, and why? These are fundamental questions about humankind that archaeologists can attempt to answer.

Archaeology is a product of Western science, and, as such, is sometimes considered irrelevant by some non-Western societies, which believe profoundly in the cyclical nature of human existence. Many Native Americans consider archaeology unnecessary, even insulting to their ancestors. But the fact remains that it offers the only scientific way of understanding the ancient world and the linear histories of Native American and other societies, many of which came into contact with literate Western civilization only in the past five centuries, during the European Age of Discovery. Before European contact, North American Indian history was not written; it consisted mostly of oral traditions handed down from generation to generation. Archaeology and archaeological sites are the only other possible sources for very early American

Indian history. More and more archaeologists are working closely with American Indian communities (Dongokse et al., 2000). Southwestern groups, among others, have retained archaeologists and anthropologists to work on land-claim cases currently in the courts. The Hopi and Zuni nations, for example, have formed their own archaeology units to investigate sites on their land (Watkins, 2003) (Chapter 19).

Archaeological excavations reveal much about the diversity of early historic American society. In Florida, Kathleen Deagan has excavated the site of Fort Mose, the first free black community in North America. This tiny hamlet of some 37 families, 2 miles (3.2 km) from Spanish St. Augustine on the Atlantic coast, was founded in 1738, overrun by the British in 1740, and rebuilt in 1753. A walled fort enclosed a large church, the priest's house, a well, and guardhouses; the villagers lived in 22 thatched houses (Figure 1.6). Many of the inhabitants were of West African origin, and excavations have recovered military artifacts and domestic items, offering the prospect that one day archaeologists will be able to identify what African, English, Native American, and Spanish cultural elements the black inhabitants assimilated. Fort Mose was occupied until the Spanish abandoned Florida in 1763 (Deagan, 1995). Other excavations in the South and the Southeast have investigated plantation life and slave communities, a rich archaeological record of very culturally diverse African American populations (L. Ferguson, 1992).

Archaeology can restore long-vanished history to peoples whose past, handed down from one generation to the next, has vanished because it was never set down in writing. Many recently independent nations, eager to foster nationalism, are encouraging archaeological research as a way to uncover the early roots of the peoples who lived there before colonial times. For years the Tanzanian and Zambian governments

Figure 1.6   Artist's impression of the Fort Mose settlement in the mid-eighteenth century.

in Africa have sponsored excavations, whose results soon appear in university text-books and schoolbooks. The primary goal of archaeology there, as in many parts of the world, is to write unwritten history, not from archives and dusty documents but from long-abandoned villages and rubbish heaps (Trigger, 1984).

Archaeology in the Contemporary World

Archaeology is unique among all the sciences in its ability to study human history over immensely long periods of time. The archaeologist's spade enables us to explore the earliest human campsites over 2.5 million years ago, to probe the densely occupied layers of late Ice Age caves of 18,000 years ago, and to reconstruct tiny farming villages and crowded urban precincts in nineteenth-century Baltimore. As a result, archaeology is important in a world where living with, and understanding, human diversity has assumed great importance.

We live in an increasingly anonymous world of large cities and multinational corporations, of instant communications and computers of unimaginable power. But we still dwell in a world of diverse people who communicate with one another daily as individuals or groups, often electronically, and frequently over distances that would have seemed impossible even a generation ago. Our technology gives us the ability to mingle freely with individuals and groups near and far away who would never have entered our lives a century ago. As technology becomes ever more important in the industrial world, so do the people who use and benefit from it. We need a far more sophisticated understanding of human diversity than did the ancient Egyptians, so we have much to learn from the past. Anatomically modern humans, *Homo sapiens sapiens,* have lived on the earth for more than 150,000 years, and the roots of human biological and cultural diversity go back at least that far. Archaeology provides us with a unique perspective on human diversity that has great value in the modern world, simply because of the sheer variety and time depth of information on human relations that is available from the scientific record of the past.

Human diversity has been a powerful political and social reality in society since human experience began. Relationships between people, between groups and individuals, were all-important in the preindustrial world, whether that of a large city like Aztec Tenochtitlán or a tiny farming village in the Mississippi Valley. Bonds of kin, long-term family ties, and links to the soil were basic adhesives for ancient societies, to the point that Chinese rulers of 4,000 years ago maintained at least fictional kin ties to their commoner subjects in their role as intermediaries with the ancestors. Eighteenth-century New York and Elizabethan London teemed with Africans and Asians. Imperial Rome was home to people from all parts of the Mediterranean and Asian worlds. Ancient Egypt and Mesopotamian cities were hubs of thriving trade routes that brought strangers from afar to early cities. Even in our urbanized and industrialized world, ties of kin and ancient social mechanisms are still important in many societies, whether in rural villages in highland Peru or among urban poor crowded into city slums in West Africa. Archaeology has vital lessons about human diversity to impart in today's world, where the messages of history are often forgotten.

Our remote ancestors knew their environments intimately and developed highly effective, and sometimes long-forgotten, ways of growing crops and protecting themselves against the hazards of frost and famine. Archaeology provides a way of reconstructing ancient farming practices and thereby contributing to modern-day economic development. As early as 1000 B.C., farmers living on the *altiplano* (high-altitude plains) along Lake Titicaca in southern Peru and Bolivia were using raised fields, elevated planting surfaces that were used to grow crops in areas that were subject to seasonal flooding. The soils were rich, and by elevating them and building a canal network, prehistoric cultivators were able to grow potatoes, quinoa, and other indigenous crops with impressive yields. Many raised fields were abandoned before the Spanish Conquest, and the modern economy of the same environment is based on pastoralism.

Archaeologists' experiments with reconstructions of ancient raised gardens showed that excellent crop yields could be obtained from the ancient plots, in areas considered marginal by modern agricultural authorities, who think in terms of large-scale industrial agriculture. The traditional system has many advantages: high yields, no need for fertilizer, and much reduced risk of frost or flood damage. Furthermore, high yields can be obtained with local, household-based labor, local crops, and no outside capital. At last count, nearly 2,125 acres (860 ha) had been rehabilitated and many more fields are planned. Archaeologists are actively involved in several other such projects in the Americas (Erickson, 1992).

Archaeology has also worked directly for contemporary American society, especially in the management of resources and waste. University of Arizona archaeologist William Rathje has studied the garbage dumps in Tucson and other cities for a long time (Rathje and Murphy, 1992). His team examines patterns in garbage disposed of by city households, uses the latest archaeological research designs and techniques to analyze evidence from the dumps, and joins to it data gleaned from interviews with householders and other sources. His study has revealed startlingly wasteful habits in Arizona households of many economic and social backgrounds, information that could be used to suggest better strategies for consumer buying and resource management. Because the objects we use shape our lives in many ways, we need to understand how they affect us to learn about the past and anticipate the future.

Archaeology and Politics

They called Tlacalel the "Woman Snake." He was the right-hand man of a series of fifteenth-century Aztec rulers in highland Mexico, a brilliant diplomat who prevailed on his masters to burn all earlier tribal records. In their place, he concocted a convincing rags-to-riches story, which recounted the Aztecs' mercurial rise from obscurity to become masters of Mexico, chosen by Huitzilopochtli, the Sun God himself. Tlacalel was not the first official in history to rewrite the past to serve the present. Archaeology has long been used to foster nationalism, to aid political propaganda. In the 1930s, the Nazis used archaeology to produce "evidence" for the existence of a white master race in Europe (B. Arnold, 1992). The Roman siege of Masada with its tragic ending has long been a focus for Israeli nationalism, and archaeology has been used to fabricate history for all kinds of European ethnic groups in recent years (Kohl and Fawcett, 1995).

Interpretations of the past are rarely value-neutral (Fowler, 1987; Hodder, 1999). Inevitably, archaeologists bring to their work values and perspectives from their own culture, even though they are more conscious of doing this than they were a generation ago (Shanks and Tilley, 1987a). Such subliminal biases are very different from the deliberate use of archaeology to establish historical fact and to support claims against governments or nationalist goals, but they still have an effect.

Who Owns the Past?

Over the past century, archaeology has become a powerful tool for studying the remote past. Nevertheless, many people question whether science offers a viable interpretation of ancient times (McBryde, 1985; Schmidt and Patterson, 1995).

All societies have an interest in the past. It is always around them, haunting, mystifying, tantalizing, sometimes offering potential lessons for the present and future. The past is important because social life unfolds through time, embedded within a framework of cultural expectations and values. In the high Arctic, Inuit preserve their traditional attitudes, skills, and coping mechanisms in some of the harshest environments on earth. They do so by incorporating the lessons of the past into the present. In many societies, the ancestors are the guardians of the land, which symbolizes present, past, and future. There are many reasons to attempt to preserve an accurate record of the past, and no one, least of all an archaeologist, should assume that she or he is unique in having an interest in the remains of that past (Layton, 1994).

We humans think of, and use, the past in different ways. Archaeologists tend to claim they are the only people qualified to reconstruct the early human past. It is true that archaeology is the only method Western science has of studying cultural change through time, but that does not give archaeologists unique authority over the past. In many societies, the past is a valued cultural commodity in ways that are fundamentally different from those of the archaeologist. The transmission of knowledge about the past lies in the hands of respected elders, who take pains to preserve the accuracy of oral traditions. Such traditions are of vital importance and are carefully controlled, for they define and preserve a group's identity from one generation to the next. The past is vested not in science but in household, community, kin groups, and territory. As both Australian Aborigines and Native Americans have pointed out, there is a fundamental incompatibility between Western scientific perspectives on the past and the perspectives of other societies.

Robert Layton points out (1994) that many non-Western societies do not perceive themselves as living in a changeless world. They make a fundamental distinction between the recent past, which lies within living memory, and the more remote past, which came before it. Most human societies of the past were nonliterate, which meant that they transmitted knowledge and history orally, by word of mouth. Many oral histories are mixtures of factual data and parables that communicate moral and political values. But to those who hear them, they are publically sanctioned history, performed before a critical group, and subject to the critical evaluation of an audience who may have heard the same stories before (M. Smith, 1996). Oral histories are subject to all kinds of bias. None can claim to be totally objective, no more than archaeology is.

Interpretation of the past requires recognition of these biases. Through the reliance on different lines of evidence and the careful evaluation of all the information presented researchers are able to evaluate the strength of different interpretations.

To the archaeologist, the past is scientific data to be studied with all the rigor of modern science. To many indigenous peoples, the past is highly personalized and the property of the ancestors. Such histories are valid alternative versions of history that deserve respect and understanding, for they play a vital role in the creation and reaffirmation of cultural identity. And they raise a fundamental question that lies behind many Native American objections to archaeological research: What do archaeologists, usually outsiders, have to offer to a cultural group that already has a valid version of their history? Why should archaeologists be permitted to dig up the burial sites of their ancestors and other sacred places or settlements under the guise of studying what is, to the people, a known history? We should never forget that alternative, and often compelling, accounts of ancient times exist, and they play an important role in helping minority groups and others maintain their traditional heritage as it existed before the arrival of the Westerner (Layton, 1994).

The Crisis in Archaeology

The archaeologist's perspective contributes not only to an understanding of our own history but also to that of the environment, the world climate, and the landscape. The long-abandoned settlements that archaeologists study are repositories of precisely dated geological, biological, and environmental data that can add a vital time depth to studies of the contemporary world. Unfortunately, archaeological sites are an "endangered species." Ancient settlements are being destroyed so rapidly that a sizable portion of the world's archaeological heritage has already vanished.

Unlike trees or animals, archaeological sites are a finite resource. Once a bulldozer or a treasure hunter moves in, archaeological evidence is destroyed. The archaeologist's archives are buried in the soil, and the only way to preserve them is to leave them alone, intact, until they can be investigated with rigorous scientific care. Both human nature and the insatiable needs of the world's growing populations have wrought terrible destruction on the archaeological record everywhere. Pothunters and treasure hunters have left thousands of archaeological sites looking like rabbit burrows and have so damaged them that archaeological inquiry is impossible. The ravages of industrial activity, strip mining, and agriculture have also taken their catastrophic toll on many sites. In some parts of the United States, damage of sites is an uncontrolled epidemic. Those of us alive today may be the last to see undisturbed archaeological sites in North America and many other parts of the world (McGimsey, 1972).

Collectors and the Morality of Collecting

Our materialistic society greatly emphasizes wealth and the possession of valuable things. Many people feel an urge to possess the past, to keep a piece of antiquity on the mantel. Projectile points, prehistoric hand axes, Benin bronzes, or Maya pots add an exotic touch to the prosaic American living room. Many archaeological artifacts, such as those Benin bronzes, have high antique and commercial value. They are "buried treasure," valued as museum pieces and by the world's major collectors, commanding enormous prices at auction and in salesrooms. High commercial prices and the human urge to own have incited unscrupulous treasure hunting and a flourishing illegal trade in antiquities, resulting in the rape of sites for gold and other precious ornaments, as well as pottery, sculpture, and other artifacts. In some countries, such as Italy and Costa Rica, tomb robbing is a full-time, if technically illegal, profession. The Italian *tombaroli* (tomb robbers) concentrate on Etruscan tombs (Meyer, 1992). Entire Inca cemeteries in the Andes have been dug up for gold ornaments. Thousands of Egyptian tombs have been rifled for papyri and statues. Massive looting of ancient cities began immediately after the Iraq war of 2003, while the Baghdad Museum was ravaged as the city fell.

Despite increasingly comprehensive legislation, illegal looting continues unabated. In a particularly scandalous episode, an undisturbed late prehistoric site at Slack Farm, close to the Ohio River in Kentucky, was looted by a group of pothunters who paid the landowner a large sum for the right to dig up Indian burials and the valuable grave goods associated with them. It was two months before their nefarious activities were halted, by which time the site looked like a battlefield (Figure 1.7). The offenders were never convicted. (See also Chapter 18 and Munson et al., 1995.)

Why do people collect antiquities? In 1921, Henri Codet, a French medical doctor, wrote a pioneering dissertation on collecting. He concluded that it has four underlying motives: "the need to possess, the need for spontaneous activity, the impulse to self-advancement, and the tendency to classify things" (Meyer, 1992:23). Another Frenchman said of collecting: "It is not a pastime, but a passion and often so violent

Figure 1.7 Slack Farm, Kentucky, showing the damage wrought by looters before archaeologists moved in.

that it is inferior to love or ambition only in the pettiness of its aims" (Meyer, 1992:67). People collect everything from beer-bottle caps to oil paintings, and collectors consider anything collectible to be portable and private and consider it their duty to preserve it. It follows that everything has a market value and can be purchased, the market value depending on the demand for the category of artifact or its rarity or aesthetic appeal (Muensterberger, 1994). The archaeological context of the artifact is often quite unimportant and information about the people who made it usually irrelevant: all that matters is the object itself (Figure 1.8).

Figure 1.8   The wrong and the right ways to dig. Archaeology is a hobby for both of these groups, but the top group is destroying evidence of the past through its digging "techniques," whereas the bottom group is preserving it. The latter, alas, happens all too rarely.

Protecting antiquities is complex and incredibly difficult, for in the final analysis it involves appealing to people's moral values and requires almost unenforceable legislation that ultimately would take away a potential source of livelihood, however illegal, from thousands of poverty-stricken peasants and more prosperous intermediaries who have some political influence. Most countries have museums, and many have antiquities services and stringent laws controlling the export of archaeological finds—at least in theory. The trouble is that the laws cost a fortune to administer and enforce, and even relatively developed countries such as Mexico are unable to police even the most famous sites. But public opinion in Egypt and other countries shows some pride in their national heritage. It is galling to see the prized sculptures and antiquities of one's past adorning museums in distant capitals. Yet the tide of public opinion cannot stem the collectors' mania or the ruthless policies of some museums. The plundering of choice objects from the Iraq Museum in Baghdad during the recent Iraq war showed the extent to which antiquities traffickers will go to obtain their loot. Changing public attitudes, more cautious policies, and a shortage of fine antiquities may slow the traffic, but terrible damage has already been done.

Pseudoarchaeologies

Modern archaeology is highly technical and—let us be honest—sometimes rather dull. In contrast, the "pseudoarchaeologies" that have appeared in recent years positively drip with romance and excitement, with "unexplained" secrets, lost civilizations, and great temples buried in dense rain forests. The Lost Continent of Atlantis, the Ten Lost Tribes of Israel, expeditions in search of Noah's Ark—all provide superb raw material for the armchair adventurer (Feder, 2001). Popular writer Erich von Däniken (1970, 1998) created a famous pseudoarchaeology by arguing that people from other worlds lived on the earth long before our civilization arose.

Von Däniken's brand of pseudoarchaeology is unusual only because he has moved into space for his heroes. Like his predecessors, and like many people fascinated by escapism and space fiction, he is intoxicated with the mystery and lure of vanished tribes and lost cities engulfed in swirling mists (Wauchope, 1972). Of course, not all pseudoarchaeologists turn to space for their explanations. British journalist Graham Hancock (1995) has claimed that a great civilization flourished under Antarctic ice 12,000 years ago. (Of course, its magnificent cities are buried under deep ice sheets, so we cannot excavate them!) Colonists spread to all parts of the world from their Antarctic home, colonizing such well-known sites as Tiwanaku in the Bolivian highlands and building the Sphinx by the banks of the Nile. Hancock weaves an ingenious story by piecing together all manner of controversial geological observations and isolated archaeological finds. He waves aside the obvious archaeologist's reaction, which asks where traces of these ancient colonies and civilizations are to be found in Egypt and other places. Hancock fervently believes in his far-fetched theory, and being a good popular writer, he has managed to piece together a best-selling book that reads like a "whodunit" written by an amateur sleuth.

This kind of pseudoarchaeology forms a distinctive literary genre in which the author is the reader's guide behind the pathetic façade put up by science along the path to the Real Historical Truth. Far more insidious are pseudoarchaeologies that masquerade as serious "alternative" histories. Some years ago, linguist Martin Bernal (1987) published a detailed scholarly analysis of Egyptian civilization in which he claimed that this earliest of states, and Western civilization for that matter, owed much to black African inspiration. Bernal's "Black Athena" hypothesis caused a sensation in African American circles and has become an important rallying point for Afrocentrists—historians who believe that Africa was at the center of world history, the fountain not only of humanity but of civilization itself. According to Egyptologists and others with detailed knowledge of Bernal's linguistic arguments, the entire Black Athena hypothesis is seriously flawed on methodological and historical grounds. Egyptian civilization was an entirely indigenous development within the narrow confines of the Nile Valley below the First Cataract, with only sporadic, usually commercial, contacts with black African kingdoms upstream until very late in Egyptian history.

Whereas von Däniken and Hancock work within a distinctive and escapist literary genre, Bernal's work appeals to very different audiences, to people whose perspectives on history are tied to establishing cultural identities in the modern world.

Unfortunately, popular attitudes toward archaeology tend toward the romantic and the exotic. A public nurtured on television, sound bites, and instant gratification prefers mystical adventure stories of lost civilizations to scientific reality. So archaeologists often fight an uphill battle to convince a wider audience of the value of their work, even if the magazine *Skeptical Inquirer* regularly debunks the more outrageous pseudoarchaeologies. Today's archaeology may be far from exotic and highly technical, but it is still extremely fascinating. This book will give you an understanding of how scientific archaeologists go about their work and of the ways in which they strive to reconstruct the past.

Archaeology, Anthropology, and History

Anthropology is the scientific study of humanity in the widest possible sense. Anthropologists study human beings as biological organisms with a unique characteristic—culture. They carry out research on human development, both biological and cultural, from the very earliest to contemporary times. This enormous field is divided into the subdisciplines listed in the Doing Archaeology box.

Many of the archaeologist's objectives are the same as those of the cultural anthropologist; the main difference is that archaeologists study ancient societies. For example, archaeologist Payson Sheets has excavated an ancient Maya village at Cerén in El Salvador that was buried in ash by a volcanic eruption in about A.D. 580. His excavations have revealed a Maya settlement so well preserved that he has recovered maize in the gardens around houses and tools that were stored in the rafters of the dwellings (Figure 4.9) (Sheets, 1992). Sheets and his colleagues are studying this long-forgotten community and its people by using the material remains of their lives,

Doing Archaeology

The Subdisciplines of Anthropology

Archaeology is part of anthropology, which itself comprises many overlapping subdisciplines and specialties. Here are the major ones:

- **Physical anthropology** involves the study of human biological evolution and the variations among different living human populations. Physical anthropologists also study the behavior of other living primates, such as the chimpanzee and the gorilla, research that can suggest explanations for behavior among the earliest human beings.
- **Cultural anthropology** deals with the analysis of human social life, both past and present. It is pri-

marily a study of human culture and how cultures adapt to the environment. Cultural anthropology involves a number of specialties:

- **Ethnography** describes the culture, technology, and economic life of living and extinct societies.
- **Ethnology** entails comparative studies of societies, a process that involves attempts to reconstruct general principles of human behavior.
- **Social anthropology** analyzes social organization, the ways in which people organize themselves.
- **Linguistics** is the study of language. Many early archaeologists were deeply concerned with such major problems as the origins of the Indo-Europeans, speakers of primeval European languages (Renfrew, 1987).

for, unlike ethnologists, they cannot talk to their subjects. One could describe an archaeologist as a special type of anthropologist, one who studies the past. This definition is somewhat inadequate, however, for archaeologists use many theoretical frameworks to link their excavated evidence to actual human behavior and do far more than merely use data different from that used by cultural anthropologists.

Archaeology and Prehistory

The term **archaeology** originally embraced the study of ancient history as a whole, but the word was gradually narrowed to its present definition: the study of material remains and human cultures using archaeological theory and techniques. **Prehistory** refers to the period of human history extending back before the time of written documents and encompasses the enormous span of human cultural evolution that extends back at least 2.5 million years.

Archaeology and History

Archaeology is our primary source of information for 99 percent of human history. Written history describes less than one-tenth of 1 percent of that enormous time span. Although written records extend back 5,000 years in southwestern Asia, the earlier portions of that period are but dimly illuminated by available documents. In other parts of the world, prehistory ended much later. Continuous written history in Britain began with the Roman conquest some 2,000 years ago; the ancient Maya of Mesoamerica (the area of Central America where civilizations emerged) developed a complex written script centuries before Spanish contact. European explorers reached the interior of East and Central Africa only in the mid-nineteenth century A.D. Parts of New Guinea and the Amazon basin in South America are still largely outside the scope of written history.

Documentary history contrasts sharply with archaeology. First, historians work with accurate chronologies. They can date an event with certainty to within a year, possibly even as closely as to the minute or the second. Second, their history is that of individuals, groups, governments, and even several nations interacting with each other, reacting to events, and struggling for power. They are able to glimpse the subtle interplay of human intellects, for their principal players have often recorded their impressions or deeds on paper. But the historian's record often has gaps. Details of political events are likely to be far more complete than those of day-to-day existence or the trivia of village life, which often mattered little to contemporary observers. Such minor details of past human behavior, reflected in abandoned artifacts and food remains, come to light in archaeological excavations that can provide astonishing detail on the lives of anonymous, humble folk living in crowded city neighborhoods or on slave plantations (Orser, 2004).

Archaeologists build theories and apply scientific techniques and theoretical concepts in studying the material remains of human culture (Renfrew and Bahn, 2004; Sharer and Ashmore, 2002; Thomas, 2003). They study all of human history, from the time of the earliest human beings up to the present. To understand what archaeology involves requires some knowledge of the material evidence we examine. As we shall see in Chapter 4, some raw materials survive much longer than others. Stone and clay vessels are nearly indestructible; wood, skin, metals, and bone are much more friable. In most archaeological sites, only the most durable remains of human material culture are preserved for the archaeologist to study. Any picture of life in ancient times derived from archaeological investigations is likely to be very one-sided. As a result, the unfortunate archaeologist is like a detective fitting together a complicated collection of clues to give a general impression and explanation of prehistoric culture and society. Often, it can be like taking a handful of miscellaneous objects—say, two spark plugs, a fragment of a china cup, a needle, a grindstone, and a candleholder—and trying to reconstruct, on the basis of these objects alone, the culture of the people who made these diverse objects.

Some people think that archaeology is an assortment of techniques, such as accurate recording, precise excavation, and detailed laboratory analysis. This narrow definition, however, deals only with "doing archaeology," the actual work of recovering data from the soil. Modern archaeology is far more than a combination of techniques. It involves not only recovering, ordering, and describing things from the past but also interpreting the evidence from the earth. In fact, it is an interactive discipline that strikes a balance between practical excavation and description and theoretical interpretation.

Theory in Archaeology

The word **theory** has many uses among social scientists. In archaeology it is the overall framework within which a scholar operates. Theory is still little developed in archaeology, as in the other social sciences, partly because working with variable human behavior is difficult and also because of inadequate research methods. Truly interactive archaeology is a constant dialogue between theory and observation, a more or less self-critical procedure that is very much based on inferences about the past, in turn built on phenomena found in the contemporary world. Theoretical approaches to archaeology are numerous; among them are the following:

- **Cultural materialism** seeks the causes behind sociocultural diversity in the modern world. Thus technoeconomic and technoenvironmental conditions exert selective pressures on society and its ideologies (M. Harris, 1968). Cultural materialism is closely associated with the teachings of Engels and Marx. It is especially attractive to archaeologists because it stresses technology, economy, and environment, for these kinds of data survive in the archaeological record. Many archaeologists would probably consider themselves cultural materialists (Chapter 3).
- **Ecological approaches** stress the study of ancient societies within their natural environments (Chapter 15). They are fundamental to contemporary archaeology.
- **Evolutionary approaches** have been popular in archaeology since the nineteenth century. The concepts that form multilinear cultural evolution are inextricable from modern archaeological research (Chapter 3).
- **Functional approaches** (**functionalism**) have long been prevalent in archaeology, the belief that a social institution within a society has a function within society as a whole. Such thinking is important to archaeologists who think of human cultures as systems made up of many interacting parts (Chapter 6).
- **Structural approaches** treat human cultures as shared symbolic structures that are cumulative creations of the human mind. Structural analyses are designed to discover the universal principles of the human mind, an approach associated in particular with famed French anthropologist Claude Lévi-Strauss. The difficulty with this approach is that the intangibles of the human mind are difficult to verify from the archaeological record (Chapter 3).

Much of archaeological research and theory are strongly influenced by contributions made by people in other academic disciplines, such as specialists in other fields of anthropology and in biology, chemistry, geography, history, physics, and computer technology.

The Diversity of Archaeologists

Because no one could possibly be expert in the entire time span of archaeology, most archaeologists specialize, pursuing one of the following major specialties.

Prehistoric archaeologists (prehistorians) study prehistoric times, from the time of the earliest human beings up to the frontiers of documentary history. Their dozens of specialties include **paleoanthropology,** which is studied by experts in the culture and artifacts of the earliest human beings. Other prehistorians are authorities in stone technology, studying the early peopling of the world and the lifeways of prehistoric hunter-gatherers. Those who specialize in the origins of agriculture and literate civilization work with pottery, domesticated grains, animal bones, and a wide range of site types and economic lifeways.

Figure 1.9   The Parthenon in Athens. Recent classical research pays close attention to the social, political, and economic contexts of ancient architecture.

Modern prehistoric archaeology covers the globe. Our knowledge of human prehistory today was gathered by hundreds of archaeologists working in all parts of the world, on small problems or large ones, on a regional survey or a ten-year excavation at one settlement. And, of course, some prehistorians are experts on soil analysis, ancient animal bones, computer applications and statistical methods in archaeology, or simply excavation itself.

Classical archaeology is the study of the remains of the great classical civilizations of Greece and Rome (Figure 1.9). Traditionally, classical archaeologists have paid much attention to art objects and buildings, but many are now beginning to study the types of economic, settlement, and social problems of interest to prehistoric archaeologists that are discussed in this book (Snodgrass, 1987; Soren and James, 1988).

Egyptologists and Assyriologists are among the many specialists who work on specific civilizations or time periods. These specialties require unusual skills. **Egyptologists** must acquire a fluent knowledge of hieroglyphs to help them study the ancient Egyptians, and **Assyriologists,** experts on the Assyrians of ancient Iraq, must be conversant with cuneiform script.

Historical archaeology is the study of archaeological sites from periods from which written records exist. Historical archaeologists examine medieval cities, such as Winchester and York in England; they excavate colonial American settlements

Figure 1.10 Foundations for the Public Hospital for the Insane at Colonial Williamsburg, Virginia, which were revealed by meticulous excavation in 1972.

(Figure 1.10), Spanish missions, and nineteenth-century forts in the U.S. West; and they study a range of historical artifacts, from bottles to uniform buttons (Orser, 2004).

Historical archaeology is concerned with the study of ancient material culture, for artifacts and technology can tell us a great deal about the diversity of historic societies. Much text-aided archaeology is a multidisciplinary enterprise; an example is the long-term research projects conducted in the historic district of Annapolis, Maryland. The excavations in the city have investigated a tavern, eighteenth-century residences, and many other sites, including a lot now occupied by a modern hotel. This property has yielded bottles, cups, and plates dating to about 1690, when the site was first occupied (Yentsch, 1994). The archaeologists revealed intricate layers of occupation, including a timber house of the early 1700s. Governor Calvert's brick house, the first floor of which now forms part of the modern hotel, was subsequently built on the same site in the 1720s. Most of this structure was drastically rebuilt in the nineteenth century, but the walls were preserved within the Victorian building. The excavations also revealed a brick heating system for channeling hot air to a greenhouse. This was partly torn up in the 1760s and filled with domestic refuse before being covered over by an addition to the 1720 house. The refuse proved a rich treasure trove for the archaeologist; it included bones, pins, buttons, hair, pieces of paper, cloth, and fish scales.

Anne Yentsch's Calvert House investigations are important because she attempted to move past the study of mere artifacts to the study of the complex culture in the house, where rich and poor, free and enslaved, men and women, lived in close juxtaposition. European cities like Winchester and York offer magnificent opportunities to combine historical records such as title deeds with excavations, making it possible to identify the owners of individual medieval houses (Keene, 1985).

Historical records can also be important in telling us about societies that had limited written records. Classic Maya civilization, which flourished in Mesoamerica between about A.D. 200 and 900, had developed a complex writing system. With it, the Maya could record religious, political, and astronomical events with elaborate glyphs sculpted on stone and wood and set down in large books. Although still only partly deciphered, these records are revealing the hitherto unknown political history of the Maya (Schele and Friedel, 1990; Schele and Miller, 1992).

Underwater archaeology is the study of sites and ancient shipwrecks on the seafloor and lake bottoms, even sunken fur-trading canoes capsized by rapids in Minnesota streams (Bass, 1970, 1988; Gould, 2000). Scuba-diving archaeologists have an array of specialist techniques for recording and excavating these underwater sites. There is a tendency to think of underwater archaeology as something different, but in fact it is not. The objectives of such archaeology remain the same: the reconstruction and interpretation of past cultures and the scientific study, through material remains, of all aspects of ancient human endeavor, in this case, seafaring. Some modern underwater excavations, such as the investigation of the Bronze Age Uluburun ship off southern Turkey (Figure 1.11) and the reconstruction of the Kyrenia ship from northern Cyprus, are superb examples of scientific archaeology (Steffy, 1994).

Figure 1.11   Recovering copper ingots from the Bronze Age shipwreck at Uluburun, off southern Turkey. The ship, dating from the fourteenth century B.C., contained objects from all over southwestern Asia, testifying to the international nature of eastern Mediterranean trade at the time.

Biblical archaeology is the study of the archaeology of a variety of ethnic groups living in Syro-Palestine, linking accounts in the Bible and Canaanite literature with archaeological sites in southwestern Asia. This complex specialization requires a detailed knowledge not only of history and several languages but of archaeology as well (R. L. Harris, 1995).

Industrial archaeologists study buildings and other structures dating to the Industrial Revolution or later, such as Victorian railway stations, old cotton plantations, windmills, and even slum housing in England (Palmer and Neaverson, 1998). Anyone entering this field needs at least some training as an architectural historian.

These are but a few of the specialties in archaeology. The modern science is so complex as to have experts in dozens of aspects of the subject, from mouse bones to soil profiles to techniques in ancient metallurgy. All are unified by their common interest in studying humanity in the past.

The Goals of Archaeology

Whether they concentrate on the most ancient human societies or those of more recent centuries, all archaeologists agree that their fundamental responsibility is to conserve the past for future generations. Their work has five broad goals:

1. Conserving and managing the world's archaeological sites for the future.
2. Studying sites and their contents in a context of time and space to reconstruct and describe long sequences of human culture. This descriptive activity reconstructs culture history.
3. Reconstructing past lifeways.
4. Explaining why cultures change or why cultures remain the same over long periods of time.
5. Understanding sites, artifacts, food remains, and other aspects of the archaeological record and their relation to our contemporary world.

By no means would every archaeologist agree that all five of these objectives are equally valid or, indeed, that they should coexist. In practice, however, each objective usually complements the others, especially when archaeologists design their research to answer specific questions rather than merely dig as a precursor to describing rows of excavated objects.

All archaeologists follow a code of professional ethics, summarized in the Doing Archaeology box, when carrying out any form of field or laboratory research.

Stewardship

Stewardship is the fundamental responsibility of all archaeologists—to ensure the conservation and survival of the finite archaeological record of artifacts and sites for posterity. In recent years, the crisis of looting and destruction that threatens archaeology has made this the most pressing and demanding of all archaeological activities, known as **cultural resource management (CRM)** (Chapter 18).

Doing Archaeology

An Archaeologist's Ethical Responsibilities

Professional archaeologists live by multiple formal and informal codes of ethics that govern the ways in which they go about their business. The Society for American Archaeology's code is simple and to the point (Lynott and Wylie, 2000). It expects professional archaeologists to do the following:

- Practice and promote the stewardship of the archaeological record for the benefit of all people.
- Consult effectively with all groups affected by their work and be sensitive to the values of other cultures.

- Avoid activities that enhance the commercial value of archaeological objects that are not readily available for scientific study or cared for in public institutions.
- Educate the public in the importance of their findings and enhance public understanding of the past.
- Publish their findings in a widely accessible form.
- Preserve their collections, records, and reports properly, as part of a permanent record of the past for future generations. They must also allow other archaeologists access to their research materials within any legal or other compelling restrictions.
- Never undertake research without adequate training, experience, and facilities to complete the task at hand.

Culture History

The expression **culture history** means, quite simply, the description of human cultures extending thousands of years into the past. An archaeologist working on the culture history of an area describes the prehistoric cultures of that region. Culture history is derived from the study of sites and the artifacts and structures in them in a temporal and spatial context. By investigating groups of prehistoric sites and the many artifacts in them, archaeologists can erect local and regional sequences of human cultures that extend over centuries, even millennia (Chapters 3 and 10). Most of the activity is descriptive, accumulating minute chronological and spatial frameworks of archaeological data as a basis for observing how particular cultures evolved and changed through prehistoric times. Culture history is an essential preliminary to any work on lifeways or cultural process.

Many archaeologists who work on culture history feel inhibited by poor preservation of artifacts and sites about making inferences on the more intangible aspects of human prehistory, such as religion and social organization. They argue that archaeologists can legitimately deal only with the material remains of ancient human behavior. Unfortunately, this rather narrow view of culture history has sent many people off in unproductive directions, into a long and painstaking preoccupation with artifact types and local chronologies that has turned much of archaeology into a glorified type of classification.

Past Lifeways

The study of past lifeways—the ways in which people made their living in the changing environments of the past—has developed into a major goal in recent years. To study artifacts and structures without environmental context gives a one-sided view of humanity and its adaptations to the environment. Studying past lifeways is a multi-disciplinary enterprise, reconstructing ancient subsistence patterns from animal bones, carbonized seeds, and other food residues recovered in meticulous excavation. Pollen analysts, soil scientists, and botanists cooperate in looking at archaeological sites in a much wider, multidisciplinary context. The context of such studies is still de-scriptive archaeology, preoccupied with space and time, but the emphasis is different: it is on changing patterns of human settlement, subsistence strategies, and ancient environments.

As long ago as 1948, Gordon Willey surveyed in detail the coastal Virú Valley in Peru, where he plotted the distributions of hundreds of prehistoric sites from different chronological periods against the valley's changing environment (Willey, 1953). This was a pioneer attempt at reconstructing prehistoric patterns of settlement, obviously a key part in any attempts to reconstruct prehistoric lifeways.

This goal of archaeology is still descriptive, within a theoretical framework that sees human cultures as complicated, ever-changing systems. These systems interact with one another and with the natural environment as well.

Cultural Process

A third archaeological goal seeks to explain the processes of culture change in the past, topics that we explore more fully in Chapter 3. The ultimate goal is to explain why human cultures in all parts of the world reached their various stages of cultural evolu-tion. Human tools are seen as part of a system of related phenomena that include both culture and the natural environment. Archaeologists design their research work within a framework of testable propositions that may be supported, modified, or rejected when they review all of the excavated and analyzed archaeological data.

This processual approach to archaeology (Chapter 3) is based on an assumption that the past is inherently knowable, provided that rigorous research methods and de-signs are used and that field methods are impeccable. It follows that archaeology is more than a descriptive science and that archaeologists can explain cultural change in the past (Binford, 2001).

Understanding the Archaeological Record

"The archaeological record is here with us in the present," wrote Lewis Binford (2001:2). He emphasized how much a part of the contemporary world the artifacts and sites that make up the remains of our past are. Our observations about the past are made today, for we are describing sites and artifacts as they come from the soil today, centuries, often millennia, after they were abandoned. In this way, the archaeologist differs from the historian, who reads a document written by a contemporary observer in, say, 1492, which conveys information that has not changed since that year. The ar-chaeological record is made up of material things and arrangements of material objects in the soil. The only way we can understand this record is by knowing something about how the individual finds came into being. Binford likens archaeological data to a kind of untranslated language that has to be decoded if we are to make statements about human behavior in the past. "The challenge that archaeology offers, then, is to take contemporary observations of static material things and, quite literally, translate them into statements about the dynamics of past ways of life and about the conditions in the past" (Binford, 2001:3). Archaeologists cannot study the past directly but must consider it with reference to the present. For this reason, controlled experiments, observations of contemporary hunter-gatherers and horticulturalists, and the formulation that Binford and others call "middle-range theory" are vital to archaeologists (Chapters 3 and 14).

Wherever they work, all archaeologists, of whatever viewpoint, would agree that we cannot hope to carry out archaeological research without sound theory, good descriptive techniques, and detailed information from both the contemporary world and prehistoric lifeways. Above all, the present and the phenomena of the world we live in are there to help us achieve better understanding of the major issues in the human past:

- What were our earliest ancestors like, and when did they come into being? How old is "human" behavior, and when did such phenomena as language evolve? What distinguishes our behavior from that of other animals?
- How and when did humanity people the globe? How can we account for human biological and cultural diversity?
- Under what conditions, and when and how, did human beings domesticate animals and plants, becoming sedentary farmers?
- What caused complex societies—the urban societies from which our own industrial civilization grew—to evolve?
- Last, a long-neglected question: How did the expansion of Western civilization affect the hunter-gatherer, agricultural, and even urban states of the world that it encountered after classical times?

In the Beginning is not meant to describe these major developments in human prehistory (Fagan, 2004; Price and Feinman, 2004). Rather, it summarizes the multitude of methods and theoretical approaches that archaeologists have used to gain a better understanding of our long past.

Summary

Modern archaeology is the scientific study of past cultures and technologies—whether ancient or recent—by scientific methods and theoretical concepts devised for that purpose.

Archaeology covers the human past, from the earliest to modern times. The discipline had its origins in treasure hunting and grave robbing, but it has evolved into a highly precise science. It has become an integral part of twentieth-century life as a component of popular culture and modern intellectual curiosity.

Archaeology provides the only viable means of discovering the history of many of the world's societies whose documented past began in recent times. As such, it is a vital support for nationalist feeling and for fostering cultural identity.

Archaeologists have major contributions to make to the resolution of modern land disputes and to modern management of resources.

The destruction of sites, fostered by greedy collectors and industrial development, is the crisis that archaeology is faced with today. Archaeological sites are a finite resource that can never be replaced. If the present rate of destruction continues, the danger is real that few undisturbed archaeological sites will remain by the end of this century.

Archaeologists also face a challenge from people who promote "pseudoarchaeologies" purporting to explain the past, such as extravagant theories that ancient Egyptians or Phoenicians landed in the New World thousands of years before Columbus.

Archaeology is part of the science of anthropology, which is the study of humanity in the widest possible sense. Archaeologists use a battery of special methods and techniques to examine human societies of the past.

There are many types of archaeologists. Prehistoric archaeologists study prehistory, that is, human history before written records; historical archaeologists use archaeology to supplement documentary history; and classical archaeologists study ancient Greece and Rome.

Modern archaeology has five basic goals: stewardship (conserving and managing archaeological sites), studying culture history, reconstructing past lifeways, explaining cultural process, and understanding the archaeological record as it relates to the contemporary world.

Key Terms

anthropology
archaeology
Assyriologist
biblical archaeology
classical archaeology
cultural anthropology
cultural materialism
cultural resource management
  (CRM)
culture history

ecological approach
Egyptologist
ethnography
ethnology
evolutionary approach
functional approach
  (functionalism)
historical archaeology
industrial archaeology
linguistics

paleoanthropology
physical anthropology
prehistoric archaeologists
  (prehistorians)
prehistory
social anthropology
stewardship
structural approach
theory
underwater archaeology

Guide to Further Reading

These books may be helpful as general reading about archaeology today, but we advise you to consult a specialist before starting on them:

BINFORD, LEWIS R. 2001. *In Pursuit of the Past.* Rev ed. Berkeley: University of California Press. A closely argued essay on archaeology that integrates ethnoarchaeology with the archaeological record. Recommended for more advanced readers. This new edition has a chapter by the author updating the original book.

BINTCLIFF, JOHN, ed. 2004. *A Companion to Archaeology.* Oxford: Blackwell. A collection of authoritative advanced essays on contemporary archaeology, which give a good impression of the discipline and its problems.

FAGAN, BRIAN M. 1995. *Time Detectives.* New York: Simon & Schuster. A popular book on archaeology that shows how science and archaeology interact.

FEDER, KENNETH L. 2001. *Frauds, Myths, and Mysteries.* 4th ed. New York: McGraw-Hill. A useful survey of the phenomenon of pseudoarchaeology.

LYNOTT, MARK, and ALISON WYLIE. 2000. *Ethics in American Archaeology.* 2d ed. Washington, DC: Society for American Archaeology. A discussion of ethics that belongs in every archaeologist's library.

ORSER, CHARLES E. 2004. *Historical Archaeology.* Upper Saddle River, NJ: Prentice Hall. An introduction to the basic principles of historical archaeology with many case examples.

RENFREW, COLIN, and PAUL BAHN. 2004. *Archaeology: Theories, Methods, and Practice.* 4th ed. New York: Thames and Hudson. A superb handbook of archaeological method and theory, comprehensively illustrated.

SCARRE, CHRIS, ed. 1988. *Past Worlds: The Times Atlas of Archaeology.* London: Times Books. A definitive atlas of ancient times, from human origins to historic times.

THOMAS, DAVID HURST. 2003. *Archaeology: Down to Earth.* 3d ed. New York: Harcourt Brace. An excellent introduction, especially to North American archaeology.

PART II

A Short History of Archaeology

Sixth Century B.C. Through A.D. 2000

The long-term future of archaeology should be in flows and networks rather than dichotomies and boundaries.

Ian Hodder, *The Archaeological Process, 1999*

Is it too late for salvation? If not, please let me have the analytical expertise of the New Archaeology—and the humility and common sense of the Old.

Kent V. Flannery, *The Early Mesoamerican Village, 1976*

No one can fully understand modern scientific archaeology without having some notion of its roots. The first archaeologists were little more than collectors and antiquarians who were searching for curiosities, buried treasure, and intellectual enlightenment. These treasure hunters were the predecessors of the early professionals, scholars who concentrated on site description and believed that human society evolved through simple stages, the final stage being modern civilization. Since World War II, archaeology has undergone a major transformation, from a basically descriptive discipline into a many-sided activity that tries to understand how human cultures changed and evolved in the past. If there is one major lesson to be learned from the history of archaeology, it is that no development in the field took place in isolation. Innovations in many other disciplines, including geology, cultural anthropology, and computer science, resulted in changes in the way archaeology was carried out in the field and, more importantly, how researchers thought about the past.

CHAPTER 2

The Beginnings of Scientific Archaeology

Sixth Century B.C. to the 1950s

Exploring the past, nineteenth-century style. French collectors brave the marshes of Cambodia to loot ancient sculptures.

Archaeologists have come a long way from the pith-helmeted professors and adventurers of cartoon and movie fame, though such characters do have their place in the history of archaeology. The great nineteenth-century archaeologists destroyed ancient cities in their reckless digging in search of the spectacular. Englishman Austen Henry Layard (1849) dug tunnels through Assyrian Nineveh. Heinrich Schliemann (1875) employed engineers who had worked on the Suez Canal to advise him on earth moving at Troy. Until the 1920s, archaeological training was highly informal, at best a short apprenticeship working alongside experienced diggers. Excavators like Leonard Woolley (1929) at Ur in Iraq or Alfred Kidder (1924) at Pecos, New Mexico, moved more earth in a week than their modern counterparts would do in over a month.

As are all scholarly disciplines, today's archaeology is a product of its own history and of the intellectual climate in which it emerged (Trigger, 1989). This chapter examines the early development of archaeology from its beginnings in the philosophical speculations of the Greeks to the advent of radiocarbon dating and theories of cultural ecology in the 1950s. We see how archaeology began as little more than treasure hunting and how successive innovations led archaeologists in new directions, away from simple description toward multilinear cultural evolutionary frameworks for ancient times.

Beginnings

People have speculated about human origins and the remote past for thousands of years. As early as the eighth century B.C., the Greek philosopher Hesiod wrote about a glorious, heroic past of kings and warriors. He described five great ages of history; the earliest one of Gold was a time when people "dwelt in ease." The last was an Age of War, when everyone worked hard and suffered great sorrow (Daniel, 1981).

Speculations of this type were widespread in classical and early Chinese writings. New Kingdom officials in ancient Egypt restored and conserved Old Kingdom monuments from 1,000 years earlier, and King Nabonidus of Babylon dug into the temples of his predecessors in search of antiquities that he displayed in his palace.

During the Renaissance, people of wealth and leisure began to travel in Greece and Italy, studying antiquities and collecting examples of classical art. These **antiquarians,** although interested in the past, conducted their activities in a haphazard, unscientific manner. Their real concern was the objects they recovered to add to their collections, not the context in which the artifacts were found or what the finds might tell them about the past. The first crude archaeological excavations were made into the depths of the Roman city of Herculaneum in 1783, one of several Roman settlements buried by mud and ash from the eruption of Vesuvius in A.D. 79 (Ceram, 1953). At Pompeii, another Roman town destroyed in the eruption, the choking ash preserved the bodies of people fleeing the eruption in panic (Figure 2.1). These early excavations—really little more than treasure hunts—recovered a wealth of classical Roman statuary and also revealed incredible details of life in ancient Rome.

Wealthy collectors toured the Mediterranean, visiting the ruins of ancient Greece and Rome and bringing back classical sculptures for their country estates. These finds—and the people that made them—were, at least in part, known through the writings of classical scholars. There were some discoveries, however, that hinted at a prehistoric past. In Britain and Europe the less wealthy antiquaries stayed at home and speculated about ancient European history and about the builders of burial mounds, fortifications, and occasionally more spectacular monuments such as Stonehenge in southern

Figure 2.1 Body of a beggar smothered by volcanic ash outside the Nucerian Gate at Pompeii, Italy.

Figure 2.2   Stonehenge, the Bronze Age ceremonial center in southern England that was an early focus of antiquarian interest.

England (Figure 2.2). When were such structures built? Had the builders resembled the American Indians, South Sea islanders, and other living nonliterate peoples?

There was only one way to find out—excavate ancient sites. These chaotic excavations yielded a mass of stone and bronze axes, strange clay pots, gold ornaments, and skeletons buried with elaborate grave goods (Figure 2.3). This jumble was confusing.

Figure 2.3   A nineteenth-century British burial mound excavation as depicted in *Gentleman's Magazine,* 1840. "Eight barrows were examined. . . . Most of them contained skeletons, more or less entire, with the remains of weapons in iron, bosses of shields, urns, beads, brooches, armlets, bones, amulets, and occasionally more vessels."

Some graves contained gold and bronze; others held only stone implements; and still others housed cremated remains in large urns. Many questions were unanswered: Which burials were earliest? Who had deposited the bodies, and how long ago? Such finds were attributed to historically documented peoples or the work of elves, trolls, or witches. No one yet had a way of putting in order the thousands of years of prehistoric times that preceded the Greeks, Romans, and ancient Egyptians of biblical fame (Daniel, 1981; Trigger, 1989).

Scriptures and Fossils

One reason early archaeologists were confused was that they had no idea how long people had been living on the earth. There were no dating techniques such as dendrochronology (tree-ring chronology) or carbon-14 that are used today (Chapter 7). In Western cultures, most people believed that Genesis, Chapter 1, provided a literal account of the Creation. God had created the world and its inhabitants in six days. The story of Adam and Eve provided both an explanation for the origin of humankind and the peopling of the world. In the seventeenth century, various clergymen used the genealogies in the Old Testament to calculate when the world had been created. However, the date reached by Archbishop James Ussher of Ireland (1581–1656) became the most pervasive, and it eventually appeared in the margin of the King James version of the Bible (Grayson, 1983). According to Ussher the world had been created on the night preceding October 23, 4004 B.C., which allowed approximately six thousand years for all of human history.

Yet new geological, anthropological, and archaeological discoveries began to cast doubt on biblical chronologies. The geological record presented evidence of gradual change over long periods of time though natural processes. The bones of extinct species of animals, such as the ancestors of the elephant and the hippopotamus, came from the gravels of European rivers, some in the same strata as carefully chipped stone axes of obvious human manufacture (Figure 2.4). But until the 1860s, the shackles of

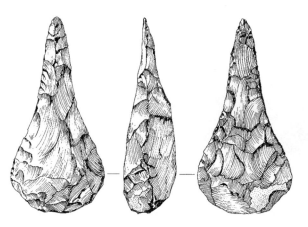

Figure 2.4   A stone hand ax of the type found in the same geological layers as the bones of extinct animals. This example was discovered by John Frere at Hoxne, England, in 1797.

theological dogma confined human existence within a few millennia, and the idea of a prehistoric past stretching back thousands of years went unrecognized.

At the same time antiquarians were digging into European burial mounds, Captain James Cook and other Western navigators were exploring the Americas and the Pacific, bringing back new information about all manner of societies very different from contemporary European society. Some, such as Native Americans, still used stone tools similar to those found in European archaeological sites. Scholars began to put prehistory in a new perspective in terms of human progress over time, from the simple to the more complex. But could all of this progress have occurred within a mere 6,000 years?

The Antiquity of Humankind

The eighteenth century saw an awakening of interest in archaeology, geology, and the natural sciences. A knowledge explosion in science coincided with the Industrial Revolution. Geologists were in the forefront, their field studies stimulated by deep cuts into the earth resulting from vast engineering projects such as railroad and canal building. William "Strata" Smith (1769–1839) was one of many field observers who studied these exposures. He observed that the fossils of different types of animals occurred in the same relative position in different geological outcrops and, in fact, the strata could be placed in the correct order on the basis of the fossils they contained. Notably, he made this observation a half century before Charles Darwin proposed his theory of evolution, which explained why animal species changed through time.

Based on their examinations of the geological record, many geologists felt that the rocks of the earth had been formed by continuous, natural geological processes. Every gale that battered the coast, every flash flood or sandstorm, and every earthquake were among the natural phenomena that had gradually shaped the earth into its modern form. James Hutton's *Theory of the Earth* (1784) was among the first works to convincingly argue that the earth was formed entirely by natural processes, not by divine floods of global proportion that earlier scientists had considered the nemesis of long-extinct animals. His work was later refined by Charles Lyell, whose book *Principles of Geology* (1833) was very influential.

Hutton's and Lyell's theories of what became known as **uniformitarianism** caused a furor, for their arguments that the earth had been formed by long-term natural processes and not by divine intervention contradicted a literal reading of biblical chronology. If one accepted these new theories, one also accepted the notion that humankind had lived on the earth for many thousands of years before written history. The debate over the antiquity of humankind culminated in 1859 with two major scientific developments: the publication of Charles Darwin's theory of evolution and natural selection and the verification of the contemporaneity of humans and extinct animals.

Charles Darwin began to formulate his theories as a result of a five-year scientific voyage around the world aboard the HMS *Beagle* in 1831–1836 on which he witnessed firsthand the incredible biological diversity of the world. Back in England,

Darwin delved more deeply into what he called the "species question." He was influenced by the work of Thomas Malthus, a nineteenth-century clergyman and economist who observed that a basic principle of nature was that most living creatures produced far more offspring than could be expected to survive and reproduce. Darwin realized that the characteristics of some individuals within a population would give them increased reproductive success, which in turn, would lead to change in the characteristics of the population as a whole. This selective force is the basis of natural selection and a principal mechanism through which new species emerge.

Darwin realized that his theory would imply that accumulated favorable variations in living organisms over long periods must result in the emergence of new species and the extinction of old ones. Darwin was a meticulous researcher and a retiring man, and he delayed publishing his results. Evolution, even more than uniformitarianism, flew in the face of the sacrosanct interpretation of the account of the Creation in Genesis. He sat on his ideas for twenty years until another naturalist (a term used at the time for biologists), Alfred Wallace, sent him an essay that reached the same conclusions. Reluctantly, Darwin penned a "preliminary sketch," as he called it, in 1859—*On the Origin of Species*.

This scientific classic described evolution and natural selection, providing a theoretical explanation for the diversity of both living and fossil species. Evolution by natural selection does not entirely explain biological phenomena, but it does provide a mechanism for biological change through time. Darwin's theories horrified many people by assuming that human beings were descended from apelike ancestors (Figure 2.5). But the basis for his conclusions and the evidence for evolution steadily accumulated, and Darwin's theories were soon widely accepted by the scientific community. They formed a theoretical background for some important contemporary archaeological discoveries (Van Riper, 1993).

Figure 2.5   A period cartoon by Thomas Nast lampooning Darwin's linking apes to human beings.

Discovery

The Somme Hand Axes, 1859

British antiquarian John Evans was a remarkable individual by any standard. A successful papermaker, he was the epitome of the Victorian businessman and believed in "Peace, Prosperity, and Papermaking" (Joan Evans, 1943). He was also a highly respected member of the scientific establishment with an impressive expertise in geology, coins, and prehistoric artifacts of all kinds. Evans and his geologist friend Joseph Prestwich were prominent members of a Royal Society committee that had supervised excavations at Brixham cave in southwestern England in 1858, where the bones of Ice Age animals lay alongside ancient stone tools. The society heard reports of de Perthes's finds and organized a party to visit him; however, Evans and Prestwich were the only committee members who went.

After a rough sea crossing, they arrived in Abbeville in the Somme Valley and inspected the voluble de Perthes's extensive collection of stone tools and fossil animal bones. After a sumptuous lunch, de Perthes took his visitors on a tour of the nearby gravel quarries. Evans and Prestwich collected axes and bones, but it was not until Evans actually removed an ancient hand ax from the same sealed level as a hippopotamus bone that they realized that de Perthes was correct. They returned to London convinced that the Somme gravels held proof of a great antiquity for humankind, something that the new theories of uniformitarianism and evolution made intellectually possible.

With characteristic Victorian industry, Evans and Prestwich prepared an immediate report for the Royal Society in which they proclaimed their support for the antiquity of humankind. All research into early human prehistory has stemmed from Evans and Prestwich's day in France a century and a half ago.

Discoveries of human artifacts in association with extinct animals were nothing new by 1859, for many such finds had been reported over the years, mostly at the hands of enthusiastic amateur diggers. One of the most persistent was French customs officer Jacques Boucher de Perthes, who collected stone tools and animal bones from sealed gravels of the Somme River near Abbeville, in northern France, between 1837 and the 1860s. De Perthes was ridiculed by the scientific establishment when he claimed that the makers of his axes had lived before the biblical flood. Rumors of his finds reached the ears of British antiquarian John Evans and geologist Joseph Prestwich. They visited de Perthes and examined his collections and sites. The two scientists were convinced that de Perthes had the proof they were looking for. Acceptance of the long antiquity of humankind followed, an established antiquity that is one of the intellectual and practical foundations of all scientific archaeology (Grayson, 1983) (see the Discovery box).

If the Somme hand axes and other such finds were of great antiquity, who were the people who had manufactured and used them? Were they modern-looking humans or apelike beings that were closer to apes than people? A piece of what became an increasingly complex picture of human origins came to light in a cave near Düsseldorf in Germany's Neanderthal ("Neander Valley") region in 1856, when quarry workers unearthed a primitive-looking human skull. It had a huge, beetling brow ridge and a squat skull cap that were quite unlike the smooth, rounded cranium of modern *Homo sapiens*. Many scientists dismissed the Neanderthal skull as that of a modern pathological idiot. But a minority, among them the celebrated English biologist Thomas Huxley (1863), believed that the skull was from a primitive human being, perhaps one of those who had made early stone tools. Scientists were finally realizing that humanity had evolved both biologically and culturally over a very long period of time indeed.

The Three-Age System

The spectacular social and economic changes during the nineteenth century generated much interest in human progress. As early as the late sixteenth century, some antiquarians were writing about prehistoric ages of stone, bronze, and iron (Daniel, 1962). Two centuries later, these general concepts were refined by Danish archaeologist Christian Jurgensen Thomsen (1788–1865), curator of the National Museum in Copenhagen, into the famous **Three-Age System** in the early nineteenth century (Gräslund 1981). He ordered the confusing collection of artifacts from bogs, burial chambers, and shell middens by classifying them into three groups, representing ages of stone, bronze, and iron, and using finds in previously undisturbed graves as a basis for his classification.

Thomsen's classification was taken up by another Dane, J. J. A. Worsaae, who proved the system's basic stratigraphic integrity. By studying archaeological finds from all over Europe, Worsaae demonstrated the widespread validity of the Three-Age System (Worsaae, 1843). A technological subdividing of the prehistoric past, this system gave archaeologists a broad context within which their own finds could be placed, a framework for dividing a prehistoric past. The Three-Age System for Old World prehistory, in modified form, survives today (see Figure 7.4).

The Three-Age System of the Scandinavians was not adopted in North America, where almost no ancient metals and no very early sites were found. Subtle changes in stone tool technology were more difficult to discern and, consequently, the past was more difficult to divide into periods. The foundations of accurate stratigraphic and chronological studies in American archaeology were laid by Thomas Jefferson, Harvard archaeologist Frederick W. Putnam in Ohio, and in the classic archaeological laboratory of the Southwest (Willey and Sabloff, 1993).

Human Progress

By the time Charles Darwin wrote *On the Origin of Species,* the Three-Age System had been well established throughout Europe. It was but a short step from the three ages to doctrines of human progress. In 1850, the sociologist Herbert Spencer (1820–1903) was already declaring that "progress is not an accident, but a necessity. It is a fact of nature" (Spencer, 1855). Darwin's theories of evolution seemed to many people a logical extension of the doctrines of social progress. The new theories opened up enormous tracts of prehistoric time for Victorian archaeologists to fill. The oldest finds were de Perthes's crude axes from the Somme Valley. Later in prehistory, apparently, other people started to live in the great caves of southwestern France, at a time when reindeer, not hippopotamuses, were living in western Europe. And the famous "lake dwellings," abandoned prehistoric villages found below the water's edge in the Swiss lakes during the dry years 1853 and 1854, were obviously even more recent than the cave sites of France (Bahn, 1996; Morlot, 1861).

What was the best theoretical framework for all these finds? Could notions of human progress be made to agree with the archaeological record? Did prehistoric peoples' technology, material culture, and society develop and progress uniformly from the crude tools of the Somme Valley to the sophisticated iron technology of the much more recent La Tène culture in Europe? Had cultures evolved naturally along with the biological evolution that lifted humanity through all the stages from savagery to civilization?

Unilinear Cultural Evolution

Early anthropological theory was influenced by several diverse intellectual ideas, including biological evolution, nineteenth-century notions of social progress, and the idea of cultural evolution. A most important influence in the development of anthropology was contact between Western civilization and other human societies with completely different social institutions. Early anthropologists, corresponding as they did with missionaries and pioneer settlers all over the world, argued that Victorian civilization was the pinnacle of human achievement. This perspective, articulated by pioneering anthropologists Sir Edward B. Tylor (1832–1917) and Lewis Henry Morgan (1818–1881), fitted anthropological and archaeological data into set stages through which all human societies progressed is called **unilinear cultural evolution.** According to this view, all human societies had the potential to evolve from a simple hunter-gatherer way of life to a state of literate—European—civilization, which nineteenth-century researchers saw as the end point of this evolutionary progression.

Tylor surveyed human development in all of its forms, from the crude stone axes of the Somme Valley in France to Maya temples and Victorian civilization. The origins of civilized institutions, he argued (1871), might be found in the simpler institutions of "ruder peoples." Tylor (1878) used accounts of contemporary non-Western peoples and archaeological findings to reemphasize a three-level sequence of human development popular with eighteenth- and early nineteenth-century scholars, including Herbert Spencer: from simple hunting ("savagery"), through a stage of simple farming ("barbarism"), to "civilization," the most complex of human conditions.

American anthropologist Lewis Henry Morgan went even farther than Tylor. He outlined no fewer than seven periods of human progress in his famous book *Ancient Society* (1877). Like Tylor, Morgan began with simple savagery and had human society reaching its highest achievements in a "state of civilization." His seven stages, he said, had developed quite rationally and independently in different parts of the world. Morgan's work, with its strong evolutionary bias, was to influence modern North

American archaeology. Even expert scientists turned to the comfortable framework of biological and social evolution to explain the astonishing diversity of humankind.

As archaeological research extended beyond Europe and into the Americas, the incredible diversity in early human experience became visible in the archaeological record. The great civilizations of southwestern Asia were uncovered by Henry Layard and others, and the great Mesoamerican religious complexes were described (see Figure 1.1). Stone Age art was accepted as authentic some years after the Altamira paintings were discovered in northern Spain in 1879 (see the Discovery box). Yet many parts of North America and Africa showed no signs of the early, complex civilizations found in other world areas. Furthermore, the American civilizations and European cave art seemed to imply to nineteenth-century scientists that humanity sometimes "regressed." Scientists became less and less certain that people had a common, consistently progressing universal prehistory.

As more and more information accumulated from all over the world, it became clear that a universal scheme of unilinear cultural evolution was a totally unrealistic and ethnocentric way of interpreting world history.

Diffusion and Diffusionists

As archaeological knowledge blossomed late in the nineteenth century—and in North America, particularly, early in the twentieth—scholars faced many hard questions. What were the origins of human culture? When and where was metallurgy introduced? Who were the first farmers? If people did not develop according to universal evolutionary rules, how, then, did culture change and cultural diversity come about? Archaeologists began to expect that population movements, migrations, and invasions would explain prehistory. Diffusion is the process by which new ideas or cultural traits spread from one person to another or from one group to another, often over long distances.

The **diffusion** of ideas and objects from one people to another was recognized early as a valid explanation for cultural change in prehistory, and it remains an important concept (see discussion in Chapter 3). It was especially popular with late nineteenth-century archaeologists, who reacted against the unilinear models of culture change. They also realized that culture change could be explained by outside influences. Many archaeologists accepted diffusion as the reason why southwestern Asian civilizations had been so much richer than the apparently poor European cultures of the same period. Furthermore, they argued, how could the brilliant American civilizations in Mexico and Peru have arisen, if not by long-distance migration from the civilized centers in southwestern Asia?

Unfortunately, some of these theories took the role of diffusion as an explanation of change too far. Early in the twentieth century, British anatomist Grafton Elliot Smith became obsessed with the techniques of Egyptian mummification, sun worship, and monumental stone architecture. The achievements of ancient Egyptian civilization were so unique, he argued in *The Ancient Egyptians* (1911), that all of world civilization and much of modern Western culture had to have diffused from the Nile Valley. It had been the "People of the Sun" who had produced and disseminated civilization, people

Discovery

The Altamira Cave Paintings, Spain, 1875

Spanish landowner Marcellino de Sautola had a casual interest in archaeology. He had visited an exhibit in Paris of some of the fine ancient stone tools from French caves. In 1875, he decided to dig for some artifacts of his own in the caverns of Altamira on his estate in northern Spain. Sautola's five-year-old daughter, Maria, begged for the chance to dig with him, so he good-naturedly agreed. Maria soon tired of the muddy work and wandered off with a flickering lantern into a low side chamber. Suddenly, he heard cries of "Toros! Toros!" ("Bulls! Bulls!"). Maria pointed excitedly at brightly colored figures of bison and a charging boar on the low ceiling. Daughter and father marveled at the fresh paintings, arranged so cleverly around bulges in the rock

that they seemed to move in the flickering light (Figure 2.6) (Daniel, 1981).

Sautola was convinced the paintings had been executed by the same people who had dropped stone tools in the cave. But the experts laughed at him and accused the marquis of smuggling an artist into Altamira to forge the bison. It was not until 1904 that the now-deceased Sautola was vindicated, when some paintings with strong stylistic links to Altamira came to light in a French cave that had been sealed since the ancient artists worked there.

Altamira was the first evidence that late Ice Age humans had been artists. The debate over the meaning of the paintings continues to this day.

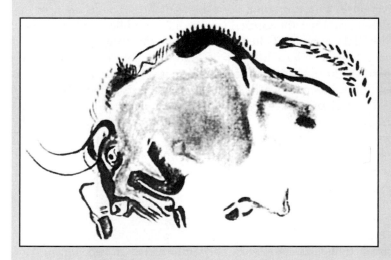

Figure 2.6 Bison in a polychrome cave painting in Altamira, Spain. The Altamira style is the ultimate artistic achievement of the late Ice Age peoples of western Europe, about 12,000 B.C.

who were not afraid of voyaging widely in search of gold, shells, and precious stones. Thus, he argued, sun worship and early civilization spread over the world.

Smith's hyper-diffusionist views of human history grossly oversimplified the past and they were at least as inadequate as unilinear cultural evolution. Nevertheless, hyper-diffusionist theories have remained popular. In their most extreme manifestations, they reach incredible heights of absurdity, as in seeking to prove that Africans colonized America before Columbus or that the Vikings settled Minnesota thousands of years ago (Chapter 1).

Historical Particularism

The first professional archaeologists and anthropologists lived at a time when many non-Western cultures were being erased by the advance of Western, industrialized society. Consequently, they felt an overwhelming priority to collect basic information about these vanishing cultures. These data were an essential preliminary to the theoretical approaches used in archaeology today. American anthropologist Franz Boas (1858–1942) and his students helped establish anthropology—and, by implication, archaeology along with it—as a form of science by applying more precise methods to collecting and classifying data. They collected an incredible amount of data on Native American kinship systems, religion, housing, pottery designs, basketry, and thousands of other cultural details. These were then meticulously studied and used to plot culture areas. This theoretical approach to cultural anthropology is referred to as **historical particularism** (Lyman and others, 1996).

This careful cataloging of cultural data was important, yet historical particularists reached some incorrect conclusions about Native American culture, which were eventually disproved by archaeological research. For instance, ethnologists of this period saw the arrival of the Europeans and their domestic horses as an event of unparalleled importance that caused the Great Plains to become filled with nomadic, horseback-mounted buffalo hunters of the type made familiar to us by Hollywood films. The Plains were thought to have been sparsely populated up to that time. The ethnologists were partly right, for the Plains population did indeed swell rapidly as horses came into use. But subsequent work by such archaeologists as Douglas Strong, who dug at Signal Butte, Nebraska, revealed that the Great Plains had been inhabited by hunter-gatherers and horticulturalists for many hundreds of years before the Europeans and horses turned the Plains into a carnival of nomads on horseback (Strong, 1935). Archaeology, then, became a source of information against which one checked the historical reconstructions produced by ethnologists.

Culture History

Historical particularism influenced how researchers interpreted archaeological data. **Culture history,** the description and chronological and spatial ordering of archaeological data, became the sole objective of archaeological research and it remained so until the 1950s. Researchers dug archaeological sites and established chronological sequences and distributions. Interpretation consisted primarily of description of the diet, technology, migrations, and lifeways of past societies; the discovery of such features remains an important aspect of archaeological research.

The synthesis of site chronologies beyond the confines of one site or local area involves not only repeating the same descriptive processes at other sites but also constantly refining the cultural sequence from the original excavations. This synthesis is cumulative, for some new excavations may yield cultural materials that are not represented in the early digs. It is here that the techniques of seriation and cross-dating come into play (Chapter 7).

The archaeological units used to aid the synthesis form an arbitrary, hierarchical classification. They represent the contents of individual sites and their distribution in time and space. The archaeological units used most widely in the Americas are those developed by Gordon Willey and Philip Phillips (1958); we describe some of them here. Throughout the world, however, the temporal framework of a culture historical approach to the past has been important in providing a means of ordering archaeological data, which can, in turn, serve as a basis for interpretation using a variety of theoretical perspectives.

Components and Phases

Components are the lowest unit in the hierarchy. They consist of a distinct artifact assemblage that distinguishes the culture of the inhabitants of a particular time and place. A site like the colonial village at Martin's Hundred, Virginia, consists of a single component representing a brief seventeenth-century occupation by Anglo-American settlers. Other sites may contain a number of distinct components, each representing a separate cultural phase. The Koster site in Illinois is an excellent example of a multi-component site, with its various layers representing different components separated by sterile layers of soil extending from 7500 B.C. to less than a thousand years ago, including evidence of the first Paleo-Indian inhabitants of the region, seasonal hunter-gatherers, and, finally, a settled, year-round village (Struever and Holton, 1979).

The definition of a component depends on stratigraphic observation, as well as the archaeologist's observational skills. Some cave sites in southwestern France contain many occupation levels, separated by sterile layers, which can be neatly isolated stratigraphically and grouped on the basis of shared artifact types, such as antler harpoons or side scrapers, that are distinctive for a certain time period and region.

Components occur at one location. To produce a regional chronology, archaeologists must synthesize them with components from other sites using the next analytical step, phases.

Phases are cultural units represented by different levels of the same site or like components on different sites, all sharing a distinctive artifact assemblage within a well-defined chronological bracket (Willey and Phillips, 1958). The characteristic assemblage of artifacts of a phase may be found over hundreds of miles within the area covered by a local sequence. Many archaeologists use the term *culture* in the same sense as phase, though it should be emphasized that archaeological cultures cannot, necessarily, be equated with ethnographically delineated cultures. Phases or cultures usually are named after a key site where characteristic artifacts are found. The Magdalenian culture of 16,000 years ago, for example, is named after the southwestern France rock shelter of La Madeleine, where antler harpoons and other artifacts so characteristic of this culture were found.

Some phases are but a few years long; others span centuries, even millennia. The Gatecliff rock shelter in Nevada was occupied for about eight thousand years; it is divided into five components, each defined by distinctive artifact types associated with particular time periods (Thomas, 1983a, 2003). The components can be compared with those from other sites and used to build up a regional chronology. The components from Gatecliff and those from other sites are combined into a phase named Yellow Blade. This period dates from about A.D. 1300 to 1850, the time of European contact. The phase applies not only to Gatecliff but to the entire region, and is the basic unit of area synthesis. At first, a phase may embrace, as the Yellow Blade phase does, five hundred years or more. But as research proceeds, chronologies become more refined, and as artifact classifications become finer, the original phase may be broken down even further into more and more chronologically precise subphases.

Culture Areas

Culture areas can be thought of as the archaeological equivalent of the broad ethnographic culture areas identified by early anthropologists. In the early twentieth century, anthropologist Franz Boas compiled catalogs of the social organization, customs, beliefs, and material culture of Native American groups that were, in turn, used to define culture areas on the basis of their shared similarities. Many areas tend to coincide with the various physiographic divisions of the world. The southwestern United States is one such area, as it is defined in part by its unique history of archaeological research and in part by cultural and environmental characteristics that lasted more than two thousand years.

Such large areas can be broken down into **subareas,** where differences within the culture of an area are sufficiently distinctive to separate one subarea from another. Gordon Willey (1966) divided the American Southwest into the Anasazi, Hohokam, and Mogollon subareas, among others (see Figure 3.1). But the term *area* implies nothing more than a very general and widespread cultural homogeneity. Within any large area, societies will adapt to new circumstances, changing in different ways and developing different economies.

Traditions and Horizons

American archaeologists use two units that synthesize archaeological data over wide areas: horizons and traditions. The term **tradition** is used to describe artifact types, assemblages of tools, architectural styles, economic practices, or art styles that distinguish an area for a long period of time. A tradition extends longer than the occupation of individual sites or phases, and may continue for thousands of years. A good example of a tradition is the Arctic Small Tool tradition of Alaska, which originated at least as early as 4000 B.C. (Dumond, 1987). The characteristic tools made by these early hunter-gatherers were so effective that they continued in use until recent times, and aspects of this tradition can be seen in the modern Eskimo technologies of the Far North.

Horizons are represented by distinctive artifacts and cultural traits that cross-cut traditions in neighboring areas. For example, a religious cult may transcend cultural boundaries and spread over an enormous area. Such cults are often associated with characteristic religious artifacts or art styles that can be identified in phases hundreds of miles apart in well-defined, contemporaneous, chronological contexts. The Chavín art style of coastal Peru, for example, was associated with distinctive religious beliefs and rituals shared by many Peruvian societies in the highlands and lowlands between 900 and 200 B.C. (Moseley, 2000). This commonality of belief is manifested in the archaeological record by Chavín art, a style that stresses exotic, jaguar-like motifs. These unique characteristics are used to define the Early Horizon in Peruvian archaeology.

Culture history remained the dominant approach in archaeology until the 1950s (Lyman and others, 1996). Archaeologists made collecting data a primary objective in both New and Old World archaeology. But archaeology itself evolved somewhat differently on each side of the Atlantic.

Old World Archaeology

The Europeans were studying their prehistoric origins, concentrating on constructing descriptive, historical schemes that traced European society from its hunter-gatherer origins to the threshold of recorded history. The ages of stone, bronze, and iron, of the Three-Age System, were further divided into shorter regional sequences. The earliest sites were the hand-ax sites in the Thames and Somme river valleys, followed by Ice Age cave dwellings in southwestern France that showed that the Neanderthals were succeeded by modern humans with a much more sophisticated hunter-gatherer culture. A similar culture history sequence was postulated for all of Europe and southwestern Asia as well.

The greatest synthesizer of European and southwestern Asian prehistory was Oxford-trained and Australian-born Vere Gordon Childe (1892–1957). A gifted linguist, he acquired an encyclopedic knowledge of the thousands of prehistoric finds in museums from Edinburgh to Cairo. Once he had mastered the data, Childe set out to describe European prehistory, using "cultures, instead of statesmen, as actors and migrations instead of battles" (Childe, 1925:7; 1958). Childe classified cultures by their surviving culture traits—pots, implements, house forms, ornaments—known to be characteristic because they were constantly found together. He reconstructed cultural successions within limited geographic areas and compared them with those from neighboring regions, checking their culture traits—presumed to have spread from one area to another.

But Childe went farther, for he was one of the few archaeologists who realized that cataloging artifacts was useless unless conducted within some frame of reference. He therefore used data from hundreds of sites and dozens of cultures to formulate a comprehensive view of Old World prehistory that became a classic.

The origins of agriculture and domestication and of urban life were, he felt, two great revolutionary turning points in world history. He described (1942) two major stages, the Neolithic and the Urban revolutions. Each so-called "revolution" saw new and vital inventions that could be identified in the archaeological record by character-istic artifacts. The idea of the Neolithic and Urban revolutions constituted a techno-logical and evolutionary model, combined with an economic one in which the way people got their living was the criterion for comparing stages of world history.

The later prehistoric peoples of southwestern Asia and temperate Europe were the logical ancestors of the Greeks, Romans, and other civilizations. It was no coinci-dence that Arnold Toynbee and other world historians adopted the archaeologists' universal schemes when they made prehistoric times the first chapter in their great his-torical syntheses. Childe dominated archaeological thinking in Europe until the late 1950s. But his ideas were less influential in the Americas because Childe himself never studied or wrote about American archaeology (Trigger, 1980).

American Archaeology

American archaeologists were in a very different position. The Three-Age System could not be used, and archaeologists initially had difficulty establishing chronologies for the archaeological record. The most logical way to do this was to work backwards in time from historically known Native American sites into prehistoric times, a method that came to be known as the **direct historical approach** (see Willey and Sabloff, 1993). The early Southwestern archaeologists adopted this approach in their 1890s research tracing modern Indian pottery styles centuries into the past. This work culminated in the excavations at Pecos Pueblo carried out by Harvard archaeologist Alfred V. Kidder between 1915 and 1929 (Kidder, 1924) (see the Site box). These ex-cavations established a cultural sequence still used in modified form today. Later re-searchers, such as Douglas D. Strong, applied similar methods to Plains archaeology with great success (Strong, 1935).

The direct historical approach has limitations. It works satisfactorily as long as one is dealing with culturally related finds. Once this continuity is lost, however, the direct historical approach can no longer be used.

The Americas: The Midwestern Taxonomic Method

Franz Boas's influence was strong from the 1920s to the 1950s among archaeologists who concentrated on collecting and classifying enormous numbers of prehistoric finds from hundreds of sites all over the Americas. They began to arrange these finds in in-creasingly elaborate regional sequences of prehistoric cultures, but they ran into trou-ble because no two archaeologists could agree on how to handle the enormous quan-tities of new data emerging from large-scale dam surveys and other depression-era "make-work" projects in the East and Midwest. Thus, no one could compare one area with another using common terminology.

Scholars in the Southwest and a group in the Midwest headed by William C. McKern wrestled with the problem, trying to find explicit and formal descriptive terms for groups of archaeological finds. McKern's group prepared definitions that

Site

Alfred Kidder at Pecos, New Mexico, 1915–1929

Harvard University archaeologist Alfred Kidder first visited the Southwest in 1907 to work on a site survey. As a student, he had been to Greece and Egypt, where he visited the complex stratigraphic excavations being conducted by Englishman Flinders Petrie, among others. This experience had convinced him of the value of the humble potsherd (pot fragments), so when he started work at Pecos Pueblo in 1915, he put ceramics to good use. He worked at Pecos every year until 1929, with a three-year gap during World War I.

Pecos Pueblo, later the site of a Spanish church, had been occupied at the time of the Spanish arrival in 1540. Kidder took advantage of this occupation with its distinctive painted pottery to work from the known present into the remote past. Graves with their offerings of pots would give him the sealed dating units he needed to develop a pottery sequence. Kidder's

workers uncovered more than 750 skeletons in the first four seasons alone. At the same time, he sifted through deep sequences of ash and occupation debris and recovered thousands of potsherds. Using the grave lots and these finds, as well as pottery from other pueblos, Kidder developed a broad outline of the Southwestern past, beginning with "Basket Makers," who were hunter-gatherers who had no pottery and did not grow crops. Eventually, they became farmers, to be followed by pre-Pueblo and Pueblo peoples, who lived in more permanent settlements.

Ultimately, Kidder identified at least six settlements lying one on top of the other at Pecos and established a broad framework for the Southwestern past that survives, albeit in much modified form, to this day. He also established the essentially indigenous development of Southwestern culture.

soon became known as the **Midwestern Taxonomic Method** (Lyman and others, 2003). By correlating sequences of artifacts and hundreds of sites through long prehistoric periods using seriation methods (Chapter 7), users of the method were able to compare cultural sequences throughout the midwestern and eastern United States. The method did provide a classificatory framework but was limited as a means of interpreting the past, simply because it relied on artifacts, many from museum collections with poor stratigraphic contexts, paying little attention to other lines of evidence about the past.

By the 1940s, James Ford, James Griffin, and Gordon Willey had begun to look farther afield than local regions. At their disposal was a mass of unpublished archaeological data from hundreds of sites excavated during the depression (Willey and Sabloff, 1993). Their studies in the eastern United States revealed steady development in prehistoric material culture over many thousands of years. They distinguished periods within which broad similarities in prehistoric culture could be found and designated them as developmental stages.

Gordon Willey and Philip Phillips extended earlier survey work in a landmark monograph (1958) that applied essentially the same techniques to archaeological materials throughout the Americas. Most important, they devised developmental stages for the entire continent. These proposed stages were defined by technology, economic data, settlement patterns, art traditions, and social factors rather than by chronology, which, to their way of thinking, was a less important consideration.

The Americas: Chronology and Time Scales

No question worried the American archaeologists of the 1920s to the 1950s more than establishing an age for their sites and finds. Once they reached the limits of direct historical ties, they had no way to date early American cultures. Typologies and classification schemes based on stratigraphy only provided the relative age of the finds, not absolute dates. The first breakthrough came in the early years of the twentieth century, when University of Arizona astronomer Andrew E. Douglass started his now-famous studies of annual growth rings in trees in the Southwest. By 1929, Douglass had developed an accurate chronology for southwestern sites that eventually extended back from modern times into the first century B.C. Unfortunately, tree-ring dating is best suited to areas such as the Southwest where trees have a well-defined annual growth season and the dry conditions favor archaeological preservation. (The method is now used successfully in northern areas.)

Elsewhere, archaeological chronology was mostly done by intelligent guesswork until 1949, when University of Chicago scientists James R. Arnold and Willard F. Libby described the radiocarbon method for dating organic materials from archaeological sites (Libby, 1955). Within a few years, radiocarbon dates were processed from hundreds of sites all over the world. For the first time, actual numerical dates superseded the guesswork of earlier years. Archaeologists could finally compare widely separated sites and cultures with a uniform time scale. They could now deemphasize chronology and classification and concentrate instead on other questions.

Cultural Ecology

Before and after radiocarbon dating arrived, new emphases in archaeology on the study of human settlement against the changing landscape developed, pioneered by Cyril Fox and other fieldworkers in Britain (Fox, 1932), and on interpretation, based on carefully studied regional sequences. One conclusion was obvious: human material culture and social organization had developed from the simple to the infinitely complex. From then on, many accounts of world prehistory or broad syntheses of large culture areas allowed for the general notion of progress in prehistory (Braidwood and Braidwood, 1983; Childe, 1942; Willey, 1966, 1971).

Multilinear Cultural Evolution

In the late 1930s, anthropologist Julian Steward asked, "Are there ways of identifying common cultural features in dozens of societies distributed over many cultural areas?"

Unlike unilineal evolutionists, who insisted that all societies passed through similar stages of cultural development, Steward assumed that certain basic culture types would develop in similar ways under similar conditions. Very few actual concrete features of culture, though, would appear in a similar, regular order repeated again and again. In other words, **multilinear cultural evolution** had proceeded on many courses and at different rates, not just on one universal track. Steward added the environment as a critical variable and also looked to it for causes of cultural variation and change. To do so, he developed a method for recognizing the ways in which culture change is caused by adaptation to the environment.

Calling his study of environment and culture change **cultural ecology,** Steward laid down three principles (1955):

1. Similar adaptations may be found in different cultures in similar environments.
2. No culture has ever achieved an adaptation to its environment that has remained unchanged over any length of time.
3. Differences and changes during periods of cultural development in any area can either add to societal complexity or result in completely new cultural patterns.

Steward used these principles as a basis for studying cultures and culture change. To study different cultures, he would isolate and define distinguishing characteristics in each culture, a nucleus of traits he called the *cultural core.* He observed, for example, that African San, Australian Aborigines, and Fuegian Indians were all organized in **patrilineal** (descent through the father) bands, forming a cultural type. Why? Because their similar ecological adaptations led to comparable social organization. Although their environments differed greatly, from desert to cold and rainy plains, the practical requirements of small bands, each with its own territory, living a hunting and gathering lifeway was fundamentally the same, despite many differences in detail. Steward employed his cultural-core device to isolate and define distinguishing characteristics of the hunter-gatherer and of other specific culture types.

Steward studied the relationships between environment and culture that form the context and, consequently, the reasons for cultural features. A culture trait, be it a new type of house or a form of social organization, might be found at one location because it had diffused there, but that did not explain why the people had accepted the trait in the first place. Steward applied cultural ecology to such questions and also to problems such as why the adjustment of human societies to different environments results in certain types of behavior. To diffusion and evolution he added a new concept: changing adaptations to the natural environment. In other words, the study of culture change involved studying human cultures and their changing environmental conditions as well.

Cultural ecology studies the whole picture of the way in which human populations adapt to and transform their environments. Human cultures are thought of as open systems because their institutions may be connected with those of other cultures and with the environment. Open-system ecology assumes a great deal of variation between individual modern and archaeological cultures. Any explanation of culture has to be able to handle the patterns of variation found in living cultures, not just the artificial ones erected by classifiers of archaeological cultures. So many factors influence cultural systems that order can be imposed only by understanding the system—those processes by which cultural similarities and differences are generated. Many complex factors are external to the culture and cannot be controlled by the archaeologist.

There are obvious difficulties in studying the interactions between people and their environments, especially when preservation conditions limit the artifacts and other data available for study. Because technology is a primary way in which different cultures adapt to their environment, models of technological subsystems allow archaeologists to obtain a relatively comprehensive picture of the cultural system as a whole. Every aspect of the cultural system has to be reconstructed separately, using the evidence specifically relevant to that facet. In time, from such reconstructions, a comprehensive picture of the whole cultural system will emerge.

Multilinear evolution recognizes that there are many evolutionary tracks, from simple to complex, the differences resulting from individual adaptive solutions (Steward, 1955). Cultural adaptations are complex processes that are fine-tuned to local conditions, with long-term, cumulative effects.

Walter Taylor's *A Study of Archaeology*

Beginning in the 1950s and 1960s some archaeologists argued that archaeologists should not simply describe the past, but rather explain why certain patterns or developments occurred. When Steward's work appeared, American archaeology was completely preoccupied with chronology and artifact description. It was as if archaeologists were classifying insects or collecting postage stamps. Then, in 1948, archaeologist Walter W. Taylor published his famed work, *A Study of Archaeology,* a devastating critique of American archaeologists' preoccupation with description and chronology.

In this landmark essay, Taylor called for shifting emphasis from chronological sequences and distributions to detailed, multilevel studies of individual sites and their features, such as cultural layers, floors, or hearths. This approach brought together all possible sources of evidence on a site—technology, artistic styles, ecological evidence, architecture, and information on social life—to focus on the people who had lived at the site and on the changes in their culture. Taylor tried to introduce into archaeology a view of culture that recognized the discipline as being integral to anthropology. He felt that the disciplines should work together to arrive at general truths about human culture (Kluckhohn, 1940).

Steward's and Taylor's research brought twentieth-century archaeology to the threshold of great theoretical change. They established, once and for all, the close relationship between archaeology and anthropology. *A Study of Archaeology* showed, with incisive clarity, that one of archaeology's primary goals must be to develop adequate explanations for human prehistory, an aim far more sophisticated than mere excavation, collection, and description. Steward's view of multilinear cultural evolution and cultural ecology greatly influenced archaeologists, and it was a principal aspect of the new archaeology of the 1960s, which is discussed in Chapter 3.

Summary

Archaeology originated in the intellectual curiosity about the past felt by a number of classical writers, such as Hesiod, who speculated about human origins and stages in early human history. After the Renaissance, this curiosity manifested itself in excavations at Herculaneum and Pompeii, where classical Roman statues were uncovered and used to decorate the estates of wealthy Europeans. There were also discoveries of far more primitive artifacts—stone tools that hinted at a more ancient, prehistoric past. But speculations about prehistory were shackled by a literal interpretation of the Bible.

With greater knowledge of human biological and cultural diversity late in the eighteenth century, people began to speculate about the relationships among different groups and about the notion of human progress from simple to complex societies. From the discoveries in the Somme Valley, France, and elsewhere, the bones of extinct animals directly associated with tools made by human beings proved that humanity had existed for far longer than the 6,000 years allowed by written history. These discoveries could not be placed in a scientific context, however, until uniformitarian geology, the new science of paleontology, and the theory of evolution by natural selection had been developed.

The notion of human social evolution followed that of biological evolution. Many archaeologists thought of prehistoric cultures as arranged in layers of progress from the simple to the complex. A simple form of unilinear cultural evolution was espoused by such pioneer anthropologists as Edward B. Tylor and Lewis Morgan, who portrayed humanity as having progressed from simple savagery to complex, literate civilization.

Unilinear cultural evolution was far too simple a scheme to satisfactorily explain prehistory. Some scholars turned to diffusion as a means of explanation, and, in the extreme, some assumed that many aspects of civilizations had emanated from Egypt or similar so-called "cradles of civilization." These hyper-diffusionist explanations, often based on limited archaeological data, proved just as unsatisfactory as unilinear models. Influenced by Franz Boas and Vere Gordon Childe, archaeologists began to describe artifacts and sites much more precisely and preoccupied themselves with culture history and chronologies.

American archaeologists used the direct historical approach to prehistory extensively, working back in time from known historical cultures to prehistoric societies. Standard taxonomic systems were also developed in the 1930s and were widely used. Radiocarbon dating arrived in the late 1940s, coinciding with greater interest in the natural environment and the study of human ecology. Anthropologist Julian Steward formulated the principles of cultural ecology, studying the relationships between human cultures and their natural environments.

W. W. Taylor's *A Study of Archaeology*, published in 1948, was a landmark critique of American archaeology, chiding archaeologists for their preoccupation with description and artifact chronologies rather than the interpretation of past social systems and the explanation of culture change. This groundbreaking work, and increasingly multilinear views of cultural evolution, helped lay the foundation for modern, explanatory archaeology.

Key Terms

antiquarians	direct historical approach	phase
component	historical particularism	subarea
cultural ecology	horizon	Three-Age System
culture area	Midwestern Taxonomic Method	tradition
culture history	multilinear cultural evolution	uniformitarianism
diffusion	patrilineal	unilinear cultural evolution

Guide to Further Reading

FAGAN, BRIAN M. 1985. *The Adventure of Archaeology.* Washington, DC: National Geographic Society. A lavishly illustrated account of the history of archaeology that is ideal for beginners.

GRAYSON, DONALD. 1983. *The Establishment of Human Antiquity.* Orlando, FL: Academic Press. A definitive and scholarly study of human antiquity based on contemporary sources. Strongly recommended for the advanced reader.

LEWIN, ROGER. 1998. *Principles of Human Evolution: A Core Textbook.* Malden, MA: Blackwell. An authoritative summary of biological and cultural evolution.

LYMAN, R. LEE, MICHAEL O'BRIEN, and ROBERT DUNNELL. 1996. *The Rise and Fall of Culture History.* New York: Plenum Press. A splendid analysis of culture history in American archaeology.

Essential reading for advanced students:

MELTZER, DAVID J., DON D. FOWLER, and JEREMY A. SABLOFF, eds. 1986. *American Archaeology Past and Future: A Celebration of the Society for American Archaeology, 1935–1985.* Washington, DC: Smithsonian Institution Press. A set of essays that review the development of American archaeology since the 1930s.

TRIGGER, BRUCE G. 1989. *A History of Archaeological Interpretation.* Cambridge: Cambridge University Press. A brilliant intellectual history of archaeology.

WILLEY, GORDON, and JEREMY SABLOFF. 1993. *A History of American Archaeology.* 3d ed. New York: W. H. Freeman. A detailed account of New World archaeology, from the Spanish Conquest until recent times.

CHAPTER 3

Science, Ecology, and the Many-Voiced Past

From the 1950s to Today

Hominid footprints, 3.5 million years old, at Laetoli, Tanzania, East Africa.

Chance preserved the earliest known human footprints. One day, about 3.5 million years ago, two hominids walked across a dry streambed where a path across soft volcanic ash led to a nearby waterhole. The ash hardened in the tropical sun and was then buried by more fine ash from another eruption. The two hominid trails, made by individuals with a rolling and slow-moving gait, with the hips swiveling at every step, came to light when the world-famous paleoanthropologist Mary Leakey excavated the streambed in the 1980s (M. Leakey and Harris, 1990). An accident of nature had preserved the footprints of the two upright-walking hominids, who had stood between 4 feet 7 inches (1.4 m) and 4 feet 11 inches (1.49 m) tall.

It is astounding what modern science can tell us about unique finds such as the Laetoli footprints in East Africa, far more than was possible even a generation ago. Archaeology has changed almost beyond recognition in four decades, as have the other social sciences. The computer, statistical methods, and the philosophy of science have transformed archaeology from a primarily descriptive discipline into a much more comprehensive study of the past. This chapter discusses modern archaeology, starting with its foundation in culture history, then going on to the processual archaeology of the 1960s, and concluding with the new theoretical approaches that developed in the following decades.

There are many different perspectives that can only be briefly considered here. As will be seen, rather than replacing one another, new ideas are often combined with or remain alongside of the old. We should stress that there is no one theoretical approach embraced by all archaeologists. Although they share an interest in the past and, necessarily, use similar methods to uncover the material record of societies, all archaeologists bring different theoretical perspectives to their views of the past. Theory is important because it structures the research questions asked, the types of data collected, and the interpretive framework the archaeologist uses in his or her work. This chapter provides a context for the emergence of modern archaeology and gives an impression of the wide diversity of theoretical perspectives in an increasingly multivocal archaeology.

Culture History

As we saw in Chapter 2, the construction of culture history has been a major preoccupation of archaeologists since the early years of the twentieth century and it remains an important aspect of research. Culture history is based on the chronological and spatial ordering of archaeological data. Its basic methods are now well established, even if they are still debated (Lyman and others, 1996). As will be seen, there are other perspectives of the past, some of which are very critical of culture history's emphasis on description and its lack of explanation (see the discussion of processual archaeology below). Nevertheless, culture history has provided an important foundation for understanding technological developments, chronology, and the archaeological record. Much of the terminology developed—culture areas, traditions, horizons, and phases, as well as the criteria for their definition—remains in use (Figure 3.1). Many parts of the world remain poorly known archaeologically, and basic description of the archaeological record is still an important concern. In addition, although new theoretical perspectives have emerged, some of the concepts employed by culture historians, such as analogy, invention, diffusion, and migration, remain important interpretive concepts.

Interpretation of Culture History

The primary basis for interpretation of culture history depends on descriptive cultural models and ethnographic analogy (Chapter 14). A number of cultural and noncultural models (like environmental change, discussed in Chapter 12) have been developed to describe culture change. The cultural models are inevitable variation, cultural selection, and the three classic processes—invention, diffusion, and migration (Trigger, 1968a).

Inevitable variation is somewhat similar to the biological phenomenon of genetic drift, except that it concerns change in human societies rather than gene frequencies in populations. As people learn the behavior patterns of their society, inevitably some small differences in learned behavior will appear from generation to generation. Although minor in themselves, these differences accumulate in a "snowball effect" over a long period of time. For instance, the variation in Acheulian hand ax technology throughout Europe and Africa between 100,000 and 150,000 years ago can be explained in part by the effects of inevitable variation.

Inevitable variation is often the result of isolation, that is, of a very low density of humans per square mile. It should not be confused with broad trends in prehistory that developed over long periods of time; and it is different from what happens when a society recognizes that certain culture changes or inventions may be advantageous. For example, many hunter-gatherer societies deliberately took up soil cultivation once they saw the advantages it gave neighboring peoples who had adopted new economies.

Cultural selection is the notion that human cultures accept or reject new traits—technological, economic, or intangible—on the basis of whether they are

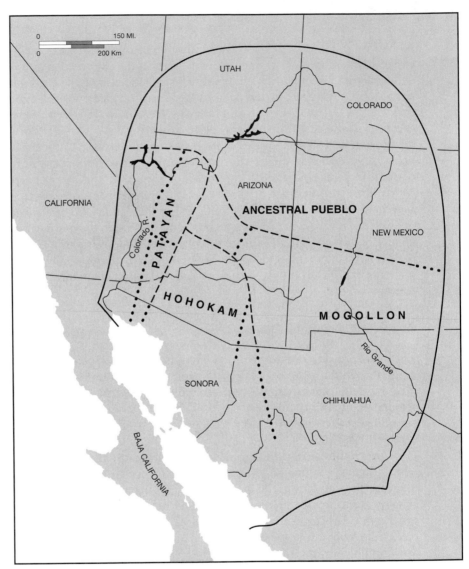

Figure 3.1   Archaeological regions and subareas in the North American Southwest.

advantageous to the society as a whole. Cultural selection results in cumulative culture change, and it operates within the constraints of the prevailing values of the society. This condition tends to make it harder for a society to accept social change as opposed to technological advances, which are less circumscribed by restrictive values. The state-organized societies in Mesopotamia and Mexico resulted from centuries of gradual social evolution, where centralized political and religious authority was perceived to be advantageous.

Invention

Invention is a new idea that either modifies an old idea or series of ideas or creates a completely new concept; it may come about by accident or by intentional research. Fire was probably the result of an accident; the atom was split by long and patient investigation with the ultimate objective of fragmentation. Inventions spread, and if they are sufficiently important, they spread widely and rapidly. Archaeologically, inventions can be seen in the emergence of new artifact types, artistic styles, construction methods, technological developments, or other tangible innovations that can be observed in the material record.

Early archaeologists often assumed that metallurgy and other major innovations were invented in only one place (Figure 3.2). But as the archaeological record became better documented, they realized that many inventions occurred separately in several parts of the world where identical adaptive processes were used. For example, agriculture is known to have developed independently in southwestern and East Asia, Mesoamerica, South America, and Africa.

Diffusion

Diffusion is the process by which new ideas or culture traits spread from one person to another or from one group to another, often over long distances, as discussed in Chapter 2. Diffusion can result from such diverse mechanisms as trade, warfare, visits between neighboring communities, and migrations of entire communities. The key factor is the formal or informal mechanisms of contact between the members of separate groups that result in the spread and acceptance of a new idea.

Several criteria must be satisfied before researchers can decide whether a series of artifacts in archaeological sites distant from one another are evidence of diffusion. First, the traits or objects must be sufficiently similar in design and typological attributes to

Figure 3.2   Iron-bladed dagger of the Egyptian pharaoh Tutankhamun, 1323 B.C. The weapon was probably made of native hammered iron. Iron metallurgy was a crucial early invention. The Egyptians tried, without success, to obtain iron tools from the Hittites in distant Anatolia after hearing of the revolutionary new metal. (Photograph by the Egyptian Expedition, The Metropolitan Museum of Art.)

indicate that they probably had a common origin. Second, it must be shown that the traits did not result from convergent evolution. The development of a trait, perhaps a form of architecture or the use of a domestic animal, must be carefully traced in both cultures. Third, distributions of the surviving traits, as well as those of their antecedents, must be carefully studied. The only acceptable evidence for diffusion of a trait is a series of sites that show continuous distribution for the trait or, perhaps, a route along which it spread when plotted on a map. Accurate chronological control is essential, with a time gradient from either end of the distribution or one from the middle.

Theoretical speculations are all very well, but they may result in completely false conclusions, sometimes supported by uncritical use of scanty archaeological evidence (R. H. Thompson, 1956). There are many valid instances of diffusion in ancient times. A well-documented instance is the religion of the Adena and Hopewell peoples of the American Midwest, who held beliefs associated with death that spread far beyond the relatively narrow confines of the Midwest. Religious beliefs are expressed in the form of distinctive rituals, which for the Adena and Hopewell involved extensive earthworks and mound building. Such monuments are found outside the Adena and Hopewell heartlands, as are the cult objects associated with Hopewell ritual (Figure 3.3).

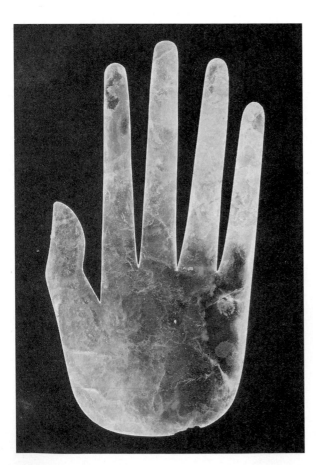

Figure 3.3   About two thousand years ago, a Hopewell artisan cut this human hand from a sheet of mica. It was found in an Ohio burial mound with the body of its owner, who lived 370 miles (595 km) from the nearest mica source. An example of the consequences of the diffusion of religious beliefs, this hand probably had powerful shamanistic associations in Hopewell society.

Diffusion itself is not a cause of the spread of culture traits; it is a way of referring to a set of phenomena caused by a wide range of cultural factors. To say that bronze sword-making diffused from one society to another is merely to describe what happened. It does not describe *how* the spread occurred. Under the culture-historical paradigm, diffusion has been invoked as a satisfactory explanation for distribution patterns of culture traits when, in fact, the factors behind the diffusion are still unexplained.

Migration

Migration is the actual movement of human populations, whether large or small. It may be peaceful, or it can be the result of deliberate aggression, invasion, and conquest (J. Chapman and Hamerow, 1997). In each case, however, people deliberately expand into new areas. English settlers moved to the North American continent, taking their own culture and society with them; the Spanish conquistadors conquered the indigenous societies of Mexico. Such population movements result not only in diffusion of ideas but also in the actual movement of people.

Perhaps the classic instance of migration in world prehistory is that of the Polynesians, who settled the remote islands of the Pacific by voyaging from archipelago to archipelago (Finney, 1994). Each time, the islands were discovered through a deliberate act of exploration by voyagers who set out with every intention of returning (see the Discovery box). Hawaii, Easter Island, and Tahiti were first settled through deliberate colonization by a small number of people to a new, uninhabited landmass. The kind of total population movement, or in some cases, population replacement, that occurs with mass migrations of this type was rare in ancient times. It is reflected in the archaeological record either by totally new components and phases of artifacts or by skeletal evidence.

A different type of migration, on a much smaller scale, occurs when a small number of foreigners moves into another region and settles there as an organized group. A group of Oaxacans may have done just that at Teotihuacán in the Valley of Mexico more than 1,500 years ago (Millon, 1973). They settled in their own precinct of the city, tentatively identified by a concentration of Oaxacan potsherds and ornaments. The Oaxacan enclave lasted for centuries.

There are other forms of migration, too. Slaves may be transported over vast areas, as Africans were in the era of the Atlantic trade, while artisans and craftsmen may wander as unorganized migrants. There are great warrior migrations, such as those of the eastern nomads in temperate Europe and the warlike Nguni tribes of southern Africa. Each of these warrior bands swept over indigenous, sedentary populations, causing widespread disruption and population shifts. But within a few generations, the warrior newcomers had adopted the sedentary way of life of their neighbors and were virtually indistinguishable from them. Such migrations may leave few traces in archaeological sites.

Interpretation of the culture-historical approach consists primarily of the description of archaeological record and what happened in the past. In itself, culture history takes little account of why certain developments occurred, why cultures changed, or the role of artifacts in the cultural system as a whole. Explanation of cultural process is a central concern of modern archaeological research.

Discovery

Ancient Pacific Navigation

When British navigator Captain James Cook visited Tahiti in 1769, he puzzled over a question that has fascinated scholars ever since. How had the Tahitians colonized their remote homeland? How had humans with only simple canoes and no metals sailed across vast tracts of open ocean to settle on the remotest islands of the Pacific? Cook met the great Tahitian navigator Tupaia and asked him how canoe navigators made their way from island to island out of sight of land. Tupaia explained how they used the sun as a compass by day and the moon and stars by night. When Cook marveled at the Polynesians' ability to sail against the prevailing winds for hundreds of miles, Tupaia pointed out that westerlies blew from November to January, and these were months when canoes could make good progress to windward. Tupaia carried a mental file of Polynesia in his head. Modern scholars believe that Tupaia could define an area bounded by the Marquesas in the northeast,

the Tuamotus to the east, the Australs to the south, and the Cook Islands to the southwest. Even Fiji and Samoa to the west lay within his consciousness, an area as large as Australia or the United States.

Later explorers did not interview Tahitian navigators. Many scholars assumed that the Pacific Islands were colonized by canoes blown accidently far offshore. But in 1965 English cruising sailor David Lewis encountered aged canoe navigators in the Carolina Islands of Micronesia. He learned how the navigators used the zenith passages of key stars to navigate far from the land, using swell direction, waves reflected off distant land, even the flights of sea and land birds to make landfall on island archipelagos far from their departure point. They were also capable of returning to their homes safely, using the same signs of sea and sky. Lewis, determined to preserve a rapidly vanishing art, sailed his ocean-going, European-designed catamaran from Rarotonga in the Cook Islands to New

The New Archaeology

Major transformations in the way archaeologists go about their business began in the 1950s, soon after the publication of *A Study of Archaeology,* by Walter Taylor in 1948 (Chapter 2). Archaeologists started to reassess what the objectives of archaeological research were and how they could use the material they excavated to explain, not just describe, what happened in the past. These new attitudes coincided with the arrival of many technological innovations, such as the computer, sophisticated statistical methods, carbon-14 and other numerical dating techniques, and new methods for locating and identifying archaeological sites (Spaulding, 1953, 1960, 1973; Willey and Sabloff, 1993). Changing ideas among researchers and the application of these new methods brought about a new approach to archaeological evidence.

One of the most influential pioneers in this revised view of the past was Lewis Binford (1983). In the 1960s, Binford wrote a number of papers that argued for a radically different approach to the past. Binford advocated the importance of theory and

Zealand using only a star map and a Polynesian navigator to help him. In the 1970s, Lewis apprenticed himself to the pilots of the Carolina Islands, learning how they made passages with the aid of sun, moon, stars, cloud and swell formations, even by watching passing birds.

In the late 1960s, anthropologist Ben Finney (1994) began long-term experiments with replicas of ancient Polynesian canoes. Finney's first replica was *Nalehia,* a 40-foot copy of a Hawaiian royal canoe. Tests in Hawaii's windy waters showed it could sail across the wind, so Finney planned a voyage from Hawaii to Tahiti and back. His second replica was built from a composite of canoe designs known throughout the Pacific Islands. *Hokule'a* is 62 feet long, with double hulls and two crab-claw-shaped sails designed by Hawaiian Herb Kawainui Kane (Figure 3.4). Finney, Satawal Island navigator Mau Piailug, and a mainly Hawaiian crew sailed *Hokule'a* from Hawaii to Tahiti and back in 1976. This journey was followed by a two-year voyage around the Pacific using only indigenous pilots. Thanks to the successful

Hokule'a experiments, ancient Polynesian navigational skills have been preserved for posterity.

Figure 3.4 The Polynesian canoe *Hokule'a.* (© Monte Costa)

underscored the close links between archaeology and cultural anthropology. The ultimate objective of archaeology, he argued, was to search for universal laws that govern culture change. Some British archaeologists, especially David Clarke (1968), also joined Binford's call for a reassessment of archaeological research. Binford and his disciples' view of archaeology was so different that it was soon called, somewhat ambitiously, the "new archaeology."

The new archaeologists were very optimistic about the potential of archaeology to contribute to anthropology as a whole. They challenged the assumption that, because the archaeological record is incomplete, reliable interpretation of the nonmaterial and perishable components of prehistoric society and culture was impossible. All artifacts found in an archaeological site, they argued, functioned in a particular culture and society. They occur in meaningful patterns that are systematically related to the economies, kinship systems, and other contexts within which they were used. Thus, artifacts are far more than mere material remnants. The archaeologist's task is to devise methods for extracting this information.

The new archaeology advocated rigorous scientific testing using formal scientific methods, an approach strongly influenced by the philosophy of science as presented by Karl Hempel (1966). Previously, inferences about the archaeological record had been made by simple induction, along with guidance from ethnographic data. Evaluation of the conclusions reached was based on how professionally competent and honest the archaeologists interpreting the past were perceived to be (Binford, 1962, 1972, 1980, 1983). Binford suggested that, although induction and inference are sound methods for understanding the past, the real need was for independent methods, commonly used in science, for testing hypotheses about the past, and that these methods must be far more rigorous than the value judgments arrived at by assessing professional competence.

Working hypotheses were nothing new in archaeology. What was different about Binford's approach was that he argued that these hypotheses be tested explicitly against archaeological data and against alternative explanations. Once a hypothesis has been successfully tested against raw data, it can join the body of reliable knowledge upon which further hypotheses can be based. These propositions in turn require additional testing and, perhaps, entirely new approaches to the excavation and collection of archaeological material. The ultimate objective was to explain past sociocultural phenomena in terms of universal laws of culture dynamics: Why did the hunter-gatherers turn to agriculture and domestic animals for their livelihood, or what cultural responses occurred under certain environmental conditions?

The new archaeology was really a synthesis of many diverse trends, among them cultural ecology, multilinear cultural evolution, and an emphasis on new scientific methods and computers. These trends were fused into what is today referred to as *processual archaeology.*

Processual Archaeology

Processual archaeology focuses on the cultural process and the explanation of culture change (Wylie, 1988). It also brings an explicitly scientific methodology to the interpretation of archaeological data. Processual archaeologists rely on the scientific method to formulate testable hypotheses and proceed to the gathering of new data to test them (Dunnell, 1982; Flannery, 1968; Watson and others, 1984; for more on archaeology as a science and the scientific method, see Chapter 5). The processual approach is firmly based on culture history. It has to be, for the chronological and spatial frameworks for prehistory come from descriptive methods developed over many generations.

The difference between the descriptive and processual approaches lies in the orientation of the research. In the early days, processual archaeologists searched for general laws of human behavior relating to the relationships between human cultures and the environment, ecological adaptation, and cultural evolution. Most of these laws were so generalized, however, that they were of little value, while the complexity of social phenomena makes it exceedingly difficult to evaluate other questions using hypothesis testing. The **deductive-nomological approach,** with an explicit focus on hypothesis testing and the identification of laws of culture dynamics, initially advocated by Binford, is now rarely used. Nonetheless, problem-oriented research, explicitly stated research questions, and a clear research design remain integral in archaeological research.

Another important aspect of processual archaeology is the **systems-ecological approach,** which involves thinking of human cultures as complicated agglomerates of components, such as technology, subsistence strategies, and social organization, that interacted with each other and, in turn, with the larger environmental systems of which they were part. Human culture was, ultimately, seen as an adaptation to the environment (Clarke, 1968; Flannery, 1968; Watson and others, 1984). It involves three basic models of culture change: systems models, which are based on **general systems theory** (Chapter 6); **cultural ecology,** which provides models of the interactions between human cultures and their environments (Chapter 2); and **multilinear cultural evolution,** which brings systems theory and cultural ecology together into a closely knit, highly flexible way of studying and explaining cultural process (Chapter 2; Sanders and Webster, 1978).

The advantage of systems theory is that it frees researchers from overemphasizing one agent of culture change, such as diffusion or migration, allowing them to focus instead on regulatory mechanisms and on the relationships between various components of a cultural system and the system as a whole and its environment. The systems approach is as valuable to archaeology as a general concept is to the study of ecology (Gibbon, 1984).

Initially, practitioners of the new archaeology believed that processual archaeology would allow researchers to investigate all aspects of human experience, including such intangibles as ideological beliefs (Binford and Binford, 1968). But very soon the focus tended toward ecology and subsistence, to the point that some processualists referred to investigations of the intangible as an inaccessible "palaeopsychology" (Binford, 1987). Processual archaeologists have made important studies of the ecological, technological, and economic constraints that act on human societies (see the Doing Archaeology box).

Postprocessual Archaeology

Inevitably, there was a reaction against the materialist approach of many processual archaeologists, which seemed to dehumanize the past in a quest for processes of culture change. Many noneconomic and nonecological factors also influence human behavior, as do the physical limitations of the human body and the nature of the human brain. So, instead of saying that the environment was responsible for culture change, one can argue that it constrained human behavior (Fish and Kowalewski, 1990). During the late 1970s and 1980s, more researchers began thinking about the entire spectrum of human behavior—the development and expression of human consciousness, religion and worldview, symbolism and iconography—as part of a more holistic archaeology.

| **Doing Archaeology** |

Hypothesis Testing at Broken K Pueblo, Arizona

The processual archaeology of the 1960s revolutionized approaches to archaeological method and theory. Practitioners of this "new archaeology" were very optimistic about the ability of archaeology to contribute to anthropology as a whole. They advocated the use of explicit research designs, which included statistical methods and the rigorous scientific testing of hypotheses using formal scientific methods. One of the best examples of the applications of the methodology of new archaeology is provided by James N. Hill's excavations at Broken K Pueblo, Arizona (1968). The Broken K site is a 95-room stone pueblo that was occupied by Native Americans from about A.D. 1150 to 1280. Hill's objective was to explain the patterning of cultural features at the site with regard to prehistoric residence patterns.

Preliminary trenching and clearing of surface levels were used to reveal most of the rooms at the site. As the pueblo was fairly large, the site could not be entirely excavated, so Hill excavated a random sample of forty-six rooms (Figure 3.5). In the course of excavation, Hill observed three different kinds of rooms. These were described in a clear and rigorous fashion, the variables noted, and the data analyzed using the chi-square test of association and the Fisher Exact Test. The variables Hill considered were room size, masonry style, and the height of the door sill, as well as the presence or absence of firepits, mealing bins, ventilators, and doorways. He also examined the number of each type of room relative to the others. Analogies with modern Zuni and Hopi pueblos allowed Hill to interpret the Broken K rooms as habitation rooms, storage rooms, and specialized rooms for rituals (*kivas*).

With these analogies in mind, Hill then developed sixteen hypotheses predicting the kinds of artifacts that would be present in the various types of rooms, which he then tested in light of the archaeological data recovered. For example, the habitation rooms would be expected to contain a wider variety and larger number of materials than other rooms, while the smaller rooms and ritual areas would contain fewer artifacts with less variation, reflecting the specialized activities that took place there. These observations also allowed Hill to estimate the number of households that likely resided at the settlement.

The clear statements of hypotheses enabled Hill to verify the analogies made, as well as to raise further hypotheses about why some expectations were not validated by the archaeological data. For example, the fact that large numbers of undecorated storage pots were not recovered from the storage rooms may suggest that the storage practices of seven hundred years ago were slightly different from those in ethnographically observed pueblos.

Thus was born **postprocessual archaeology,** a sometimes extreme antidote to its predecessor—in general terms, a reaction against the relatively anonymous, processual approach, which emphasized cultural processes and adaptation to the environment over groups of people and individuals (Bintcliff, 1991, 1993; Earle and Preucel, 1987; Trigger, 1989; Yoffee and Sherratt, 1993). Defined by the perspective that preceded it, the term *postprocessual archaeology* actually embraces a variety of

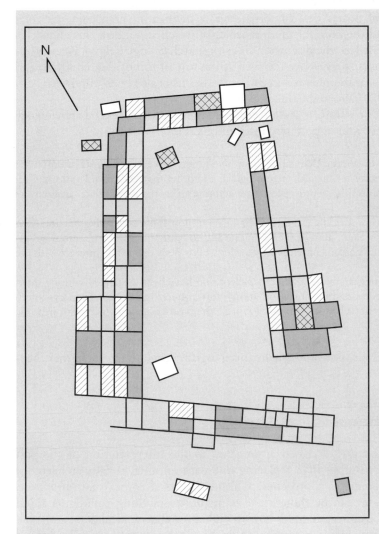

Figure 3.5 Different kinds of rooms at Broken K Pueblo. Black areas represent "large rooms"; hatched areas are "small rooms"; and crosshatched areas are "special rooms." Blank areas were not excavated. James Hill developed a number of testable hypotheses about the types of artifacts that would be recovered from the different rooms.

Source: Based on James N. Hill, "Broken K Pueblo: Patterns of Form and Function." In Lewis and Sally Binford, eds., *New Perspectives in Archaeology,* pp. 103–42.

Although archaeologists now make use of many different theoretical and methodological approaches, a clear research design and the assumptions made during interpretation remain important.

different theoretical perspectives, vantage points, and views of the potential methodologies of scientific inquiry.

Some of the passions raised by postprocessual archaeology are a reflection both of Western society in transition and an interdisciplinary field made up of dozens of specialties. It incorporates several often compellingly expressed intellectual developments that parallel "postmodernist" schools of thought in science, literature, and anthropology (Hodder, 1986; Shanks and Tilley, 1987a, 1987b). A particularly important aspect of some postprocessual perspectives is delineating archaeologists' roles in modern society and the need for the archaeologist to reflect on how this affects his or her views of the past (see the discussion of critical archaeology below). Agency/individualism and feminist perspectives, as well as the role of minorities, children, and other groups under- or unrepresented in earlier studies have also been important concerns (Ferguson, 1992; Gero and Conkey, 1991).

For all its constantly shifting and diverse paradigms, postprocessual archaeology has made three positive and important contributions (Hodder, 1999):

1. Meaning is more important than materialism. No longer can archaeologists interpret the past in terms of purely ecological, technological, and other material considerations. Culture is interactive. In other words, people are actors who create, manipulate, and remake the world they live in.
2. Archaeologists must critically examine their social responsibilities, looking beyond their specialties to the broader aims of the discipline and to issues of moral and emotional involvement with the past in contemporary society. How does the public interact with the past?
3. There are many perspectives on ancient society that have been neglected, among them those of women, ethnic minorities, and anonymous, often illiterate commoners—often called "people without history." In other words, the past has many voices, not just one (Hodder, 1999).

In the final analysis, postprocessualism is a logical development of earlier theoretical approaches.

Some Schools of Archaeological Theory

To varying extent, the just-discussed approaches to the interpretation of the past remain with us today. Rather than replacing one with another, today's archaeology embraces myriad theoretical approaches. Culture-historical, processual, and post-processual archaeologies can be thought of as major, overarching paradigms about how the past should be conceptualized, how to evaluate archaeological data, and what the objectives of archaeological research should be. To see these as rigidly divided schools of thought is misleading, for in practice each often takes something of the other. (For a discussion of the radical differences in new explanatory paradigms, see Bintcliff, 1991, 1993.)

To explain past cultures, researchers also draw on a variety of other theories and concepts to model social, economic, political, and cultural systems and to contextualize their work. Many of these theories come from philosophy and cultural anthropology, but sociology, political science, evolutionary biology, and even literary criticism have also been employed as sources. These varying perspectives help archaeologists conceptualize and model past social systems. Although some may be better suited to processual or postprocessual views of the past, none can be easily compartmentalized. For example, while much of processual archaeology may have grappled with human adaptation to the environment, the interpretation of past ideology, religion, and worldview are of central concern to the **cognitive-processual approach** (Flannery and Marcus, 1993). Gender roles have also been the focus of both processual and postprocessual researchers (Hays-Gilpin and Whitley, 1998). Theoretical approaches to archaeology are numerous; among them are the following.

Evolutionary approaches have been integral to archaeology since the nineteenth century. While the idea of the unilinear evolution of human societies has been discarded (Chapter 2), the concept of multilinear cultural evolution is inextricably linked with modern archaeological research. This is a useful way of conceptualizing change in past societies (see, for example, Earle, 1997).

Some researchers have also employed ideas of evolutionary processes to examine social and cultural adaptations, as well as adaptations to the natural environment. Archaeologists of this persuasion maintain that natural selection constrained human thought and action. Consequently, the way in which people behave can be understood by understanding the constraints placed on the human mind during its long evolutionary heritage. From this viewpoint, natural selection produced culture by conferring a reproductive advantage on its bearers. Thus, thought and action were channeled by natural selection in directions that were adaptive for an evolving *Homo sapiens* (Mithen, 1989, 1996). The legacy of natural selection is a tendency for humans to think and act in certain ways and not in others. The result is a trend toward conformity in thought and action among very diverse human societies with very different institutions and beliefs.

Ecological approaches stress the study of ancient societies within their natural environments. As seen in the discussion of cultural ecology, culture change as an adaptation to the environment emerged as an important area of study in the mid-twentieth century, and it was subsequently important in the emergence of processual archaeology, which primarily saw culture as an **extrasomatic** adaptation to the environment (Crumley, 1994).

Marxist perspectives, derived from the writings of Friedrich Engels and Karl Marx, have also had a long and important influence on archaeological theory. Classical Marxist perspectives stress the contradictions between economic relations (especially production and exchange), class conflict, and inequality as the primary forces behind sociocultural evolution. Indeed, Marx and Engels saw the unilinear evolutionary framework outlined by Lewis Henry Morgan (discussed in Chapter 2) as a model for the evolution of ancient human societies, just their own work detailed the evolution of capitalism, socialism, and communism. V. Gordon Childe also was greatly influenced by Marxist perspectives, which focused on major changes in the relations of productions, such as occurred with the transition to agriculture and with the rise of sociopolitical complexity, to understand changes in social organization (Trigger, 1980).

Some researchers turn to Marxism for framing their discussions and for analytical concepts, some introduced by Marxist scholars such as Antonio Gramsci, H.

Lefebvre, and Claude Meillassoux (McGuire, 1992). Dialectical Marxism, for example, underscores an understanding of the interconnected relationships among phenomena within a society. Hence, subsistence, gender, class, and race are seen as integrated parts of the entire social system, rather than independent constructs. Marxist perspectives and analytical concepts have been very important for historical archaeologists examining the archaeology of capitalism and the expansion of Europe into the non-Western world (M. Johnson, 1993; Orser, 1996). Another branch of Marxist archaeology focuses on the modern contexts in which archaeologists operate and is integral to critical archaeology.

Critical archaeology assumes that because archaeologists are actors in contemporary culture, they must have some active impact on society (Shanks and Tilley, 1987a, 1987b). One extreme is the Marxist view of archaeology, which states that all knowledge is class-based, so archaeology composes history for class purposes (McGuire, 1992). Thus, reconstructions of the past have a social function and, consequently, archaeology cannot be a neutral, objective science. By engaging in critical analysis, an archaeologist can explore the relationship between a reconstruction of the past and the ideology that helped create that reconstruction.

Critical archaeology is a process of archaeologists becoming more critical of their own place in the unfolding intellectual development of Western scholarship (Trigger, 1984, 1989). Much critical archaeology focuses on understanding the pasts of people who have been "denied" a history—women, blacks, the Third World, and so on. In other words, we should be concerned with the cultural roots of our work.

Cultural materialism is derived from Marxist perspectives, but the role of subsistence and subsistence technology as the principal source of sociocultural phenomena is emphasized. At the base of all sociocultural phenomena is the infrastructure, which includes the means of subsistence and basic needs such as food, clothing, and shelter. These phenomena exert selective pressures on the rest of society, including family structure, division of labor, class, religion, science, customs, and ideologies (M. Harris, 1968, 1979, 1999). Although other cultural phenomena may influence cultural evolution, infrastructural factors are viewed as being far more important.

Cultural materialism is especially attractive to archaeologists because it stresses technology and the environment, aspects of past societies that survive well in the archaeological record and can be evaluated.

World systems theory, developed by sociologist Immanuel Wallerstein (1974, 1979, 1980), maintains that the socioeconomic differences between societies are the product of an interlocking global economy. All societies are placed in one of three general categories: core societies are powerful industrial nations that dominate other regions or nations; semiperipheral societies are somewhat industrialized but lack the power of the core; and peripheral societies lie outside the core and can do little to control the economic expansion of the core. Relationships between industrialized and developing countries in the modern world are seen in terms of core-periphery relations.

Not surprisingly, world systems theory has provided an important model for historical archaeologists examining the intersection of Europe with the non-Western world (DeCorse, 2001a, 2001b). However, archaeologists working on precapitalist societies have also found some of the concepts useful in examining the relations in older, smaller "world systems," such as the emergence of sociopolitical complexity in Mesopotamia and Mesoamerica (Chase-Dunn and Hall, 1991).

From an archaeological perspective, the term ***cognitive archaeology*** covers the spectrum of human behavior, especially religion and belief, but also the development and expression of human consciousness, sometimes called the "archaeology of mind."

Some archaeologists employ a cognitive-processual approach, with a new framework for archaeology drawing on both old and new models and methods. It stresses the careful evaluation of data that characterize processual archaeology. Cognitive processualists never claim they can establish what people thought, but they can gain insights into *how* they thought (Renfrew, 1993a, 1993b; Skibo and others, 1995).

Structural approaches (**structural archaeology**) treat human cultures as shared symbolic structures that are cumulative creations of the human mind. In other words, people think and order their world by using similar "central, powerful, and pliable symbols" (Leone and others, 1987). Structural analyses aim to discover these universal principles of the human mind, an approach associated in particular with French anthropologist Claude Lévi-Strauss. They are an attempt to get at the conscious and unconscious of human thinking. Lévi-Strauss argued that human thinking is based on binary oppositions (1966); that is, we classify things into opposing types—hot and cold, raw and cooked, nature and culture. These binary contrasts are found in all societies, and can be identified through analysis.

The cognitive-nonmaterial nature of structuralism makes it difficult to examine in the material record and, consequently, structuralism has had limited application. However, some poststructuralists are less concerned with cultural universals and focus more on the cognitive structure within individual societies (Kirch and Sahlins, 1992). Archaeologist Ian Hodder studied the Nuba agriculturalists of the Sudan and showed that all aspects of their material culture, including burial customs, settlement patterns, and artifact styles, could be understood in the context of a set of rules that perpetuated their beliefs in "purity, boundedness, and categorization" (1982a, 1982b). Thus, Nuba society is the result of structured, symbolizing behavior and has fundamental utility. But it also has a logic of its own, which generated the material culture that is observed by the archaeologist.

What Lies Ahead?

Archaeology is a curious social science, since archaeologists are "unable either to observe human behavior or to learn about human thoughts at first hand from their primary data," wrote Bruce Trigger (1991). Therein lies the crux of current theoretical debates. Trigger and others believe that the processual approach may lend a better understanding of what archaeologists know, but this is useless without a better comprehension of what human behavior produced the archaeological record (Wylie, 1988).

Processual and postprocessual archaeology flourish alongside each other. Processual archaeology is most successful in dealing with long-term constraints on culture change and larger-scale social structures. Such topics, as well as hunter-gatherer and farmer settlement studies, are well suited to broader, often dispassionate analysis based on statistical data. Postprocessual advocates tend to focus on individuals and small groups, on "interpretation, multivocality, meaning, agency, history" (Hodder, 1999). Such themes are best studied in complex historical societies where a great deal of written and archaeological information is available, or when researching cultural heritage for social purposes.

Where does the future lie? The answer can only be that archaeologists are uncertain. Today, many archaeologists believe that there is much greater variation in human behavior than processual archaeologists have allowed for. In other words, human behavior is less orderly than many cultural evolutionists would lead us to believe, yet not entirely random, as some postprocessual scholars assume. There are sufficient regularities in cultural developments in different regions, such as, for example, in the development of agriculture and village life in southwestern Asia and Mesoamerica, to suggest that recurrent operations of cause and effect result in the evolution of similar forms of behavior in widely separated areas.

The rich diversity of human society results from the interaction between universal psychological propensities of humankind and the varied circumstances that cause each individual to adapt to different social, ecological, and historical situations. Hence, explanation lies in varying levels of analysis between the poles of cultural universals and individual adaptations. Neither alone can explain the great differences and similarities between ancient and modern societies. Thus, the most useful evolutionary perspective in archaeology, concerned as it is with change through time, is one that focuses on individuals who are constantly adjusting their behavior as their social and physical environments change.

Hodder makes a case for a "multivocal" archaeology, for "flows of the past, continua of interpretation" (see the Site box). He thinks archaeology is a way of breaking established patterns of thought and domination in the twenty-first century. Herein lies the challenge for the archaeologists of the future—not to dominate interpretations of the past with sterile reporting and standardization but to encourage what Hodder calls "an open and diverse engagement of the past, a participation from multiple perspectives and interests." Hodder is right, for the future of archaeology lies in networks of information and diverse interpretations that celebrate and foster the remarkable diversity of humankind.

The debate over a new, more human-centered archaeology has barely begun, but we predict that more holistic approaches to the past will replace the somewhat polarized viewpoints so characteristic of archaeology today (Ucko, 1995). At the same time, new realities engage archaeology more closely with the contemporary world: new technologies such as the World Wide Web and burgeoning global tourism. On the other hand, environmental deterioration, the rapid destruction of archaeological sites, and the responsible management of cultural resources will likely be of increasing concern (Chapters 18 and 19). Archaeologists can no longer afford to live in academic ivory towers, divorced from the industrial world.

Site

Çatalhöyük, Turkey

Çatalhöyük, in central Turkey, was one of the largest communities in the world in 7000 B.C. The settlement was a large village or small town of numerous small houses built of sun-dried brick, constructed to back onto one another and occasionally separated by a court-yard (Figure 3.6). The outside walls of the flat-roofed houses served as a convenient defense wall.

The village was rebuilt at least twelve times after 7000 B.C., and owed its size and increasing prosperity to agriculture and widespread trade in obsidian (volcanic glass) quarried in nearby mountains. Obsidian was widely prized for its toolmaking qualities and was often used for ornaments because of its beauty. Volcanic glass from Turkish quarries has been traced deep into Syria and along the eastern Mediterranean coast (Chapter 16).

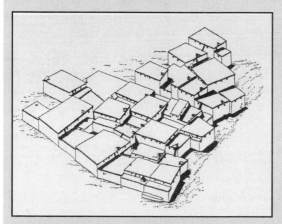

Figure 3.6 Artist's reconstruction of houses at Çatalhöyük, Turkey.

British archaeologist James Mellaart (1967) dug a series of houses and remarkable village shrines in the site that tell us much about the religious beliefs of the inhabitants. The shrine walls bear friezes of vultures and ancestors, scenes of birth and shamanistic dances, and sculptures depicting women or bulls' horns. We know little of the religious beliefs at Çatalhöyük, but the people worshiped a female deity who may have been a form of mother goddess, and they clearly revered their ancestors.

Since 1993, another British archaeologist, Ian Hodder, and an international team of researchers have been excavating Çatalhöyük as a long-term project, using a multidisciplinary perspective and innovative methods that address both the theory of excavation and many basic issues in postprocessual archaeology (Hodder, 1999).

Çatalhöyük promises to be one of the most important excavations of the early twenty-first century, both because of its innovative methodologies and because it will provide unique information on the early religious beliefs and ideologies of Stone Age farmers. The initial work by Mellaart is a good example of the importance of establishing a chronological framework and also some of the archaeological data that may be used to infer past religious beliefs. The ongoing work by Ian Hodder underscores postprocessual ideas about the importance of the modern context in which archaeologists work and the subjective perspective of the excavators.

Summary

Interpretation in modern archaeology has gone through dramatic changes since the 1950s. Based on a culture-historical foundation, a variety of processual and postprocessual perspectives are now employed by archaeologists. These represent very different ideas about the objectives and potential of archaeological research.

The process of synthesis in culture history is based on constructing precise chronological sequences. Interpretation depends on analogy and descriptive cultural models that are used to identify variables that operate when culture change takes place. These models include inevitable variation, cultural selection, invention, diffusion, and migration. They may provide a useful means of describing what happened in past societies but, in themselves, they do not explain culture change.

In the 1960s, Lewis Binford formulated new approaches to archaeology using explicitly scientific methods. He emphasized the evaluation of archaeological data using formal hypotheses and clearly stated research designs for planning all inquiries. He also drew on statistical methods long used in the natural and physical sciences. Binford's "new archaeology" was the basis of processual archaeology.

Processual archaeology embraces a systems-ecological approach that deals with the ways in which cultural systems function, both internally and in relation to external factors, such as the environment. This approach is based on general systems theory, cultural ecology, and multilinear cultural evolution.

Some archaeologists rebelled against the somewhat anonymous, impersonal depictions of the processes of culture change engendered by the processual approach. Postprocessual archaeology developed as a reaction against the ardent materialism of processual archaeology. Postprocessual archaeologists point out that archaeology is the study of human behavior, individual as well as collective. People are actors, they argue, who assume an active role in shaping their culture, their society. Some postprocessual approaches underscore the role of archaeology within modern society and with the multivocal archaeology of individuals and groups.

Modern archaeology consists of a variety of theoretical perspectives and approaches that share aspects of culture-historical, processual, and postprocessual archaeology. The archaeology of the future cannot afford to remain aloof from a real and increasingly networked world, where many human voices can contribute to new models of the human past.

Key Terms

cognitive archaeology
cognitive-processual approach
critical archaeology
cultural ecology
cultural materialism
cultural selection
deductive-nomological
    approach

diffusion
extrasomatic
general systems theory
inevitable variation
invention
migration
multilinear cultural evolution

postprocessual archaeology
processual archaeology
structural archaeology
systems-ecological approach

Guide to Further Reading

BINFORD, LEWIS R. 1983. *Working at Archaeology.* Orlando, FL: Academic Press. Binford's major papers arranged in historical order. Read in conjunction with *In Pursuit of the Past.*

———— . 2001. *In Pursuit of the Past.* Rev. ed. Berkeley: University of California Press. A first-hand account of the development of processual archaeology by its originator. The revised version features an introductory, updating chapter by the author. Essential for serious students.

GERO, JOAN, and MARGARET CONKEY, eds. 1991. *Engendering Archaeology.* Oxford: Blackwell. Thought-provoking essays on the study of gender in the archaeological record.

HAYS-GILPIN, KELLEY, and DAVID S. WHITLEY, eds. 1998. *Reader in Gender Archaeology.* New York: Routledge. A useful collection of essays on this important subject.

HEGMON, MICHELLE. 2003. "Setting Theoretical Egos Aside: Issues and Theory in North American Archaeology." *American Antiquity* 68(2): 213–244. An invaluable summary of the current status of theory in North American archaeology.

HODDER, IAN. 1999. *The Archaeological Process: An Introduction.* Oxford: Blackwell. A short, clearly written analysis of the process of archaeological research that reflects much current thinking on theory.

TRIGGER, BRUCE G. 1989. *A History of Archaeological Interpretation.* Cambridge: Cambridge University Press. An authoritative account of the development of explanation in archaeology.

WHITLEY, DAVID S., ed. 1998. *Reader in Archaeological Theory: Post-Processual and Cognitive Approaches.* New York: Routledge. A comprehensive set of readings by some of the principal figures in the development of postprocessual approaches to archaeology.

Basic Processes and Principles

Excavators, as a rule, record only those things which appear to them important at the time, but fresh problems in archaeology and anthropology are constantly arising. . . . Every detail should, therefore, be recorded in the manner most conducive to facility of reference, and it ought at all times to be the chief object of an excavator to reduce his own personal equation to a minimum.

General Augustus Lane Fox Pitt Rivers,
Excavations in Cranborne Chase (1887)

Part III describes the basic processes and principles of archaeological research. What is the archaeological record? How do archaeologists carry out their research? What are the basic principles upon which archaeology is based? In these chapters, we define the archaeological record, look at factors that affect it, and examine the concept of culture in archaeology, the nature of archaeological data, and the ways in which people have established archaeological contexts. Fundamental to context are methods of defining human activities in space and, especially, of measuring prehistoric time. We describe the various methods that have been devised for dating prehistoric cultures from the very earliest times.

CHAPTER 4

Matrix and Preservation

Chimu ceremonial knife from the northern coast of Peru,
c. twelfth to thirteenth centuries A.D.

Archaeologists study ancient human behavior using the surviving material remains of the past. The archives of this past are archaeological sites and artifacts, food remains, and many other categories of finds that make up the **archaeological record.** As we have already mentioned, this record is finite and easily destroyed. Even under the best preservation conditions, the record is incomplete, but it is the basis of all research into the remote past. Our discussion of the basic principles of archaeology begins with this record of sites, artifacts, and other phenomena. This record is incomplete and biased, for complex and still little-understood processes have transformed the abandoned artifacts, structures, and sites of our forebears. In this chapter, we examine the makeup of the archaeological record, site-formation processes, and the nature of archaeological data.

Archaeological Data

Archaeological data consist of any material remains of human activity—a scatter of broken bones, a ruined house, a gold mask, a vast temple plaza. Archaeological data result from two processes. One is human behavior, the result of human activity. The other is what are often called transformational processes. As we have seen, the archaeologist identifies and reconstructs ancient human behavior, such as the occupation of a hunter-gatherer camp. The band decides on a location, gathers building materials—sticks, brush or sod, mammoth bones—erects a dwelling, occupies it, and then destroys or just abandons the settlement. Archaeologists reconstruct sequences of ancient human behavior not only from archaeological data but also from the circumstances under which they are found.

Human behavior is the first stage in the formation of the archaeological record. But what happens when the site is deserted? The collapsed brush shelters, a scatter of stone tools, the remains of a ceremony are abandoned, being of no further use to their owners. All manner of natural processes take hold. The bodies of the buried dead decay; toppled shelters rot away in the sun. Subsequently, a nearby lake may rise and cover the remains, or windblown sand may accumulate over the stone artifacts.

Discovery

The Dead Sea Scrolls, Jordan, 1947

Dry conditions often preserve remarkable finds. Mohammed Adh-Dhib had lost a goat that hot day in 1947. The Bedouin teenager chased the errant beast as it skipped into the craggy hills near Qumran by the Dead Sea. The sun grew hotter, so he lay down under a rocky overhang to rest. His curiosity aroused by a small hole in the cliff face, he threw a stone into the opening. He heard it strike a clay vessel in the dark. He pulled himself up to the hole and saw several cylindrical objects standing in rows. They were wide-necked jars. Next day, Mohammed returned with a friend. They examined the jars and found bundles of tarry rags and folds of smooth leather. Back in camp, they unrolled one roll and found it stretched from one side of their tent to the other. Eventually, the roll and other finds ended up in the hands of a Christian cobbler, who thought he might use the leather for shoes. When he saw the writing on them, he took them to a Jerusalem convent and then ransacked the Qumran caves in search of more scrolls. The first scholars to see the scroll realized it was a copy of the book of Isaiah in the Old Testament and of priceless value. Months of careful negotiations and detective work passed before the fragmentary Dead Sea Scrolls passed into scientific hands and years of scholarly research began.

The Dead Sea Scrolls are important religious texts that bear witness to the historical environment in which Christianity first emerged. They were buried in a remote cave by the members of an austere Jewish community at Qumran in about A.D. 58, when Roman persecution made life impossible. The Scrolls soon became political symbols of immense value, now on view to tourists in Israel's Shrine of the Book. Their study and interpretation continue to occupy dozens of experts.

Another group may come and build a farming village on the same spot or may simply reuse some of the artifacts left by the earlier occupants.

All these cultural and noncultural developments are **transformational processes**—continuous, dynamic, and unique processes that vary with each archaeological site. Of course, there are wide differences in the preservation of various artifacts, raw materials, and other finds. Thus, the archaeologist's data are always biased and incomplete, altered by a variety of transformational, or site-transformation, processes. It follows that anyone investigating an archaeological site has to look closely at both natural and human agents of transformation. For example, World Wars I and II destroyed thousands of archaeological sites, whereas wet conditions in Scandinavian bogs have preserved prehistoric corpses in excellent condition.

Site-Formation Processes

The objects from the past that survive come down to us in two forms, either as historically documented artifacts, such as Orville and Wilbur Wright's first airplane, or in the archaeological record as culturally deposited artifacts that are no longer part of a living society. This past, in the form of artifacts, does not come to us unchanged, for complex processes have acted upon these objects, be they tools, dwellings, burials, food remains, or other human-manufactured or -modified items. In their study of these artifacts, archaeologists must also untangle the many events and processes that contributed to the great variation in the archaeological record as we know it today (Butzer, 1982; Schiffer, 1987).

The factors that create the historical and archaeological records are known as site-formation processes. **Site-formation processes** are those agencies, natural or cultural, that have transformed the archaeological (or historical) record since a site was abandoned. There are two basic forms of site-formation processes: cultural and noncultural.

Cultural transformations are those in which human behavior has transformed the archaeological record. They can vary widely in their impact and intensity. For example, later occupants of a site that was a hunter-gatherer camp in southwestern Asia may have been farmers and goatherders rather than hunters. The foundations of their houses cut deeply into underlying strata, and the hooves of their penned goats trampled on and scattered small stone artifacts lying on the surface. And, of course, the archaeologist's excavations are cultural processes, too.

On a more specific level, people reuse artifacts—to conserve precious tools and valuable raw materials—changing the use of an artifact from a knife to a scraper, recycling a projectile point to another use. Sometimes prestigious or valuable objects become prized heirlooms passed down from generation to generation or buried with the dead, as soapstone pipes and other precious artifacts were with Hopewell kin leaders in the Midwest more than 2,000 years ago. Reuse, especially of commodities such as building materials, can become a potent factor in settlements that are occupied for long periods of time, where people recycle old bricks and other materials for new dwellings. Then there is the dumping of trash, some of it underfoot, much of it elsewhere in secondary locations where trash heaps may form. These heaps often tend to cluster in specific locations—perhaps a convenient, abandoned storage pit or an old dwelling—that can be used for many generations. Disposal of the dead can be viewed as another form of discard behavior. The archaeologist must decipher the complicated behavioral processes—the logic, if you will—behind the accumulation of trash heaps, the disposal of the dead, and many other activities. In short, the archaeological record is not a safe place for artifacts, for myriad human activities can disturb them after deposition—plowing, mining, digging of foundations, clearing land, even artillery bombardment, to say nothing of pot hunting and site looting.

Noncultural processes are the events and processes of the natural environment that affect the archaeological record. The chemical properties of the soil or bacteria may accelerate the decay of organic remains such as wooden spears or dwellings or may even increase the chances of superb preservation. Rivers may overflow and inundate a settlement, mantling the abandoned remains with fine silt. A great earthquake can topple a settlement in a few minutes, as happened to the Roman town at Kourion in Cyprus on July 21, A.D. 365 (Soren and James, 1988). Windblown sands, ice disturbances, and even the actions of earthworms can disturb the archaeological record.

Whether site-formation processes are cultural or noncultural, the important point is that the archaeological record can never be taken at face value. In other words, what you see in the ground is not necessarily a direct reflection of human behavior. In recording, analyzing, and interpreting the archaeological record, the archaeologist must also consider and investigate the formation processes that altered the record from the moment of its deposition.

Site-formation processes are always important in archaeology, but they assume special importance when it is necessary to document precise associations between, say, human activity and extinct animals. This necessity is especially evident in the ongoing debates about the date of the first human settlement of the Americas (Meltzer, 2003). The earliest, well-attested occupation of the Americas dates to about 13,000 years ago, perhaps a couple of millennia earlier, documented by an archaeological record that is beyond question. It is a different matter with earlier claims, claims as early as 40,000 years ago or more, notably from sites in South America. The Boqueirão da Pedra Furada site in northeastern Brazil is claimed to contain evidence of human occupation, including hearths, dating to before 40,000 years ago. However, the excavators failed to scrutinize the site-formation processes that acted on the artifacts from the lower levels of the site (Guidon and Delibrias, 1986). Natural geological phenomena such as water action, which filled the lower levels of the cave, resulted in the appearance of a 32,000-year-old occupation and associated artifacts (Meltzer and others, 1994).

The natural environment is a hostile place for human artifacts, for the process of interacting with it causes deterioration and drastic modification of the many properties of artifacts, affecting everything from color and texture to weight, shape, chemical composition, and appearance. The environmental agents of deterioration can be grouped into chemical, physical, and biological categories, and some agents produce more than one type of change; for example, water and sunlight produce both chemical and physical changes (Schiffer, 1987).

Chemical agents are universal, for the atmosphere contains water and oxygen, which create many chemical reactions; corrosion of some metals is an example. Different water temperatures, irradiation of materials by sunlight, and atmospheric pollutants all cause chemical reactions. Buried objects are often subject to rapid chemical change, especially as a result of dampness. Soils also contain reactive compounds, such as acids and bases, that contribute to many deterioration processes. Acidic soils dissolve bones, for example. Many archaeological deposits are somewhat salty, a condition caused by salts derived from wood ash, urine, and the neutralization of acids and bases. Such saline conditions can retard some decay, but they can severely accelerate the decay of copper, iron, and silver.

Physical agents of deterioration are also universal: water, wind, sunlight, and earth movement. Water is especially potent, for it can tumble artifacts on the shores of oceans or lakes or from riverbank encampments, sometimes even fracturing them in ways that suggest human manufacture. Rainwater can cascade off roofs and tunnel deep grooves into walls. The cycle of wetness followed by drying cracks many woods and causes rot; melting and freezing ice cracks rocks, even concrete. Physical agents operate on scales small and large. For example, the effects of the Kourion earthquake flattened the small port and also affected the landscape for miles around.

Living organisms are the main agents of biological decay. Bacteria occur almost everywhere and are usually the first to colonize dead organic matter and begin the processes of decay. Fungi also occur widely and are especially destructive to wood and other plant matter, particularly in damp, warm climates. Beetles, ants, flies, and termites infest archaeological sites, especially middens and abandoned foods. Animals such as dogs and hyenas chew, gnaw, and scavenge bones and other organic materials from the surfaces of abandoned sites and game kills.

In summary, archaeological sites are affected by all the processes within their natural environment. The first human activity at any site took place on a natural surface, on natural sediments themselves sitting on underlying bedrock. Sometimes this underlying sediment was weathered over a long time and may contain pollen grains, plant remains, or other sources of environmental information. For instance, some Bronze Age burial mounds in Europe were erected on undisturbed soils that contained forest pollen grains, giving a picture of the local environment at the time of construction (Chapter 12). After a site is abandoned, additional sediments usually accumulate on top of the archaeological remains through the action of wind or water, such as the windblown sands that accumulate in the rooms of Southwestern pueblos. Human feet or animal paws, burrowing animals, earthworms, wall flakings from overhanging cliffs, and the deteriorating elements of artifacts and structures contribute to the alteration of archaeological deposits. Rock shelters in southwestern France, for example, were occupied intermittently by hunter-gatherer groups between 30,000 and 15,000 years ago. Some of the larger ones contain densely packed layers of hearths, ash accumulations, boulders, and decaying structures (Laville and others, 1980). Untangling how these levels were formed is a complex process.

The site-formation processes at each individual site must be considered separately, usually in the context of the different deposits within the site. The first stage is to identify the specific cultural and noncultural transformation processes that created each deposit or set of deposits. This identification involves thinking of the artifacts as an integral part of the deposits in which they are found. The investigator records and analyzes such phenomena as reductions in size, patterns of damage, and distribution within the deposit as clues to understanding the complex "package" of materials that make up that deposit. In other words, the archaeologist has to establish what cultural and noncultural processes led to the formation of each deposit in the site.

The fundamental point about studying site-formation processes is that they have to be identified before behavioral or environmental inferences can be made about any archaeological site. Identifying specific site-formation processes is difficult, even under ideal circumstances, and involves not only geological research but also data acquired from ethnoarchaeology, controlled experiments, and other sources. It is not enough, then, to observe conditions of unusually good preservation or to describe the complex layers of a prehistoric rock shelter. One must also analyze and interpret the ways in which the archaeological record was created through site-formation processes.

The Matrix: Preservation and Human Activity

All archaeological finds, from a humble worker's stone chopper to an Egyptian pharaoh's tomb, occur within a **matrix** (the physical substance that surrounds the find), from natural phenomena such as a river flood or from human behavior such as the building of a new community on top of an older one. The chemical and physical characteristics of the matrix can have a profound effect not only on the provenance (the precise three-dimensional position of the find in the matrix as recorded by the archaeologist) of an archaeological find but also on its context and association with other subjects. For example, the physical characteristics of the deposits in which dozens of Stone Age hand axes were found tell us that fast-running waters of the River Thames in England rolled them downstream from where they were originally dropped by their makers and deposited them in river gravels, to be recovered by archaeologists more than 250,000 years later. Human behavior also determines the context and provenance of archaeological finds in the matrix. Many Hopewellian culture burials of 1,800 years ago were deposited in mound platforms in the Ohio Valley. Careful excavation of the surrounding deposits shows that many people were laid to rest before a large earthwork was erected over the sepulchral platform where the dead lay (Fagan, 2005).

Evaluating the natural formation processes that have contributed to the archaeological record involves geological and archaeological research combined. Deciphering human activities from artifact patterns in the matrix requires careful evaluation of many subtle behaviors from the remote past. The following are some common instances of human activity that affect the archaeological record.

Discarding

The patterns of artifact discard can be very subtle; understanding them often requires knowledge that is still beyond our grasp. For example, at the Maya trading center on Cozumel, off the coast of the Yucatán Peninsula, the people invested very little material wealth in temples, tombs, or other permanent monuments (Friedel and Sabloff, 1984). Their capital in obsidian (volcanic glass) was kept fluid and on hand, an investment in resources different from that found at other Maya ceremonial centers, which invested heavily in religious monuments and tangible displays of wealth. The different investments in resources reflect the activities and their significance in each type of locality. Deciphering such patterns of discard—the remains that are left for interpretation after the long centuries and millennia of natural destruction have taken place—presents huge difficulties for archaeologists.

Recycling

People discard artifacts, and they recycle them as well. A stone ax can be sharpened again and again until the original, large artifact is just a small stub that has been recycled into extinction. It takes a great deal of effort to build a mud-brick house from scratch. Very often, an old house is renovated repeatedly, its precious wooden beams used again in the same structure or in another building. Such recycling can distort the archaeological record, for what appears to be a one-time structure might in fact have been used again and again. Tree-ring dating of pueblos in the Southwest is complicated by the constant reuse of wooden beams. Sometimes, too, the Pueblo Indians would cut beams and stockpile them for later use.

Not only individual artifacts but also entire archaeological sites can be recycled. A settlement flourishes on a low ridge in southwestern Asia. After a generation or two the site is abandoned, and the inhabitants move. Later, people return to the site, level the abandoned houses, and build their own dwellings on top of the site. This type of recycling can seal and preserve earlier levels, but it can also result in the reuse of building materials from earlier houses.

Preserving Ceremonial Artifacts and Heirlooms

Successive generations may find a structure or an artifact so valuable that they consciously preserve it for the benefit of their descendants. The great temple, or *ziggurat,* of the city of Eridu in Mesopotamia was first erected around 5000 B.C. This important shrine was visible for miles around and was rebuilt on the same site time and time again for more than 2,000 years. Tracing the complex history of this mud-brick structure has consumed many hours of excavation time (Lloyd, 1963).

Many ancient societies valued ritual objects, such as masks, ceremonial axes, and other symbolic artifacts that were associated with ancestor worship. These ceremonial artifacts were sometimes buried with a dead priest or leader, as with Tutankhamun and with the lords of Sipán in Peru (see the Doing Archaeology box). It is easy enough to tell their age and association with a grave dug at a particular period. In other instances, ceremonial artifacts can be treasured for generations, displayed only on special occasions or kept in a special relic hut. By treasuring such objects, however, the owners can unwittingly distort the archaeological record. Fortunately, in most cases it is possible to identify instances of curation, or preservation, by the style of the artifacts. In Tutankhamun's tomb, Howard Carter found objects that had belonged to earlier pharaohs. Presumably, they had been placed in the tomb to fill in gaps in the royal inventory caused by the king's unexpected death (Reeves, 1990).

Deliberate and Accidental Destruction

The many other potential causes of human distortion of the archaeological record can include deliberate destruction of cemeteries, erasure of inscriptions from temples at royal command, or the ravages of warfare, both ancient and modern. Even more destructive are depredations by treasure hunters and antiquities dealers to satisfy the greed of museums and private collectors (Meyer, 1992).

Preservation Conditions: Inorganic and Organic Materials

We now examine preservation conditions, some of the circumstances under which the archaeological record comes down to us in exceptional condition. Under highly favorable circumstances, many kinds of artifacts are preserved, including such perishable items as leather containers, baskets, wooden arrowheads, and furniture. But under normal circumstances, only the most durable artifacts survive. In general, the

Doing Archaeology

The Ur Lyre, Iraq

The Royal Cemetery at Ur, in southern Iraq, was excavated by British archaeologist Leonard Woolley in 1931, some years after he had located a royal burial pit with gold artifacts. He waited deliberately for about five years before he felt he had the skills and the trained personnel to recover a royal burial and its ceremonial artifacts. The excavation yielded remarkably complete details of a royal funeral in 2900 B.C., but Woolley's greatest triumph was his recovery of a wooden lyre, despite all the wooden parts having rotted in the ground.

While excavating the burial of Prince Pu-abi, Woolley noticed a small, vertical hole in the ground and some fragments of ivory inlay. Suspecting that he had located a precious artifact, he mixed plaster of paris and water and poured the solution into the hole, so that it filled all the hollows below ground. Once the plaster had hardened, he removed the block of soil around the mysterious artifact for careful excavation in the laboratory. Back at the British Museum, in London, Woolley removed the soil from around his plaster cast with meticulous care, recording the position of every tiny inlay fragment exposed during the process. His plaster cast reproduced the wooden parts of a superb musician's lyre with timber box inlaid with ivory and semiprecious stone that lay on the bodies of three women, perhaps musicians, placed atop them after they had died. He was able to build an accurate reconstruction of one of the earliest known musical instruments in the world from his inspired piece of archaeological detective work (Figure 4.1).

Ur's Royal Cemetery, like the tomb of the Egyptian pharaoh Tutankhamun, offered a rare opportunity to study ceremonial artifacts, perhaps some of them heirlooms as they were laid out in the original sepulcher. In the case of Pu-abi, Woolley reconstructed the entire funeral process, from the digging of the deep burial pit to the mass suicide of the royal court in its depths. Unfortunately, the surviving records of the Ur excavation do not allow us to check the accuracy of Woolley's remarkable story of a royal funeral 5,000 years ago.

Figure 4.1   The wooden lyre reconstructed by Leonard Woolley from the Royal Cemetery at Ur.

objects found in archaeological sites are of two broad categories: inorganic and organic materials.

Inorganic materials include stone, metals, and clay. Prehistoric stone implements, such as the choppers of the earliest humans made 2.5 million years ago, have survived in perfect condition for archaeologists to find. Their cutting edges are just as sharp as they were when abandoned by their makers. Clay pots are among the most durable artifacts, especially if they were well fired. It is no coincidence that much of prehistory is reconstructed from chronological sequences of changing pottery styles. Fragments (potsherds) of well-fired clay vessels are practically indestructible; they have lasted as long as 10,000 years in some Japanese sites.

Organic materials are objects made of plant- or animal-derived substances, such as wood, leather, bone, or cotton. They rarely survive in the archaeological record. When they do, the picture of ancient life they give us is much more complete than that from inorganic finds.

Organic Materials and the Archaeological Record

Most of the world's archaeological sites preserve little more than the inorganic remains of the past. Sometimes, however, especially favorable preservation conditions result in the survival of highly informative organic materials. Conditions of moisture and temperature extremes have preserved many archaeological sites.

Waterlogged Environs and Wetlands

Waterlogged or peat-bog conditions are particularly favorable for preserving wood or vegetal remains, whether the climate is subtropical or temperate. Tropical rain forests, such as those of the Amazon basin and the Congo, are far from kind to wooden artifacts. In contrast, a significant number of archaeological sites occur near springs or in marshes where the water table is high and perennial waterlogging of occupation layers has occurred since they were abandoned (Coles and Coles, 1986, 1989; Purdy, 1988). Numerous shipwrecks have yielded valuable archives of information, for conditions under water have preserved even insignificant artifacts. English King Henry VIII's warship *Mary Rose* yielded priceless information on Tudor ship construction and gunnery, as well as the skeletons of archers, their weaponry, and various day-to-day artifacts, large and small. The Uluburun Bronze Age ship from southern Turkish waters provided a unique portrait of eastern Mediterranean trade more than 3,300 years ago, and the ship's timbers will add much to our knowledge of early marine architecture (see Figure 1.11 and Chapter 16).

Wetlands—dreary, waterlogged countryside—are far from appealing. In ancient times, wetlands were often used just for hunting or were traversed by pathways. Others were exploited for crops, for grazing, or even for settlement and such industries as gathering thatching grass. Wetlands come in an infinite variety, each type formed by unique depositional processes, and encompass a highly varied archaeological content. Many wetland sites have been well protected from the ravages of animal and human

Figure 4.2 Bronze Age track in the Somerset Levels, southwestern England.

scavengers and from the severe noncultural processes that act on more exposed locations. In some cases, as in the Somerset Levels of southwestern England, archaeologists have been able to reconstruct entire landscapes traversed by wooden walkways; their reconstruction methods have included not only walking but also use of aerial photographs, remote sensing, and subsurface boring (Coles and Coles, 1986).

     Somerset Levels, England. The Somerset Levels in England were once a bay of the nearby Severn River, a bay filled with thick peat deposits between 6,000 and 1,500 years ago (Coles and Coles, 1986). Conditions on the Levels fluctuated constantly, so the inhabitants built wooden trackways that traversed their traditional routes across the Levels (Figure 4.2). Some 6,000 years ago, the Neolithic builders of the Sweet Track needed a raised walkway to join two islands in a marsh. They felled trees on dry ground, prepared them as required, and carried the wood to the marsh edge. Then they placed long poles end to end on the marsh surface along the preferred route. They usually used alder, ash, or hazel trunks pegged into the underlying wet ground with stout stems about every 3 feet (1 m). The pegs were driven in obliquely in pairs, crossing over the poles in a **V** shape. The builders then lodged planks into these crossed pegs on top of the poles, forming a mile-long walkway about 16 inches (41 cm) wide and about the same height above the poles.

     The Sweet Track excavations have provided a unique opportunity for paleoenvironmental reconstruction and also for tree-ring analyses. A chronology from the ash trees has established that all the timber for the track was expertly felled at one time, with the track being used for about ten years. So detailed were the investigations that the excavators were able to show that part of the track, over a particularly wet portion, was repaired several times. Wooden wedges, wooden mallets, and stone axes were used

Figure 4.3   Tollund Man, preserved for 2,000 years in a Danish bog.

for splitting the planks; other artifacts came from the crevices of the track, among them stone arrowheads, complete with traces of shaft, glue, and binding; hazelwood bows; and imported stone axes.

Tollund Man, Denmark.   Danish bogs have yielded a rich harvest of wood-hafted weapons, clothing, ornaments, traps, and even complete corpses, such as that of Tollund Man (Glob, 1969). This unfortunate individual's body was found by two peat cutters in 1950, lying on its side in a brown peat bed in a crouched position, a serene expression on his face and eyes tightly closed (Figure 4.3). Tollund Man wore a pointed skin cap and a hide belt—nothing else. We know that he had been hanged, because a cord was found knotted tightly around his neck. The Tollund corpse has been shown to be about 2,000 years old and to belong to the Danish Iron Age. A formidable team of medical experts examined his cadaver, among them a paleobotanist who established that Tollund Man's last meal consisted of a gruel made from barley, linseed, and several wild grasses and weeds, eaten twelve to twenty-four hours before his death. The reason for his execution or sacrifice is unknown.

Ozette, Washington.   Richard Daugherty of Washington State University worked at the Ozette site on the Olympia Peninsula in the Pacific Northwest for more than a decade (Kirk, 1974). The site first came to his attention in 1947 as part of a survey of coastal settlements. Ozette had been occupied by Makah Indians until twenty or thirty years before, and traces of their collapsed houses could be seen on top of a large midden. It was not until 1966 that Daugherty was able to start excavations at the site, which was being threatened with obliteration by wave action and mud slides. A trial trench revealed large deposits of whale bones and yielded radiocarbon samples

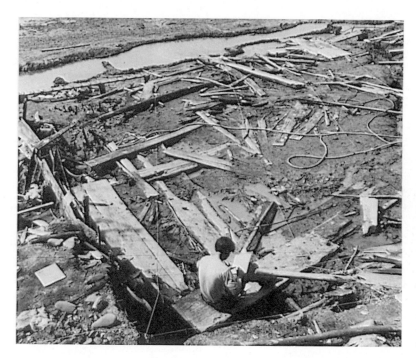

Figure 4.4 Ozette, Washington. Excavation of the walls, sleeping benches, and planks of a prehistoric house uncovered by a mud slide. The waterlogged conditions preserved wood and fiber perfectly.

dating back 2,500 years. Most important, the muddy deposits had preserved traces of wooden houses and the organic remains in them. Then, in 1970, a call from the Makah Tribal Council alerted Daugherty to a new discovery. High waves had cut into the midden and had caused the wet soil to slump, revealing collapsed wooden houses buried under an ancient landslide.

Daugherty and his colleagues worked for more than ten years to uncover the remains of four cedarwood longhouses and their contents (Figure 4.4). The excavations were fraught with difficulty. High-pressure hoses and sprays were needed to clear the mud away from the delicate woodwork. All the finds were then preserved with chemicals before final analysis. The wet muck that mantled the houses had engulfed them suddenly in a dense, damp blanket that preserved everything except flesh, feathers, and skins. The houses were perfectly preserved; one, uncovered in 1972, measured 69 feet long and 46 feet wide (21 m by 14 m). There were separate hearths and cooking platforms, and hanging mats and low walls served as partitions. More than 40,000 artifacts came from the excavations, including conical rain hats made of spruce roots, baskets, wooden bowls still impregnated with seal oil, mats, fishhooks, harpoons, combs, bows and arrows, even fragments of looms, and ferns and cedar leaves. The finds included a whale fin carved of red cedar and inlaid with 700 sea otter teeth (see Figure 11.17).

The Ozette site is a classic example of how much can be recovered from an archaeological site in waterlogged conditions. But Ozette is important in other ways, too, for the Makah Indians who lived there had a tangible history extending back at least 2,000 years before the Europeans came. Oral traditions and written records for

Figure 4.5   Moccasins from Hogup cave, Utah.

the Makah go back no farther than A.D. 1800. The Makah abandoned Ozette only in modern times, to move nearer to a school in the 1920s. The archaeological excavations have traced the continuity of this village of whale catchers and fisherfolk far back into the past, giving a new sense of historical identity to the Makah of today.

Dry Conditions

Very arid environments, such as those of the American Southwest or the Nile Valley, are even better for preservation than waterlogged localities. The caves of the arid North American Great Basin have preserved such organic finds as moccasins (Figure 4.5).

The Tomb of Tutankhamun, Egypt.   One of the most famous of all archaeological discoveries is the amazing tomb of Tutankhamun (c. 1323 B.C.), unearthed by Lord Carnarvon and Howard Carter in 1922 (H. Carter and others, 1923–1933; Reeves, 1990). The undisturbed burial chamber was opened, revealing the grave furniture in exactly the same state as it had been laid out by the king's mourners. Gilded wood chests, cloth, ivory caskets, models of chariots and boats, and the mummy were all perfectly preserved, together with a bewildering array of jewelry and paintings shining as brightly as the day they were painted, even showing the somewhat hasty execution accorded them by the artist. Tutankhamun's sepulcher provides as vivid a glimpse of the past as we are ever likely to obtain (see photo on chapter 1 opening page and Figure 4.6).

Chinchorro Mummies, Chile.   The Chinchorro culture flourished along the southern Peruvian and Chilean coasts of South America at least as early as 7000 B.C. The Chinchorro were a hunter-gatherer society that subsisted off the rich Pacific inshore fisheries and local patches of wild plant foods (Arriaza, 1995). They settled in permanent villages, burying their dead in cemeteries such as one at the El Morro site near Arica. More than 280 Chinchorro mummies have been recovered from coastal cemeteries, astonishingly well preserved in one of the driest environments on the

Figure 4.6 The jumble of well-preserved artifacts, including chariots, funerary beds, and personal effects, in the antechamber of Tutankhamun's tomb. (Egyptian Dynasty XVIII, Thebes: Valley of the Kings, Tomb of Tut-ankh-amun: Antechamber south end. Photography by Egyptian Expedition, The Metropolitan Museum of Art)

earth. Beginning in about 5000 B.C., the people dismembered the dead, skinned and eviscerated them, then packed the bodies with plant material and reinforced them with sticks. Then they sewed them together with human hair and cactus needles. With red-painted ash paste, they attached wigs of human hair, like helmets, to the skulls and often painted the faces of the mummies black. Sometimes the mourners reattached the skin like bandages around the trunks and legs. The mummified bodies were displayed and cared for, then eventually wrapped in shrouds of twined reeds and buried in shallow graves, sometimes in family groups of six or more. Mummification ceased among the Chinchorro in about 1500 B.C., centuries before Tutankhamun ruled Egypt. The bone chemistry and bowels of the Chinchorro mummies reveal a diet heavy in seafood and evidence of tapeworm infestations and auditory exostosis, caused by diving in deep water.

Extreme Cold Conditions

Arctic sites, too, are excellent for preserving the human past. The circumpolar regions of Siberia and the Americas have acted like a giant freezer in which the processes of decay have been held in check for thousands of years. Close to the Arctic Ocean, dozens of deep-frozen mammoth carcasses have survived for millennia in a state of perennial refrigeration. Perhaps the most famous is the Beresovka mammoth, which became mired on the swampy banks of a Siberian river one spring some 10,000 years ago. The Russian expedition that recovered the carcass in 1901 found the meat so fresh that the scientists fed it to their dogs. The mammoth's hair was perfectly preserved, and the remains of its last meal were found on its tongue and in its stomach (Digby, 1926).

"The Ice Man," Italian Alps.   A combination of dry winds and extreme cold dried out and preserved a 5,300-year-old Bronze Age corpse found high on the Similaun glacier in the European Alps in 1991 (Barfield, 1994; Spindler, 1994) (Figure 4.7). The forty-year-old man's body was first dried out by cold winds, then

Figure 4.7   A reconstruction of "Otzi the Ice Man" from the Similaun glacier in the European Alps.

buried by snow and ice before being exposed in modern times when the glacier melted in warm weather. The man carried a copper ax with a wooden shaft, a leather quiver with fourteen bone- and wood-pointed arrows, and replacement arrowheads and a puttylike substance for mounting them. He wore leather boots lined with hay for warmth, a stone necklace, and leather and fur garments. His knee and back bore small tattoos. The cause of death has been the source of considerable speculation. Recently, an arrowhead was found buried deep in his right shoulder, while a dagger wound, perhaps resulting from a hand-to-hand fight, had crippled his left hand. Severely wounded, perhaps he escaped from his enemy (enemies), then collapsed and died in the small gully where he was found. An international team of experts is examining the body, deciphering its DNA, and analyzing its connective tissues. The Similaun corpse has been radiocarbon-dated to between 3350 and 3300 B.C.

Inca Mountain Sacrifices, Peru and Argentina.   The Inca people of South America carried out human sacrifices on mountain peaks high in the Andes, for they regarded such mountains as sacred. Fortunately for science, the bitterly cold conditions at high altitude preserved the mummies of young boys and girls in near-perfect conditions. Anthropologist Johan Reinhard (1996) and his Peruvian colleague Miguel Zarate found the mummy bundle of a girl at an altitude of 20,700 feet (6,210 m) in the southern Peruvian Andes. The fourteen-year-old Inca girl died as a sacrificial victim five centuries ago and was buried on a summit ridge of the sacred Nevado Ampato mountain (Figure 4.8). Her well-preserved body was wrapped in a rough outer garment over a brown-and-white striped cloth. Underneath, she wore a finely woven dress and a shawl fastened with a silver pin. Her feet bore leather moccasins, but her head was bare. She may originally have worn a fanlike feather headdress, which was dislodged when the summit ridge collapsed and her mummy bundle fell down a slope. Computerized tomography (CT) scans of her skull revealed fractures by her right eye.

Figure 4.8   The Nevado Ampato mummy, Peru.

She died from a massive hemorrhage resulting from a swift blow to the head. Blood from the wound pushed her brain to one side of her skull.

Reinhard (1999) later discovered three more mummies—two girls and a boy—in the Argentinian Andes, in such good condition that their organs are intact. The researchers could even see the fine hair growing on the victims' arms. Frozen blood may still fill the heart of one mummy. The children were between eight and fourteen years old when they died, but their cause of death has not yet been established. The clothed victims were buried with a rich collection of three dozen gold, silver, and shell ritual figures, half of them clothed. Bundles of ornate textiles, moccasins, and clay vessels, some even containing food, accompanied the children. These were remote sacrifices, lying at the summit of a volcano at least 124 miles (200 km) from the nearest village.

Tragedy at Utqiagvik, Alaska.   Another spectacular discovery, this time on a bluff overlooking the Arctic Ocean near Barrow, Alaska, also records a tragedy, this one from more recent times. Two Inupiat women, one in her forties, the other in her twenties, were asleep in a small driftwood-and-sod house on a bluff overlooking the ocean on a stormy night in the 1540s (Hall et al., 1990). A teenage boy and two young girls slept nearby. The sea ice was crashing against the shore, the ice pack driven against the coast by high waves. Suddenly, a giant mass of ice chunks broke free in a violent surge and was carried over the bluff, crashing tons of ice down on the tiny house. The roof collapsed, killing the inhabitants immediately. At dawn, the neighbors found the house silent and left it buried under the ice. Later, members of the family removed some utensils and food from the ruins, and the timber uprights projecting through the ice were salvaged. The rest was undisturbed for four centuries, a deep-frozen prehistoric tragedy.

Five centuries ago, Utqiagvik was a sizable settlement (there are at least 60 house mounds), but it is now buried under much of an expanding Barrow, Alaska. In 1982, the remains of the winter house of the two Inupiat women came to light, intact and still mostly frozen. The house was formed of hand-hewn driftwood used for both floorboards and wall panels. Everything was held together with a matrix of frozen earth, and the house was insulated with a sod roof. The well-preserved bodies of the women were autopsied. Both had been in reasonably good health, although their lungs were blackened with anthracosis, a condition caused by inhaling smoke and oil-lamp fumes in closed-in winter houses. They ate a heavy diet of whale and seal blubber, which had narrowed their arteries and caused atherosclerosis. The older woman had given birth about two months before the disaster and was still lactating. Both of them had suffered periods of poor nutrition and illness. The older had recovered from pneumonia and a painful muscle infection called trichinosis, perhaps contracted from eating raw polar bear meat. The women had slept naked under their bed robes, probably to avoid moisture buildup in their everyday garments, which would freeze when they went outside.

Outside, they had worn caribou parkas, snow goggles, mittens, and waterproof sealskin inner boots, all found in the entrance tunnel to the house. Much of their time was spent making and repairing clothing and maintaining the hunting gear that was well preserved in the ruins. There were bone harpoon heads for hunting seals and other sea mammals, with the remains of a bola, a sinew throwing device weighted with bone weights used to snare birds in flight. A wooden bucket stitched together with baleen and a wood-and-bone pick for clearing ice were recovered near the house entry.

Volcanic Ash

Everyone has heard of Roman Herculaneum and Pompeii, entire towns overwhelmed in A.D. 79 by an eruption of nearby Vesuvius. The volcanic ash and lava buried both communities, even preserving the body casts of fleeing victims (see Figure 2.1). Such sites are rare, but when they are discovered they yield remarkable finds. In about A.D. 580, a volcanic eruption in San Salvador suddenly buried a small Maya village at Cerén (Sheets, 1992). The people had eaten their evening meal but had not yet gone to bed. They abandoned their houses and possessions and fled for their lives. Not only did the ash bury the village, it also smothered the nearby crops, burying corn and agave plants in the fields. Payson Sheets and a multidisciplinary research team have recovered entire dwellings and outhouses and the artifacts within them just as they were abandoned, for the ash was too thick for the people to rescue their possessions.

Each Cerén household had a building for eating, sleeping, and other activities, as well as a storehouse, a kitchen, and sometimes other structures (Figure 4.9). Substantial thatched roofs projected beyond the walls, providing not only covered walkways but also places for processing grain and for storage. Each household planted maize, cacao, agave, and other crops in gardens close to the house, setting most crops in neat rows. Grain was stored in clay vessels with tight lids. Some corn and chilis were suspended from the roof, and many implements were also kept in the rafters. So far, the excavations have uncovered three public buildings, one of which may have been a community center. Also found were outlying maize fields, where the plants were doubled over, with the ears still attached to the stalk—a "storage" technique still used in parts of Central America. The mature maize plants indicate that the eruption occurred at the end of the growing season, in August.

Figure 4.9   Artist's reconstruction of the dwelling, kitchen, workshop (*right*), and storehouse (*left*). (Household 1, Cerén, San Salvador.)

Cerén provides an unusually complete look at life in a humble Maya settlement far removed from the great ceremonial centers where the elite lived. It is remarkable for its complete artifact inventories and food supplies, finds so well preserved that even minute details of village architecture are evident. We even know where the Cerén people kept their sharp knives away from curious children—in the rafters of their houses.

Summary

Site-formation, or transformational, processes are factors that create the historical and archaeological records, natural or cultural agencies that have changed the archaeological record during and since a site was abandoned.

There are two basic types of site-formation processes. Cultural transformations are those in which human behavior has changed the archaeological record through such acts as rebuilding houses or reusing artifacts. Noncultural processes are events and processes of the natural environment that affect the archaeological record, such as the chemical properties of the soil and natural phenomena such as earthquakes and wind action.

Later human activity can radically affect archaeological preservation. People may selectively discard or preserve some types of artifacts, and many variables can affect the layout of settlements and other considerations. Some people, such as the Southwestern Indians, recycled wooden beams and other materials, distorting the archaeological record. Sites are reused, lower strata are often disturbed, and succeeding generations may preserve an important building, such as a temple, for centuries. Modern warfare, industrial activity, even deep agriculture and cattle grazing can affect the preservation of archaeological remains.

Preservation conditions depend mostly on the soil and general climatic regime in the area of a site. Inorganic objects, such as stone and baked clay, often survive almost indefinitely. But organic materials, such as bone, wood, and leather, survive only under exceptional conditions, such as in dry climates, in permafrost areas, and in waterlogged areas.

Waterlogged and peat-bog conditions are especially favorable for preserving wood and vegetal remains. In this context we discussed the Somerset Levels, Danish bog corpses, and the Ozette village in Washington State as sites of these types.

Dry conditions can preserve almost the full range of human artifacts, the best examples being the remarkably complete preservation of ancient Egyptian culture and the finds made in desert caves in the American West and in South America.

Arctic conditions can refrigerate organic materials in the soil. We described the discovery of the "Ice Man" in the European Alps as well as Inca mountain sacrifices in South America, a buried Eskimo family in Alaska, and modern findings on the fate of the Franklin expedition.

Volcanic ash preserved the Maya village at Cerén in San Salvador. A sudden eruption mantled the settlement in thick ash, so that entire houses and their contents, as well as gardens, survived intact.

Key Terms

archaeological data	inorganic materials	organic materials
archaeological record	matrix	site-formation processes
cultural transformations	noncultural processes	transformational processes

Guide to Further Reading

BEATTIE, O., and J. GEIGER. 1986. *Frozen in Time: The Fate of the Franklin Expedition.* London: Bloomsbury. The fascinating story of the Franklin burials told for a popular audience. An excellent case study of the difficulties of working in a cold environment.

COLES, BRYONY, and JOHN M. COLES. 1986. *Sweet Track to Glastonbury.* New York: Thames and Hudson. An exemplary account of the Coles's excavations in England's Somerset Levels. Excellent illustrations.

REEVES, NICHOLAS. 1990. *The Complete Tutankhamun.* London: Thames and Hudson. All you need to know about this most famous of archaeological discoveries, superbly illustrated.

SCHIFFER, MICHAEL B. 1987. *Site Formation Processes of the Archaeological Record.* Tucson: University of Arizona Press. A synthesis of site-formation processes in archaeology and some of the research problems associated with them. Comprehensive bibliography.

SHEETS, PAYSON D. 1992. *The Cerén Site: A Prehistoric Village Buried by Volcanic Ash.* New York: Holt, Rinehart & Winston. A short case study of this Maya village buried by volcanic ash. Ideal for readers unfamiliar with archaeological methods.

CHAPTER 5

Doing Archaeological Research

Moai statues at Ahu Nau Nau on the north coast of Easter Island in the South Pacific. These ancestral figures bear topknots of red volcanic rock.

One of the most essential qualities of an archaeologist is an ability to function as a member of a team. A century ago, most archaeologists worked virtually alone. Today, archaeologists work much more carefully and never alone. They work not only with other archaeologists but with scientists from other disciplines as well. All archaeological research is a complex process involving research design, field surveys, excavation, and lengthy laboratory analyses of many types of finds.

After discussing the qualifications of a good archaeologist, we look at the relationship between science and archaeology and at inductive and deductive reasoning. We then examine the process of archaeological research itself. This short chapter is an important preliminary to later discussions of archaeological data acquisition.

The Archaeologist's Skills

Today's archaeologists need specialist training in administrative, technical, and academic skills of many types. Modern archaeology has become so complex that few individuals can master all the skills needed to excavate a large city or even a medium-sized settlement where preservation conditions are exceptionally complete. In the 1920s, Woolley excavated Ur with a handful of Europeans, three expert Syrian foremen, and several hundred workers. An expedition to an equivalent site today would consist of a carefully organized team of experts whose skills would reflect the complexity and environmental setting of the site. Furthermore, as stewards of a fragile resource, we have an obligation to preserve the past for the future, to acquire the maximum amount of information for the minimal disturbance of the resource. Let us examine, then, some of the basic skills an archaeologist needs.

Theoretical Skills

The archaeologist must be able to define research problems in their context: everything that is known about them. This knowledge includes the current status of

Discovery

A Saxon Ship Burial at Sutton Hoo, England, 1939

When British archaeologist James Brown asked landowner Elizabeth Pretty in 1939 which of the burial mounds on her property at Sutton Hoo in eastern England she wanted opened, she pointed to the largest. "What about this?" she remarked. Her casual choice epitomized the archaeology of sixty years ago but led to a remarkable feat of archaeological excavation.

The work began that very afternoon with the cutting of a wide trench across the mound. Brown soon found five iron ship nails and suspected at once that he had found a funerary boat. With trowels and brushes, he and his workers cleared the bow and eleven frames of an Anglo-Saxon vessel. When he reached a sealed bulkhead, Brown wisely stopped the excavation and called in Charles Phillips of Cambridge University, an expert on Anglo-Saxon sites and on ancient timber structures. Phillips was a meticulous excavator. He followed gray discolorations in mound soil and traced the lines of the boat

and the planked burial chamber that lay amidships (Figure 5.1). The diggers even found evidence of repairs to the hull. With infinite care, they opened the burial chamber, recording and conserving each find, however small. The chamber contained the treasure buried with a long-vanished body of a nobleman, which included metal cauldrons, bowls, spears, axes, bottles, and thirty-seven coins dating to about A.D. 650. The boat was one of two in the burial mound. Eighty-nine feet (27 m) long, it had no mast or sails and was propelled by thirty-eight oars and had been dragged overland 0.3 mile (1 km) to its final resting place.

Phillips excavated Sutton Hoo with great skill, but later generations of archaeologists have been able to use far more sophisticated technology—metal detectors to find small buttons, ground-penetrating radar to map subsurface features, and ultraviolet light to detect the fragile outlines of bodies in the soil (Carver, 1998).

Figure 5.1   The Sutton Hoo ship exposed by excavating gray discolorations and iron nail fragments in the soil. (Copyright The British Museum)

research on a specific problem, such as the origins of humanity or the earliest human settlement of Ohio, and the latest theoretical and methodological advances in archaeology that could affect the definition and solution of the problem. The research problem will be defined by the specific objectives to be achieved. The archaeologist must have the expertise to formulate the precise hypotheses to be tested in the research. As the research proceeds, he or she has to be able to evaluate and put together the results of the work in the context set by the original objectives.

Methodological Expertise

Every archaeologist must have the ability to plan the methods to be used in the research to achieve the theoretical goals initially laid out. Methodological skills include being able to select among methods of data collection and to decide which analytical methods are most effective for the data being handled. Excavating sites and conducting field surveys require a large range of methodological skills, from deciding which sampling or trenching systems to use to devising recording methods to dealing with special preservation conditions where fragile objects have to be removed intact from their matrix.

One important aspect of methodological expertise requires selecting and working with specialists from other disciplines. Teamwork between experts is especially important on cultural resource management (CRM) projects, where it is a daily reality, and deadlines for completing field and laboratory research are often short. Every team member needs to understand multidisciplinary research and must know the uses and limitations of the work done by, say, geologists or zoologists for the specific problems being investigated.

Technical Skills

Methodological and technical skills overlap, especially in the field. The scientific excavation of any site or a large-scale field survey requires more than the ability to select a method or a recording system; one also needs to execute it under working conditions. Archaeological excavations require great precision in measurement and excavation, deployment of skilled and unskilled labor, and implementation of find-recovery systems that keep artifacts in order from the moment they are found until they are shipped to the laboratory for analysis. At issue here is the provenance of the artifacts and the features of the associated **ecofacts**—nonartifactual materials such as food residues and other finds that shed light on human activities. The field archaeologist has to assume the roles of supervisor, photographer, surveyor, digger, recorder, writer, and soil scientist and must be able to deal with any unexpected jobs, such as uncovering the delicate bones of a skeleton or setting up details of a computer program. On large sites, expertly trained students or fellow archaeologists may assume such specialist tasks as photography; on small sites, the archaeologist must often perform this and all other tasks single-handedly.

Administrative and Managerial Skills

Modern archaeology, whether academic research or CRM, requires that its practitioners exercise high-level administrative and managerial skills. Today's archaeologist has to be able to coordinate the activities of specialists from other disciplines, organize and deploy teams of volunteer students and paid laborers, and raise and administer research funds obtained from outside sources. He or she must always be aware of all aspects of a research project as it progresses, from arranging for permits and supplies of stationery and digging tools to keeping the accounts. CRM archaeologists have to be able to negotiate and carry out project contracts and ensure compliance with legal requirements (Chapter 18).

Above all, anyone working on an archaeological project has to be an expert in human relations, keeping people happy at demanding work that is often carried out under difficult and uncomfortable conditions. The diplomatic side of archaeological excavations is often neglected. But the folklore of archaeology abounds with stories of disastrous excavations run by archaeologists with no sensitivity toward their fellow workers. A truly happy excavation is a joy to work on, a dig on which people smile, argue ferociously over interpretations of stratigraphic profiles through an endless day, and enjoy the companionship of a campfire or a nearby bar in the evenings.

Writing and Analytical Skills

If there is one basic lesson to be learned at the beginning of any archaeological endeavor, it is that all excavation is destruction of finite archives in the ground that can never be restored to their original configuration. Every archaeologist is responsible not only for analyzing the finds in the laboratory but also for preparing a detailed report on the fieldwork that has been done—an important part of the permanent record of archaeological research. Regrettably, the shelves in museums the world over are filled with finds from sites that have been excavated but never written up. An unpublished site is effectively destroyed. Prompt publication is an ethical responsibility for all archaeologists.

At first glance, the list of qualifications a professional archaeologist needs can be formidable. In practice, though, sound classroom training combined with a great deal of fieldwork experience provide the necessary background.

Archaeology and Science

At various places we have referred to scientific archaeology, the scientific method, and the testing of hypotheses against data collected in the field (Kelley and Hanan, 1988). It is now time to ask a fundamental question: Is archaeology a science? The answer is a qualified yes. In the sense that archaeologists study human societies of the past by scientifically recovering and analyzing data that consist of the material remains of these societies, it is a science. But in the sense that archaeology, as part of anthropology, studies the intangible philosophical and religious beliefs of a society, it is not a science.

What do we mean by scientific? **Science** is a way of acquiring knowledge and understanding about the parts of the natural world that can be measured. It is a disciplined and carefully ordered search for knowledge, carried out in a systematic manner. This is a far cry from the ways in which we acquire our personal experience of religious philosophies, social customs, or political trends. Science involves using methods of acquiring knowledge that are not only cumulative but also subject to continuous testing and retesting.

The Scientific Method

Over the years, scientists have developed general procedures for acquiring data, known as the scientific method, which have come into wide use. Even though the **scientific method** may be applied in somewhat different ways in botany, zoology, and anthropology, the basic principles are the same: the notion that knowledge of the real world is both cumulative and subject to constant rechecking. The scientific method has many applications to archaeological data, and its use classifies much of archaeology as a science. Science establishes facts about the natural world by observing objects, events, and phenomena. In making these observations, the scientist proceeds by using both inductive and deductive reasoning.

Inductive reasoning takes specific observations and makes a generalization from them. I (BMF) once found nearly 10,000 wild vegetable remains in a 4,000-year-old hunter-gatherer camp in central Zambia. More than 42 percent of them were from the bauhinia, a shrub currently prized for its fruit and roots and flowers from October to February. The bauhinia is still eaten by San hunter-gatherers in the Kalahari today. From these observations, I used the process of induction to hypothesize that bauhinia has been a preferred seasonal food for hunter-gatherers in this area for thousands of years (Fagan and Van Noten, 1971).

Deductive reasoning follows from hypotheses formulated through induction. That is, the researcher postulates specific implications from the generalized hypotheses. In the Kalahari, I would have formulated a hypothesis (or series of hypotheses) about bauhinia eating by San and prehistoric hunter-gatherers and then tested it with ethnographic fieldwork and archaeological investigations based on the specific implications of the hypothesis. My hypothesis would then be confirmed, rejected, or refined.

A classic example of applying the scientific method comes from field studies done in the Great Basin in the western United States by anthropologist Julian Steward and the archaeologists who expanded on his work. Steward spent much of the 1920s and 1930s working on Shoshonean ethnography. The mass of field data he collected led him to formulate hypotheses about the ways in which the Shoshoneans moved their settlements throughout the year (Steward, 1938).

In the late 1960s this pioneering work was greatly refined by David Hurst Thomas, who deduced densities and distributions of artifacts in the various ecological zones of the Great Basin from Steward's hypotheses about Shoshonean settlement patterns. "If the late prehistoric Shoshoneans behaved in the fashion suggested by Steward, how would the artifacts have fallen on the ground?" he asked (Thomas, 1983a, 1983b:14). Thomas constructed more than 100 predictions relating to Steward's original hypotheses and then devised tests to verify or invalidate his predictions. He expected to find specific forms of artifacts associated with particular types of activity, such as hunting, in seasonal archaeological sites where hunting was said to be important. Aware of local preservation conditions, he strongly emphasized the distribution and frequency of artifact forms. Then he collected in the field the ar-chaeological data needed for his tests. Finally, Thomas tested each of his predictions against the field data and rejected about 25 percent of his original ones. The remain-der were supported by the data and provided a major refinement of Steward's origi-nal hypotheses. Later fieldwork gave him abundant opportunities to refine these hy-potheses and to collect more data to test them further. Thomas's Great Basin research is a good example of the benefits of the scientific method in archaeological research.

The importance of the scientific method, however, should not be overestimated. A balanced view is this: "Science advances by disproof, proposing the most adequate explanations for the moment, knowing that new and better explanations will later be found. This continuous self-correcting feature is the key to the scientific method" (Doran, 1987:65).

Remarkably, there is almost no literature on how archaeologists come to their conclusions (Hodder, 1999), but, clearly, archaeology, with its concerns with social and political structures and other human behavior, is not nearly as potentially empir-ical as, say, physics. The controlled progress from hypothesis to testing to conclusion associated with the scientific method simply does not work in much archaeology, where researchers spend a lot of time in the field fitting together different pieces of ev-idence, such as, say, stratified layers and ruined dwellings. A great deal of archaeology is about physical relationships, between features and finds, layers and environmental data, and so on. It is also about using comparisons from other sites and modern data **(analogy).** Above all, though, it is about constructing narratives, which can involve everything from recording the layers in a trench wall to interpreting an entire site (Hodder and Evans, 1999).

The Process of Archaeological Research

We now describe the process of archaeological research from formulation of the re-search design to publication of the final report. Figure 5.2 illustrates the process.

Research Design and Formulation

A **research design,** simply defined as a working plan for a research project, whether simple or complex, is intended to direct the execution of an archaeological investigation. It has multiple objectives, among them to ensure that the results will be scientifically valid and to carry out the research as efficiently and economically as pos-sible with minimal disturbance of the record (Binford, 1964). There are also issues of stewardship, of ensuring that the views of specialists in other disciplines and others with a stake in the site or sites are taken into consideration, as is the case with, for example, a well-known site like Stonehenge or the 9,000-year-old farming settlement at Çatalhöyük in Turkey (Hodder, 1999).

The process of archaeological research, then, is controlled by the research design, which takes the project through stages. These stages are by no means common to all research projects, for, although "research design" sounds rigid and inflexible, in

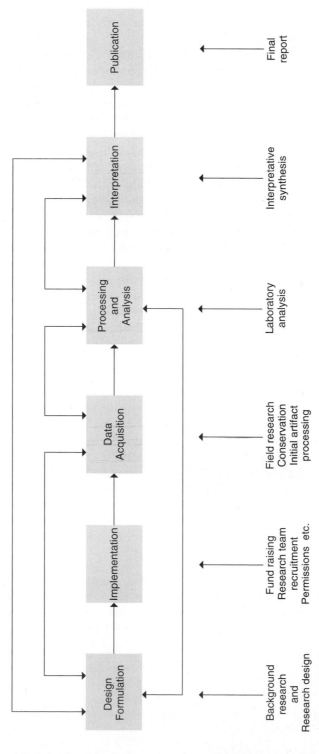

Figure 5.2 The process of archaeological research.

practice the design for any project has to be flexible enough to allow changes in the overall project as field research proceeds.

Any archaeological research begins with fundamental decisions about the problem or area to be studied. A research problem can be as grandiose as determining the origins of agriculture in the American Southwest—a truly enormous project—or as specific as determining the date of the second phase in Stonehenge's construction or surveying a small lot in New York City. The initial decisions will identify both the problem and the geographic region in which it will be investigated. The latter can be one site or an entire region. These decisions immediately limit the scope of the research design.

Once the problem and the area have been identified, the researcher must do a great deal of background research, involving both library work and field investigations. He or she must read up on previous archaeological research on the problem and study the geology, climate, ecology, anthropology, and general background of the area. Several field visits are essential, both to examine fieldwork conditions and to get a feel for the region. Water supplies, campsites, and sources of labor have to be identified. Landowners' permissions to dig and survey are essential, and government permits may be needed. At least some preliminary fieldwork is needed to aid in formulating the research design, especially in areas where no archaeology has been carried out before. This reconnaissance is really designed to see what is there and to evaluate the potential significance of the site or area. Does it offer an opportunity for providing new knowledge? What kinds of research will be needed to minimize impact on the sites involved? What conservation work will be needed, and are site management issues in the future involved?

The objective directing all this initial work is to refine the problem being investigated until the archaeologist can begin to define specific research goals. These goals will almost inevitably include testing fairly specific hypotheses, which can be related to research carried out by previous investigators or can be entirely new hypotheses that come out during the preliminary formulation of the research problem. More goals will be added as the research work proceeds. Generating hypotheses at this stage is vital, for they determine the types of data that will be sought in the field. These types must be defined, at least in general, before one goes into the field.

Let us take two hypotheses designed as part of a research project involving early food production in Egypt:

1. The earliest cereal agriculture near Kom Ombo developed among hunter-gatherers who had been exploiting wild vegetable foods very intensively.
2. The emergence of agriculture came about as a result of the intensification of gathering and rapid population growth, causing shortages of wild cereals. So people began to grow wild cereals for themselves.

What sorts of data would be needed to test these hypotheses at Kom Ombo? The archaeologist formulating the project of which this hypothesis is a part would be looking for:

- Sites in areas where wild cereals could have grown, where preservation conditions would allow for survival of vegetal remains.

- Food residues in the form of carbonized and discarded vegetable foods and the bones of domesticated animals.
- Implements used for harvesting and processing both wild and domesticated grains— grindstones, sickles, and so on.
- Evidence for such features as storage pits or baskets, indicating deliberate conservation of food supplies.
- Sites that were occupied longer than the relatively short periods favored by most hunter-gatherers, since farmers have to watch over their crops.

Armed with both hypotheses and lists of the types of evidence likely to be encountered in the field, the archaeologist can plan for the equipment, facilities, and people needed to carry out the job. Even more important, the project can be formulated with advice from experts, whose specialist knowledge will be needed either in the field or in the laboratory. The necessary contacts with experts are best made before the fieldwork begins and funds are obtained. A surprising number of specialists are needed for even quite simple investigations. The Kom Ombo hypothesis could ideally require the long- or short-term services of these experts:

- A geologist to assist in geological dating of sites in the Nile Valley
- A soil scientist to study occupation levels and organic soils
- A radiocarbon-dating laboratory to date carbon samples
- A botanist to supervise recovery of vegetal remains and to identify them
- An expert on pollen analysis to work on any such samples recovered in the excavations
- A zoologist to study the animal bones

The larger-scale project may take an integrated team of experts from several disciplines into the field—an expensive enterprise that often yields important results. The study of early agriculture in southwestern Asia was revolutionized by Robert Braidwood of the University of Chicago in the 1950s when he took such a team of experts with him to the Zagros Mountains. The research team was able to trace agriculture and animal domestication from their beginnings among nomadic hunter-gatherers on the highlands more than 9,000 years ago (Braidwood and Braidwood, 1983).

Research design has a critical role in cultural resource management (Chapter 18). Regional research designs for large areas such as the San Juan basin in Colorado provide a long-term framework for hundreds of small environmental impact studies and research projects. These designs are not cast in concrete; they are ever-changing documents that are updated regularly to accommodate changing methodologies and new circumstances in the field (Fowler, 1982). In CRM projects, the research design often incorporates recommended courses of action to mitigate damage caused by construction work and other nonarchaeological activities.

The final stage in formulating an academic research project is acquiring the necessary funding. This can be frustrating and time-consuming, for sources of money for archaeological fieldwork are always in short supply. Most purely academic excavations organized in the Americas are funded either by the National Science Foundation or, if within the United States, by some other government agency, such as the National Park Service. CRM contracts now provide most archaeological funding in North America and in many other countries. Some private organizations, such as the National Geographic Society and the Wenner Gren Foundation for Anthropological Research, support excavations. Many excavations, such as the regular seasons at Aphrodisias in Turkey or Crow Canyon in the U.S. Southwest, rely heavily on private donations. The organizers spend much time seeking private gifts to support each field season and the laboratory work that follows it.

Data Collection

Once the field team has been assembled and the funds are in hand, actual implementation of the project begins. The first stage is to acquire equipment, set up a base, and organize the research team in the field. Once that preparatory phase has been completed, collection of archaeological data can begin.

Data collection involves two basic processes: locating and surveying sites and scientifically excavating carefully selected sites. Locating archaeological sites is obviously the first stage in collecting data. As we discuss in Chapter 8, reconnaissance can be carried out on foot, in vehicles, or even on the back of a mule. A variety of techniques are used to ensure that a representative sample of the sites is located and investigated before excavation. Then the surfaces of the sites are carefully examined, and samples of artifacts at ground level are collected to record as much as possible about the location without the expense of excavation. This recording can include photographs, some surveying and measurement, and, often, especially on CRM projects, some probing of the site with borers or electronic devices (Chapter 8). Obviously, much less information is collected from surface surveys than from excavations.

Archaeological excavations are ultimately a recording of subsurface features and the provenance, or precise spatial relationships, of the artifacts within the site. Varied techniques are used to collect and record archaeological data from beneath the ground, as described in Chapter 9. The scope of archaeological excavation can range from a small test pit to a large-scale investigation at an ancient city.

Data Processing, Analysis, and Interpretation

The end products of even a month's excavation on a moderately productive site are a daunting accumulation. Box upon box of potsherds, stone tools, bones, and other finds are stacked in the field laboratory and must be cleaned, labeled, and sorted. Hundreds of digital images, slides, and photographs must be processed and cataloged. Computer records and rolls of drawings with information on the provenance of finds from the trenches must also be cataloged. Then there are radiocarbon and pollen samples, burials, and other special finds that need examination by specialists. The first stage in processing the data, then, occurs at the site, where the finds are washed, sorted, and given preservation treatment sufficient to transport them to the archaeological laboratory for more thorough examination.

The detailed analysis of the data is carried out, often for many months, in a laboratory with the facilities for such research work. These analyses include not only

Doing Archaeology

Ancient Wine at Abydos, Egypt

Much archaeological research combines excavation with high-technology laboratory analysis, which may change radically the original interpretations of a site. In 1988, German Egyptologist Günter Dreyer excavated the tomb of one of Egypt's first leaders at Abydos on the Middle Nile. Scorpion I lived in about 3150 B.C. His elaborate tomb contained four rooms stocked with at least 700 jars that held a total of about 1,200 gallons (4,550 liters) of wine. Forty-seven of the jars contained wine pips, together with remains of sliced figs that had been suspended on strings in the wine, probably to sweeten it. The crusty residues adhering to the insides of the pots were analyzed with an infrared spectrometer and liquid chromatography, which revealed the remains of tartaric acids (found naturally in grapes), and of terebinth resin, which ancient vintners used to prevent wine from turning into vinegar. Neutron activation analysis of the clay jar yielded trace element clusters that were compared against a large database of samples from Egypt and the eastern Mediterranean. The database pointed to the southern hill country of Israel and Transjordan as the source of the vessels, an area where vine growing was well established in 3100 B.C. The wine probably traveled the Nile across an ancient trade route, "the Way of Horus," that linked southern Israel with Egypt via the Sinai Desert. By 3000 B.C., wine growing had been well established in the Nile Delta in northern Egypt, the source of the pharaoh Tutankhamun's wines 1,500 years later.

classifying artifacts and identifying the materials from which they were made but also studying food remains, pollen samples, and other key sources of information. All these analyses are designed to provide information for interpreting the archaeological record. Some tests, such as radiocarbon dating or pollen analysis, are carried out in laboratories with the necessary technical equipment. We describe various approaches to archaeological analysis in Chapters 10 through 17.

Interpreting the resulting classified and thoroughly analyzed data involves not only synthesizing all the information from the investigation but also final examination of the basic questions formulated at the beginning of the project. These tests produce models for reconstructing and explaining the prehistory of the site or region, as illustrated by the Abydos investigation (see the Doing Archaeology box). We look at some of these models and interpretations in Part VII.

Publication

The archaeologist's final responsibility is publishing the results of the research project. Archaeological excavation destroys all or part of a site; unless the investigator publishes the results, vital scientific information will be lost forever. The ideal published scientific report includes not only the research design and hypotheses that have been formulated but also the data used to test them and to interpret the site or region so that the tests can be replicated by others.

All archaeological research is cumulative, in the sense that everyone's investigations are eventually superseded by later work, which uses more refined methods of recovery and new analytical approaches. But unless every archaeologist publishes the results of his or her completed work, the chain of research will be incomplete, and a fragment of human history will vanish into oblivion. It is sad that the pace of publication has been far behind that of excavation. The reason is not hard to discern: excavating is far more fun than writing reports!

In recent years, more and more researchers are turning to the World Wide Web and digital publication as a way of making basic data available to both fellow archaeologists and other interested parties. At Çatalhöyük, Turkey, Ian Hodder and his research team have made each season's data freely accessible through the site's Web page to generate discussion of their research (Hodder, 1999; http://catal.arch.cam.ac.uk/catal/catal.html). Today, most excavations of any size make an effort to share their results with the public, both during and after the fieldwork.

Summary

Modern archaeology makes use of scientific methods devised by archaeologists and by scientists in many other disciplines.

A well-qualified archaeologist commands many skills, both in archaeological method and theory and in practical methodology. This expertise includes the ability to select and work with specialists in other academic disciplines. Practical fieldwork experience and considerable administrative and managerial skill are also required on even the smallest research project. All archaeologists have to acquire precise analytical and writing skills to enable them to communicate their results and record them for posterity.

Archaeologists use science as a means of acquiring knowledge and understanding about the parts of the natural world that can be observed. They do so by working with two forms of reasoning: inductive reasoning, which takes specific observations and makes a generalization from them, and deductive reasoning, which starts with a generalization and proceeds to specific implications.

The process of archaeological research begins with formulating highly specific research designs that are flexible enough to allow changes in the overall project as field research proceeds. The research project is formulated to fit the problem to be investigated and the geographic area involved. Formulation means carrying out background research and then developing hypotheses to be tested against data acquired in the field.

Once the field team has been assembled, members acquire data by reconnaissance, site survey, and excavation. This acquisition requires them to record provenance, archaeological context, and a great deal of basic information about the site, its natural environment, and its archaeological finds.

The processing of archaeological data requires analyzing and interpreting the archaeological finds, which involve sorting, classifying, and ordering the finds, then testing the hypotheses developed as part of the research design.

The final stage in archaeological research is publishing the results as a permanent record for posterity.

Key Terms

analogy   inductive reasoning   science
deductive reasoning   research design   scientific method
ecofact

Guide to Further Reading

DANCEY, WILLIAM S. 1981. *Archaeological Field Methods: An Introduction.* Minneapolis, MN: Burgess. Probably the best manual on American field methods around. Especially good on research design.

HESTER, THOMAS R., HARRY J. SHAFER, and KENNETH L. FEDER. 1997. *Field Methods in Archaeology.* 7th ed. Palo Alto, CA: Mayfield. A basic field manual on survey and excavation for the beginner.

RENFREW, COLIN, and PAUL BAHN. 2004. *Archaeology: Theories, Methods, and Practice.* 4th ed. New York: Thames and Hudson. A comprehensive discussion of archaeological methods that explores the issues raised in this chapter in more detail.

CHAPTER 6

Culture, Data, and Context

Victorian excavation at its most dramatic—and unscientific. M. De Morgan lifts a golden crown from the mummy of Queen Khnemit at Dahshur, Egypt, 1896.

In this chapter we introduce some basic concepts of archaeological research: to culture, to data in the form of artifacts and their matrix, provenance, and context (see also Sharer and Ashmore, 2002; Thomas, 2003). The provenance and context of all archaeological data are based on two fundamental laws: association and superposition. From basic concepts, we move on to discuss spatial context—not the limitless frontiers of the heavens but a precisely defined location for every find made during an archaeological survey or excavation.

The Concept of Culture

In Chapter 1, I (BMF) stated that "anthropologists study human beings as biological organisms with a distinctive and unique characteristic—culture." Few concepts in anthropology have generated as much controversy and academic debate as those expressed in that statement (A. Kroeber and Kluckhohn, 1952). All definitions of culture, one of the most elusive of theoretical formulations, are a means of explaining societies and human behavior in terms of the shared ideas a group of people may hold. One of the best definitions of culture was proposed by the great Victorian anthropologist Sir Edward Tylor more than a century ago. He stated that **culture** is "that complex whole which includes knowledge, belief, art, morals, law, custom, and any other capabilities and habits acquired by man as a member of society" (1871). To that definition, modern archaeologists would add that culture is our primary means of adapting to our environment. Tylor's definition, and all other such formulations, agree on one important point: culture and human behavior are shared ideas a group of people may hold.

Culture is a distinctively human attribute, for we are the only animals to use our culture as our primary means of adapting to our environment. It is our adaptive system. Although biological evolution has protected the polar bear from Arctic cold with dense fur and has given the duck webbed feet for swimming, only human beings make thick clothes and igloos in the Arctic and live with minimal clothing under light, thatched shelters in the tropics. We use our culture as a buffer between ourselves and the environment, a buffer that became more and more elaborate through the long millennia of prehistory. We are now so detached from our environment that removal of our cultural buffer would render us almost helpless and would probably lead to extinction of the human species in a very short time.

Thus, human cultures are made up of human behavior and its results; they obviously consist of complex and constantly interacting variables. Human culture, never static, is always adjusting to both internal and external change, whether environmental, technological, or societal (Deetz, 1967). Increasingly, humans have modified the natural environment to such an extent that they have created their own.

The Nature of Culture

Culture can be subdivided in all sorts of ways—into language, economics, technology, religion, political or social organizations, and art. But human culture as a whole is a complex, structured organization in which all our categories shape one another. All cultures are made up of myriad tangible and intangible traits, the contents of which result from complex adaptation to a wide range of ecological, societal, and cultural factors. Much of human culture is transmitted from generation to generation by sophisticated communication systems that permit complex and ceaseless adaptations to aid survival and help rapid culture change take place—as when less advanced societies come into contact with higher civilizations.

Everyone lives within a culture of some kind, and every culture is qualified by a label, such as "middle-class American," "Eskimo," or "Masai." The qualification conjures up characteristic attributes or behavior patterns typical of those associated with the cultural label. One attribute of a middle-class American might be the hamburger; of the Eskimo, the kayak; of the Masai, a long-handled, fine-bladed spear. Elite members of Maya society are associated with elaborate cities and intricate **hieroglyphs,** ancient writing featuring picture or ideographic symbols. Our mental images of cultures are associated with popular stereotypes, too. To many Americans, Chinese culture conjures up images of paper lanterns and willow-pattern plates; French culture, good eating and fine wines. We are all familiar with the distinctive "flavor" of a culture that we encounter when dining in a foreign restaurant or arriving in a strange country. Every culture has its individuality and recognizable style, which shape its political and judicial institutions and morals.

Unfortunately, cultural labels often become simplistic and sometimes demeaning stereotypes, such as that of the Native Americans as "feathered braves" or of the French as romantic, consummate lovers. Cultural reality is much more complex and often deeply challenging for an outsider to penetrate and comprehend.

Discovery

Celebrating Finds at Carchemish, Syria

Some early archaeologists in Egypt and parts of southwestern Asia worked with enormous teams of workers by modern standards. The work force on Flinders Petrie's Egyptian digs in the 1890s numbered in the hundreds, as did those at Ur in Iraq in the 1920s and 1930s. Leonard Woolly of Ur fame excavated the Hittite city at Carchemish on the Euphrates River in Syria just before World War I. He and his colleague T. E. Lawrence (later to achieve worldwide fame as "Lawrence of Arabia") not only excavated the great city; they also spied on German engineers building a nearby railroad to Baghdad.

Woolley was a born leader of Arab workers. He worked closely with his foreman Hamoudi, famous among archaeologists of the day for his ability to lead Arab workmen and for his swearing. The mood at the Carchemish excavations was always lighthearted. Woolley and Hamoudi celebrated each important discovery with a rifle volley, the number of cartridges denoting the significance of the find. The volleys became a form of competition that were a badge of honor for the workers and a celebration of discovery. The workers labored in teams, with the job of pick-man being especially prized, for the chance of receiving a volley was much higher. But Woolley made sure that basket carriers who found something of significance were given an extra large volley, to ensure that eyes were always open.

Woolley himself admitted that the system appeared childish, but he encouraged it as a way of making the excavation proceed smoothly, more than what he called "a mere business." He hated dull excavations and enjoyed the company of workers who were fiercely loyal to him. The process of discovery was a game pursued with deadly seriousness and on a scale and with methods that would never be tolerated today.

Archaeologists think of culture as possessing three components:

1. The individual's own version of his or her culture—the diversified individual behavior that makes up the myriad strains of a culture. Individual decisions play a vital role in changing even elaborate cultures.
2. Shared culture—elements of a culture shared by everyone. These can include cultural activities such as human sacrifice or ritualized warfare or any other human activity, as well as the body of rules and prescriptions that make up the sum of the culture (Figure 6.1). Language is critical to this sharing; so is the cultural system.
3. The cultural system—the system of behavior in which every individual participates. The individual not only shares the cultural system with other members of society but also takes an active part in it.

Culture, then, can be viewed as either a blend of shared traits or a system that permits a society to interact with its environment. To do anything more than merely work out chronological sequences, the archaeologist has to view culture as a group of

Figure 6.1   The Aztec Indians of Mexico sacrificed hundreds of human victims to the sun god Huitzilopochtli each year in the belief that the blood of human hearts nourished the sun on its journey across the heavens. This belief was part of the shared culture of this society, even if such sacrifices were totally alien to other societies.

complex, interacting components. These components remain static unless the processes that operate the system are carefully defined. Archaeologists are deeply involved with cultural process, the processes by which human societies changed in the past.

The notion of cultural systems has come into use in archaeology purely as a general concept to help us understand the ever-changing relationship between human cultures and their environment. It is derived from general systems theory, a body of theoretical concepts formulated as a means of searching for general relationships in the empirical world (Watson and others, 1984). A **cultural system** was well defined by archaeologist Stuart Struever (1971:188): "Culture and its environments represent a number of articulated [interlinked] systems in which change occurs through a series of minor, linked variations in one or more of these systems." For example, an Eskimo cultural system is part of a much larger Arctic ecosystem. The cultural system itself is made up of dozens of subsystems: an economic subsystem, a political subsystem, and many others. Let us say that the climate changes suddenly. The Eskimo now switch from reindeer hunting to fishing and sealing. The change triggers all sorts of linked shifts, not only in the economic subsystem but in the technological and social subsystems as well.

A cultural system is in a constant state of adjustment within itself and with the ecosystem of which it is a part.

Many of the interacting components of culture are highly perishable. So far, no one has been able to dig up an unwritten language. Archaeologists have to work with the tangible remains of human activity that still survive in the ground. But these surviving remains of human activity are radically affected by intangible aspects of human culture. For example, the Hopewell people of the American Midwest traded finely made ornaments fashioned out of hammered copper sheet over enormous distances 1,800 years ago. These ornaments turn up in Hopewell burial mounds. The copper technology that made them was simple, but the symbolism behind the artifacts was not. They were probably exchanged between important individuals as symbolic gifts, denoting kin ties, economic obligations, and other intangible social meanings that are beyond the archaeologist's ability to recover (Fagan, 2005).

The notion of cultural systems is a useful conceptual framework, provided one does not take it too far and apply it like a rigid, mechanistic formula. We should never forget that our forebears were human beings like ourselves. They made decisions as individuals and as groups, as friends, enemies, neighbors, lords, or commoners, so it is impossible to apply universal rules of cultural behavior to humanity. The archaeologist thus faces much greater limitations in research than the ethnographer, who works with living societies and can talk to individuals.

Models of Culture

Normative Models

Anthropologist Franz Boas had a profound influence on early American archaeology, for he developed what is often called a **normative view** of culture. This was the first concept of culture to be applied to archaeology, the notion that all human behavior is patterned, the forms of the patterns being determined very largely by culture. This rubric envisages a set of rules, or norms, for behavior within any society that pass from one generation to the next. There are, of course, individual variations, for all the norms do is define the range of acceptable behavior.

Boas applied the normative view of culture to contemporary societies, but archaeologists often use it to examine societies evolving over long periods of time. Anthropologists try to abstract the norms of human behavior by observing societies over many months, even years. They are searching, as it were, for the "grammar" of a society. Archaeologists use the material remains of the archaeological record, such as pottery or stone tools, to infer human behavior, arguing that such durable artifacts represent norms of technological behavior, if nothing else. They assume that implicit rules governed the manufacture of all kinds of artifacts over many generations.

This descriptive approach allowed archaeologists to reconstruct and observe variations and changes in what they called behavioral norms. It has been very successful in working out detailed, descriptive outlines of human prehistory at the local and regional levels. However, it does not address two critical goals of archaeology: reconstructing past lifeways and explaining culture change.

Functional Models

Bronislaw Malinowski was one of the great anthropologists of the early twentieth century, famous for his observations of the Trobriand Islanders in the western Pacific and for his functional model of culture (functionalism). Culture to Malinowski and other functionalist anthropologists, like E. E. Radcliffe-Brown (1931), who worked among the Nuer of the Sudan, was "inherited artifacts, goods, technical processes, ideas, habits, and values." He went much farther than Boas, arguing that each human culture was a set of closely interrelated mechanisms designed to satisfy both social and survival needs, not just for individuals but for society as a whole. Thus, the nature of any society could be understood only by looking at the network of complex relationships that formed the underlying structure of that society. Each component of a cultural system, living or prehistoric, has a specific function, be it stone technology, ways of growing crops, or residence rules after marriage. Each function is connected to myriad others by a network of relationships, forming an ever-adjusting cultural system.

Functionalism can be a somewhat a historical way of looking at human societies, but archaeologists have found it of considerable use in examining individual artifacts and culture traits as part of a much larger network of functional relationships. However, in one aspect functionalism diverges greatly from more recent ecological models of culture, which view cultural systems not as self-regulating but as undergoing constant change as they adapt to their natural environments.

Processual Models

The changing models of culture in archaeology reflect a gradual shift in emphasis from mere description of the past to often-used processual models based on hypothesis-testing strategies, cultural ecology, and multilinear cultural evolution (Chapter 3). Some archaeologists are even toying with the idea of not using the concept of culture at all.

Systems theory deals with relationships and variations in relationships; in other words, it deals with precisely the phenomena involved in explaining the processes by which cultures change. Modern scientific archaeology analyzes the causes of culture change, that is, cultural process.

The word *process* implies a patterned sequence of events that leads from one state of affairs to another. This patterned sequence is determined by a decision-making process that sets the order of events. A 40-foot (12-m) sailing yacht starts as a pile of materials—wood, aluminum, copper, bronze—and then a patterned sequence of manufacturing events turns the material into a gleaming new ship. Archaeology is a process, too. It involves designing the research project, formulating the hypothesis from prior research, collecting and interpreting new data to test the hypothesis, and, finally, publishing the results.

Conditions are events that force people to make decisions about how to deal with new situations. As such, they are distinct from the actual process of decision making, the mechanism that lead to any kind of change. A change in the natural environment from year-round rainfall to a seasonal pattern is a condition.

In archaeology, **cultural process** refers to the "identification of the factors responsible for the direction and nature of change within cultural systems" (Sharer and Ashmore, 1999:56). Processual archaeology is analysis of the conditions of culture change, which involves looking at relationships among variables that could lead to culture change. These possible conditions are then tested against actual archaeological data, sometimes in a systems theory context.

Clearly, no one element in any cultural system is the primary cause of change; instead, a complex range of factors—rainfall, vegetation, technology, social restrictions, population density—interact with and react to changes in any element in the system. It follows, then, that human culture, from the ecologist's viewpoint, is merely one element in the ecosystem, a mechanism of behavior whereby people adapt to an environment (Figure 6.2) (Dunnell, 1980).

Figure 6.2 A San hunter-gatherer in the Kalahari Desert searches in the bole of a tree for honey. Human culture is, from the ecologist's point of view, merely one element in the ecosystem.

Postprocessual Models

Archaeologists who work with postprocessual theory are little interested in cultural systems. Their primary concern is to find out what ideas people were trying to express through their material culture. Under this approach, archaeological sites are texts to be read rather than merely materials to be analyzed in order to decipher the cultural system behind them. They were often constructed as a form of self expression—Stonehenge with the intricate beliefs behind it is a good example. Thus, much archaeological research is interpretation rather than merely just observation of the operation of a cultural system.

Such approaches are reflexive, that is to say, they are constantly self-critical and allow for many different viewpoints—a *multivocality* (Hodder, 1999). The task for the archaeologist is to define stratigraphic units, not discover them, for what we call the archaeological record is made by archaeologists, not just something that occurs.

The Archaeological Record

The **archaeological record** (or, as it is sometimes called, the "archaeological resource") is the general name denoting the more or less continuous distribution of artifacts over the earth's surface, in highly variable densities. Variations in artifact densities reflect the character and frequency of land use, making them an important variable that the archaeologist can measure (Dunnell and Dancey, 1983). Some high-density clusters of artifacts may be subsumed under the term *site*. Although archaeological record refers specifically to distributions of artifacts, it can include:

- **Artifacts:** in the strict sense, objects manufactured or modified by humans.
- **Features:** artifacts and artifact associations that cannot be removed intact from the ground, such as postholes and ditches.
- **Structures:** houses, granaries, temples, and other buildings that can be identified from standing remains, patterns of postholes, and other features in the ground.
- **Ecofacts:** sometimes refers to food remains, such as bones, seeds, and other finds, which throw light on human activities.

Data are the materials recognized by the archaeologist as significant, all of which are collected and recorded as part of the research. Data are different from "facts," which are simply bits of observable information about objects, conditions, and so on. Archaeological data are sometimes referred to as *evidence*. Archaeological data do not consist of artifacts, features, structures, and ecofacts alone, however; they also include their context in space and time.

Matrix and Provenance

All scientifically collected or excavated archaeological finds, be they a complete site or a lone object, occur within a matrix and have a specific provenance. The *matrix* (described in Chapter 4) is the physical substance that surrounds the find. It can be gravel, sand, mud, or even water. Most archaeological matrices are of natural origin; passing time and external phenomena, such as wind and rainfall, create them. The early bone caches at Olduvai Gorge in Tanzania were at the edge of a shallow and ever-fluctuating lake 1.75 million years ago. The scatters of tools and bones left by the departing hominids were soon covered by a layer of thin lake sand carried by advancing shallow water. This matrix preserved the tools in their original positions for thousands of millennia (L. S. B. Leakey, 1971). An archaeological matrix can also be humanly made, such as the huge earthen platforms of Hopewell burial mounds in the American Midwest.

Provenance (or provenience) is the precise three-dimensional position of the find within the matrix as recorded by the archaeologist. It is derived from accurate records kept during excavations and site surveys, from evidence that is inevitably destroyed as a site is dug or artifacts are collected from a surface site. Every human artifact has a provenance in time and space. The provenance in time can range from a radiocarbon date of $1,400 \pm 60$ years before the present for a Maya temple to a precise reading of A.D. 2004 for a dime released by the United States Mint.[1] Frequently, it can simply be an exact position in an archaeological site whose general age is known. Provenance in space is based, finally, on associations between tools and other items that were results of human behavior in a culture. Provenance is determined by applying two fundamental archaeological principles: the principle of association and the principle of superposition.

The Principle of Association

The archaeological principle of **association** (Figure 6.3) was first stated by Danish archaeologist J. J. A. Worsaae when he was excavating prehistoric burials in 1843:

> The objects accompanying a human burial are in most cases things that were in use at the same time. When certain artifact types are found together in grave association after grave association, and when more evolved forms of the same tools are found in association with other burials, then the associations provide some basis for dividing the burials into different chronological groups on the basis of association and artifact styles.

Instances of archaeological associations are legion (Figure 6.4). The first evidence of high antiquity for humankind came from associations of stone axes and the bones of extinct animals discovered in the same geological layers. Many early Mesoamerican farmers' houses are associated with storage pits for maize and other crops. In this and many other cases, the horizontal association between artifacts and houses, dwellings and storage pits, or artifacts and food residues provides the archaeological association. Much of the most valuable archaeological data are derived from precise studies of associations between different finds in the ground.

---

[1] Conventional archaeological usage is B.P. (years before present), "present" being A.D. 1950 by international agreement, and also A.D./B.C., dates calculated relative to the date of Christ's birth. Some archaeologists use C.E./B.C.E. ("Common Era," "Before Common Era") instead of A.D./B.C.

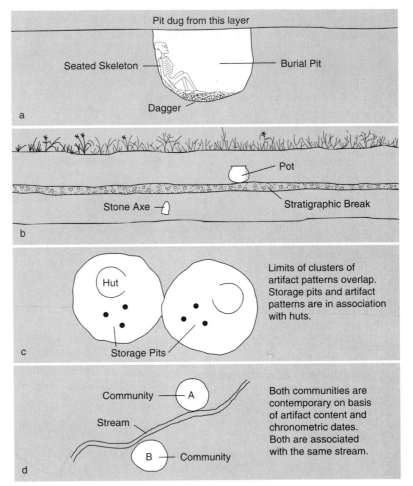

Figure 6.3 Some instances of archaeological associations. (a) The burial pit, dug from the uppermost layer, contains not only a skeleton but also a dagger that lies close to its feet. The dagger is associated with the skeleton, and both finds are associated with the burial pit and the layer from which the grave pit was cut into the subsoil. (b) In contrast, a pot and a stone ax are found in two different layers, separated by a sterile zone, a zone with no finds. The two objects are not in association. (c) Two different household clusters with associated pits and scatters of artifacts. These are in association with one another. (d) An association of two contemporary communities.

The Principle of Superposition

The time dimension of archaeology is erected on basic principles of stratigraphic geology and the principle of superposition set down by the uniformitarians early in the nineteenth century (Chapter 2). The principle of **superposition** states that the geological layers of the earth are stratified one upon another, like the layers of a cake. Cliffs by the seashore and quarries are easily accessible examples. Obviously, any

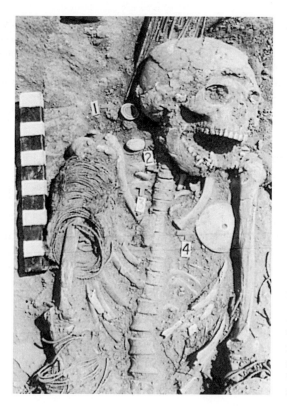

Figure 6.4 A case of association: burial from Ingombe Ilede in the Middle Zambezi Valley, Zambia, Central Africa, dating to around the fifteenth century A.D. The *conus* shells around the neck came from the Indian Ocean coast, 600 miles (965 km) away, and were of great prestige value.

object found in the lowermost levels, whether a stone or something humanly made, was deposited there before the upper levels were accumulated. In other words, the lower strata are earlier than the upper strata. The same principle applies to archaeological sites: the tools, houses, and other finds in one layer of a site can be dated relative to the other layers (see Figure 6.3). The basis of all scientific archaeological excavation is the accurately observed and carefully recorded stratigraphic profile (Chapter 9).

Archaeological Context

Archaeological **context** is derived from careful recording of the matrix, provenance, and association of the finds. Context is far more than just a find spot, a position in time and space. It involves assessing how the find got to its position and what happened after its original owners abandoned it. Anyone wanting to reconstruct human behavior or ancient cultural systems must pay careful attention to the context of every find.

Context is affected by three factors:

1. The manufacture and use of the object, house, or other find by its original owners. The orientation of a house may be determined by the position of the sun on summer afternoons. Because the archaeologist's objective is to reconstruct ancient behavior, this aspect of context is vital.

2. The way in which the find was deposited in the ground. Some discoveries, such as burials or caches of artifacts, were deliberately buried under the ground by ancient people; others got there as a result of natural phenomena. Houses that have been abandoned are slowly covered by blowing sand or rotting vegetation, or houses may be buried quickly, as was the Roman city of Herculaneum in Italy, which was covered by volcanic ash in an eruption of Vesuvius in August A.D. 79.
3. The subsequent history of the find in the ground. Was the burial disturbed by later graves, or was the site eroded away by water?

Primary and Secondary Context

The context of any archaeological find can be affected by two processes: the original behavior of the people who used or made it and events that came later.

Primary context is the original context of the find, undisturbed by any factor, human or natural, since it was deposited by the people involved with it. The Iron Age warrior depicted in Figure 6.5, who was buried at Maiden Castle in A.D. 43, died from his wounds in a battle against a Roman legion (see Site box). The survivors buried him swiftly in a shallow grave. The skeleton survived intact in its primary context until Sir Mortimer Wheeler excavated the undisturbed burial late in the 1930s (R. Wheeler, 1943).

Secondary context refers to the context of a find whose primary context has been disturbed by later activity. Very frequently, excavators of a burial ground will find incomplete skeletons whose graves were disturbed by deposition of later burials. For example, in 500 B.C., a group of Chumash Indians camped by a rocky peninsula on

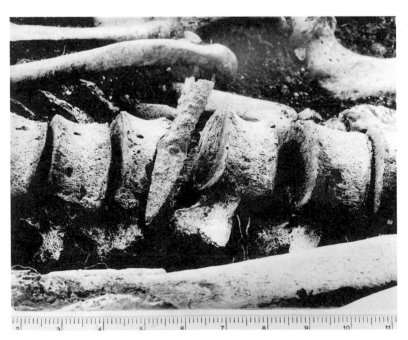

Figure 6.5   An iron arrowhead embedded in the backbone of a man killed in the Roman attack on Maiden Castle, Dorset, England, in A.D. 43. The artifact (the arrowhead) comes from a Roman cultural context; the skeleton, native British. Nevertheless, they are associated in the archaeological record.

Site

The Siege of Maiden Castle

Maiden Castle is an Iron Age hill fort that was occupied by a Celtic tribe at about the time of Christ. The fort lies on a ridge, visible from a long way off because of its serried, steep-sided earthworks and ditches. Two thousand years ago, the now-grass-covered fortifications would have gleamed brightly, even on a cloudy day, the white soil of the exposed chalk subsoil standing out in the grassy landscape. By the standards of its time, Maiden Castle was a powerful fortress, with entrances protected by multiple earthworks topped with wooden palisades designed to protect the inhabitants from arrows, slingshots, and other long-distance weapons. Inside, the local tribespeople lived in a large settlement of circular, thatched houses on the site of a much older Stone Age camp. In A.D. 43, the Roman general Vespasian's Second Legion attacked the fort in an assault on the lower, eastern end. The successful attack killed many of the villagers; survivors dispersed elsewhere.

Nineteen hundred years later, in 1934, archaeologist Mortimer Wheeler excavated Maiden Castle in one of the classic archaeological digs of all time. Wheeler and his then-wife Tessa brought refined digging methods to Maiden Castle. The site was so complex that Wheeler developed horizontal and verti-

cal trenching systems to investigate the history of the earthworks and to expose a large area at the eastern end of the fort. (For one of his exemplary trenches, see Figure 9.4.) He dug with paid laborers and volunteers, many of whom went on to become prominent archaeologists in their own right. In 1937, Wheeler uncovered traces of the Roman attack, which were reconstructed in a classic piece of archaeological writing. He described (1943) how Vespasian brought up siege artillery, which laid down a barrage as the infantry advanced, cutting its way from rampart to rampart, tower to tower. A huddle of dwellings found in the excavations lay just outside the sealed gates. The Romans set fire to them and stormed the gates under the cover of the smoke. "The fury of the attackers was aroused. Men and women, young and old, were savagely cut down before the legionaries were called to heel and the work of systematic destruction began." Wheeler tells how the survivors returned after dark and hastily buried their dead, one with an iron arrowhead deep in his spine (Figure 6.5).

Few archaeological excavations can tell such a vivid tale. Although details of Wheeler's reconstruction have been challenged, his account still stands.

the south side of Santa Cruz Island off southern California. Their ancestors had collected shellfish and hunted sea mammals at this location for untold generations. They camped for several days, nursing a sick man. After he died, they buried his body in the large shell heap downwind of their camp, and moved away. Fifty years later, another group visited the same spot and buried two children in the same mound. As they dug their graves into a corner of the original sepulcher, they disturbed the bones of the long-forgotten ancestor. When archaeologists uncovered the burials centuries later, they referred to the later interments as secondary burials. Incomplete skeletons can also occur when a group exposes the dead until the corpse has decomposed, then buries the bones in a bundle in a communal burial chamber, such as a British Stone Age long barrow or a Hopewell mound in the Ohio Valley.

As in the tomb of pharaoh Tutankhamun, tomb robbers may disturb the original grave furnishings, searching for gold or precious oils. In still other instances, finds can be shifted by the natural forces of wind and weather. Many of the Stone Age tools found in European river gravels were transported by floodwaters to a location far from their original place of deposition. All these disturbed finds are in a secondary context.

Spatial Context

Spatial context is the distance between different objects or features, between entire settlements, or between settlements and key vegetational zones and landmarks. Important distances can be a few inches of level ground between a dagger and the associated skeleton of its owner, a mile separating two seasonal camps, or a complicated series of interrelated distance measurements separating dozens of villages that are part of an elaborate trading system carrying goods through several geographic regions hundreds of miles apart.

One can identify four dimensions of variability in human behavior reflected in spatial context:

1. *Artifact:* individual human activity.
2. *Structure:* household or group activities (structures can, of course, include public buildings, such as temples, which are used by more than one household).
3. *Site:* community activity, groups of contemporary houses, stores, temples, and other structures.
4. *Region:* the activities of groups of people reflected by the distribution of sites on the landscape, sometimes referred to as a settlement pattern.

These four levels of spatial context are closely tied to actual cultural behavior (Figure 6.6). An artifact itself can provide valuable information on technology and actual use. But, to infer cultural behavior, we must know the artifact's association, both with other artifacts and with the matrix in which it was found. The patterning of artifacts in space around an abandoned iron-smelting furnace or near the bones of a slaughtered bison kill is tangible evidence for specific human behavior. An unassociated projectile point will never indicate anything more specific than the inference that it was used as a weapon. But a patterning of projectile points, scraping tools, and large boulders associated with a bison skeleton has a context in time and space that allows much more detailed inferences.

The basic assumption behind all studies of artifacts in space is that they were used for different purposes, and that characteristic groups of them were used for specific activities, such as ironworking, butchery, and hunting. It follows that similarly patterned groups of artifact types found on other sites resulted from similar activities, even if they show differences in detail. During the earlier millennia of the Stone Age,

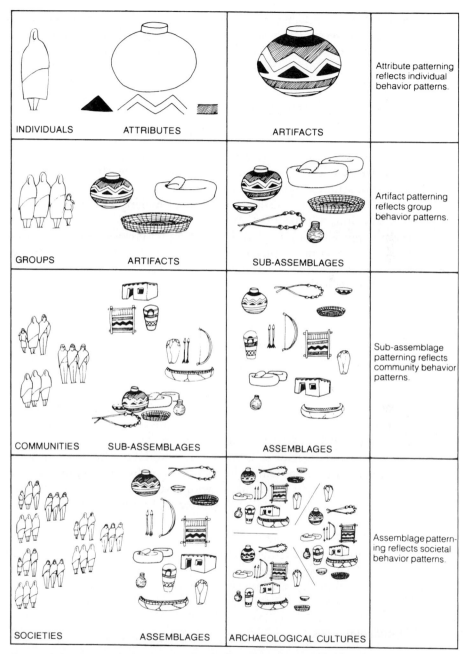

Figure 6.6   Human behavior as reflected in archaeological classification. The hierarchy begins with attributes and artifacts and ends with entire archaeological cultures.

Source: James Deetz, *Invitation to Archaeology* (New York: Doubleday, 1967). Copyright © 1967 by James Deetz. Used by permission of Doubleday, a division of Random House, Inc.

people enjoyed much the same level of hunting and gathering culture throughout Africa, Europe, and India. This parallel is reflected in thousands of similar-looking stone axes found in sites as widely separated as the Thames Valley in England and the Cape of Good Hope in South Africa.

Artifacts, Subassemblages, and Assemblages

As we saw in Chapter 4, archaeological data comprise the material remains of ancient human behavior. These data come in many forms, and a fundamental part of archaeological research involves classifying and interpreting the data, creating order out of a jumble of artifacts and other finds.

The process of classification involves making judgments about different categories of finds (Chapter 10). Archaeologists have terms that define these remains for research purposes, arbitrary groupings used for archaeological analysis, which may, or more often may not, represent "real" things in the past. In other words, data groups are instruments used in research, not actual cultural phenomena, even if sometimes they coincide with them.

Artifacts

Artifacts are commonly defined as items that exhibit any physical attributes that can be assumed to be the result of human activity. This definition implies that the term *artifact* covers every form of archaeological find, from stone axes, bronze daggers, and clay pots to butchered animal bones, carbonized seeds, huts, and all other manifestations of human behavior that can be found in archaeological sites. Some archaeologists define artifacts by breaking them down into four categories: portable artifacts, features, structures, and ecofacts. Whichever definition is preferred, all assume that any object or any event of manufacture or consumption is a product of human activity if its location or any other of its features cannot be accounted for by natural processes (Deetz, 1967). In other words, artifacts are compared with natural objects and distinguished from them, not by individual features but by a patterning of different, human-caused features. It is this patterning that is important. A simple flake removed from an elaborate ceremonial obsidian knife blade may not necessarily show evidence of human modification. But the patterned, consistently repeated finding of several dozen or hundreds of small flakes—the pattern forming a knife—is highly diagnostic of human activity. Normally there is no difficulty in telling artifacts made or caused by humans from those caused by water action, fire, animal kills, or other natural phenomena (but see Lyman, 1994).

Subassemblages

An artifact, such as an arrowhead or a basket, is made up of a combination of *attributes* (minor features) (Chapter 10) that make up a constant pattern of behavior reflected in the finished artifact. When such artifacts are found in patterned associations reflecting the shared cultural behavior of minimal groups, they are commonly classified in **subassemblages.** A hunter uses a bow, arrows, and a quiver; a blacksmith uses hammers, tongs, and bellows; and so on. Subassemblages represent the behavior of individuals and are often tool kits.

Assemblages

When a number of subassemblages of artifacts—say, a collection of hunting weapons, baskets, pounders, and digging sticks, traces of windbreaks, and stone vessels—are found in a contemporaneous association, they reflect in their patterning the shared activities of a total community and are known as **assemblages.** With assemblages, one is looking at the shared behavior of a community as a whole, which frequently is reflected in the remains of houses, the features associated with them, and community settlement patterns.

Archaeological Sites

Sites are places where traces of past human activity are to be found. They represent accumulations of the remains of human behavior over periods of time. Sites are normally identified by the presence of artifacts. They can range in size from a large city, such as Teotihuacán in the Valley of Mexico, to a tiny scatter of hunter-gatherer artifacts in Death Valley, California. There are millions of archaeological sites in the world, many of them still undiscovered. Some were occupied for a few hours, days, or weeks; some for a generation or two and then abandoned forever. Other localities, such as Mesopotamian occupation mounds, or *tells,* were occupied again and again for hundreds, even thousands, of years and contain many stratified layers. In contrast, the occupation site may contain little more than a surface scatter of potsherds or stone tools or an occupation layer buried under a few inches of topsoil. In a sense, archaeological sites are a paradox. They may represent long-term communal behavior over, say, 300 or 1,000 years, but what the archaeologist actually finds may be the remains of a very brief episode of such behavior, perhaps the filling of a storage pit, which took ten minutes on July 4, A.D. 1250.

Archaeological sites can be classified in these ways:

- *By archaeological context.* The context of artifacts in the site can be used to distinguish between sites such as surface locations, single-level occupations, and stratified settlements.
- *By artifact content.* The site is labeled according to its specific artifact content: pottery, stone tools, milling stones, and so on. The associations, assemblages, and subassemblages of artifacts in the site are used to label it as Stone Age, Maya, and so on.
- *By geographic location.* Most human settlements have been concentrated in well-defined types of geographic locations, and these sites can be referred to as cave sites, valley bottom sites, foothill sites, and the like.
- *By artifact content* related to site function. Because subassemblages reflect individual human behavior, sites can be classified by the characteristic patterning of the artifacts found in them, such as kill sites and habitations.

Using these criteria, researchers identify several broad site functions, which are commonly used by archaeologists everywhere (see the Doing Archaeology box).

Doing Archaeology

Common Site Functions

Living or habitation sites are the most important sites, for they are the places where people have lived and carried out a multitude of activities. The artifacts in living sites reflect domestic activities, such as food preparation and toolmaking. Dwellings are normally present. The temporary camps of California fisherfolk are habitation sites, as are Stone Age rock shelters, Southwestern pueblos, and Mesopotamian tells. Habitation sites of any complexity are associated with other sites that reflect specialized needs, such as agricultural systems, cemeteries, and temporary camps.

Kill sites are places where prehistoric people killed game and camped around the carcasses while butchering the meat. They are relatively common on the Great Plains; the Olsen-Chubbock site is a good example (see Figure 8.5). Projectile points and butchery tools are associated with kill sites.

Ceremonial sites may or may not be integral to a living site. The Mesopotamian ziggurat (temple mound) dominated its mother city, and Maya cities such as Tikal boasted imposing ceremonial precincts surrounded by habitation areas. Other famous ceremonial sites, such as Stonehenge in England and the Great Serpent Mound in Ohio, are isolated monuments.

Ceremonial artifacts, such as stingray spines used in mutilation rituals, and statuary may be associated with sacred sites.

Burial sites include both cemeteries and isolated tombs. People have been burying their dead since at least 50,000 years ago and have often taken enormous pains to prepare them for the afterlife. Perhaps the most famous burial sites of all are the pyramids of Giza in Egypt. Royal burials, such as that of the Egyptian pharaoh Tutankhamun, absorbed the energies of hundreds of people in their preparation. Many burials are associated with special grave furniture, jewelry, and ornaments of rank.

Trading, quarry, and art sites form a special category in that some kind of specialist activity was carried out. The special tools needed for mining obsidian, copper, and other metals identify quarry sites. Trading sites are identified by large quantities of exotic trade objects and by their strategic position near major cities. The Assyrian market that flourished outside the Hittite city of Kanesh in 1900 B.C. is an example. Art sites, which abound in southwestern France, southern Africa, Australia, California, and other areas, are identified by paintings on the walls of caves and rock shelters.

Cultures, Areas, Regions, and Settlement Patterns

The spatial units we have referred to thus far are all confined to the boundaries of one community. They reflect the activities of the maximum number of people who occupied a settlement at some time during a cycle of settlement. Although a great deal of archaeological research is carried out on single sites, archaeologists often seek to understand the prehistory of a much wider area. Several communities or a scattered population living in a well-defined region may be linked in the same subsistence or settlement system. Such commonly held systems, and the human activities that derive from them, make up an entire culture. Cultural behavior is identified by the patterning that appears in an entire assemblage. Studying an entire culture involves working with much larger bodies of archaeological information, as well as with background geographic and environmental data. A number of units commonly subsume such larger-scale information (Willey and Phillips, 1958). Cultures, areas, regions, and settlement patterns are both spatial and integrative units that involve chronological, social, and cultural dimensions as well.

Archaeological cultures are consistent patternings of assemblages, the archaeological equivalents of human societies. Archaeological cultures consist of the material remains of human culture preserved at a specific time at several sites.

Culture areas are large geographic areas in which artifacts characteristic of an archaeological culture exist in a precise context of time and space. One can refer to both a Maya cultural system and a Maya culture area.

Archaeological regions are generally described as well-defined geographic areas bounded by conspicuous geographic features, such as an ocean, a lake, or mountains. Once having defined a region geographically, the researcher will try to identify its ecological and cultural boundaries throughout prehistoric times. Most regional approaches involve far more than comparing the artifacts from a few scattered settlements. They are based on a research strategy aimed at sampling the entire region and on objectives intended to reconstruct many more aspects of prehistoric life than those uncovered at a single site. These include both social organization and economic strategies.

A **settlement pattern** is the distribution of sites and human settlement across the natural landscape (Chapter 15). Settlement patterns are determined by many factors, including the environment, economic practices, and technological skills. Settlement archaeology is part of the analysis of interactions between people and their environment.

In determining spatial relations, archaeologists base their studies of the behavior of a human society as a whole on models and hypotheses tested by data from many disciplines. These data bear on the ways in which communities and their associated assemblages are grouped into larger units on the landscape. They bear, too, on the ways in which prehistoric societies interacted with the ever-changing natural environment.

Spatial context is vital to scientific archaeology, for it provides one of the critical dimensions of archaeological data. Time, the other critical dimension, is considered in Chapter 7.

Summary

Culture is humanity's primary means of adapting to the environment. Human culture is made up of our behavior and its results; it is also the way in which we assign meaning to our lives. Our culture is always adjusting to both internal and external change.

Archaeologists work with the tangible remains of human activity that survive in the ground. Archaeological finds are not culture in themselves but products of it, and they are linked to culture in a systematic way.

Archaeologists often think of human cultures as complex systems of interacting variables. This viewpoint is based loosely on principles of general systems theory, a way of searching for general relationships in the empirical world.

A major objective of archaeology is to understand the complex linkages between human cultures and the environments in which they are found.

Cultural process involves identifying the factors responsible for the direction and nature of change within cultural systems. Processual archaeology is the analysis of the causes behind cultural change.

In this chapter we defined the archaeological record, data, and provenance; discussed the fundamental principles of association and superposition; and examined context in archaeology.

Key Terms

archaeological culture	cultural system	provenance
archaeological record	culture	secondary context
archaeological regions	culture areas	settlement pattern
artifact	data	sites
assemblage	ecofacts	spatial context
association	feature	structures
condition	hieroglyphs	subassemblage
context	normative view	superposition
cultural process	primary context	

Guide to Further Reading

The literature on basic archaeological concepts is sketchy at best, but these are some key works.

CHILDE, V. GORDON. 1956. *Piecing Together the Past.* London: Routledge and Kegan Paul. A little-known classic that describes the basic principles of culture history for the beginner. Still useful.

DEETZ, JAMES. 1967. *Invitation to Archaeology.* Garden City, NY: Natural History Press. A classic exposition of basic archaeological concepts.

RENFREW, COLIN, and PAUL BAHN. 2004. *Archaeology: Theories, Methods, and Practice.* 4th ed. New York: Thames and Hudson. A comprehensive handbook on archaeological method and theory. Hundreds of illustrations.

SHARER, ROBERT J., and WENDY ASHMORE. 1999. *Archaeology: Discovering the Past.* 4th ed. New York: McGraw-Hill. A comprehensive text with good coverage of the subject matter of this chapter.

THOMAS, DAVID HURST. 2003. *Archaeology: Down to Earth.* 4th ed. New York: Harcourt Brace. An excellent basic text for beginning readers.

WATSON, PATTI JO, STEVEN A. LE BLANC, and CHARLES L. REDMAN. 1984. *Archaeological Explanation: The Scientific Method in Archaeology.* 2d ed. New York: Columbia University Press. A fundamental source that describes processual archaeology in rather technical language.

WILLEY, GORDON R., and PHILIP PHILLIPS. 1958. *Method and Theory in American Archaeology.* Chicago: University of Chicago Press. A classic essay on basic cultural history in North American archaeology.

CHAPTER 7

How Old Is It?

The might of ancient Rome. Hadrian's Wall, near the border of England and Scotland, built by the Emperor Hadrian to keep the Scots out of the northernmost Roman province in the first century A.D.

Consider for a moment how you view time. What is the earliest date you can remember? BMF's is his third birthday; I remember balloons, birthday cake, ice cream, and lots of people. My continuous memory of people as individuals and of day-to-day events begins at age eight. My parents saw Queen Victoria in her extreme old age driving in an open carriage in London in 1898. Our collective family history encompasses the twentieth century—over a hundred years. Most adults have a similar span of recollection and have a chronological perspective on their lives extending back into early childhood. Our sense of personal involvement in human history, too, extends only over our lifetimes. We have only indirect involvement with the lives of our parents, relatives, or friends, some of whom may have been alive fifty to seventy years before we were born. Perhaps our most profound involvement with time occurs toward the end of our lives, with a period covering the lives of our immediate family. But we also have a marginal sense of longer chronologies and a perspective on events within them—our family ancestry, the history of our community, of our nation, and in these days of ardent internationalism, of the world as well—though few people have a sense of perspective for the whole span of human experience.

The measurement of time and the ordering of prehistoric cultures in chronological sequence have been one of the archaeologist's major preoccupations since the very beginnings of scientific research. In this chapter we examine the ways in which archaeologists establish chronological relationships among artifacts, sites, and other features. How does one classify the past and measure the age of the great events of prehistory?

Cyclical and Linear Time

Westerners think of the passage of the human past as having occurred along a straight, if branching, highway of time. The great nineteenth-century German statesman Otto von Bismarck called this the "stream of time," upon which all human societies ride through good times and bad. The analogy is apt, if you think of time in a linear fashion, as archaeologists do. They use a variety of chronological methods to date the millennia of the remote past.

Discovery

Human Sacrifice at Teotihuacán, Mexico, 1998

Teotihuacán, on the edge of the Valley of Mexico, had grown from a series of small villages into a huge metropolis with more than 200,000 inhabitants by A.D. 650 (see Figure 15.12). A vast ceremonial complex dominated by the Pyramids of the Sun and Moon formed the core of the city, but little is known of the builders or of the rituals once celebrated there. In 1998, a team of American and Mexican archaeologists headed by Saburo Sugiyama excavated into the heart of the Pyramid of the Moon, where they unearthed four stratified substructures and a human burial dated to about A.D. 150. The grave contained more than 150 artifacts that surrounded a male skeleton: clay vessels, jade artifacts, figurines, fine obsidian (volcanic glass)

blades, and jadeite ear ornaments. The skeletons of several hawks and a jaguar, perhaps buried alive in their cages, lay nearby.

At first Sugiyama and his colleagues thought they had unearthed the burial of a noble. But the man's hands were bound behind his back and he lay at the edge of what is obviously a much larger burial complex. They believe that he was a sacrificial victim, killed as part of a ceremony to dedicate either a ruler or an important structure. Sugiyama believes that more burials await discovery deeper in the pyramid, including, perhaps, the undisturbed sepulcher of one of Teotihuacán's rulers. Such a discovery would be of the highest importance, as nothing is known of the great city's powerful rulers.

An unfolding, linear past is not the only way of conceptualizing ancient times. Many societies, ancient and modern, think of time as a cyclical phenomenon, or sometimes as a combination of the linear and the cyclical. The cyclical perspective stems from the passage of the seasons and of heavenly bodies, from the close relationships that foragers and village farmers have with their natural environments. It is also based on the eternal realities of human life: fertility and birth, life, growth, and death. The endlessly repeating seasons of planting and harvest, of game movements or salmon runs, and of ripening wild foods governed human existence in deeply significant ways. The ancient Maya developed an elaborate cyclical calendar of interlocking secular and religious calendars to measure the passage of the seasons and to regulate religious ceremonies (Coe, 2002; Schele and Friedel, 1990).

But we should not assume that societies with cyclical views of time did not have linear chronologies as well. The celebrated Maya "Long Count" was a linear chronology that formed an integral part of the close relationship between Maya rulers and the cosmos. The ancient Egyptians developed a linear chronology for administrative purposes. But, in general, societies develop linear chronologies only when they need them. For example, Western societies use linear time to regulate times of prayer, to control the working day, and for airline schedules. It is hard to generalize, but societies with centralized political systems tend to use the reigns of chiefs or kings as signposts along a linear time scale (Figure 7.1).

Figure 7.1 Art as history. A brass plaque from Benin city, West Africa, showing a seated oba (king) with his attendants. These artifacts served as important historical records of royal reigns and genealogy and were stored in the royal palace. (National Museum of African Art, Smithsonian Institution, Washington D.C., U.S.A. Aldo Tutino/Art Resource, NY)

Relative Chronology

Archaeologists refer to two types of chronology:

1. **Relative chronology** establishes chronological relationships between sites and cultures.
2. **Absolute chronology** (sometimes called chronometric chronology) refers to dates in years.

BMF's aged tortoiseshell cat has just come into his study. Bulging with breakfast, she gives me a plaintive miaow and looks for a patch of sunlight on the carpet. She spots one, just where I have laid down a pile of important papers. Thump! With a sigh, she settles down right on top of the documents and passes out blissfully as I write. Time passes and I realize that I need one of the articles in the pile under my faithful beast. I debate whether to have a cup of coffee and procrastinate or to disturb her, knowing there will be angry claws. In the end, writing deadlines prevail. I gently elevate the cat and slip the papers out from under her. She protests halfheartedly and settles down again, as I congratulate myself on escaping grievous injury.

The case of the cat and the papers is a good example of stratigraphy in action (Figure 7.2). Consider the sequence of events. I sit at my computer, consult some documents, then lay them to one side on the floor. This is the first event in the sequence. Some time later, the second event takes place: the cat settles on the papers and

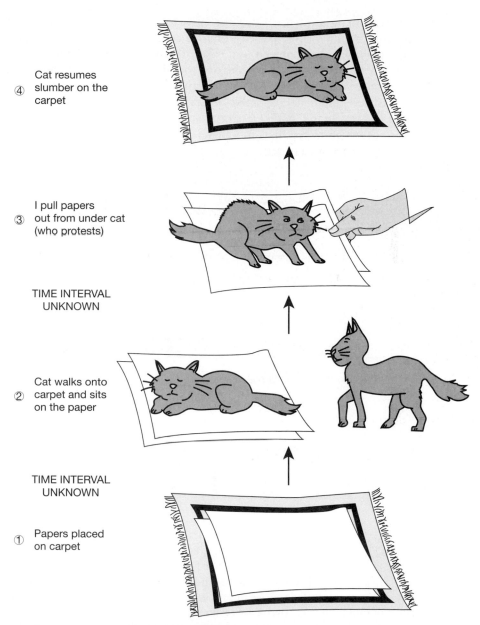

④ Cat resumes slumber on the carpet

③ I pull papers out from under cat (who protests)

TIME INTERVAL UNKNOWN

② Cat walks onto carpet and sits on the paper

TIME INTERVAL UNKNOWN

① Papers placed on carpet

Figure 7.2   A case of feline chronology.

goes to sleep. More time passes. I need an article in the pile, lift the cat, and remove the papers. This third event is followed by the final act of this stirring drama, as the cat settles down again. An outside observer could use the law of superposition (Chapter 6) to reconstruct the sequence of events from the earliest (the dropping of papers on the floor) to the latest (the cat's settling down again). However, although the observer can establish the sequence of events relative to one another in time, he or she cannot tell how long a span of time passed from one event to the other. Nor can he or she know the age of the various objects in the pile. For instance, a document compiled in 1970 might lie in a folder under another one containing a letter written ten years earlier.

Relative chronology is a foundation of all archaeological research, a time scale established either by stratigraphic observation or by placing artifacts in chronological order. As we saw in Chapter 6, stratigraphic observation is based on the law of superposition, which states that, in general, the earliest layers lie below later ones (Figure 7.3). Many ancient settlements, such as long-occupied caves and rock shelters or

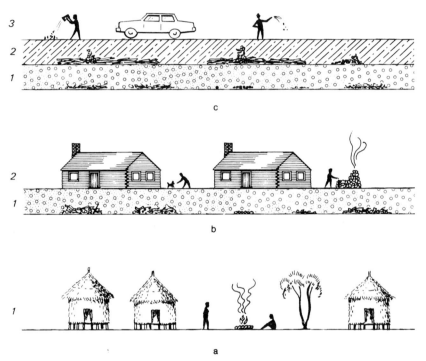

Figure 7.3 Superposition and stratigraphy. (a) A farming village flourishes five thousand years ago. After a time, the village is abandoned and the huts fall into disrepair. Their ruins are covered by accumulating earth and vegetation. (b) After an interval, a second village is built on the same site, with different architectural styles. This village in turn is abandoned; the houses collapse into piles of rubble and are covered by accumulating earth. (c) Twentieth-century people park their cars on top of both village sites and drop litter and coins that, when uncovered, reveal to the archaeologist that the top layer is modern. An archaeologist digging this site would find that the modern layer is underlain by two prehistoric occupation levels; that square houses were in use in the upper of the two, which is the later (principle of superposition); and that round huts are stratigraphically earlier than the square ones. Therefore, village 1 is earlier than village 2, but when either was occupied or how many years separate village 1 from village 2 cannot be established without additional data.

huge city mounds in southwestern Asia, can contain dozens of occupation levels, sometimes separated by layers of sterile soil.

Stratigraphy and Relative Chronology

Stratigraphic observation can sometimes yield remarkably long cultural sequences, which can be dated by radiocarbon and other methods. Most relative chronology in archaeology has its basis in large- or small-scale stratigraphic observations in archaeological sites of all ages. These were the types of observations that led to the wide acceptance of the Three-Age System in the Old World (Chapter 2), and Willey and Phillips's system (1958) of Paleo-Indian, Formative, Classic, and Postclassic in the Americas (Figure 7.4).

Superposition is fundamental in studying archaeological sites, for many settlements, such as southwestern Asian mounds, Native American villages in the Ohio Valley, or cave sites, contain multilevel occupations whose decipherment is the key to their relative chronology (see Figure 7.3).

Stratigraphy, as applied to archaeological sites, is on a much smaller scale than that of geology (E. C. Harris, 1989). Most archaeological relative chronology employs careful observation of sequences of occupation levels as well as correlation of these with cultural sequences at other sites in the same area. Successive occupation levels may be found at the same spot, as in a cave, fort, or mound site, where many generations of settlers lived within a circumscribed or restricted area (Figure 7.5). In other sites, however, the chronological sequence can be horizontal, as when economic or

Approximate Age	Geological Epoch	Three-age Terminology	Important Events
3000 B.C. — 7800 B.C. —	HOLOCENE	Iron Age Bronze Age Neolithic Mesolithic	Writing in the Near East Origins of food production
12,000 B.C. — 35,000 B.P. —	END OF PLEISTOCENE	Upper Paleolithic	Settlement of the Americas Origins of blade technology
70,000 B.P. — 400,000 B.P. —	PLEISTOCENE	Middle Paleolithic	Emergence of *Homo sapiens sapiens* (150,000 B.P.) Hand axes in widespread use
1.75 million B.P. — 5 million B.P. —		Lower Paleolithic	Origins of toolmaking (2.5 million B.P.)
13 million B.P. —	PLIOCENE		
25 million B.P. —	MIOCENE		No humans
34 million B.P. —	OLIGOCENE		

Figure 7.4   Some common nomenclature of Old World archaeology and geology.

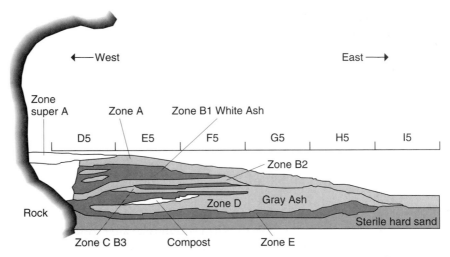

Figure 7.5   An idealized section through Guilá Naquitz Cave, Valley of Oaxaca, Mexico, showing the different occupation zones. Most cave and rock shelter sections are more complex than this one.

Source: Bruce Smith, *The Emergence of Agriculture.* © Bruce D. Smith. Reprinted by permission of the author.

political conditions dictate regular movement of villages when fields are exhausted or residence rules are modified. In this case, a cultural sequence may be scattered throughout a series of single-level occupation sites over a large area and can be put together only by judicious survey work and careful analysis of the artifacts found in the different sites.

The stratigraphy of the Koster site in the American Midwest was much less complex than that of ancient cities, where people lived in houses for a generation or more, then knocked them down and rebuilt on the same spot. They lost beads and ornaments, trampling them into the earth. They laid new floors, a layer of tile or a few centimeters of liquid cattle dung, over earlier living surfaces. Buildings crumble, a flood may demolish them, or a fire may consume an entire city block. People dig graves and storage pits, resurface streets, enlarge temples, and build open plazas. The archaeologist's relative chronology comes from deciphering these kinds of chronological jigsaw puzzles.

The law of association also comes into play, for the artifacts, food remains, and other finds that come from different occupation layers are as vital as the stratigraphy itself. Each layer in a settlement, however massive or however thin, has its associated artifacts, the objects that archaeologists use as chronological indicators and evidence of cultural change. Stratigraphic observation is rarely straightforward. Some key questions are never far from the observer's mind: Was the site occupied continuously? Was the sequence interrupted by a natural catastrophe such as a flood, or was it abandoned,

Site

Koster, Illinois

Few archaeological sites have such exceptional stratigraphy as the well-known Koster site in the Midwest's Illinois River valley (Struever and Holton, 1979). There, human occupations are separated by sterile layers from before 7500 B.C. right into the past millennium. The excavators isolated fourteen stratified occupation levels in their large-scale excavations (see Figure 9.2) that provide an extraordinary chronicle of human exploitation of the river valley environment from about 7500 B.C. to A.D. 1200.

The excavators were able to isolate different occupations and expose large areas of them, starting with transitory Paleo-Indian visitors, then a seasonal camp covering about 0.75 acre (0.3 ha) with temporary dwellings built in about 6500 B.C. They traced repeated visits by an extended family group of about twenty-five people to the same site over many centuries, perhaps timed to exploit rich fall nut harvests. Between 5600 and 5000 B.C., a large permanent camp with longhouses covered in hides or mats came into use; the inhabitants focused on a narrow spectrum of abundant foods throughout much of the year. By 3900 B.C., people lived at Koster year-round in a village covering 5 acres (2 ha). The excavations identified at least six houses with sunken earthen floors, whose inhabitants lived off fish from backwater lakes and fall nut harvests. Koster was abandoned in about 2800 B.C., then was reoccupied briefly about 800 years later. The Koster excavations yielded a treasure trove of chronological information, which provided a framework for studying major changes in Native American society over many thousands of years.

then reoccupied generations later? Far more is involved than merely observing different layers. Basically, the excavator has to reconstruct both the natural and cultural transformations that have affected the site since it was abandoned.

Natural transformations result from natural phenomena, such as the volcanic eruption that buried Roman Pompeii in A.D. 79, or the earthquake that devastated another Roman town, Kourion, on Cyprus, in A.D. 365 (see Figure 15.4). In the case of the Kourion quake, excavator David Soren was able to use historical records to identify the exact moment of the earth movement (Soren and James, 1988). The orientation of collapsed roof tiles gave him the general direction of the epicenter, which lay to the southwest of the town in deep water. Both Roman Herculaneum and Pompeii have yielded graphic evidence of the awful destruction wrought by the sudden ash clouds, including casts of fleeing people frantically trying to escape the ash and fumes (see Figure 2.1). In these cases, volcanic ash sealed a precise moment in time, providing unique opportunities for observing life in a city at a single period.

Mud slides, floods, windstorms, and sand dunes can seal off occupation layers from later horizons. At the other end of the spectrum, burrowing animals can tunnel through soft ash layers and transform beautifully stratified layers into confused mazes.

Relative chronology depends on precise, and thorough, observation and interpretation. (There is more on stratigraphic observation in Chapter 9.)

Artifacts and Relative Chronology

Manufactured artifacts of all kinds are the fundamental data archaeologists use to study past human behavior. Artifacts are reflections of ancient human behavior, so it follows that they change as peoples' technologies, lifeways, and activities shift over the millennia. Consider the simple, sharp-edged flake knives and choppers used by our earliest ancestors 2.5 million years ago (see Figure 11.3). Modern-day experiments have shown that such artifacts were highly effective for slicing through fresh meat and butchering animals. Compare such tools with the highly sophisticated supercomputers used by banks and credit card companies today. In the final analysis, you could argue that one evolved from the other, but millions upon millions of minor technological and behavioral changes took place along the way as the simple artifacts of yesteryear branched into more and more sophisticated tools for all kinds of specialized purposes. Most changes were small, sometimes almost imperceptible: a more efficient method for edge-sharpening a stone tool; changes in the lip angle or decoration on a clay bowl, which led ultimately to an entirely different vessel; new alloys such as tin added to copper to make much tougher bronze. Such cumulative changes are an excellent way of establishing relative chronologies.

Sequence dating is now known as **seriation,** a technique for ordering artifacts by their structure and design. Seriation has achieved a high degree of sophistication since the 1920s. **Frequency seriation** employs percentages of artifacts and their features to develop cultural sequences (L. Johnson, 1968; Marquardt, 1978).

We live in a world of whirlwind fashions. Automobiles acquire fins. A few years later, fins are gone and rounded contours are the rage. Whitewall tires are all the fashion; a decade later you never see them. Minivans replace station wagons; then sport utility vehicles reign supreme. The miniskirt suddenly descends to midcalf or even the ankle before rising to new heights. Fashions of all kinds are volatile and ever-changing, including CDs in the top 40 or the colors of glass beads traded in remote African villages. In contrast, Stone Age hand axes took hundreds of thousands of years to assume more sophisticated shapes. All these changes, dizzyingly fast or mind-numbingly slow, have one thing in common; at some period in time, they enjoyed a brief, or long, moment of maximum popularity. All artifact seriations start with this assumption.

Two historical archaeologists, Edwin Dethlefsen and James Deetz, set out (1966) to verify this assumption against known historical data. They chose dated New England colonial gravestones from Stoneham, Massachusetts, for this purpose. Three decorative styles had come into fashion at different times: death's heads, cherubs, and urn and willow motifs. Dethlefsen and Deetz recorded the percentages of the three motifs at nine-year intervals from 1720 to 1829. They found that the

Doing Archaeology

Flinders Petrie and Sequence Dating

In the 1880s and 1890s, a remarkable Egyptologist named Flinders Petrie (1889) unearthed hundreds of shallow graves in desert cemeteries at Diospolis Parva, close to the Nile River. These villagers had farmed along the river many centuries before the first pharaoh, Menes, unified Egypt into a single state in about 3100 B.C. Historical dates in Egypt went back to Menes, but then petered out. Petrie's "Predynastic" burial subjects wore few ornaments, but they lay with groups of jars, pots, and bowls. Flinders Petrie had an eye for smaller objects. He hit on the brilliant idea of using the groups of clay vessels from the graves to place the graves in chronological order, by arranging the pots so that their stylistic differences reflected gradual design changes. The jar handles were especially informative, for they changed over time from mere ledgelike appendages to more decorative and functional handles before they degenerated into little more than painted lines. Petrie spent months dividing the grave lots into no fewer than fifty stages, which he called "sequence dates." His stages started with SD30, for he rightly assumed he had not found the earliest Predynastic pottery. SD80 linked the cemeteries to dynastic Egypt in about 3100 B.C.

Flinders Petrie's sequence dates provided an admirable way of placing Predynastic burials and sites throughout the Nile Valley into relative chronological order. Over half a century passed before anyone could provide calendar year dates for Predynastic Egyptian cultures with radiocarbon dates. The Diospolis Parva graves provided one of the first instances where artifacts provided a reliable relative chronology.

death's head was universally popular until 1760, when it began to give way to the cherub. Cherubs enjoyed high fashion until about 1809, when they suddenly went out of favor as the urn and willow became the style of the day. When they plotted the percentages as horizontal bar graphs (Figure 7.6), they acquired a series of profiles, which looked very much like an old-fashioned battleship seen from above with its thick belt of armor amidships. The "battleship" curves of the Stoneham gravestones followed one upon the other with almost perfect symmetry. This classic and oft-quoted example of changing artifacts illustrates the principle of frequency seriation perfectly.

The so-called battleship curve frequency seriation method is widely used in American archaeology. Let us say you have nine excavated archaeological sites, each containing different percentages of different pottery forms. You classify the vessels from each location into three distinct types with characteristic decoration, calculating the percentages of each in every site. Next, you apply the battleship curve principle, placing the sites in order by placing the horizontally arranged percentage bars in order (Figure 7.7). This arrangement will give you a relative chronology for the sites. Then, later on, you excavate two more settlements, where, again, you calculate the

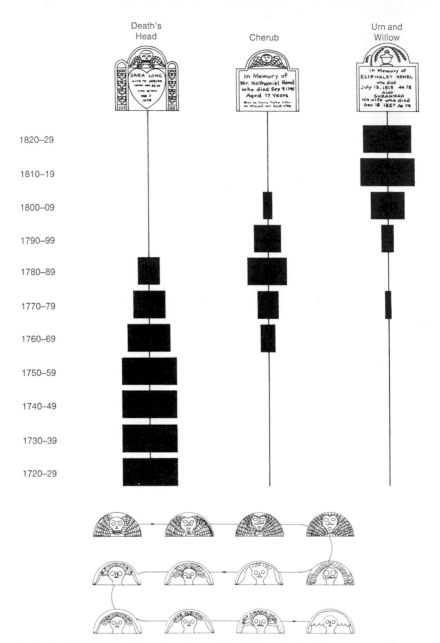

Figure 7.6 (*top*) Seriation. The changing styles of New England gravestones, from Stoneham, Massachusetts, between A.D. 1720 and 1829, seriated in three styles. Notice how each style rises to a peak of maximum popularity and then declines as another comes into fashion. The cherub style shows the classic "battleship curve." Each horizontal bar represents the percentage of a gravestone type at that date; for example, between 1720 and 1729, death's heads were at 100 percent. (*bottom*) Seriation of a stylistic change within one New England gravestone motif. This type of seriation deals with the minute changes in the death's head motif and shows how cultural traits change very gradually over time.

Source: James Deetz, *Invitation to Archaeology* (New York: Doubleday, 1967). Artist Eric G. Engstrom. Copyright © 1967 by James Deetz. Used by permission of Doubleday, a division of Random House, Inc.

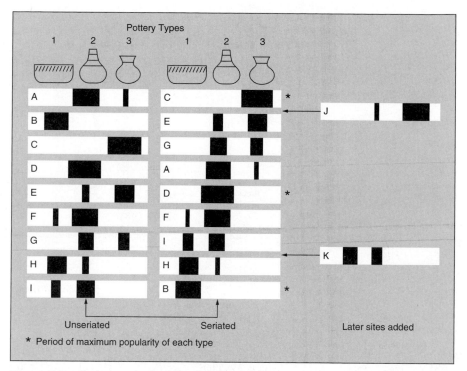

Figure 7.7   Seriation. At the left, nine excavated sites (A to I) contain different percentages of three distinct pottery types. At the right, the nine sites have been seriated by rearranging the bars of type percentages into battleship curve order. At the far right, later excavations are eventually fitted into the sequence.

percentages of decorated pots. On the assumption that closely similar artifacts were made at approximately the same time at all sites within a restricted order, you can fit these new percentages into your master sequence and obtain a relative date for the extra sites.

Figure 7.8 shows a classic example of pottery seriation combined with stratigraphic observation from Mexico's Tehuacán Valley, famous for its evidence of early maize farming. Archaeologist Richard MacNeish (1970) worked before radiocarbon dating was a highly refined dating method. He had excavated or surface-collected dozens of stratified and unstratified sites and needed to develop a relative chronology based on changing pottery styles. He used a combination of stratigraphy and seriation of many distinctive pottery types to place three stages of Tehuacán culture in a relative chronology. Notice that MacNeish used no absolute dates to develop this sequence (which has subsequently been confirmed by radiocarbon dating).

Artifact seriation has obvious limitations and works best when pottery types or other tool forms change predictably over a long period of time. Today's seriators use sophisticated statistical methods to produce the seriation and to test the validity of their conclusions (Dunnell, 1970; Marquardt, 1978).

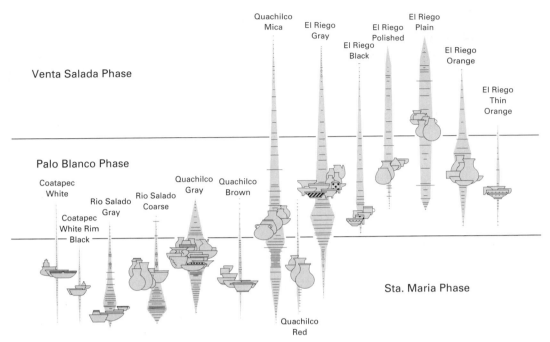

Figure 7.8 Seriation of pottery styles from the Tehuacán Valley, Mexico, showing many sites ordered into a single sequence. Richard MacNeish classified the different pottery types at each site, then placed them in chronological order on the basis of stratigraphic observations and periods of maximum popularity for each pottery type represented. Here the battleship curve principle is used to develop a sequence of changing pottery forms, each site being "fitted" into the sequence on the basis of the percentage of each pottery type represented.

Source: R. S. MacNeish, *The Prehistory of the Tehuacán Valley,* Vol. 3. Copyright 1970, University of Texas Press. Reprinted by permission of the Andover Foundation for Archaeological Research.

Absolute Chronology

Many of our most fundamental questions about the past involve chronology (Taylor and Aitken, 1998). How old is this stone ax? Are these villages contemporaneous? When was this woman buried? Relative chronology is comparatively straightforward compared with actual dating in calendar years. More effort has gone into inventing methods of dating the past than into almost any other aspect of archaeology (Geyh and Schleicher, 1990).

The landscape of the human experience stretches back more than two- and one-half million years into the past. Relative dating allows us to people this landscape with myriad long- and short-lived human cultures, ordered in local, regional, and continentwide sequences. The relatively dated past is like a branching tree, but a tree whose branches and limbs never grew evenly or sprouted at the same time. Relative dating allows us to erect the tree, to plot its boughs and twigs in reasonably accurate order. We have a sense of a changing landscape but no perspective of passing years.

Without absolute dates, we do not know the precise dates when humanity originated, when specific cultures began and ended, or how fast they changed. Nor do we have any inkling of when different major developments, such as the changeover from hunting and gathering to farming, took place in the Americas as opposed to southwestern Asia, or in China relative to tropical Africa. Absolute chronology is essential if we are to measure the rates of culture change over long and short periods of time.

Dates in calendar years are the force that causes the stationary body of the past to come alive in the archaeologist's hands. Extremely precise tree-ring dates from the American Southwest tell the story of a prolonged drought cycle that affected the Ancestral Pueblo people in the twelfth century, perhaps causing them to disperse from large pueblos into small villages. Radiocarbon dates calibrated with tree rings from Abu Hureyra, Syria, tell us that people switched from foraging to farming within a remarkably short time, perhaps a few generations. We now know that urban civilizations developed first in Egypt and Mesopotamia in about 3100 B.C., by 2000 B.C. in northern China, and in Central and South America shortly thereafter.

Figure 7.9 shows the chronological span of the major absolute dating methods used to date the immense span of the human past. Let us now work our way back into the remote past, as we examine these major methods.

Historical Records, Calendars, and Objects of Known Age (c. 3000 B.C. to Present)

Everyone learns the dates of major events in recent history in elementary school: the date of the Declaration of Independence (A.D. 1776) or the year when Roman general Julius Caesar landed in Britain (55 B.C.). Such years are landmarks that anchor the formation of modern nations, recorded in many documents. Unfortunately, however, written history has a short time span of only about 5,000 years; therefore, it is useful only for dating sites and artifacts from about 3000 B.C. to the present.

Historical Documents.   In 1290 B.C., the Egyptian king Seti I inscribed a king list on the walls of his temple at Abydos by the Nile River. His scribes recorded the names of seventy-five royal ancestors. His successor, Rameses II, ordered his scribes to prepare yet another complete list of rulers, which survives as the so-called Turin Canon (Kemp, 1989). This remarkable document appears to contain the list of every pharaoh from Rameses back to Narmer (Menes), the first ruler of a unified Egypt in about 3100 B.C. The scribes who compiled the two king lists were less concerned with chronology than with making a political statement about the long continuity and stability of Egyptian civilization since the remotest past. Today, both the Seti list and the Turin document provide Egyptologists with a priceless record of the chronology of ancient Egyptian civilization.

Writing began in Mesopotamia and Egypt sometime just before 3000 B.C. At first, simple clay tokens and other marking systems recorded increasingly complex dealings between people living at some distance from one another. Eventually, the tokens became picture representations and then written scripts such as Sumerian cuneiform (Greek *cuneus,* "wedge"), with its wedgelike symbols punched into wet clay,

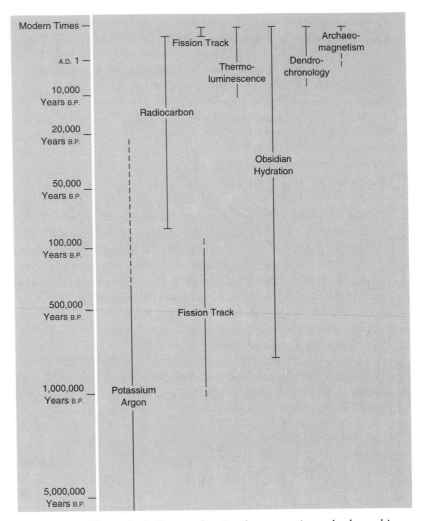

Figure 7.9   Chronological span of major chronometric methods used in archaeology. The column at the left shows the immense span of prehistory when compared with historic times, illuminated by written documents, which began about 5,000 years ago.

and Egyptian hieroglyphs (Robinson, 1995). The earliest written records were little more than merchants' transactions and accounts, but early scribes soon widened their activities. Sumerian and Egyptian literature includes epics; love poetry; legal, political, and religious documents; and even school texts. Ancient scripts dating from 2500 B.C. provide valuable chronological information.

Historical records provide dates for early eastern Mediterranean civilizations, for Chinese states after 2000 B.C., and for Europe after the Roman occupation just before Christ. However, document-based history came to parts of tropical Africa and Asia only in the late nineteenth century A.D. In the Americas, the Maya developed a complex written script just over 2,000 years ago and an intricate calendar system that provides an accurate chronology for major events in later Mesoamerican history (Schele and Friedel, 1990). Written sources for Native American societies elsewhere begin with European expansion after the fifteenth century.

Thus, documents provide accurate dates for only a tiny span of human history, most of it concentrated in the Mediterranean and eastern Asian worlds. We know the precise date when the Pilgrims settled Plymouth Plantation in Massachusetts and when galleons from the battered Spanish Armada foundered on the rocks of western Ireland. But history covers but the blink of a chronological eye in the larger landscape of a two-and-one-half-million-year-old past.

Calendars. People maintain calendars for many reasons: to commemorate the dates when rulers ascended to their thrones, to time important festivals, or to mark the passage of the seasons. Few ancient societies developed calendars as elaborate as those of the ancient Mesoamericans. The Maya calendar is justly famous. Once used to regulate the agricultural and religious years, the gear wheel of intersecting sacred and secular calendars organized every aspect of Maya life in repeating cycles (Coe, 2002). At the same time, their priests maintained a linear calendar known as the Long Count, recorded on stone uprights. Experts have linked this to the Christian calendar and placed its span to be between 3114 B.C. and A.D. 909, although it lasted in places until the Spanish Conquest of the sixteenth century. Much of this time scale unfolded before the Maya themselves lived in organized states, but their unique calendar provides a useful check on the dates of cities such as Copán, Palenque, and Tikal.

Like written documents, ancient calendars cover relatively short time brackets within the past 5,000 years. Nevertheless, they are invaluable for detailed studies of such topics as Aztec or Egyptian civilization.

Objects of Known Age (Cross-Dating). Objects of known age, such as Roman coins or Chinese porcelain, can be used to date archaeological sites hundreds, if not thousands, of miles away from their point of origin. Sir Arthur Evans, who discovered Minoan civilization on the island of Crete in 1900, established the chronology of the Bronze Age Palace of Knossos, home of the legendary King Minos, using cross-dating in reverse (Joan Evans, 1943). He developed an elaborate relative chronology of Minoan painted pottery at the palace, then consulted Egyptologists, who showed him examples of precisely similar vessels excavated from Egyptian sites dating to before 1500 B.C. Evans anchored Minoan chronology with these historical links, which resulted from an active trade in timber, olive oil, and other commodities between Crete and the Nile Valley (Figure 7.10).

Historical archaeologists make extensive use of objects of known age to date sites and structures (Orser, 2004). One of the most useful colonial American artifacts is the imported English kaolin pipe (Figure 7.11). Not only were pipes manufactured, imported, smoked, and thrown away within a very short time, but the shape of the pipe body changed in an easily recognizable evolutionary chain. Clay pipes were so cheap that everyone, however poor, used and discarded them almost like cigarettes. Not only

Figure 7.10 Palace of Minos at Knossos, Crete, c. 1450 B.C.

1730-1770

1780-1820

1800-1830

Figure 7.11 Representative evolutionary changes in the designs of English clay tobacco pipes dating to between A.D. 1730 and 1830.

Source: Ivor Noël Hume, *Artifacts of Colonial America.* Copyright © 1969 by Ivor Noël Hume. Used by permission of Alfred A. Knopf, a Division of Random House, Inc.

the bowl but the length of the stem and the diameter of the hole changed between A.D. 1620 and 1800. These characteristics have been used to date these artifacts and the sites associated with them with considerable precision.

The potential range of historic objects that can be dated to within surprisingly narrow chronological limits is enormous (Orser, 2004). Many people collect beer cans, bottle caps and openers, barbed wire, firearms, uniform buttons, and even horseshoes. All these artifacts, to say nothing of such prosaic objects as forks, electrical switch plates, and scissors, can be dated to within a few years with mail-order catalogs, U.S. patent records, and a great deal of patient detective work. Bottles, buckets, and horseshoes may be the unrespectable artifacts of archaeology, but, unlike many of their prehistoric equivalents, they can be dated with great accuracy.

What better way to learn about archaeology than to study and date our own material culture!

Cross-dating uses objects of known historical age to date archaeological sites found far from the known objects' place of origin. This dating method is useful for a chronological span from about 3000 B.C. to the present. Such objects as Chinese porcelain, Roman glass, cotton and flax fabrics, bronze daggers, and Greek amphorae traveled far from their homelands in the Old World. European coins and medals sometimes passed deep into the American interior along well-established trade routes. Such objects provide chronological horizons for dating hitherto undated pottery styles and other artifacts in remote areas such as, for example, western Europe during the Iron Age, after 3,000 years ago.

Cross-dating is also effective when you can date a single long cultural sequence comprising numerous archaeological sites using seriated artifacts, then date the same sites and artifact forms with blocks of tree-ring or radiocarbon dates. You can then extrapolate the master chronology to nearby sites in the same region by seriating distinctive artifact types and matching them to the master sequence. Richard MacNeish (1970) used this approach with great success in Mexico's Tehuacán Valley, as have many other researchers in North America.

Tree-Ring Chronology (10,000 Years Ago to Present)

Everyone is familiar with tree rings—concentric circles, each circle representing annual growth—visible in the cross section of a felled tree's trunk. All trees form such rings, but they are better defined when the tree grows in an environment with well-marked seasons (winter and summer temperatures or dry and wet months). In about 1913, Arizona astronomer Andrew E. Douglass started counting tree rings as a way of dating sunspot activity. He soon realized the potential of **dendrochronology,** a method of using tree rings to date ancient Southwestern pueblos (Baillie, 1982). At first he developed two tree-ring sequences. One was based on slow-growing and long-lived sequoias and California bristlecone pines; the latter eventually provided a chronology of 8,200 years. His second sequence used ancient, long-dead trunks, many of them pueblo door lintels and beams. Douglass was unable to link his "floating" chronology of pueblo beams to his master sequence until 1929, when he located the missing few years in a beam from Show Low, Arizona. Since then, Southwestern archaeologists have enjoyed a remarkably accurate chronology, so precise it can date not only entire pueblos but sometimes individual rooms within them. The principles of tree-ring dating are discussed in the Doing Archaeology box.

Extremely accurate chronologies for Southwestern sites come from correlating a master tree-ring sequence from felled trees and dated structures with beams from Indian pueblos. The beams in many such structures have been used again and again, and thus some are very much older than the houses in which they were most recently used. The earliest tree rings obtained from such settlements date to the first century B.C., but most timbers were in use between A.D. 1000 and historic times.

In one classic example, Jeffrey Dean (1970) collected numerous samples from wooden beams at Betatakin, a cliff dwelling in northeastern Arizona dating to A.D. 1270.

Site

Cross-Dating at Great Zimbabwe, Zimbabwe, Central Africa

A classic example of cross-dating comes from Central Africa. Back in 1929, British archaeologist Gertrude Caton-Thompson found herself confronted by a first-rate archaeological mystery. Great Zimbabwe was a complex of freestanding stone ruins clustered below a low hill where the ancient builders had erected stone-walled enclosures high above the valley floor (Figure 7.12).

The high granite walls of the oval Great Enclosure, adorned with a chevron pattern and an enigmatic conical tower, dwarfed the diminutive Caton-Thompson, who had never seen anything like them before. Great Zimbabwe was unique and was such a sophisticated structure that early European archaeologists who ransacked the buildings for treasure refused to believe they had been built by black Africans. Caton-Thompson searched for patches of undisturbed occupation deposits missed by earlier excavators and sunk carefully placed stratigraphic trenches in the hilltop enclosures and in the Great Enclosure. Almost at once, she discovered fragments of imported Chinese porcelain, which had reached Zimbabwe in the hands of traders from the distant Indian Ocean coast. From her researches in Egypt and elsewhere, she knew that experts could date Chinese porcelain within remarkably narrow chronological limits in their places of origin. She sent the porcelain to London's Victoria and Albert Museum, where specialists in Chinese artifacts assigned her imported potsherds to the Ming dynasty, specifically to the fourteenth and early fifteenth centuries A.D.

The Chinese porcelain provided Caton-Thompson with a solid cross-date from China to Africa, thereby placing the heyday of Great

He used 292 samples to reconstruct the history of the cliff dwelling, room by room. He found that three room clusters were built in 1267, and a fourth was added a year later. In 1269, the inhabitants trimmed and stockpiled beams for later use, which were not used until 1275, when ten more room clusters were added. Such intrasite datings are possible when a large number of samples can be found. Similar research at Walpi Pueblo, a Hopi site in Arizona founded in A.D. 1400 and still inhabited today, proved the essential validity of Dean's methods but also highlighted the difficulties of dating complex sites where beams are reused frequently, as when salvaged beams have been trimmed and reused (Ahlstrom and others, 1991).

Use of dendrochronology was once confined to the American Southwest but is now widely used in many other parts of the world, including Alaska, Canada, parts of the eastern United States, England, Ireland, continental Europe, the Aegean Islands, and the eastern Mediterranean (Kuniholm, 2001). The Europeans have worked with oak trees with ages of 150 years or more to develop master chronologies for recent times. Using visual and statistical comparisons, they have managed to link living trees to dead specimens serving as church and farmhouse beams and others found well

Zimbabwe between A.D. 1350 and 1450. She concluded that indigenous Africans had built the stone structures. Although radiocarbon dates have refined Caton-Thompson's chronology, no scientist has challenged her cross-dating (Garlake, 1973).

Figure 7.12 The Great Enclosure, Great Zimbabwe, Zimbabwe.

preserved in bogs and waterlogged peats or prehistoric sites. The resulting tree-ring sequences go back at least 10,021 years in Germany and 7,289 years in Ireland. The Aegean Dendrochronology Project has developed a tree-ring sequence covering 6,000 of the last 8,500 years, which is leading to much more precise dates for the Minoan and Mycenaean civilizations than those suggested by cross-dating or radiocarbon readings. So precise are the master sequences that an expert can date even short ring cycles to within a few years. Art historians even use tree rings to date the oak boards used by Dutch old masters as a means of authenticating paintings. And two British scholars used tree rings from a Stradivarius violin known as "the Messiah," thought to be a forgery, to show that it was made in about 1716 and from the same batch of spruce as two other Stravidarius instruments (Topham and McCormick, 2000)!

Tree-ring chronologies have far wider importance than merely dating the past. They can provide records of short-term climatic change in areas such as the American Southwest, where cycles of wetter and drier weather can cause radical changes in settlement patterns. Southwestern chronologies are accurate to within a year, a level of accuracy rarely achieved with archaeological chronologies anywhere. In recent years,

Doing Archaeology

The Principles of Tree-Ring Dating

As a rule, trees produce growth rings each year, formed by the cambium, or growth layer, lying between the wood and the bark. When the growing season starts, large cells are added to the wood. These cells develop thicker walls and become smaller as the growing season progresses; by the end of the growth season, cell production has ceased altogether. This process occurs every growing year, and a distinct line is formed between the wood of the previous season, with its small cells, and the wood of the next, with its new, large cells. The thickness of the rings may vary according to the tree's age and annual climatic variations; thick rings are characteristic of good growth years.

Weather variations within a circumscribed area tend to run in cycles. A decade of wet years may be followed by five dry decades. One season may break a forty-year rainfall record. These cycles of climate are reflected in patterns of thicker or thinner tree rings, which are repeated from tree to tree within a limited area. Dendrochronologists have invented sophisticated methods of correlating rings from different trees so they can build up long master sequences of rings from a number of trunks that may extend over many centuries.

Samples are normally collected by cutting a full cross section from an old beam no longer in a structure, by using a special core borer to obtain samples from beams still in a building, or by V-cutting exceptionally large logs. Delicate or brittle samples are impregnated with paraffin or coated with shellac before examination.

In the laboratory, the surface of the sample is leveled to a precise plane. Analyzing tree rings consists of recording individual ring series and then comparing them against other series. Comparisons can be made by eye or by plotting the rings on a uniform scale so that one series can be compared with another. The series so plotted can then be computer-matched with the master tree-ring chronology for the region (Figure 7.13).

the Laboratory of Tree Ring Research at the University of Arizona has used tree-rings to reconstruct climatic variability in the Southwest from A.D. 680 to 1970. By mapping decade-long tree-ring sequences like contour maps, experts can correlate vacated large and small pueblos with short-term climatic fluctuations (see Doing Archaeology box in Chapter 12).

Radiocarbon Dating (From 40,000 Years Ago to A.D. 1500)

In 1949, University of Chicago scientist Willard Libby (1955) revolutionized archaeology with the radiocarbon dating method of dating wood, bone, and other organic materials up to 40,000 years old. Libby's discovery was a direct offshoot of the development of the atomic bomb during World War II. At first, he tested his new method against organic objects of known historical age, such as Egyptian mummies, but he soon started dating archaeological sites that had been occupied thousands of

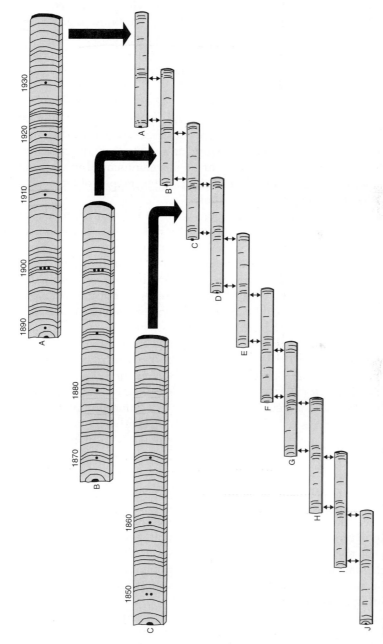

Figure 7.13 Building a tree-ring chronology. (A) Boring taken from a living tree after the 1939 growing season. (B through J) Specimens taken from old houses and progressively older ruins. The ring patterns match and overlap back into the past.

Source: Adapted from D. R. Brothwell and Eric Higgs, eds. *Science in Archaeology* (London: Thames and Hudson, 1961).

years earlier. Today, radiocarbon dating based on **accelerator mass spectrometry (AMS)** allows the dating of objects as tiny as a fleck of charcoal inside a tool socket or an individual seed from an early farming village (Gowlett, 1987; Taylor et al., 1992). Thanks to AMS radiocarbon dating, we know that farming first began in southwestern Asia in about 8,800 radiocarbon years B.C.—and we have the dated seeds to prove it. And calibrations based on tree rings, corals, and geological phenomena such as icebergs convert these radiocarbon ages into calendar chronologies, in the case of agriculture about 10,000 B.C.

Radiocarbon dating is the most widely used dating method for dating the past from 40,000 years ago until A.D. 1500 and provides a global radiocarbon chronology for world prehistory and the late Ice Age. It enables us to measure rates of culture change in different regions of the world and to compare the chronology of such major developments as the first farming or the development of urban civilization in widely separated locations (B. D. Smith, 1992). The principles of radiocarbon dating are discussed in the Doing Archaeology box.

Libby made a false assumption when he originally formulated the radiocarbon method. He had argued that the concentration of radiocarbon in the atmosphere remained constant as time passed, so that prehistoric samples, when alive, would have contained the same amount of radiocarbon as living things today. In fact, changes in the strength of the earth's magnetic field and alterations in solar activity have considerably varied the concentration of radiocarbon in the atmosphere and in living things. For example, samples of 6,000 years ago were exposed to a much higher concentration than are living things today. It is possible, fortunately, to correct radiocarbon dates by using accurate dates from tree rings dating to between about 10,000 B.C. and A.D. 1950 (Stuiver and others, 1998). The discrepancies between radiocarbon and calibrated dates are wide. Here is an example: a radiocarbon age of 1,007 radiocarbon years B.C. is a calibrated date of 1267 B.C. (standard deviations are omitted here) (Figure 7.14, p. 158). Radiocarbon ages around 10,000 B.P. may be as much as 2,000 years too young.

Earlier dates are still uncalibrated. Recently, though, scientists have used a new, highly accurate technique based on the decay of uranium into thorium to date fossil coral near Barbados in the Caribbean and other deposits in the south Pacific (Stuiver and others, 1998). They compared these dates with radiocarbon results and found that radiocarbon dates between 10,000 and 25,000 years ago may be as much as 3,500 years too recent. The new coral researches, combined with ice core and deep-sea core data, are beginning to provide calibrations for radiocarbon ages back to 25,000 years ago, which is about 28,000 years ago in calibrated years.

In the early days of radiocarbon dating, the carbon-14 laboratory required as much as a handful of charcoal or other organic material for a single date. Today, accelerator mass spectrometry (AMS) allows radiocarbon dating to be carried out by direct counting of carbon-14 atoms (Figure 7.15, p. 159). Accelerator dating distinguishes between carbon-14 and carbon-12 and other isotopes through their mass and energy characteristics, requiring only tiny organic samples such as a seed to do so. The samples needed are so small that it is possible, for example, to date an individual tree ring, a plant fragment, or an artifact. This technology has enabled archaeologists such as Bruce Smith (1992) and Andrew Moore (2000) to date single maize cobs or wheat seed

Doing Archaeology

The Principles of Radiocarbon Dating

The **radiocarbon dating** method is based on the fact that cosmic radiation produces neutrons that enter the earth's atmosphere and react with nitrogen. They produce carbon-14, a carbon isotope with eight rather than the usual six neutrons in the nucleus. With these additional neutrons, the nucleus is unstable and is subject to gradual radioactive decay. Willard Libby calculated that it took 5,568 years for half the carbon-14 in any sample to decay, its so-called **half-life.** (The half-life is now more accurately measured to be 5,730 years.) He found that the neutrons emitted radioactive particles when they left the nucleus, and he arrived at a method for counting the number of emissions in a gram of carbon.

Carbon-14 is believed to behave exactly like ordinary carbon from a chemical standpoint, and together with ordinary carbon it enters into the carbon dioxide of the atmosphere. The rate of the process corresponds to the rates of supply and disintegration. Because living vegetation builds up its own organic matter through photosynthesis and by using atmospheric carbon dioxide, the proportion of radiocarbon present in it is equal to that in the atmosphere. As soon as an organism dies, no further radiocarbon is incorporated into it. The radiocarbon present in the dead organism will continue to disintegrate slowly, so that after 5,730 years only half the original amount will be left; after about 11,100 years, only a quarter; and so on. Thus, if you measure the rate of disintegration of carbon-14 relative to nitrogen, you can get an idea of the age of the specimen being measured. The initial amount of radiocarbon in a sample is so small that the limit of detectability is soon reached. Samples older than 50,000 years contain only minuscule quantities of carbon-14.

A date received from a radiocarbon dating laboratory for a particular sample would be in this form: 3,621 ± 180 radiocarbon years before the present (B.P.). The figure 3,621 is the probable statistical age of the sample (in radiocarbon years) before the present (the present being A.D. 1950). Notice that the sample reads in radiocarbon years, not calendar years. Corrections from tree rings must be applied to make this a chronometric date.

The radiocarbon age has the reading ±180 attached to it. This is the standard deviation, an estimate of the amount of probable error. The figure 180 years is an estimate of the 360-year range within which the date falls. Statistical theory provides that there is a two-out-of-three chance that the correct date is within the span of one standard deviation (3,441 and 3,801). If we double the deviation, chances are nineteen out of twenty that the span (3,261 and 3,981) is correct. Most dates in this book are derived from carbon-14–dated samples and should be recognized for what they are—statistical approximations.

fragments, which obviously give far more accurate dates for such developments as the origins of agriculture than samples that reflect a whole occupation layer do.

Radiocarbon dates reach their outer limits around 40,000 years ago, which means they are useful for dating the all-important developments of the late Ice Age and more recent times. Earlier prehistory is far harder to date, because of the large periods of time involved and the lack of reliable dating methods that cover much of the Ice Age.

Radiocarbon Date	Tree-Ring Calibrations
A.D. 1760	A.D. 1945
1505	1435
1000	1105
500	635
1	15
B.C. 505	B.C. 767
1007	1267
1507	1867
2007	2477
3005	3795
4005	4935
5005	5876
6050	7056
7001	8247
8007	9368
9062	9968
AMS Radiocarbon Date	*Uranium/Thorium Calibration (Barbados)*
B.C. 7760	B.C. 9140
8270	10,310
9320	11,150
10,250	12,285
13,220	16,300
14,410	17,050
15,280	18,660
23,920	28,280

Differences increase beyond 25,000 B.C. (calibrated).

Calibrations are based on tables in Stuiver and others (1998). It should be stressed that these calibrations are provisional, statistically based, and subject to modification, especially before 7000 B.C.

Figure 7.14   Calibration table for radiocarbon ages.

Potassium-Argon Dating (Earliest Times to c. 50,000 Years Ago)

The only viable means of chronometrically dating the earliest archaeological sites is the **potassium-argon dating** method (Dalrymple and Lamphere, 1970). Geologists use this radioactive counting technique to date the age of the earth from rocks as much as 2 billion years old and as recent as 50,000 years old.

Fortunately, many early human settlements in the Old World are found in volcanic areas, where such deposits as lava flows and tuffs are found in profusion. The first archaeological date obtained from this method came from Olduvai Gorge, Tanzania, where Louis and Mary Leakey found a robust australopithecine skull (*Australopithecus boisei*), stone tools, and animal bones in a lake bed of unknown age. Lava samples from the site were dated to about 1.75 million years, doubling the then-assumed date for early humans (Tobias, 1971). Stone flakes and chopping tools of undoubted human manufacture have come from Koobi Fora in northern Kenya, potassium dated to about 2.6 million years, the earliest date for human artifacts. Still earlier ***Australopithecus*** fossils have been dated to about 4.5 million years ago by the

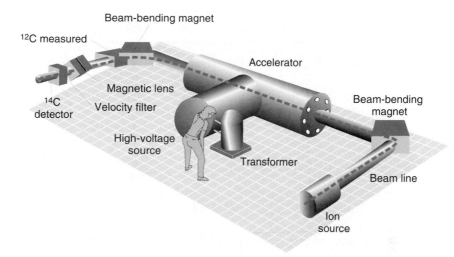

Figure 7.15   Accelerator mass spectrometry (AMS) radiocarbon dating. Ionized carbon atoms from the sample are first pulled in beam form toward the accelerator. As the beam passes through the first beam-bending magnet, lighter atoms turn more sharply than heavier ones. They move to the inside of the diverging beam, where a filter blocks the further progress of all charged particles except those of atomic mass 14. When the beam enters the accelerator, it is stripped of all molecules of mass 14 that might be indistinguishable from single carbon-14 atoms. The accelerator pushes the remaining ions through a second beam-bending magnet, filtering out more non-carbon-14 particles. Then the beam is focused before reaching an extremely sensitive detector that counts the number of remaining ions.

Source: Bruce Smith, *The Emergence of Agriculture.* © Bruce D. Smith. Reprinted by permission of the author.

same method at Aramis near the Hadar in Ethiopia. A team of Berkeley scientists have dated **Homo erectus**–bearing levels at Modjokerto in southeastern Asia to 1.8 million years using a new laser fusion technique (Swisher and others, 1994). The principles of potassium-argon dating and laser fusion are discussed in the box on page 160.

Other Absolute Dating Methods

Accurate dating of the past remains one of the greatest challenges of archaeology, partly because of the enormous time scales involved, and also because each archaeological site is unique and there are so many stratigraphic and other variables that affect the formation of archaeological deposits. The specialist literature is full of well-established dating methods and still-experimental methods that are destined to become part of the archaeologist's tool kit or vanish into scientific oblivion (Aitken, 1990). The following are some of the more common dating methods.

Doing Archaeology

The Principles of Potassium-Argon Dating

Potassium (K) is one of the most abundant elements in the earth's crust and is present in nearly every mineral. In its natural form, potassium contains a small proportion of radioactive potassium-40 atoms. For every hundred potassium-40 atoms that decay, eleven become argon-40, an inactive gas that can easily escape from material by diffusion when lava and igneous rocks are formed. As volcanic rock forms through crystallization, the concentration of argon-40 drops to almost nothing. But regular and reasonable decay of potassium-40 will continue, with a half-life of 1.3 billion years. It is possible, then, to measure with a spectrometer the concentration of argon-40 that has accumulated since the rock formed. Because many archaeological sites were occupied during a period when extensive volcanic activity occurred, especially in East Africa, it is possible to date them by associations of lava with human settlements.

Potassium-argon dates have been obtained from many igneous minerals, of which the most resistant to later argon diffusion are biotite, muscovite, and sanidine. Microscopic examination of the rock sample is essential to eliminate the possibility of contamination by recrystallization and other processes. The samples are processed by crushing the rock, concentrating it, and treating it with hydrofluoric acid to remove any atmospheric argon from the sample. The various gases are then removed from the sample and the argon gas is isolated and subjected to mass spectrographic analysis. The age of the sample is then calculated using the argon-40 and potassium-40 content and a standard formula. The resulting date is quoted with a large standard deviation—for early Pleistocene sites, on the order of a quarter of a million years.

In recent years, computerized argon laser fusion has become the technique of choice. By steering a laser beam over a single irradiated grain of volcanic ash (feldspar), a potassium-argon specialist can date a lake bed layer or even a small scatter of tools and animal bones left by an early hominid. The grain glows white hot and gives up a gas, which is purified, then charged by an electron beam. A powerful magnet accelerates the charged gas and hurls it against a device that counts its argon atoms. By measuring the relative amounts of two isotopes of the element, researchers can calculate the amount of time that has elapsed since the lava cooled and the crystals formed.

Obsidian Hydration Dating.   This method can be used over the entire span of human existence. Obsidian is a natural glass substance formed by volcanic activity (Leute, 1987). It has long been prized for its sharp edges and other excellent qualities for toolmaking. Obsidian hydration dating makes use of the fact that a freshly made surface of obsidian will absorb water from its surroundings, forming a measurable hydration layer that is invisible to the naked eye (no other known artifact material has this property). Because the freshly exposed surface has a strong affinity for water, it keeps absorbing until it is saturated with a layer of water molecules. These molecules then slowly diffuse into the body of the obsidian. This hydration zone contains about 3.5 percent water, increasing the density of the layer and allowing it to be measured accurately under polarized light. Each time a freshly fractured surface is prepared, as when a tool is being made, the hydration begins again from scratch. Thus the depth of hydration achieved represents the time since the object was manufactured or used. Hydration is observed with microscopically thin sections of obsidian sliced from artifacts and ground down to about 0.003 inch (76 mm). Neutron activation analysis is now commonly used; it provides not only dates but also sourcing information that can be used to monitor changes in trade networks (Chapter 16).

Obsidian hydration dating has been used with great success in Mesoamerica, notably in a ten-year dating campaign at the Maya city of Copán (Freter, 1993). The researchers were careful to collect information on such critical environmental variables as temperature, rainfall, and soil acidity from weather stations, from wet and dry thermal cells buried at various depths in the sites to be dated, and from soil composition measurements, collected for as many years as possible. Ann Corinne Freter calls this a "conjunctive approach" that brought all kinds of chronological data and a formal investigation of all the variables that could affect hydration into a single chronological project. Thus, the accuracy of obsidian hydration dates was checked at every turn.

The Copán Obsidian Dating Project began in 1984 and has yielded more than 2,300 dates from 252 sites, over 17 percent of the sites in the Copán Valley (Freter, 1994). The method was ideal for Copán, where radiocarbon and archaeomagnetic dates are rare and expensive, whereas obsidian hydration is relatively cheap. At the same time, the abundance of obsidian in both the central core and in outlying rural settlements allowed the economical dating of large numbers of sites. Thus, Freter and her research team were able to plot changing settlement patterns from A.D. 500 to 1150 with such chronological accuracy that they were able to show that the collapse of the Copán state was rapid between 800 and 850 (more on the Copán survey in Chapter 15). Freter points out that, given constant environmental conditions within a site, obsidian hydration has great potential for providing relative chronologies and identifying sites with disturbed occupation layers.

Thermoluminescence (TL) Dating.

Thermoluminescence (TL) Dating.   This method is based on the fact that every material on earth receives a low level of radiation from the radioactive elements in the environment (Aitken, 1984, 1990). Many solid materials store small fractions of this energy, which accumulates steadily over time. When the solid is heated, the stored energy is released and emits light, a phenomenon called *thermoluminescence.* The age of the sample is assumed to be the length of time since the object was heated to a very high temperature. Thermoluminescence dating has obvious applications for dating volcanic rocks and other geological formations, but it can also be applied to humanly heated objects such as clay vessels, heat-treated stone artifacts, or fired bricks.

Samples are taken by crumbling an object such as a potsherd or by drilling tiny holes in it for core samples. The laboratory measures the natural thermoluminescence of the object with an alpha radiation counter, the rate at which the sample has been obtaining radiation from the environment (by monitoring the location where it was found), and the amount of thermoluminescence produced by known amounts of radiation. All this assumes that humanly manufactured objects were heated to a sufficiently high temperature originally, which is not always the case.

Thermoluminescence dating is claimed to have an accuracy of 67 percent and is most commonly used to date pottery or clay-fired objects between 50 and about 20,000 years old. Thermoluminescence dates have also been applied to burnt flint and other silicious toolmaking materials found in Stone Age rock shelters and burials, such as Neanderthal graves in Israel, which date to more than 40,000 years ago. A related dating method uses laser technology to date the emissions from quartz and feldspar grains in archaeological layers. This optically stimulated luminescence (OSL) method can date sites in the 100- to 100,000-year range and is claimed (very controversially) to date the first settlement of Australia to as early as 60,000 years ago.

Thermoluminescence sometimes provides absolute dates, but it is more often used to produce relative readings that allow archaeologists to establish whether a clay vessel is actually of the same relative age as the known age of similar pots—a useful approach for unmasking forgeries. Although thermoluminescence has been used to date such developments as the appearance of anatomically modern humans in southwestern Asia and early Australian colonization, most authorities agree that independent verification from radiocarbon or other approaches is advisable.

Electronic Spin Resonance (ESR) Dating.   This technique measures radiation-induced defects or the density of trapped electrons within a bone or shell sample without the need to heat them. This promising dating method is somewhat similar to thermoluminescence dating and has the advantage of being nondestructive. It is especially effective on tooth enamel and bone, allowing investigators to date fossil fragments up to about a million years old. Electronic spin resonance has important applications for the study of early human evolution and has been used to date Neanderthal teeth in southwestern Asia to nearly 90,000 years ago.

Uranium Series Dating.   This dating method measures the steady decay of uranium into various daughter elements inside any formation made up of calcium carbonates, such as limestone or cave stalactites. Since many early human groups made use of limestone caves and rock shelters, bones and artifacts embedded in calcium carbonate layers can sometimes be dated by this method, using techniques somewhat similar to those used in radiocarbon dating. Uranium series dating is most effective when applied to sites between 50,000 and a million years old (Shreeve, 1992).

Fission-Track Dating.   Many minerals and natural glasses, such as obsidian, contain tiny quantities of uranium that undergo slow, spontaneous decay (Fleischer, 1975). The age of any mineral containing uranium can be obtained by measuring the amount of uranium in the sample. This measurement is done by counting the fission tracks in the material, which are narrow trails of damage in the sample caused by the fragmentation of massive, energy-charged particles. The older the sample, the more tracks it has. Volcanic rocks, such as are commonplace at Olduvai Gorge and other early human sites, are ideal for fission-track dating. The volcanic level under the earliest hominid sites at Olduvai has been fission-track dated to 2.03 ± 0.28 million years, which agrees well with potassium-argon dates from the same location.

Archaeomagnetic Dating.   We know that the direction and intensity of the earth's magnetic field have varied throughout ancient times. Many clays and clay soils contain magnetic minerals, which when heated to a dull red heat will assume the direction and intensity of the earth's magnetic field at the moment of heating. Thus, if the changes in the earth's magnetic field have been recorded over centuries or even millennia, it is possible to date any suitable sample of clay material known to have been heated by correlating the thermoremnent magnetism of the heated clay with records of the earth's magnetic field (Wolfman, 1984). Archaeologists frequently discover structures with well-baked clay floors—ovens, kilns, and iron-smelting furnaces, to name only a few—whose burned clay can be used for archaeomagnetic dating. Of course, reheated clays (clays used again after their original heating) will change their magnetic readings and are thus useless for archaeomagnetic dating.

Thermoremnent magnetism (the alignment of magnetic particles fixed by heating) results from the ferromagnetism of magnetite and hematite, minerals found in significant quantities in most soils. When the soil containing these minerals is heated, the magnetic particles in magnetite and hematite change from a random alignment to one that conforms with that of the earth's magnetic field. In effect, the heated lump of clay becomes a very weak magnet that can be measured by a parastatic magnetometer. A record of the magnetic declination and dip similar to that of the earth's actual magnetic field at the time of heating is preserved in the clay lump. An absolute date for the sample can then be obtained if the long-term, or secular, variation of the earth's field for the region is known.

From an archaeological point of view, archaeomagnetism still has but limited application because systematic records of the secular variation in the earth's magnetic field have been kept for only a few areas. Declination and dip have been recorded in London for 400 years, and a very accurate record of variations covers the period from A.D. 1600 to the present. France, Germany, Japan, and the southwestern United States have received some attention. Highly accurate AMS radiocarbon or tree-ring dates offer potential for longer magnetic time scales. In the Southwest, clay samples associated directly with dendrochronological or radiocarbon samples have been tested, with one set of readings from sixteen pre-Columbian villages extending back almost 2,000 years.

Summary

Absolute (chronometric) dates are expressed in years. In contrast, relative dates represent relationships in time that are used to correlate prehistoric sites or cultures with one another, which are based on the law of superposition.

Early archaeologists studied the evolution of artifact styles over time. This approach developed into the technique of seriation. Seriation is based on the assumption that artifacts come into fashion, have a period of maximum popularity, and then slowly go out of style. Tested against the evidence of New England tombstones and other modern artifacts, seriation has become an effective way of ordering sites in chronological sequence.

Historical records and calendars developed by the ancient Egyptians and the Maya are of immense value for dating their literate civilizations. A great deal of valuable chronological information can also be obtained from objects of known age, such as clay pipes or coins. But, again, these objects are confined to the most recent periods of human history. Cross-dating, widely applied in Europe and Mesoamerica, uses artifacts of a known age, such as coins and other items that were widely traded, to provide relative dates for sites in areas that have no historical chronology.

Dendrochronology (tree-ring dating) provides an accurate chronology for about two thousand years of prehistory of the American Southwest and can be used on sites as early as 8000 B.C. in Europe. Dendrochronologists count the annual growth rings in trees such as the bristlecone pine and correlate them into long sequences of growth years that are joined to a master chronology. Wooden beams and other archaeological wood fragments are correlated with this master chronology to provide accurate dates for pueblos and other sites.

Radiocarbon dating is the most widely used method. It can be applied at sites from 40,000 to 400 years before the present. Based on the rate at which carbon-14 decays to nitrogen in organic objects, it can be used to date such materials as charcoal and bone and even skin and leather.

Today, accelerator mass spectrometry (AMS) dates provide a much higher degree of accuracy and use tiny fragments of organic materials. The accuracy of radiocarbon dating is subject to statistical errors. Dates up to 30,000 years ago are calibrated against tree-ring chronologies, ice cores, and coral growth sequences, owing to variations in the carbon-14 content of the atmosphere.

Potassium-argon methods are used for dating the earliest human beings. These can be used to determine dates from the origins of the earth up to about 50,000 years ago. This radioactive counting method is based on measuring accumulations of argon-40 in volcanic rocks.

Thermoluminescence may prove to be a method for dating potsherds, in which the baked clay has trapped electrons; these are released for measurement by sudden and intense heating under controlled conditions. The visible light rays emitted during heating are known as thermoluminescence. Thermoluminescence can also be applied to burnt flint artifacts of much greater age.

Electron spin resonance and uranium series dating are also experimental chronometric methods that date sites between a million and 50,000 years old.

Fission-track dating is done by measuring the uranium content of many minerals and volcanic glasses and examining the fission tracks left in the material by fragmentation of massive concentrations of energy-charged particles. It can be applied in sites between three million and 100,000 years old, where volcanic rocks are found in human-occupied levels.

Key Terms

absolute chronology
accelerator mass spectrometry (AMS) dating
archaeomagnetic dating
Australopithecus
cross-dating
dendrochronology (tree-ring dating)

electronic spin resonance (ESR) dating
fission-track dating
frequency seriation
half-life
Homo erectus
obsidian hydration dating
potassium-argon dating

radiocarbon dating
relative chronology
seriation
thermoluminescence (TL) dating
thermoremnent magnetism
uranium series dating

Guide to Further Reading

AITKEN, MARTIN J. 1990. *Science-Based Dating in Archaeology.* New York: Longmans. An introduction to scientific dating methods for the general reader.

DEETZ, JAMES. 1967. *Invitation to Archaeology.* Garden City, NY: Natural History Press. Deetz's little volume on the basics of archaeology is one of the best ever written. His discourse on seriation, complete with New England tombstones, is a classic.

TAYLOR, ROBERT E., and MARTIN J. AITKEN, eds. 1998. *Chronometric Dating in Archaeology.* New York: Plenum Press. Authoritative descriptions of the major dating methods used for earlier prehistory. For the more advanced reader.

TAYLOR, R. E., A. LONG, and R. S. KRA, eds. 1992. *Radiocarbon Dating after Four Decades: An Interdisciplinary Perspective.* New York: Springer Verlag. Essays on radiocarbon dating that offer an excellent overview of this all-important dating method.

WINTLE, ANN G. 1996. "Archaeologically-Relevant Dating Techniques for the Next Century." *Journal of Archaeological Science* 23: 123–138. An up-to-date survey of the current state of absolute dating methods in archaeology. Includes a comprehensive bibliography.

Recovering Archaeological Data

Archaeology is the only branch of anthropology where we kill our informants in the process of studying them.

Kent V. Flannery, *The Golden Marshalltown*

A mere hole in the ground, which of all sights is perhaps the least vivid and dramatic, is enough to grip their attention for hours at a time.

P. G. Wodehouse, *A Damsel in Distress*

Part IV deals with the ways in which archaeologists acquire data. As we stressed earlier, the gathering of such data is done in a systematic way that depends on a sound research design. Archaeologists are then able to obtain the information best suited to address the specific research questions they are interested in. Our knowledge of the past is limited by the materials that are preserved in the ground and by our own methods for recovering data. Chapters 8 and 9 describe some of the fundamental principles and processes of archaeological fieldwork, as well as some of the special problems encountered by archaeologists. Rather than draw on a single case study, we have used many examples, as well as relying on your instructors to use examples from their own experiences, to illustrate the diversity of situations archaeologists face.

CHAPTER 8

Finding and Assessing Archaeological Sites

Gudea, a Sumerian ruler of Lagash, Iraq.

In 1649, a gentleman antiquarian named John Aubrey galloped into the middle of the village of Avebury in southern England while fox hunting (Figure 8.1). He found himself surrounded by a deep ditch and mysterious, weathered stones erected in a circle inside the earthwork. Aubrey was "wonderfully surprized at the sight of these vast stones, of which I had never heard before" and returned later to sketch and explore (Fagan, 1998:117). Aubrey never excavated at Avebury, but he made the first survey of one of Britain's most remarkable sacred monuments. He speculated that it had been built by ancient Britains, "who were, I suppose, two or three degrees less savage than the Americans." Today, the Avebury stone circles are one of the most famous archaeological sites in Europe.

Some archaeological sites, such as the pyramids of Giza in Egypt (Figure 16.5) or the stone circles at Stonehenge, 23 miles (37 km) south of Avebury (Figure 2.2), are so conspicuous that they have never been "discovered" by archaeologists. Avebury was well known to local farmers in Aubrey's day, but he was the first person to draw the site to the attention of a wider scientific community. Earthworks, burial mounds, and entire cities are relatively easy to find, for they form an easily identifiable part of the modern landscape. But how do archaeologists locate inconspicuous Stone Age foraging camps, tiny farming villages, and sites that leave no traces on the surface whatsoever?

Until fairly recently, archaeologists paid relatively little attention to the techniques for locating archaeological sites and assessing them without actual excavation. Although excavation remains central to archaeological research, new emphasis on regional archaeological studies, innovative remote-sensing techniques, and, above all, the urgent need to save and record sites before they are destroyed by development has added a new dimension to archaeological research.

Data on the location and distribution of archaeological sites, combined with the assessment of archaeological material recovered from sites, can be used to address a diversity of research questions, ranging from change in subsistence strategies and ancient

Figure 8.1   Aerial photograph of the stone circles at Avebury in southern Britain, built around 2000 B.C.

trade patterns to the origins of iron technology. In some instances, data are gathered to protect and manage archaeological resources. Cultural resource management (CRM) archaeologists spend much of their time evaluating the potential impact of development projects, such as road and building construction. Federal and state laws in the United States now mandate archaeological investigations before construction or other disturbance begins on publicly owned land and on private property if government funds are involved. Many cities and counties have similar regulations, designed to prevent the destruction of chance finds. The identification and evaluation of archaeological resources prior to development allow decisions to be made as to whether sites should be further investigated or protected.

   In the pages that follow, we review some of the archaeologists' techniques for locating, studying, and assessing archaeological sites with little or no excavation. The interpretation of archaeological field data involves two interrelated processes:

1. **Archaeological survey** is the systematic attempt to locate, identify, and record the distribution of archaeological sites on the ground and in relation to their natural environment.
2. **Site assessment** is the evaluation of each site's archaeological significance. Assessment considers site location and evaluates data from controlled surface collections and, in some cases, information from subsurface detection using electronic and limited subsurface testing.

Both these aspects of archaeological study are *nonintrusive,* in the sense that they do not, for the most part, destroy archaeological context. Archaeological excavation (Chapter 9), in contrast, involves the investigation of the site by means of actual digging. In the process, artifacts, features, and, in some instances, entire structures are removed from their stratigraphic context and must be meticulously recorded by the archaeologist. In these days of wholesale destruction of archaeological sites through industrial activity, deep plowing, and illegal excavation, archaeologists do all they can to avoid disturbing subsurface levels. This destruction, and the need for management of archaeological resources of all kinds (Chapter 18), make the assessment of archaeological sites a critical concern.

Finding Archaeological Sites

Archaeological sites manifest themselves in many ways. Some may be quite evident, as in the case of city mounds, which are literally man-made mountains made up of occupation debris. Others may be identified by conspicuous ruins or the presence of middens, which are mounds of food remains and trash. But many others are far less easily located, perhaps displaying no more than a small scatter of stone tools or a patch of discolored soil. Still other sites leave no traces of their presence above the ground and may come to light only when the subsoil is disturbed. Let us examine some key indicators of archaeological sites.

- Conspicuous earthworks, stone ruins, or other surface features are among the most obvious indicators. Good examples are the fortified *pa,* or defensive earthworks, built by the Maori in New Zealand, or massive megalithic structures such as Avebury. The **tells** (city mounds) of southwestern Asia, occupied by generation after generation of city dwellers, were easily recognized by early travelers, and the temples and monuments of ancient Egypt have attracted antiquarian and plunderer alike for many centuries (Figure 8.3). Archaeological sites in the Americas, such as Teotihuacán, were described by some of the first conquistadors. Maya sites were vividly cataloged by John Lloyd Stephens and Frederick Catherwood in the mid-nineteenth century (see Figure 8.6) (Bahn, 1996).

- Surface finds of artifacts, bones, pottery and other materials may be the principal surface indicator of some archaeological sites. A variety of factors, including vegetation, plowing, and water and wind erosion, as well as the nature of the artifacts themselves, can affect the visibility of surface materials. Such remains may consist of a thin scatter of artifacts or show up as dense concentrations of debris that stand out from the surrounding ground. In some cases, wind erosion may remove the soil surrounding artifacts and leave them exposed on the surface. Burrowing animals living in sites can also bring artifacts to the surface.

- Vegetation is also a useful indicator, for plants may grow more lushly on areas where the subsoil has been disturbed or the nitrogen content of the soil is greater. Conversely, many California shell **middens** are covered with stunted vegetation, a result of the artifact-filled, alkaline soil, which contrasts sharply with the surrounding green grass at the end of the rainy season. Sometimes, specific types of trees or brush are associated with archaeological sites. One is the breadnut, or ramon, tree, which was once cultivated by the Maya. These trees are still common near ancient settlements and have been used as guides in locating many archaeological sites.

Discovery

African American Burial Ground, New York City, 1991

In 1991, the federal government planned to build a thirty-four-story office building in the heart of Lower Manhattan, New York. The responsible agency, the General Services Administration, retained a team of archaeologists to study the cleared site. When they examined eighteenth-century city maps of the area, the researchers found that the proposed construction site was located in an area that surveyors of the day had called the "Negro Burial Ground." They assumed that the basements of nineteenth-century buildings had destroyed most, if not all, the graves in the abandoned cemetery and thus concluded that it was safe to proceed with construction.

Unfortunately, much of the cemetery had been buried beneath thick layers of fill, and many burials remained intact beneath the basements of the nineteenth-century buildings (Figure 8.2). Just weeks before the contractors were due to start construction, dozens of undisturbed burials were discovered. Four hundred and twenty graves, some stacked one on top of the other, were eventually recovered from one small portion of the cemetery. The discovery provides the largest American skeletal collections and one of the most significant eighteenth-century sites studied by archaeologists.

Intense controversy erupted over the discovery, as New York's black community expressed outrage at the way in which the survey, excavations, and human remains had been handled without consultation with African Americans. The site itself became a focus of community protests and cultural inspiration. Eventually, the skeletons were handed over to biological anthropologist Michael Blakey of Howard University for study and eventual reburial.

Few archaeological discoveries are as controversial as the Negro Burial Ground, where much bitterness and political activity could have been avoided by more thorough field research well ahead of time. Nevertheless, this celebrated find highlights the great complexity of archaeological survey, especially in urban areas, where historical records and sites of all kinds form a tangled archive for the modern scholar. Many of the world's largest cities, among them Amsterdam, London, and San Francisco, have offices specifically concerned with the identification and preservation of archaeological resources.

Figure 8.2 The African American burial ground in New York City.

Figure 8.3   The temple of the sun god Amun at Karnak, near Thebes, Egypt, a famous tourist destination since Roman times.

- Soil discolorations can also be a sign of archaeological sites. In many cases, the dark midden soils of long-abandoned villages show up in plowed land as dark zones, often associated with potsherds and other artifacts.

Chance Discoveries

Whole chapters of the past have been exposed by accidental discoveries of sites, artifacts, or burials. Farming, industrial activity, highway construction, urban renewal, airport expansion, and other destructive actions of twentieth-century life have unearthed countless archaeological sites, many of which have to be investigated hurriedly before the bulldozers remove all traces. Development is a bitter enemy of the past. Yet dramatic discoveries have resulted from our despoiling of the environment.

Mexico City is built on the site of Tenochtitlán, the capital city of the Aztecs. Tenochtitlán, destroyed by the Spanish under Hernán Cortés in 1521, was a wonderful city whose markets rivaled those of most major Spanish cities in size. Little remains of Tenochtitlán on the surface today, but the contractors digging tunnels for the city's Metro found more than 40 tons of pottery, 380 burials, and even a small temple dedicated to the Aztec god of the wind, Ehecatl-Quetzalcoatl. The temple is now preserved on its original site in the Pino Suárez station of the Metro system, part of an exhibit commemorating Mexico City's ancestor. Another accidental discovery of a ceremonial stone depicting the sun led to the uncovering and excavation of the Temple of the Sun and Rain gods of the Aztecs, Huitzilopochtli and Tlaloc, which lay in the heart of the Aztec capital (R. Townsend, 1992).

Many other spectacular finds result from human activity. In June 1968, a detachment of China's People's Liberation Army on patrol among the barren hills near Man-Zh'ieng in central China stumbled on a subterranean burial chamber. They found themselves inside a vast rock-cut sepulcher where their flashlights caught the glint of gold, silver, and jade. Bronze and clay pots stood in orderly rows. Fortunately for science, the soldiers reported their find to the Academy of Sciences in Beijing, which had experts on-site in hours. They rapidly identified the tomb as that of Liu Sheng, a prominent Han nobleman, elder brother of the emperor and governor of the principality of Zhou-shan until his death in 113 B.C. A few days later, the nearby tomb of Liu Sheng's wife, Tou Wan, came to light. The Han emperors were the longest-lived dynasty of Chinese rulers, assuming power in 206 B.C. and reigning for four hundred years. Han rulers developed the Great Silk Road across Central Asia and sent trading missions deep into Southeast Asia, making China a major power. The two tombs reflected the prestige and wealth of a man and woman at the pinnacle of Han society. Both wore jade suits made up of hundreds of thin plaques sewn together with gold wire (Figure 8.4).

Nature itself sometimes uncovers sites for us, which may then be located by a sharp-eyed archaeologist looking for natural exposures of likely geological strata. Erosion, flooding, tidal waves, low lake levels, earthquakes, and wind action can all lead to the exposure of archaeological sites. Some of the most famous sites to be exposed in this manner are in Olduvai Gorge, in Tanzania, a great gash in the Serengeti Plains where earth movement and erosion have sliced through hundreds of feet of Pleistocene lake beds to expose numerous site locations of early human ancestors. It is the unique natural environmental setting of Olduvai, which has brought so many finds to light, that makes the gorge so unique.

In 1957, an amateur archaeologist reported what initially appeared to be five piles of bison bones and a few projectile points exposed in an arroyo near the town of Kit Carson in southeastern Colorado (Wheat, 1972). The dense concentration of bone, subsequently known as the Olsen-Chubbuck site, lay in a filled bison trail of the

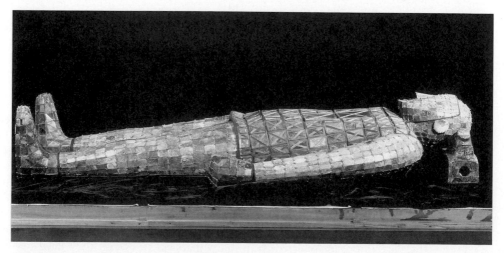

Figure 8.4 The jade suit of Prince Liu Sheng, China.

Figure 8.5   A layer of bison bones from the Olsen-Chubbuck site in Colorado, a Paleo-Indian kill site found by a cowboy.

type that crisscrossed the plains in early frontier days (Figure 8.5). The remains of nearly two hundred bison were eventually excavated from the arroyo, many of which had been butchered. Clearly, the arroyo was a trap into which the beasts had been stampeded. Bison have a keen sense of smell but poor vision; a lumbering herd of these gregarious beasts can be readily stampeded into an abrupt declivity, and the leaders have no option but to plunge into the gully and be immobilized or disabled by the weight of those behind them. So vivid a reconstruction of the Paleo-Indians' hunt could be made that excavators could even guess at the direction of the wind on the day of the stampede. The dramatic evidence of this hunt of 8,500 years ago was buried in the arroyo by nature and exposed again in our time, to be discovered by the vigilant eye of an amateur archaeologist.

Documentary Records and Oral Traditions

For archaeologists working on more recent time periods, documentary records and oral traditions may provide important sources of information. Classical Greek and Roman texts, Egyptian hieroglyphs, or cuneiform inscriptions may refer to archaeological sites and, in some instances, actually preserve maps showing the location of ancient sites. A written account of the destruction of the classical Roman town of Pompeii during the eruption of Vesuvius on August 24, A.D. 79 was recorded in letters by Pliny the Younger to Tacitus, and inscriptions excavated at the site in the eighteenth century confirmed the town's location (Daniel, 1981). Famous sites like the Parthenon are referred to in many classical texts and they have never been lost

(Figure 1.9). The Acropolis at Athens was remembered even when Athens itself had become an obscure medieval village.

Historical archaeologists working on the more recent past often have quite detailed records to help them locate archaeological sites. For example, in studying colonial St. Augustine, a Spanish creole town in Florida, archaeologist Kathleen Deagan was able to rely on maps to chart the town's growth, the location of the principal buildings, and even the names and ethnicity of some of the house owners (1983). Yet written records and plans cannot necessarily be taken at face value. The major African trading entrepot of Elmina, Ghana, which flourished following the arrival of the Portuguese in the late fifteenth century, is depicted in numerous illustrations and plans, but many of these are lacking in scale and perspective and others are entirely spurious (DeCorse, 2001b). Despite the presence of written records, it was archaeological data that provided the details of the town's arrangement.

Oral traditions have been particularly important in African archaeology. While there are some indigenous African writing systems, *oral traditions*—memories passed on from generation to generation—are important in many cultures. Stories, songs, and epics recount rulers and important events, as well as the location of sites. A striking example is Begho in central Ghana, which reached its peak between the fifteenth and the eighteenth centuries A.D. This important African trading settlement was divided into four quarters, the names of which were recalled in the oral traditions of the modern village of Hani.

In other instances, sites ranging from early twentieth-century California mining towns to Native American villages have been located using oral histories: the personal memories, reminisces, and accounts of individuals who lived, worked or visited the sites. In addition to location, oral histories may also provide important information about activities, events, and the identities of the inhabitants of a settlement.

Archaeological Survey

Although chance and nonarchaeological sources play an important part of discovery, the greater part of archaeological research involves researchers actively looking for sites. Most of the world's archaeological sites are far less conspicuous than the Parthenon, and, unlike Homeric Troy, they have no historical records to testify to their existence. Early antiquarians discovered sites primarily by locating burial mounds, stone structures, hill forts, and other conspicuous traces of past human activity on the landscape. Archaeological surveys were aimed at identifying individual sites for excavation. Monumental architecture, spectacular sculptures, and ceramic sequences were consistent with early antiquarian objectives and later culture-historical concerns (Chapters 2 and 3). Although such finds provide important information, the haphazard, unsystematic approach to locating sites yielded an incomplete view of the past.

Systematic site survey did not become a serious part of archaeology until twentieth-century archaeologists began to realize that people had lived their lives against the background of ever-changing cultural and natural landscapes, modified by ecological change and human activities. Individual sites cannot be evaluated without taking this broader background into consideration. As archaeologists have grown more intent on explaining cultural processes, they have increasingly focused on entire regions rather than individual sites. Although archaeologists still search for sites to excavate, most do so with broader research questions in mind.

Archaeological surveying is one of the most important components of archaeological investigation, for it is concerned with the archaeological record of ancient settlement patterns, with ancient peoples' imprints on the land. An archaeological survey seeks to identify ancient landscapes, which are far more than merely site dots or settlement patterns plotted on a map. A landscape is both material and symbolic, for every society has given meaning to its surroundings. For example, ritual sites such as the Avebury stone circles or the great pyramids never functioned in isolation. They were part of a much wider landscape and a complex relationship between living people, the forces of the spiritual world, and the environment. Archaeologists have only the material remains of such relationships to study, so many of them refer to landscape "signatures," the material imprints left on the earth's surface by past human groups.

This approach makes archaeological surveying a much more important component of archaeological investigation than ever before, especially when studying hunter-gatherers or herders, who enjoyed a highly mobile lifeway and left few traces behind them. Like experts on ancient scripts, we are in the decipherment business, but our "script" is a mosaic of sites and many other conspicuous, and inconspicuous, remains of human activity.

In recent years archaeologists have paid increasing attention to what they call **off-site areas,** places with a low density of artifacts or features such as plow marks or irrigation ditches. These locations may not represent major occupation areas, but such areas are of vital importance because they may reveal important clues about activities such as farming, food processing, and technology that took place in areas spatially separated from the areas where people lived. For example, hunter-gatherers often killed and butchered wild game some distance from settlements. In West Africa, iron smelting furnaces were often located well away from villages. Entire field systems may be spotted only from faint traces visible in aerial photographs. At Céide Fields, in northwestern Ireland, for example, more than 5,000 acres (2,023 ha) of field systems dating to about 5000 B.C. are preserved, and they are as revealing about the society that created them as the associated settlements, because they provide vital environmental and social information (see Figure 15.1).

Partly because regional studies have become more fashionable and partly because of the growing demands of cultural resource management, archaeologists have become deeply interested in economical methods for collecting survey data. Many of them now use a variety of remote sensing methods, techniques that allow them to determine, or partially assess, the presence of archaeological features without visiting the site.

Approaches to Archaeological Survey

A survey can vary from searching a city lot for historical structures or a tiny river valley with a few rock shelters in its walls to a large-scale survey of an entire river basin or water catchment area—a project that would take several years to complete. Often, the theoretical ideal is the same: to recover all or nearly all traces of ancient settlement in the survey area. This is often, however, impractical.

Many people make a fundamental distinction between two types of survey (Hester and others, 1997):

1. **Reconnaissance survey** is just that, a preliminary examination of a survey area to identify major sites, to assess potential, and to establish tentative site distributions. Reconnaissance survey also involves background research, such as examining archives if historical properties are involved, talking to landowners, and acquiring general environmental information.
2. **Intensive survey** is a systematic, detailed field survey that covers an entire area. It may include subsurface testing.

Most surveys are in the reconnaissance category, especially if large areas are involved. Archaeological features are located in a variety of ways. The survey area can be traversed by automobile, horseback, mule, camel, bicycle, or—most effectively—foot. Footwork is important, for it enables the archaeologist to acquire an eye for topography and the relationships of human settlement to the landscape. However, as discussed below, various types of subsurface testing, aerial photographs, and remote-sensing methods are increasingly used.

As noted, it would be ideal if archaeologists could map out and identify all archaeological resources within a region. Such holistic surveys are sometimes attempted. For example, William Sanders and his colleagues carried out a long-term archaeological survey of the Basin of Mexico in which they tried to locate every site in the area over many seasons of fieldwork. At the end of the project, Sanders argued that this approach was far more effective than any sampling of the area, for it gave a much clearer picture of site variability on the ground (Sanders and others, 1979). Undoubtedly he is right—if one has the time and the money. Yet, in these days of limited budgets and short-term archaeological contracts dictated by impending site destruction, the examination of an entire region or an entire site is often impossible, and was always unrealistic in most settings.

For this reason, archaeologists have increasingly turned to both sampling and a variety of new surveying techniques to locate and identify sites. The comprehensiveness of any survey is affected by other factors, too. Many are carried out in intensively populated areas or on private farmland. Thousands of sites lie inaccessible, buried under suburban housing and parking lots. Site survey can be further complicated by dense vegetation, crops, and floodwaters. In many parts of California, Mexico, and Africa, the obvious months for surveys are at the end of the dry season, when the vegetation is dry or even burned off. But in lush, lowland floodplains, such as those of the American South, large tracts of the survey area may be totally inaccessible all year, except to shovel testing and controlled surface collecting of known sites. Only the most conspicuous sites, such as mounds, show up under these conditions.

In the Mesoamerican and Amazonian rain forests, where the vegetation is so thick that even new roads are in constant danger of being overgrown, it is no coincidence that many archaeological sites are found near well-trodden roads and tracks.

Doing Archaeology

Basic Types of Ground Survey

Archaeological surveys range from intensive surveys that seek to identify all archaeological sites within a region to reconnaissance surveys that provide only preliminary information for an area. In practice, actually fieldwork spans a continuum of levels in between. There are four basic types of intensive ground survey:

1. *Conspicuous and accessible sites* are located by superficial survey, such as that used by Catherwood and Stephens for Maya sites in the Yucatán in the 1840s (Figure 8.6). The investigator visits only very prominent and easily reachable sites.

2. *Relatively conspicuous sites* at accessible locations are studied in the next level of survey, with the assistance of local informants such as landowners. This approach was used frequently in the 1930s for the classic river basin surveys in the lower Mississippi Valley, when archaeologists worked on depression-era survey projects. Such surveys, although effective, give a rather narrow view of the archaeological sites in an area.

3. *Limited-area survey* involves door-to-door inquiries, supported by actual substantiation of claims that a site exists by checking the report on the ground. This type of survey, with its built-in system of verification, may yield more comprehensive information

Figure 8.6 Copán in Honduras, a conspicuous archaeological site found by the Spanish in 1576 and made known by Stephens and Catherwood in the nineteenth century. This photograph shows the reconstructed ball court.

on sites. But it still does not give the most critical information of all, data on the ratios of one site type to another within an area, nor does it assess the percentage of accessible sites that have been found.

4. *Intensive foot survey* occurs when a party of archaeologists covers an entire area by walking over it, perhaps with a set interval between members of the party. This is about the most rigorous method of survey, but it does work. When Paul Martin and Fred Plog surveyed 5.2 square miles (13.5 sq. km) of the Hay Hollow Valley in east-central Arizona in 1967, they supervised a team of eight people who walked back and forth over small portions of the area. Workers were 30 feet (9 m) from each other, their pathways carefully laid out with compass and stakes. Two hundred and fifty sites were recorded by this survey, at the cost of thirty person-days per square mile. One would think every site would have been recorded. Yet two entirely new sites were discovered in the same area in 1969 and 1971; prehistoric irrigation canals were

spotted by an expert on some aerial photographs, and some sandstone quarry sites were also found.

The chances of any archaeological survey recording every site, in even a small area, is remote. Obviously, though, total survey of an area is desirable, and sometimes nearly total coverage can be achieved by combining remote sensing and ground survey. The excavators of the Roman town of Wroxeter in central England are surveying the topography of the now-vanished town using a combination of aerial photographs and ground survey. Volunteers are taking measurements every 33 feet (10 m) and combining their survey with systematic surface collections of potsherds and other finds (Figure 8.7).

Figure 8.7 Surface electronic survey in fields near the Roman city of Wroxeter, England.

The early archaeologists working in these regions located sites by following narrow paths through the forest cut by *chicleros,* local people who collected resin from forest trees and guided researchers to sites. Even today, archaeologists can pass right through the middle of a large site in the forest or within a few feet of a huge pyramid and see nothing.

No surface survey, however thorough and sophisticated, will achieve complete coverage. In the past, archaeological survey was often a haphazard, hit or miss process. Researchers would visit known sites or examine areas adjacent to existing paths cleared by farmers or fortuitously exposed by construction. These opportunities revealed archaeological sites but left many potential rich areas totally unexplored.

In contrast to the work of early antiquaries, modern archaeological surveys are typically systematic; that is, they approach sites using some consistent, predetermined method to ensure that all parts of the proscribed survey area are examined. Rather than attempting to identify all of the sites within a particular area, modern archaeologists also make use of sampling, for archaeologists are only too aware that many site distributions reflect the distribution of archaeologists rather than an unbiased sampling of the archaeological record.

Sampling in Archaeology

Sampling is an enormous subject that cannot be discussed in detail here. But systematic and carefully controlled sampling of archaeological data is essential if we are to rely heavily, as we do, on statistical approaches in the reconstruction of past lifeways and cultural processes. If we are interested in past adaptations to environmental conditions, we must systematically sample many types of sites in each environmental zone, not merely those that look important or seem likely to yield spectacular finds. (For more details, see Hester and others, 1997; Mueller, 1974; Orton, 2000.)

Statistical sampling methods occupy an important place in archaeological research, and some training in statistics is now integral to every professional's training. The key to effective archaeological surveying lies in proper research designs and in rigorous sampling techniques to provide a reliable basis for extending the findings of the survey from a sample zone to a wider region. Archaeologists generally use **probability sampling,** a means of mathematically relating small samples of data to much larger populations. Classic examples of this method are public opinion polls, which may use tiny samples, say, 1,500 people, to draw more general conclusions on major political issues.

Sampling enables researchers to obtain a statistically reliable slice of archaeological data from which to make generalizations, the assumption being that the sample observations are a mathematical representation of the whole (see the Doing Archaeology box). Portions of a region, area, environmental zone, site, or even the artifacts recovered are selected to serve as a representative sample of the larger area. Probability sampling improves the chance that the conclusions reached on the basis of the sample will be relatively reliable. The outcome depends, of course, on very carefully drawn research designs and precisely defined sample units.

Doing Archaeology

Probability Sampling Schemes

Three basic probability sampling schemes are common in archaeological survey and excavation:

1. **Systematic sampling** chooses one unit at random, then selects others at equal intervals from the first one. This method is useful for studying artifact patterning on a surface site. However, because the samples occur at regular intervals, it may produce a biased sample if archaeological material also falls at regular intervals.
2. Simple **random sampling** identifies a percentage of the survey area or site to be sampled; numbers are assigned to a grid drawn over the survey area and the units to be sampled are determined by means of a table of random numbers. The space between the sample units are, therefore, irregular. The data recovered from the sample are used to evaluate the archaeological resources of the entire survey area. This approach treats all samples as absolutely equal, a useful approach when surveying an unknown area or site.
3. **Stratified sampling** is used when sample units within an area are not uniform. They are divided into separate groups, or strata, that reflect observed

variation within the area, such as different ecological zones, activity areas, artifact classes, and so on. This approach ensures that an adequate sample is obtained from each type of feature or environmental zone represented. Alternatively, such units permit intensive sampling of some areas and less detailed work on others.

Simple random sampling is the most common sampling strategy used in survey and excavation. Under ideal circumstances, however, the other two probability sampling methods make for more precise comparisons between and within sites. But field survey means dealing with such realities as patches of open and thickly vegetated terrain, uncooperative landowners, and urban sprawl. There is rarely a perfect world in the field, so the researcher has to watch carefully for bias in the data and select a sampling strategy that provides a truly representative sample of the total data universe.

Remote Sensing

Increasingly, archaeologists are relying on technology and elaborate instrumentation to help them discover the past. Some archaeologists are beginning to talk about **nonintrusive (nondestructive) archaeology,** the analysis of archaeological phenomena without excavation or the collecting of artifacts, both of which destroy the archaeological record. The major methods in this approach are generally called remote sensing (Scollar and others, 1990).

Remote-sensing techniques include aerial photography, various magnetic prospecting methods, and side-scan radar. These methods have revolutionized some aspects of archaeological research, but they probably will never completely supersede the traditional task of the archaeologist: investigating archaeological sites on the ground. The primary purposes of many remote-sensing surveys are to map concentrations of sites and, on larger projects, to identify where maximal efforts in ground surveying and excavation should be concentrated. Remote sensing—particularly aerial photography—has also been extremely useful in mapping large and complex sites that are more clearly viewed from the air.

Aerial Photography

Aerial photography gives an unrivaled overhead view of the past. Indeed, numerous sites that have left almost no surface traces on the ground have come to light through the air photograph (D. N. Riley, 1987). Whole field systems and roadways have been incorporated into panoramas of prehistoric and Roman landscapes in Italy and North Africa. Well-known sites such as Stonehenge and many Mesoamerican and South American ceremonial centers have been mapped using aerial photographs. At Chaco Canyon, New Mexico, for example, a prehistoric road system was plotted, using both side-scan radar and aerial photographs (Sever and Wiseman, 1985).

A classic application of aerial photography was provided by Gordon Willey, who used a standard Peruvian Air Force photographic mosaic of cultivated valley bottoms and margins of the Virú Valley in northern coastal Peru to survey changing settlement patterns (Willey, 1953). Employing these photographs as the basis for a master site distribution map of the valley, Willey was able to plot many archaeological features. Three hundred and fifteen sites in the Virú Valley were eventually located, many of them stone buildings, walls, or terraces that showed up very well on the mosaics. Some much less conspicuous sites were also spotted, among them midden heaps without stone walls, refuse mounds that appeared as low hillocks on the photographs, and small pyramid mounds of insignificant proportions. The aerial photographs enabled Willey and his team to pinpoint many sites before going out in the field. The result was a fascinating story of shifting settlement patterns in Virú over many thousands of years, a classic of its kind.

The interpretation of aerial photographs requires careful study. Archaeological features may be difficult to discern, or may be revealed in unexpected ways. Most aerial photographs—at least those most readily available to archaeologists—are taken with black-and-white film, which, fortunately, gives definition superior to that of color film and is cheaper to buy and reproduce than color. The wide range of filters that can be used with black-and-white also gives the photographer great versatility. Different kinds of photography yield different kinds of details that, separately or in conjunction, may be used to identify archaeological sites. For instance, sites can be photographed obliquely or vertically, at different seasons or times of day, from varying altitudes, and with diverse types of lenses. Under certain conditions, subtle variation in topography, vegetation, or soil color may reveal archaeological sites or features.

Shadow Marks.   **Shadow marks** are caused by slight variations in topography. Many earthworks, ditches, roads, and structures have been leveled by plow or erosion, but their reduced topography still shows up clearly from the air. The rising or setting sun can set off long shadows, emphasizing the relief of almost-vanished banks or ditches, so that the features of the site stand out in the oblique light, thus the term *shadow marks.*

Figure 8.8 A crop mark site, a series of enclosures, from Thorpe, Huntingdonshire, England. Under favorable circumstances, such marks can be seen clearly from the air.

Crop Marks. Variation in crop growth sometimes provides an indication of buried archaeological features (Figure 8.8). Such **crop marks** may be detected on the surface, but under favorable circumstances they may be seen especially clearly from the air. Crop marks result from the fact that the growth and color of plants are mainly determined by the amount of moisture they can derive from the soil and the subsoil. Topsoil depth can be increased when features such as pits and ditches have been filled in or when additional earth has been heaped up to form artificial banks or mounds. Crops growing over such abandoned structures are tall and well nourished. The converse is true where topsoil has been removed and the infertile subsoil is near the surface, or where impenetrable features, such as paved streets, are buried just below ground level. Crops in these areas are stunted. Thus, dark healthy plants may indicate a ditch or a pit; a lighter line of vegetation will define a buried wall or building foundation.

Soil Marks. These features result from the exposure of distinctive soil types on the surface that are indicative of archaeological features. Plowing or ground clearing may reveal dark patches of organic soil associated with midden deposits. On the other hand, traces of brick walls or earthen banks, built from sub-soil, may show up lighter in color than that of the darker, deeper soil around them. While such traces may be visible on the ground, aerial photographs may reveal patterns virtually invisible on the surface.

Infrared, False Color Photographs. Infrared film, which has three layers sensitized to green, red, and infrared, detects reflected solar radiation at the longer wavelength radiation of the electromagnetic spectrum, some of which is invisible to the human eye. The different reflections from cultural and natural features are translated by the film into distinctive false colors. Bedrock comes up blue on infrared film, but vigorous grass growth on alluvial plains shows up bright red. Experiments at the famous Snaketown site in the American Southwest, a great Hohokam Indian pueblo, trade center, and ceremonial center, did not show up new cultural features, but tonal contrasts within a color indicated various cultural components. Vigorous plant growth showing up red on infrared photographs has been used to track shallow subsurface water sources where springs were used by prehistoric peoples (Harp, 1978).

Nonphotographic Methods

Archaeological sites can be detected from the air, even from space, by nonphotographic techniques as well. But aerial photography is the last of the "do-it-yourself" types of remote sensing, a technique whose cost is within the reach of even a modest archaeological expedition. Aerial sensor imagery, using aircraft, satellites, and even manned spacecraft, involves instrumentation that is astronomically expensive by archaeological standards. Thus, these exciting techniques are only occasionally used, and then only when the collaboration of NASA and other interested experts can be enlisted.

Aircraft-Borne Sensor Imagery. Aircraft-borne instrumentation of several types can be used to record images of the electromagnetic radiation that is reflected or emitted from the earth's surface. A multispectral scanner, for example, measures the radiance of the earth's surface along a scan line perpendicular to the aircraft's line of flight. A two-dimensional image is processed digitally. Multispectral scanners are ideal for mapping vegetation and for monitoring bodies of water when more complete data are needed than can be obtained from aerial photographs. Thermal infrared line scanners were originally used for military night survey but now have many applications in the environmental sciences. The line scanners have thermal devices that record an image on photographic film. The temperature data obtained from such scans is combined with aerial photographs to reveal tiny thermal patterns that may indicate different kinds of vegetation, the distribution of range animals, or variations in soil moisture and groundwater, both ancient and modern.

Sideways-Looking Airborne Radar (SLAR). This technique senses the terrain to either side of an aircraft's track by sending out long pulses of electromagnetic radiation. The radar then records the strength and time of the pulses' return to detect objects and their range from the aircraft. Because SLAR is not dependent on sunlight, it has great potential for archaeology. The flying aircraft enables the observer to track the pulse lines in the form of images, no matter what obscures the ground. The SLAR images are normally interpreted visually, using radar mosaics or stereo pairs of images, as well as digital image processors. Sideways-looking airborne radar was originally used for oil exploration, geology, and geomorphology, applications that justify its high cost.

Figure 8.9   A Spaceborne Imaging Radar-C/X-band Synthetic Aperture Radar photograph of the city of Angkor, Cambodia, taken from the space shuttle *Endeavour* on September 30, 1994. The image shows an area about 34 miles by 53 miles (55 by 85 km). The principal complex, Angkor Wat, is the rectangle at the lower right, surrounded by a dark line, which is a reservoir. Cambodia's great central lake, the Tonle Sap, lies at the lower right. A network of ancient and modern roads can also be seen. The data from these images are being used to establish why the site was abandoned in the fifteenth century A.D. and to map the vast system of canals, reservoirs, and other works built during the city's heyday.

SLAR is useful for mapping surface soil moisture distributions, something that has great potential for the study of ancient roads, such as the Silk Road between China and the West, and of ancient Angkor (Figure 8.9). It can also show where changes in topography have taken place or where the subsoils of large sites have been disturbed. It can also be applied to underwater sites to locate wrecks on the seafloor. So far, applications of this exciting technology to the past have been few and far between, but experiments in the Mesoamerican lowlands have hinted that SLAR may be able to identify buildings beneath dense rain forest canopy. Scans of the Maya lowlands have shown that areas of wet-season swamp often have irregular grids of gray lines and curvilinear patterns. These patterns have been compared with known ancient canal systems and are thought to represent long-forgotten large-scale irrigation schemes (Adams and others, 1981). The field testing of these data has hardly begun, but surface investigations at Pulltrouser Swamp in northern Belize have shown that Maya farmers exploited the edges of seasonally flooded swamps between 200 B.C. and A.D. 850. A rising population of farmers brought under cultivation more than 740 acres (300 ha) of raised field plots, linked with interconnecting canals. These fields were hoed, mulched, and planted with maize, amaranth, and perhaps cotton (Fedick, 1996; Turner and Harrison, 1983).

The space shuttle *Columbia* used an imaging radar system to bounce radar signals off the surfaces of the world's major deserts in 1981. This experiment was designed to study the history of the earth's aridity, not archaeology, but it identified bedrock valleys in the limestone up to 20 feet (6 m) under overlying sand sheets in the eastern Sahara Desert. Such identifications were possible because of the arid deposits. Wetter soils do not permit such deep access, for the water table blocks the radar eye completely.

A team of geologists, including archaeologist C. Vance Haynes of the University of Arizona, journeyed into the desert to investigate the long-hidden watercourses. About the only people to have worked in this terrain were British soldiers in World War II and Egyptian oil companies. The oil companies arranged for a skip loader to be transported into the desert. To Haynes's astonishment, the skip-loader trenches yielded some 200,000-year-old stone axes, dramatic and unexpected proof that early Stone Age hunter-gatherers had lived in the heart of the Sahara when the landscape was more hospitable than it is today. The Haynes find is of cardinal importance, for African archaeologists now believe that the Sahara was a vital catalyst in early human history that effectively sealed off both Archaic and modern Africans from the rest of the Ice Age world for many millennia.

The most accurate space images of all are, of course, in the closely guarded hands of the military. Despite the veil of secrecy, some astonishingly clear black-and-white satellite photographs have proved a bounty to geologists, who are expert in analyzing subtle tone, texture, and light reflections given off by rock formations on the earth. Herein lies a remarkable bonus for archaeology, for potential hominid fossil beds in Ethiopia and other parts of East Africa can be detected from shuttle images. Paleoanthropologists traditionally spend months on end combing hundreds of square miles of potentially fossil-bearing landscapes to locate promising deposits. John Fleagle of the State University of New York at Stony Brook, however, used shuttle photographs to investigate fossil beds in the Fejeji region of the Ethiopian Rift Valley. He returned months later with some 3.7-million-year-old hominid teeth from one of the earliest australopithecines yet discovered. Ethiopian archaeologists are now using images from space to develop an inventory of potential fossil deposits in their country.

Satellite Sensor Imagery. This method is well known for its military applications, but earth resources technology satellites, both manned and unmanned, have proved extremely valuable for environmental monitoring. The most famous of these satellites are the LANDSAT series, which scan the earth with sensors that record the intensity of reflected light and infrared radiation from the earth's surface. The data from scanning operations are converted electronically into photographic images and from these into mosaic maps. Normally, however, these maps are taken at a scale of about 1:1,000,000, far too imprecise for anything but the most general archaeological surveys. The first LANDSAT images could detect images about 200 feet (61 m) wide. The pyramids and plazas of Teotihuacán in the Valley of Mexico might appear on such a map, but certainly the types of minute archaeological distribution information that the average survey seeks would not. The latest images pick up features only 90 feet wide, although the French SPOT satellites can work to within 60 feet (18 m).

The latest generations of the LANDSAT and SPOT satellites have great potential for archaeological use. Both are expensive, especially when complex image-processing equipment is required. At a cost of up to $3,000 an image or even more, only the most well-heeled researchers can make free use of this revolutionary technology—and few archaeologists have access to that kind of money. The LANDSAT imagery offers an integrated view of a large region and is made up of light reflected from many components of the earth: soil, vegetation, topography, and so on. Computer-enhanced LANDSAT images can be used to construct environmental cover maps of large survey regions that are a superb backdrop for both aerial and ground survey for archaeological resources.

Recording Archaeological Sites

Once sites have been identified, whether by field survey or satellite imagery, their location, features, and extent are carefully recorded. These data can be used to address various research questions or cultural resource management concerns. For example, studies of changing settlement distributions plotted against environmental data provide significant information on changing human exploitation of the landscape (Chapter 15). Thus, recording the precise global location of archaeological phenomena revealed by a survey is a high priority.

Information on site location can be recorded in a variety of ways. It is not enough just to record the precise latitude, longitude, and map grid reference. Special forms are used to record the location of the site, as well as information about surface features, the landowner, potential threats to the site, and so on. Every site in the United States is given a name and a number. Sites in Santa Barbara County, California, for example, are given the prefix CA-SBa- and are numbered sequentially. So many sites are now known in North America that most states and many large archaeological projects have set up computer data banks containing comprehensive information about site distributions and characteristics. Arkansas, for example, has a statewide computer bank that is in constant use for decisions on conservation and management.

Maps

Maps are a convenient way of storing large quantities of archaeological information. Mapping specialists, called cartographers, use many methods to record and communicate information graphically, devices that are very useful inclusions in archaeological reports. Sites may be recorded at different scales depending on their size and location, and different features or phenomena may be highlighted. Large archaeological sites such as road systems or major settlements can sometimes be easily plotted using aerial photographs and placed on large-scale maps, but very small phenomena such as artifact scatters or middens are generally impossible to find on even the most detailed maps. Traditionally, recording was done entirely by hand, but the increasing availability of a variety of computer mapping programs has facilitated both site recording and data storage.

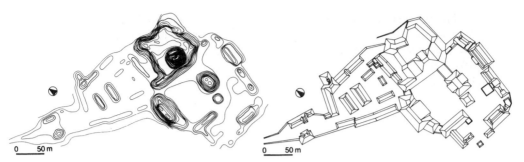

Figure 8.10   Examples of archaeological maps of Nohmul, a Maya ceremonial center. (*left*) The topographic map shows the relationship between sites and the landscape; elevation is indicated by concentric lines called contour lines. (*right*) A planimetric map showing the features of a site.

Source: Corozal Project. Drawing by Richard Bryant. Used by courtesy of Norman Hammond.

Topographic Maps.   Distributions of archaeological sites are usually plotted on large-scale **topographic maps** that relate the ancient settlements to the basic features of the natural landscape, such as hills, valleys, mountains, and rivers, as well as settlements, roads, railroads, quarries, and trails (Figure 8.10, *left*). Topographic maps indicate elevation by concentric lines that provide the experienced surveyor with a detailed idea of the survey areas terrain. These base maps can then be overlaid with plots that show vegetation cover—either prehistoric or modern—and soil types, site distributions, and even prehistoric trade routes.

Global Positioning Systems.   An important advance in recent years has been the advent of low-cost Global Positioning Systems (GPS), which locate sites using satellite positioning systems. Hand-held GPS units can be used in a variety of environmental settings and enable fieldworkers to locate sites within a few feet. They are especially advantageous in settings where roads and other identifiable features are limited, or where vegetation makes plotting sites on topographic maps challenging. With larger regional investigations, and extensive CRM projects, especially in the western United States, remote sensing and Global Positioning Systems are used to record and manage archaeological sites (Chapter 18).

Archaeologists make use of three general categories of maps:

Site Plans.   Site plans are specially prepared maps made by archaeologists to record the provenance of artifacts, food residues, and features present at an archaeological site. Site plans are keyed to topographic and other survey information from a carefully selected, fixed point called a **datum point.** A datum point is usually located on a prominent feature, such as a survey beacon, structure, or survey marker that appears on a large-scale map, but it may also be fixed by GPS. The datum point provides a reference from which a grid of squares can be laid over the area of the site, normally open-ended so that it can be extended to cover more ground if necessary. A site grid is critical for recording surface finds and, during excavation, for use in three-dimensional recording (Chapter 9).

Planimetric Maps. In addition to site plans, a variety of more specialized maps are used to record archaeological data. On large sites, structures and monumental architecture may be plotted on **planimetric maps,** which relate different archaeological features to each other and contain no topographic information (Figure 8.10, *right*). Idealized reconstructions of a site's principal features may be shown to provide a graphic representation of what the site may have looked like.

The Geographic Information System (GIS)

More and more survey and site data are now entered into the **Geographic Information System (GIS).** Computer-aided mapping came into being during the 1970s as a means of presenting cartographic information rapidly and accurately. The Geographic Information System is a revolutionary technology that goes beyond mapping. It is a computer-aided system for the collection, storage, retrieval, analysis, and presentation of spatial data of all kinds (Gaffney and Stancic, 1991; Wheatley and Gillings, 2002). The GIS incorporates computer-aided mapping, computerized databases, and statistical packages and is best thought of as a computer database with mapping capabilities. It also has the ability to generate new information based on the data within it. GIS has enormous potential for the study of site distributions and spatial problems in archaeology, especially of artifacts, settlements, and cultures distributed over a landscape (Kvamme, 1989).

From an archaeological perspective, the GIS has the advantage of allowing the manipulation of large amounts of data, which is especially useful for solving complex settlement analysis problems (Chapter 15). Information on environment, topography, archaeological features, artifact distributions, chronology, development work, and diverse other data can be added to the same database. Analyses that once took years can be done in minutes, even seconds. Until the advent of the GIS, most archaeological surveys and settlement studies were confined to the site itself. Now the archaeologist can move away from the narrow confines of the site and examine, for example, the environmental potential of areas where no sites have been found—as a way of assessing the overall distribution of sites within the environment.

GIS applications are still relatively new in archaeology, but their value is clear. Vincent Gaffney and Zoran Stancic (1991) incorporated GIS technology into their regional survey of the island of Hvar off the Adriatic coast. They created an environmental database for the island by covering it with a grid of 66-foot- (20-m-) square pixels, for a total of 3.8 million pixels. Then they entered modern data on elevation, soils, geology, and microclimate. In the field, they visited and recorded every known archaeological site on the island from early farming villages to post-Roman settlements, entering the data into a computer database. They then combined this database with the GIS data for a series of studies on the extent of site territories, analysis of land use within the same territories, and the factors that affected site location. For instance, they were able to show that Roman villas were located near good agricultural soils (Figure 8.11). The GIS also allows archaeologists to model different environmental scenarios and to study such problems as the ways in which different settlements controlled valuable land.

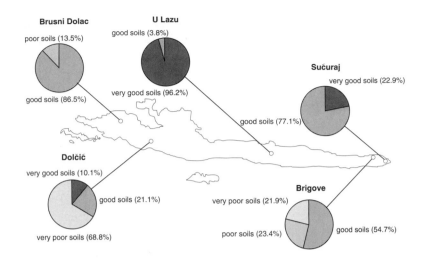

Figure 8.11   Roman sites on Hvar, Jugoslavia, with pie charts illustrating the proportions of soil types within catchment areas derived from GIS analysis.

Source: Reprinted by permission of Vincent Gaffney.

The most comprehensive North American GIS project is the National Archaeological Archive. It provides U.S. archaeologists with access not only to archaeological site distribution data from all parts of the United States but also with the ability to consult a bibliographic database and review site distribution data against a background of topographic, climatic, and other information, even seasonal changes. The Arkansas Archaeological Survey, among others, uses this database in its field research (Sabo and others, 1990). Historical archaeologists and CRM projects are using GIS on a regular basis. The Historic Annapolis Foundation has used GIS extensively in mapping the historic district of the city.

Assessing Archaeological Sites

Archaeological surveys are designed to solve specific research problems or to address cultural resource management concerns. Once sites have been located, they are carefully surveyed and the data recorded. **Site survey** includes the mapping of archaeological features, as well as the collection and assessment of surface material recovered (see the Site box). These data are used to provide an evaluation of the archaeological site's age, significance, and integrity. Site survey has specific objectives in mind (Hester and others, 1997):

- To collect and record information on subsurface features, such as walls, buildings, and fortifications, traces of which may be detected on the surface. Such features may include ancient roads, agricultural systems, and earthworks, which are first detected from the air and then investigated on the ground.
- To record and collect information on artifacts and other finds lying on the surface of the site.
- To use both of these categories of data to evaluate the age, significance, and function of the site.

Site

Teotihuacán, Mexico

Perhaps the largest site survey project ever undertaken was the Teotihuacán Mapping Project directed by George Cowgill and René Millon. Teotihuacán lies northeast of Mexico City and is one of the great tourist attractions of the Americas. This great pre-Columbian city flourished from about 250 B.C. until A.D. 700. Up to 150,000 people lived in Teotihuacán at the peak of its prosperity. Huge pyramids and temples, giant plazas, and an enormous market formed the core of the well-organized and well-planned city. The houses of the priests and nobles lay along the main avenues; the artisans and common people lived in crowded compounds of apartments and courtyards.

Cowgill and Millon realized that the only effective way to study the city was to make a comprehensive map of all of the precincts; without it, they would never have been able to study how Teotihuacán grew so huge (Cowgill and others, 1984). Fortunately, the streets and buildings lay close to the surface, unlike the vast city mounds of southwestern Asia, where only excavation yields settlement information.

The mapping project began with a detailed ground survey, conducted with the aid of aerial photographs and large-scale survey maps. The field data were collected on 147 map data sheets of 500-meter squares at a scale of 1:2,000. Intensive mapping and surface surveys, including surface collections of artifacts, were then conducted systematically within the 8-square-mile (20-sq.-km) limits of the ancient city defined by the preliminary survey. Ultimately, the architectural interpretations of the surface features within each 1,640-foot (500-m) square were overprinted on the base map of the site. These architectural interpretations were based on graphic data and surface data collected on special forms and through artifact collections, photographs, and drawings. Extensive use of sophisticated sampling techniques and quantitative methods was essential for successful completion of the map.

By the end of the project, more than five thousand structures and activity areas had been recorded within the city limits. The Teotihuacán maps do not, of course, convey to us the incredible majesty of this remarkable city, but they do provide, for the first time, a comprehensive view of a teeming, multifaceted community with vast public buildings, plazas, and avenues, where thousands of small apartments and courtyards formed individual households and workshops for production of pottery, figurines, and obsidian items. The survey also revealed that the city had been expanded over the centuries according to a comprehensive master plan. (For more on Teotihuacán, see Chapter 15.)

Site survey has the great advantage of being much cheaper than excavation, provided that the methods used are based on explicit research designs. Many of the most exciting recent studies of cultural process and changing settlement patterns have depended heavily on archaeological survey and site survey. The large-scale field surveys around the Maya city of Copán have used remote sensing, field survey, and obsidian hydration dating to chart changing settlement patterns before and during the collapse of Maya civilization (Freter, 1993). The data from the survey show a concentration of population in the urban core during the height of Classic Maya civilization, followed by a slow dispersal into rural communities, which caused the environment to become overexploited at the time of the collapse.

Surface Collections

The artifacts and other archaeological finds discovered on the surface of a site are a potentially vital source of information about the people who once lived there. Surface finds are often the first materials examined from a site and, consequently, frequently provide preliminary information on the age, cultural associations, and types of activities represented. Surface collection has these objectives (Hester and others, 1997):

- To gather representative samples of artifacts from the surface of the site to establish the age of the area and the various periods of occupation.
- To establish the types of activity that took place on the site.
- To gather information on the areas of the site that were most densely occupied and that might be most productive for either total or sample excavation.
- To locate major structures that lie, for the most part, below the surface.

Some archaeologists distrust surface collection, arguing that artifacts are easily destroyed on the surface and can be displaced from their original positions by many factors. But this viewpoint neglects a truth: all archaeological deposits, however deep, were once surface deposits, subject to many of the same destructive processes as those resting on the surface today (Dunnell and Dancey, 1983). Experiments have shown that even more than a century of cultivation may scatter artifacts over no more than a radius of 20 feet (6 m). This relatively small "halo" area makes total collection feasible, especially for small hunter-gatherer settlements.

Surface levels contain abundant information about artifact patterning if one can separate cultural patterns from those caused by natural formation processes that have occurred since the site was abandoned. With the increased emphasis on regional surveys and settlement archaeology in recent years, many fieldworkers have demonstrated that surface deposits can provide much information on artifact distributions and other phenomena found underground. This is provided, of course, that they have not been subjected to catastrophic industrial activity, strip mining, or other drastic alteration from natural weathering, erosion, and rainfall.

Natural processes and human activity may result in the pulverizing of potsherds, stone tools, and bone fragments. But surface data have two major advantages: they are a body of information that can be obtained on a regional scale, not site by site, and the cost of obtaining the data is but a fraction of that for excavation. Increasingly, archaeologists are thinking of surface data as primary archaeological information essential to understanding regional prehistories (Lewarch and O'Brien, 1981). There are various ways of collecting artifacts from the surface of a site, but the process is always carefully controlled, and the provenance of the finds is plotted on a map at the time of collection.

Sampling

Controlled surface collection sometimes involves meticulous recording of all finds, using a grid laid over the surface of the site, an approach especially effective on plowed fields. But as in the case of archaeological survey, surface collections may involve a variety of sampling strategies. Certain areas, representing different time periods, activity areas, or cultural materials, may be selected for collection. One may also collect only diagnostic artifacts, items such as potsherds, stone artifacts, or other characteristic finds that are easily classified and identified. These key finds may enable the archaeologist to assess what periods of occupation, activity areas, or cultural associations are represented at the site.

A common controlled surface collection method involves **random sampling.** Because total collection is impossible on sites of any size where surface finds are abundant, some type of sampling technique is used to obtain a random sample of the surface artifacts. One often used random-sampling approach involves laying out a grid of squares on the surface of the site and then collecting everything found in randomly selected units. Once such a controlled collection has been made, the rest of the site is covered for highly diagnostic artifacts. Rigorous sampling techniques are essential to obtain even a minimal sample of finds at the individual site level. Surface collection and sampling are often combined with systematic, small test-pit excavations to get preliminary data on stratigraphic information.

Subsurface Detection

Evidence of the past activities of a region's inhabitants can be obtained from surface collections, but only when the relationship between remains found on the surface and present below the ground is clearly understood. Sometimes the surface finds may accurately reflect site content; at other times they may not. It is reasonable to assume that, on shallow sites, such as many prehistoric settlements in the American West, the artifacts on the surface accurately reflect those slightly below the ground (Millon, 1973). This assumption provides a basis for studying activities from surface finds. In other cases, natural processes and cultural factors impact the integrity and the depth of archaeological deposits. Obviously, almost no finds from the lowest levels of a 30-foot- (9-m-) deep village mound will lie on the surface today, unless erosion, human activity, or animal burrows bring deeply buried artifacts to the surface (McManamon, 1984). In any case, the conclusions derived from any surface collections must be verified by excavation.

Because archaeological remains may lie deeply buried below ground surface, determining the presence of archaeological resources and site assessment must rely on some type of subsurface testing or evaluation. These include both nonintrusive methods, which do not impact subsurface remains in any way, to increasingly intrusive techniques like excavation and subsurface testing.

Nonintrusive Methods

Every archaeologist dreams of a way of exploring sites without the labor of excavating them. Some subsurface detection methods are very simple, but most are expensive;

some are very time-consuming. Many of the more sophisticated techniques were originally developed for oil or geological prospecting (A. Clark, 1997; Hester and others,
1997; Weymouth, 1986). These methods can sometimes save many weeks of expensive excavation and, on occasion, can aid in formulating an accurate research design
before a dig begins.

Bowsing.   In this low-tech, nonmechanical method, the surface of the site is
thumped with a suitable heavy pounder. The earth resonates in different ways, so
much so that a practiced ear can detect the distinctive sound of a buried ditch or a
subsurface stone wall. *Bowsing,* more an art than a geophysical method, really works—
with practice. In particular, features such as buried walls may be identified in this way.

Resistivity Survey.   The electrical resistivity of the soil provides some clues to
subsurface features on archaeological sites (Carr, 1982; Leute, 1987). Soils vary in
their ability to conduct electricity, mainly because the different soils or structural features have varying moisture containing mineral salts in solution. For example, clay
soils provide the least resistance to current flow; sandy soils, much more. A **resistivity
survey** meter can be used to measure the variations in the resistance of the ground to
an electrical current. Stone walls or hard pavements retain less moisture than a deep
pit filled with soft earth or a large ditch that has silted up. These differences can be
measured accurately so that disturbed ground, stone walls, and other subsurface features can be detected by systematic resistivity survey. Surveying a site requires only the
resistivity meter, which is attached to four or five probes. A grid is laid over the site,
and the readings taken from the probes are plotted as contour lines. These show
the areas of equal resistance and the presence of features such as ditches and walls (see
Figure 8.14). This method was, for example, employed to identify subsurface features at the late Woodland and early Historic Howorth-Nelson site in southwestern
Pennsylvania (Adovasio and Carlisle, 1988; see Chapter 18).

Magnetic Survey.   Variation in magnetic fields is used to find buried features
such as iron objects, fired clay furnaces, pottery kilns, hearths, and pits filled with rubbish or soft soil (Leute, 1987). The principle is simple: the subtle variation in the magnetic fields of buried materials is used to identify archaeological features. Rocks, boulders, and soil will acquire magnetism if iron oxides are present when they are heated.
Any mass of clay heated to about 1,292°F (700°C) and then cooled acquires a weak
magnetism. When the remnant magnetism of fired clay or of other material is measured, it will give a reading different from that of the intensity of the earth's magnetic
field normally obtained from undisturbed soils.

The proton magnetometer is the instrument most commonly used to magneti-
cally detect archaeological features. A site is surveyed by laying out 50-foot-square
(15-sq.-m) units, each divided into a grid of 5-foot (1.5-m) squares. The measurement is taken with a staff, to which are attached two small bottles filled with water or
alcohol enclosed in electrical coils. The magnetic intensity is measured by recording
the behavior of the protons in the hydrogen atoms in the bottle's contents. The magnetometer itself amplifies the weak signals from the electrical coils. Features are traced

by taking closely spaced measurements over areas where anomalies in the magnetic readings are found. Computers record the field data and convert them into a display on a television screen or a printout. Sophisticated software allows the operator to screen out nonarchaeological variation in soil magnetism. **Magnetometer surveys** have been used successfully to record pits, walls, and other isolated features in the middle of large forts or plazas, where total excavation is clearly uneconomical. This method has been used widely in Europe and on Olmec pyramids at La Venta, Mexico. However, it is subject to some error because of interference from such modern features as barbed wire fences, electric trains, and power cables (Kaczor and Weymouth, 1981).

Ground-Penetrating Radar (GPR). Magnetic and resistivity surveys are somewhat crude. In recent years, ground-penetrating radar has come to the fore as a major instrument for nonintrusive archaeology, especially in cultural resource management. **Ground-penetrating radar (GPR)** reflects radar waves off subsurface features by propagating distinct pulses of radar waves from a surface antenna. The velocity of the radar waves depends on the electrical and magnetic properties of the soil through which they are passing. When the travel times of the pulses are measured and their velocity through the ground is known, then the depth of a feature below the ground can be measured accurately.

Early ground-penetrating radar units were cumbersome but have become much lighter and can be loaded into several backpacks and taken to remote locations. Most systems can be powered from car batteries or portable electrical generators. Some of the latest generation of machines are even powered by small rechargeable batteries. The same machines allow immediate computer processing of the data in the field. Although much depends on mineralogy and ground moisture, modern computer enhancement tools allow GPR to be used even in seemingly unfavorable situations.

When using ground-penetrating radar, the operator moves the antennas along the ground. Two-dimensional profiles of a large number of reflections are produced along lines, creating a profile of subsurface stratigraphy and buried archaeological features. The data are acquired in a series of transects within a site grid; the reflections are correlated and processed, and an accurate three-dimensional picture of buried features and their stratigraphy results (for an excellent discussion, see Conyers and Goodman, 1997). Anomalies spotted by GPR can be plotted with good accuracy, and pits as small as 12 inches (30 cm) in diameter and 4 inches (10 cm) deep have been located. Individual metal objects can also be detected using this method, which holds great promise for the future.

Intrusive Subsurface Testing

In many instances equipment such as a magnetometer may not be available or is unsuitable for particular local conditions. Also, data from magnetometer or resistivity surveys must be verified and evaluated against the archaeological record. Consequently most archaeological surveys and site assessments incorporate some limited subsurface testing. It is incorporated into the research design and carried out following a specified pattern.

Techniques used range from the very simple to increasingly sophisticated methods and substantial excavation. For example, a simple probe, consisting of a solid metal rod welded to a T-bar handle, may be stuck into the ground at intervals to determine if buried features or walls are present (Noël Hume, 1983). The amount of resistance encountered or the sound made by the probe scraping against artifacts may help determine the presence of buried features. On the other hand, archaeologists evaluating buried tombs or the interiors of monuments have also used sophisticated periscopes and robot-guided video cameras. In some cases, earthmoving equipment such as backhoes must be used to determine if cultural materials lie buried beneath thick layers of sterile alluvial soil in river basins.

Shovel Test Pits.   A common method of subsurface testing involves the use of shovel **test pits (STPs),** a technique in which shallow holes of a proscribed size and depth are made with a shovel. Material excavated from the STPs is typically screened to recover any artifacts, and features or changes in soil color are recorded. STPs are commonly used when large areas need to be tested or when time is short, as in the case of CRM surveys.

The Auger, or Core Borer.   The auger is a hand-operated or power tool used to bore through subsurface deposits to find the depth and consistency of archaeological deposits. As in the case of STPs, auger samples can recover artifacts and allow for an evaluation of buried deposits to be made. This technique has the disadvantage that the auger or borer may destroy artifacts. Nevertheless, it lends itself to situations where time is limited and large areas are involved.

Augers were used successfully at the Ozette site in Washington to establish the depth of midden deposits (Kirk, 1974). Some specialized augers are used to lift pollen samples. Augers with a camera attached to a periscope head are also used to investigate the interiors of Etruscan tombs (Figure 8.12). The periscope is inserted through a small hole in the roof of the tomb to inspect the interior. If the contents are undisturbed, excavation proceeds. But if tomb robbers have already emptied the chamber, many hours of fruitless labor have been saved.

Examples of Subsurface Detection

Many new, innovative approaches to archaeological survey and site assessment no doubt lie ahead. For example, Kent Weeks and a team of fellow Egyptologists have embarked on a long-term project to map all of the royal tombs in Thebes's Valley of the Kings. They are using a hot-air balloon, X rays, and sonic detectors to map subterranean features and hidden chambers in royal tombs; recently, they located a large tomb that once housed Rameses II's sons (Weeks, 1998). The application of radar and other electronic devices is proliferating in archaeology. However, evaluation of an archaeological site typically continues to rely on a combination of methods that may

Figure 8.12 A periscope being used to investigate an Etruscan tomb.

range from the simple to the sophisticated and from nonintrusive remote sensing to subsurface testing.

The excavations at the Maya village of Cerén in San Salvador offer an instructive example of coordinated use of innovative geophysical methods to locate subsurface features (Sheets, 1992). The site was buried under up to 16 feet (5 m) of volcanic ash and was first located by a chance bulldozer cut. Obviously, it was uneconomical to bulldoze large areas, so Payson Sheets called in geophysicist Hartmut Spetzler, who analyzed the properties of the volcanic ash at Cerén and of the adobe buildings buried beneath it. There were considerable differences in porosity and density between the ash and the adobe, so Spetzler recommended deploying a portable seismograph, ground-penetrating radar equipment, and a resistivity meter.

The survey started with the seismograph, which records shock waves passing through the earth. Instead of the usual dynamite, Sheets struck a steel plate set in the soil with a hammer, recording the resulting waves with a set of twelve sensitive microphones. Buried hut floors conducted shock waves faster than the surrounding ash, and the seismograph did indeed locate some structures, but, designed as it was for detecting huge geological anomalies, the results were somewhat haphazard. Sheets then turned to ground-penetrating radar, using an instrument developed for studying permafrost melting along the Alaska oil pipeline. Instead of attaching it to a pickup truck, he enlisted the services of an ox cart, which eliminated all background vibration. The ox-cart driver simply drove slowly and steadily along a carefully marked straight line (Figure 8.13). The machine itself sent microwave energy deep into the soil and

Figure 8.13 Ground-penetrating radar slung behind an ox cart being used at Cerén, San Salvador.

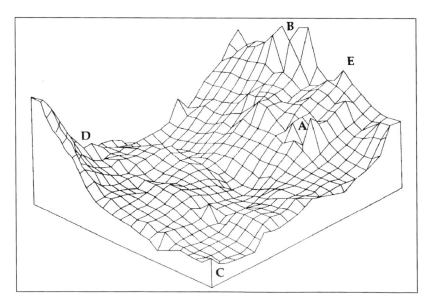

Figure 8.14 A three-dimensional computer plot of a resistivity survey at the Maya village at Cerén, San Salvador. The anomalies resulting from different electrical resistance show up as sharp peaks (A to E), of which A and B have been investigated and shown to be prehistoric structures.

Source: Payson Sheets, *The Cerén Site: A Prehistoric Village Buried by Volcanic Ash in Central America.* Copyright © 1992. Reprinted by permission of Wadsworth, a division of Thomson Learning: www.thomsonrights.com. Fax 800-730-2215.

detected it as it was reflected back. The subsurface stratigraphy was recorded on special paper and revealed some strong reflectors, some of which turned out to be the clay surfaces of hut floors covered by ash.

Using a drill rig, Sheets tested some of the anomalies. Some were the result of eroded and redeposited volcanic ash; others were large structures. The radar was still unable to detect smaller features, although it may be able to do so once the data are digitized and the original ground surface is mapped.

Resistivity surveys over Cerén recorded the resistance of subsurface deposits to electricity. Sheets expected that house floors would conduct electricity better than the surrounding ash, for they are constructed of dense, fired clay. His researchers recorded measurements along a grid over the site and fed the data into a laptop computer. The three-dimensional software revealed interesting double-peaked anomalies, which, when tested with a drill rig, turned out to be large prehistoric structures (Figure 8.14). Thus a combination of geophysical methods provided an effective and economical way to locate subsurface features at Cerén, at a fraction of what it would have cost to bulldoze away acres of ashy overburden.

Summary

Two interrelated processes are involved in locating archaeological sites: archaeological survey and site assessment. Site survey is concerned with locating and identifying archaeological sites; site assessment evaluates sites in terms of their age, integrity, potential, and cultural affiliations.

Many famous archaeological sites, such as the Parthenon, have never been lost to human knowledge. But other, less conspicuous locations are only discovered by accident or by planned archaeological survey. Archaeological sites are sometimes identified by features such as mounds, structural remains, or monumental architecture that are prominent on the landscape. Yet, many more are much less obvious and are located only by soil discolorations or surface finds.

Archaeological surveys are done at different levels of complexity, ranging from preliminary, reconnaissance surveys leading to location of only the largest sites, to intensive surveys aimed at covering an entire area in detail. In most instances, even an intensive survey may not be able to locate all of the archaeological resources within an area, and all survey is, at best, only a sampling of the research area. Consequently, archaeologists rely on probabilistic sampling methods to obtain unbiased samples of the research area.

A battery of new survey techniques involves aerial photography and remote sensing. Photographs taken from the air can be used to locate sites spread over huge areas. Pioneer efforts have been made with side-scan aerial radar and scanner imagery.

Site assessment involves mapping, controlled surface collection, and subsurface detection methods designed to assess the significance of the site without intrusive excavation.

Controlled surface collection is designed to collect and record artifacts and other surface finds. These categories of data are used to test hypotheses about the age, significance, and function of the site.

Surface collections may be made by gathering every artifact on the surface of the site, by selecting for diagnostic artifacts, or by random sampling. Surface collections are used to establish the activities that took place on the site, to locate major structures, and to gather information about the most densely occupied areas of the site.

Geographic Information System (GIS) technology offers great potential as a way of mapping archaeological data and analyzing them in a wider environmental context.

Subsurface features are often detected with subsurface radar and with resistivity surveys, which measure the differences in electrical resistivity of the soil between disturbed and undisturbed areas. Proton magnetometers are used to locate iron objects, fired clay furnaces, and other features.

Key Terms

archaeological survey	nonintrusive (nondestructive)	site assessment
crop marks	archaeology	site survey
datum point	off-site areas	soil marks
Geographic Information	planimetric maps	stratified sampling
System (GIS)	probability sampling	systematic sampling
ground-penetrating radar	random sampling	tells
(GPR)	reconnaissance survey	test pits
intensive survey	remote sensing	topographic maps
magnetometer survey	resistivity surveying	
middens	shadow marks	

Guide to Further Reading

CLARK, ANTHONY. 1997. *Seeing Beneath the Soil.* London: Batsford. A basic description of remote-sensing methods with an emphasis on European sites.

GAFFNEY, VINCENT, and ZORAN STANCIC. 1991. *GIS Approaches to Regional Analysis: A Case Study of the Island of Hvar.* Ljubljana, Yugoslavia: Znanstveni institut Filozofske fakultete. An exemplary case study in the use of Geographic Information System technology in archaeology. It is also readable!

HESTER, THOMAS R., HARRY J. SHAFER, and KENNETH L. FEDER. 1997. *Field Methods in Archaeology.* 7th ed. Mountain View, CA: Mayfield. A classic field manual aimed at American archaeologists that contains much valuable information on field survey and remote sensing.

MILLON, RENÉ. 1973. *The Teotihuacán Map: Urbanization at Teotihuacán, Mexico.* Vol. 1. Austin: University of Texas Press. A prime example of a complicated survey and mapping project.

ORTON, CLIVE. 2000. *Sampling in Archaeology.* Cambridge: Cambridge University Press. A comprehensive account of statistical sampling as applied to archaeology. Essential for intending professionals.

SANDERS, WILLIAM T., JEFFREY R. PARSONS, and ROBERT S. SANTLEY. 1979. *The Basin of Mexico: Ecological Processes in the Evolution of a Civilization.* 2 vols. Orlando, FL: Academic Press. The best description of a long-term survey project and of survey problems.

WEEKS, KENT R. 1998. *The Lost Tomb.* New York: William Morrow. A popular account of site survey and mapping in the Valley of the Kings that focuses on the tomb of Rameses II's sons. This is a marvelous example of the detective work that is modern-day Egyptology.

A useful Website for remote sensing methods is **http://www.ads.ahs.ac.uk/project/goodguides/gis**

CHAPTER 9

Archaeological Excavation

The ultimate in archaeological excavation: King Henry VIII's Privy Garden at Hampton Court, England, was restored after archaeological excavations by Brian Dix of Northamptonshire Archaeology located the outlines of flower beds and other features.

"The wonder of touching something that had lain buried and unmoving for so long came over me. . . . But I thought of it this way: the little head, wedged in that rubble, up against a ruined wall in this silent, sunny place in Egypt, had been lying there, face downwards, while Troy was burning; while [Assyrian King] Sennacherib was ransacking cities beyond his borders; on through the slow centuries, while the greatness of Athens came and went, and while Christ lived out his days on earth" (Chubb, 1954:110). The excitement of discovery that comes with excavation is one of the profound pleasures of archaeology. Even the smallest object can spark deep emotions and provide astonishingly detailed information about the remote past.

Excavation! The very word conjures up romantic images of lost civilizations and royal burials, of long days in the sun digging up inscriptions and gold coins. Yet, though the image remains, the techniques of modern excavation are far less romantic than they are rigorous, requiring long training in practical field techniques (Roskams, 2001). Unlike reconnaissance and surface survey, excavations recover data from beneath the surface of the ground, where conditions for preservation are best, and accurate information on provenance, context, and association can be recovered intact. Excavation is a creative activity, not just the standardized recording of the archaeological record. It requires constant interpretation, flexible research designs, and an ability to improvise.

In this chapter we discuss some of the basic principles of archaeological excavation: the organization, planning, and execution of a scientific dig.

Organizing Archaeological Excavations

The director of a modern archaeological field expedition needs skills beyond those of a competent archaeologist. He or she also must be able to fill the roles of accountant, politician, doctor, mechanic, personnel manager, and even cook. Cultural resource

202

management project directors require expertise in compliance with legal requirements (Chapter 18). On a large dig, though manual labor may not be the director's responsibility, logistical problems are compounded, and he or she will head a large excavation team of site supervisors, artists, photographers, and specialists (Dancey, 1981; Joukowsky, 1981; Hester and others, 1997). Above all, the field director has to be the leader of a multidisciplinary team of specialist fieldworkers (Hodder, 1999).

Multidisciplinary Research Teams

Modern archaeology is so complex that all excavation projects, whether purely academic or CRM, now require multidisciplinary teams of archaeologists, botanists, geologists, zoologists, and other specialists to work together on closely integrated research problems. The team approach is particularly important where environmental problems are most pressing, where the excavations and research seek the relationships between human cultures and the rest of the ecosystem.

A good interdisciplinary or multidisciplinary study is based on an integrated research design bringing a closely supervised team of specialists together to test carefully formulated research questions against data collected by all of them. Notice that we say "data collected by all of them." An effective multidisciplinary archaeological team must be just that—a team whose combined findings provide an integrated view of a site. This approach is logical, but it is rarely carried to its complete extreme, where the experts design their research together, share an integrated field mission, and communicate daily about their findings and research problems (Isaac and Isaac, 1989).

The most thorough multidisciplinary excavation must be that at Çatalhöyük, Turkey, where Ian Hodder has embarked on a long-term project to investigate this important farming village (see the Site box in Chapter 3). He enlisted a large team of archaeologists from different countries who are using different approaches to excavation, as well as a small army of specialists in everything from ceramics to zooarchaeology and all kinds of environmental data. Hodder has specialists who are working on communicating the results of the work to the public; he even has a resident anthropologist who studies not only local communities and the workers but the dynamics of the excavation team as well. This remarkable excavation is based on the belief that the best results in the field come from sustained dialogue between team members and from an integration of theory and observation from the first day of the dig. "Theory begins at the edge of the trowel," Hodder tells us (1999). The Çatalhöyük excavation carries the multidisciplinary approach to extremes by networking all the archaeologists and specialists by computer and requiring them to keep research diaries, which are posted on the Internet and are read by everyone (Hodder, 1999).

Excavation Staff

Large, elaborate excavations that take several seasons to complete are staffed by a director and other specialist experts and by several technicians as well. Among the technicians are these:

Site Supervisors.   Skilled excavators are responsible for excavating trenches and recording specific locations. The large-scale digs of medieval York in northern England were divided into localities, each with a skilled excavator who supervises the volunteers doing the actual digging.

Recording Experts.   Some very large excavations will have a full-time surveyor who does nothing but draw and record the stratigraphic profiles and structures found in the dig. Expert archaeological artists and photographers are in great demand, and will take thousands of digital images, slides and black-and-white photographs during even a short season. Their task is to create a complete record of the excavation from beginning to end (Adkins and Adkins, 1989; Dorrell, 1994). Today, much of these activities are carried out electronically, using three-dimensional mapping systems.

Laboratory Staff.   Even a small excavation can yield a flood of artifacts and floral and faunal remains that can overwhelm the staff of a dig. A basic laboratory staff to bag the finds and wash, rough-sort, and mark them for eventual transport to the laboratory is vital on any but the smallest excavation. Some knowledge of preservation techniques is essential as well.

Foremen.   Paid foremen are common on larger Mediterranean excavations. They can become skilled archaeological excavators in their own right, but their primary responsibility is to manage paid laborers. Some devote their entire working lives to archaeology.

CRM Staff.   Many CRM excavations are part of survey projects, where sites are excavated before destruction. Larger CRM organizations in the public and private sectors hire professional excavators, often people with bachelor's and master's degrees in archaeology, to carry out both basic labor and more specialized excavation, recording, and laboratory tasks.

In these days of rising costs and limited budgets, most excavations are conducted on a comparatively small scale. A team of students or paid laborers works under the overall supervision of the director and perhaps one or two assistants. The assistants may be graduate students with some technical training in archaeological fieldwork who can take some of the routine tasks from the director's shoulders, allowing him or her to concentrate on general supervision and interpretative problems. But on many sites, the director will not only be in charge of the research and arrangements for the excavation but will also personally supervise all trenches excavated. On that one person, therefore, devolve the tasks of recording, photography, drawing, measurement, and supervision of labor. The director may also take a turn at recovery of fragile burials and other delicate objects that cannot be entrusted to students or workers; he or she is also responsible for the maintenance of the excavation diaries and find notebooks, the storage and marking of artifacts, and the logistics of packing finds and shipping them to the laboratory.

So varied are the skills of the excavator that much of a professional archaeologist's training in the field is obtained as a graduate student working at routine tasks and gaining experience in the methods of excavating and site survey under experienced

Discovery

The Princess of Khok Phanom Di, Thailand, 1984

Charles Higham of the University of Otago in New Zealand is one of the world's experts on the archaeology of southeastern Asia. Working closely with Thai archaeologists, he has made spectacular discoveries of early rice-farming villages and well-established Bronze Age settlements. In 1984, he began excavations at the large Khok Phanom Di mound on the floodplain of the Bang Pakong River. From a previous test excavation carried out by a Thai colleague, he knew that the occupation deposits were nearly 30 feet (9 m) deep, the mound resting on layers of shell midden debris. In the trial pit, Higham spotted "the hollow eye sockets of some prehistoric person," so he knew he would probably find burials.

After digging through the uppermost levels, he found lighter, sandier soil about 3 feet (1 m) below the surface. He cleaned the surface of the deposit carefully and spotted the telltale outline of the dark filling of a grave. Soon the excavators uncovered a row of graves close to the foundation of a raised platform with a building on it. Their trowels traced the walls of beautifully polished black vessels, many of them decorated with curvilinear designs. Higham's excitement mounted as he uncovered fourteen burials. From the platform, "I could look down the row of skeletons and see the remains of men, women, and children, and even a tiny grave with the intertwined bones of two newly born infants, probably twins. It looked like a family group running through a couple or more generations" (Higham, 1996:283).

The excavation penetrated downward into a large burial chamber, uncovering a pyramid of circular clay cylinders, once destined to become pots. When the pyramid was removed, the skeleton of a woman in her mid-thirties appeared, her wrist muscles well formed, probably from kneading clay. She had borne one or two children. Her chest was covered with tiny shell beads and a necklace of large, white I-shaped beads. Higham lifted the top half of the body in a single block of soil and dissected it in the laboratory, where he recovered no less than 120,787 shell beads, once sewn onto two ornate upper garments. The princess must have shimmered in the sunlight, her wealth and social position coming from her expertise at potmaking, evidenced by the burnished polishing pebbles found by her feet and the broken vessels covering her legs. Just 6 feet (2 m) away, Higham found another, identical grave covered by another heap of clay cylinders; this was the grave of an infant only fifteen months old. The child was adorned with the same decoration as that of her mother and lay with a tiny potmaking anvil, a smaller version of the anvils used by adults, by her side. Higham is convinced that this was the princess's daughter.

By the time the excavation finished six months later, Higham had recovered another 139 burials, representing seventeen to twenty generations of expert potters who had traded pots to obtain exotic shell ornaments. But none of them rivaled the splendor of the Princess of Khok Phanom Di.

supervision. For the director, such students provide not only useful supervisory labor but also an admirable sounding board on which to try out favorite theories and discuss in great detail the interpretation of the site. The camaraderie and happiness of a well-run, student-oriented excavation is one of the most worthwhile experiences of archaeology.

Planning an Excavation

Excavation is the culminating step in the investigation of an archaeological site. It recovers from the earth data obtainable in no other way (Barker, 1995; Hester and others, 1997). Like historical archives, the soil of an archaeological site is a document whose pages must be deciphered, translated, and interpreted before they can be used to write an accurate account of the site's inhabitants.

Excavation is destruction. The archaeological deposits so carefully dissected during any dig are destroyed forever, and their contents are removed. Here, again, there is a radical difference between archaeology and the sciences and history. A scientist can readily re-create the conditions for a basic experiment; the historian can return to the archives to reevaluate the complex events in a politician's life. But all that we have after an excavation are the finds from the trenches, the untouched portions of the site, and the photographs, notes, and drawings that record the excavator's observations for posterity. Thus, accurate recording and observation are overwhelmingly vital in the day-to-day work of archaeologists, not only for the sake of accuracy in their own research but also because they are creating an archive of archaeological information that may be consulted by others. Archaeological sites are nonrenewable resources. Thus, unfocused excavation is useless, for the manageable and significant observations are buried in a mass of irrelevant trivia. Any excavation must be conducted from a sound research design intended to solve specific and well-defined problems.

Research Designs

Archaeological excavation is not digging by formula, but a carefully managed process that requires constant creative thinking. There are general methodologies for excavation, but the appropriate one varies from site to site and from moment to moment as an excavation proceeds. In a way, excavation is a process of negotiation that balances acquiring the maximum amount of information against potential destruction and the needs of contemporary society. Specific, yet flexible research designs are essential (Figure 9.1).

Excavation costs are so great that problem-oriented digging is now the rule rather than the exception, with the laboratory work forming part of the continuing evaluation of the research problem. The large piles of finds and records accumulated at the end of even a small field season contain a bewildering array of interdigitating facts that the researcher must evaluate and reevaluate as inquiry proceeds—by constantly rearranging propositions and hypotheses, correlating observations, and reevaluating interpretations of the archaeological evidence. Finds and plans are the basis of the researcher's strategy and affect fieldwork plans for the future, the basis for constant reevaluation of research objectives. The need for sound planning and design is even more acute in ecological research in archaeology, in which archaeologists try to understand changes in human culture in relation to human environmental systems. In many respects a research design resembles a business plan—the general blueprint for the investigation.

Let us take the example of the Koster excavation in Illinois, one of the largest and most complex academic digs undertaken in North America. (Koster is not,

Figure 9.1 An organized horizontal-grid excavation on the Iron Age hill fort at Danebury, England. The Danebury research was carried out over many years and its research designs were constantly modified.

of course, the only site with a long, stratified sequence, but it is the most completely published.)

The Koster Site

The Koster site lies in the lower Illinois Valley, a deep accumulation of 26 prehistoric occupation layers extending from about 10,000 years ago to around A.D. 1100 to 1200 (Struever and Holton, 1979). The wealth of material at Koster first came to light in 1968 and has been the subject of very large-scale excavation. The dig involved collaboration by three archaeologists and six specialists from other disciplines such as zoology and botany, as well as use of a computer laboratory (Figure 9.2). Even superficial examination of the site showed that a very careful research design was needed, both to maximize the use of funds and to ensure adequate control of data. In developing the Koster research design, James Brown and Stuart Struever (1973) were well aware of the numerous, complex variables that had to be controlled for and the need to define carefully their sampling procedure and the size of the collecting units.

They faced formidable difficulties. Thirteen of the Koster cultural horizons are isolated from their neighbors by a zone of sterile slopewash soil, which makes it possible to treat each as a separate problem in excavation and analysis—as if it were an individual site—although, in fact, the thirteen are stratified one above another. Because the whole site is more than 30 feet (9 m) deep, the logistical problems were formidable, as in all large-scale excavations. One possible strategy would have been to sink test pits, obtain samples from each level, and list diagnostic artifacts and cultural items.

Figure 9.2 General view of the Koster excavations in southern Illinois.

But this approach, though cheap and commonly used, was inadequate to the systems model the excavators drew up to study the origins of cultivation in the area and culture change in the lower Illinois Valley. Large-scale excavations were needed to uncover each living surface so that the excavators could not only understand what the living zones within each occupation were like but could also, after studying in detail the sequence of differences in activities, make statements about the processes of culture change.

From the large scale of the excavations, Brown and Struever saw the need for immediate feedback from the data flow from the site during the excavation. Changes in the excavation method would no doubt be needed during the season's fieldwork to ensure that maximum information was obtained. To accomplish this flexibility, they combined excavation and data-gathering activities into a data flow system (Figure 9.3) that would ensure nearly instantaneous feedback to the excavators. The categories of data—animal bones, artifacts, vegetable remains—were processed in the field, and the information from the analyses was then fed by remote access terminal to a computer in Evanston, Illinois, many miles away. Pollen and soil samples were sent directly to specialist laboratories for analysis. The results of the data flow system are very worthwhile. The tiresome analysis of artifacts and food residues is completed on the site, and the data are available to the excavators in the field in a few days, instead of months

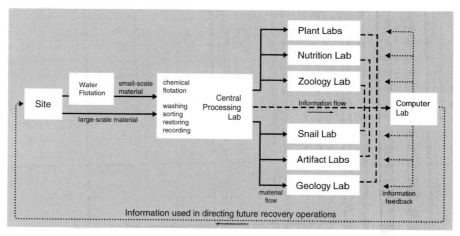

Figure 9.3   Data flow system of the Koster site.

Source: Redrawn from Stuart Struever and James A. Brown, "The Organization of Research: An Illinois Example," in Charles A. Redman, ed., *Research and Theory in Current Archaeology,* p. 128. Copyright © 1971 John Wiley and Sons, Inc. Reprinted by permission of John Wiley and Sons, Inc.

later, as is usual. The research design can be modified in the field at short notice, with ready consultation among the team members in the field. A combination of instant data retrieval; comprehensive and meticulous collecting methods involving, among other things, flotation methods (Chapter 13); and a systems approach to both excavation strategy and research planning has made the Koster project an interesting example of effectively used research design in archaeology.

Tremendous advances in computer technology and software since the 1970s have made the Koster example look simple compared with even small-scale excavations and surveys today. The advent of the World Wide Web, of laptops, and highly portable desktop computers has made it easy for excavators to develop on-site networks, to remain in constant touch with laboratories many miles away, to develop digital maps and plans and stratigraphic profiles, and to find location diagrams almost instantaneously. But the Koster dig stands as a fine example of an ideal model.

Types of Excavation

Archaeological excavation balances destruction against acquiring as much information as possible and available funds against the needs of society. When undertaken, its ultimate objective is to produce a three-dimensional record of an archaeological site in which the various artifacts, structures, and other finds are placed in their correct provenance and context in time and space. And when this process is completed, the record has to be published in full for posterity.

Total and Selective Excavation

Total excavation of a site has the advantage of being comprehensive, but it is expensive and is undesirable because it leaves none of the site intact for excavation at a later date with, perhaps, more advanced techniques. Total excavation is commonly used on CRM projects when a site is threatened by imminent destruction.

Selective excavation is much more common, especially on CRM projects when time is often of the essence. Many sites are simply too large for total excavation and can be tested only selectively, using sampling methods or carefully placed trenches. Selective excavation is used to obtain stratigraphic and chronological data as well as samples of pottery, stone tools, and animal bones. From this evidence, the archaeologist can decide whether to undertake further excavation.

Vertical and Horizontal Excavation

Invariably, **vertical excavation** is selective digging, uncovering a limited area on a site for the purpose of recovering specific information. Most vertical excavations are probes of deep archaeological deposits, their real objective being to reveal the chronological sequence at a site. **Horizontal (area) excavation** is used to expose contemporaneous settlement over a larger area. However, it should be stressed that all excavation strategies are based on decisions made as an excavation and a research design unfold. The illustrations in this and other texts, for that matter, invariably show completed excavations. Thus, an archaeologist may legitimately switch back and forth from test pits to horizontal or vertical excavation during even a short dig.

Vertical Excavation.　Almost invariably, vertical excavation is used to establish stratigraphic sequences, especially in sites where space is limited, such as small caves and rock shelters, or to solve chronological problems, such as the sequences across sets of ditches and earthworks (Figure 9.4). Some vertical trenches reach impressive size, especially those sunk into city mounds. However, most such excavation is on a much smaller scale.

Test pits, sometimes given the French name *sondages,* or referred to as "telephone booths," are a frequently used form of vertical excavation. They consist of small trenches just large enough to accommodate one or two diggers, and are designed to penetrate to the lower strata of a site to establish the extent of archaeological deposits (Figure 9.5). Test pits are dug to obtain samples of artifacts from lower layers. Augers or borers may augment this method.

Test pits are a preliminary to large-scale excavation, for the information they reveal is limited, at best. Some archaeologists will use them only outside the main area of a site, on the grounds that they will destroy critical strata. But carefully placed test pits can provide valuable insights into the stratigraphy and artifact content of a site before larger-scale excavation begins. They are also used to obtain samples from different areas of sites, such as shell middens, where dense concentrations of artifacts are found throughout the deposits. In such cases, test pits are excavated on a grid pattern, their position being determined by statistical sampling or by a regular pattern such as alternate squares. A set of pits laid out like a chess board is especially effective when

Figure 9.4   A classic example of vertical excavation from Sir Mortimer Wheeler's excavations at Maiden Castle, Dorset, England, before World War II. The recording posts on either side of the cutting and the worker in the trench give an idea of the scale of the dig.

Figure 9.5   A line of test pits at Quirigua, a Maya ceremonial center, laid out at 49.2-foot (15-m) intervals and aligned with the site grid.

excavating earthworks, for the walls of the pit separated by unexcavated blocks provide a continuous stratigraphic sequence across the fortification.

Vertical trenches have been widely used to excavate early village sites in southwestern Asia (Moore, 2000). They may also be used to obtain a cross section of a site threatened by destruction or to examine outlying structures near a village or a cemetery that has been dug on a large scale. Vertical excavations of this kind are almost always dug in the expectation that the most important information to come from them will be the record of layers in the walls of the trenches and the finds from them. But, clearly, the information to be obtained from such cuttings is of limited value compared with that from a larger excavation.

Horizontal (Area) Excavation. Horizontal, or area, excavation is done on a much larger scale than vertical excavation and is the next thing to total excavation. An area dig implies covering wide areas to recover building plans or the layout of entire settlements, even historic gardens (Figure 9.6; see also the chapter-opening photograph). The only sites that almost invariably are totally excavated are very small hunting camps, isolated huts, and burial mounds.

A good example of horizontal excavation comes from St. Augustine, Florida (Deagan, 1983; Milanich and Milbrath, 1989). St. Augustine was founded on the east coast of Florida by the Spanish conquistador Pedro Menéndez de Avilés in 1565. Sixteenth-century St. Augustine was plagued with floods, fire, and hurricanes and was plundered by Sir Francis Drake in 1586. He destroyed the town, which was a military

Figure 9.6 Horizontal excavation of an open area: a Middle Iroquoian longhouse c. A.D. 1400, at Crawford Lake, Ontario. The small stakes mark the house's wall posts; hearths and roof supports are found inside the house.

presidio and mission designed to protect Spanish treasure fleets passing through the Florida Straits. In 1702, the British attacked St. Augustine. The inhabitants took refuge in the Castillo de San Marcos (which still stands). The siege lasted six weeks before the attackers retreated, after burning the wooden buildings of the town to the ground. The colonists replaced them with masonry buildings as the town expanded in the first half of the eighteenth century.

Kathleen Deagan and a team of archaeologists investigated eighteenth-century and earlier St. Augustine on a systematic basis, combining historic preservation with archaeological excavation. Excavating the eighteenth-century town is a difficult process on many accounts, partly because the entire archaeological deposit for three centuries is only about 3 feet (0.9 m) deep at the most, and it has been much disturbed. The excavators have cleared and recorded dozens of barrel-lined wells. They have also used horizontal excavations to uncover the foundations of eighteenth-century houses built of tabby, a cementlike substance of oyster shells, lime, and sand. The foundations of oyster shell or tabby were laid in footing trenches in the shape of the intended house (Figure 9.7). Then the walls were added. The tabby floor soon wore out, so another layer of earth was added and a new floor was poured on top. Because the deposits outside the house had been disturbed, the artifacts from the foundations and floors were of great importance, and selective, horizontal excavation was the best way to uncover them.

Figure 9.7 Horizontal excavation at St. Augustine, Florida, showing oyster-shell house footings from an early eighteenth-century building.

The problems with horizontal digs are exactly the same as those with any excavation: stratigraphic control and accurate measurement. Area excavations imply exposure of large, open areas of ground to a depth of several feet. A complex network of walls or postholes may lie within the area to be investigated. Each feature is related to other structures, a relationship that must be carefully recorded so that the site can be interpreted correctly, especially if several periods of occupation are involved. If the entire area is uncovered, it is obviously difficult to measure the position of the structures in the middle of the trench, far from the walls at the excavation's edge. Better control of measurement and recording can be achieved by using a system that gives a network of vertical stratigraphic sections across the area to be excavated. This work is often done by laying out a grid of square or rectangular excavation units, with walls several yards thick between one square and the next (Figure 9.8). Such areas may average 12 feet (3.6 m) square or larger. As Figure 9.8 shows, this system allows stratigraphic control of large areas.

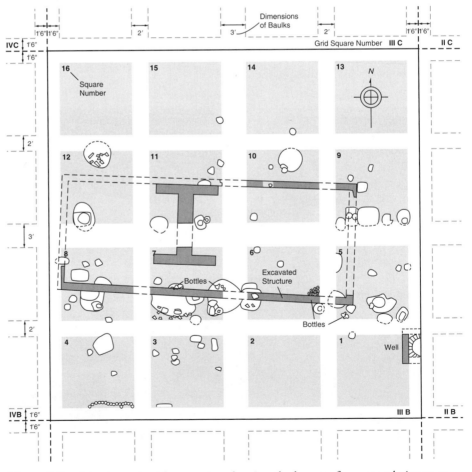

Figure 9.8   A horizontal-grid excavation showing the layout of squares relative to an excavated structure at Colonial Williamsburg, Virginia.

Figure 9.9   Using a backhoe to strip sterile overburden at the Lohmann site, Illinois. The mechanical stripping is followed by manual scraping.

Large-scale excavation with grids is extremely expensive and time-consuming; it is also difficult to use where the ground is irregular. However, grid excavation has been employed with great success at many sites, being used to uncover structures, town plans, and fortifications. Many area digs are "open excavations," in which large tracts of a site are exposed layer by layer without a grid (see Figure 9.1). Electronic surveying methods have solved many recording problems on large horizontal excavations, but the need for tight stratigraphic control remains.

Stripping off overlying areas of no archaeological significance to expose buried subsurface features is another type of large-scale excavation. Stripping is especially useful when a site is buried only a short distance below the surface and the structures are preserved in the form of postholes and other discolorations in the soil. Almost invariably, excavators use earthmoving machinery to clear large areas of topsoil, especially on CRM projects, a task that requires both skilled operators and a clear knowledge of the stratigraphy and soil texture (Figure 9.9).

Horizontal excavation depends, of course, on precise stratigraphic control. It is normally combined with vertical trenches, which provide the information necessary for careful and accurate peeling off of successive horizontal layers.

Tools of the Trade

Indiana Jones went into the field with gangs of laborers armed with shovels; and, of course, he had his favorite bullwhip. Today's archaeologist uses more refined tools of the trade.

Earthmoving equipment is an essential part of CRM excavations and large digs. Such equipment is now widely used, especially when sites are threatened with destruction and time is short. Everything depends, however, on the archaeologist's close supervision of the operation. An expert operator can work wonders with a backhoe, front-end loader, removing even a few centimeters of soil with a delicate touch.

The traditional archaeological symbol is the spade, which has a flat back and a straight edge and is used for cleaning walls. Shovels, with their scooplike shape, are used for piling up earth in a trench preparatory to its being examined; they have innumerable applications in cleaning straight edges and tidying trenches, and they are the principal working tool of the archaeologist when much ground is to be uncovered. Systematic shoveling by teams of excavators is an excellent way of removing layers of plow soil to expose the archaeological deposits below. This works especially well when the horizon beneath the plow soil contains traces of postholes and dwellings, such as is often the case, for example, with early farming settlements in Europe (Grygiel and Bogucki, 1997).

Tools for loosening soil are the mattock, the pick, and the fork. The mattock and the pick may be considered together because they are variants on the same type of tool; when used with care, they are delicate gauges of soil texture, for softer earth may come from pit fillings and other structures. The traditional Mediterranean excavation used teams of pickmen, shovelers, and basket carriers to remove the soil and dump it off the site.

The most common archaeological tool is the diamond-shaped trowel, its straight edges and tip having innumerable uses: it can ease soil from a delicate specimen; the edges can scrape a feature in sandy soil into higher relief; and, as an instrument of stratigraphic recording, it can trace a scarcely visible stratum line or barely discernible feature. It is also used for clearing postholes and other minor work, so much so that it is rarely out of a digger's hand on small sites.

Brushes are very useful, especially for dry sites. The most commonly used is the household brush, which has fairly coarse bristles; it can be held by the handle or by the bristles. Wielded with short strokes, it effectively cleans objects found in dry, hard soil. The excavator uses various paintbrushes for more delicate jobs. The one-inch or half-inch domestic paintbrush has wide application in cleaning animal bones and coarser specimens. Fine camel hair artists' brushes are best for most delicate bones, beads, and fragile ironwork.

Small tools, some improvised on the site, aid in clearing delicate finds. Six-inch nails may be filed to a point and used for delicate cleaning jobs on bones and other fragile artifacts. The needle is another tool used to clear soil from such delicate parts of skeletons as the eye sockets and cheekbones. One of the most useful digging tools is the dental pick, available in a variety of shapes.

Screens are essential tools because many finds, such as coins, glass beads, shells, small tacks, nails, and other artifacts, are minuscule. Most deposits from sites where small artifacts are likely to occur are laboriously sifted through fine screens with openings of one-quarter to one-eighth inch or smaller. Flotation techniques are also widely used (Chapter 13).

Doing Archaeology

A Personal Excavation Tool Kit

I (BMF) always like to take my own small tools on an excavation or survey, simply so that I always have familiar equipment on hand. Here are the contents of my tool kit, which live in a small backpack:

- *Diamond-shaped pointing trowel,* the true archaeologist's trademark. The Marshalltown brand is widely used in the United States, with a one-piece blade and stem. Refuse all cheap substitutes. The pointing trowel is a highly versatile tool for uncovering small items or clearing soil near small features such as hearths. It is also a superb scraping tool in expert hands, ideal for tracing the dark outlines of postholes or complex stratigraphic layers in a trench wall. A holster for your trowel is convenient.
- *A small whisk broom* for cleaning up.
- *An ice pick or small set of dental picks* for delicate excavation work, such as cleaning bones in the soil.

Some excavators prefer handmade bamboo picks, said to be more delicate on bone.

- *Three or four paintbrushes* of 2-inch (50-mm) width or less are essential for fine cleaning.
- *A 25-foot steel measuring tape (or metric equivalent).* I always carry my own because the excavation tapes are always in use. Most digs are now metric, so you should come equipped accordingly.
- *Pencils, erasers, permanent ink pens* for note taking and marking artifacts.
- *A personal notebook.*
- *Ziplock plastic bags of various sizes.* Never be without them!
- Don't forget a broad-brimmed hat, sunscreen, sunglasses, and good, sturdy boots, as well as gloves and knee pads if you feel a need for them. If hardhats are required, the excavation will provide them. Some Band-Aids are advisable.
- A light computer notebook is an increasingly commonplace, if relatively expensive, convenience.

Surveying tools normally include lines or metal tapes, plumb bobs, string, spirit levels, drawing boards, drawing instruments, a plane table, and a surveyor's level and compass—all essential for accurate recording of site plans and sections for setting up the archaeological archive. Increasingly, fieldworkers use laser surveying equipment tied into a laptop computer, a technology that enables the production of three-dimensional plans, even architectural renderings of buildings.

Laptop computers are widely used instead of conventional notebooks for site records and diaries. Some excavators have gone as far as to link all site supervisors and specialists to a site computer network, to encourage dialogue among them.

Storage containers are vital on any excavation to pack and transport the finds to the laboratory, as well as to store them permanently. Paper and plastic bags are essential for pottery, animal bones, and other small finds; vegetal remains and other special items may require much more delicate packaging. Cardboard cartons, supermarket bags, even large oil drums can be used for storing finds.

The Process of Archaeological Excavation

Archaeological excavation is an extremely precise, usually slow-moving process that is far more than mere digging. The actual mechanics of archaeological excavation are best learned in the field. There is an art in the skillful use of the trowel, brush, and other implements to clear archaeological deposits. Stripping off layers exposed in a trench requires a sensitive eye for changing soil colors and textures, especially when excavating postholes and other features; and a few hours of practical experience are worth thousands of words of instructional text.

The excavator's aim should be to explain the origin of every layer and feature encountered in the site, whether natural or humanly made. It is not enough just to excavate and describe the site; one must also explain how the site was formed. This process is achieved by removing and recording the superimposed layers of the site one by one.

The fundamental approach for digging any site usually involves one of two basic methods, but both can be used on the same site:

- *Excavation by Visible Layers.* This method involves removing every visible layer in the site separately (Figure 9.10). This slow-moving approach is commonly used in cave sites, which often have complex stratigraphy, and also on open sites such as bison kills on the North American Plains, where bone layers and other levels can be distinguished relatively easily in preliminary stratigraphic test pits.
- *Excavation by Arbitrary Levels.* Here the soil is removed in standard-sized arbitrary levels, which vary in size depending on the nature of the site (from 3 to 12 inches (5 to 20 cm) is normal). This approach is used when there is little discernible stratigraphy or variation in the occupation layers; each level is screened carefully to recover artifacts, animal bones, seeds, and other small finds.

Figure 9.10   General view of a major cutting at Cuello, a stratified Maya site in Belize. The labels mark the identified layers.

Ideally, of course, one would like to excavate every site according to natural stratigraphic layers, but in many instances, such as California coastal shell middens and some large occupation mounds, one simply cannot see the natural layers, if there ever were any. The deposits are often too fine or ashy to form discrete layers, especially when riffled by wind or trampled by later occupants or cattle. I (BMF) have excavated a series of African farming villages up to 12 feet (3.6 m) deep that were most logically excavated in arbitrary levels, for the few visible occupation layers were marked by obvious concentrations of wall fragments from collapsed houses. Most levels merely yielded counts of potsherds, occasional other artifacts, and numerous fragmentary animal bones.

Deciding Where to Dig

All archaeological excavation begins with making a precise surface survey and an accurate topographic map of the site. A grid is then laid over the site. The surface survey and the collections of artifacts made as part of it help determine the working hypotheses that the archaeologist uses as a basis for deciding where to dig.

The first decision to be made is whether to carry out a total or a selective excavation. Which one depends on the size of the site, its possible imminent destruction, the hypotheses to be tested, and the time and money available. Most excavations are selective. Anyone contemplating a selective dig is faced with choosing the areas of the site to be dug. The choice can be clear-cut and nonprobabilistic, or it can be based on complex sampling approaches. A selective excavation to determine the age of one of the stone uprights at Stonehenge (see Figure 2.2) obviously will be at the foot of the stones. But excavation of a shell midden with no surface features may be determined by sampling and selection of random grid squares that are excavated to obtain artifact samples.

In many cases, an excavation can involve both probabilistic and nonprobabilistic choices. For the Maya ceremonial center at Tikal in Guatemala (see Figure 15.2), the archaeologists were eager to learn something about the hundreds of mounds that lay in the hinterland around the main ceremonial precincts (Coe, 2002). These mounds extended at least 6 miles (10 km) from the center of the site and were identified along four strips of carefully surveyed ground extending out from Tikal. Because, obviously, excavation of every mound and structure identified on the surface was impossible, a test-pit program was designed to collect random samples of datable pottery so that the chronological span of the occupation could be established. By using a well-designed sampling strategy, the investigators were able to select about a hundred mound structures for testing and obtain the data they sought.

The choice of where to dig can also be determined by logistical considerations, such as access to the trench, which may be a problem in small caves; by the time and funds available; or, regrettably, often by the imminent destruction of part of a site that is close to industrial activity or road construction. Ideally, though, the archaeologist will dig where the results will be maximal and the chances of acquiring data to test working hypotheses are best.

Stratigraphy and Sections

We touched briefly on archaeological stratigraphy in Chapter 7, where we said that the basis of all excavation is the properly recorded and interpreted stratigraphic profile (R. Wheeler, 1954). A section through a site gives a picture of the accumulated soils and occupation levels that constitute the ancient and modern history of the locality. Obviously, anyone recording stratigraphy needs to know as much about the history of the natural processes that the site has undergone since abandonment as about the formation of the ancient site itself (Stein, 1987, 1992). The soils that cover archaeological finds have undergone transformations that have radically affected the ways in which artifacts were preserved or moved around in the soil. Burrowing animals, later human activity, erosion, wind action, grazing cattle—all can modify superimposed layers in drastic ways (Schiffer, 1987).

Archaeological stratigraphy is usually much more complicated than geological layering, for the phenomena observed are much more localized and the effects of human behavior tend to be intensive and often involve constant reuse of the same location (Villa and Courtin, 1983). Subsequent activity can radically alter the context of artifacts, structures, and other finds. A village site can be leveled and then reoccupied by a new community that digs the foundations of its structures into the lower levels and sometimes even reuses the building materials of earlier generations. Postholes and storage pits, as well as burials, are sunk deep into older strata; their presence can be detected only by changes in soil color or the artifact content.

Here are some factors to be taken into account when interpreting stratigraphy (E. C. Harris and others, 1993):

- Human activities at the times in the past when the site was occupied and their effects, if any, on earlier occupations.
- Human activities, such as plowing and industrial activity, subsequent to final abandonment of the site (Wood and Johnson, 1978).
- Natural processes of deposition and erosion at the time of prehistoric occupation. Cave sites were often abandoned when the walls were shattered by frost and fragments of the rock face were showering down on the interior (Courty and others, 1993).
- Natural phenomena that have modified the stratigraphy after abandonment of the site (floods, tree uprooting, animal burrowing).

Interpreting archaeological stratigraphy involves reconstructing the depositional history of the site and then analyzing the significance of the natural and occupation levels observed. This analysis means distinguishing between types of human activity; between deposits that result from rubbish accumulation, architectural remains, and storage pits; between activity areas and other artifact patterns; and between human-caused and natural effects.

Philip Barker, an English archaeologist and expert excavator, advocated a combined horizontal and vertical excavation for recording archaeological stratigraphy (Figure 9.11). He pointed out that a vertical profile gives a view of stratigraphy in the vertical plane only (1995). Many important features appear in the section as a fine line and are decipherable only in the horizontal plane. The principal purpose of a stratigraphic

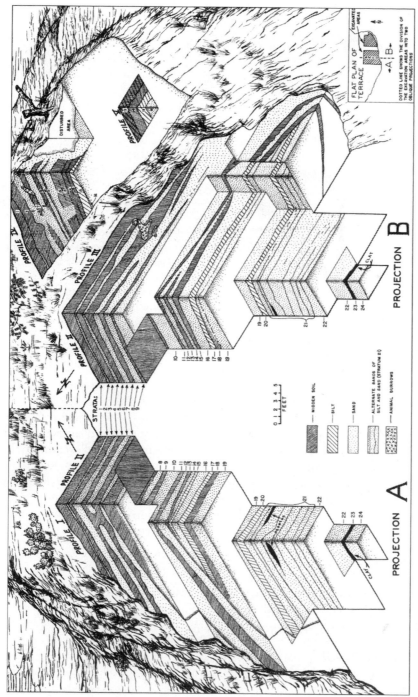

Figure 9.11 Three-dimensional stratigraphic profile from the Devil's Mouth site, Armistad Reservoir, Texas. The complex deposits are correlated from one pit to the next.

Source: Le Roy Johnson, Jr., *Devil's Mouth Site, 1964.* Department of Anthropology, University of Texas at Austin.

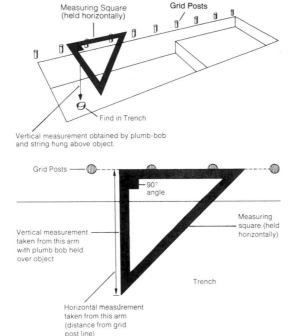

Figure 9.12   Three-dimensional recording the traditional way. (*top*) Using a measuring square. (*bottom*) A close view of the square from above. A horizontal measurement is taken along the edge, perpendicular to the grid post line; the vertical measurement, from that arm with a plumb bob. Electronic instruments are now commonly used for three-dimensional recording.

profile is to record the information for posterity so that later observers have an accurate impression of how it was formed. Because stratigraphy demonstrates relationships— among sites and structures, artifacts, and natural layers—Barker preferred cumulative recording of stratigraphy, which enables the archaeologist to record layers in section and in plan at the same time. Such recording requires extremely skillful excavation. Various modifications of this technique are used in both Europe and North America.

All archaeological stratigraphy is three-dimensional; that is to say, it involves observations in both the vertical and horizontal planes (Figure 9.12). The ultimate objective of archaeological excavation is to record the three-dimensional relationships throughout a site, for these are the relationships that provide the provenance.

Archaeological Recording

Archaeological records come in three broad categories: written records, photographs and digital images, and measured drawings. Notebooks or computer files are an important part of record keeping.

Written Records.   An archaeologist maintains a number of notebooks throughout the excavation, including the site diary or daybook. The site diary is where he or she records all events at the site—the amount of work done, the daily schedule, the number of people on the digging team, and any labor problems. Dimensions of all sites and trenches and all observed data are recorded. The site diary purports to be a complete record of the procedures and proceedings of the excavation. It is more than just an aid to the fallible memory of the excavator; it is a permanent record of the dig for future generations of scientists who may return to the site to amplify the original findings. For this reason, site records need to be recorded digitally and on archivally stable paper. A clear distinction is made between observation and interpretation. Any interpretations or ideas on the interpretations, even those considered and then discarded, are meticulously recorded in the site diary or on a computer file. Important finds and significant stratigraphic details are also noted carefully, as is much apparently insignificant information that may later prove to be vital in the laboratory.

Site Plans. Site plans may vary from a simple contour plan for a burial mound or occupation midden to a complex plan of an entire town or of a complicated series of structures (Barker, 1995). Accurate plans are important, for they provide a record not only of the site's features but also of the measurement recording grid set up before excavation to provide a framework for the trenching. The advent of computer-aided mapping (CAM) programs has made the production of accurate plans much easier in expert hands. For example, Douglas Gann (1994) has produced a three-dimensional AutoCad map of Homol'ovi Pueblo near Winslow, Arizona, which is a far more vivid reconstruction of the 150-room pueblo than any two-dimensional map. Combined with animations made with visualization software, it enables someone unfamiliar with the site to envisage what it must have been like when in use.

Stratigraphic records can be drawn in a vertical plane, or they can be drawn axonometrically using axes. Any form of stratigraphic record is complex and requires not only skill in drawing but also considerable interpretative ability. The difficulty of recording varies with the site's complexity and with its stratigraphic conditions. Often, the different occupation levels, or geological events, are clearly delineated in the stratigraphic sections. On other sites, the layers may be much more complex and less visible, especially in dry climates where the soil's aridity has leached out colors. Some archaeologists have used scaled photographs or surveying instruments to record sections, the latter being essential with large sections, like those through city ramparts.

Three-Dimensional Recording. Three-dimensional recording is the recording of artifacts and structures in time and space. The provenance of archaeological finds is recorded with reference to the site grid. Three-dimensional recording is carried out with an electronic recording device or with tapes and plumb bobs. It assumes particular importance on sites where artifacts are recorded in their original positions or on those where different periods in the construction of a building are being sorted out.

High technology is adding new accuracy to three-dimensional recording. By using theodolites equipped with laser beams, an excavation team can cut recording times dramatically. Many excavators now use recording devices and software that instantly convert their digitized records into contour plans or three-dimensional representations. They can call up distributions of individually plotted artifacts almost instantaneously, to the point that the data can be used to plan the next day's excavation.

Grids, units, forms, and labels are the backbone of all recording efforts. Site grids are normally laid out with painted pegs and strings stretched over the trenches when recording is necessary. Small-scale recording of complex features may involve using an even smaller grid that covers but one square of the entire site grid.

```
┌─────────────────────────────────┐
│              Site               │
└─────────────────────────────────┘
```

Tunneling at Copán, Honduras

Tunneling is rarely used in archaeological excavation, except in structures such as Maya pyramids, where the history of the structure can be deciphered only by tunneling into the otherwise inaccessible interior. Slow-going and expensive, tunneling is extremely difficult and presents complex problems in interpreting stratigraphic layers, which are both on either side of the trench and on each wall.

The most extensive tunneling project of recent times is that used to study the sequence of Maya temples that make up the great Acropolis at Copán, Honduras (Figure 9.13) (Fash, 1991). Here, the excavators tunneled into an eroded slope of the pyramid worn away by the nearby Río Copán. They were aided in their task by deciphered Maya glyphs, which date this political and religious precinct to between A.D. 420 and 820. The archaeologists followed ancient plaza surfaces and other features buried under feet of compacted earth and rock fill. They used computer-based surveying stations to create three-dimensional representations of changing building plans.

Maya rulers had a passion for commemorating their architectural achievements and the rituals that accompanied them with elaborate glyphs. The tunnelers had a valuable reference point in an inscription on a ceremonial altar called Altar Q, which provides a textual guide to the ruling dynasty at Copán, sponsored by the sixteenth ruler, Yax Pac. The glyphs on Altar Q record the arrival of the founder Kinich Yak K'uk Mo' in A.D. 426 and portray the subsequent rulers who embellished and expanded the great city.

Fortunately for the archaeologists, the Acropolis is a compact royal precinct, which made it relatively easy to decipher the sequence of buildings and rulers. In the end, the tunneling project linked individual structures with the recorded history of Copán's sixteen rulers. The earliest building belonged to the reign of Copán's second ruler, but the buildings fall into three separate political, ritual, and residential complexes. By A.D. 540, these complexes were linked into a single Acropolis. Just unraveling the complex histories of all the demolished buildings has taken years of

At Boomplaas cave in South Africa, Hilary Deacon (1979) used a precise grid laid out using the cave roof to record the position of minute artifacts, features, and environmental data (Figure 9.14, p. 227). Similar grids have been erected over underwater wrecks in the Mediterranean (Bass, 1966), although laser recording is gradually replacing this technique. The various squares in the grid and the levels of the site are designated by grid numbers, which provide the means for identifying the location of finds, as well as a basis for recording them. The labels attached to each bag or marked on the find bear the grid square numbers, which are then recorded in the site notebook.

Analysis, Interpretation, and Publication

The process of archaeological excavation ends with filling in the trenches and transporting the finds and site records to the laboratory. The archaeologist retires from the field with a complete record of the excavations and with the data needed to test the

tunneling and stratigraphic analysis. Today, we know the core of the Acropolis evolved from a small masonry structure decorated with brightly painted murals, perhaps the residence of the founder Kinich Yax K'uk Mo' himself. His successors elaborated the ceremonial complex beyond recognition.

Copán's Acropolis is an extraordinary chronicle of Maya royal power and dynastic politics, rooted firmly in a complex spiritual world revealed by deciphered glyphs. It is also a triumph of careful excavation and stratigraphic interpretation under very demanding conditions.

Figure 9.13   Artist Tatiana Prokouriakoff's reconstruction of the central precincts at Copán, Honduras.

hypotheses that were formulated before going into the field. But with this step, the job is far from finished; in fact, the work has hardly begun. The next stage in the research process is analyzing the finds, a topic covered in Chapters 10–17. Once the analysis has been completed, interpretation of the site can begin (Chapter 3).

In these days of high printing costs, it is impossible to publish in complete detail the finds from any but the smallest sites. Fortunately, many data retrieval systems enable us to store data on CD-ROM and microfilm so that they will be available to the specialists who need them. Digital publishing on the World Wide Web is also becoming commonplace, but there are interesting issues about just how permanent cyberarchives actually are.

Beyond publication, the archaeologist has two final obligations. The first is to place the finds and site records in a convenient repository where they will be safe and readily accessible to later generations. The second is to make the results available to a general audience as well as fellow professionals.

Doing Archaeology

Site Records

I (BMF) keep all kinds of notebooks on an excavation, of which the following are all-important:

A day-to-day journal of the excavation, which begins the day we reach camp and ends when we pull out at the end of the dig. This is a general diary in which I write about the progress of the excavation, record general thoughts and impressions, and write spontaneously about the work I am engaged in. This is also a personal account in which I will write about conversations, discussions, and other people-related matters, such as theoretical disagreements between members of the research team. This journal is absolutely invaluable when you are in the laboratory or writing up the excavation for publication, for it contains many forgotten details, first impressions, and passing thoughts that would otherwise not have been set down. I use a journal for all my research, even when visiting sites. For example, my journal reminded me about details of my visit to the excavations at the Maya center at Xunantunich in Belize that had escaped my memory.

At Çatalhöyük, archaeologist Ian Hodder (1999) not only asks his colleagues to keep daily diaries but also to put them on the site computer network, so that everyone knows what other people are thinking, and also as a basis for continual discussion about individual trenches, finds, and excavation problems. From my own experience, I suspect that this is a wonderful way to ensure that theoretical dialogue keeps pace with practical recording and actual excavation.

The site notebook is the formal record of the excavations, which contains technical details of the dig, information on excavation and sampling methods, stratigraphic data, records of unusual finds, and major features, among other things. This is a much more organized document, really a logbook of the day-to-day operation of the dig. The site notebook is also the entry point into all site records and is cross-referenced accordingly. I usually use loose-leaf notebooks, so that I can insert single-page forms for recording features and other important discoveries at the correct place in the book. Your site notebook should be compiled on archival paper, as it is the permanent record of the excavation.

The logistical notebook is self-evident, the place where I record mundane details of accounts, key addresses, and other data relating to the administration and domestic life of the excavation.

When I first started in archaeology, everyone used pencils and paper. Many excavators now use laptops and send their notes and data back to base by modem. Using computers has the advantage of instant duplication of vital information and gives you the ability to meld your notes with survey data and other materials while still on-site. The Çatalhöyük excavations are networked for free interchange of data, something impossible with paper and pencil. If my excavation recordings are computer-based, I am very careful to back up everything every quarter hour or so, and to print out a hard copy at the end of the day, to guard against the kind of catastrophic computer crash that can destroy weeks of work in seconds. If using pencil and paper, I photocopy all the site records as soon as possible and put the originals in a safe to guard against loss.

Figure 9.14 Meticulous recording of an excavation at Boomplaas cave in South Africa, where the researchers were recovering dozens of transitory Stone Age occupation horizons and fragile environmental data. The excavation removed tiny layers of deposit, recording the positions of individual artifacts with the aid of a grid suspended from the cave roof.

Special Excavation Problems

Not all excavation consists of sifting through shell mounds or uncovering huge palaces. A great deal of archaeological fieldwork is dull and monotonous, but occasionally archaeologists face unexpected and exciting challenges that require special excavation techniques. Imagine being confronted with a royal grave, such as that of Tutankhamun, which took Howard Carter nearly ten years to excavate (see Figure 1.2), or with the incredible complexities of the burials of the lords of Sipán (see Figure 1.4). In both sites, the excavators had to find special techniques for dealing with these fragile discoveries. Let us examine some of the most common problems in excavation.

Fragile Objects

Narratives of nineteenth-century excavation abound with accounts of spectacular and delicate discoveries that crumbled to dust on exposure to the air. Regrettably, similar discoveries are still made today, but many spectacular recoveries of fragile artifacts have been made. In almost every find, the archaeologist responsible has had to use great ingenuity, often with limited preservation materials on hand.

Leonard Woolley faced very difficult recovery problems when he excavated the Royal Cemetery at Ur-of-the-Chaldees in the 1920s (Woolley, 1954). In one place, he recovered an offering stand of wood, gold, and silver, portraying a he-goat with his front legs on the branches of a thicket, by pouring paraffin wax over the scattered remains. Later, he rebuilt the stand in the laboratory to a close approximation of the original.

Conservation of archaeological finds has become a highly specialized field that covers every form of find, from textiles to leather, human skin, and basketry (Cronyn, 1990). Many conservation efforts, such as those used to preserve the Danish bog corpses, can take years to complete (see Figure 4.3) (Glob, 1969). One of the largest conservation efforts was mounted at Ozette, Washington, where the sheer volume of waterlogged wooden artifacts threatened to overwhelm the excavators (see Figure 4.4). The finds that needed treatment ranged from tiny fishhooks to entire planks. A large conservation laboratory was set up in Neah Bay, where the finds were processed after transportation from the site. Many objects were left to soak in polyethylene glycol to replace the water that had penetrated the wood cells, a treatment that takes years for large objects. The results of this major conservation effort can be seen in the Neah Bay Museum, where many of the artifacts are preserved (Kirk, 1974).

Burials

Human remains can be encountered either as isolated finds or in the midst of a settlement site. Some projects are devoted to excavating an entire cemetery. In all cases in which graves are excavated, the burial and its associated grave, funerary furniture, and ornamentation are considered as a single excavation unit or grave lot.

Human skeletons are a valuable source of information on prehistoric populations. The bones can be used to identify the sex and age of a burial, as well as to study ancient diseases and, in some cases, diets. A whole series of new techniques, including DNA analysis, are revolutionizing studies of prehistoric humans (Larsen, 1997; Stirland, 1987).

Excavation of burials is a difficult and routine task that must be performed with care because of the delicacy and often bad state of the bones. The record of the bones' position and the placement of the grave goods and body ornaments is as important as the association of the burial, for the archaeological objective is reconstructing burial customs as much as establishing chronology (Simon, 1997; T. White, 1999). Although the Maya lords of Mesoamerica were sometimes buried under great pyramids, as at Palenque, where the Lord Pacal lay under the Temple of the Inscriptions (Coe, 2002), most burials are normally located by means of a simple surface feature, such as a gravestone or a pile of stones, or through an accidental discovery during excavation. Once the grave outline has been found, the skeleton is carefully exposed from above. The first part of the skeleton to be identified will probably be the skull or one of the limb bones. The main outline of the burial is then traced before the delicate backbone, feet, and finger bones are uncovered. The greatest care is taken not to displace the bones or any of the ornaments or grave goods that surround them (Stirland, 1987). Normally, the undersurfaces of the bones are left in the soil so that the skeleton may be recorded photographically before removal (Figure 9.15). Either the burial is removed bone by bone, or it is removed as a single unit to the laboratory, where it is cleaned at leisure. Removal of the entire unit is expensive and is done only when a skeleton is of outstanding scientific importance.

Figure 9.15 A classic Maya collective tomb at Gualan in the Motagua Valley of Guatemala. Note the clean excavation, the carefully brushed skeletons, and the stone lining of the tomb.

Some burials are deposited in funerary chambers so elaborate that the contents of the tomb may reveal information not only on the funeral rites but also, as in the Sumerian royal burials at Ur, on the social order of the royal court (Chapter 16). The great royal tombs of the Shang civilization of northern China are an example of complex tombs, where careful excavation made possible recording of many chariot features that otherwise would have been lost (Barnes, 1999). The shaft, axle, and lower parts of the chariot wheels were visible only as discolored areas in the ground.

Excavation of American Indian burials has generated furious political controversy in recent years, with Native groups arguing that it is both illegal and unethical to dig up even the prehistoric dead. Reburial and repatriation legislation now restricts the excavation of ancient burials, and many collections are now being returned to their historic owners for reburial (Bray and Killion, 1994; Powell and others, 1993; see also Chapter 18). In some states, such as California, it is now illegal to disturb ancient Native American burial grounds.

Structures and Pits

Open excavations are normally used to uncover structures of considerable size (Barker, 1995). Grids allow stratigraphic control over the building site, especially over the study of successive occupation stages. Many such structures may have been built of perishable materials such as wood or matting. Wooden houses are normally recognized by the

Doing Archaeology

Some Problems in Archaeological Excavation

Archaeological excavation involves a wide range of sites and different research problems, only a few of which we can cover in these pages. Figure 9.16 illustrates how an excavator dates a structure or building by its associated artifacts. A brick wall was built in a foundation trench that was filled with brick dust and clay. Someone dropped a coin dating to 1723 into the clay as the trench was being filled. Obviously, then, the building of which the wall forms a part dates to no earlier than 1723.

The excavation of individual features like storage pits involves careful dissection of the pit fill, as shown in Figure 9.17. A double storage

pit at Maiden Castle, Dorset, England, was cut into the chalk subsoil; the fill was identified by its dark and soft texture and then sectioned and removed.

The same principles of meticulous vertical and horizontal excavation are applied to all manner of sites, among them some of the earliest human kill sites and camps in the world. The FxJj50 site at Koobi Fora in northern Kenya (Figure 9.18), an early hominid site, is a scatter of broken animal bones and stone artifacts more than 2 million years old. The horizontal excavations revealed associations between the stone tools and bones. Every

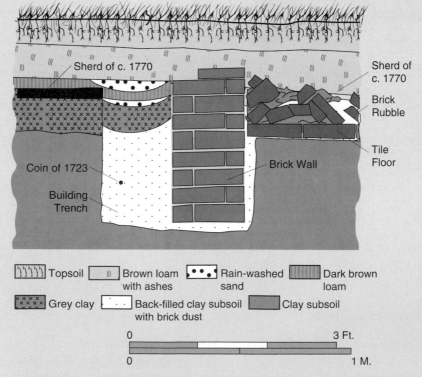

Figure 9.16   Dating construction of a building by its associated artifacts and stratigraphy.

Figure 9.17 A double storage pit at Maiden Castle, Dorset, England, that was cut into the chalk subsoil.

Figure 9.18 Excavation at the FxJj50 site, Koobi Fora, Kenya.

find, however small, was plotted in position before removal, to ensure recording of the precise content of every object on the site.

Shell middens can reveal important information on water's edge adaptations. A midden is a dump of remains and occupation debris, including shells, fish bones, ash, and occasional artifacts, piled up over many years. The Galatea Bay shell midden near Auckland, North Island, New Zealand, excavated by Wilfred Shawcross in the 1960s, is a classic example of how to dig such a site (Figure 9.19). Galatea Bay yielded shells, fish bones, and artifacts used for processing mollusks, as well as evidence for seasonal occupation, from fish remains. On larger shell middens, many archaeologists use sampling methods to test the dense concentration of shells and other materials.

Excavations through entire city mounds or large structures like temples and forts require complex vertical excavations, like that in Figure 9.20, which shows a stratigraphic profile through the ramparts of the ancient city of Harappa in the Indus Valley, Pakistan, dating to about 2000 B.C.

Whatever the size and complexity of the excavation—whether it be a CRM excavation conducted in advance of road construction or a multiseason investigation of a Mesopotamian city or Maya center—it is based on careful recording, so that no artifact, no structure, not even the smallest of food remains is taken out of its context in time and space. The archaeologist's archives, drawings, notes, photographs, and the final report on the site represent the only permanent record. Archaeological excavation, even in its most refined approaches, is destruction of a finite resource.

Figure 9.19 Galatea Bay shell midden, North Island, New Zealand.

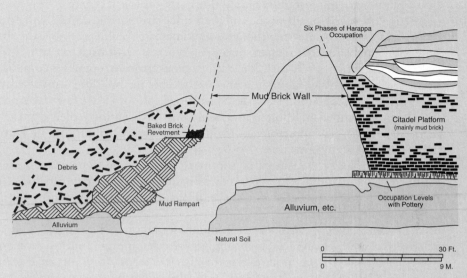

Figure 9.20a   Stratigraphic profile through the ramparts of the ancient city of Harappa in the Indus Valley, Pakistan.

Source: A. M. Rosen, *Cities of Clay*. Copyright © 1986 University of Chicago Press. Reprinted by permission of University of Chicago Press.

Figure 9.20b   Photograph of the actual excavation, a deep probe into the depths of the city's citadel. The right of the top illustration is the back of the back of this picture.

postholes of the wall timbers and, sometimes, foundation trenches. Clay walls collapse into a pile when a hut is burned or falls down; thus the wall clay may bear impressions of matting, sticks, or thatch. Stone and mud-brick structures are often better preserved, especially if mortar was used, although sometimes later builders remove the stone, and only foundation trenches remain. Stratigraphic cross sections across walls give an insight into the structure's history. The dating of most stone structures is complicated, especially when successive rebuilding or occupation of the building is involved. Some of the most spectacular buildings in the archaeological record leave few traces on the surface. Figure 9.6 shows an Iroquois longhouse that was identified solely from subsurface markings in the soil. Numerous longhouses from early farming sites in Europe have been identified in the same way.

The pueblos of the American Southwest offer another type of problem in excavation. The many rooms of the pueblos contain complicated deposits full of occupation debris and many artifacts. Such assemblages can be used to identify the activities carried out in different spaces.

Storage and rubbish pits are commonly found on archaeological sites and may reach several meters in depth. Their contents furnish important information on dietary habits, data gleaned from food residues or caches of seeds. Trash pits are even more informative. Garbage pits and privies at Colonial Williamsburg have yielded a host of esoteric finds, including wax seals from documents that were used as toilet tissue (Noël Hume, 1983). Some historic pits can be dated from military buttons and other finds.

Storage and trash pits are normally identified by circular discolorations in the soil. The contents are then cross-sectioned, and the associated finds are analyzed as an associated unit. Large pits, which may contain thousands of seeds and other informative materials, are excavated with particular care.

Postholes are normally associated with houses and other such structures. The posts they once contained were buried in holes that were dug larger than the base of the post itself. When the structure was abandoned, the post might have been left to rot, might have been removed, or might have been burned or cut off. The traces each of these outcomes leaves in the ground differ sharply and can be identified with careful excavation. Sometimes it is possible to find fragments of the post or of the charcoal from its burning, which enables archaeologists to identify the type of wood used.

Each archaeological site offers challenges to the investigator, including preservation, recording, or interpretation. Though individual methods may vary from site to site, from area to area, and even along national boundaries, the fundamental objective is the same: to recover and record data from below the ground as systematically and scientifically as possible.

Summary

Excavation is a primary way in which archaeologists acquire subsurface data about the past. Modern archaeologists tend to carry out as little excavation as possible, however, because digging archaeological sites destroys a finite resource—the archaeological record.

Modern excavations are often conducted by multidisciplinary research teams made up of specialists from several disciplines who work together on a carefully formulated research design.

All archaeological excavation is destruction of a finite resource. Accurate methods for planning, recording, and observation are essential. Today, excavation is the strategy of last resort, as it is potentially destructive.

The Koster site in Illinois, where the excavators devised a sophisticated data flow system to keep their research design up-to-date, illustrates the essential details of a research design.

Sites can be excavated totally or, as is more common, selectively. Vertical excavation is used to test stratigraphy and to make deep probes of archaeological deposits. Test pits, often combined with various sampling methods, are dug to give an overall impression of an unexcavated site before major digging begins. Horizontal or area excavation is used to uncover far wider areas and especially to excavate site layouts and buildings.

The process of archaeological excavation begins with a precise site survey and establishment of a site recording grid. A research design is formulated, and hypotheses are developed for testing. Placement of trenches is determined by locating likely areas or by sampling methods. Excavation involves not only digging but also recording of stratigraphy and the provenances of finds, as well as observations of the processes that led to the site's formation.

Careful stratigraphic observation in three dimensions is the basis of all good excavation and is used to demonstrate relationships among layers and between layers and artifacts.

Excavation is followed by analysis and interpretation and, finally, publication of the finds to provide a permanent record of the work carried out.

Among the special excavation problems are the recovery of fragile objects, human skeletons, and structures and pits.

Key Terms

horizontal (area)
  excavation

selective excavation
test pit (*sondage*)

total excavation
vertical excavation

Guide to Further Reading

BARKER, PHILIP. 1986. *Understanding Archaeological Excavation.* London: Batsford. An expert guide to excavation; strong British orientation.

BRAY, TAMARA L., and THOMAS W. KILLION, eds. 1994. *Reckoning with the Dead: The Larsen Bay Repatriation and the Smithsonian Institution.* Washington, DC: Smithsonian Institution Press. A superb discussion of a controversial case study in repatriation, which includes valuable information on the Native American perspective.

DANCEY, WILLIAM S. 1981. *Archaeological Field Methods: An Introduction.* Minneapolis, MN: Burgess. An excellent brief survey of American fieldwork approaches.

HESTER, THOMAS R., HARRY J. SHAFER, and KENNETH L. FEDER. 1997. *Field Methods in Archaeology.* 7th ed. Mountain View, CA: Mayfield. A volume of essays on all aspects of archaeological fieldwork for students.

HODDER, IAN. 1999. *The Archaeological Process.* Oxford: Blackwell. Hodder insists that excavation and theory are closely intermingled. A thought-provoking and useful perspective on the subject, which every excavator should read.

JOUKOWSKY, MARTHA. 1981. *Complete Manual of Field Archaeology.* Englewood Cliffs, NJ: Prentice Hall. A comprehensive survey of excavation methods in both New World and Old World contexts. Recommended for general reading.

WHEELER, R. E. MORTIMER. 1954. *Archaeology from the Earth.* Oxford: Clarendon Press. An archaeological classic that is outdated but which describes excavation on a grand scale with verve and elegance. A must for every archaeologist's bookshelf, if only for its commonsense information.

Analyzing the Past

Artifacts and Technology

People who [have] looked with the archaeological eye will never see quite normally. [They] will be wounded by what other [people] call trifles. It is possible to refine the sense of time until an old shoe in the bunch grass or a pile of nineteenth-century beer bottles in an abandoned mining town tolls in one's head like a hall clock. This is the price one pays for learning to read time from surfaces other than an illuminated dial. It is the melancholy secret of the artifact, the humanly touched thing.

Loren Eiseley, *The Night Country*, 1971

Part V begins our exploration of archaeology's ultimate objectives: constructing culture history, reconstructing past lifeways, and studying cultural process. Chapters 10 and 11 discuss the classification of artifacts and the ways in which ancient peoples used organic and inorganic raw materials. Proper understanding of technology, its uses, and its limitations is an essential preliminary to any discussion of ancient lifeways, our relationships to the changing environment, and culture change in the past.

CHAPTER 10

Classifying Artifacts

Unknown man, perhaps a priest or ruler from Mohenjodaro, Pakistan, c. 1800 B.C.

Technology. We are obsessed with it. Our society can land someone on the moon, aim cruise missiles at small targets hundreds of miles away and hit them, transplant human hearts, and send pilotless aircraft powered by the sun high above the earth. Technology has changed history. The harnessing of fire just after 2 million years ago enabled our remote forebears to settle in bitterly cold climates. About 25,000 years before the present, small ivory needles with perforated eyes led to the development of layered clothing that allowed people to survive comfortably in subzero winters. The development of the outrigger canoe enabled people living in the southwestern Pacific to colonize offshore islands hundreds of miles beyond the horizon 3,000 years ago.

Since the earliest times, our cultures and technological inventiveness have allowed us to adapt to a great range of natural environments and to develop ingenious ways of intensifying the food quest of fishing and sea-mammal hunting and of farming the land in a world of growing population densities. All modern humanity's myriad technologies are ultimately descended from the first simple tools made by human beings over 2.5 million years ago.

We know more about ancient technologies than any other aspect of the societies of the past because we study the material remains of long-forgotten behavior. Thus, it is hardly surprising that the analysis of artifacts is a major part of archaeological research and the follow-up from site surveys or excavations, whatever the size of the project. This chapter describes the processes of classifying artifacts. Chapter 11 discusses artifact analysis and the major technologies used in ancient times.

Artifact analysis starts in the field alongside excavation—processing and organizing the finds so that they can be analyzed and interpreted. At the same time, the excavator keeps an eye on the data flowing from the trenches and plans further excavation to obtain larger samples, if they are required.

These first stages in processing newly excavated archaeological data are entirely routine. Most excavations maintain some form of field laboratory. It is here that the major site records are kept and developed, stratigraphic profile drawings are kept up to date, and radiocarbon samples and other special finds are packed for examination by specialists. A small team staffs the field laboratory. They ensure that all finds are cleaned, processed promptly, packed carefully, and labeled and recorded precisely. A successful laboratory operation allows the director of the excavation to evaluate the available data daily, even hourly. It is here, too, that basic conservation work is carried

Discovery

The Tarim Mummies, China, 1988

Only rarely do archaeologists gaze on the bodies of ancient people dressed in their original raiment. The Tarim Basin in extreme northwestern China has yielded several thousand mummies and tens of thousands of human skeletons, preserved by exceptionally arid conditions and local soils with a very high salt content. These spectacular burials first came to Western attention in 1988, when American scholar Victor Mair entered a new gallery of the Ürümchi Museum. To his astonishment, he found himself in a room of mummies dressed in their everyday clothes. The bodies of men, women, and children looked as if they were asleep. One man with blond hair lay on his back, his head on a white pillow, his hands bound together over his stomach with a red-and-blue bracelet. He wore a reddish purple woollen shirt trimmed with fine red piping and wool pants. His knee-high socks were colored with horizontal stripes of red, yellow, and faint blue. White leather boots came up to his thighs.

Since then, teams of researchers have collaborated on a detailed study of some of the Tarim mummies, whose cultural and ethnic identity is still a mystery (Mallory and Mair, 1999). One of the earliest of the Tarim mummies is a woman, known locally as the "Beauty of Krorän," who was buried in about 1800 B.C.

She had blondish brown hair and was dressed in fur and wool. Her hair was rolled in a felt headdress topped with two goose feathers. About forty to forty-five years of age, she was about 5 foot 2 inches (1.56 m) tall and weighed between 104 and 115 pounds (47–52 kg). Her skin was red-brown and very smooth, and her muscle tissue was better preserved than if her body had been immersed in formaldehyde. She suffered from head lice, which were still in the roots of her hair, and her eyebrows and eyelashes were inflicted with nits, to the point that the Chinese scientists who examined her wondered how she tolerated them. Her lungs contained large quantities of charcoal and silicate dust, the result of sitting close to indoor hearths and living in an arid, windy environment. The Beauty of Krorän was wrapped in a woollen shroud and wore leather boots, with the fur turned inward. A large winnowing basket protected her head and chest, with layers of branches and reeds above the body. A comb and a long, narrow straw basket lay in the grave.

Few archaeological discoveries offer such unique portraits of the remote past. Unfortunately, dozens of the Tarim mummies have been looted or are being destroyed before they have been studied for their unique biological and cultural information.

out—reassembling fragmented pots, hardening bones with chemicals, or stabilizing fragile objects. Computers play an important role in the field laboratory, for they are used to code vast quantities of information for later use.

The analysis continues back in the home laboratory, whether a small ceramic study for a CRM project or an enormous, years-long activity that results from a large-scale survey or excavation. You need a good eye for detail, an orderly mind, and, above all, infinite patience. It takes weeks to sort and classify even a relatively small artifact collection. We have colleagues who have spent years analyzing a single medium-sized excavation.

Successful artifact analysis revolves around classification and typology, two fundamental archaeological skills.

Classification

Our attitude toward life and our surroundings involves constant classification and sorting of massive quantities of data. We classify types of eating utensils: knives, forks, and spoons—each type has a different use and is kept in a separate compartment in the drawer. We group roads according to their surface, finish, and size. A station wagon is classified separately from a truck. In addition to classifying artifacts, lifestyles, and cultures, we make choices among them. If we are eating soup, we choose to use a spoon.

All people classify, because doing so is necessary for abstract thought and language. But everyday classes are not often best for archaeological purposes. In our daily life we habitually use classification as a tool for our lifestyle. Like the computer, however, it should be a servant rather than a master. Sometimes our classifications of good and bad—those based on color of skin or on our definitions of what is moral or immoral—are made and then adhered to as binding principles of life without ever being questioned or modified, no matter how much our circumstances may change. The dogmatism and rigidity that result from these attitudes are as dangerous in archaeology as they are in daily life. In archaeology, **classification** is a research tool, a means for ordering data.

Classifications used by archaeologists follow directly from the problems they are studying. Let us say that our excavator is studying changes in pottery designs over a 500-year period in the Southwest. The classification he or she uses will follow not only from what other people have done but also from the problems being studied. How and even what you classify stem directly from the research questions asked of the data. Because the objectives of classifications may change according to the problems being investigated, archaeologists must be sensitive to the need for revising their classifications when circumstances require it.

Taxonomy and Systematics

Taxonomy is the name given to the system of classifying concepts, materials, objects, and phenomena used in many sciences, including archaeology. The taxonomies of biology, botany, geology, and some other disciplines can be highly sophisticated. Archaeology has built its own taxonomy of specialist terminologies and concepts quite haphazardly. Universal comparisons and classifications have been virtually impossible. British archaeologists refer to cultures; North American scholars refer to phases; and the French to civilizations. Each term has basically the same meaning as the others, but the subtle differences stem from cultural traditions and from different field situations (Dunnell, 1986).

Systematics is essentially a way of creating units of classification that can be used to categorize things as a basis for explaining archaeological or other phenomena (Dunnell, 1971). It is a means of creating units of classification within a scientific discipline. Biologists classify modern human beings within a hierarchical classification developed by Carl Linnaeus in the eighteenth century. It begins with the kingdom Animalia and proceeds in increasingly specific units through the phylum Chordata (animals with notochords and gill slits), the subphylum Vertebrata (animals with backbones), the class Mammalia, the subclass Eutheria, the order Primates, the suborder Hominoidea (apes and hominids), the family Hominidae, the genus *Homo*, the species *sapiens*, and, finally, the subspecies *sapiens*. This hierarchy is gradually refined until only *Homo sapiens sapiens* remains in its own taxonomic niche. The biological classification just described is based on each form's having common progenitors or just similarities. It consists of empirically defined units (kingdom, phylum, and so on) in which each element is defined and related to the others, whereas in archaeology, classification is based on the relation of the elements to the problem being studied.

Objectives of Classification

Although classification in archaeology depends on the problem being studied, four major objectives that are common to all archaeological studies can be identified:

1. *Organizing Data into Manageable Units.* This step is part of the preliminary data-processing operation, and it commonly involves separating finds on the basis of raw material (stone, bone, and so on) or artifacts from food remains. This preliminary ordering allows much more detailed classification later on.
2. *Describing Types.* By identifying the individual features of hundreds of artifacts, or clusters of artifacts, the archaeologist can group them, by common attributes, into relatively few types. These types represent patterns of separate associations of attributes. Such types are economical ways of describing large numbers of artifacts. Which attributes are chosen depends on the purpose of the typology.

   Artifact types (sometimes called archaeological types) are based on criteria set up by archaeologists as a convenient way of studying ancient tool kits and technology. They are a useful scientific device that provides a manageable way of classifying small and large collections of prehistoric tools and the by-products from manufacturing them.
3. *Identifying Relationships between Types.* Describing types provides a hierarchy, which orders the relationships between artifacts. These stem, in part, from the use of a variety of raw materials, manufacturing techniques, and functions.

These three objectives are much used in culture-historical research. Processual archaeologists may use classification for a fourth:

4. *Studying Assemblage Variability in the Archaeological Record.* These studies are often combined with middle-range research on dynamic, living cultural systems (Chapter 14).

Archaeological classifications are artificial formulations based on criteria set up by archaeologists. These classificatory systems, however, do not necessarily coincide with those developed by the people who made the original artifacts (Dunnell, 1986; Willey and Phillips, 1958).

Typology

Typology is a system of classification based on the construction of types. A **type** is a grouping of artifacts based on form, chronology, function, or style. Typology is a search for patterns among either objects or the variables that define those objects, a search that has taken on added meaning and complexity as archaeologists have begun to use computer technology and sophisticated statistical methods (W. Adams and E. Adams, 1991). This kind of typology is totally different from arbitrarily dividing up the objects and variables.

Typology enables archaeologists to construct arbitrarily defined units of analysis that apply to two or more samples of artifacts, so that these samples can be compared objectively. These samples can come from different sites or from separate levels of the same site. Typology is classification to permit comparison, an opportunity to examine underlying patterns of human design and behavior (W. Adams and E. Adams, 1991; J. A. Brown, 1982). Typology, as James Deetz put it, has one main aim: "classification which permits comparison. . . . Such a comparison allows the archaeologist to align his assemblage with others in time and space" (1967:74).

For accurate and meaningful comparisons to be made, rigorous definitions of analytical types are needed, to define not only the "norm" of the artifact type but also its approximate range of variation, at either end of which one type becomes one of two others. Conventional analytical definitions are usually couched in terms of one or more attributes that indicate how the artifact was made, the shape, the decoration, or some other feature that the maker wanted the finished product to display. These definitions are set up following carefully defined technological differences, often bolstered by measurements or statistical clusterings of attributes. Most often, the average artifact, rather than the variation between individual examples, is the ultimate objective of the definition. A classifier who finds a group, or even an individual artifact, that deviates at all conspicuously from the norm often erects a new analytical type. "Splitters" tend to proliferate types, and "lumpers" do the opposite. The whole operation is more or less objective (Dunnell, 1971).

Types

All of us have feelings and reactions about any artifact, whether it is a magnificent wooden helmet from the Pacific Northwest coast (Figure 10.1) or a simple acorn

Figure 10.1   Tlingit carved ceremonial wooden helmet from the Pacific Northwest coast, a "natural" type, classified as such when found in an archaeological context. This artifact would obviously be classified as a helmet from the perspective of our cultural experience. (Height, 9 inches; width, 10 inches [23 by 25 cm].)

Doing Archaeology

Artifact Classification

The difficulties of artifact classification are well demonstrated by this classic example of a basketry tray for parching acorns (Deetz, 1967) (Figure 10.2). This finely made basket was produced by the Chumash Indians of southern California by weaving plant fibers. The design was formed in the maker's mind by several factors, most important of which was the tremendous reservoir of learned cultural experience that the Chumash had acquired, generation by generation, through the several thousand years they lived in southern California. The designs of their baskets were learned and were related to the feeling that such and such a form and color were "correct"

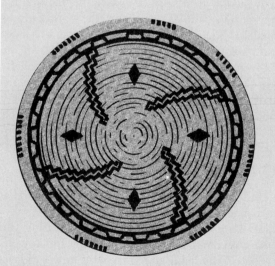

Figure 10.2   A Chumash parching tray.

and traditionally acceptable. But there were more pragmatic and complex reasons, too, including the flat, circular shape that enabled the user to roast seeds by tossing them with red embers.

Each attribute of the basket had a good reason for its presence—whether traditional, innovative, functional, or imposed by the technology used to make it. The band of decoration around the rim is a feature of the Chumash decorative tradition and occurs on most of their baskets. It has a rich red-brown color from the species of reed used to make it. The steplike decoration was dictated by the sewing and weaving techniques, but the diamond pattern is the unique and innovative stamp of one weaver and might or might not have been adopted by other craftspeople in later generations.

The problem for the archaeologist is to measure the variations in human artifacts, to establish the causes behind the directions of change, and to find what those variations can be used to measure. This fine parching tray is a warning that variations in human artifacts are both complex and subtle.

The Chumash hunter-gatherers occupied the Santa Barbara Channel region of southern California. At the time of European contact in the fifteenth century, they dwelt in permanent villages, some housing as many as 1,000 people. They were ruled by chiefs and enjoyed a complex ritual and social life.

pounder from the southern California interior. Our immediate instinct is to look at and classify these and other prehistoric artifacts from our own cultural standpoint. That is, of course, what prehistoric peoples did as well. The owners of the tools that archaeologists study classified them into groups for themselves, each one having a definite role in their society. We assign different roles in eating to a knife, a fork, and a spoon. Knives cut meat; steak knives are used in eating steaks. The prehistoric arrowhead is employed in the chase; one type of missile head is used to hunt deer, another to shoot birds, and so on. The use of an artifact may be determined not only by convenience and practical considerations but also by custom or regulation. The light-barbed spearheads used by some Australian hunting bands to catch fish are too fragile for dispatching a kangaroo, but the special barbs permit the impaled fish to be lifted out of the water. Pots are made by women in most African and Native American societies, which have division of labor by sex; each has formed complicated customs, regulations, or taboos, which, functional considerations apart, categorize clay pots into different types with varying uses and rules in the culture.

Furthermore, each society has its own conception of what a particular artifact should look like. Americans have generally preferred large cars; Europeans, small ones. These preferences reflect not only pragmatic considerations of road width and longer distances in the New World but also differing attitudes toward traveling and, for many Americans, a preoccupation with prestige manifested in gold-leaf lettering and custom colors, hubcabs, and style. The steering wheel is on the left, and the car is equipped with turn signals and seat belts by law. In other words, we know what we want and expect an automobile to look like, even though minor design details change—as do the length of women's skirts and the width of men's ties.

Because archaeologists devise archaeological types that are appropriate to the research problems they are tackling and that facilitate comparison with other groups, a type may or may not coincide with the actual groupings designated by the original makers or with their uses for the tools. A good example comes from the world-famous Olduvai Gorge site in East Africa, where Louis and Mary Leakey excavated a series of cache sites used by very early humans, *Homo habilis*. Mary Leakey studied the stone tools and grouped them in the **Oldowan** tradition, a tradition characterized by jagged-edged chopping tools and flakes (M. D. Leakey, 1973). She based her classifications on close examination of the artifacts, and an assumption that the first human tool kit was based on crude stone choppers soon became archaeological dogma.

Subsequently, Nicholas Toth of Indiana University took a radically different approach to classifying Oldowan artifacts (Toth and Schick, 1993). He has spent many hours not only studying and classifying the original artifacts but also learning Oldowan technology for himself, replicating hundreds of artifacts made by *Homo habilis* two million years ago. His controlled experiments have shown that *H. habilis* was not using chopping tools at all. The primeval stone workers were more interested in the sharp-edged flakes they knocked off lumps of lava for cutting and butchering the meat they scavenged from predator kills. The "chopping tools" were, in fact, just cores or the end product of knocking flakes off convenient lumps of lava. Controlled experiments like Toth's provide useful insights into how prehistoric peoples manufactured the tools they needed. Toth and other experts are now trying to study the telltale patterns of edge wear on the cutting edges of Oldowan flakes; for the polish, striations, and microflake scars left by working, for example, fresh bone as opposed to hide or wood are highly distinctive. With controlled experimentation and careful examination of edge wear, they hope to achieve a closer marriage between the ways in which the first humans used stone tools and the classifications devised by archaeologists hundreds of thousands of years later.

Everyone agrees that a type is based on clusters of similar attributes or on clusters of objects. Although patterns of attributes may be fairly easy to identify, how do archaeologists know what is a type and what is not? Should they try to reproduce the categories of pot that the makers themselves conceived? Or should they just go ahead and create "archaeological" types designed purely for analytical purposes? Herein lies the hub of the controversy about types in archaeology.

The archaeologist constructs typologies based on the recurrence of formal patterns of physical features of artifacts. Many of these formal types have restricted distributions in space and time, which suggests that they represent distinctive "styles" of construction or tasks that were carried out in the culture to which they belong. For example, the so-called **Chavín** art style was widespread over much of coastal and highland Peru after 900 B.C. The jaguar, snake, and human forms of this art are highly characteristic and mark the spread of a distinctive iconography over a large area of the Andean region. Chavín art, and the characteristic styles associated with it, had a specific role in Peruvian society of the time.

Processes of Archaeological Classification

As we have emphasized, archaeological classification is the ordering of data on the basis of shared characteristics. But how do archaeologists go about this process? Traditionally, classification has been based on the archaeologist's "concept of types," subject of one of the great controversies in archaeology (Dunnell, 1986). On a formal level, a type can be defined as "a group or class of items that is internally cohesive and separated from other groups by one or more discontinuities" (Whallon and Brown, 1982). Until the late 1950s, almost all archaeological classification was qualitative, based to a great extent on instinct and experience rather than on numerical methods or empirical testing. The new perspectives on the archaeological record that emerged in the 1960s coincided with a new generation of quantitative techniques that bear on the traditional problem of archaeological classification, techniques that are revolutionizing typology. (For a comprehensive discussion, see Shennan, 1988.)

Quantitative Methods

The concept of quantitative methods has great breadth in archaeology. It refers not only to the standard techniques of statistical analysis and inference that readily come to mind but also to various techniques of numerical analysis and numerical manipulation, as well as graphical techniques for displaying data so that the patterns in the data are more readily apparent. Modern archaeology relies heavily on all manner of quantitative methods. In fact, quantitative methods are now central to archaeology in that the descriptive and explanatory power inherent in those methods and the carefully structured reasoning behind the methods provide us with powerful tools for answering such fundamental questions as "How old is it?" "Where does it come from?" and "What was it used for?"

An understanding of the process of applying quantitative methods to archaeological problems and a basic level of computer literacy are fundamental skills for all

Doing Archaeology

Archaeological Types

Archaeologists tend to use three "types of types," described briefly here, which, in practice, are rarely separated one from another, for experts tend to draw this kind of information from more general classifications of artifacts (Steward, 1955) (Figure 10.3).

Descriptive types are based solely on the form of the artifact—physical or external properties. The descriptive type is employed when the use or cultural significance of the object or practice is unknown. Descriptive types are commonly used for artifacts from early prehistory, when functional interpretations are much harder to reach.

Chronological types are also defined by decoration or form, but they are time markers. They are defined in terms of attributes that show change over time. For example, on the Great Plains of North America, Clovis and Folsom points were used for short periods of prehistoric time, the former for about three and a half centuries from about 11,300 to 10,950 B.C. (see Figure 11.7d). Folsom dates to between about 9880 to 8250 B.C. Projectile points have long been used as chronological markers in North American archaeology.

The great Egyptologist Flinders Petrie used chronological types when he studied the

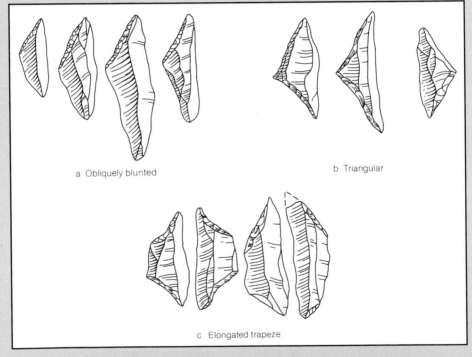

a Obliquely blunted

b Triangular

c Elongated trapeze

Figure 10.3 Some 9,000-year-old stone artifacts from Star Carr, England (actual size). You can classify these by descriptive type as geometric stone tools; by chronological type as Mesolithic microliths, Star Carr forms; and by functional type as microlithic arrowhead barbs.

pre-Dynastic jars from Diospolis Parva on the Nile (Chapter 7). Chronological types figure prominently in archaeology of the American Southwest and were used by Alfred Kidder (1924) in his classic excavations at Pecos. Such types have the disadvantage that they are often hard for an archaeologist other than their originator to duplicate owing to poor definitions of different types, except under favorable conditions or by archaeologists who have received identical extensive training (Sackett, 1977).

Functional types are based on cultural use or role in their user's culture rather than on outward form or chronological position—for example, "weapons," "clothing," "food preparation," and so on. Ideally, functional types should reflect the precise roles and functional classifications made by the members of the society from which they came. Needless to say, such an objective is very difficult to achieve because of incomplete preservation and lack of written records. We have no means of visualizing the complex roles that some artifacts achieved in prehistoric society. Although in some cases obvious functional roles, such as that of an arrowhead for hunting or warfare or of a pot for carrying water, can be correctly established in the laboratory, functional classifications are necessarily restricted and limited.

Let us consider a Scandinavian flint dagger (Figure 10.4)—a beautifully made, pressure-flaked tool that was a copy of the bronze daggers so fashionable about 2000 B.C. in central Europe. This tool has been classified by generations of archaeologists as a dagger, by implication a weapon of war and defense, worn by Scandinavian farmers who still had no metal and made a slavish imitation of a more advanced metal tool. This instinctive designation may seem obvious, but we really do not know whether our functional classification is correct. Does use-wear on the blade show that a dagger was actually used in warfare and for personal defense? Was it a weapon, or was it purely an object of prestige for the owner, perhaps with some religious function?

Stylistic types are best exemplified by items such as clothing, because style is often used to convey information through public display. The Aztecs of central Mexico lived in a ranked society in which everyone's dress was carefully regulated by sumptuary laws (Anawalt, 1981). Thus, a glance at the noble in the marketplace could reveal not only his rank but also the number of prisoners he had taken in battle and many other subtle distinctions. Even the gods had their own regalia and costumes that reflected their roles in the pantheon (R. F. Townsend, 1992). Stylistic types, which may result in a grouping entirely different from a grouping based on functional types, are not used often in archaeological classification, except when historical records are available (Conkey and Hastorf, 1990; Plog, 1983).

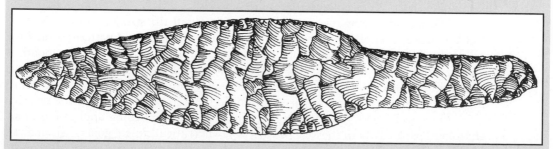

Figure 10.4   A pressure-flaked Scandinavian flint dagger (one-half actual size). (Copyright The British Museum)

modern archaeologists (Drennan, 1996). In general, however, some sophisticated techniques are performed almost routinely by most practicing archaeologists today.

There are three fundamental issues in applying quantitative methods to archaeological problems. The first is realizing when quantitative methods can aid in resolving a problem. The second is being familiar enough with various techniques and their underlying assumptions to know which techniques are appropriate to specific kinds of archaeological problems. Finally, the third is being familiar enough with the data, the methods, and general anthropological theory to formulate a reasonable interpretation of the analytical results that has meaning in terms of the ultimate topic of archaeology—human behavior.

Quantitative methods are valuable in archaeology in three broad areas: data exploration and characterization, data description, and hypothesis testing or confirmation. It is important to keep in mind the distinction between descriptive techniques and confirmatory, or inferential, techniques. The former term applies to economical methods of describing sets of data in ways that are useful to other researchers and that preserve the inherent structure of the data. The latter refers to methods aimed at inferring the characteristics of an unobservable population on the basis of the characteristics of a sample taken from that population and providing some guide as to the reliability of the inference.

Exploration.   In recent years, a new suite of analytical tools has been added to the archaeologist's repertoire. These tools rely on a slightly different way of thinking about archaeological data, as well as new ways of looking at the data. Collectively known as **exploratory data analysis (EDA),** these techniques have been specifically designed to aid in detecting patterns and deviations in sets of data by relying heavily on visual displays of data rather than on summary statistics and statistical significance tests.

Two basic principles lie behind these techniques. First, the fastest, most sophisticated pattern-recognition hardware and software known are the human eye and brain. To the extent that large quantities of data can be reorganized and presented in a graphical rather than numerical form, the researcher can more readily detect patterns and deviations in the data that may have important implications for the problem at hand. The proliferation of microcomputers and minicomputers with graphics capabilities in the 1980s dramatically accelerated the development and acceptance of these techniques among archaeologists and other scientists.

The second principle is a basic assumption about the structure of data sets. In EDA parlance, a set of observations can be divided into a general pattern, sometimes called the "smooth," and deviations from that pattern, the "rough." The smooth is important for understanding the general distribution of the data and the phenomena responsible for the observed regularity. The rough is important for potentially pointing out either unique events or perturbations in the normal operation of the system.

These techniques for analyzing data have a very compelling application in archaeology, particularly in the area of typology, where the ultimate goal of the analysis is to identify regular patterns in the artifactual data that may reveal patterning in the human behavior that produced or distributed the artifacts. Exploratory data analysis is useful for reducing masses of data to some kind of observable order, usually in the form of frequency distributions, to obtain an initial impression of the rough and the smooth. Any number of graphical devices may be used, including bar charts, histograms, frequency curves, box plots, and stem-and-leaf plots. These graphics can give the researcher valuable insights into the structure of the data, point up possible relationships between variables, and suggest appropriate techniques for later descriptive or confirmatory analysis. (For an excellent discussion of EDA, see Shennan, 1988.)

Description. **Descriptive statistics** aid in the economical presentation of facets of the archaeological record. These techniques provide a means for organizing and quantifying archaeological data in a manner that facilitates objective comparison while preserving the inherent structure of the data. Descriptive statistics provide archaeologists with an economical way of indicating the numbers and kinds of artifacts found at a site or the dimensions of artifacts and the degree of variation in those dimensions. They provide a means of taking masses of data stored in computer databases and summarizing them in a readily digestible form. Today, descriptive statistics are often employed on-site as an aid to excavation or survey. The basic data are often collected and entered into a computer database in the field laboratory on a daily basis. Those data can then be quickly summarized using basic descriptive techniques to indicate differences in the frequency of artifacts between excavation areas or levels or to indicate emergent patterns in survey data that can then be used to refine field techniques and strategies. Use of descriptive statistics generally involves summarizing sets of data using very straightforward measures of the structure of the data. They include such things as measures of central tendency (mean, median, mode) and measures of dispersion (standard deviation, spread, range), as well as basic graphical devices such as bar graphs, histograms, and line graphs.

In archaeology, the ultimate goal of descriptive statistics is to organize data into a more manageable form in order to facilitate comparison and indicate patterning. It is one of the oldest and simplest sets of techniques of quantitative analysis for archaeologists and remains one of the most frequently used because of its simplicity and its power. In innumerable archaeological problems, basic descriptive statistics is all that is required to characterize the data adequately and to provide meaningful interpretive information on the problem.

Hypothesis Testing (Confirmation). **Confirmatory (inferential) statistics** are designed to allow the researcher to make informed inferences about the characteristics of a population or the relationship between variables on the basis of data collected from a sample of the population of interest. All the various confirmatory techniques provide a summary statistic that indicates how reliable the inference is likely to be. Archaeologists are concerned with making inferences about the past on the basis of patterns and relationships evident in the archaeological record. However, because the relationship between the observable phenomena (the archaeological record) and the unobservable phenomena of real interest (past human behavior) is often a very imperfect one, archaeologists need to know how reliable their inferences are. Since we cannot go back in a time machine to see for ourselves whether our inferences are valid, we must rely on mathematics and the

---

Site

Olduvai Gorge, Tanzania

Olduvai Gorge is a deep gash cut into the Serengeti Plains of Tanzania, East Africa, by an ancient earth movement (Figure 10.5). By chance, the gash cuts through the deposits of a long-dried-up shallow lake, where very early humans once scavenged for food. German paleontologist Hans Reck was the first scientist to visit Olduvai. He collected the bones of fossil elephants and other mammals from the lake beds in the 1920s. In 1931, Louis Leakey visited the gorge for the first time and soon collected magnificent stone axes from the same deposits. From that year until the 1950s, Louis and Mary Leakey worked occasionally at Olduvai, recovering thousands of stone artifacts, which Mary studied in relation to the stratified lake beds where they were found (L. S. B. Leakey, 1951; M. D. Leakey, 1973).

The gorge cuts through the shores of the lake, where hominids scavenged on predator kills by the shallow water for tens of thousands of years. There are four major, stratified lake bed formations at Olduvai, the lowest of them lying on a bed of hardened volcanic ash potassium-argon dated to about 2 million years ago. *Zinjanthropus boisei* and *Homo habilis* come from the lowest formation, known as Bed I, both found in association with small scatters of stone fragments and broken animal bones, places where the hominids broke up bones and ate fresh meat before moving on.

Over many years, Mary Leakey developed a remarkable artifact sequence at Olduvai, based on thousands of stratified tools. The earliest visitors to Olduvai made the simple flakes and crude "choppers" described in this chapter. Subsequently, hominid technology became more refined as the first crude stone axes appeared and were succeeded by progressively more refined axes and cleaving tools, multipurpose artifacts used for butchering animals. Mary's studies chronicled the slow evolution of stone technology in East Africa,

---

known laws of probability. As Stephen Shennan (1988) put it, "The area where mathematics meets the messier parts of the real world is usually statistics."

The tricky part about employing any of the various univariate and multivariate techniques of inferential statistics is that the test statistic (Student's t, F test, chi square, and so on) is only measuring the reliability of the mathematical relationship between variables in a data set, between a sample and its presumed population, or among data sets. How inferences about those mathematical relationships are interpreted in terms of the actualities of the archaeological record or human behavior depends on the archaeologist.

In the final analysis, quantitative methods enable archaeologists to organize their artifact and other data in intelligent, efficient, and replicable ways, allowing them to view the data more clearly and objectively as they work toward the goal of discerning patterns that relate to past human behavior. These techniques also allow archaeologists to evaluate objectively the reliability of their inferences from small samples to larger populations of archaeological entities, as well as inferences about the interrelations among variables. To the extent that these techniques are applied to

from soon after the first toolmaking more than 2.5 million years ago until long after more advanced Archaic humans such as *Homo erectus* flourished on the African savanna. Olduvai is still the longest known sequence of stone tool technology in the world.

Figure 10.5   Olduvai Gorge, Tanzania.

attribute and object pattern recognition, they are extremely valuable aids to artifact classification.

Quantitative methods have been applied to two contrasting approaches to artifact classification, both of which were in use before the advent of computers and statistical methods in archaeology: attribute analysis and object clustering.

Attribute Analysis.   **Attribute analysis** emphasizes combinations of attributes that distinguish and isolate one artifact type from another. The physical characteristics or features of significance used to distinguish one artifact from another are known as **attributes** (Whallon and Brown, 1982). As archaeologists work out their typologies, they find themselves examining hundreds of individual fragments, each of which bears several distinctive attributes (Figure 10.6). Every commonplace artifact we use can be examined by its attributes. The familiar glass beer mug has a curved handle that extends from near the lip to the base, often fluted sides, a straight, rounded rim, and dimensions that are set by the amount of beer it is intended to contain. It is manufactured of clear, relatively thick glass (the thickness can be defined by precise measurement).

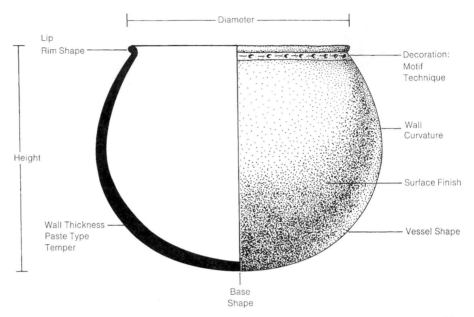

Figure 10.6   Some common attributes of a clay vessel. Specific attributes that could be listed for this pot are concave shoulder, dot-and-drag decoration, mica temper, round base, and thickness of wall at base.

You can find numerous attributes on any human artifact, be it a diamond ring or a prehistoric pot. For example, a collection of fifty potsherds lying on a laboratory table may bear black-painted designs; eight of them may have red panels on the neck, ten may have shallow bowls, and so on. An individual potsherd may come from a vessel made of bright red clay mixed with powdered seashells so that the clay would fire better. It may come from a pot with a thick rim made by applying a rolled circle of clay before firing, and a crisscross design cut into the wet clay with a sharp knife during manufacture. Each of the many individual features is an attribute, most of which are obvious enough. Only a critically selected few of these attributes, however, will be used in classifying the artifacts. (If all were used, then no classification would be possible: each artifact would be an individual object identified by its unique combination of attributes.) Thus, the archaeologist works with only those attributes considered most appropriate for the classificatory task at hand.

Three broad groups of attributes are in common use:

- **Formal attributes** are such features as the shape of the artifact, its measurable dimensions, and its components. Usually they are fairly obvious.
- **Stylistic attributes** involve decoration, color, surface finish, and so on (Sackett, 1977, 1981).
- **Technological attributes** include the material used to make an artifact and the way it was made.

The selection of attributes normally proceeds through a close examination of a collection of artifacts. Exploratory data analysis techniques can be useful in helping to determine which attributes provide the most diagnostic discrimination. A group of potsherds can be divided into different decorative styles based on shape, surface, and color. The selected attributes are then hand-recorded, and a series of artifact types is erected from them. The definition of the type here can depend on the order in which the attributes are examined and on the researcher's decision as to which are important.

Statistical typologies are derived from attribute clusters, usually coded on a computer, which are then used to divide the artifact collection into categories defined by statistically derived attribute clusters. James Sackett (1966) used this approach on 32,000-year-old Aurignacian end scrapers from Upper Paleolithic sites in southwestern France and found that the extent and location of trimming on the edges and the angle between the two longer sides were important variables that may have defined classes of artifacts used for different purposes.

Object Clustering.   The **object clustering** approach to classification begins with a series of so-called **operational taxonomic units (OTUs),** usually artifacts (Cowgill, 1982). The archaeologist calculates the similarities between all possible pairs of objects, using similarity coefficients. On the basis of similarity scores, the analyst can then link the OTUs into a hierarchical structure, which ranges all the way from complete uniqueness of all artifacts (an unanalyzed collection) to complete unity, when all OTUs are in the same cluster. Object clustering does use attributes, but, in contrast to attribute approaches, it uses them to assess the similarity between objects, not the associations between attributes. (Cowgill, 1982, describes the differences between the two approaches.) Object clustering classifications are based on a quantitative approach known as *cluster analysis,* a form of numerical taxonomy.

Each approach to classification supplies different information about the very structure of archaeological data, all of which is valuable. In a sense, the approaches are descriptions of the structure in archaeological data, based, in their quantitative guises, on a greater concern for techniques for discovering variations in artifacts than on the actual selection of attributes for comparison. At present there is still little theoretical justification for selecting the attributes that are used to classify artifacts or to cluster them.

Assemblages and Patterns

Culture history in archaeology is based on classification of artifacts and assemblages, defined as associations of artifacts that are thought to be contemporaneous. This was the approach espoused by V. Gordon Childe in the 1930s and 1940s and was also popular in North America. "We find certain types of remains . . . constantly recurring together," Childe (1925:15) wrote. "Such a complex of regularly associated traits we shall term . . . a 'culture.' We may assume that such a complex is the material expression of what would today be called a 'people.'" This assumption was virtually archaeological law until the 1950s, when a number of prehistorians began using statistical methods to look at assemblages of artifacts.

These earlier archaeologists had assumed a steady, almost inevitable progression of human culture through the ages. They assumed that artifact assemblages with recurring patterns were merely traces of cultural "species" that extended far back into antiquity. This "organic" view of culture history regarded assemblages of artifacts as distinct categories, like organic species that did not modify their form from one context to the next (Sackett, 1981). The argument went on to assume that a specific cultural tradition leads to only one characteristic type of industry in the archaeological record that is circumscribed in time and space.

What Do Assemblages and Patterns Mean?

The "organic" view of the past is a highly organized scheme, rather like the medieval "Chain of Being" in early biology, in which every living thing had its place in the general scheme of things. American archaeologists have generally preferred a more "cultural" perspective, making considerable use of data on artifacts and other culture traits known to have been used by living societies in North America. Observation of these data has shown a strong correlation between the distributions of distinctive cultural forms and different environments. For example, plank houses and an elaborate canoe technology are characteristic of the peoples of the Pacific Northwest coast, where readily split cedar and other trees flourished in abundance. In contrast, desert peoples in the Great Basin lived in much more transitory settlements of brush shelters and houses, using a highly portable tool kit adapted to a mobile desert lifeway. It is all very well to say that such correlations were true of historic times, but what about earlier prehistory? Can one say that artifact assemblages from the Great Basin dating to 5,000 years ago reflect similar adaptations, similar social groups? Were conditions different in the past from today? Can one use modern artifact patternings as a basis for interpreting ancient behavior?

Observations of living societies, such as Lewis Binford's research on the Nunamiut caribou hunters in Alaska, have shown that it may not be possible to distinguish among ethnic and cultural groups from artifact assemblages alone (Binford, 1978, 1983). Thus the role of classification in archaeology is shifting away from organic viewpoints that consider artifacts and cultures as finite in time and space to problem-oriented classifications that concentrate not just on individual tools but on entire assemblages and their patterns in archaeological sites. In other words, classification alone is meaningless, unless the classifications are interpreted in terms of other data. This is where middle-range theory comes in (Chapter 14).

Artifact classifications are still carried out, for the most part, using approaches meant for reconstructing culture history, formulations of time and space that owe much to functional classifications of artifacts based on common sense (Dunnell, 1978). Thus, the same classificatory units have remained in use, while archaeologists pay lip service to newer approaches. As Dunnell (1986) pointed out, the question of questions is a simple one: Can style be explained within a scientific and evolutionary framework, using laws of culture change? So far, such a theoretical framework does not exist.

Summary

The first stage in laboratory analysis is processing field data into a form that will enable one to analyze and interpret them. The finds are also inventoried during this stage.

Classifying artifacts in archaeology is somewhat different from our day-to-day classification of the objects around us. Two systems of classification are taxonomy and systematics. Taxonomy is a classification system of concepts and terms used by many sciences, archaeology among them. Systematics is a way of creating units of classification that can be used to categorize things as a basis for explaining archaeological or other phenomena.

The objectives of archaeological classification are to organize data into manageable units, to describe types, and to identify relationships among types. Archaeological types are groupings of artifacts created for comparisons with other groups. These groupings may or may not coincide with the actual tool types designed by the manufacturers.

Types are based on clusters of attributes. Four "types of types" are commonly used today:

1. Descriptive types are based on the form of the artifacts, using physical or external properties.
2. Chronological types are defined by form but are time markers.
3. Functional types are based on cultural use or role rather than outward form or chronological position.
4. Stylistic types use changing styles for classification purposes.

Archaeological classification begins with identifying artifact attributes, the characteristics that distinguish one artifact from another. Formal attributes are such features as the shape of an artifact, and technological attributes include the materials used to make an artifact and manufacturing methods. Attributes can be selected by closely examining a collection of artifacts, or they can be derived statistically.

Statistically based classifications are now in common use, based on quantitative analyses, including the use of exploratory data analysis (EDA). Attribute and object-cluster classifications are two major approaches now based on quantitative methods.

Culture history in archaeology is based on classification of artifacts and assemblages, defined as associations of artifacts that are thought to be contemporaneous. This "organic" view of culture history has been replaced by a more "cultural" viewpoint in which environment and culture play important roles.

Key Terms

attribute
attribute analysis
Chavín
chronological types
classification
confirmatory (inferential)
  statistics
descriptive statistics
descriptive types

exploratory data analysis
  (EDA)
formal attributes
functional types
object clustering
Oldowan
operational taxonomic units
  (OTUs)
statistical typologies

stylistic attributes
stylistic types
systematics
taxonomy
technological attributes
type
typology

Guide to Further Reading

The literature on archaeological classification is both complex and enormous. We strongly advise you to obtain expert advice before delving into even key references. Here, however, are some useful starting points.

COWGILL, GEORGE L. 1982. "Clusters of Objects and Associations between Variables: Two Approaches to Archaeological Classification." In Robert A. Whallon and James A. Brown, eds., *Essays in Archaeological Typology,* pp. 30–55. Evanston, IL: Center for American Archaeology. An excellent comparison of attribute-based and object cluster-based classifications in archaeology.

DRENNAN, ROBERT. 1996. *Statistics for Archaeologists.* New York: Plenum. An excellent introduction to quantitative archaeology.

DUNNELL, R. C. 1971. *Systematics in Prehistory.* New York: Free Press. A highly technical introduction to systematic classification in archaeology.

————. 1986. "Methodological Issues in Americanist Artifact Classification." *Advances in Archaeological Method and Theory* 10: 149–208. A specialist essay on artifact classification that summarizes the major controversies surrounding the subject.

SHENNAN, STEPHEN. 1988. *Quantifying Archaeology.* Orlando, FL: Academic Press. An introduction to quantitative archaeology for the advanced student. Includes simple exercises.

CHAPTER 11

Technologies
of the Ancients

Gold mask of a Mycenaean king, called Agamemnon's mask, c. 1300 B.C. (National Archaeology Museum, Athens, Greece. Copyright Giraudon/Art Resource, NY)

The technological achievements of humanity over the past 3 million years of cultural evolution have been both impressive and terrifying. Today we can land an astronaut on the moon, transplant human hearts, and build sophisticated computers. Yet, in the final analysis, our contemporary armory of lasers, atomic bombs, household appliances, and every conceivable artifact designed for a multitude of specialized needs has evolved in a direct, albeit branching, way from the first simple tools made by the earliest human beings. In this chapter we examine some of the main technologies used by prehistoric peoples to adapt to, and extend their use of, their natural environments and look at some of the ways in which archaeologists study them (Cotterell and Kamminga, 1989).

Stone

Bone, plant fiber, wood, and some kinds of rock have been the primary raw materials for human technology for most of human existence. Metallurgy is but a recent development, and stone tools have provided the foundation for classification of many prehistoric cultures since scientific archaeology began. The raw material itself set severe limits on peoples' technological achievements for much of history, and the evolution of stoneworking over the millions of years during which it has been practiced was infinitely slow. Nonetheless, people eventually exploited almost every possibility afforded by suitable rocks for making implements (Odell, 1996).

Working Stone

The manufacture of stone tools is what is called a **reductive** (or **subtractive**) **technology**, for stone is acquired, then shaped by removing flakes until the desired form is achieved. Obviously, the more complex the artifact, the more reduction is required to make it (Swanson, 1975). Basically, the process of tool manufacture is linear. The

Discovery

Zinjanthropus boisei at Olduvai Gorge, Tanzania, East Africa, 1959

It was a blazing hot day at Olduvai Gorge, East Africa, in 1959. Back in camp, Louis Leakey lay in his tent, suffering from a bout of influenza. Meanwhile, Mary Leakey, sheltered by a beach umbrella, was excavating the small scatter of broken animal bones and crude stone artifacts deep in the gorge. For hours, she brushed and pried away dry soil. Suddenly, she unearthed part of an upper jaw with teeth so humanlike that she took a closer look. Moments later, she jumped into her Land Rover and sped up the rough track to camp. "Louis, Louis," she cried, as she burst into their tent. "I've found Dear Boy at last."

Louis leapt out of bed, his flu forgotten. Together, they excavated the fragmentary remains of a magnificent robust hominid skull. The Leakeys named it *Zinjanthropus boisei* ("African human of Boise," a Mr. Boise being one of their benefactors), now known as *Australopithecus boisei.*

Zinjanthropus was the first of a series of very early human fossils discovered by Louis and Mary Leakey at Olduvai Gorge in the years that followed. Between them, they unearthed another, much more lightly built human that they named *Homo habilis,* "Handy Person," as they were convinced it was the first human toolmaker.

The Leakeys worked with shoestring budgets until their *Zinjanthropus* discovery gave them access to National Geographic Society funding. Since their magnificent discovery, the search for our earliest ancestors has become an international enterprise, which is revealing a far greater variety of prospective early human ancestors than anyone imagined back in 1959.

stoneworker acquires the raw material, prepares a lump of stone (the **core**), then carries out the initial reduction by removing a series of flakes. These flakes are then trimmed and shaped further, depending on the artifact required. Later, after use, a tool may be resharpened or modified for another use.

Principles of Manufacture. The simplest way of producing a stone that will cut or chop, surely the basic tool produced by prehistoric peoples, is simply to break off a piece and use the resulting sharp edge. But to make a tool that has a more specialized use or can be employed for several purposes requires a slightly more sophisticated flaking technique. First, an angular fragment or smooth pebble of suitable rock can be brought to the desired shape by systematically flaking it with another stone. The flakes removed from this core are then primarily waste products, whereas the core becomes the implement that is the intentional end product of the toolmaker. Furthermore, the flakes struck from the core can themselves be used as sharp-edged knives, or they can be further modified to make other artifacts. From this simple beginning, many complex stone industries have evolved, the earliest tools being simple—many of them virtually indistinguishable from naturally fractured rock (D. Crabtree, 1972).

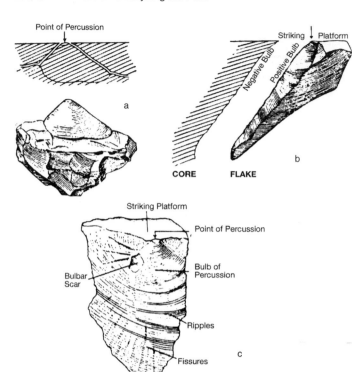

Figure 11.1   How stone fractures when a blow is struck on homogeneous types of rock. (a) When a blow is struck, a core of percussion is formed by the shock waves rippling through the stone. (b) A flake is formed when the block (or core) is hit at the edge and the stone fractures along the edge of the ripple. (c) Features of a struck flake.

In general, Stone Age people and other makers of stone tools chose flint, obsidian, and other hard, homogeneous rocks from which to fashion their artifacts. All these rocks break in a systematic or predictable way, like glass. The effect is similar to that of a hole in a window produced by a BB gun. A sharp blow by percussion or pressure directed vertically at a point on the surface of a suitable stone dislodges a flake, with its apex at the point where the hammer hit the stone. This method results in a **conchoidal fracture** (Figure 11.1). When a blow is directed at a stone slab obliquely from the edge, however, and the break occurs conchoidally, a flake is detached. The fractured face of the flake has a characteristic shape, with a bulge extending from the surface of the piece outward down the side. This is known as the **bulb of percussion** (or of force); there is a corresponding hollow, or flake scar, on the core from which the flake has been detached. The bulb of percussion is readily recognized, as Figure 11.2 shows, not only by the bulge itself but also from the concentric rings that radiate from the center of the impact point, gradually widening away from it.

Such deliberate human-made fractures are quite different from those produced by such natural means as frost, extreme heat or cold, water action, or stones falling from a cliff and fracturing boulders below. In these types, the rock sometimes breaks in a similar manner, but most of the flake scars are irregular, and instead of concentric rings and a bulb of percussion, often a rough depressed area is left on the surface with concentric rings formed around it.

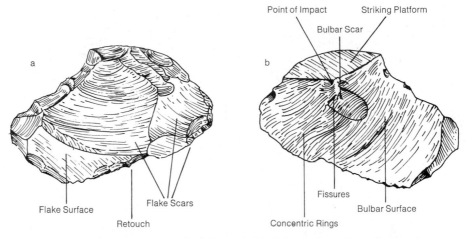

Figure 11.2   The components of a flake tool. (a) Flake surface. (b) Bulbar surface.

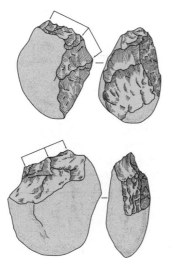

Figure 11.3   These cores, from Olduvai Gorge, Tanzania, are some of the earliest human tool forms. Arrows show the working edges.

Distinguishing human-worked from naturally fractured stones requires long experience with stone tool manufacture, especially when handling very early human artifacts. Our earliest ancestors used the simplest of hard hammer percussion techniques, removing two or three sharp-edged flakes from lava pebbles (Figure 11.3). Several famous controversies have raged over alleged "artifacts" found in early Ice Age deposits in Europe and Africa that are contemporary with periods when hominids were already flourishing elsewhere. Under such circumstances, the only sure identification of human-fractured stone implements is to find them in association with fossil human remains and broken animal bones, preferably on living sites.

Methods.   Figures 11.4 through 11.6 show some of the major stone-flaking methods prehistoric peoples used. The simplest and earliest was direct fracturing of the

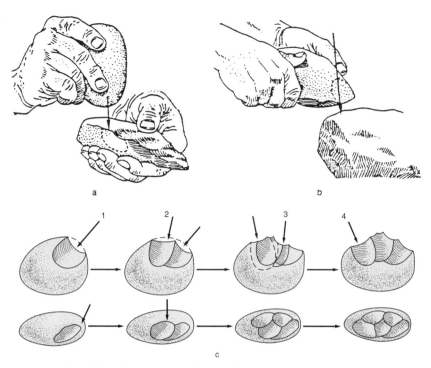

Figure 11.4   The earliest stoneworking techniques. (a) Using a hammerstone. (b) A variant on the hammerstone: striking a core against a stone block, the so-called anvil technique. (c) The earliest stone tools were made by a simple method. The top row shows the side view: First, two flakes were struck off (1 and 2); second, the stone was turned over, and two more flakes were removed (3); third, a fifth flake completed the useful life of the core (4). The bottom row shows the process from above.

stone with a hammerstone (Figure 11.4). After thousands of years, people began to make tools flaked on both surfaces, such as Acheulian hand axes (named after the town of St. Acheul in northern France, where they were first found). As time went on, the stoneworkers began to use bone, "soft" antler, or wood hammers to trim the edges of their hand axes. The hand ax of 150,000 years ago had a symmetrical shape; sharp, tough working edges; and a beautiful finish. As people became more skillful and specialized, such as the hunter-gatherers of about 100,000 years ago, they developed stone technologies producing artifacts for highly specific purposes. They shaped special cores that were carefully prepared to provide one flake or two of a standard size and shape (Figure 11.5).

About 35,000 years ago, some stoneworkers developed a new technology based on preparing cylindrical cores from which long, parallel-sided blades were removed by indirect percussion with a punch and hammerstone (Figure 11.6). These regular blanks were then trimmed into knives, scraping tools, and other specialized artifacts (Figure 11.7). This **blade technology** was so successful that it spread all over the world. It has been shown to be highly efficient. Controlled experiments resulted in

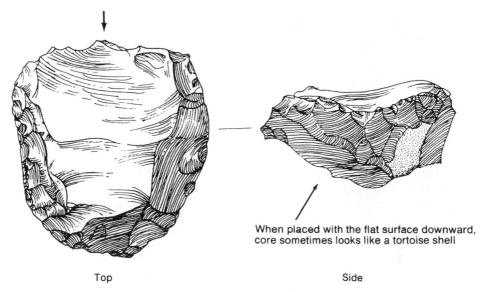

When placed with the flat surface downward,
core sometimes looks like a tortoise shell

Top   Side

Figure 11.5   A special core shaped to produce one thin flake. The arrow indicates where the flake was removed. Archaeologists call these Levallois cores, so-named after a suburb of Paris, France, where such cores were first discovered. (One-half actual size.)

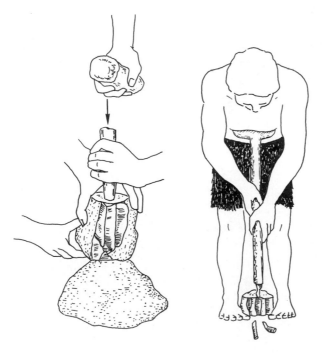

Figure 11.6   Two uses of the blade technique, employing a punch.

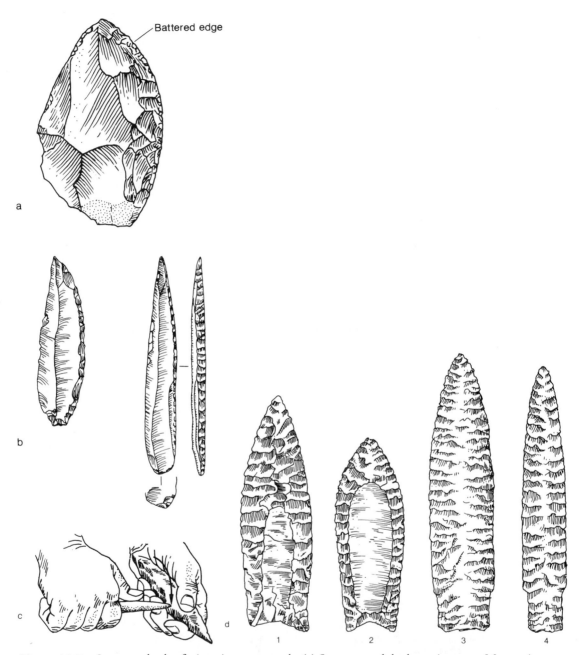

Figure 11.7   Some methods of trimming stone tools. (a) Steep retouch by battering, on a Mousterian, Middle Paleolithic, side scraper. (One-half actual size.) (b) Specialized blade tools made by pressing and sharpening the edges. These are backed blades used as spearpoints about 22,000 years ago. (Actual size.) (c) The pressure-flaking technique. (d) Paleo-Indian pressure-flaked points: (1) Clovis point, (2) Folsom point, (3) Scottsbluff point, (4) Eden point.

6 percent of the raw material being left on one exhausted blade core; 91 percent of it formed 83 usable blades (Sheets and Muto, 1972). Once blades had been removed from their cores, they were trimmed into shape by a variety of techniques. In some, the blade's side was pressure-flaked with an antler or a piece of wood to sharpen or blunt it. Sometimes the flake would be pressed against another stone, a bone, or a piece of wood to produce a steep, stepped edge or a notch (Figure 11.7a and b).

Pressure flaking became so refined that it became the most common technique of later prehistory, especially in the Americas (Figure 11.7c and d). The stoneworker used a small billet of wood or antler pressed against the working edge to exert pressure in a limited direction and remove a fine, thin, parallel-sided flake. Eventually, many flake scars formed in this way covered most of the implement's surfaces. Pressure flaking facilitates the production of many standardized tools with extremely effective working edges in a comparatively short time. In southwestern Asia, Europe, and many parts of Africa and southern and eastern Asia, small blades were fashioned into minute arrowheads, barbs, and adzes, known as microliths, often made using a characteristic notching technique (see Figure 10.4). A variant of this technique also evolved in Arctic America and in Australia, where small cores were produced to manufacture diminutive microblades or bladelets.

The blade technologies of later times could produce far more tools per pound of material than earlier methods. Later Stone Age peoples ground and polished stone when they needed a sharp and highly durable blade. They shaped the edges by rough flaking and then laboriously polished and ground them against a coarser rock, such as sandstone, to produce a sharp, tough working edge. Modern experiments have demonstrated the greater effectiveness of polished stone axes in felling forest trees, the toughened working edge taking longer to blunt than that of a flaked ax (W. H. Townsend, 1969). Polished stone axes became important in many early farming societies, especially in Europe, Asia, Mesoamerica, and parts of temperate North America. They were used in New Guinea as early as 28,000 years ago and in Melanesia and Polynesia for the manufacture of canoes, which were essential for fishing and trade (J. White and O'Connell, 1982).

Expert stoneworkers still fashion artifacts to this day, especially gunflints for use in flintlock muskets. Gunflint manufacture was a flourishing industry in Britain and France into the twentieth century, and it is still practiced in Angola, Africa, where flintlock muskets are used for hunting.

Stone Tool Analysis

Lithic Analysis.   **Lithic analysis** is the term used to describe the study of stone technologies. Early attempts at stone tool analysis used finished tools, or "type fossils," which were thought to be representative of different human cultures. This type-fossil approach was abandoned gradually as more sophisticated typological methods came into use, methods that named well-defined artifact types according to their shape, dimensions, and assumed use, such as the Acheulian hand ax and the Mousterian side scraper (named after the village of Le Moustier, France) (see Figure 11.7a). This approach led, like the type-fossil concept before it, to searches for perfect, "typical"

Doing Archaeology

Blade Technology:
The Swiss Army Knife of the Late Ice Age

The bright red Swiss Army Knife is a common artifact in the pockets of travelers throughout the world. Not limited to merely cutting and opening bottles, the most elaborate forms of the tool boast of scissors, tweezers, screwdrivers, nail file, toothpick, and corkscrew for just a start. I have eaten meals with this remarkable knife, extracted thorns, spliced ropes at sea, even sawn my way through animal fibers. All of this is possible because the Swiss Army Knife is basically a strong-hinged chassis with all manner of implements attached to it.

Late–Ice Age blade technology had its own Swiss Army Knife in the blade core, the carefully shaped nodule of fine-grained rock from which a stoneworker would strike off numerous parallel-sided, thin blades (Figure 11.8). Carry around the core like a pocket knife and you could fabricate a convenient stone tool any time you wished. The repertoire of late–Ice Age blade artifacts included a broad array of blunt-backed knives for spears, cutting tools, woodworking implements such as simple spokeshaves, and, most important of all, the **burin,** a blade with a chisel facet on the end, which opened up another range of artifact possibilities.

The burin could groove through the thick outer surface of fresh deer and reindeer antler, allowing late Ice Age people to extract long, thin strips of antler, which they turned into barbed fish and hunting spear points (see Figure 11.8). Larger antler fragments became spearthrowers used to propel spears much longer distances, thong straighteners, and many other artifacts used for specialized purposes. Most important of all, fine burins and borers enabled men and women to fashion the first perforated needles, needed for making the tailored, layered clothing that was essential for survival in long, subzero winters.

All this technological artistry stemmed from a simple blade technology that, like the Swiss Army Knife, allowed endless innovation and ingenuity.

The same technologies of burins and grooved antlers persisted long after the Ice Age and was a staple of hunter-gatherer societies in Europe as recently as 7000 B.C. By this time, stone technology was so refined that a stoneworker relied on much smaller cores to produce microblades that were snapped, then often mounted in wooden handles to serve as arrowbarbs and for other purposes.

artifacts. Many functional labels such as "projectile point" remain in use in modern stone tool studies, but they are no considered anything more than a generalized description of the form of an artifact. Functional analyses of this type have achieved great refinement in western Europe, where many varieties of Stone Age tools are to be found (Bordaz, 1970). As with other artifact forms, recent classifications have a sophisticated concern with analyses based on attributes chosen for their ability to throw light on manufacturing technology or function.

In recent years, the focus of lithic analysis has shifted dramatically from a preoccupation with finished tools to a broader concern with prehistoric lithic technology in a context of human behavior. Modern studies of stone technology rely on a combination

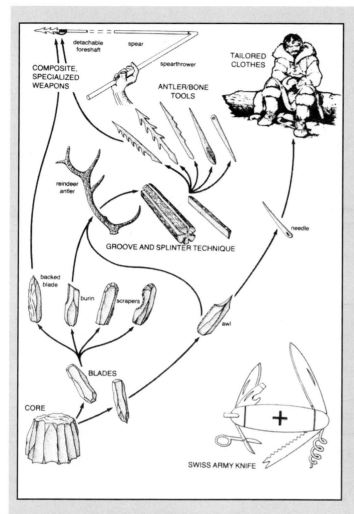

Figure 11.8 The "Swiss Army Knife" technology of the European late Ice Age.

of several approaches that focus as much on the processes of manufacture of artifacts as they do on the artifacts themselves.

Debitage Analysis. The making of any stone artifact is the result of a **reduction sequence,** a series of steps that begins with the selection of a core of fine-grained rock and ends with the completion of a finished artifact. Reconstructing these reduction sequences is one way in which archaeologists achieve an understanding of artifact manufacturing processes in prehistory.

Ancient stone tool manufacture can be reconstructed in several ways, for the clues lie in abandoned cores, in flake scars, in striking platforms, in the dimensions of flakes and blades, and even in the obvious and not-so-obvious mistakes made by ancient artisans. For example, a blow struck at the wrong point on a carefully prepared core can shatter it in distinctive ways easily recognized by someone familiar with lithic technology. Most steps in stone tool manufacture can be recognized by studying finished artifacts, cores, and, above all, the debris, often called **debitage,** left behind by the stoneworker. By close examination of debitage, an expert lithic technologist can separate primary flakes, flakes resulting from the rough blocking out of the core, from the finer flakes that were removed as the artisan prepared the striking platform on the top or sides of the core. Then there are the flakes that all this preparatory work was aimed at—the artifact blanks struck from the core. Finally, there are the fine retouching flakes that turn the blank into the finished projectile point, scraper, or whatever other implement was needed (A. Sullivan and Rozen, 1985).

> ***Lithic Experimentation.***   Archaeologists have experimented with the making of stone tools since the mid-nineteenth century. Today many archaeological laboratories ring with the sound of people trying to make stone tools and replicate ancient technology—and cutting their fingers in the process (Flenniken, 1984). Experimental work began with general attempts to compare the stone tool making methods of living peoples such as the Australian Aborigines with those of prehistoric cultures. Modern experimenters have drawn on both experimentation and ethnographic observation to work out prehistoric techniques (Swanson, 1975). Recent research has focused on reconstructing reduction sequences and also on locating and studying quarry sites; both approaches attempt to reconstruct prehistoric trade in obsidian and other rocks that can be traced back to their source (Chapter 16) (Torrence, 1986) and to understand better the relationships between human behavior and lithic technology (Ericson and Purdy, 1984).

There is another side to experimental lithic technology as well. Obsidian flake and blade edges are so sharp that they are widely used by modern eye surgeons, on the grounds that such cutting tools are superior to modern steel!

> ***Petrological Analyses.***   **Petrological analyses** have been applied with great success to the rocks from which stone tools are made, especially ground stone axes in Europe. Petrology is the study of rocks (Greek, *petros;* "stone"). A thin section of the ax is prepared and examined under a microscope. The minerals in the rock can then be identified and compared with samples from quarry sites (Ericson and Purdy, 1984). British archaeologists have had remarkable success with this approach and have identified more than twenty sources of ax blade stone (Bradley and Edmonds, 1993). Spectrographic analysis of distinctive trace elements in obsidian has yielded remarkable results in southwestern Asia and Mesoamerica, where this distinctive volcanic rock was traded widely from several quarry centers (Torrence, 1986) (Chapter 16).

> ***Refitting.***   Watch someone making stone tools and you will find that the person is sitting in the middle of a pile of ever-accumulating debris—chips, flakes, abandoned cores, and discarded hammerstones. Ancient stoneworkers produced the same sort of debris—hundreds, if not thousands, of small waste fragments, by-products of

toolmaking that are buried on archaeological sites of all ages. Vital information on prehistoric lithic technology comes from careful excavation of all the debitage from a place where a prehistoric artisan worked, then trying to fit the pieces together one by one, to reconstruct the procedures used—a process called **refitting.**

Refitting taxes the patience of even the most even-tempered archaeologist but can yield remarkable results. At the 9,000-year-old Meer II site in northern Belgium, Daniel Cahen and Lawrence Keeley (1980) combined edge-wear analysis with refitting to reconstruct a fascinating scenario. They used the evidence from three borers that were turned counterclockwise to show that a right-handed artisan walked away from the settlement and made some tools, using some prepared blanks and cores he brought with him. Later, a left-handed artisan came and sat next to him, bringing a previously prepared core, from which he proceeded to strike some blanks that he turned into tools. Reconstruction in this sort of fine detail is often impossible, but it has the advantage that the artifact pattern revealed in the archaeological record can be interpreted with extreme precision because the refitting shows that no modification has affected the evidence displayed in the archaeological record.

Sometimes, lithic specialists trace the movement of individual fragments or cores horizontally across a site, a process that requires even more patience than simple refitting. This procedure is of great value in reconstructing the functions of different locations in, say, a rock shelter site, where a stoneworker might make tools in one place, then carry a core to a nearby hearth and fashion another blade for a quite different process. This approach works well on Folsom Paleo-Indian sites on the Great Plains, where individual flakes have been refitted to their cores after having been excavated from locations as much as 12 feet (3.6 m) away.

Use-Wear Analysis.   **Use-wear analysis** involves both microscopic examination of artifact working edges and actual experiments using stone tools, in an effort to interpret telltale scratches and edge luster resulting from their use (Hayden, 1979; Keeley, 1980). Many researchers have experimented with both low- and high-power magnification and are now able to distinguish with considerable confidence among the wear polishes associated with different materials such as wood, bone, and hide (Phillips, 1988; Vaughan, 1985). The approach is now reliable enough to allow one to state whether a tool was used to slice wood, cut up vegetables, or strip meat from bones, but relatively few archaeologists are trained in using the microscopes and photographic techniques required for analyzing wear. Cahen and Keeley's study (1980) of stone tools from the Meer II site in Belgium showed that two people had used the tools they made to bore and grave fragments of bone. In instances like this, tool-wear analysis offers exciting opportunities for studying the behavior of individual stoneworkers thousands of years ago. There are many examples of distinctive microwear patterns, among them polishes that can be identified with high-powered microscopes. One instance is the flint sickle blade used for harvesting wild or domesticated grasses, which often shows a gloss caused by the silica in the grass stems.

Marvin Kay of the University of Arkansas is using three-dimensional Nomarski optics, which enables him to examine artifact surfaces with different colors of polarized light, to focus on polishes and on microscopic striations that result not only from hafting projectile points but also from the impact on the head when it strikes an animal. Nomarski optics also distinguishes other uses, such as butchery and woodworking. Kay compares the use wear on prehistoric artifacts with different use patterns resulting from modern experiments with artifact replicas against elephants and other animals. He has found, for example, that Clovis points from North America display minute scratches near the base that result when the head absorbs the shock of impact during the hunt. Not only that, but there are clear signs that many of them were used, then reshaped and used again, often serving as knives after their usefulness as points was over. Kay's methodology is so sophisticated that he can even detect planing effects on tough stone like quartzite, the planing resulting from use of the artifact for butchery. This research will allow archaeologists to develop histories of individual artifacts as part of a larger-scale analysis of activities on archaeological sites (Kay, 1996, 2000).

The important thing about lithic analysis is not just the study of the implements themselves; it is understanding of what the implements mean in terms of human behavior. And the new, multifaceted approaches to lithic analysis offer a real chance that methods such as edge-wear analysis will provide definitive ways of classifying stone tools in terms of their original functions.

Clay (Ceramics)

Objects made of clay are among the most imperishable of all archaeological finds, but pottery is a relatively recent innovation. From the very earliest times, people used animal skins, bark trays, ostrich eggshells, and wild gourds for carrying loads beyond the immediate surroundings of their settlements. Such informal vessels were ideal for hunter-gatherers, who were constantly on the move. Pottery appeared before 6000 B.C. at such early agricultural settlements in southwestern Asia as Çatalhöyük, Jarmo, and Jericho (Moore, 1985). In contrast, in Japan, pottery was made by hunter-gatherers before 10,000 B.C. (Akazawa and Aikens, 1986). The inhabitants of the Tehuacán Valley in highland Mexico began cultivating crops before the first pottery appeared in North America, in about 2500 B.C. (B. D. Smith, 1999).

The invention of pottery seems to have coincided with the beginnings of more lasting settlement. Fired clay receptacles have the advantage of being both durable and long-lived. We can assume that the first clay vessels were used for domestic purposes: for cooking, carrying water, and storing food. They soon assumed more specialized roles in salt making, in ceremonial activities, and as oil lamps and burial urns. Broken ceramic vessels are among the most common archaeological finds. Their shape, style, and form have provided the foundations for thousands of archaeological analyses (Olin and Franklin, 1982; Orton and others, 1993; Rice, 1987).

Pottery Technology

Modern industrial potters turn out dinnerware pieces by the millions, using mass-production methods and automated technology. Prehistoric artisans created each of their pieces individually, using the simplest of technology but attaining astonishing skill in shaping and adorning their vessels.

The clay used in potmaking was invariably selected with the utmost care; often, it was even traded over considerable distances. The consistency of the clay is critical; it is pounded meticulously and mixed with water to make it entirely even in texture. By careful kneading, the potter removes the air bubbles and makes the clay as plastic as possible, allowing it to be molded into shape as the pot is built up. When the clay is fired, it loses its water content and can crack, so the potter adds a *temper* to the clay, a substance that helps reduce shrinkage and cracking. Although some pot clays contain a suitable temper in their natural state, potmakers commonly added many other materials such as fine sand, powdered shell, or even mica as artificial temper.

Potmaking (ceramics) is a highly skilled art, with three major methods:

1. *Coil.* The vessel is built up with long coils or wedges of clay that are shaped and joined together with a mixture of clay and water (Figure 11.9). Sometimes the pot is built up from a lump of clay. Hand methods were common wherever potmaking was a part-time activity satisfying local needs.
2. *Mold.* The vessel is made from a lump of clay that is either pressed into a concave mold or placed over the top of a convex shape. Molding techniques were used to make large numbers of vessels of the same size and shape, as well as figurines, fishing net weights, and spindle whorls. Sometimes, several molds were used to make the different parts of a vessel.
3. *Potter's Wheel.* Wheel-made pots came into wide use after the invention of the potter's wheel in Mesopotamia about five thousand years ago. The vessel is formed from a lump of clay rotating on a platform turned by the potter's hands or feet. The wheel method has the

Figure 11.9 Pueblo Indian woman making pots using the coil method.

advantage of speed and standardization and was used to mass-produce thousands of similar vessels, such as the bright red Roman Samian ware (Shepard, 1971). Wheel-made pots can sometimes be identified by the parallel rotation marks on their interior surface.

Surface finishes provided a pleasing appearance and also improved the durability of the vessel in day-to-day use. Exterior burnishing and glazing made vessels watertight or nearly so. The potter smoothed the exterior surface of the pot with wet hands. Often, a wet clay solution, known as a *slip,* was applied to the smooth surface. Brightly colored slips were often used and formed painted decorations on the vessel (Figure 11.10). In later times, glazes came into use in some areas. A *glaze* is a form of slip that turns to a glasslike finish during high-temperature firing. When a slip was not applied, the vessel was allowed to dry slowly until the external surface was almost like leather in texture. Many utilitarian vessels were decorated with incised or stamped decorations, using shells, combs, stamps, and other tools. Some ceremonial pots were even modeled into human effigies (Figure 11.11) or were given decorations imitating the cords used to suspend the pot from the roof.

Figure 11.10   A painted Zuni bowl, ca. 1880. (22.7882; Height, 9¾ inches [25 cm]. (N21678). Zuni Pueblo, New Mexico. Courtesy, National Museum of the American Indian, Smithsonian Institution. Photo by Carmelo Guadagno.)

Figure 11.11   A spouted Moche bottle from Peru. (South America, Peru, North Coast, Moche culture, Portrait vessel of a ruler. Earthenware with pigmented clay slip, A.D. 300–700, 35.6 by 24.1 cm. Kate S. Buckingham endowment, 1955.2338 frontal view. Photograph © 1999, The Art Institute of Chicago. All Rights Reserved.)

The firing of clay objects requires careful judgment on the part of the potter. Most early pottery was fired over open hearths. The vessels were covered with fast-burning wood, whose ash would fall around the vessels and bake them evenly over a few hours. Far higher temperatures were attained in special ovens, known as **kilns,** which would not only bake the clay and remove its plasticity but would also dissolve carbons and iron compounds. Kilns were used to fire vessels at high temperatures and also for glazing, when two firings were needed. Once fired, the pots were allowed to cool slowly, and small cracks were repaired before they were ready for use.

The making of clay vessels was circumscribed by all manner of social and other variables (P. Arnold, 1991). Archaeological literature is rich in descriptions of pot-making techniques among people all over the world. Unfortunately, however, few of these studies go beyond technology and processes of manufacture. They may tell us something about the division of labor in making pots, but they reveal little about the potters' status in their own society, their artistic attitudes, or changing ceramic fashions. In many societies, pottery has a well-defined economic role, and the training of potters is long and elaborate. The analysis of ceramics in archaeology must, however, depend on an understanding of the cultural influences that lie behind the variations in pottery in the archaeological record (Rice, 1987).

Ceramic Analysis

An enormous expenditure of archaeological energy has gone into **ceramic analysis,** and a sophisticated literature covers the common analytical methods (Olin and Franklin, 1982; Rice, 1987; Shepard, 1971).

Analogy and Experiment. Controlled experiments to replicate prehistoric ceramic technology have been undertaken to acquire data on firing temperatures, properties of tempers, and glazing techniques (Shepard, 1971). Ethnographic analogy has been a fruitful source of basic information on potters and their techniques (Kramer, 1985, 1997), and the direct historical approach traces modern pottery styles back to the prehistoric past.

Form and Function and Stylistic Analysis. Two features of ancient pottery are immediately obvious when we examine a collection of vessels: shape and decoration. Generations of archaeologists have used ethnographic analogy to assign specific functions to different vessel forms. Bowls are commonly used for cooking and eating, but globular vessels are most suitable for storing liquids. Sometimes, associations of clay vessels and other artifacts, such as cooking utensils, leave no doubt as to their function. But such instances are rare, and archaeologists usually must rely on analysis of the vessel's form to infer its function.

Form analysis depends on the common assumption that the shape of a vessel directly reflects its function. This assumption, which is based on ethnographic analogies, can be dangerous, for many intangibles affect the function of pottery. Intangibles include the properties of the clay used, the technological devices available, and perhaps most important, the cultural values that constrain not only the technology but also the uses and fashions of the vessels. Changes in vessel form can sometimes reflect a change in economic activities, but the economic evidence must be complete before such conclusions can be drawn. The functional distinction between utilitarian (see Figure 10.6) and ceremonial vessels (see Figure 11.11) is one of the most evident, but it must be supported by vessel form and by direct association with other artifacts.

Form analysis is based on careful classification of clusters of different vessel shapes. These shapes can be derived from complete vessels or from potsherds that preserve the rim and shoulder profiles of the vessel. It is possible to reconstruct the pot form from these pieces by projecting measurements of diameter and vessel height. Such analyses produce broad categories of vessel form that are capable of considerable refinement (Sabloff, 1975).

Stylistic analysis is much more commonly used, for it concentrates not on the form and function of the vessel but on the decorative styles used by the potters. These are assumed to be independent of functional considerations and so reflect more accurately the cultural choices made by the makers. In areas such as the American Southwest, pottery styles have been used to trace cultural variations over thousands of years.

Even a cursory glance at pottery reports from different parts of the world will show you that archaeologists have used dozens of different stylistic classifications to study their potsherds. Only in recent years have people tried to standardize stylistic classifications, using clusters of easily recognized attributes to produce hierarchies of types, varieties, and modes. With this approach, small numbers of distinctive attributes from different pottery assemblages are recorded. These attributes commonly appear in associated sets of features that provide the basis for erecting types and varieties of pottery styles, which are assumed to represent the social system behind the pots studied. For instance, Classical Attic and Corinthian pottery from Greece reflect standardized styles that can be dated accurately. Although a *variety* may represent only the activities of one family of potters, a *type* can represent the work of several villages or an entire community. Thus, goes the argument, standardized pottery types reflect a fairly rigid social system that prescribes what pottery styles are used, but less formal designs are characteristic of a less restrictive society. However, can one really assume that pottery styles reflect social behavior? The answer must await the day when many more standardized typologies from different areas of the world are available.

Technological Analysis.   The more elaborate, computer-generated classifications of today reveal that many of the archaeologist's classificatory cornerstones, such as pottery temper, are in fact subject to complex behavioral and environmental factors rather than the simple barometers of human behavior they were once thought to be. For example, Marian Saffer found that classifications developed for pottery from the Georgia coast in the southeastern United States were based on simple criteria, among them tempers of sand, grit, and ground-up potsherds. There appeared to have been little variation in the style and decoration in Georgia coastal pottery for two thousand years. Therefore, archaeologists used variations in temper as criteria for distinguishing new cultures and phases. Saffer used clay samples from the islands and the mainland, as well as many decorative and stylistic attributes, together with a sophisticated computer analysis, to show that variations in temper could be correlated with the qualities of different potting clays. Thus, variations in temper are due not only to cultural factors but to environmental conditions as well (Rice, 1987).

Technological analysis of pottery focuses on the fabric and paste in potting clays and relates ceramic vessels to locally available resources. It also provides useful, statistically based yardsticks for interpreting variability between different pottery forms and for developing much more sophisticated pottery classifications. Furthermore, the current interest in regional studies of prehistoric cultures and in trade and exchange encourages the analysis of pottery clays as a means of tracing centers of ceramic manufacture. Throughout later prehistory, clay vessels were major trade commodities, not only for their own qualities but also because they were convenient receptacles for such products as olive oil, wine, or salt.

Tell el Amarna in Egypt was founded by the heretic Egyptian king Akhenaten in 1348 B.C. and was occupied only until his death, fifteen years later. It is famous for its fine artworks, for the immortal head of Queen Nefertiti, and for its diplomatic correspondence. Egyptologist Flinders Petrie found more than 1,300 Mycenaean potsherds in rubbish dumps from el Amarna's palace and nearby noble residences. Most of them were from containers used to carry imported, scented oils, which were traded widely from the Aegean across the eastern Mediterranean at the time. By using neutron activation analysis of thirty-seven elements in the clays used to make these vessels, and comparing them with samples taken from Mycenaean vessels discovered in Greece, German scientists have pinpointed their original place of production as a major pottery workshop in the Mycenae-Berbati region of the eastern Peloponnese in mainland Greece—a remarkable piece of archaeological detective work now being expanded with computer databases (Mommsen and others, 1992).

Numerous other procedures yield valuable information on ancient ceramics, including X-ray diffraction studies and ceramic petrology. These approaches can be used in combination to study what can be called **ceramic ecology,** the interaction of resources, local knowledge, and style that ultimately leads to a finished clay vessel (Stimmell and others, 1982). For instance, Mississippian pottery, manufactured in the southern and southeastern United States between A.D. 800 and 1500, was fired to a temperature between 1,472°F (800°C) and 1,652°F (900°C). The Mississippians used crushed shell to temper their pots, so their vessels should not have vitrified at these temperatures. But they did, and scanning electron microscope photographs reveal that the potters may have added salt to their raw clay, perhaps even tasting the clay during manufacture to see if it was correctly mixed. Mississippian settlement was concentrated in valley bottoms, where the potters used clay heavy in montmorillonite, adding crushed shell so that they could work the clay more easily. This technique created another problem, that of poor firing. So the potters added salt to improve the firing qualities. However, salt was available in relatively few locations, so a complex trading system in this newly vital commodity developed.

Technological analyses of pottery offer useful ways to amplify manufacturing data obtained from archaeological sources and ethnographic analogy (D. E. Arnold, 1985). Even the sediment found inside ancient pots can be examined spectrographically, and sometimes identified, as was a wine-storage jar from Iran dating to 4000 B.C. (Biers and McGovern, 1990).

Metals and Metallurgy

The study of metallurgy and metals found in archaeological sites is limited both by the state of preservation and by our knowledge of prehistoric metallurgy as a whole (Muhly and Wertime, 1980; Tylecote, 1992). Preservation of metal tools in archaeological horizons depends entirely on the soil's acidity. In some circumstances, iron tools are preserved perfectly and can be studied in great detail; in other cases, soil acids have reduced the iron to a rusty mass that is almost entirely useless. Copper, silver, and gold normally survive somewhat better.

Metals first became familiar to people in the form of rocks in their environment. Properties of metal-bearing rocks—color, luster, and weight—made them attractive for use in the natural state. Eventually, people realized that heat made such stone as flint and chert easier to work. When this knowledge was applied to metallic rocks, stoneworkers discovered that native copper and other metals could be formed into tools by a sequence of hammering and heating. Of the seventy or so metallic elements on the earth, only eight—iron, copper, arsenic, tin, silver, gold, lead, and mercury—were worked before the eighteenth century A.D. Properties of these metals that were important to ancient metalworkers were, among others, color, luster, reflecting abilities (for mirrors), acoustic quality, ease of casting and welding, and degrees of hardness, strength, and malleability. Metal that was easily recycled had obvious advantages (Craddock, 1995).

We know much about ancient metallurgy because prehistoric artifacts preserve traces of their thermal and mechanical history in their metallic microstructure. This structure can be studied under an optical microscope. Each grain of the metal is a crystal that forms as the metal solidifies. The shape and size of the grains can reveal whether alloys were used and indicate the cooling conditions and the type of mold used. At first, prehistoric metallurgists used "pure" metals, which could be worked easily but produced only soft tools. Then they discovered how to alloy each of these metals with a second one to produce stronger, harder objects with lower melting points.

The basic data for studying prehistoric alloys come from *phase diagrams,* which relate temperature and alloy composition, showing the relative solubility of metals when combined with other metals. Phase diagrams are developed under controlled conditions in a laboratory and tend to reflect ideal conditions. By examining the object under an optical microscope, researchers can often spot differences in chemical composition, such as the cored, treelike structure that is characteristic of cast copper-tin alloys. Metals contain insoluble particles that can give clues to the smelting procedures and types of ores used. An energy-dispersive X-ray spectrometer and a scanning electron microscope are used to identify the particles. This impressive battery of analytical techniques has enabled archaeologists to study how six thousand years of experimentation took humanity from simple manipulation of rocks to the production of steel in about 1000 B.C. The record of these millennia is read in the lenses of the microscope and reveals the triumphs and frustrations of the ancient smith.

Copper

The earliest metal tools were made by cold-hammering copper into simple artifacts. Such objects were fairly common in southwestern Asian villages by 6000 B.C. Eventually, some people began to melt the copper. They may have achieved sufficiently high temperatures with established methods used to fire pottery in clay kilns. The copper was usually melted or smelted into shapes and ingots within the furnace hearth itself. Copper metallurgy was widespread by about 4000 B.C. European smiths were working copper in the Balkans as early as 3500 B.C. In contrast to high-quality stone and iron, copper ores are rare and concentrated in well-defined regions. The metal was normally, but not invariably, alloyed with tin, which is even rarer. In the New World, copper-working was well developed among the Aztecs and the Inca. The Archaic peoples of Lake Superior exploited the native deposits of copper ore on the southern shores of the lake, and the metal was widely traded and cold-hammered into artifacts from Archaic to Woodland times (Figure 11.12).

Bronze

The real explosion—it was nothing less—in copper metallurgy took place midway through the fourth millennium B.C., when southwestern Asian smiths discovered that they could improve the properties of copper by alloying it with a second metal, such as arsenic, lead, or tin. Perhaps the first alloys came about when smiths tried to produce different colors and textures in ornaments. But they soon realized the advantages of tin, zinc, and other alloys that led to stronger, harder, and more easily worked

Figure 11.12 Mississippian copper repoussé plate of a human head, perhaps a portrait, c. A.D. 1100. (20.699 LeFlore County, Oklahoma (N21678). Courtesy, National Museum of the American Indian, Smithsonian Institution.)

artifacts. There is reason to believe that they experimented with the proportions of tin for some time, but most early bronzes contain about 5 to 10 percent tin (10 percent is the optimum for hardness). An extraordinary development in metallurgical technology occurred during the third millennium B.C., perhaps in part resulting from the evolution of writing and the expansion of trade in raw materials. By 2500 B.C., practically every type of metallurgical phenomenon except hardening of steel was known and used regularly. The use of tin alloying may have stimulated much trading activity, for the metal is relatively rare, especially in southwestern Asia. Bronze-working was developed to a high pitch in northern China after 2000 B.C. (Chang, 1984).

Gold

Gold-decked burials fascinate many people, but in fact they are rare finds in archaeological excavations. Gold did, however, have a vital part in prestige and ornamentation in many prehistoric societies. Thus Tutankhamun is sometimes described as the "Golden Pharaoh": his grave was rich in spectacular gold finds (Reeves, 1990). The burials of Moche lords of A.D. 400 under an adobe platform at Sipán, on the northern coast of Peru, revealed the remarkable wealth of this desert civilization. One shroud-wrapped warrior-priest wore a pair of gold eyes, a gold nose, and a gold chin-and-neck visor; his head was lying on a gold, saucerlike headrest (see Figure 1.4). Hundreds of minute gold and turquoise beads adorned the lord of Sipán, who wore sixteen gold disks as large as silver dollars on his chest. There were gold-and-feather headdresses and intricate ear ornaments, one of a warrior with a movable club (Alva and Donnan, 1993). The later Sicán and Chimú peoples of coastal Peru were master goldsmiths of pre-Columbian Latin America (see Site box). The Aztecs and the Inca also were talented goldsmiths whose magnificent products were shipped off to Europe and melted down for royal treasuries in the sixteenth century (Hosler, 1995).

Gold rarely forms compounds in its natural state. It was collected in its pure form or in grains gathered by crushing quartz and concentrating the fine gold by washing. The melting point of gold is about the same as that of copper, so no elaborate technology was needed. Gold is easily hammered into thin sheets without **annealing**—heating and cooling of metal to make it less brittle. Prehistoric smiths frequently used such sheets to sheath wooden objects such as statuettes. They also cast gold, used appliqué techniques, and alloyed it with silver and other ores. Gold was worked in southwestern Asia almost as early as copper, and it was soon associated with royal prestige. The metal was widely traded in dust, ornament, and bead form in many parts of the Americas and the Old World.

Iron

Bronze Age smiths certainly knew about iron. It was a curiosity, of little apparent use. They knew where to find the ore and how to fashion iron objects by hammering and heating. But the crucial process in iron production is *carburization,* in which iron is converted into steel. The result is a much harder object, far tougher than bronze tools. An iron object is carburized by heating it in close contact with charcoal for a

Site

The Lord of Sicán at Huaca Loro, Peru

In 1990–1992, archaeologist Izumu Shimada and a team of researchers excavated the Huaco Loro pyramid in the Lambayeque Valley area of Peru's north coast to investigate the little known Sicán culture, successor to the flamboyant Moche state in the region. The archaeologists unearthed a tomb at the north base of the pyramid that comprised a 10-foot-square (3-m-square) burial chamber at the base of a 33-foot (10-m) vertical shaft sunk into the clay of the river floodplain.

A man of forty to fifty years of age lay in an inverted position in the chamber, surrounded by his full ceremonial regalia. This included a large textile shawl with almost two thousand small gold foils sewn to the now-vanished cloth. The owner would have glittered and shimmered in the sun when he wore the mantle. A pair of ceremonial gloves were fashioned of gold, silver, and copper, one holding a golden cup, the other a wooden staff ornamented with gold and gold-silver-copper alloy. The man owned several golden headdresses, a semicircular bladed ceremonial knife with silver working edge, and a formal standard. He wore a gold mask with dripping nostrils, symbolic of his role as a shaman and a living personification of the Sicán deity, who is depicted in similar regalia.

The burial chamber included the skeletons of two young women and two juveniles who were sacrificial victims; a disassembled litter, which had carried the lord to his grave; imported seashells; clusters of beads; and bundles of copper, metal scrap, and thousands of copper sheet fragments, thought to have been a simple form of currency.

The Sicán lord's grave shows the extraordinary skills of Peruvian metalsmiths centuries before the Spanish Conquest. They were well aware of alloying, had developed ways of joining metal sheets without solder, and made ornaments by cutting out metal and by hammering decoration into sheets for a repoussé effect. As did other Andean metalworkers, they used depletion gilding, a technique that used acids to deplete baser metals from the surface of alloyed metal objects, leaving them high in gold concentration and with a golden appearance.

considerable period of time. The solubility of carbon in iron is very low at room temperature but increases dramatically at temperatures above 1,670°F (910°C), which could easily be achieved with charcoal and a good Bronze Age bellows. It was this technological development that led to the widespread adoption of iron technologies in the eastern Mediterranean area at least by 1000 B.C. (Muhly and Wertime, 1980).

Iron tools are found occasionally in some sites as early as 3000 B.C., but widespread smelting does not seem to have begun until the second millennium B.C. Use of iron was sporadic at first, for objects made of the metal were still curiosities. Iron tools were not common until around 1200 B.C., when the first iron weapons appeared in eastern Mediterranean tombs. The new metal was slow to catch on, partly because of the difficulty of smelting it. Its widespread adoption may have coincided with a period of disruption in eastern Mediterranean trade routes as a result of the collapse of several major kingdoms, among them that of the Hittites, after 1200 B.C. Deprived of tin, the smiths turned to the much more readily available substitute—iron. It was soon in use even for utilitarian tools and was first established on a large scale in continental Europe in the seventh century B.C. by Hallstatt peoples (Collis, 1997).

In earlier times iron had a comparatively limited economic role, most artifacts being slavish copies of bronze tools before the metal's full potential was realized. Weapons such as swords and spears were the first artifacts to be modified to make use of the new material. Specialized ironworking tools, such as tongs, as well as wood-working artifacts, began to be used as soon as the qualities of iron were recognized.

Iron ore is much more abundant in the natural state than copper ore. It is readily obtainable from surface outcrops and bog deposits. Once its potential was realized, it became much more widely used, and stone and bronze were relegated to subsidiary, often ornamental, uses.

The influence of iron was immense, for it made available abundant supplies of tough cutting edges for agriculture. With iron tools, clearing forests became easier, and people achieved even greater mastery over their environment. Ironworking profoundly influenced the development of literate civilizations. Some peoples, such as the Australian Aborigines and the pre-Columbian Americans, never developed iron metallurgy.

Metal Technologies

Copper technology began with the cold-hammering of the ore into simple artifacts. Copper smelting may have originated in the accidental melting of some copper ore in a domestic hearth or oven. In smelting, the ore is melted at a high temperature in a small kiln and the molten metal is allowed to trickle down through the charcoal fuel into a vessel at the base of the furnace. The copper is further reduced at a high temperature, then cooled slowly and hammered into shape. This annealing adds strength to the metal. Molten copper was poured into molds and cast into widely varied shapes.

Copper ores were obtained from weathered surface outcrops, but the best material came from subsurface ores, which were mined by expert diggers. Copper mines were in many parts of the Old World and provide a fruitful field for the student of metallurgy to investigate. The most elaborate European workings were in the Tyrol and Salzburg areas, where many oval workings were entered by a shaft from above (Cunliffe, 1997). At Mitterburg, Austria, the miners drove shafts into the hillside with bronze picks and extracted the copper by means of elaborate fire-setting techniques.

Many early copper workings have been found in southern Africa, where the miners followed surface lodes under the ground (Figure 11.13) (Bisson, 1977). Fortunately, the traditional Central and East African processes of copper smelting have been recorded. The ore was placed in a small furnace with alternating layers of charcoal and was smelted for several hours at high heat maintained with goatskin bellows. After each firing, the furnace was destroyed and the molten copper was dripped onto the top of a sand-filled pot buried under the fire. Bronze technology depended on *alloying*, the mingling of small quantities of such substances as arsenic and tin with copper. With its lower melting point, bronze soon superseded copper for much metalwork.

Figure 11.13 Excavation in a prehistoric copper mine at Kansanshi, Zambia, Central Africa. The miners followed outcrops of copper ore deep into the ground with narrow shafts, the earth fillings of which yielded both radiocarbon samples and artifacts abandoned by the miners.

Some of the most sophisticated bronze work was created by Chinese smiths, who cast elaborate legged cauldrons and smaller vessels with distinctive shapes and decoration in clay molds (Figure 11.14).

Ironworking is a much more elaborate technology that requires a melting temperature of at least 2,799°F (1,537°C). (For traditional African technology, see Schmidt, 1996a. See also the essays in Norbach, 1997.) Ancient smiths normally used an elaborate furnace filled with alternating layers of charcoal and iron ore that was maintained at a high temperature for many hours with a bellows. A single firing often yielded only a spongy lump of iron, called a bloom, which then had to be forged and hammered into artifacts. It took some time for the metallurgists to learn that they could strengthen working edges by quenching the tool in cold water. This process gave greater strength, but it also made the tool brittle. The tempering process, reheating the blade to a temperature below 1,340°F (727°C), restored the strength. Iron technology was so slow in developing that it remained basically unchanged from about 600 B.C. until medieval times (Piggott, 1985).

Analysis of Metal Artifacts

Typological Analyses. In Europe, metal tools have been analyzed for typology since the early nineteenth century. Stylistic features of bronze brooches, swords, and

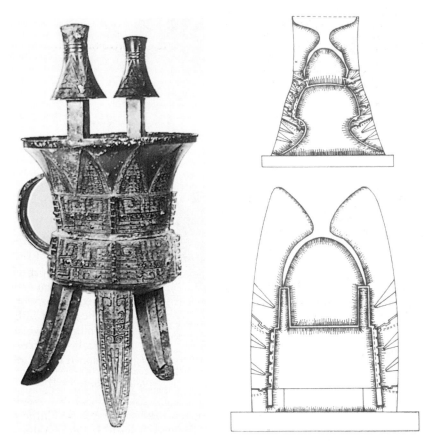

Figure 11.14   Shang ceremonial bronze vessel from about the twelfth century B.C. and diagrams of clay molds for casting such vessels. (Chinese bronze; 12th Century B.C., Shang dynasty; ceremonial vessel of the type chia; 52.8 by 30.5 cm (20^{13}⁄$_{16}$ × 12 in.), 23.1. Freer Gallery of Art, Smithsonian Institution, Washington, D.C.: Purchase, F1923.1)

axes and of iron artifacts were very sensitive to fashion and to changing trading patterns. As a result, the evolution of bronze pins or of iron slashing swords, for example, can be traced across Europe, with small design changes providing both relative dating and occasional insights into the lifeways of the people who used them (Cunliffe, 1997). In many ways, such studies are similar in intent to those carried out with stone implements or potsherds.

Technological Analyses.   In many respects, technological analyses are more important than the study of finished artifacts. Many of the most important questions relating to prehistoric metallurgy involve manufacturing techniques. Technological studies start with ethnographic analogies and actual reconstructions of prehistoric metallurgical processes. Chemists study iron and copper slag and residues from excavated furnaces. Microscopic examination of metal structure and ores yields valuable information not only on the metal and its constituents and alloys but also on the methods used to produce the finished tool. The ultimate objective of the technological analyses is to reconstruct the entire process of metal tool production, from the mining of the ore to the production of the finished artifact.

Bone

Bone as a material for toolmaking probably dates to the very beginnings of human history, but the earliest artifacts apparently consisted of little more than fragments of fractured animal bone used for purposes that could not be fulfilled by wood or stone implements (M. Leakey, 1973). The earliest standardized bone tools date from later prehistoric times. Splinters of bone were sharpened and used as points in many societies, but bone and antler artifacts were especially favored by the Upper Paleolithic peoples of southwestern France from 30,000 to 12,000 years ago and by postglacial hunter-gatherers in Scandinavia (Gamble, 1999). In both the Old World and the New, later bone implements were ground and scraped from long bones, hardened in the fire, and polished with beeswax to produce arrowheads, spearpoints, needles, and other artifacts. Bone was also carved and engraved, especially during Upper Paleolithic times in western Europe, as was reindeer antler (Bahn and Vertut, 1988).

Deer antler was an even more important material than bone for some later hunter-gatherers. Fully grown deer antler is particularly suitable for making barbed or simple harpoons and spearpoints. Bone and antler were much used in prehistoric times for harpoons for fishing and for conventional hunting. Numerous harpoons are found in Magdalenian sites in western Europe (Figure 11.15) and in Eskimo settlements in the Arctic, where they form a valuable index of cultural development, analogous to that of pottery in the American Southwest (Dumond, 1987).

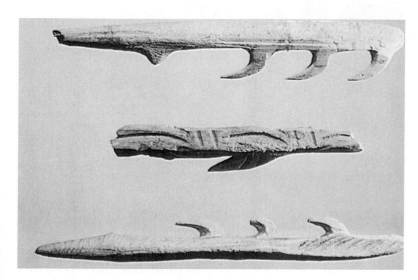

Figure 11.15
Magdalenian antler harpoons from France, about 15,000 years old. (About two-thirds actual size.) (Photograph by Jean Vertut, taken at the British Museum. Copyright The British Museum.)

The humble bone or ivory needle may have been a revolutionary artifact in prehistory, for it enabled humans to manufacture layered, tailored clothing. Such garments were essential for colonizing periglacial latitudes of the Old World, an event that occurred at least 25,000 years ago (Fagan, 1991).

Bone Tool Analysis

In the Arctic, where bone and ivory are critical materials, elaborate typological studies have been made of the stylistic and functional changes in such diverse items as harpoons and the winged ivory objects fastened to the butts of harpoons (Figure 11.16). Other artifacts include picks made of walrus tusk and snow shovels and wedges of ivory and bone, as well as drills and domestic utensils. Studying such a range of bone artifacts is complicated by the elaborate and variable engraved designs applied to some, but Henry B. Collins and others have been able to trace the development of the harpoon of the Northern Maritime Eskimo from the elaborate types of the Okvik and Old Bering Sea phases to the simpler forms characteristic of the Punuk phase and the modern Eskimo weapons (Fagan, 2005).

Bone technology was of the simplest, so technological analyses are rudimentary. The most basic bone technologies involved splitting and flaking bones. Fine points were produced by polishing slivers of bone against grinding surfaces. The Magdalenians used fine lengths of reindeer antler, which they removed from the beam by grooving through the hard outer core of the antler with stone burins or engraving tools. It is no coincidence that their material culture included a wide range of scraping and graving tools (Fagan, 1991).

Figure 11.16   Bone and ivory artifacts. (*left*) Harpoon socket piece, Old Bering Sea style. (3.7 inches [9.5 cm] long.) (*right*) Turreted ivory object of the Punuk phase. (2.7 inches [7 cm] wide.)

Wood

Nonhuman primates sometimes use sticks to obtain grubs, or for other purposes, so it is logical to assume that since the earliest times, humans also may have used sticks. Wood implements form a major part of many modern hunter-gatherer tool kits; occasional tantalizing glimpses of prehistoric wood artifacts have come down to us where preservation conditions have been favorable. The oldest known wooden tools are a series of sophisticated, large wooden throwing spears from Schoningen in northern Germany, dating to about 400,000 years ago. Numerous wood artifacts, as well as basketry, have come from dry sites in western North America.

The Ozette village on the Olympia Peninsula in Washington was buried by a prehistoric landslide that covered up not only several wood longhouses but also many domestic artifacts, baskets, boxes, and other fine wooden tools (Chapter 4). The waterlogged conditions preserved fibers and delicate halibut fishhooks complete with their bindings. Richard Daugherty's most important wooden find was a ritual whale fin carved in cedar wood, decorated with 700 sea otter teeth (Figure 11.17) (Kirk, 1974).

Wood Technology and Analysis

The manufacture of wood tools involves such well-understood mechanical processes as cutting, whittling, scraping, planing, carving, and polishing. Fire was often used to harden sharpened spearpoints, and oil and paint imparted a fine sheen and appearance to all kinds of wood artifacts. On the rare occasions when wood artifacts are preserved, important clues to their manufacture can be obtained by closely examining the objects

Figure 11.17 A whale fin carved from cedar wood and inlaid with more than 700 sea otter teeth, found at Ozette, Washington. The teeth at the base are set in the design of a mythical bird with a whale in its talons.

themselves. Unfinished tools are very useful, especially handles and weapons that have been blocked out but not finished (Coles and Coles, 1986). Even more revealing are wood fragments from abandoned buildings, fortifications, and even track walkways. Microscopic analysis of wood fragments and charcoal can provide information on the woods used to build houses, canoes, and other such objects. On very rare occasions, stone projectile heads and axes have been recovered in both waterlogged and dry conditions in which their wooden handles and shafts have survived, together with the thongs used to bind stone to wood. The Ozette excavations yielded complete house planks and even some wooden boxes that had been assembled by skillful grooving and bending of planks (Kirk, 1974).

In many instances, the only clues to the use of wood come from stone artifacts, such as spokeshaves and scrapers used to work it, or from stone ax blades and other tools that were once mounted in wooden handles. Only the form of the artifact and occasional ethnographic analogies allow researchers to reconstruct the nature of the perishable mount that once made the artifact an effective tool.

Wood was probably the most important raw material available to our ancestors. The thousands upon thousands of ground stone axes in the archaeological record all once had wooden handles. Wood was used for house building, fortifications, fuel, canoes, and containers. Most skilled woodworking societies used the simplest technology to produce both utilitarian and ceremonial objects. They used fire and the ringing of bark to fell trees, stone wedges to split logs, and shells and stones to scrape spear shafts.

Basketry and Textiles

Basket production is one of the oldest crafts (Adovasio, 1979). Basketry includes such items as containers, matting, bags, and a wide range of fiber objects. Textiles are found in many later, dry sites, and they are well preserved along the Peruvian coast (Moseley, 2000).

Some scholars believe that basketry and textiles are among the most sensitive artifacts for the archaeologist to work with, culturally speaking, on the grounds that people lived in much more intimate association with baskets and textiles than with clay vessels, stone tools, or houses. Furthermore, even small fragments of basketry and textiles display remarkable idiosyncrasies of individual manufacture.

Patricia Anawalt is a textile expert who has spent many years studying pre-Columbian garments depicted on Mexican Indian codices. This research has enabled her to work out some of the complicated sumptuary rules that governed military uniforms and other clothing. For example, the length, material, and decoration of Aztec men's cloaks were regulated precisely by the state. Even the type of knot was specified (Anawalt, 1981).

The dry climate of the Peruvian coast has preserved the wardrobes of Paracas nobles buried between 600 and 150 B.C. Paracas rulers wore mantles, tunics, ponchos, skirts, loincloths, and headpieces. These garments were embroidered with rows of brightly colored anthropomorphic, zoomorphic, and composite figures (Figure 11.18). Interpreting the iconographic patterns that appear on these ancient garments tells us

Figure 11.18 Cotton funerary textile from the Paracas Peninsula, Peru, dating to c. 300 B.C. ("Cloth with Procession of Figures," Peru, South Coast, Nasca Style, 100 B.C. – 200. Cotton, plain weave and pigment [field]; camelid fiber, plain weave [border], 69.8 × 280.7 cm. © The Cleveland Museum of Art, 2003. The Norweb Collection, 1940.530)

something of Paracas religious and social customs (Paul and Turpin, 1986). One of the important functions of a Paracas ruler was to mediate between people and the supernatural forces that influenced and determined life's events. Many of the rulers' garments were adorned with shaman figures, showing that the wearer had a special relationship to the supernatural (Anton, 1988). (For study methods, see M. E. King, 1978.)

It is easy for archaeologists to become preoccupied with technology and artifacts, but the potential is great for insights into ancient society and subsistence from such research, provided that the ultimate objective is to study people rather than inanimate objects.

Summary

One of the main inorganic materials used by prehistoric peoples was stone, especially hard, homogeneous rock, which fractures according to the conchoidal principle. We described the basic techniques for manufacturing stone tools, starting with the stone-on-stone technique, the cylinder-hammer method, and the prepared cores used to produce blanks for Middle Paleolithic artifacts. Blade technology came into use about 45,000 years ago. Lithic experimentation and ethnoarchaeology have leading roles in the study of stone technologies; edge-wear and petrological studies throw light on the trade in raw materials and the uses to which tools were put.

Ceramics (clay objects), which date to the last 10,000 years of prehistory, are a major preoccupation of archaeologists. We described the process of pottery manufacture, the various methods used, and the surface finishes employed. Ceramic analysis proceeds by analogy and experiment, research in which controlled experiments with firing and the properties of clay have had leading parts. The vessels themselves are studied through form and functional analyses. Many archaeologists prefer to use stylistic analyses. Clusters of attributes are used now, also, in attempts to standardize stylistic classifications.

Metallurgy is a phenomenon of the past six thousand years. We described the basic properties of copper, bronze, gold, and iron, and some of the cultural contexts in which metallurgy developed. Typological and technological analyses are used to study prehistoric metallurgy.

Bone tools are thought to be among the earliest of all artifacts. They are important in some areas, particularly the Arctic, as indicators of typological change. The functional analysis of bone tools is somewhat easier than that of stone tools or ceramics.

The manufacture of wood tools involves well-understood mechanical processes, such as cutting and whittling, and these can often be identified even from unfinished artifacts. Stone artifacts and other materials that have been found mounted in wooden handles provide insights into the uses of composite artifacts.

Basketry and textiles offer unique opportunities for studying individual idiosyncrasies in the archaeological record; they also provide useful chronological markers.

Key Terms

annealing	core	reduction sequence
blade technology	debitage	reductive (subtractive)
bulb of percussion	form analysis	technology
burin	kiln	refitting
ceramic analysis	lithic analysis	stylistic analysis
ceramic ecology	petrological analysis	technological analysis
conchoidal fracture	pressure flaking	use-wear analysis

Guide to Further Reading

ARNOLD, DEAN E. 1988. *Ceramic Theory and Cultural Process.* Cambridge: Cambridge University Press. A well-written and closely argued discourse on ceramic ecology.

CRABTREE, DON E. 1972. *An Introduction to Flintworking.* Pocatello: Idaho State Museum. The best simple account of basic lithic technology ever written, by an expert with a lifetime of experience. Valuable glossary and clear illustrations.

HOSLER, DOROTHY. 1995. *The Sounds and Colors of Power.* Cambridge, MA: MIT Press. An authoritative study of metallurgy in the Americas. For the advanced reader.

KEELEY, LAWRENCE H. 1980. *Experimental Determination of Stone Tool Uses.* Chicago: University of Chicago Press. An especially valuable monograph on use wear and stone tools.

MUHLY, JAMES D., and THEODORE A. WERTIME, eds. 1980. *The Coming of the Age of Iron.* New Haven, CT: Yale University Press. Essays on early metallurgy, covering much more than just ironworking. Although somewhat outdated, a good starting point.

RICE, PRUDENCE M. 1987. *Pottery Analysis: A Sourcebook.* Chicago: University of Chicago Press. An excellent reference book for anyone interested in ceramics.

SHEPARD, ANNA O. 1971. *Ceramics for the Archaeologist.* 2d ed. Washington, DC: Smithsonian Institution. The classic work on ceramics in the Americas. Technical and informative.

Environments, Lifeways, People, and the Intangible

And I prophesied as I was commanded; and as I prophesied, there was a noise, and behold, a rattling; and the bones came together, bone to its bone. And as I looked, there were sinews on them, and flesh had come upon them, and skin had covered them.

Ezekiel 37:10

In Part VI we discuss how archaeologists study the ways in which people have solved the problems of making a living and adapting to their environment. Chapter 12 examines the many ways in which researchers can now reconstruct both short- and long-term climatic and environmental change. Chapter 13 describes the analysis of food remains, animal bones, vegetable foods, and evidence of prehistoric diet. Archaeologists rely very heavily on ethnographic analogies for interpreting prehistoric subsistence and past lifeways. In Chapter 14 we examine some of the latest work in experimental archaeology and ethnoarchaeology, approaches that involve both controlled experiments and observations in the field. Human settlements changed radically through prehistory. In Chapter 15 we survey the ways in which archaeologists study ancient settlement patterns, with special reference to recent research in Mesoamerica. Trade, social organization, and religious beliefs are the topics of Chapters 16 and 17, which make the point that much information on these subjects can be obtained through careful research design and meticulous analysis of field data. The study of all facets of ancient lifeways is an essential preliminary to interpretation of culture change.

CHAPTER 12

Ancient Environments

Eland scene painted by San hunter-gatherers in a rock shelter. The elongated hunters are probably dancing around the animal, which is superimposed on the humans intentionally.

In 4500 B.C., a patch of woodland in northern England boasted of mature oak, ash, and elm trees, interspersed with occasional patches of open grassland and swamp. In 3820 B.C., some foragers set fire to the forest, to encourage fresh green shoots for feeding deer. Birch and bracken then appeared. About thirty years later, the landscape was cleared even more. Numerous charcoal fragments indicate that fire swept through the undergrowth, leaving fine ash to fertilize the soil. Then wheat pollen and pollen of a cultivation weed, *Plantago lanceolata,* appeared. Fifty years of wheat farming ensued. These years saw only two fires, one after six years; the other, nineteen years after that. Then, seventy years passed, during which agriculture ceased and the land stood vacant. Hazel, birch, and alder became more common and oak resurged, as woodland rapidly gained ground.

This scenario of brief clearance, slash-and-burn agriculture, then abandonment and regeneration was repeated at thousands of locations in ancient Europe in the early years of Stone Age farming. Over a few centuries, the natural environment of mixed oak forest was transformed beyond recognition by gardens and domesticated animals. Until a few years ago, we could only have guessed at these environmental changes. Today, analysis of fine-grained pollen and other highly sophisticated methods allow the reconstruction of even short-lived climatic and environmental changes in the remote past.

Archaeology is unique in its ability to study culture change over very long periods of time. By the same token, it is a multidisciplinary science that also studies human interactions with the natural environment over centuries and millennia. This chapter describes some of the ways archaeologists study long- and short-term environmental change from a multidisciplinary perspective.

Long- and Short-Term Climatic Change

Climatic change comes in many forms. The long cycles of cold and warm associated with the Ice Age occur on a millennial scale and have long-term effects on human existence. For example, the existence of a low-lying land bridge between Siberia and

Discovery

Eruption at Akrotiri, Greece, 1967

Only rarely do archaeologists find sites associated with direct evidence of ancient climatic or natural phenomena. A half century ago, Greek archaeologist Spyridon Marinatos speculated that the flamboyant Minoan civilization of Crete was severely damaged by a huge volcanic eruption that blew the center of the island of Santorini (Thera), 62 miles (100 km) north, into space in about 1688 B.C. Few archaeologists agreed with his theory. Undeterred, Marinatos searched diligently for Minoan sites on Santorini, but he found that everything was buried under massive volcanic ash deposits. In 1967, he heard reports from farmers of masses of stones close underground in the fields around Akrotiri in the south of the island. So dense were the boulders that the farmers could not plow their land. Marinatos began digging into places where the ground

had collapsed between the subterranean masonry and promptly discovered the Greek Pompeii, an island town of 3,500 years ago completely buried by pumice and ash when the volcano erupted (Figure 12.1).

Akrotiri's houses are remarkably well preserved, their stone and timber walls often two stories high. Brilliant polychrome frescoes still adorn some of the rooms, depicting religious and military scenes, the island landscape, animals, and plants. Food storage jars still stand in the basements of the houses. But there was no trace of the inhabitants, who had fled when ominous subterranean rumblings began. The imported Minoan pottery at Akrotiri is at least twenty to thirty years earlier than that from the latest levels of Cretan villages, proving that Marinatos was wrong. The Santorini eruption did not destroy Minoan civilization.

Figure 12.1   Two-story houses perfectly preserved under volcanic ash at Akrotiri, Santorini Island, Aegean Sea, Greece.

Alaska during much of the late Ice Age may have allowed humans to forage their way from Asia into the Americas before 15,000 years ago, but the actual formation of the shelf that linked the two continents would have taken many centuries and human generations.

Short-term climatic change, such as the floods or droughts caused by El Niño episodes or the volcanic eruptions that dump ash into the atmosphere, are another matter. Memories of catastrophic famines and other results associated with such events would have endured for generations, for they had immediate impact on hundreds, if not thousands, of people. Throughout human history, people have developed strategies to deal with sudden climatic shifts, which bring drought, hunger, or unexpected food shortages. Humans have always been brilliant opportunists, capable of improvising solutions to unexpected problems caused by environmental change. Thus, environmental reconstruction and climatic change are two major concerns for archaeologists wherever they work.

Geoarchaeology

Geoarchaeology, the study of archaeology using the methods and concepts of the earth sciences, plays a major role in reconstructing ancient environments and long- and short-term climatic change (Butzer, 1974, 1982; Waters, 1993). This is a far wider enterprise than geology and involves at least four major approaches:

1. Geochemical, electromagnetic, and other remote-sensing devices to locate sites and environmental features (Chapter 8)
2. Studies of site-formation processes (Chapter 4) and of the spatial contexts of archaeological sites, a process that includes distinguishing human-caused phenomena from natural features
3. Reconstructing the ancient landscape by a variety of paleogeographic and biological methods, including pollen analysis
4. Relative and chronometric dating of sites and their geological contexts (Chapter 7)

People are geomorphic agents, just as the wind is. Accidentally or deliberately, they carry inorganic and organic materials to their homes. They remove rubbish, make tools, build houses, abandon tools. These mineral and organic materials are subjected to all manner of mechanical and biochemical processes while people live on a site and after they abandon it. The controlling geomorphic system at a site, whatever its size, is made up not only of natural elements but of a vital cultural component as well. The geoarchaeologist is involved with archaeological investigations from the very beginning and deals not only with formation of sites and with the changes they underwent during occupation but also with what happened to them after abandonment. Working closely with survey archaeologists, geoarchaeologists locate sites and other cultural features in the natural landscape using aerial photographs, satellite images, and even geophysical prospecting on individual sites. As part of this process, they examine dozens of natural geological exposures, where they study the stratigraphic and sedimentary history of the entire region as a wider context for the sites found within it. The ultimate objective is to identify not only the microenvironment of the site but also the environmental conditions of the region as a whole—to establish ecological and spatial frameworks for the socioeconomic and settlement patterns that are revealed by archaeological excavations and surveys (Broschier and others, 1992; see also Chapter 15).

Long-Term Climatic Change: The Great Ice Age

About 1.8 million years ago, global cooling marked the beginning of the **Pleistocene Epoch,** or more popularly, the Great Ice Age (Goudie, 1992; Lowe and Walker, 1997). (The term **Quaternary Period** is commonly used to cover both the Pleistocene Epoch and the Holocene Epoch [postglacial times, discussed later in this chapter].) It was remarkable for dramatic swings in world climate. On numerous occasions during the Pleistocene, great ice sheets covered much of western Europe and North America, bringing arctic climates to vast areas of the Northern Hemisphere. Scientists have identified at least eight major glacial episodes over the past 780,000 years, alternating with shorter warm periods, when the world's climate was sometimes warmer than it is today. The general pattern is cyclical, with slow coolings culminating in a relatively short period of intense cold, followed by rapid warming. For 75 percent of the past three-quarters of a million years, the world's climate has been in transition from one extreme to another. We still live in the Ice Age, in a warm interglacial period. If current scientific estimates are correct and human-caused global warming does not interfere, we will probably begin to enter another cold phase in about 23,000 years.

No one knows exactly what causes the climatic fluctuations of the Ice Age, but they are connected with oscillations in the intensity of solar radiation and the trajectory of the earth around the sun. Such climatic changes are of great importance to archaeologists, for they form a long-term environmental backdrop for the early chapters of our past. Although almost no human beings lived on, or very close to, the great ice sheets that covered so much of the Northern Hemisphere, they did live in regions affected by geological phenomena associated with the ice sheets: coastal areas, lakes, and river floodplains. When human artifacts are found in direct association with Pleistocene geological features of this type, it is sometimes possible to tie in archaeological sites with the relative chronology of Pleistocene events derived from geological strata (Gamble, 1999).

Glacial Geology and Sea Levels

Ice Age glaciers and ice sheets formed in mountainous, high-latitude areas and on continental plains during the Pleistocene. Prolonged periods of arctic climate and abundant snowfall caused glaciers to form over enormous expanses of northern Europe, North America, and the alpine areas of France, Italy, and Switzerland. These alternated with shorter interglacial phases, when world climate was considerably warmer than it is today. Glacial geologists have identified the rubble deposits left by advancing and retreating ice sheets throughout the Northern Hemisphere. However, the processes of advance and retreat were so destructive of earlier deposits in most places that we have a clear picture of only the last two or three glacial advances.

Every ice sheet had a **periglacial** zone, an area affected by glacial climatic influences. For example, at the height of the late Ice Age some 20,000 years ago, the persistent glacial high-pressure zone centered over the northern ice sheet caused dry, frosty winds to blow over the periglacial regions of central Europe. The dry winds blew fine dust, called **loess,** onto the huge, rolling plains of central and eastern Europe and northern North America (Figure 12.2).

About 18,000 years ago, a hunter-gatherer band lived on the edge of the shallow Dnepr Valley at Mezhirich in southern Ukraine (Soffer, 1985). These people dug the floors of their semisubterranean dwellings into the soft loess soil, then roofed them with lattices of mammoth bones, using the enormous jawbones to support the roofs. Once covered with sod, the domelike houses hugged the ground and offered excellent protection from the bitter cold winds of winter. Both radiocarbon dates and the stratified loess deposits date the Mezhirich site to within close chronological limits. Much later, around 6000 B.C., Danubian peoples, the first farmers of temperate Europe, settled almost exclusively on these same light loess soils, for they were eminently

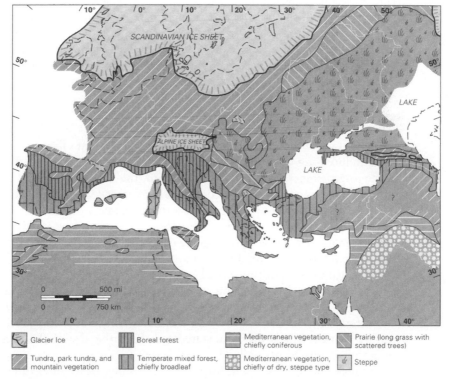

Figure 12.2   Europe during the height of the last Ice Age glaciation.

Source: Karl W. Butzer, *Archaeology as Human Ecology: Method and Theory for a Contextual Approach.* © 1982. Reprinted by permission of Cambridge University Press.

suitable for the simple slash-and-burn agriculture practiced by these pioneer farmers (Figure 12.3) (Cunliffe, 1997).

The ice sheets growing on land had effects beyond the formation of loess plains. The water that fell as snow to form the ice sheets and glaciers ultimately came from the oceans. When large areas in the northern latitudes were covered with ice, enormous quantities of water—enough to reduce the general level of the oceans by many yards, more than 295 feet (90 m) at the height of the last glaciation 18,000 years ago—were immobilized on land. This **eustatic** effect was accompanied by an **isostatic** effect as well. The sheer deadweight of the massive ice sheets sank the loaded continental blocks of the landmasses into the viscous underlying layers of the earth that lie some 6 miles (10 km) below the surface. In interglacial times, the world's sea levels rose sharply to levels higher than they are today. As the water levels retreated once again, they left their abandoned beaches raised high above later sea levels, high and dry where geologists can study them today.

Many prehistoric settlements that were occupied during periods of low sea levels are, of course, buried deep beneath the modern ocean waters. Numerous sites on ancient beaches have been found dating to times of higher sea levels. American archaeologist Richard Klein excavated a coastal cave at Nelson's Bay in the Cape Province of South Africa that now overlooks the Indian Ocean (Deacon and Deacon, 1999). Large quantities of shellfish and other marine animals are found in the uppermost levels of the cave. But in the lower levels, occupied roughly 11,000 to 12,000 years ago, fish bones and other marine resources are very rare. The seashore was many miles away at that time, for world sea levels were much lower during a long period of arctic climate in northern latitudes. Today the cave is only 50 yards (45 m) from the sea.

Deep Sea and Ice Cores

The world's ocean floors are a priceless archive of ancient climatic change. Deep-sea cores produce long columns of ocean-floor sediments that include skeletons of small marine organisms that once lived close to the ocean's surface. The planktonic foraminifera (protozoa) found in deep-sea cores consist largely of calcium carbonate. When alive, their minute skeletons absorbed organic isotopes. The ratio of two of these isotopes—oxygen-16 and oxygen-18—varies as a result of evaporation. When evaporation is high, more of the lighter oxygen-16 is extracted from the ocean, leaving the plankton to be enriched by more of the heavier oxygen-18. When great ice sheets formed on land during glacial episodes, sea levels fell as moisture was drawn off for continental ice caps. During such periods, the world's oceans contained more oxygen-18 in proportion to oxygen-16, a ratio reflected in millions of foraminifera. A mass spectrometer is used to measure this ratio, which does not reflect ancient temperature changes but is merely a statement about the size of the oceans and about contemporaneous events on land.

You can confirm climatic fluctuations by using other lines of evidence as well, such as the changing frequencies of foraminifera and other groups of marine microfossils in the cores. By using statistical techniques, and assuming that relationships

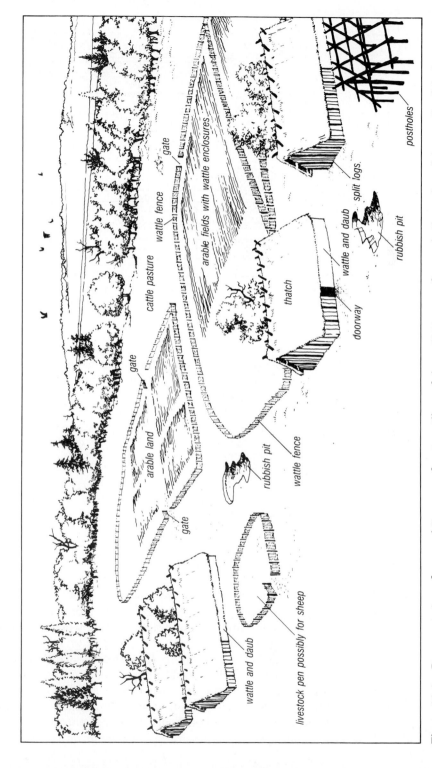

Labels within figure:
cattle pasture — wattle fence — gate — arable fields with wattle enclosures — postholes — split logs — wattle and daub — rubbish pit — thatch — doorway — gate — arable land — gate — rubbish pit — wattle fence — wattle and daub — livestock pen possibly for sheep

Figure 12.3 Reconstruction of a central European farming village of about 6000 B.C., of a type built on the soft loess soils of the late Ice Age.

Source: Grahame Clark, *World Prehistory, 3/e,* p. 140. Copyright © 1978 Cambridge University Press. Reprinted by permission of Cambridge University Press.

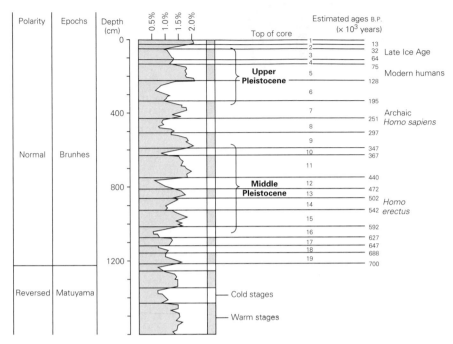

Figure 12.4   The deep-sea core that serves as the standard reference for the past 780,000 years comes from the Solomon Plateau in the southwestern Pacific Ocean. The Matuyama-Brunhes event occurs at a depth of 39.3 feet (11.9 m). Above it, a sawtoothlike curve identifies at least eight complete glacial and interglacial cycles.

Source: Nicholas John Shackleton and Neil D. Opdyke, "Oxygen Isotope and Paleomagnetic Stratigraphy of Equatorial Pacific Ocean Core V28-238," *Quarternary Research* 3(1973), 39–55. Copyright © 1973 by University of Washington. Reprinted by permission.

between different species and sea conditions have not changed, climatologists have been able to turn these frequencies into numerical estimates of sea surface temperatures and ocean salinity over the past few hundred thousand years and to produce a climatic profile of much of the Ice Age (Figure 12.4). These events have been fixed at key points by radiocarbon dates and by studies of paleomagnetism (ancient magnetism). The Matuyama-Brunhes magnetic reversal of 780,000 years ago (when the world's magnetic field suddenly reversed) is a key stratigraphic marker, which can be identified both in sea cores and in volcanic strata ashore, where it can be dated precisely with potassium-argon samples.

One of the finest deep-sea cores comes from the Carioco Basin off the coast of Venezuela in the southeastern Caribbean. The uppermost 5.5 meters of the 170-meter Carioco core cover the past 14,000 years, with a sedimentation rate of about 30 centimeters per 1,000 years. So precise was the definition of the Carioco sedimentation that an X-ray fluorescence scanner could read measurements of bulk titanium concentrations at a 2-mm spacing, representing intervals of only four years. Titanium concentrations reflect the amount of terrestrial sediment flowing into the Carioco Basin, and thus provide a sequence of changing river flow and variations in rainfall through time. A high concentration signals rainfall; a lesser one, drier conditions. Because dry conditions in northern South America are mainly caused by El Niño events, titanium fluctuations are an accurate reflection not only of drought but of El Niños. The Carioco core has thrown fascinating light on the collapse of ancient Maya civilization in the southern Mesoamerican lowlands after the eighth century A.D. The exceptional definition in the core reveals a series of four major droughts, in about A.D. 760, 810, 860, and 910, the latter lasting about six years, spaced at about forty- to forty-seven-year intervals, which coincides well with an estimate of a fifty-year interval obtained from lake cores taken in the heart of the Maya homeland (Haug et al., 2003).

Deep-ice cores are the equivalent of seabed cores, but they pose very different interpretative problems. Paleoclimatologists have drilled deep into the Greenland ice, into the Antarctic ice sheet, and into mountain glaciers and ice caps in locations as widely separated as China and Peru. Many of the interpretative problems revolve around the complex process by which annual snowfall layers are buried deeper and deeper in a glacier until they are finally compressed into ice. Scientists have had to learn the different textures characteristic of summer and winter ice so that they can assemble a long record of precipitation that goes back deep into geological time. They also use various indicators of temperature, such as carbon dioxide and methane content and other chemical properties of the ice, to estimate changes over time. Snowfall changes are especially important, for they can provide vital evidence on the rate of warming and cooling during sudden climatic changes. Researchers can now read ice cores like tree-ring samples, with very good resolution back for 12,000 years and improving accuracy back to 40,000 years. Ice cores have been especially useful for studying not so much the long-term fluctuations of Ice Age climatic change but the short-term episodes of warmer and colder conditions that occurred in the middle of glaciations, which had profound effects on humanity. For example, scientists now suspect that there were bursts of human activity in late Ice Age western Europe about 35,000 and 25,000 years ago, when conditions were relatively warm for short periods of time (van Andel, 1997).

Ice cores reveal complex climatic changes, among them long-term changes that result from the 100,000- and 23,000-year periodicities in the earth's orbit. The Greenland cores take the story back some 150,000 years from the present, through two glacial and interglacial cycles. The same cores also chronicle rapid global warming between 15,000 and 10,000 years ago and numerous minor shifts since then (Alley, 2000).

In 2000, an international team of scientists finished drilling the deepest ice core of all, to a depth of 3,623 meters through the Antarctic ice sheet at the Russian Vostok Station. The drillers stopped 120 meters short of the vast subglacial lake that lies under the ice, to avoid contaminating it with drilling fluid (Petit and others, 1999). The Vostok ice core takes us to about 420,000 years ago, through four transitions from glacial to warm periods. These shifts came at about 100,000-year intervals, the first about 335,000 years before present, then at 245,000, 135,000, and 18,000 years

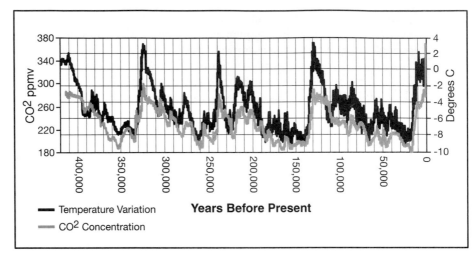

Figure 12.5   Climatic fluctuations over the past 420,000 years, as revealed by the Vostok ice core, Antarctica.

ago—a cyclical rhythm. There seem to be two periodicities involved, a primary one of about 100,000 years and another, weaker one of about 41,000 years. Together, they support the long-held theory that changes in the orbital parameters of the Earth—eccentricity, obliquity, and precession of axis—cause variations in the intensity and distribution of solar radiation. These in turn trigger natural climatic changes on a grand scale (Figure 12.5).

The Greenland and Vostok cores also document major changes in atmospheric concentrations of CO_2 (carbon dioxide) and CH_4 (methane), the most important greenhouse gases. All of the four Vostok transitions from glacial to warmer periods were accompanied by *increases* in atmospheric CO_2 from about 180 to 300 parts per million by volume. (The present level, in a world warmed by human activity, is around 365 parts per million.) At the same time, atmospheric CH_4 rose from about 320 to 350 parts per billion per volume to 650 to 770 parts per billion. Why CO_2 levels increased so rapidly during these four transitions is unknown, but many experts believe that sea surface temperatures in the Southern Ocean played a key role in triggering changes in the atmosphere. The Greenland ice cores show clearly that shifts in CH_4 levels coincide with fast and major temperature changes in the Northern Hemisphere.

If these connections are correct, we can discern a sequence of events that unfolded not only at the beginning of the Holocene but in earlier transitions as well. First, changes in orbital parameters of the earth triggered the end of a glacial period. Next, an increase in greenhouse gasses amplified the weak orbital signal. As the transition progressed, the decreased albedo (solar reflection) caused by rapid melting of the vast ice sheets in the Northern Hemisphere amplified the rate of global warming.

In providing a detailed record of the beginnings and endings of all the glacial periods of the past 420,000 years, the Vostok core shows us that the world's climate has almost always been in a state of change over these 420 millennia. But until the Holocene, it has always oscillated. The Holocene climate breaks through these boundaries. In duration, in stability, in the degree of warming, and in concentration of greenhouse gases, the warming of the past fifteen millennia exceeds any in the Vostok record. Civilization arose during a remarkably long summer. We still have no idea when, or how, that summer will end.

Ice cores also provide evidence of medium-range shifts between 5,000 and 10,000 years in duration and data of particular importance to archaeologists but still little understood: high-frequency climatic changes with periodicities of about 1,000 years. All three types of climatic change interact in the ice-core record, which looks rather like a wave diagram of a radio playing three stations at once.

Some paleoclimatologists believe that changes in arctic climate may have triggered changes elsewhere in the world, reflected in such phenomena as pollen records in Florida lakes, glacial records in the Andes, and ocean-bottom sediments in the Santa Barbara Channel, California. Ice-core research is also providing convincing evidence of drought cycles and other climatic fluctuations during the Holocene (discussed later in this chapter).

Ice and sea cores, combined with pollen analysis, have provided a broad framework for the Pleistocene, which is in wide use by archaeologists. It is worth summarizing here (Figure 12.6).

The Pleistocene Framework

The Pleistocene began about 1.8 million years ago, during a long-term cooling trend in the world's oceans. These millennia were ones of constant climatic change. The Pleistocene is conventionally divided into three long subdivisions.

The *Lower Pleistocene* lasted from the beginning of the Ice Age until about 730,000 years ago. Deep-sea cores tell us that climatic fluctuations between warmer and colder regimes were still relatively minor. These were critical millennia, for it was during this long period that humans first spread from tropical regions in Africa to other regions and then into temperate latitudes in Europe and Asia.

The *Middle Pleistocene* began with the Matuyama-Brunhes reversal in the earth's magnetic polarity, about 780,000 years ago, a change that has been recognized geologically not only in deep-sea cores but also in volcanic rocks ashore, where it can be dated by potassium-argon samples.

Since then, there have been at least eight cold (glacial) and warm (interglacial) cycles, the last cycle ending about 12,000 years ago. (Strictly speaking, we are still in an interglacial today.) Typically, cold cycles have begun gradually, with vast continental ice sheets forming on land—in Scandinavia, on the Alps, and over the northern parts of North America (Figure 12.7). These expanded ice sheets locked up enormous quantities of water, causing world sea levels to fall by several hundred feet during glacial episodes. The geography of the world changed dramatically, and large

Temperature ← Lower Higher →	Dates (B.P.)	Periods	Epochs	Subdivisions	European Glacials/ Interglacials	North American Glacials/ Interglacials	Human Evolution	Prehistory	Three-Age System
		Holocene	Holocene	Holocene	Holocene	Holocene		Cities, agriculture Settlement of New World	Iron Age Bronze Age Neolithic Mesolithic
	10,000								
	118,000	Quaternary	Brunhes (Pleistocene)	Upper Pleistocene	Weichsel (Würm) Eemian Saale (Riss)	Wisconsin Sangamon Illinoian	Homo sapiens sapiens		Upper Paleolithic
	128,000			Middle Pleistocene	Holstein Elster (Mindel)	Yarmouth Kansan	Homo sapiens	Hunter-gatherers	Lower and Middle Paleolithic
	730,000		Matuyama (Pleistocene)	Lower Pleistocene			Homo erectus		
		Tertiary	Olduvai Event (Pliocene)						
	1,600,000						Early hominids and Australopithecus		

Uncertain climatic detail before 130,000 years ago

Figure 12.6 Provisional chronology and subdivisions of the Ice Age.

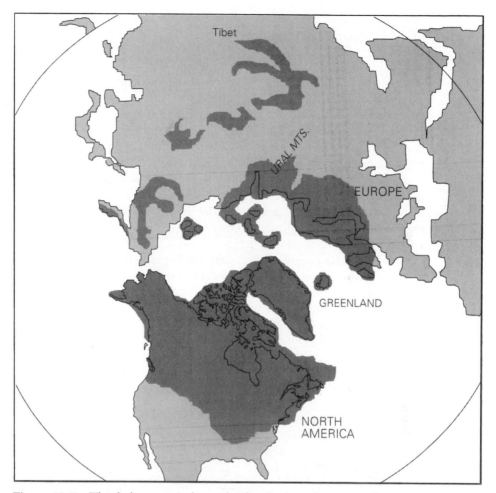

Figure 12.7 The darker areas indicate the distribution of major ice sheets in Europe and North America during the maximum Ice Age glaciation, and the lighter areas show the extent of land exposed by low sea levels.

continental shelves were opened up for human settlement. When a warming trend began, deglaciation occurred very rapidly and rising sea levels flooded low-lying coastal areas within a few millennia. During glacial maxima, glaciers covered a full one-third of the earth's land surface, whereas during interglacials, they were as extensive as they are today.

Throughout the past 780,000 years, vegetational changes have mirrored climatic fluctuations. During glacial episodes, treeless arctic steppe and tundra covered much of Europe and parts of North America but gave way to temperate forest during interglacials. In the tropics, Africa's Sahara Desert may have supported grassland during interglacials, but ice and desert landscape expanded dramatically during dry, cold spells.

The *Upper Pleistocene* stage began about 128,000 years ago, with the beginning of the last interglacial. This period lasted until about 118,000 years ago, when a slow cooling trend brought full glacial conditions to Europe and North America. This Würm glaciation, named after a river in the Alps, lasted until about 15,000 years ago, when there was a rapid return to more temperate conditions.

The Würm glaciation was a period of constantly fluctuating climatic change, with several episodes of more temperate climate in northern latitudes (see Figure 12.4). It served as the backdrop for some of the most important developments in human prehistory, notably the spread of anatomically modern *Homo sapiens sapiens* from the tropics to all parts of the Old World and into the Americas. Between about 30,000 and 15,000 years ago, northern Eurasia's climate was intensely cold but highly variable. A series of Stone Age hunter-gatherer cultures evolved both on the open tundra of central Europe and Eurasia and in the sheltered river valleys of southwestern France and northern Spain, cultures famous for their fine antler and bone artifacts and exceptional artwork.

The world's geography was dramatically different 18,000 years ago during the last glacial maximum. These differences had a major impact on human prehistory; one could walk from Siberia to Alaska across a flat, low-lying plain, the Bering Land Bridge (Figure 12.8). This was the route by which humans first reached the Americas some time before 12,000 years ago—although some scholars espouse a coastal settlement instead (Dillehay, 2000). The low-lying coastal zones of Southeast Asia

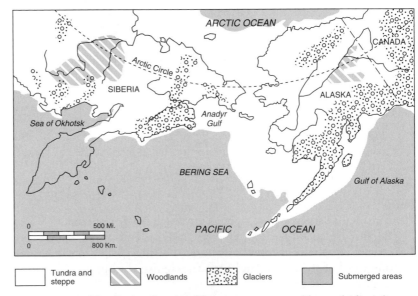

Figure 12.8 The Bering Land Bridge, as reconstructed by multidisciplinary research. Alaska finally separated from Siberia about 11,000 years ago as sea levels rose in response to warmer conditions.

Source: Jason W. Smith, *Foundations of Archaeology* (New York: Macmillan, 1974). Copyright © 1974 by Jason W. Smith. Reprinted by permission.

were far more extensive 15,000 years ago than they are now, and they supported a thriving population of Stone Age foragers. The fluctuating distributions of vegetational zones also affected the pattern of human settlement and the course of human history.

Pollen Analysis

As long ago as 1916, Swedish botanist Lennart von Post used fossil pollen grains from such familiar trees as birches, oaks, and pines to develop a sequence of vegetational change for northern Europe after the Ice Age (Dimbleby, 1985). He showed how arctic, treeless tundra gave way to birch forest, then mixed oak woodland in a dramatic sequence of change that survived in pollen samples from marshes and swamps all over Scandinavia. Since then, **pollen analysis (palynology)** has become a highly sophisticated way of studying both ancient environments and human impacts on natural vegetation (see the Doing Archaeology box).

Pollen analysis reconstructs ancient vegetational change and gives insights into the ways people adapted to shifting climatic conditions. For instance, palynology is providing new perceptions of Stone Age life at the height of the last glaciation in southwestern France, some 15,000 to 20,000 years ago (Gamble, 1999) (see Figure 12.2). This was, we have been told, a period of extreme arctic cold, when Europe was in a deep freeze, and people subsisted on arctic animals and took refuge in deep river valleys such as the Dordogne and the Vézère, where some of the earliest cave art in the world has been discovered. In fact, pollen grains from the rock shelters and open camps used by Stone Age hunter-gatherers of this period paint a very different picture of the late Ice Age climate in this area. It is a portrait of a favored arctic environment in which the climate fluctuated constantly, with surprisingly temperate conditions, especially on the south-facing slopes of deep river valleys. Here, people used rock shelters that faced the winter sun, where snow melted earlier in the spring, within easy reach of key reindeer migration routes and of arctic game that wintered in the valleys. The vegetational cover was not treeless, as is commonly assumed, but included pine, birch, and sometimes deciduous trees, with lush summer meadows in the valleys.

The late Ice Age was a period of continual, and often dramatic, short- and long-term climatic change. Some of these changes lasted millennia, bringing intervals of near-modern conditions to temperate Europe, interspersed with much colder winters. Other cold and warm snaps extended over a few centuries, causing human populations to adapt to dramatically new conditions. Just as there are today, there were much shorter climatic episodes, which endured for a year or more, bringing unusually warm summers, floods, droughts, and other short-term events.

Holocene Environmental Reconstruction

With the rapid retreat of late Ice Age glaciers 15,000 years ago, the world entered a period of profound environmental change that saw the great ice sheets of northern

Doing Archaeology

Pollen Analysis

The principle is simple. Large numbers of pollen grains are dispersed in the atmosphere and survive remarkably well if deposited in an unaerated geological horizon. The pollen grains can be identified microscopically (Figure 12.9) with great accuracy and can be used to reconstruct a picture of the vegetation, right down to humble grasses and weeds that grew near the spot where the pollen grains are found.

Pollen analysis begins in the field. The botanist visits the excavation and collects a series of closely spaced pollen samples from the stratigraphic sections at the site. Back in the laboratory, the samples are examined under a very powerful microscope. The grains of each genus or species present are counted, and the resulting numbers are subjected to statistical analysis. These counts are then correlated with the stratigraphic layers of the excavation and data from natural vegetational sequences to provide a sequence of vegetational change for the site. Typically, this vegetational sequence lasts a few centuries or even millennia (Figure 12.10). It forms part of a much longer pollen sequence for the area that has been assembled from hundreds of samples from many different sites. In northern Europe, for example, botanists have worked out a complicated series of vegetational time zones that cover the past 12,000 years. By comparing the pollen sequences from individual sites with the overall chronology, botanists can give a relative date for the site.

Palynology has obvious applications to prehistory, for sites are often found in swampy deposits where pollen is preserved, especially fishing or fowling camps and settlements near water. Isolated artifacts, or even human corpses (such as that of Tollund Man, found in a Danish bog; see Figure 4.3), have also been

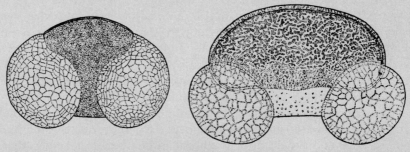

Figure 12.9   Pollen grains: spruce (*left*), silver fir (*right*). (Both 340 times actual size.)

Source: Adapted from Kenneth P. Oakley, *Frameworks for Dating Fossil Man* (Chicago: Aldine, and London: Weidenfeld & Nicholson, 1964), Figure 7.

discovered in these deposits; pollen is sometimes obtained from small peat lumps adhering to crevices in such finds. Thus, botanists can assign relative dates even to isolated finds that would otherwise remain undated.

Until recently, pollen analysts dealt in centuries. Now, thanks to much more refined methods and accelerator mass spectrometry (AMS) radiocarbon dating, they can study even transitory episodes, such as the brief farming incident described at the beginning of this chapter (see also Chapter 7). For example,

dramatic declines in forest tree pollens at many locations in Europe chronicle the first clearances made by farming cultures with almost decade-long accuracy—at a moment when characteristic cultivation weeds such as *Plantago lanceolata* appear for the first time. In the United States, Southwestern archaeologists now have a regional pollen sequence that provides not only climatic information but also valuable facts about the functions of different pueblo rooms and different foods that were eaten by the inhabitants.

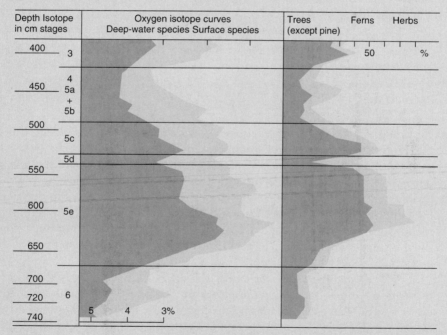

Figure 12.10   A long-term pollen sequence for the Ice Age from Spain (*right*) compared with oxygen isotope curves taken from a deep-sea core in the nearby Bay of Biscay (*left*), showing the close correlation between the two.

Source: Colin Renfrew and Paul Bahn, *Archaeology* (London: Thames and Hudson, 2000). Reprinted by permission.

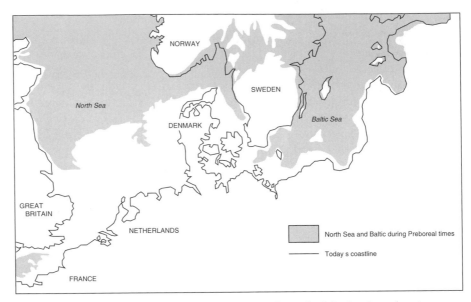

Figure 12.11   Great Britain and Scandinavia at the end of the Ice Age, showing sea levels around 7000 B.C.

Source: Grahame Clark, *Star Carr* Figure 27b. Copyright © 1954. Reprinted by permission of Cambridge University Press.

latitudes melt and world sea levels rise to modern levels (Figure 12.11). Thus dawned the **Holocene Epoch** (Greek *holos,* "recent"), which saw massive global warming, sudden cold episodes, periods of warmer climate than today, and the appearance of both food production and civilization, as well as the Industrial Revolution. Many people believe this warming has been continuous and is reflected in the record warm temperatures of today. In fact, the world's climate has fluctuated just as dramatically as it did during the late Ice Age. Recent research is revolutionizing our knowledge of these changes, which started new chapters in human history, overthrew civilizations, and caused widespread disruption (Fagan, 2004).

We can identify Holocene climatic changes from ice cores, sedimentary records in caves, tree rings, and pollen samples with a chronological resolution that improves every year as analytical methods become ever more refined. For example, the famous Stone Age Star Carr forager camp in northeastern England has been dissected with the aid of highly refined pollen analysis (Mellars and Dark, 1999), AMS radiocarbon dating, and minute studies of wood charcoals and soils. Researchers believe that the site was occupied repeatedly for about 350 years around 8500 B.C. The inhabitants burned the lakeside vegetation repeatedly and built a substantial wooden platform in the reeds. The platform was part of a much larger settlement on nearby dry land than was originally thought when the site was excavated in the late 1940s (see the Doing Archaeology box on pp. 314 to 315).

The onset of the Holocene coincided with a period when Stone Age foragers had occupied virtually all inhabitable parts of the Old World, except the offshore Pacific

A.D./B.C.	Episodes	Conditions
A.D. 1950 1850	Trend to warmer conditions	Warming
	Little Ice Age	Unpredictable, sometimes cooler than today
1400		
	Medieval Warm Period	Warmer, or as warm as, today
980		
A.D. 1	Cooler and wetter	Cold winters
5000 6000	Black Sea formed	Warming
11,000 13,000 B.C.	Younger Dryas End of the Pleistocene	Near-glacial conditions

Figure 12.12   Major climatic and historical events of the Holocene. (This is, of course, a gross simplification of reality.)

Islands. By this time, too, a tiny number of humans had probably foraged their way into the Americas. Wherever they flourished, the people of the early Holocene had to adjust to radically new, and often very challenging, environmental conditions. Over a period of a mere five thousand years, hundreds of familiar, large Ice Age animals such as the mammoth, Ice Age bison, and arctic rhinoceros became extinct. People turned to far more intensive exploitation of local environments. Many became specialized hunters or fishers or concentrated on plant foods to the virtual exclusion of all other resources. And some became farmers, changing the course of human history (Fagan, 2004).

Centuries-Long Climatic Changes: The Younger Dryas and the Black Sea

At least three major cold episodes have cooled global temperatures since 15,000 years ago (Figure 12.12). The last of these was the so-called Little Ice Age, a global event of sometimes markedly colder conditions that lasted from A.D. 1400 to 1850. The earlier two of these cold intervals, the Younger Dryas and the Black Sea episode, had major effects on the course of human history, which we can now assess with new deep-sea core, ice-core, and pollen researches.

The Younger Dryas.   This period lasted from 11,000 to 10,000 B.C. For some still little understood reason, global warming abruptly ceased, perhaps as a result of sudden changes in the warm water circulation in the Atlantic Ocean. Within a century or so, Europe again shivered under near–Ice Age conditions, as forests retreated and widespread drought affected areas such as southwestern Asia. This catastrophic drought after centuries of ample rainfall may have been a major factor in the appearance of agriculture and animal domestication in such areas as the Euphrates and Jordan River valleys, where dense forager populations had long subsisted off abundant food resources.

What happened next has been documented by botanist Gordon Hillman with plant remains at the Abu Hureyra site (Hillman and others, 1989; Moore, 2000)

(Chapter 13). When the drought came, nut harvest yields plummeted, game populations crashed, and wild cereal grasses were unable to support a dense human population. So the foragers turned to cultivation to supplement their food supplies. Within a few generations, they became full-time farmers.

The Younger Dryas–induced drought was not the only cause of the development of agriculture, but the sudden climate change was of great importance. The same economic shift was repeated at many locations, and, within a few centuries, agriculture was widespread throughout southwestern Asia. Thanks to accurate radiocarbon dating of individual seeds and pollen grains from freshwater lakes, archaeologist Andrew Moore and his colleagues were able to tie the changeover to farming to the 1,000-year-long Younger Dryas (Moore, 2000).

The Black Sea.   This was an enormous freshwater lake (often called the Euxine Lake) isolated from the Mediterranean by a huge natural earthen levee in the Bosporus Valley between Turkey and Bulgaria during the early Holocene. Four centuries of colder conditions and drought again settled over Europe and southwestern Asia between 6200 and 5800 B.C. Many farmers abandoned long-established villages and settled near the great lake and other permanent water sources. Deep-sea cores and pollen diagrams chronicle what happened next as the climate warmed up again after 5800 B.C. Sea levels resumed their inexorable rise toward modern high levels, and salty Mediterranean waters climbed ever higher on the Bosporus levee. Then, in about 5500 B.C., the rising water breached the barrier. Torrents of saltwater cascaded into the Euxine Lake 500 feet (150 m) below. Within weeks, the great waterfall had carved a deep gully and formed the narrow strait that now links the Black Sea to the Mediterranean. The former lake not only became a saltwater sea but also rose sharply, flooding hundreds of agricultural settlements on its shores, perhaps with great loss of life. This long-forgotten event has recently been reconstructed from deep-sea cores, taken in the Mediterranean and in the Black Sea, which chronicle not only the cold episode and drought but also the sudden change in the now-drowned lake (Ryan and Pitman, 1998).

The Black Sea discoveries are so new that archaeologists still have to assess their full consequences. The flooding of the huge lake does coincide with the spread of farmers across temperate Europe from the Balkans. Some experts believe the environmental catastrophe and the spread of farming were connected, as people fled their once-fertile homelands.

Short-Term Climatic Change: El Niño

The Younger Dryas and Black Sea drought and flood were centuries-long events but are considered short by geological and early prehistoric standards. It is only now that we are beginning to understand their profound impact on ancient societies. As research into these and other centuries-long events has intensified, scholars have paid increasing attention to violent, year-long episodes such as monsoon failures, volcanic eruptions, and, most important of all, El Niños.

Identifying ancient short-term climatic change requires extremely precise and sophisticated environmental and climatic evidence, much of it obtained from ice cores, pollen diagrams, and tree rings. Ice cores, in particular, are revolutionizing our knowledge of ancient climatic shifts, for they are now achieving a resolution of five years or less, which allows one to study drought cycles and major El Niño events of the past.

El Niños like those in 1982–1983 and 1997–1998 have grabbed world headlines, and with good reason (Fagan, 1999; Glantz, 2001). Billions of dollars of damage resulted from drought and flood. California experienced record rains; Australia and northeastern Brazil suffered through brutal drought; enormous wildfires devastated rain forests in Southeast Asia and Mexico. Once thought to be a purely local phenomenon off the Peruvian coast, El Niños are now known to be global events that ripple across the entire tropics as a result of a breakdown in the atmospheric and oceanic circulation in the western Pacific. From the archaeologist's point of view, El Niños are of compelling interest, for they had drastic effects on many early civilizations living in normally dry environments, where flooding may have wiped out years of irrigation agriculture in hours. Humanity was not that vulnerable to El Niños until people settled in permanent villages, then cities, when the realities of farming and growing population densities made it harder for them to move away from drought or flood.

A classic example of such vulnerability comes from the northern coast of Peru, where the Moche civilization flourished around A.D. 400, ruled by authoritarian warrior-priests (see Figure 1.4). The Moche survived in one of the driest environments on earth by using elaborate irrigation schemes to harness spring runoff from the Andes in coastal river valleys. Everything depended on ample mountain floodwaters. When drought occurred, the Moche suffered (Moseley, 2000).

The Quelccaya ice cap in the Cordillera Occidental of the southern Peruvian highlands lies in the same zone of seasonal rainfall as the mountains above Moche country. Two ice cores drilled in the summit of the ice cap in 1983 provide a record of variations in rainfall over 1,500 years (L. Thompson, 1986; L. Thompson and others, 1984) and, indirectly, an impression of the amount of runoff that would have reached lowland river valleys during cycles of wet and dry years. In the southern highlands, El Niño episodes have been tied to intense short-term droughts in the region and on the nearby altiplano, the high-altitude plains around Lake Titicaca. The appearance of such drought periods in the ice cores may reflect strong El Niño events in the remote past. However, it is more productive to look at long-term dry and wet cycles.

The two ice cores, 508 and 537 feet (154.8 and 163.6 m) long, each yielded clear layering and annual dust layers that reflected the yearly cycle of wet and dry seasons, the latter bringing dust particles from the arid lands of the west to the high Andes; they are accurate to within about 20 years. The cores show clear indications of long-term rainfall variations. A short drought occurred between A.D. 534 and 540. Then, between A.D. 563 and 594, a three-decade drought cycle settled over the mountains and lowlands, with annual rainfall as much as 30 percent below normal. Abundant rainfall resumed in 602, giving way to another drought between A.D. 636 and 645.

The thirty-year drought of A.D. 563 to 594 drastically reduced the amount of runoff reaching coastal communities. The effect of a 25 or 30 percent reduction in the water supply would have been catastrophic, especially to farmers near the coast, well downstream from the mountains. Moche society apparently prospered until the mid-sixth century's severe drought cycle. As the drought intensified, the diminished runoff barely watered the rich farming lands far downstream. Miles of laboriously maintained irrigation canals remained dry. Blowing sand cascaded into empty ditches. By the third or fourth year, as the drought lowered the water table far below normal, thousands of acres of farmland received so weak a river flow that unflushed salt accumulated in the soil. Crops withered. Fortunately, the coastal fisheries still provided ample fish meal—until a strong El Niño came along without warning, bringing warmer waters and torrential rains to the desert and mountains.

We do not know the exact years during the long drought when strong El Niños struck, but we can be certain that they did. We can also be sure they hit at a time when Moche civilization was in crisis—grain supplies running low, irrigation systems sadly depleted, malnutrition widespread, and confidence in the rulers' divine powers much diminished. The warmer waters of the El Niño reduced anchovy harvests in many places, decimating a staple both of the coastal diet and highland trade. Torrential rains swamped the Andes and coastal plain. The dry riverbeds became raging torrents, carrying everything before them. Levees and canals overflowed and collapsed. The arduous labors of years vanished in a few weeks. Dozens of villages vanished under mud and debris as the farmers' cane-and-adobe houses collapsed and their occupants drowned. The floods polluted springs and streams, overwhelmed sanitation systems, and stripped thousands of acres of fertile soil. As the water receded and the rivers went down, typhoid and other epidemics swept through the valleys, wiping out entire communities and eroding fertile soils. Infant mortality soared.

The Moche's elaborate irrigation systems created an artificial landscape that supported dense farming populations in the midst of one of the driest deserts on the earth, where farming would be impossible without technological ingenuity. The farmers were well aware of the hazards of droughts and El Niños, but technology and irrigation could not guarantee the survival of a highly centralized society driven as much by ideology as by pragmatic concerns. There were limits to the climatic shifts Moche civilization could absorb. Ultimately, the Moche ran out of options and their civilization collapsed.

We do not know how long El Niños have oscillated across the globe, but they have descended on Peru for at least 5,000 years. A new generation of climatic researches from ice cores and other data shows that short-term climatic shifts played a far more important role in the fate of early civilizations than was once realized.

Tree Rings: Studying Southwestern Drought

Many ancient societies lived in environments with unpredictable rainfall, where agriculture was, at best, a chancy enterprise. The ancient peoples of the southwestern United States farmed their semiarid environment with brilliant skill for more than three thousand years, developing an extraordinary expertise at water management and plant breeding. One central philosophy of modern-day Pueblo Indian groups surrounds movement, the notion that people have to move to escape drought and survive. Until recently, archaeologists did not fully appreciate the importance of movement in Southwestern life and were at a loss to explain the sudden dispersal of the Ancestral Pueblo people of Chaco Canyon and the Four Corners region in the twelfth and thirteenth centuries A.D.

The Ancestral Pueblo dispersal can be better understood by dividing the relationship between climatic change and human behavior into three broad categories.

Certain obvious stable elements in the Ancestral Pueblo environment have not changed over the past two thousand years, such as bedrock geology and climate type. Then there are low-frequency environmental changes—those that occur in cycles longer than a human generation of twenty-five years. Few people witnessed these changes during their lifetimes. Changes in hydrological conditions, such as cycles of erosion and deposition along watercourses, fluctuations in water table levels in river floodplains, and changes in plant distributions, transcend generations, but they could affect the environment drastically, especially in drought cycles.

Shorter-term, high-frequency changes were readily apparent to every Ancestral Pueblo: year-to-year rainfall shifts, decade-long drought cycles, seasonal changes, and so on. Over the centuries, the Ancestral Pueblo were probably barely aware of long-term change, because the present generation and its immediate ancestors experienced the same basic adaptation, which one could call a form of "stability." Cycles of drought, unusually heavy rains, and other high-frequency changes required temporary and flexible adjustments, such as farming more land, relying more heavily on wild plant foods, and, above all, movement across the terrain.

Such strategies worked well for centuries, as long as the Ancestral Pueblo farmed their land at well below its carrying capacity. When the population increased to near carrying capacity, however, as it did at Chaco Canyon in the twelfth century, people became increasingly vulnerable to brief events such as El Niños or droughts, which could stretch the supportive capacity of a local environment within months, even weeks. Their vulnerability was even more extreme when long-term changes—such as a half century or more of much drier conditions—descended on farmlands already pushed to their carrying limits. Under these circumstances, a year-long drought or torrential rains could quickly destroy a local population's ability to support itself. So the people dispersed into other areas, where there were ample soil and better water supplies. Without question, the Ancestral Pueblo dispersed from Mesa Verde and Chaco Canyon because drought forced them to do so. Unlike the Moche in distant Peru, they had the flexibility to move away.

The coming decades will see a revolution in our understanding of ancient environments and short-term climatic change, as scientists acquire a better knowledge both of climates in the past and of the still little known forces that drive the global weather machine. Like our predecessors, we still live in the Ice Age, which, some estimates calculate, will bring renewed glacial conditions in about 23,000 years. So it is hardly surprising that, like our forebears, we have had to adjust to constant short-term climatic changes. And, as human-induced global warming accelerates, these changes may become more frequent and violent, spelling danger for an overpopulated world.

Reconstructing Human-Caused Environmental Change

One of the great misconceptions of history proclaims that most preindustrial societies lived in exquisite ecological balance with their natural environments. Although it is true that the imprint of a small forager group on the landscape is rarely catastrophic, many early societies used fire to burn off dead grass and stimulate new growth for game to feed on or to grow edible grasses, with long-term effects on the natural

Doing Archaeology

Climatic Variability in the Ancient American Southwest

Dendrochronologies for the Ancestral Pueblo are now accurate to within a year, giving us the most precise time scale for any early human society anywhere. In recent years, the Laboratory of Tree-Ring Research at the University of Arizona has undertaken a massive dendroclimatic study that has yielded a reconstruction of relative climatic variability in the Southwest from A.D. 680 to 1970 (Dean, 1988; Dean and Funkhauser, 1994). The same scientists, headed by Jeffrey Dean, are now producing the first quantitative reconstructions of annual and seasonal rainfall and of temperature, drought, and stream flow for the region. Such research involves not only tree-ring sequences but also intricate mathematical expressions of the relationships between tree growth and such variables as rainfall, temperature, and crop yields. These calculations yield statistical estimations of the fluctuations in these variables on an annual and seasonal basis.

By using a spatial grid of twenty-seven long tree-ring sequences from throughout the Southwest, Dean and his colleagues have compiled maps that plot the different station values and their fluctuations like contour maps, one for each decade. These maps enable them to study such phenomena as the progress of what Dean sometimes calls the "Great Drought" of A.D. 1276 to 1299 from northwest to southeast across the region. In 1276, the beginnings of the drought appear as negative standard deviations from average

rainfall in the northwest, while the remainder of the region enjoys above-average rainfall. During the next ten years, very dry conditions expand over the entire Southwest before improved rainfall arrives after 1299. This form of mapping allows close correlation of vacated large and small pueblos with short-term climatic fluctuations (Figure 12.13).

When the research team looked at the entire period from A.D. 966 to 1988, they found that the tree-ring stations in the northwestern region accounted for no less than 60 percent of the rainfall variance. In contrast, stations in the southeastern part of the Southwest accounted for only 10 percent. This general configuration, which persisted for centuries, coincides with the modern distribution of seasonal rainfall in the Southwest: predictable summer rainfall dominates the southeastern areas, while the northwest receives both winter and summer precipitation. Winter rains are much more uncertain. When the scientists examined this general rainfall pattern at 100-year intervals from 539 to 1988, they observed that it persisted most of the time, even though the boundary between the two zones moved backward and forward slightly.

But this long-term pattern broke down completely from A.D. 1250 to 1450, when a totally aberrant pattern prevailed in the northwest. The southeast remained stable, but there was major disruption elsewhere. For nearly two centuries, the relatively simple long-term pattern of summer and winter

vegetation. However, the relationship between humans and their environments changed dramatically with the advent of agriculture and animal domestication.

Back in 1944, a Danish botanist named Johannes Iverson noticed that pollen diagrams from Scandinavian bogs showed a dramatic falloff in forest cover at about

rains gave way to complex, unpredictable precipitation and severe droughts, especially on the Colorado Plateau. This change to an unstable pattern would have had a severe impact on Ancestral Pueblo farmers, especially since it coincided with the Great Drought of A.D. 1276 to 1299.

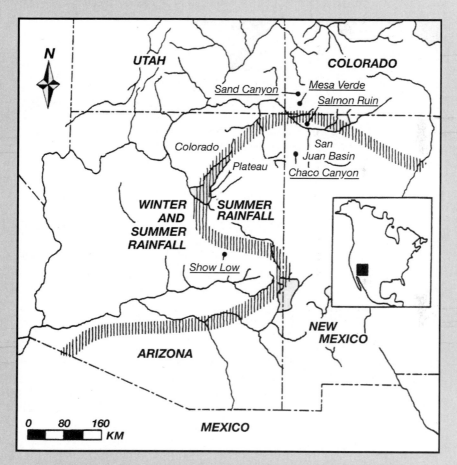

Figure 12.13   The climatic regimes of the American Southwest, showing the general configuration of rainfall across the region, reconstructed with tree-ring data. The northwest receives both summer and winter rainfall; in the southeast, only summer rainfall is predictable.

the time when farmers first settled in northern Europe. Simultaneously, pollen counts for grasses of all kinds rose rapidly. He also found evidence for *Plantago lanceolata,* a little known weed that grows on cultivated fields. Iverson's discovery produced confirmation of the changes wrought by forest clearance. Herds of grazing

Site

Environmental Archaeology at Easton Down, England

Obtaining evidence of ancient landscapes requires careful excavation and sample collection, most often of the original land surfaces under burial mounds and earthworks. When archaeologist Alisdair Whittle excavated some test trenches into a burial mound at Easton Down in southern England, he exposed the original land surface as well as the core of stacked sod, chalk, and topsoil under the mound, all of which gave him an unusual opportunity to obtain a portrait of the local vegetation in about 3200 B.C. (Whittle and others, 1993). First, he turned to pollen analysis. Small amounts of pollen grains from the land surface were predominantly from grasses, showing that no woodland grew close to the tumulus (mound) when it was built. A well-sealed section of the premound soil yielded eleven mollusk samples, which chronicled a dramatic change from woodland to open grassland forms over a short period of time. Whittle located an ancient tree hollow under the mound, which, hardly surprisingly, contained woodland mollusks. A sudden increase in open-country mollusks followed, a change so rapid that human clearance of the land seems the only logical explanation. Interestingly, soil scientists found signs of lateral movement of the soil below the mound, which can have resulted only from cultivation before the mound was built.

Excavations such as Easton Down can only give us snapshots of the complex mosaic of cleared and uncleared land that characterizes any agricultural landscape. For example, mollusks and soil samples under the famous stone circles at Avebury, near Easton Down, tell us that the great temple of 2550 B.C. rose on long-established but little-grazed natural grassland close to a forest that had regenerated after having been cleared for farming.

animals can also change the landscape dramatically. Goats, for example, are voracious feeders that can strip bushes and trees and tear out plants by their roots. Many archaeologists believe that the natural environment of southwestern Asia was stripped of much tree and natural grass cover by overgrazing a few centuries after animal domestication.

As did the mollusks at Easton Down, beetles can provide remarkably precise information about the habitats in which they flourished (see the Site box). Many species feed off specific host plants, some of which grow as a result of human activity. There are, for example, distinct beetle forms associated with stored and decaying organic material such as human food or feces. When another British archaeologist, Francis Pryor (1991), discovered an artificial platform of 1350 B.C. in the middle of waterlogged Flag Fen in eastern England, he was anxious to determine if the jumble of ancient timbers in the midst of the water included actual dwellings. Biologist Mark Robinson took core samples from organic sediments adjacent to the platform and from sealed layers on the structure itself. The beetles from the side samples were predominantly those that flourished in marsh habitats and in stagnant water. Robinson also found the remains of dung beetles, which feed on cattle droppings. The same species came from the platform itself, but no insects that typically feed on damp thatch, old

This kind of environmental archaeology is now so precise that we can fix the exact seasons when monuments were built or buildings were erected. For example, soil samples from carefully cut sod laid under the original ground surface of 130-foot (40-m) Silbury Hill, built in about 2200 B.C. close to Easton Down, show that the builders started work in the late summer, most likely after the harvest, when people had time for construction work. We know this because the well-preserved sods contain ants and anthills. The ants were beginning to grow wings and fly away from their anthills, as they do in late summer (Figure 12.14).

Figure 12.14   Silbury Hill.

straw, stored grain, or foul matter such as settlement refuse were found. Robinson concluded that no active human settlements had been within 164 feet (50 m) of any of his samples. He also believes that the timbers became waterlogged rapidly, because they contained almost no woodworm beetles, which feast off fresh, dry wood.

The most powerful reconstructions come from a combination of lines of evidence. A medieval town at Uppsala, Sweden, was burnt down in 1543, leaving a treasure trove of ecological data for archaeologists. A team of researchers studied the wood, mollusks, and plant remains, as well as the insects, which were among the most informative ecological finds. Magnus Hellqvist and Geoffrey Lemdahl identified eighty-one insect forms dating from the twelfth to fifteenth centuries; almost all of them were beetles found in a row of oak barrels. The beetles were varieties that flourished in moist habitats, open areas, and cultivated fields, suggesting that the settlement, mainly of farm buildings, lay in an open landscape. Several of the beetle forms were species that live in habitats in and around farm buildings, suggesting that towns such as Uppsala were more rural than urban. Some of the beetles do not occur as far north as Uppsala today, suggesting that summers were one or two degrees warmer than the 63°F (17°C) of modern times; the difference is not surprising, for the history of the town spans the end of the medieval warm period of A.D. 900 to 1300 as well as the subsequent Little Ice Age.

Summary

The study of long- and short-term climatic and environmental change is of vital importance to archaeologists concerned with human societies' changing relationships with their surroundings. This chapter described ways of studying such changes.

Geoarchaeology is a multidisciplinary approach to the study of human adaptations that reconstructs ancient landscapes using such approaches as remote sensing and paleographical and biological methods such as pollen analysis.

Deep-sea cores and ice drillings provide us with a broad framework of climatic change during the Pleistocene (Ice Age) Epoch that chronicle at least nine glacial periods during the past 730,000 years. The Pleistocene itself is divided into three broad subdivisions, the last of which coincides with the spread of modern humans across the world from Africa.

The Holocene covers postglacial times and has witnessed not only global warming but at least three short periods of much colder conditions as well. The Younger Dryas brought drought and cold conditions and may have helped trigger the development of agriculture in southwestern Asia. The catastrophic flooding of the Black Sea lake in approximately 5500 B.C. by saltwater from the Mediterranean caused major population movements in Europe.

Short-term events such as El Niños and drought cycles are studied with the aid of ice cores, geological observations, and tree rings, methods that are achieving increasing precision. We are now beginning to realize that short-term climatic change played a vital role in the rise and fall of many human societies.

Key Terms

eustatic
geoarchaeology
Holocene Epoch

isostatic
loess
periglacial

Pleistocene Epoch
pollen analysis (palynology)
Quaternary Period

Guide to Further Reading

BUTZER, KARL. 1974. *Environment and Archaeology.* 3rd ed. Hawthorne, NY: Aldine.

———. 1982. *Archaeology as Human Ecology.* Cambridge: Cambridge University Press. Butzer's two books are still fundamental sources on geoarchaeology and environmental reconstruction, even if outdated in detail.

DAVIS, MIKE. 2001. *Late Victorian Holocausts.* New York: Verso. Davis has written a truly sobering account of the impact of short-term climatic change on tropical societies in the nineteenth century. Every archaeologist should read this book.

FAGAN, BRIAN. 2004. *The Long Summer: Climate Change and Civilization.* New York: Basic Books.

A popular account of the impact of climatic change on human societies, 15,000 years ago to the present.

MELLARS, PAUL, and PETRA DARK. 1998. *Star Carr in Context.* Cambridge: McDonald Institute Monographs and the Vale of Pickering Research Trust. A state-of-the-art monograph on environmental reconstruction in the context of one of the world's most famous hunter-gatherer sites.

ROBERTS, NEIL. 1999. *The Holocene: An Environmental History.* 2d ed. Oxford: Blackwell. An excellent introduction to postglacial climate change for general readers.

Subsistence and Diet

Finely constructed Inca walls at Cuzco, Peru.

Take the forelimb of a deer, a handful of wild grass seeds, a corncob, and a few grinding implements, study them closely in a laboratory, and come up with a reconstruction of the diet of the people who lived at the site where you found those few food remains. This is basically what archaeologists attempt to do when they study the subsistence practices of ancient societies.

We can boast of some remarkable progress in the study of ancient lifeways. We know, for example, that the earliest hominids scavenged meat from predator kills under the noses of lions and other formidable cats. Late Ice Age Cro-Magnon people of 20,000 years ago followed spring and fall reindeer migrations and butchered animals in their prime. In a remarkable piece of detective work, from the feces of infants recovered from small hearths, botanist Gordon Hillman was able to reconstruct the plant foods eaten by a group of foragers who lived at Wadi Kubbaniya on the banks of Egypt's Nile River in 16,000 B.C. They relied on at least thirteen edible plants, most commonly wild nut grass, which is still a staple for Egyptian villagers to this day (Hillman, 1989). Similarly, we know that some of Thomas Jefferson's slaves at Monticello, Virginia, ate better cuts of meat than some of the field servants. Food remains open unusual and often fascinating windows into the past and tell us a great deal about social conditions and adaptations to changing environments. This chapter describes some of the methods archaeologists use to study ancient subsistence and diet.

Studying Subsistence

Archaeologists reconstruct ancient lifeways from the surviving material remains of subsistence activities, which come in many forms. As it is in every other form of

Discovery

Hiram Bingham at Machu Picchu, Peru, 1911

The "Lost City of the Incas" was one of the great archaeological mysteries of the late nineteenth century, a legend of a last Inca stronghold where their rulers found refuge from rapacious Spanish conquistadors after Francisco Pizarro overthrew their empire in 1534. A young Yale University graduate named Hiram Bingham fell under the spell of the mystery and penetrated to the remote Vilcabamba site high in the Andes and realized that this was not the settlement. He persuaded his wealthy Yale classmates to finance a second expedition to the Andes.

Tough and intensely curious, the young Bingham was a competent mountaineer and had a sound historical background. He left Cuzco in 1911 with a well-equipped mule train and traveled along the Urubamba River, admiring the extraordinary vista of snowy peaks, mountain streams, mist, and tropical vegetation. A chance encounter with a local farmer named Melchor Arteaga brought a report of some ruins on a hillside across the river. On July 24, 1911, Bingham and the farmer, accompanied by a Peruvian sergeant, crossed the Urubamba by a log bridge. There was little margin for error. Bingham got down on his hands and knees and crawled across, 6 inches at a time. Then he climbed 2,000 feet (600 m) up a narrow path through the forest on the other side of the river. After pausing for lunch in an Indian homestead high above the valley, Bingham set out reluctantly to climb farther. Just round a spur, he sighted a flight of a hundred recently cleared stone terraces climbing about 1,000 feet (300 m) up the hillside. Above the terraces, which the Indians had

cleared, he plunged into thick forest and found himself wandering among building after building, including a three-sided temple with masonry as fine as that at Cuzco or Ollantaytambo. He found himself confronted with the walls of ruined houses built with the highest quality of Inca stonework. He plunged through the undergrowth and entered a semicircular building whose outer wall, gently sloping and slightly curved, bore a striking resemblance to the famous Temple of the Sun in Cuzco. Bingham had stumbled on the most famous of all Inca ruins, Machu Picchu (Figure 13.1).

Figure 13.1 Machu Picchu, Peru.

archaeological research, the perspective is multidisciplinary, for we rely on the expertise of scientists from many other fields, among them botanists, ecologists, and zoologists.

- *Environmental Data.* Background data on the natural environment is essential for studying subsistence. The data can include information on such phenomena as climate, animal distributions, ancient and modern flora, and soils—the range of potential resources to be exploited (Chapter 12).
- *Animal Bones (Faunal Remains).* These are a major source of information on hunting practices and domestic animals.
- *Plant Remains (Floral Remains).* Plant remains can include both wild and domestic species, obtained using flotation methods and from actual seeds found in dry sites or carbonized by fire.
- *Human Bones.* Stable carbon isotopes of skeletal collagen from human bones provide vital information on ancient diets. Bones also give evidence of anatomical anomalies, ancient diseases, and dietary stress.
- *Feces (Coprolites).* These yield vital evidence for reconstructing prehistoric diet in both animals and humans.
- *Artifacts.* The picture of human subsistence yielded by artifacts can be incomplete because of poor preservation, but implements such as plow blades can be useful sources of evidence.
- *Rock Art.* Occasionally, rock art depicts scenes of the chase, fishing, and food gathering and can provide useful information on subsistence activities.

Most reconstructions of ancient lifeways rely on evidence from several different sources. For instance, the excavators of the Wadi Kubbaniya site found Nile catfish bones, the bones of gazelle (a desert antelope) and wild oxen, plant remains preserved in infant feces, and the bones of winter-migrating waterfowl. They painted a composite portrait of foragers who moved along the Nile in search of different seasonal foods 11,000 years before the pharaohs founded ancient Egyptian civilization (Hillman, 1989). As we saw earlier, archaeologists have long considered humans and their culture as merely one element in a complex ecosystem. The study of prehistoric subsistence, then, has developed hand in hand with attempts to understand the complex interrelationships between the way people make their living and their environment.

Animal Bones (Zooarchaeology)

The Old Testament prophet Ezekiel unwittingly defined the task of the zooarchaeologist: "And I prophesied as I was commanded; and as I prophesied, there was a noise, and behold, a rattling; and the bones came together, bone to its bone" (Ezekiel 37:10). Zooarchaeologists literally put the flesh on long-dead animals, reconstructing the environment and behavior of ancient peoples to the extent that animal remains allow. Zooarchaeology is a specialized expertise that requires a background in paleontology or zoology.

Zooarchaeology is the study of animal bones found in the archaeological record. Its goal is to reconstruct the environment and behavior of ancient peoples to the extent that animal remains allow (Klein and Cruz-Uribe, 1984). Although some zoologists specialize in the study of animal bones from archaeological sites, most zooarchaeologists have a background either in paleontology or in the study of prehistoric faunas (faunal analysis). (For general discussions, see L. Binford, 1981b; S. J. M. Davis, 1987; O'Connor, 2000; and Reitz and Wing, 1999.)

Taphonomy

The word **taphonomy** (Greek *taphnos,* "tomb"; *nomos,* "law") is used to describe the processes that operate on organic remains to form fossil deposits (Lyman, 1994; Shipman, 1981). Simply put, it is the study of the transition of animal remains from the biosphere to the lithosphere.

A fossil fauna goes through several stages as it passes from the biosphere into the hands of the archaeologist. The bones originally come from what scientists call the **life assemblage,** the community of live animals in their natural proportions. The animals that are killed or die of natural causes become the **deposited assemblage,** the carcasses or portions of carcasses that come to rest in a site. The fossil assemblage consists of the animal parts that survive in a site until excavation or collection by a scientist. The **sample assemblage,** however, is what reaches the laboratory, the part of the fossil assemblage that is actually excavated or collected (Klein and Cruz-Uribe, 1984). Anyone carrying out faunal analysis must solve two problems: the statistical problem of estimating the characteristics of a fossil assemblage from a sample and the taphonomic problem of inferring the nature of the deposited assemblage from the fossil assemblage.

Taphonomy involves two related avenues of investigation. The first is actual observation of recently dead organic remains as they are transformed gradually into fossils; the other is the study of fossil remains in the light of this evidence. This field of investigation came into fashion during the 1960s and 1970s, when archaeologists became interested in the meaning of animal bone scatters at such early sites as Olduvai Gorge in East Africa and especially in the celebrated *Australopithecus* caves of South Africa (Brain, 1981).

Many questions about the processes that transform living organisms into "archaeological" bones remain unanswered, despite some research into such topics as ways in which bones can be transported and disarticulated by both carnivores and natural agents such as water. For example, experiments with captive hyenas have shown that they first choose backbones and hipbones, which they usually destroy completely. Limb bone ends are often hewed off, while shafts are often intact. These experiments are of importance because they tell us that the early hominid bone caches at Olduvai Gorge were picked over by hyenas after their human owners had abandoned them, a process that led to the destruction of many body parts, thereby making it impossible to tell whether the hominids had selectively transported some parts of animal kill and not others (Marean and others, 1992). Humans disarticulate animals with tools long before the carcasses are dispersed by natural phenomena or by carnivores, so their systematic activities are at least a baseline for examining patterns of damage on archaeological bones. Interpretation of prehistoric living floors and kill sites has to be undertaken with great care, for the apparent patterns of bones and artifacts on such a prehistoric land surface represent not only human activity but complex and little-understood natural processes as well.

Many zooarchaeologists worry that interpretations of bone assemblages from archaeological sites will never reconstruct the actual living population environment. However, Klein and Cruz-Uribe (1984) believe that viable paleoecological reconstructions can be made when several fossil assemblages can be compared using statistical measures, provided that both the quality of bone preservation and the sedimentary conditions of the bones at the study locations are similar. Each situation must be assessed with great care.

Sorting and Identification

Animal remains are usually fragmentary, coming from dismembered carcasses butchered either at the archaeological site or at the hunting grounds. To some degree, how much of the carcass is carried back to camp depends on the animal's size. Small deer may be taken back whole, slung from the shoulder. Hunter-gatherers sometimes camped at the site of the kill of a large animal, where they ate parts of the carcass and dried parts for later use. Almost invariably, however, the bones found in occupation sites have been broken into splinters. Every piece of usable meat was stripped from the bones; sinews were made into thongs, and the skin was formed into clothing, containers, or sometimes housing. Even the entrails were eaten. Limb bones were split for their marrow; some bones were made into tools such as harpoon heads, arrow tips, and mattocks (Figure 13.2).

It would be a mistake to assume that the fragmentary bones found in an archaeological deposit will give an accurate count of the number of animals killed by the inhabitants or accurate insights into the environment at the time of occupation (Grayson, 1984). The fragmentary bones found in an archaeological deposit have been subjected to many diverse processes since their deposition. Taphonomic processes often result in major changes in buried bone, perhaps even destroying the bones of smaller animals, though not of larger ones. Then there are human factors: people may carry in some game from far away, yet kill all of their goats at the village. We have no way of knowing what spiritual role some animals possessed in ancient societies or what taboos and other prohibitions may have caused certain animals to be hunted and others to be ignored. Nor, as we have already pointed out, have we any means of knowing precisely what the relative frequencies of different animal species were in the prehistoric environment. Certainly, researchers cannot use animal bones from archaeological sites for this purpose. The difference between what one might call the "actual animal" and the "archaeological animal" identified by the archaeologist is always unknown (S. J. M. Davis, 1987; Grayson, 1981). The archaeological animal consists of a scatter of broken bones that have been shattered by a butcher, then subjected to hundreds or thousands of years of gradual deterioration in the soil.

Most bone identification is done by direct comparison with bones of known species. It is fairly simple and easily learned by anyone with sharp eyes (S. J. M. Davis, 1987). But only a small proportion of the bones in a collection is complete enough for

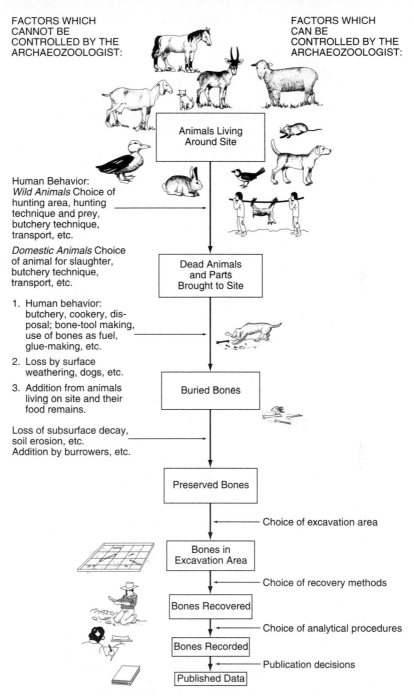

FACTORS WHICH CANNOT BE CONTROLLED BY THE ARCHAEOZOOLOGIST:

FACTORS WHICH CAN BE CONTROLLED BY THE ARCHAEOZOOLOGIST:

Animals Living Around Site

Human Behavior:
Wild Animals Choice of hunting area, hunting technique and prey, butchery technique, transport, etc.

Domestic Animals Choice of animal for slaughter, butchery technique, transport, etc.

Dead Animals and Parts Brought to Site

1. Human behavior: butchery, cookery, disposal; bone-tool making, use of bones as fuel, glue-making, etc.

2. Loss by surface weathering, dogs, etc.

3. Addition from animals living on site and their food remains.

Buried Bones

Loss of subsurface decay, soil erosion, etc.
Addition by burrowers, etc.

Preserved Bones

Choice of excavation area

Bones in Excavation Area

Choice of recovery methods

Bones Recovered

Choice of analytical procedures

Bones Recorded

Publication decisions

Published Data

Figure 13.2 Analysis of bones from the archaeological record. This figure shows some of the factors that affect the data. Factors that the archaeologist cannot control are on the *left;* those that the archaeologist can control are on the *right.*

Source: Adapted from Simon J. M. Davis, *The Archaeology of Animals* (London: Batsford, 1987.)

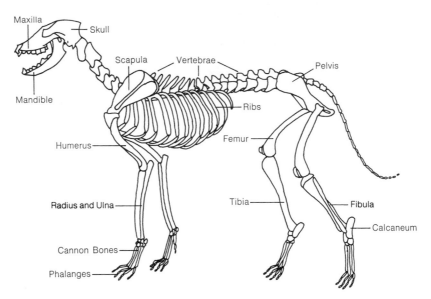

Figure 13.3   Skeleton of a dog, showing the most important body parts from the osteological viewpoint.

this purpose. The drawing of a dog in Figure 13.3 illustrates a typical mammalian skeleton. Small skull fragments, vertebrae, ribs, scapulae, and pelvic bones are normally of little use in differentiating a domestic animal from a wild one or one species of antelope from another. Upper and lower jaws and their dentition, individual teeth, the bony cores of horns, and sometimes the articular surfaces of long bones are easy to identify. Teeth are identified by comparing the cusp patterns on their surfaces with those on comparative collections carefully taken from the site area (Figure 13.4).

In some parts of the world, the articular ends of long bones can be used as well, especially in southwestern Asia or parts of North America, where the indigenous mammalian fauna is somewhat restricted. It is even possible to distinguish the fragmentary long bones of domestic stock from those of wild animals of the same size in southwestern Asia, provided that the collections are large enough and the comparative material is sufficiently complete and representative of all ages of individuals and of variations in size from male to female. But in other areas, such as sub-Saharan Africa, the indigenous fauna is so rich and varied, and has such small variations in skeletal anatomy, that only horn cores or teeth can help distinguish among species of antelope and separate domestic stock from game animals. Even the dentition is confusing, for the cusp patterns of buffalo and domestic cattle are remarkably similar, often distinguishable only by the smaller size of the latter. Experts disagree as to what constitutes identifiability of bone, so it is best to think in terms of levels of identifiability rather than simply to reject many fragments out of hand. For example, you can sometimes identify a fragment as having come from a medium-sized carnivore even if you have no way of telling that it is from a wolf.

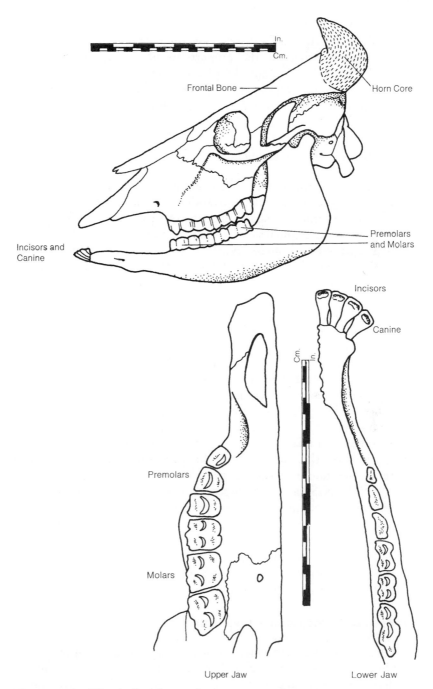

Figure 13.4 The skull and jaw of a domestic ox, showing important osteological features. (One-fourth actual size.)

The identification stage of a bone analysis is the most important, for several fundamental questions need answering: Are domestic and wild species present? If they are, what are the proportions of each group? What types of domestic stock did the inhabitants keep? Did they have any hunting preferences that are reflected in the proportions of game animals found in the occupation levels? Are any wild species characteristic of vegetational associations no longer found in the area today?

Comparing Bone Assemblages

Zooarchaeologists Richard Klein and Kathryn Cruz-Uribe (1984) describe measures of taxonomic abundance for assessing whether differences between assemblages are real or the result of biased collecting or other factors. They also use the same measures to make estimates of the relative abundance of different species. The **number of identified specimens (NISP)** is a count of the number of bones or bone fragments from each species in a bone sample. This measure has obvious disadvantages, especially since it can overemphasize the importance of one species that has more bones than another or has carcasses that were butchered more thoroughly than those of other species. Both human activities, such as butchering, and natural processes, such as weathering, can affect the NISP. The NISP does have a certain value, however, especially when used in conjunction with an estimate of the minimum number of individuals from which the identified bones have come. The **minimum number of individuals (MNI)** is a count of the number of individuals necessary to account for all the identifiable bones. This count is smaller than the NISP and is often based on careful counts of such individual body parts as heel bones. The MNI overcomes many limitations of the NISP because it is a more accurate estimate of the actual number of animals present. However, everything depends on the experts' using the same method of calculating the MNI—which they often do not (Grayson, 1984).

The NISP and MNI together permit us to estimate the number of animals present in a bone sample, but they are highly imperfect ways of measuring abundance of animals in an archaeological sample, let alone of providing a means for relating the bone materials to a living animal population in the past. Klein and Cruz-Uribe, among others, have developed sophisticated computer programs to overcome some of the limitations of NISP and MNI, programs that lay out the basic information that is vital for intersample comparisons.

Species Abundance and Culture Change

Climatic rather than culture change was probably responsible for most long-term shifts in animal species abundance in the Ice Age. Some shifts must reflect human activity, changes in the way in which people exploited other animals (Klein and Cruz-Uribe, 1984). These changes are, however, very difficult to distinguish from environmental changes. One of the few places where it has been possible to document such shifts is in South Africa (see the Doing Archaeology box).

Doing Archaeology

Changing Hunting Practices in Ancient South Africa

Zooarchaeologist Richard Klein has tackled the problem of species abundance and culture change by studying large faunal samples from two coastal caves in the Cape Province of South Africa. The Klasies River cave was occupied by Middle Stone Age hunter-gatherers between about 130,000 and 95,000 years ago, during a period of warmer climate, and thereafter until about 70,000 years ago, when the weather had become much cooler. The seashore was close to the cave during the earlier, warmer millennia. Numerous mollusks, seal bones, and penguin remains tell us much about Middle Stone Age diet in the cave. Seabird and fish remains are rare. The remains of eland, a large antelope, are the most common large mammal remains, more than twice as common as those of the Cape buffalo. The rest of the land mammal remains are of species common in the area during modern historic times. In contrast, the nearby Nelson's Bay cave contains evidence of later Stone Age occupation, dating to after 20,000 years ago, much of it at a time when the sea was some miles from the cave, during the coldest part of the last Ice Age glaciation. Bones of flying seabirds and fish are abundant in this cave, and those of eland are only a third as common as buffalo.

Klein points out that tool kits are quite different in the two caves. The Middle Stone Age people of the Klasies River cave used large flake tools and spears. In contrast, the later Nelson's Bay hunters had bows and arrows and a rich tool kit of small stone tools and bone artifacts, many of them for specialized purposes such as fowling and fishing. These innovations allowed Late Stone Age hunters to kill dangerous or more elusive species with greater frequency. Thus, the reason that the Middle Stone Age people took more eland was not that eland were more abundant in earlier times but that more elusive creatures, such as birds and fish, were captured less frequently. There is every indication that the Klasies people were less advanced behaviorally than the Nelson's Bay people (Klein and Cruz-Uribe, 1984).

Klein combines some other faunal evidence with his mammalian and climatic data. The Klasies River site contains larger tortoise and limpet remains, as if these creatures were permitted to grow to a larger size than in later times. This evidence implies less pressure on the tortoise and shellfish populations from a smaller human population before technologically more advanced people arrived.

Game Animals

Though the listing of game animals and their habits gives an insight into hunting practices, in many cases the content of the faunal list gains particular significance when we seek to explain why the hunters concentrated on certain species and apparently ignored others.

Taboos.   Dominance by one game species can result from economic necessity or convenience, or it can simply be a matter of cultural preference. Many societies restrict hunting of particular animals or consumption of certain game meat to one or the other sex. The modern-day !Kung San of the Dobe area of Botswana have

Figure 13.5   The aurochs as depicted by S. von Herbenstain in 1549.

complicated personal and age- and sex-specific taboos on eating mammals (Lee, 1979). No one can eat all twenty-nine game animals regularly taken by the San; indeed, no two individuals will have the same set of taboos. Some mammals can be eaten by everyone, but with restrictions on what part they may eat. Ritual curers will set personal dietary restrictions on other animals; no one eats primates and certain carnivores. Such complicated taboos are repeated with innumerable variations in other hunter-gatherer and agricultural societies and have undoubtedly affected the proportions of game animals found in archaeological sites.

Examples of specialized hunting are common from ancient times, even if the reasons for the attention given to one or more species are rarely explained. The specialized big-game hunting economies of the Plains Indians are well known (Frison, 1978). Another factor is overhunting, or the gradual extinction of a favorite species. One well-known example is *Bos primigenius* (Figure 13.5), the European aurochs or wild ox, which was a major quarry of Upper Paleolithic hunters in western Europe and was still hunted in postglacial times and after food production began (Kurtén, 1968). The last aurochs died in a Polish park in 1627. We know from illustrations and descriptions what these massive animals looked like. The bulls were large, up to 6 ½ feet (2 m) at the shoulder, and often with very long horns. The male's coat was black with a white stripe along the back and white curly hair between the horns. Through careful, long-term breeding and selecting for the physical features of the aurochs, German and Polish biologists have "reconstituted" these beasts successfully. Reconstituted aurochs are fierce, temperamental, and extremely agile if allowed to run wild. The experiments have provided a far more convincing reconstruction of a most formidable Pleistocene mammal than could any number of skeletal reconstructions or artists' impressions.

Changes in Hunting Activities.   Hunting activities have changed drastically in recent times. Richard Lee (1979) records how the older members of the San say that in earlier times there were more game animals and more hunters in the central interior of Botswana. Their forefathers used to hunt in large groups, killing buffalo, giraffe, and elephants. Today, their descendants have a predominantly gathering economy, supplemented by the meat of twenty-nine mammals, mostly those whose carcasses have a relatively high meat yield. Hunting is a common pursuit, with the warthog being the most important source of meat, together with small game. This change in hunting habits results directly from the importation of rifles and from early hunting safaris, which decimated the wonderful African fauna within three generations.

Seasonal Occupation. Many prehistoric hunter-gatherers and farmers, like their modern counterparts, lived their lives in regular, seasonal cycles in which subsistence activities changed according to the seasons of the year. The Pacific Northwest Indians congregated near salmon rivers when the summer runs upstream took place. They would catch thousands of salmon and dry them for consumption during the winter. The early dry season in Central Africa brings into season an abundance of wild fruit, an important part of early farmers' diet 1,500 years ago. How do archaeologists study seasonal activities and reconstruct the "economic seasons" of the year?

Every aspect of ancient hunter-gatherer life was affected by seasonal movements. The Northwest Indians enjoyed a complex ceremonial life during the sedentary winter months. The settlement pattern of the Khoe Khoe pastoralists of the Cape of Good Hope changed radically between dry and wet seasons (Elphick, 1977). During the dry months they would congregate at the few permanent water holes and near perennial rivers. When the rains came, the cattle herders spread out over the neighboring arid lands, watering their herds in the standing waters left by rainstorms. How do archaeologists study seasonality? A variety of approaches have been used with some success (Monks, 1981). The simplest method uses bones or plant remains to establish the season a site was visited. For example, bird bones were used to establish that a 1,000-year-old San Francisco Bay site was visited each year about June 28, when cormorants were young (Howard, 1929) (see the discussion on birds, later in the chapter). The presence of cod bones in early Norwegian fishing sites indicates that they were occupied during the winter and early spring, the optimal time for drying fish. This type of analysis is fine, provided that the habits of the animals or the availability of the plants being examined are well known or have not changed through time. Some plants are available for much of the year but are edible only during a few short weeks.

Knowledge about the ecology of both animals and plants is essential, for the "scheduling" of resource exploitation, though perhaps not explicit, was certainly a major factor in ancient societies (see the Doing Archaeology box). Some species such as deer are relatively insensitive to seasonal changes, but people sometimes exploited them in different ways at different times of the year. For instance, the Coast Salish of the Pacific Northwest took bucks in the spring and does in the fall (Monks, 1981).

Then there are physiological events in an animal's life that an archaeologist can use to establish seasonal occupation. During the fifteenth century A.D., a group of Plains hunters regularly took bison near a water hole at Garnsey, New Mexico (Speth, 1983). John Speth analyzed the body parts at the kill site and discovered that the hunters had a strong preference for male beasts during the spring, the season at which the hunts took place. The butchers had abandoned at the kill site body parts with a low meat yield, such as skulls and upper neck bones. In contrast, bones that yielded a great deal of meat, marrow, or grease were underrepresented at Garnsey. Many more

Doing Archaeology

Environment and Seasonality at Star Carr, England

The Star Carr site in northeastern England was occupied by a small band of Stone Age hunter-gatherers in about 8500 B.C. This tiny settlement, with its well-preserved, and rare, bone and wooden artifacts, excavated half a century ago, is world-famous for its remarkably complete portrait of Stone Age life in northern Europe immediately after the last Ice Age. Between 1949 and 1951, Cambridge University archaeologist Grahame Clark (1954) excavated a tiny birchwood platform crammed with stone tool fragments, bone and wooden artifacts, and a wealth of food remains. Using carefully recorded artifact counts, animal bones, pollen analysis, and all manner of esoteric identifications, as well as a liberal dose of traditional European folklore, Clark reconstructed a small hunting camp set in a patch of reeds by a lake. Pollen samples placed Star Carr to a time when birch forests first spread into northern Britain and much of the southern North Sea was still dry land. Clark and his experts argued, because of the red deer antlers, that the site was occupied in winter. He analyzed the methods used to make bone spearpoints, linked the technology of the stone tools to those made in Scandinavia at the time, and described a remarkable series of bone and wooden tools, including elk antler mattock heads (one with the tip of its wooden handle still in place), a single wooden canoe paddle, awls, even bark rolls and lumps of moss used for firelighting (Figure 13.6).

Star Carr has become an important testing ground for new ideas on ancient hunter-gatherer societies over the past half-century. Archaeologists Paul Mellars and Petra Dark (1999) have recently completed twelve years of highly selective paleoecological and archae-ological investigations at the site that have used all the resources of modern science to reinterpret the site.

When Clark originally excavated Star Carr, he concentrated on a small waterlogged area in a gully. After three seasons, he interpreted the site as a small settlement, perhaps used irregularly by four or five families. The new excavations extended onto drier areas and showed that the site was of far greater extent than Clark had suspected. By fieldwalking and careful test pitting, the excavators plotted flint artifact scatters over more than 400 feet (12 m) of the ancient lake shore. Thus, Star Carr saw much more widespread activity than Clark had originally suspected. By carefully surveying the original topography of the site, Mellars and Dark and their colleagues located a clay-filled channel that once flowed through the center of the site, separating Clark's wetland area from the drier locations.

Clark had claimed that the inhabitants of Star Carr had had little impact on their surroundings. Dark was able to use much higher resolution microscopes to examine the distribution of charcoal particles associated with a new array of accelerator mass spectrometry (AMS) radiocarbon dates. She showed that there was an initial period of intense charcoal deposition that lasted for about eighty years, then a century with little activity, followed by fairly continuous distribution for another 130 years. Botanist Jon Hather identified the charcoals as lakeside reeds, burnt off when they were dry between autumn and spring, when the new growth begins. Mellars and Dark believe that the reeds were fired repeatedly by humans, largely because the samples of high charcoal frequency are localized at the site, as if burning had been tightly controlled. Such conflagrations could have provided people with a better view of the lake and surrounding terrain, as well as a convenient landing place for canoes, and could have fostered new plant growth, which would attract feeding animals.

Clark's original report described Star Carr as a winter settlement. Now X-ray analysis of unerupted teeth deep in deer jawbones and comparisons with modern samples have identified many ten- to eleven-month-old animals, which would have been killed in March or April (R. Carter, 1998). This new seasonality data agree with minute finds of tightly rolled leaf stems of reeds burnt in early growth between March and April and with aspen bud scales, which date to the same time of year. No winter settlement, Star Carr may have been occupied from March until at least June or early July.

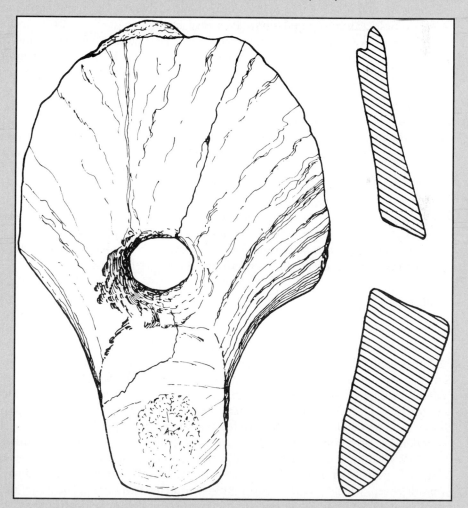

Figure 13.6   Elk antler mattock from Star Carr, England. (Two-thirds actual size.)

high-utility bones were taken from males than from females. Speth believes that the hunters concentrated on males because their meat had a higher fat content and they were in better condition than females after the winter.

Growth patterns in animal bones can sometimes yield clues on seasonal occupation. The epiphyses at the ends of limb bones are slowly joined to the main bones by ossification as an animal ages. Their study can certainly give some clues as to the general age of an animal population in, say, a hunting camp, but such variables as nutrition, even castration in domesticated animals, can affect the rate of fusion. Some species, such as ducks, mature much faster than others, such as deer. Clearly, knowledge of the different ages at which epiphyses fuse is essential to this approach.

Everyone knows that teeth erupt from upper and lower jaws as one grows into adulthood, often causing problems with wisdom teeth in people. Teeth are such durable animal remains that many archaeologists have tried to use them to age game and domestic animal populations. It is easy enough to study tooth eruption from complete or even fragmentary upper and lower jaws, and it has been done with domesticated sheep and goats and wild deer. Again, factors of nutrition, even domestication, can affect eruption rates, and the rate at which teeth wear can vary dramatically between one population and another (Monks, 1981).

Interpretation of seasonal occupation depends heavily on ethnographic analogies. One classic example is wild wheat. Botanist Gordon Hillman has studied the gathering of wild wheat in southwestern Asia and has shown that the collectors must schedule their collecting activities very precisely if they are to gather the harvest before the ears fall off the stems or the grain is consumed by birds and other animals (Hillman and Davis, 1990). It is reasonable to assume that the same precise scheduling was essential during prehistoric times, an analogy that has enabled southwestern Asian archaeologists to interpret seasonal occupations on sites in Syria and elsewhere.

By studying not only large mammals and obvious plant remains but also tiny mollusks and even fish bones and fish scales, one may be able to narrow the window of seasonal occupation at many sites to surprisingly tight limits.

Domestic Animals

Nearly all domestic animals originated from a wild species with an inclination to be sociable, facilitating an association with humans (Clutton-Brock, 1981, 1989). Domestic animals did not all originate in the same part of the world; they were domesticated in their natural area of distribution in the wild. Scholars have assumed that domestication of wild animals takes place when a certain level of cultural achievement is reached. Domestication everywhere seems to begin when a growing population needs a more regular food supply to feed larger groups of people; domestication is dependent on such conditions and is a prerequisite for further population growth.

Wild animals lack many characteristics that are valuable in their domestic counterparts. Thus, wild sheep have hairy coats, but their wool is not the type produced by domestic sheep, which is suitable for spinning; aurochs, ancestors of the domestic ox, and wild goats produce sufficient milk for their young but not in the quantities so important to humans. Considerable changes have taken place during domestication, as people develop characteristics in their animals that often render them unfit for survival in the wild.

The history of domestic species is based on fragmentary animal bones found in the deposits of innumerable caves, rock shelters, and open sites (Clutton-Brock, 1989). Osteological studies of wild and domesticated animals are inhibited both by fragmentation of the bones in most sites and by the much greater range of sexual and growth variation in domestic populations than in wild ones (Zeder and Hesse, 2000; Zeder et al., 2002). Nevertheless, a number of sites have produced evidence of gradual osteological change toward domesticated animals. If the bones of the wild species of some prehistoric domesticated animals are compared with those of the domestic animals throughout time, the range of size variations first increases, and eventually selection in favor of smaller animals and less variation in size appears. This transition is fluid, however, and it is difficult to identify wild or domestic individuals from single bones or small collections.

The bones of domestic animals demonstrate that a high degree of adaptability is inherent in wild animals. People have found it necessary to change the size and qualities of animals according to their needs, with corresponding effects on the animals' skeletal remains. Different breeds of cattle, sheep, and other domestic animals have been developed since the beginning of domestication.

Slaughtering and Butchery

Some insights into peoples' exploitation of wild and domestic animals can be obtained by studying not only animal bones themselves but also their frequency and distribution in the ground.

Sex, Age, and Slaughter Patterns. Clearly, determining the sex of an animal and the age at which it was killed may provide a way of studying the hunting or stock-raising habits of the people who did the slaughtering. Archaeologists have used a variety of methods for establishing sex and age from fragmentary bones (S. J. M. Davis, 1987).

Males and females of many mammal species vary considerably in size and build. For example, male horses have canine teeth, but females usually lack them. In humans, the female pelvis is very different from that of the male, in order to accommodate childbirth. We can estimate the proportions of males and females in sites such as the Garnsey bison kill by comparing the ratio of male to female body parts; in this case the differences between male and female beasts are known. Such analyses are much harder when less is known about size differences, or when bones are very fragmentary. Zooarchaeologists use a variety of bone measurements to distinguish sex, but such approaches are fraught with statistical and practical difficulties; they work best on complete bones. Even then, it may only be possible to identify different measurement distributions that may or may not reflect differences between the sexes.

How old were these cattle when they were slaughtered? Did the inhabitants concentrate on immature wild goats rather than on fully grown ones? These are the kinds of questions that are of importance on many sites. To answer them, researchers must establish the age of the animals in the faunal sample at death. The skeletal parts most commonly used to determine the age of an animal at death are teeth and the epiphyses at the ends of limb bones. In almost all mammals, bones where the epiphyses are not fused come from younger animals. This fact enables us to construct two age classes: immature and fully grown. If we know the ages at which epiphyses fuse, as is sometimes the case in species such as domestic cattle, we can add additional classes. Unfortunately, epiphyseal fusing is too gross a method to provide the kind of data that archaeologists need.

Fortunately, teeth and upper or lower jaws provide a more accurate way of establishing animal age. Teeth provide an almost continuous guide to the age of an individual from birth to old age. Complete upper and lower jaws allow us to study immature and mature teeth as they erupt, so we can identify not only the proportion of young animals but the very old animals as well.

Individual teeth can also be a mine of information on animal age. Some biologists are using growth rings on teeth, but this method is still highly experimental. A far more promising approach measures the height of tooth crowns. Richard Klein, an expert on African bones, has measured crown heights on Stone Age mammal teeth found at the Klasies River and Nelson's Bay caves in the Cape Province of South Africa. Taken as two groups, the teeth measurements give interesting general impressions of the hunting habits of middle and late Stone Age peoples in this area (Klein, 1977). Klein compared the mortality distributions from the Cape buffalo and other large and medium-sized species with mortality curves from modern mammal populations. He identified two basic distributions for the Stone Age bones (Klein and Cruz-Uribe, 1983). The **catastrophic age profile** has fewer older individuals. It is the normal distribution for living ungulate populations (Figure 13.7, left column) and is normally found in mass game kills achieved by driving herds into swamps or over cliffs, and in populations that perished of natural causes. The **attritional age profile**

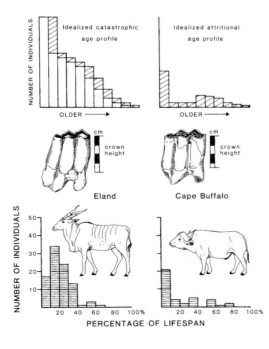

Figure 13.7   Idealized mortality data from modern animal populations based on molar crowns of two common South African mammals, the eland and the Cape buffalo: (*left column*) idealized catastrophic age profile; (*right column*) idealized attritional age profile.

(Figure 13.7, right column) shows an underrepresentation of prime-age animals relative to their abundance in living populations, but young and old are overrepresented. This profile is thought to result from scavenging or simple spear hunting.

Klein found that the Cape buffalo age distributions from both sites were close to those observed for modern buffalo killed by lions, and may be because both young and old males are vulnerable to attack because they are isolated from the large herds of formidable prime animals. Thus, he argued, the Stone Age hunters at both caves enjoyed a lasting, stable relationship with their prey populations of buffalo. The distributions for eland and bastard hartebeest (smaller, gregarious antelopes) were much more similar to the catastrophic profile. Klein speculates that they were similar because these species were hunted in large game drives, as were the bison on the American Great Plains. Thus, entire populations would be killed at one time. Age distributions can reflect all kinds of other activities as well. The Star Carr site in northeastern England contains no young red deer. Most of the animals were three or four years old, inexperienced subadults killed as they were leaving their mothers (Legge and Rowley-Conwy, 1988).

Hunting and slaughter patterns are subject to all manner of subtle variables, many of which were described by Lewis Binford (1978, 1981b). While studying hunting practices among the Nunamiut of Alaska, he found that the hunters butcher animals as part of a much broader subsistence strategy. The Nunamiut rely heavily on stored meat for most of the year and thus orient their hunting practices toward storage objectives, as well as many other considerations. In the fall, they may hunt caribou calves to obtain skins for winter clothing, and the heads and tongues of these animals provide the meat for the people who process the skins. Binford stressed that it is difficult to interpret slaughter patterns without closely understanding the cultural systems of which hunting was a part.

Domestic animals are a controllable meat supply and subject to quite different selection criteria. In more advanced agricultural societies, cattle or horses might be kept until old age for draught purposes, surplus males being castrated and females being retained until they stopped lactating or were of no further use for breeding or plowing. Even if riding or work animals were not kept, the problem of surplus males persists. This surplus is an abundant source of prime meat, and these animals were often slaughtered in their early adulthood. Cattle stood for wealth in many traditional societies, as they do in some today; and they were slaughtered on such special occasions as funerals or weddings. The herd surplus was consumed in this manner, and the owner's obligations were satisfied.

Butchery. The fragmentary bones in an occupation level are the end product of the killing, cutting up, and consumption of domestic or wild animals. To understand the butchery process, one must examine the articulation of animal bones in the levels where they are found, or a close study must be made of fragmentary body parts. The Olsen-Chubbock kill site in Colorado yielded evidence of a slaughtered bison herd. The hunters camped beside their kill, removing the skin and meat from a carcass and perhaps drying some surplus meat for later consumption. The butchering tools used by the skinners are found in direct association with the bones, so the excavations preserve the moment of butchery for posterity (Wheat, 1972).

Interpreting butchery techniques is a complicated matter, for many variables affected the way in which carcasses were dismembered. The Nunamiut rely heavily on stored meat, and the way they dismember a caribou varies according to storage needs, meat yield of different body parts, and proximity of the base camp. At any base site, the animal's size may affect the number of bones found: goats, chickens, or small deer could have been carried to the village as complete carcasses, but only small portions of larger beasts often are brought in. Sometimes animals with high meat yield are consumed where they are killed, and every scrap of flesh and entrails is utilized. Even with the NISP and MNI indices, interpretation is difficult.

Once again, the problem is to establish the meaning of archaeological distributions in terms of human behavior. Just how complicated this is in the context of butchery can be appreciated from Binford's comment (1978) that the Nunamiut criteria for selecting meat for consumption are the amount of usable meat, the time required to process it, and the quality of the flesh.

Plant Remains

Wild vegetable foods were a staple of the ancient world from the earliest times up to the moment when people first began to cultivate the soil some 12,000 years ago and long afterward. Unfortunately, the foods that were collected or cultivated are very hard to find in the archaeological record, so our knowledge of prehistoric foraging and the early history of food crops is very incomplete (Hawkes, 1983). Seeds, fruits, grasses, and leaves are among the most fragile of organic materials and do not survive long unless they are carbonized or preserved under very wet or arid conditions. Fortunately, new flotation methods and radiocarbon dating techniques (Chapter 7) are yielding a wealth of new information.

Carbonized and Unburned Seeds

Carbonized and unburned seeds are normally found in cooking pots, in midden deposits, or among the ashes of hearths, where they were dropped by accident. Though the preservation conditions are not ideal, researchers can identify domestic and wild plant species from such discoveries (Pearsall, 1989; B. D. Smith, 1999). Much early evidence for cereal cultivation in southwestern Asia comes from carbonized seeds. Many more unburned vegetable remains occur in waterlogged sites and in dry caves.

The extremely dry conditions of the North American desert West and of the Peruvian coast have preserved thousands of seeds, as well as human coprolites that contain a wealth of vegetal material. Hogup cave in Utah was occupied as early as 7000 B.C. From about 6400 to 1200 B.C., the inhabitants relied so heavily on pickleweed seeds in their diet that the early deposits are literally golden with the chaff threshed from them (Aikens, 1970; Madsen and O'Connell, 1982). Deposits of pickleweed and the milling stones used to process it from after 1200 B.C. decline rapidly. An abrupt rise in the nearby Great Salt Lake may have drowned the marsh where the seed was collected, so the cave was only visited by hunting parties.

Four 19,000- to 17,000-year-old hunter-gatherer camps at the Wadi Kubbaniya site in the Egyptian desert have yielded remarkable collections of charred plant foods, some apparently roasted seeds preserved in human infant feces. The inhabitants brought back more than twenty types of food plant. The most common were nutgrass tubers, which are easily collected by the ton with simple digging sticks and are used as famine food when crops fail in West Africa and India today. Indeed, harvesting the wild tubers each year fosters new growth. When cooked to make it nontoxic, nutgrass can serve as a staple, and may, in fact, have fulfilled such a purpose at Wadi Kubbaniya (Hillman, 1989; Wendorf and others, 1980).

Tehuacán

The Tehuacán Valley in the state of Puebla, Mexico, has provided a record of continuous human occupation, from the earliest times to the Spanish Conquest, and a unique chronicle of early maize cultivation (Byers, 1967; MacNeish, 1970). Early inhabitants of the valley lived mainly by hunting rabbits, birds, and turtles. Later, about 6700–5000 B.C., their successors subsisted mostly on wild plants such as beans and amaranth. These people were seasonally mobile hunter-gatherers who eventually added the deliberate cultivation of plants to their seasonal round without making radical changes in their lifeways. The dry valley caves document a gradual shift from wild-plant foraging to an almost total dependence on cultivated crops, including maize and beans. And within a few centuries of full domestication of maize, the people had moved into permanent village settlements anchored to their fields.

The wild ancestor of maize was an indigenous grass, teosinte (*Zea mays* subspecies *parviglumis*), which still grows in Central America. Botanists believe that both maize and beans were domesticated from identifiable wild ancestors in the Guadalajara region, some 155 miles (250 km) west of the Tehuacán Valley, where both teosinte and a population cluster of wild beans still flourish (B. D. Smith, 1999). Richard MacNeish excavated more than a dozen sites in Tehuacán, five of which contained the remains of ancient corn; 80,000 wild-plant remains and 25,000 specimens of corn came from the sites. Early maize cobs came from the lowest occupation level in San Marcos cave, dried ears no more than three-quarters of an inch (20 mm) long. This was fully domesticated maize, incapable of dispersing its kernels naturally, as wild plants do to regenerate. The mature plants would have stood about 4 feet (1.2 m) high with one to five ear-bearing lateral branches, each plant producing ten to fifteen small corn ears (Figure 13.8). Originally, MacNeish estimated their age at between 7,000 and 5,500 years ago, but AMS radiocarbon dating on actual cobs from San Marcos and Coxcatlán caves indicates only as early as 4,700 to 4,600 years ago (about 2700 B.C.), a thousand years or so later than originally thought.

Flotation Recovery

Flotation techniques have been employed systematically to recover seeds in recent years. The method uses water or chemicals to free the seeds, which are often of microscopic size, from the fine earth or occupation residue that masks them; the vegetal

Figure 13.8 The evolution of maize through the various stages in the transformation from teosinte to maize. The earliest teosinte form is (a); the stabilized maize phenotype is (e). The harvesting process increased the condensation of teosinte branches and led to the husks' becoming the enclosures for corn ears.

Source: Walter Galinat, "Domestication and Diffusion of Maize," in Richard I. Ford, ed., *Prehistoric Food Production in North America* (Ann Arbor: University of Michigan Museum of Anthropology, 1984).

remains usually float and the residue sinks. Although this technique enables us to recover seeds from many sites where doing so was once impossible, by no means can it be applied universally, for its effectiveness depends on soil conditions. Using flotation, Stuart Struever and his colleagues recovered more than 36,000 fragments of carbonized hickory nutshells from ovens, hearths, and storage-refuse pits in the Apple Creek site in the lower Illinois Valley. This settlement also yielded 4,200 fragments of

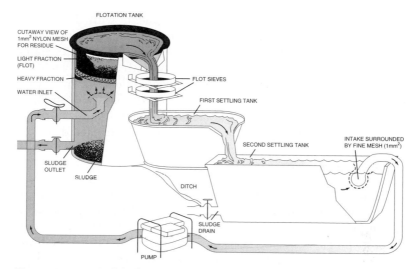

FLOTATION TANK

CUTAWAY VIEW OF 1mm² NYLON MESH FOR RESIDUE

LIGHT FRACTION (FLOT)

HEAVY FRACTION

WATER INLET

FLOT SIEVES

FIRST SETTLING TANK

SECOND SETTLING TANK

INTAKE SURROUNDED BY FINE MESH (1mm²)

SLUDGE OUTLET

SLUDGE

DITCH

SLUDGE DRAIN

PUMP

Figure 13.9 Model of a water flotation device for recovering plant remains using recycled water, developed by botanist Gordon Hillman. The lightest remains float to the surface and are caught in flot sieves. The heavier material sinks and is caught in light nylon mesh.

acorn shell, as well as more than 2,000 other seeds from at least three species. Few cultivated seeds were found, indicating that the inhabitants relied on hickory nuts and acorns for much of their vegetable diet (B. D. Smith, 1992).

Flotation has revolutionized the study of prehistoric vegetal remains. The methods used are being refined as more experience is gained with them under varied field conditions. A number of ingenious machines have been developed to carry out large-scale flotation (Figure 13.9). The sample of earth is poured into the screened container and agitated by the water pouring into the screen. The light plant remains and other fine materials float on the water and are carried out of the container by a sluiceway that leads to fine mesh screens, where the finds are caught, wrapped in fine cloth, and preserved for the botanists to study. The heavy sludge, in the meantime, sinks to the bottom of the container.

Flotation is rewriting the early history of farming in all parts of the world, partly because it yields much larger samples of domestic and wild seeds to work with. Andrew Moore used flotation with great efficiency on the Stone Age farming village at Abu Hureyra on the Euphrates River in Syria. He acquired 712 seed samples from soil deposits that comprised a bulk of more than 132 U.S. gallons (500 liters). Each sample contained as many as 500 seeds from over 150 plant taxa, many of them edible. By studying these large samples, botanist Gordon Hillman was able to document the retreat of oak forests in the region, and the changes in plant gathering that accompanied environmental change. He showed that Abu Hureyra had been in the grip of a prolonged drought in about 10,500 B.C. At first, the people turned to drought-resistant small-seeded grasses. Then they abandoned Abu Hureyra, probably moving to places close to permanent water, where experiments with the cultivation of cereal crops began. As more favorable conditions returned, in about 9700 B.C., a farming settlement appeared at Abu Hureyra, based on the cultivation of emmer, einkorn, and barley, staple cereal crops that were rotated with legumes such as lentils, vetches, and chick-peas. But the people still supplemented their diet by collecting significant quantities of wild vegetable foods (Moore, 2000). They lived in the same place for a long period of time because they rotated their crops and used a simple fallow system that allowed exhausted fields to recover before being replanted.

Grain Impressions

Apart from the seeds themselves, which reveal what the food plants were, grain impressions in the walls of clay vessels or adobe brick help to uncover the history of agriculture or gathering. The microscopic casts of grains that adhered to the wet clay of a pot while it was being made are preserved in the firing and can be identified with a microscope. Numerous grain impressions have been found in European handmade pottery from the end of the Stone Age. Grain impressions have been studied in southwestern Asia and the western Sahara Desert; some related work on adobe bricks has been carried out in the western United States.

Palynology

Pollen analysis has been an extremely valuable tool for analyzing European forest clearance (see also Chapter 12) (Figure 13.10). About 4000 B.C., in northern Europe the components of high forest—oak, ash, beech, and elm—simultaneously declined, while the pollen of grasses increased sharply. At many locations, charcoal layers underlie the zone where forest trees declined. The increase in grass pollen was also associated with the appearance of several cultivation weeds, including *Plantago,* which is associated with cereal agriculture in Europe and went with European farmers throughout the world, even to North America. The tree cover vanished as a direct result of farming activity—humanity's first major imprint on the environment. Similar pollen curves have been plotted from data gathered elsewhere in Europe.

The Chilean wine palm (*Jubaia chilensis*) is the largest in the world, growing to a height of at least 65 feet (20 m). The tree yields a valuable sap to make honey or potent wine, and the nuts have a prized oily kernel. At the time of its first settlement by Polynesian voyagers in the eighth or ninth century A.D., Easter Island in the South Pacific supported forests of wine palms. Pollen diagrams from the island show that deforestation and depletion of the environment through burning and cutting destroyed the palm forests, diminished water supplies, and cut the people off from the outside world by destroying the timber used for offshore canoes (Bahn, 1992).

Plant Phytolith Analysis

Opal phytoliths, minute particles of silica from plant cells, are produced from hydrated silica dissolved in groundwater that is absorbed through a plant's roots and

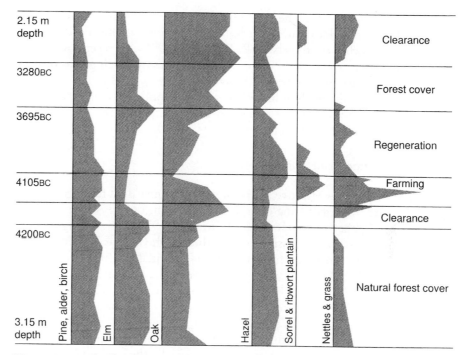

Figure 13.10   Pollen diagram from northern Ireland that documents the impact of farmers on the prehistoric landscape. About 4150 B.C., tree pollen counts fall dramatically as farmers first clear the forest. At the same time, grasses and field weeds take over. Subsequently, the farmers abandon the fields and the forest regenerates before being cleared again after 3280 B.C.

carried through its vascular system (Piperno, 1988). Silica production is continuous throughout the growth of a plant. Phytolith samples are collected in much the same way as pollen samples, and then they are studied by identifying individual species. Most research in the field has been with grasses, so the archaeological applications are obvious, especially in the study of prehistoric agriculture.

Archaeological applications of phytolith research are still at an early stage, but the method shows promise. Anna Roosevelt used phytolith analysis on sites in the Orinoco River valley of Venezuela. She found that the percentages of grass phytoliths had increased dramatically at the very time when maize was introduced to the area, as indicated by carbon-13 and carbon-12 analysis of skeletal material and actual seeds. Deborah Pearsall and Dolores Piperno have developed a complex formula for distinguishing between phytolith samples produced by modern maize and those produced by wild grasses (Pearsall and Piperno, 1990). They analyzed soil samples from radiocarbon sites in coastal Ecuador and found phytolith evidence for the presence of maize in layers radiocarbon-dated to as early as 8,000 to 7,000 years ago. When these results were first announced, they seemed in broad agreement with the earlier chronology for maize at Tehuacán. But AMS dating of actual Mexican cobs has shortened the time frame considerably. There are no cobs in the Ecuadorian sites, and the average size of wild and possible domesticated phytoliths was tiny. Thus Pearsall and Piperno's results are somewhat controversial (B. D. Smith, 1999). In recent years, much research has focused on tropical root crops, where analyses of starch grains on stone tools offers a potential avenue of research (Piperno and Holt, 1998).

Phytolith analysis has many potential applications in archaeology in the study of diet, through the use of coprolites and even phytoliths embedded in jawbones, but research is still in its infancy.

Interpreting Plant Evidence

No matter how effective the recovery techniques used for vegetal remains, the picture of either food gathering or agriculture is bound to be incomplete. A look at modern hunter-gatherers reveals the problem (Lee, 1979). The !Kung San of the Kalahari in southern Africa are classic hunter-gatherers who appear in every book on ethnography. Many early writers on hunter-gatherers assumed that the !Kung relied on game alone and lived in perennial starvation that was relieved periodically by meat-eating orgies. In fact, nothing could be farther from the truth. Much subsistence activity of the San and other hunter-gatherers is conducted by the women, who gather wild vegetable foods that constitute a substantial part of their diet. The San know of at least eighty-five species of edible fruit, seeds, and plants; of this enormous subsistence base, they eat regularly only some nine species, especially the bauhinia. In a famine year or when prime vegetable food sources are exhausted, they turn to other species, having an excellent cushion of edible food to fall back on when their conventional diet staple is scarce. Theoretically, therefore, the San can never starve, even if food is scarce at times. Their territory, of course, is delineated in part by available sources of vegetable foods as well as by water supplies; its frontiers in many cases represent a day's walking distance to the gathering grounds and back to the base camp.

Agriculture and Domestic and Wild Animals

Very few subsistence-farming peoples have ever relied on agricultural products or their herds alone to provide them with food year-round. The rate of domestic herd growth is affected by many factors, among them endemic stock disease, nutrient qualities of grazing grass, availability of water supplies, and in some areas, distribution of the dreaded tsetse fly, carrier of trypanosomiasis, which is fatal to cattle and harmful to humans. Similar factors also affect the growth rate of domestic stock because the size of cattle or smaller stock can vary widely from one environment to another. Hunting, fishing, and gathering have always supplemented the diet, and in famine years or times of epidemic the people have fallen back on the natural resources of their environment for survival.

Since food production has led to increased population densities, however, famine often ensues because the resource base of wild foods for farmers is smaller than that which may have supported a smaller hunter-gatherer population in comfort

(Scudder, 1962). Even in times of plenty, most food producers rely on game for some of their meat, as evidenced by the bones of wild animals in faunal collections where cattle and small stock are also present. The changeover from hunting and gathering to full-fledged agriculture and animal domestication took place remarkably rapidly in many places—witness the Abu Hureyra site in Syria (see the Site box).

Birds, Fish, and Mollusks

Birds

Bird bones have been sadly neglected in archaeology, although some early investigators did realize their significance. In 1902, the famous Peruvianist Max Uhle dug a large shell mound at Emeryville on the eastern shores of San Francisco Bay. The site was excavated again in 1926, and Hildegarde Howard studied a large collection of bird remains from the dig. Her report (1929) illustrates the potential importance of bird faunas in archaeology. She found that waterbirds were the predominant species, especially ducks, geese, and cormorants, and that land birds distinctive of hill country were absent. All the geese were winter visitors, mostly found in the bay area between January and April of each year. The cormorant bones were nearly all immature, suggesting that the Indians had been robbing cormorant rookeries; most of the cormorant bones equaled an adult bird's in size, but ossification was less complete, equivalent to that in modern birds about five to six weeks old. Howard examined rookery records and estimated that a date of June 28 each year would be the approximate time when the rookeries could be raided. Thus, from the evidence she concluded that the Emeryville mound was occupied during both the winter and the early summer, and probably all year.

Bird hunting has often been a sideline in the struggle for subsistence. In many societies, boys have hunted winged prey with bow and arrows while training for hunting larger game. A specialized bird-hunting kit is found in several cultures, among them the Holocene hunter-gatherer cultures of northern Europe. Though bows and spears were used in the chase, snaring was obviously practiced regularly.

Waterfowl were of great significance in the American Midwest and Southeast and also in the Great Basin. Archaic and later peoples exploited the vast annual migrations of waterfowl, which flew in spring and fall along the Mississippi flyway, shooting them with bow and arrow and trapping them with nets. The carcasses were then dried for later consumption. Archaic hunter-gatherers in the Great Basin often congregated near shallow lakes, where they preyed on waterfowl with cunning decoys, which are preserved in dry caves (Fagan, 2000).

The birds found in some African hunting and farming sites are almost invariably species, such as guinea fowl, that rarely fly and are easily snared. No traces of the snares have been found in excavations, for they would have been made of perishable materials. Surprisingly little has been written on prehistoric fowling, perhaps because bird bones are fragile and present tricky identification problems (Avery and Underhill, 1986; Gilbert and others, 1985; Klein and Cruz-Uribe, 1984).

Site

Abu Hureyra, Syria

Abu Hureyra, one of the earliest farming villages in the world, was excavated by Andrew Moore and a team of researchers in the 1970s. Thanks to state-of-the-art science, especially flotation, we know much about the transition from foraging to farming at Abu Hureyra (Hillman, 1989; Moore, 2000).

The first village of pit houses with reed roofs was built about 11,500 B.C. and flourished for five hundred years. The climate was damper and warmer than today. Abu Hureyra lay in well-wooded steppe, where animals and wild cereals were abundant. The hamlet lay close to woodland and open country and to the fertile river floodplain, where wild cereal grasses could be harvested. Each spring, Abu Hureyra's hunters preyed on thousands of migrating Persian gazelle, which moved northward with the changing season (Figure 13.11). They killed thousands of them and dried the meat for later use (Legge and Rowley-Conwy, 1987).

With such a favorable location, Abu Hureyra increased in size to 300–400 people, until a long drought cycle, and perhaps deforestation due to heavy firewood consumption, caused abandonment of the settlement. About 9700 B.C., another village rose on the same site. This was a much larger village that grew to cover nearly 30 acres (12 ha). At first the inhabitants still hunted gazelle intensively. Then, about 9000 B.C., within the span of a generation or so, they switched over to herding domesticated sheep and goats and to growing cereal crops. Visitors to the village would have found themselves wandering through a closely knit community of rectangular, one-story, mud-brick houses, joined by narrow lanes and courtyards.

Andrew Moore's very thorough excavations show us that each gradual or rapid change in the subsistence pattern or environment of Abu Hureyra instituted by humans led to a complicated chain reaction affecting every sector of the inhabitants' culture.

Fish

Fishing, like fowling, became increasingly important as people began to specialize in different and distinctive economies and as their environmental adaptations became more sophisticated and their technological abilities improved. Evidence for this activity comes from both artifacts and fish bones (Colley, 1990; A. Wheeler and Jones, 1989).

Freshwater and ocean fish can be caught in various ways. Nets, basket traps, and dams were widely used from 10,000 years ago on, but their remains rarely survive in the archaeological record except in dry sites or waterlogged deposits (Petersen and others, 1984). Basket fish traps have been found in Danish peat bogs, dating to earlier than 4000 B.C. (J. G. D. Clark, 1952). The ancient Egyptians employed somewhat similar traps, depicted in Old Kingdom tomb paintings (2575–2134 B.C.). Nets remained the most popular fishing device and were used in northern Europe in Holocene times, too. A larger fish weir, constructed of vertical sticks 4 to 16 feet

Figure 13.11   Abu Hureyra, Syria.

(1.2 to 4.9 m) long and sharpened at one end with a stone ax, enclosed an area of 2 acres (0.8 ha) at Boylston Street, Boston. The weir was built about 2500 B.C. and was probably the work of coastal Archaic people. Such traps were evidently widely used along the Atlantic Coast, built in estuary areas where tidal currents were strong. In the Boston weir, brush and flexible withies—twigs or branches—were placed between the stakes; fish were diverted into the enclosure by "leaders," also made of brush, leading to the trap mouth. Some days' work must have been necessary to build this weir, which provided an almost inexhaustible food supply for its designers.

Fishhooks, harpoons, and barbed spearheads are frequent finds in lakeside or riverside encampments. The earliest fishhooks had no barbs, but they did have a U-shaped profile (Figure 13.12). Postglacial hunting peoples, such as the Maglemose folk of Denmark, used such artifacts in the seventh millennium B.C., in all probability to hunt pike, a prized freshwater fish in prehistoric times (J. G. D. Clark, 1952).

Artifacts alone tell us little about the role of fish in the prehistoric economy or about the fishing techniques of prehistoric peoples. Did they fish all year or only when

Figure 13.12   Bone fishhooks of the Maglemose culture in northern Europe. (Two-thirds actual size.)

salmon were running? Did they concentrate on bottom fish or rely on stranded whales for protein? Such questions can be answered only by examining the fish bones themselves, or actual fish scales. Perhaps the most effective method of collecting fish remains is to take samples from each level, an approach advocated by Richard Casteel, who found that this was one-ninth as time-consuming as normal collection methods. Furthermore, he succeeded in identifying 30 percent more fish types from his column samples. He used this approach at the Glenrose Cannery site on the Fraser River Delta in British Columbia, where salmon and sturgeon were taken for thousands of years, from at least 5,700 years ago (Casteel, 1976; Matson, 1981).

Since fish are a relatively predictable food resource, lakeside or seaside fishing
The Chumash Indians of southern California were remarkably skillful fishers, venturing far offshore in frameless plank canoes and fishing with hook and line, basket, net, and harpoon (J. Arnold, 2001). The piscatory skill of California Indians is reflected in the archaeological sites of Century Ranch, Los Angeles, where the bones of such deep-sea fish as the albacore and oceanic skipjack were found, together with the remains of large deep-water rockfish that live near the sea bottom in water too deep to be fished from shore (C. King and others, 1968). Five other species normally occurring offshore, including the barracuda, were found in the same midden. The bones of shallow-water fish, among them the leopard shark and the California halibut, were discovered in the same sites, indicating that both surf fishing and canoe fishing in estuaries with hook and line, basket, or net were also practiced.

Since fish are a relatively predictable food resource, lakeside or seaside fishing encampments tend to be occupied longer than hunting camps, for the food supply, especially when combined with collection of shellfish, is both reliable and nourishing.

Mollusks

Shellfish from seashores, lakes, or rivers formed an important part of the prehistoric diet for many thousands of years (Waselkov, 1987). The identification of the mollusks in shell middens is a matter for expert conchologists, who possess a mine of information on the edibility and seasons of shellfish.

Freshwater mollusks were important to many Archaic bands living in the southeastern United States, but, because each mollusk in itself has limited food value, the amount of mollusks needed to feed even a small band of about twenty-five people must have been enormous. It has been calculated that such a band would need between 1,900 and 2,250 mussels from the Meramec River each day, and a colossal accumulation of between 57,000 and 67,000 each month (Parmalee and Klippel, 1974). A group of 100 persons would need at least 3 tons of mussels each month. In many regions such as California, marine and freshwater shellfish mollusks were a valuable supplemental food at times of scarcity during the year or a source of variety in a staple diet of fish, game, or vegetable foods (Waselkov, 1987).

When freshwater or seawater mollusks were collected, the collectors soon accumulated huge piles of shells at strategic places on the coast or on the shores of lakes, near rocky outcrops or tidal pools where mollusks were commonly found (Meehan, 1982). Modern midden analysis involves systematic sampling of the deposits and counting and weighing the various constituents of the soil. The proportions of different shells are readily calculated, and their size, which sometimes changes through time, is easily measured. California shell middens have long been the subject of intensive research, with the changes in frequency of mollusks projected against ecological changes in the site areas.

The La Jolla culture middens of La Batiquitos Lagoon in San Diego are a notable example of such analysis. Claude N. Warren took column samples from one shell mound and found that the remains of five species of shellfish were the dominant elements in the molluscan diet of the inhabitants (see R. M. Crabtree, 1963). The changes in the major species of shellfish were then calculated for each excavated level. They found that *Mytilus,* the bay mussel, was the most common in the lower levels and was gradually replaced by *Chione,* the Venus shell, and *Pecten,* the scallop, both of which assumed greater importance in the later phases of the site's occupation, which has been radiocarbon-dated from the fifth to the second millennia B.C. Warren found that *Ostrea,* the oyster, a species characteristic of a rocky coast, was also common in the lower levels, indicating that the San Diego shore was rocky beach at that time, with extensive colonies of shellfish. By about 6,300 years ago La Batiquitos Lagoon was silted to the extent that it was ecologically more suitable for *Pecten* than the rock-loving *Mytilus.* Soon afterward, however, the lagoons became so silted that even *Pecten* and *Chione* could no longer support a large population dependent on shellfish. The inhabitants then had to relocate. Similar investigations elsewhere in California have also shown the great potential of mollusks in the study of prehistoric ecology.

Many peoples collected mollusks seasonally, but it is difficult to identify such practices from the archaeological record. Growth bands in mollusk shells have been used to measure seasonality, but the most promising approach is to measure the oxygen-isotopic ratio of its shell carbonate, which is a function of the water temperature (Lightfoot and Cerrato, 1988). Using a mass spectrometer, you can measure the oxygen-18 composition at the edge of a shell, obtaining the temperature of the water at the time of the mollusk's death. It is difficult to determine actual temperatures, but you can gain an idea of seasonal fluctuations, thereby establishing whether a mollusk was taken in winter or summer (Deith, 1983; Killingley, 1981).

Both freshwater and seawater shells had ornamental roles as well. Favored species were traded over great distances in North America. Millions of *Mercenaria* and *Busycon* shells were turned into wampum belts in New England in early colonial times. *Spondylus gaederopus,* a mussel native to the Black Sea, the Sea of Marmara, and the Aegean, was widely distributed as far north and west as Poland and the Rhineland by European farmers in the fifth millennium B.C. Andean lords in both coastal and highland states prized *Spondylus* as a sacred shell, which was buried with the lord of Sicán, among others (see the Site box in Chapter 11). The *Conus* shell, common on the East African coast, was widely traded, finding its way into the African interior and becoming a traditional perquisite of chieftainly prestige. The nineteenth-century missionary and explorer David Livingstone recorded that, on his visit to Chief Shinte in western Zambia in 1855, the going price for two *Conus* shells at that time was a slave; for five, a tusk of elephant ivory.

Subsistence Data from Rock Art

Rock art is a major source of information on economic activities. Upper Paleolithic cave art in southwestern France depicts dozens of mammal species, perhaps meant to represent large, meaty animals that were economically (and symbolically) valuable (Bahn and Vertut, 1988).

Much more detailed information comes from southern Africa. Nearly half a century ago, African archaeologist J. Desmond Clark (1959) published an account of late Stone Age hunting and gathering practices in southern Africa in which he drew heavily on the rock art of Zimbabwe and South Africa. The paintings depict the chase, weapons, collecting, and camp life.

The rock paintings of Natal, South Africa, provide fascinating information on fishing practices and the boats associated with them. Patricia Vinnecombe (1960) recorded a famous fishing scene in the Tsoelike River rock shelter in Lesotho, southern Africa (Figure 13.13). The fishermen, armed with long spears, are massed in boats, apparently cornering a shoal of fish that are swimming around in confusion. Some boats have lines under their hulls that may represent anchors; the fish cannot be identified with certainty, but they may be freshwater catfish or yellowfish. Such vignettes of prehistoric hunting life add insight into data obtained from the food residues recovered from caves and rock shelters, but the actual interpretation of the art is subject to many sophisticated variables, among them the symbolic meaning of the paintings (see Lewis-Williams, 1981, 1995).

Not only rock art but even pottery can throw light on prehistoric subsistence. The Mimbres culture developed in southwestern New Mexico in the late first millennium A.D. and is famous for its black-on-white painted pottery that was produced mainly between A.D. 950 and 1150 in some twenty villages along the Mimbres River. The potters depicted humans, other mammals, birds, reptiles, fish, insects, and mythical creatures. About 11 percent of the images are fish, many of them species that

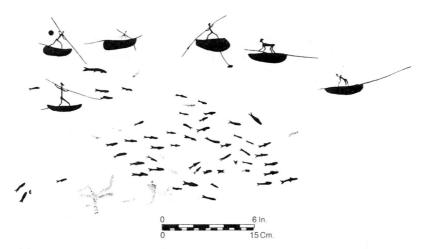

Figure 13.13   A rock painting depicting a fishing scene from Lesotho, southern Africa.

Source: Patricia Vinnicombe, "A Fishing Scene from the Tsoelike River, Southeastern Basutoland," *South African Archaeological Bulletin* 15 (March 1960): 15. Reprinted by permission.

Figure 13.14   Mimbres painted bowl depicting a man spearing a large fish, sometimes interpreted as a whale.

can be identified as being native to the Gulf of California, more than 450 miles (724 km) away. Both the distribution of modern fish species and the marine mollusks found in Mimbres villages strongly suggest that the people had visited the ocean, perhaps to collect marine shells for making beads (Figure 13.14) (Jett and Moyle, 1986).

Ancient Diet

The ultimate objective of the archaeology of subsistence is not only to establish how people obtained their food but also to reconstruct their actual diet. Dietary reconstruction is difficult, mainly because of incomplete economic information. Yet the problems involved are fundamental. What proportion of the diet was meat? How diverse were dietary sources? Did the principal sources of diet change from season to season? To what extent did the people rely on food from neighboring areas? Was food stored? What limitations or restrictions did technology or society place on diet? All these questions lie behind any inquiry into prehistoric subsistence (Gilbert and others, 1985).

Diet (what is eaten) and **nutrition** (the ability of a diet to maintain the body in its environment) must be studied in close conjunction, for they are quite distinct from subsistence, the actual process of obtaining resources. The baseline for any study of prehistoric diet and nutrition must be surveys of modern hunter-gatherers, subsistence cultivators, and pastoralists. Unfortunately, however, lack of agreement among dietary experts is so widespread that it is difficult to estimate the caloric needs of prehistoric peoples. So many cultural, medical, and physiological factors must be weighed, even in modern situations, that research of prehistoric nutrition and food consumption will often be little more than inspired guesswork. Despite such recovery methods as flotation, it is still impossible to assess the intake of vitamins, minerals, and milk products in prehistoric diets. Nor do we have adequate data on the waste of food during preparation and storage or on the effects of different cooking techniques. Archaeological data can only indicate some of the foods eaten by prehistoric communities and show, at least qualitatively, how important some of them were generally. We are far from being able to ascribe precise food value to animal and plant remains, as would be demanded for precise studies of diet and nutrition.

Sources of Data on Diet and Nutrition

There are only a few sources of data on prehistoric diet and nutrition, and these are subject to serious limitations. Human skeletal remains can sometimes provide evidence of ancient malnutrition and other conditions attributable to diet (Larsen, 1987). For example, the parish church of Rothwell in Britain's Midlands has a massive bone crypt that houses the remains of more than 20,000 people disinterred from the graveyard when the church was expanded in the thirteenth century A.D., as well as skeletons from a nearby sixteenth-century hospice. A preliminary study of some of the bones has shown that many of these medieval and later people suffered from malnutrition, as well as from arthritis, tuberculosis, and other infections. Fractures were also common (Shackley, 1985).

Physical anthropologist Jane Buikstra has studied diet and health among the prehistoric populations of the lower Illinois Valley. As early as 5500 B.C., the inhabitants of this area began harvesting hickory and other nuts on an ever-larger scale. Nuts provided a high-quality food resource, but to support large numbers of people, they had to be harvested over large areas. As time went on, the growing population of the valley turned more and more to wild seeds, especially oily ones such as marsh elder, that were high in protein and a concentrated source of food energy. In time, they actually cultivated marsh elder as well as sunflowers, whose seeds had equivalent food value. They supplemented the oily species with starchy seeds such as knotweed that were highly dependable and easily stored. In the last half of the first millennium A.D., the starchy seeds gave way to cultivated maize. Buikstra observes that, as much more complex social organization and regional trade evolved, dental diseases became much more common and tuberculosis spread among the dense village populations. The introduction of maize appears to have coincided with a deterioration in child health, too (Buikstra, 1984; Cook, 1984).

Stable carbon isotope analysis involves identifying types of plant foods from the isotopic analysis of prehistoric bone and hair (De Niro, 1987). By using the ratio between two stable carbon isotopes—carbon-12 and carbon-13—in animal tissue, researchers can establish the diet of the organism. Research on controlled animal populations has shown that as carbon is passed along the food chain, the carbon composition of animals continues to reflect the relative isotopic composition of their diet. Carbon is metabolized in plants through three major pathways: C_3, C_4, and Crassulacean acid metabolism. The plants that make up the diet of animals have distinct carbon-13 values. Maize, for example, is a C_4 plant. In contrast, most indigenous temperate flora in North America is composed of C_3 varieties. Thus, a population that shifts its diet from wild vegetable foods to maize will also experience a shift in dietary isotopic values. Because carbon-13 and carbon-12 values do not change after death, you can study archaeological carbon from food remains, soil humus, and skeletal remains to gain insight into ancient diet. This approach is of great importance to archaeologists studying dietary patterns, especially when combined with information from other sources.

For example, excellent organic preservation at the Windover burial grounds in eastern Florida allowed a team of researchers to combine an archaeobotanical analysis with bone-collagen stable carbon isotope and nitrogen-isotopic studies of human skeletal remains. They were interested in the degree of reliance on marine as opposed to terrestrial food resources among the people buried at Windover between about 6000 and 5000 B.C. A comparison of nitrogen-isotopic values from human bone collagen at Windover with values from coastal sites shows that the inhabitants of the former made little use of marine resources. Many C_3 plants were part of the Windover diet, with duck and catfish, with intermediate C_3/C_4 values also significant. The plant remains, such as elderberry, from the site included virtually all C_3 plants, confirming the isotopic data and data from well-preserved stomach contents. The research team believes it has evidence for seasonal foraging based on wild plant foods and freshwater and estuarine resources over a long period of time (Tuross and others, 1994).

A detailed bone chemistry analysis of adult burials from Grasshopper Pueblo in east-central Arizona shows the great potential of this approach. Joseph Ezzo (1993) was able to show that between A.D. 1275 and 1325 males had greater access to meat and cultivated plants, while females had greater access to wild plants. Between 1325 and 1400, men and women ate virtually the same diet, one in which meat and wild plant foods were less important. This change may have resulted from a combination of social and environmental factors: increased population, drought cycles, or use of marginal farming land, which compelled the Grasshopper people to live on agricultural products. The people responded to food stress by increasing storage capacity, reducing household size, and eventually moving away.

The stable carbon isotope method is not restricted to use with agriculture; it has been applied with success to measure the reliance on marine species of prehistoric Northwest Coast populations in British Columbia (Chisholm and others, 1983). Forty-eight samples from prehistoric human skeletons from fifteen sites along the coast revealed a dietary reliance of about 90 percent on marine sources, a figure much higher than crude ethnographic estimates. The same data suggest that there has been little dietary change along the British Columbia coast for the past five thousand years, which is hardly surprising, given the rich maritime resources of the shoreline.

Isotopic and elemental analyses of prehistoric skeletons have been useful in the study of the origin and spread of maize in the New World, by using stable carbon isotopes of skeletal collagen and as a way of detecting the consumption of marine foods. For instance, isotope analyses show that about 70 percent of the diet of the Maya inhabitants of Copán, Honduras, came from maize. There remain important potential avenues of inquiry. Can one, for example, establish the importance of meat in early hominid diets?

Concentrations of strontium, a stable mineral component of bone as opposed to calcium, can be used to measure the contribution of plants to diet. For instance, it has been shown that prehistoric people in the eastern Mediterranean ate much the same proportions of meat and plant foods from 100,000 years ago up to the end of the Ice Age. Then there was a significant shift toward the consumption of plant foods.

Stomach contents and feces provide unrivaled momentary insights into meals eaten by individual members of a prehistoric society. Dietary reconstructions based on these sources, however, suffer from the disadvantage that they are rare and represent but one person's food intake. Furthermore, some foods are more rapidly digested than others. But even these insights are better than no data at all. The stomach of Tollund Man, who was executed around the time of Christ, contained the remains of a finely ground meal made from barley, linseed, and several wild grasses; no meat was found in the stomach contents (Glob, 1969).

Many American scholars have studied human **coprolites** (droppings) from dry caves in the United States and Mexico (Figure 13.15). Such researches include analyses of microscopic food remains found in the feces and also of pollen, phytoliths, and parasites (Reinhard and Bryant, 1992). Since the 1980s, researchers in southwestern Texas have obtained coprolite evidence for a basically stable hunter-gatherer diet over nine thousand years of hunting and gathering in this arid region. Dry conditions in coastal Peru have also provided valuable information on changing diet along the Pacific Coast.

Some coprolite studies in North America have analyzed pollen grains found in human feces. Fifty-four samples from Glen Canyon in Utah showed that the pollen ingested by their owners could yield valuable information on plants eaten, seasonal occupation, and even the medicinal use of juniper stem tea (Bryant, 1974). Vaughn Bryant analyzed coprolite pollen from a site near the mouth of the Pecos River in southwestern Texas. He found that the inhabitants of the site between 800 B.C. and A.D. 500 spent the spring and summer at this locality. During their stay, they ate many vegetable foods, including several types of flowers. One danger of using pollen grains is that of contamination from the background pollen "rain" that is always with us. But

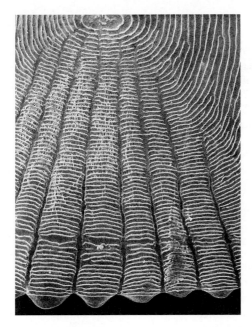

Figure 13.15   Fish scale found in human coprolite.

Bryant was able to show that all but two of the species represented in the pollen were local plants. In all these instances, too, valuable insights were obtained into minor details of prehistoric diet, as well as into intestinal parasites that were commonplace among peoples living on a diet of game meat that was often slightly rotten ("high") (Horne, 1985).

Summary

Archaeologists rely on many sources to reconstruct prehistoric subsistence methods. These include environmental data, animal bones, vegetal remains, human feces, artifacts, and prehistoric art.

Zooarchaeology involves the study of animal bones. Bone identification is carried out by direct comparison between modern and ancient bones.

Game animal remains can give insights into prehistoric hunting practices. The proportions of animals present can be affected by cultural taboos, the relative meat yields of different species, and hunting preferences. Overhunting and extinction can also affect the numbers of animals in a site.

Early domesticated animals are very difficult to distinguish from their wild ancestors. Domestication alters both the characteristics of an animal and its bone structure.

Slaughtering and butchery practices can be derived from the frequency and distribution of animal bones in the ground. Teeth can be used to establish the age of animals slaughtered, but hunting and slaughter patterns are subject to all manner of subtle variables, including convenience and season of the year. Understanding the cultural systems of which the food remains are a part is essential for interpreting slaughter and butchery patterns.

Carbonized and unburned plant remains are recovered from hearths and pits, often using a flotation method to separate seeds from the matrix around them. Dry sites, such as the rock shelters and camps in the Tehuacán Valley of Mexico, provide abundant evidence for early crop domestication. Grain impressions on European pots are studied to reconstruct prehistoric agriculture in the Old World. Danish archaeologists have used pollen analysis to study forest clearance in temperate zones during early farming times.

Bird bones provide valuable information on seasonal occupation; fish remains reflect specialized coastal adaptations that became common in later prehistoric times. Hooks, nets, and other artifacts, as well as fish remains themselves, provide insights into both coastal and offshore fishing practices.

Freshwater and saltwater mollusks were both consumed as food and traded over enormous distances as prestigious luxuries or ornaments.

Ancient diet and nutrition must be studied together, for they are distinct from subsistence, which is the actual process of obtaining food. It is difficult to estimate the caloric needs of modern peoples, let alone those of ancient groups. Archaeological data can indicate only some of the foods eaten by prehistoric communities and show their importance in general. But this is far from ascribing their true caloric importance to ancient societies.

Human skeletal remains, stomach contents, and feces are the few direct sources available for information on ancient diet.

Key Terms

attritional age profile
catastrophic age profile
coprolite
deposited assemblage
diet
flotation

life assemblage
minimum number of
   individuals (MNI)
number of identified
   specimens (NISP)
nutrition

opal phytoliths
sample assemblage
stable carbon isotope analysis
taphonomy
zooarchaeology

Guide to Further Reading

BINFORD, LEWIS R. 1981. *Bones: Ancient Men and Modern Myths.* Orlando, FL: Academic Press. A provocative essay on animal bones, concentrating on both ethnographic analogy and faunal analysis.

DAVIS, SIMON J. M. 1987. *The Archaeology of Animals.* London: Batsford. A superbly illustrated, definitive book on zooarchaeology for beginners. Strongly recommended; comprehensive.

KLEIN, RICHARD G., and KATHRYN CRUZ-URIBE. 1984. *The Analysis of Animal Bones from Archaeological Sites.* Chicago: University of Chicago Press. Statistical approaches to faunal analysis; for more advanced readers.

MOORE, ANDREW. 2000. *Village on the Euphrates.* New York: Oxford University Press. An exemplary, and definitive, monograph on one of the earliest farming settlements in the world.

PEARSALL, DEBORAH. 1989. *Paleoethnobotany: A Handbook of Procedures.* Orlando, FL: Academic Press. A useful introduction for more advanced students.

SMITH, BRUCE D. 1999. *The Emergence of Agriculture.* New York: Scientific American Library. A superb introduction to this complex subject for the layperson.

CHAPTER 14

Analogy, Middle-Range Theory, and the Living Past

A jade mask of a Maya lord at Palenque, Mexico. Jade was the most prized raw material in Maya society.

Even today, you can sometimes get a glimpse of ancient life, long before Western industrial civilization. Sailing up the Nile River, you see Egyptian villages looking virtually unchanged from two thousand years ago. In the heart of Central Africa, the rhythm of farming life with its endless cycles of planting and harvest, of life and death is virtually unchanged from centuries ago. Our modern world gives archaeologists many opportunities to look from the present into the past far more convincingly than one might think. So far, we have considered the processes of archaeological research—data acquisition, analysis, and interpretation. We now look more closely at the tools that archaeologists use to bridge the gap between the world of the past and the archaeological record of the present: analogy, middle-range theory, ethnoarchaeology, and experimental archaeology.

Early Comparisons

Archaeologists have long recognized the value of comparisons between prehistoric and modern cultures. In Chapter 2 we discussed the evolutionists of the late nineteenth century, who considered living tribes to be good examples of successive stages of development in culture history. Each stage of cultural development was correlated with a stage of technology, a form of the family, a kind of religious belief, and a type of political control that could be observed in some group of people. Thus, the Australian Aborigines, the Eskimo, and the San, who retained a hunter-gatherer way of life, manufactured stone tools, and had no knowledge of metallurgy, were considered to be living representatives of Paleolithic peoples. Many early investigators thought that the most primitive Stone Age peoples were matriarchal, had no government, and believed in numerous spirits. They thought that it was perfectly in order to turn to the literature on Eskimo or other living gatherers for the "correct" interpretation of artifacts in the archaeological record.

Discovery

Early Ancestor: *Australopithecus garhi* in Ethiopia, 2001

As scientists delve ever more deeply into the earliest chapters of human evolution, they find that changing primate behavior was a critical driving force in the emergence of tool-making humans. The spectacular discoveries of recent years have shown that a great variety of hominid forms flourished on the East African savanna 2.5 million years ago. But when paleoanthropologist Tim White and his colleagues found *Australopithecus garhi,* they discovered a hominid with a remarkable mix of human and more apelike features. (The word *garhi* means "surprise" in the local Afar dialect.) The new find, believed to be about 3.2 million years old, has a primitive-looking projecting face and a small brain case but exceptionally large back teeth, a unique feature. Other fossilized bones at the same site show that *Australopithecus garhi* had long, human-like legs and stood about 4 feet 10 inches (1.47 m) tall (Figure 14.1). However, its forearms were still apelike and long. These features place the new hominid find midway between the even more primitive, and older, *Australopithecus afarensis,* represented by paleoanthropologist Don Johanson's famous "Lucy," and the earliest known forms of true humans.

Adjacent to the hominid fossil site, a team of archaeologists found broken and crushed antelope and wild horse bones bearing cut marks and gouges, perhaps made by stone tools, although none were found at the site. The fossilized bones were crushed at the ends, as if hominids had used hammerstones to get at the marrow. Although this is not direct

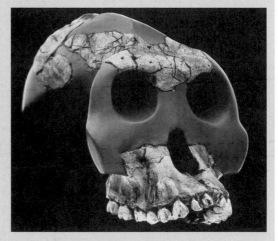

Figure 14.1 *Australopithecus garhi.*

evidence that the hominids actually used stone tools and butchered the animals, it is certainly strong circumstantial evidence for such practices over 3 million years ago. Using stone tools to obtain meat and marrow could have been a major breakthrough in early hominid evolution, for such artifacts improved our remote ancestors' ability to feed themselves in a much wider range of settings. Regular access to highly nutritious foods such as bone marrow may have contributed to the evolution of larger hominid brain sizes.

Controlled experiments and observations on East Africa's Serengeti Plains have moved archaeologists away from early interpretations of our first ancestors as hunters. Most experts now believe they scavenged for meat from predator kills.

Analogy

Analogy is a process of reasoning that assumes that if objects have some similar attributes, they will share other similarities as well. It involves using a known, identifiable phenomenon to identify unknown ones of broadly similar type. It implies that a particular relationship exists between two or more phenomena because the same relationship may be observed in a similar situation. As Ian Hodder has pointed out (1999), analogy is central to archaeological research, which is much concerned with relationships between different finds and pieces of evidence. Our abilities to reason by analogy are often tested in aptitude examinations by such questions as this: "A fish is to water as a bird is to: (a) a tree, (b) a house, (c) air, (d) grass seed." Obviously, if we grasp the relationship between fish and water, we will have no trouble completing the question.

Analogy in archaeology involves inferring that the relationships among various traces of human activity in the archaeological record are the same as or similar to those of similar phenomena found among modern "primitive" peoples. Analogies in archaeology only suggest what modern human behavior is capable of and what the boundaries of prehistoric behavior might have been. Researchers can use them to generate hypotheses that can then be tested by real archaeological data.

Archaeologists use analogy on many levels. In a simple one, a researcher infers that small, pointed pieces of stone are projectile points because there are ethnographic records of peoples who make small, pointed pieces of stone for the tips of lances or arrows. People often make use of an ethnographic name, such as arrowhead, as a label for an artifact. In doing so, they are assuming that their artifact type, which they recognize by attributes whose presence cannot be explained by natural processes, is identical in form to other, known arrowheads used by the people who made the kind of artifact in question (Figure 14.2). But this simple analogy is a far cry from claiming similarities—or analogies—between the ways in which the prehistoric culture referred to used the arrowhead and the ways in which a living society uses it. To do the latter is to assume that the relationship between the form and the function of the artifact has remained static through the ages. If you explain the past simply by analogy with the present, you are assuming that nothing new has been learned by many generations of people and that the past was not much—if any—different from the present.

Many archaeologists make use of analogies based on the technology, style, and function of cultures as they are defined archaeologically. J. G. D. Clark (1952) wrote an economic prehistory of Europe in which he made systematic and judicious use of analogy to interpret such artifacts as freshwater fish spears that were still common in historical European folk culture. This type of analogy is secure enough, as are those about small, pointed pieces of stone claimed to be arrowheads (Wylie, 1985). Enough of these have been found embedded in the bones of animals and people for us to safely acknowledge that such tools were most likely projectile points. Still, we have no way of knowing if the points were part of ritual activity as well as the hunt. Similarly, archaeologists will have information about how houses were constructed and what they looked like, what plants were grown and how these were prepared for food, and perhaps some facts on grave furniture. But they will not know what the people who lived at this site thought a proper house should look like, which relatives would be invited

Figure 14.2 Eskimo demonstrating a sinew-backed bow and an ivory-tipped arrow at Chicago's Columbian Exposition in 1893. Archaeologists often make use of an ethnographic name, such as arrowhead, assuming that their artifact is identical to arrowheads used by the people who made the artifact. This is a simple example of an archaeological analogy.

to help build a house, what spirits were responsible for making crops grow, who in the house customarily prepared the food, or whether the people believed in life after death. Most analogies drawn from the ideas and beliefs of present-day people are probably inadequate.

Archaeologists develop analogies in many ways. One approach is direct historical analogy, using the simple principle of working from the known to the unknown. In archaeological problems, the known is the living people with written records of their way of life, and the unknown is their ancestors for whom we have no written records. Text-aided analogies involve using written records to interpret archaeological data. Ivor Noël Hume, working at the colonial settlement on Martin's Hundred, Virginia, found some short strands of gold and silver wire in the cellar of one of the houses. Each was as thick as a sewing thread, the kind of wire used in the early seventeenth century for decorating clothing. Noël Hume turned to historical records for analogies. He found European paintings showing military captains wearing clothes adorned with gold and silver wire and a resolution of the Virginia governor and his council in 1621 forbidding "any but ye Council & heads of hundreds to wear gold in their cloaths" (Noël Hume, 1982). Using this and other historical analogies, he was able to identify the owner of the house as William Harewood, a member of the council and the head of Martin's Hundred.

According to the proponents of the direct historical approach, confidence in interpretation of past lifeways diminishes as we move from historic to prehistoric times.

Analogies to living peoples become less and less secure as we become remote from written records. Nevertheless, many archaeologists have taken a functionalist approach to analogy.

Functionalist ethnographies integrate various aspects of culture with one another and with the adaptation of the culture as a whole to its environment. Functionalism stresses the notion that cultures are not made up of random selections of traits but that culture traits are integrated in various ways and influence each other in fairly predictable ways. Much of processual archaeology, with its emphasis on adaptation and cultural systems, falls under the general title of functionalist archaeology. Functionalist thinking is evident in the way in which many archaeologists select analogies from the ethnographic data to help them interpret their archaeological finds. Because several ethnologically known cultures might provide reasonable analogies, functionally oriented scholars suggest selecting the ones that most resemble the archaeological culture in subsistence, technology, and environment—and are least removed from the archaeological culture in time and space.

We might want to know about the role of sandal making among the Great Basin Indians of six thousand years ago. Were sandals produced by men, women, individuals on their own initiative, or formal groups working together? If we consider sandal making as an aspect of technology, we might turn to the ethnographic literature on Australian and San material culture, in which sandals are sometimes featured. Among both the San and the Australian Aborigines, domestic tasks are generally done by women working alone or with one or two helpers. The analogy might lead us to argue that sandal making was regarded as a domestic task by Great Basin people and was carried out by women who usually worked alone. Conversely, weaving is men's work among the Pueblo Indians and is done in special ceremonial rooms; because much ritual performed there today reflects very ancient Pueblo Indian practices, we might be led to infer by analogy that the Great Basin people of six thousand years ago did not regard weaving as domestic work, so it was carried out by men. No matter which alternative we chose, we probably would not have much confidence in our choice.

The selection of possibly appropriate analogies from the ethnographic literature is increasingly being seen as only the first step toward interpretation. Once several analogies have been chosen, the implications of each are explicitly stated and then are tested against the archaeological data. In our example of sandal making among Great Basin peoples, the ethnographic literature provided conflicting analogies. If we want to gain confidence in selecting one analogy over the other, we must state explicitly the implications each would have for the archaeological data and then examine the latter again in the light of each implication. If sandal making were a domestic task done by women working alone, we might expect to find the raw materials for sandal manufacture associated with tools that more surely represent women's work, such as grinding stones for food preparation. We might also expect to find tools for sandal making (such as awls and scrapers for preparing fiber) among the debris of more domestic sites. We could anticipate that women working alone might introduce more variation into the finished product than might be done in products made by group effort or by individuals working in the company of other specialists. A contrasting list of implications for the possibility that men produced sandals could also be made, and both sets could be tested against the archaeological data.

Devising test implications is not an easy task. To find a measure for the amount of variation in a finished product that one would expect under specific production conditions requires sophisticated measurements, various statistical tests, and often experimentation among groups of people. Archaeologists willing to make the effort entailed in this approach, however, have found that they are able to discover more about ancient societies than was previously thought possible. Reasoning by analogy is, of course, an important part of this process, but it is only one step in the archaeologist's task. Analogies provide the material from which test implications are drawn; they are not ends in themselves. Thus, analogy is not necessarily misleading, provided that the right criteria and research strategies are used to strengthen and evaluate inferences made from ethnographic and other analogies (Wylie, 1985).

A great deal of archaeological analogy is based on the assumption that because an artifact is used in a specific way today, it was used in that way millennia earlier. The great contribution of the processual archaeologists has been not in their search for general laws but in their insistence that independent data should be used to test and verify conclusions from surveys, excavations, and laboratory analyses. The basic objective in using hypotheses and deductions—the scientific method, if you will—is not to formulate laws but to explore the relationship between past and present. This relationship is assumed to have two parts. The first is that the past is dead and knowable only through the present. The second is that accurate knowledge of the past is essential to understanding the present (Leone, 1982).

Whatever one's approach to archaeology, the leading problem in archaeological analogy is to let the present serve the past. Many archaeologists try to achieve this end with three interlocking approaches that help them study the past by using the present:

1. *Middle-Range Theory:* methods, theories, and ideas from the present that can be applied to any time period and anywhere in the world to explain what we have discovered, excavated, or analyzed from the past.
2. *Ethnoarchaeology:* the study of living societies to aid in understanding and interpreting the archaeological record.
3. *Experimental Archaeology:* controlled, modern experiments with ancient technologies and material culture that can serve as a basis for interpreting the past.

Middle-Range Theory

The sociological term **middle-range theory** is used to characterize the body of theory that is emerging as archaeologists develop methods of inference that bridge the gap between what actually happened in the past and the archaeological record of today, which is our chronicle of ancient times (Binford, 1977). Middle-range theory is based on the notion that the archaeological record is a static and contemporary phenomenon—what survives today of the once-dynamic past. How can researchers make inferences about the past unless they know linkages between dynamic causes and static consequences? The dynamic elements of the past are long gone. Binford (1981b:211) and others have searched for "Rosetta stones . . . that permit the accurate conversion from observation on statics to statement about dynamics."

Middle-range theory begins with three fundamental assumptions:

1. The archaeological record is a static contemporary phenomenon—static information preserved in structured arrangements of matter.
2. Once energy ceased to power the cultural system preserved in the archaeological record, a static condition was achieved. Thus, the contents of the archaeological record are a complex mechanical system, created both by long-dead human interaction and by subsequent mechanical forces and formation processes (Schiffer, 1987; see also Chapter 4).
3. To understand and explain the past, we must comprehend the relationship between static, material properties common to both past and present and the long-extinct dynamic properties of the past.

According to Binford, middle-range theory helps explain the transformation from past cultural dynamic to present physical residues. It helps reconstruct a long-defunct cultural system by aiding in reconstructions based on appropriate interpretation of the archaeological record. In contrast, general theory seeks to provide a basis for interpreting and explaining a succession of cultural systems, showing how they changed over time, again based on archaeological evidence read across the consecutive cultures. General theory builds on information obtained through middle-range theory.

Middle-range theory is often described as actualistic because it studies the coincidence of the static and the dynamic in cultural systems in the only time frame in which it can be achieved—the present. It provides the conceptual tools for explaining artifact patterns and other material phenomena from the archaeological record. Michael Schiffer (1987) argues, in contrast, that the subject matter of archaeology is the relationship between human behavior and material culture in all times and places. Binford (1981a, 1981b) considers the archaeological record to be static and material, containing no direct information on the subject whatsoever. Middle-range theory is one way of mediating between the past and the present (Shanks and McGuire, 1996), and, as Harold Tschauner (1996) has argued, both processual and postprocessual archaeologists make use of independent sets of information for reconstructing the past. (For a critique of the subject, see Hodder, 1999, and Trigger, 1995.)

Ethnoarchaeology

Middle-range research is important to archaeology, whether one believes that this research is meant to specify the relationships between behavior and material remains or to understand the determinants of patterning and structural properties of the archaeological record.

How can the present, with its rich data on modern subsistence, climate, soil qualities, and myriad other phenomena, be used to interpret the past? A related question is: Do we need to study the present to understand the past? Under our world, with its varied landscape, lies the archaeological record: thousands of sites and artifacts buried since they were abandoned by their makers thousands of years ago. Theoretically, at any rate, we have a wealth of data that could be used to interpret the past, to bridge the gap between sites and peoples as they were in ancient times and the surviving archaeological record of today.

This form of living archaeology, **ethnoarchaeology,** came into its own in the 1970s (David and Kramer, 2001; see the bibliography in David and others, 1999). Richard Lee was among the anthropologists who studied the !Kung San of the Kalahari, one of the world's last hunter-gatherer groups. He realized archaeologists' difficulties and arranged to take an archaeologist, John Yellen, to study the remains of long-abandoned campsites and compare them with modern settlements (Lee, 1979; Yellen, 1977). At about the same time, Lewis Binford was working among the Nunamiut Eskimo and the Navajo, comparing living cultures and archaeological materials and trying to develop workable models of culture as rigorous yardsticks for studying variability (Binford, 1978). More recent research has focused on hunter-gatherer groups such as the Hadza of northern Tanzania; on farming societies, such as the Kalinga of the Philippines (Longacre, 1991); and on several southwestern Asian groups.

Ethnoarchaeology is the study of living societies to aid in understanding and interpreting the archaeological record. By living in, say, an Eskimo hunting camp and observing the activities of its occupants, the archaeologist hopes to record archaeologically observable patterns, knowing what activities brought them into existence. Sometimes historical documents can be used to amplify observations in the field. Archaeologists have actually lived on San campsites, then have gone back later and recorded the scatter of artifacts on them or have excavated them (Yellen, 1977). The earliest ethnoarchaeological work focused on specific artifact patterings and on studies of hunter-gatherer encampments that might provide ways of interpreting the very earliest human sites at Olduvai Gorge and elsewhere. But a major focus of later work has been to develop archaeological methods of inference that bridge the gap between past and present (Cameron and Tomka, 1993).

Many archaeologists regard ethnoarchaeology simply as a mass of observed data on human behavior from which they can draw suitable hypotheses to compare with the finds from their excavations and laboratory analyses (Gould, 1980). This interpretation is totally wrong, for, in fact, ethnoarchaeological research deals with dynamic processes in the modern world (Layton, 1994).

Ethnoarchaeology among the San and the Hadza

Much ethnoarchaeological research has been among hunter-gatherers, especially those perceived as having ancestry among earlier, prehistoric peoples (Gamble and Boismier, 1991). Both the San of southern Africa's Kalahari Desert and the Australian Aborigines fall into this category.

Anthropologist Richard Lee (1979) has spent many years studying the human ecology of the !Kung San of the Kalahari and has accumulated a mass of information of use to archaeologists. Archaeologist John Yellen (1977) worked with Lee, collecting data on house and camp arrangements, hearth locations, census information, and bone refuse. Yellen pointed out that a San camp develops through conscious acts, such as the construction of windbreaks and hearths, as well as through such incidental deeds as the discarding of refuse and manufacturing debris (Figure 14.3). He recognized communal areas in the campsites, often in the middle of the settlement, that belonged to no one in particular and family areas focused on hearths that belonged to

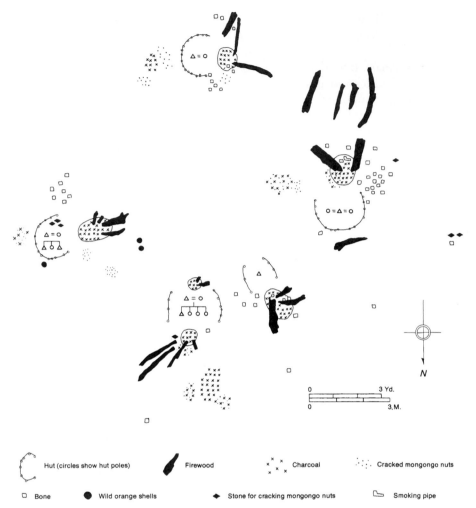

Figure 14.3   A San camp in Botswana, southern Africa, as plotted by John Yellen to show the layout of activity areas and artifacts.

Source: Reprinted from *Archaeological Approaches to the Present: Models for Predicting the Past* by John Yellen. Copyright © 1977, with permission from Elsevier.

individual families. The communal activities of the camp members, such as dancing and the first distribution of meat, took place in the open spaces that belonged to no one family. Such activities leave few traces in the archaeological record. Cooking and food processing as well as manufacturing of artifacts normally take place around family hearths. Yellen points out some interesting variations on this pattern: manufacturing activities taking place at one hearth will sometimes involve people from other families; large skins will normally be pegged out for treatment away from main living areas because of vermin and carnivores. The San study showed that it is dangerous to

Figure 14.4   A team of archaeologists and anthropologists records details of a successful hunt by Hazda hunter-gatherers in northern Tanzania. Data from surveys like this are of great value for interpreting the archaeological record of prehistoric hunter-gatherers.

assume that activities with the greatest archaeological visibility, such as preparing meat or cracking nuts, take place in special places. The activity patterning at San campsites is related, for the most part, directly to family groups. Hypothetically, Yellen argues, it should be possible to use artifact clusters through time to study the development and evolution of such social structures.

Since 1984, archaeologist James O'Connell and his research team have recorded more than seventy incidents of large mammal butchery by Hadza hunter-gatherers in East Africa (Figure 14.4). The Hadza hunt animals when they encounter them and also ambush them from specially built blinds near water holes in the late dry season. They are very determined hunters, tracking their wounded prey for hours, even days. They also scavenge meat from predator kills at every opportunity. O'Connell recorded kill rates for a single camp of seventy to eighty large animals a year, or about one for forty to sixty man-days of foraging, with scavenging accounting for about 15 to 20 percent of the total. The researchers were mainly interested in time allocation, food choice, and food-sharing activities, so they routinely recorded site location, distance from residential bases, method of acquiring the prey, carcass condition, details of the butchery, and the sexes and ages of the people involved. In addition, they collected comprehensive "archaeological" data from each location, where possible, including the positions of broken bones and abandoned artifacts.

The Hadza research yielded a mass of basic ethnoarchaeological data that casts serious doubt on many of the assumptions made by archaeologists about hunter-gatherer

Maya Stone Metate Manufacture

Brian Hayden took advantage of a unique opportunity to record and understand the conception, life, death, and discard of lithic artifacts (or their substitutes). He combined descriptive research with highly exploratory, new theoretical approaches based on design analysis theory, among other things. The research was broad-based, concerned with the properties of the stone collected for tool manufacture, the efficiency of stone technology, and the evolution of the forms of stone tools as they were used and reused. The researchers looked closely at patterns of waste deposition and site-formation processes and at the social and economic positions of stoneworking artisans. They were able to work closely with a fifty-year-old specialist metate maker named Ramon Ramos Rosario, one of the few full-time specialists still working (Figure 14.5).

Because his lands cannot support his family, Ramon makes his living manufacturing manos (pounders) and metates and selling them over a wide area of western Guatemala. He can sell more widely today because of improved public transport. In earlier years, he and other specialists would sell locally. Hayden followed Ramon through the entire manufacturing process, from the selection of the material to the final surface smoothing of the artifact. Time and motion studies showed that it took this expert two and one-half days to rough out and smooth a metate blank using only stone tools, and four and one-half to five and one-half days to finish both a metate and a mano.

Finally, Hayden examined the characteristics of the picks used to chip and peck the rock as if they were archaeological finds, combining these studies with use-wear analysis. Hayden seriated the picks on the basis of the intensity of edge-wear development as a way of estimating the relative length of use of comparable tools. He compared his results

kill sites. O'Connell's team found that 75 to 80 percent of the Hadza's large mammal prey were underrepresented in their bone samples, by virtue of the people's hunting and butchering practices. Furthermore, most prehistoric kill sites have been excavated on a small scale, whereas many Hadza butchery sites occupy a large area, through which the hunters scatter the bones, often to find shade in which to work. Sometimes, too, bones from different animals are left in separate locations. The disarticulation of animal bones follows a similar pattern, whether carnivores or humans are involved—the limbs first, then the backbone, with differences being more the result of individual animal anatomy than deliberate cultural choice. The Hadza findings cast doubt on many interpretations of animal butchery and highlight the vital importance of ethnoarchaeology and middle-range theory (O'Connell and others, 1992).

Lithic Technology among the Highland Maya

Although ethnoarchaeological investigations have tended to focus on hunter-gatherers, there are numerous instances of fascinating research on more complex societies, even our own. A major long-term study of modern urban garbage in Tucson, Arizona, for

with prehistoric artifacts and was able to show that many blunt-edged Maya celts in archaeological sites, tools that were of no use for woodworking, were probably used by women to repeck (roughen) used manos and metates.

The study also threw interesting light on site-formation processes. For example, the stoneworker removes as much waste material from the metate blank at the quarry as possible to save weight. At the same time, he carefully conserves the stone tools used in roughing out blanks, caching them at the quarry and resharpening them to prolong their life. Observations like these, combined with specific environmental conditions, could one day provide a body of what Hayden calls "robust" middle-range theory.

Figure 14.5   Ramon Ramos Rosario manufactures a stone metate.

example, is based on the latest archaeological methods and research designs (Rathje and Murphy, 1992). The project is investigating the relationships between resource management, urban demography, and social and economic stratification in a modern context, where some control data from interviews and other perspectives are available to amplify an archaeological study of a type that might be conducted at an ancient urban center. The Tucson garbage study, which is more strictly ethnography than ethnoarchaeology, has produced remarkable results, showing widely different patterns of resource management from one segment of the city's population to another, with the middle class being the most wasteful.

Long-term observations in modern-day peasant societies are providing unexpected dividends, as was the case when Canadian archaeologist Brian Hayden was studying stone tool making among the ancestors of the modern-day Coxoh Maya Indians near the Mexico-Guatemala border. He discovered that some present-day Maya-speaking communities in the area still made and used stone artifacts. Even after four and a half centuries of European contact, a few people were making metates (grinders) in the traditional way, and simple stone tools still fulfilled many basic functions (Hayden, 1987) (see the Doing Archaeology box).

The Maya lithic study demonstrates the power and potential of a many-sided approach to ethnoarchaeology, using data from the dynamic present to evaluate archaeological evidence from the static archaeological record.

Other Studies

Ethnoarchaeological studies of many kinds abound, some of them conducted over many years. In the Philippines, William Longacre has spent years studying Kalinga potmakers, examining not only the actual process of potmaking using materials science but also the transmission of ideas, the organization of production, and trade (Longacre and Skibo, 1994). Nicholas David has spent many field seasons working among the Madara of northern Cameroon and Nigeria in West Africa. David and his colleagues have studied changes in material culture among these upland people, who traded with people around Lake Chad to the north over many centuries. The years of study focused both on potting and ironworking and also on the symbolic meaning of changing artifact styles. The researchers identified what they call a "symbolic reservoir" of fundamental beliefs and integrative social processes that led to broad similarities in material culture over a wide area (David et al., 1991).

Nunamiut Eskimo

Lewis Binford and his students undertook ethnoarchaeological studies to help begin construction of middle-range theory. He decided to study the Nunamiut Eskimo of Alaska, 80 percent of whose subsistence comes from hunting caribou. His aims were to find out as much as he could about "all aspects of the procurement, processing, and consumption strategies of the Nunamiut Eskimo and relate these behaviors directly to their faunal consequences" (Binford, 1978:61). He chose to concentrate on animal bones rather than on artifacts because, although the bones were not human-manufactured, the patterns of their use were the result of cultural activity.

The Nunamiut depend more heavily on meat than do any other known hunter-gatherers. Indeed, Binford estimated that each adult eats around a cup and a half of vegetable foods a year, supplemented by the partially digested stomach contents of caribou. In an environment that has a growing season of only twenty-two days, the Eskimo rely on stored food entirely for eight and a half months a year and partly for an additional month and a half. Fresh meat is freely available for only two months a year. Binford soon realized that the strategies the Eskimo use to feed themselves are based not only on game distributions but on other considerations as well. With such a heavy reliance on stored food, the problem of bulk is always important. Is it easier to move people to where fresh meat is available or to carry the meat back to a base camp where precious stored food is kept? It is no coincidence that the Nunamiut move around most in late summer and early fall, when stored foods are at their lowest levels. The Nunamiut's way of life involves complicated and interacting decisions related to the distribution of food resources at different seasons, the storage potential of different animals and of different parts of an animal, and the logistics of procuring, carrying, and storing meat.

By close study, not only of the Nunamiut's annual round of activities but also of their butchery and storage strategies, Binford was able to develop indices that measured, in exhaustive detail, the utility of different body parts of caribou and to describe the butchering techniques, distribution of body parts, and methods of food preparation used. He showed that the people have an intimate knowledge of caribou anatomy with regard to meat yield, storage potential, and consumption needs—relative to the logistical, storage, and social needs of the moment. The field study also included analysis of forty-two archaeologically known locations that dated to earlier times.

The Nunamiut adaptation depended on long-term storage strategies that were keyed to two aggressive periods of caribou hunting, in spring and fall. That the Nunamiut were able to hunt the caribou twice a year was linked to the topography in their homeland, which lies close to the borders of both summer and winter caribou feeding ranges (Figure 14.6). The movement of the people was keyed to seasonal game movements and to storage and other needs. Fall hunting was directed toward calves, whose skins were used to make winter clothing. Small, mobile parties of Nunamiut would pursue them, knowing that their prey would yield not only skins but also the added bonus of heads and tongues to feed the people who processed the skins. Without taking account of this fact, the Nunamiut would have been unable to maintain a viable cultural system.

What is the importance of the Nunamiut research? First, it provides a mass of empirical data on human exploitation of animals that is applicable not only to the Nunamiut and other caribou hunters but also to the interpretation of different types of archaeological sites in many parts of the world. Binford showed how local any cultural adaptation is—that the Nunamiut depended on interacting topographic, climatic, logistical, and other realities. The result is considerable variation in archaeological sites and in artifact frequencies and forms.

Such ethnoarchaeological studies show that archaeologists can no longer assume that all variability in the archaeological record is directly related to cultural similarity and difference (David and Kramer, 2001). They have profoundly affected archaeological studies of prehistoric hunter-gatherers, both of the earliest hominids and in more recently occupied areas such as the Great Basin. So far, the main influence of middle-range theory and ethnoarchaeology has been on the archaeology of hunter-gatherers. One exception to that rule is Harriet Blitzer's long-term study of eighteenth- and nineteenth-century Greek jars (*pithoi*). Blitzer's study has important implications for the study of ancient Aegean trade, which has deep roots in antiquity (Blitzer, 1990; for other exceptions, see David and Kramer, 2001, and Kramer, 1997).

Structures and Symbols

Ian Hodder (1982b) took a somewhat different structural and symbolic tack in ethnoarchaeological studies of farming and hunter-gatherer societies in tropical Africa. He studied the Nuba farmers of the Sudan and the Lozi of western Zambia, among other peoples. "Symbols are actively involved in social strategies," he wrote. Every society, he believes, has a set of general conceptual principles that form a "structure" that

Figure 14.6   The Mask site, a Nunamiut Eskimo hunting stand. (*top*) The hunting stand in its environmental setting. (*bottom*) Caribou remains at the stand.

runs through each society. Structuralism has long been debated in anthropology but is new to archaeology. Under this approach, Hodder would have archaeologists looking for the principles and concepts that played a part in all social and ecological actions in individual ancient societies, a structure that affected the patterning of the material culture found in the archaeological record.

There is little actual difference between the structure of the Binford and Hodder approaches (David and Kramer, 2001). Middle-range theories relate the empirical to the real, as do Hodder's structuring principles, themselves middle-range theories. Where the two schools of thought differ is in their styles of analysis. More science-based approaches rely more heavily on statistics and numerical data, focusing on behavior rather than on its meaning and on cross-cultural laws more than on cultural patterns. For most archaeologists, ethnoarchaeology is a way of raising analogical consciousness, of sensitizing them to the dimensions of variability and the richness of the relationship between human beings and their artifacts. But, combined with experimental archaeology, and integrating history and science, it can be a valuable way of approaching the realities of the past, which are often hard to discern from the archaeological record alone (Hammersley, 1992).

In recent years, ethnoarchaeologists have become increasingly interested in ideology, notably in West Africa (David et al., 1991) and in subsistence (Hudson, 1993) (Figure 14.7).

Ethnoarchaeology is gradually broadening its scope and sharpening its analytical tools as it moves into new and important areas such as landscape analysis and ideologies. It is an increasing important tool for archaeological research with, also, numerous applications in today's world with its inexorable shifts toward cultural homogeneity.

Experimental Archaeology

Controlled experiments with the dynamics of material culture can be a fruitful source of data to test middle-range theory. **Experimental archaeology** began in Europe during the eighteenth century, when people tried to blow the spectacular bronze horns recovered from peat bogs in Scandinavia and Britain. One ardent experimenter, Robert Ball of Dublin, Ireland, blew an Irish horn so hard that he was able to produce "a deep bass note, resembling the bellowing of a bull." Sadly, a subsequent experiment with a trumpet caused him to burst a blood vessel, and he died several days later (J. Coles, 1979). Ball is the only recorded casualty of experimental archaeology. It was not until the early years of the twentieth century that experimental archaeology took on more immediate relevance. One reason that it did was the capture and observation of Ishi, one of the last California Indians to follow a traditional way of life (Figure 14.8).

Stone Technology

Only the sketchiest historical accounts of stoneworking and other craft activities survive in the records of early explorers. Some of the Spanish friars, notably Juan de Torquemada, saw Indian stoneworkers flaking obsidian knives. In 1615, he described how the Indians would take a stick and press it against a stone core with their "breast." "With the force of the stick there flies off a knife," he wrote. But until recently, no one knew just how pressure flaking, as it is called, was done (J. Coles, 1979).

It was an Idaho rancher named Don Crabtree who worked out some of the ways in which the Paleo-Indians had made the beautiful Folsom projectile points found on the Plains. He experimented for more than forty years and was able to describe no fewer than eleven methods of reproducing the "flute" at the base of the artifact

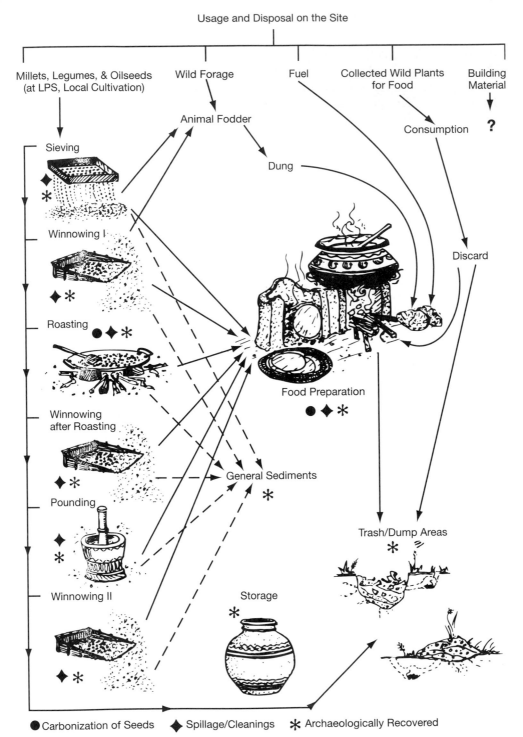

Usage and Disposal on the Site

Millets, Legumes, & Oilseeds
(at LPS, Local Cultivation)

Wild Forage

Fuel

Collected Wild Plants
for Food

Building
Material

?

Animal Fodder

Consumption

Dung

Sieving

Winnowing I

Roasting

Winnowing
after Roasting

Pounding

Winnowing II

Food Preparation

General Sediments

Storage

Discard

Trash/Dump Areas

● Carbonization of Seeds   ◆ Spillage/Cleanings   ✳ Archaeologically Recovered

Figure 14.7   Seetha Reddy's analysis of processing cereals at the Harappan site of Babor Kot, Gujerat, India.
This is an excellent example of the application of ethnoarchaeology to the interpretation of ancient subsistence.

Source: Nicholas David and Karen Kramer, *Ethnoarchaeology in Action* Figure 5.6, page 133. Copyright © 2001.
Reprinted by permission of Cambridge University Press.

Figure 14.8   Ishi hunts with a bow and arrow. Studies of Ishi's archery (Pope, 1923) and technological practices (T. Kroeber, 1965) had important implications for archaeology.

(D. E. Crabtree, 1972). Eventually, he came across Torquemada's account of pressure flaking and used a chest punch to remove flakes from the base of unfinished points gripped in a vise on the ground. The result was points that were almost indistinguishable from the prehistoric artifacts. Many other researchers have followed in Crabtree's footsteps and have successfully replicated almost every kind of stone artifact made by pre-Columbian Indians.

Does the production of an exact replica mean, in fact, that modern experimentation has recovered the original technique? The answer, of course, is that we can never be certain. Lithic expert Jeff Flenniken has replicated dozens of Paleo-Indian projectile points and argues that many of the different "types" identified by Plains archaeologists are in fact simply heads that were modified for reuse after they were broken in their original use. By reducing an existing head, he argues, the Paleo-Indian artisan produced a different but convenient shape that did the job just as well as the original. The same reduction process might lead the worker to the same shape again and again, but he certainly did not design it that way (Flenniken, 1984). David Hurst Thomas (1986), a Great Basin specialist, disagrees. He argues that modern stoneworkers must not interpret prehistoric artifacts in terms of their own experience, for to do so is to ignore the vast chronological gap that separates us from prehistoric times. Thomas believes that a strictly technological approach to stone tool experimentation restricts the questions to be asked about lithic technology. Lithic experimentation is a valuable approach to the past, but only if combined with other approaches, such as retrofitting or edge-wear analysis.

Criteria for Experimental Archaeology

Experimental archaeology can rarely provide conclusive answers (Ingorsoll and others, 1977). It can merely provide some insights into the methods and techniques perhaps used in prehistory, for many of the behaviors involved in, say, prehistoric agriculture have left no tangible traces in the archaeological record. But some general rules must be applied to all experimental archaeology. First, the materials used in the experiment must be those available locally to the prehistoric society one is studying. Second, the methods must conform with the society's technological abilities. Obviously, modern technology must not be allowed to interfere with the experiment. Experiments with a prehistoric plow must be conducted with a plowshare made correctly, with careful reference to the direction of wood grain, the shape and method of manufacture of working edges, and all other specifications. If the plow is drawn by a tractor, the experiment's efficiency will be radically affected; thus, for accuracy, you will need a pair of trained oxen. The results of the experiment must be replicable, and the experiment must consist of tests that lead to suggested conclusions.

Some Examples of Experimental Archaeology

One of the best-known instances of experimental archaeology is the *Kon Tiki* expedition, on which Thor Heyerdahl attempted to prove that Polynesia had been settled by adventurous Peruvians who sailed rafts across thousands of miles of ocean (Heyerdahl, 1950). He did succeed in reaching Polynesia, and his expedition showed that long ocean voyages in rafts were possible; but he did not prove that the Peruvians settled Polynesia.

Most experimental archaeology is far more limited in scope, often involving experiments with spears or bows against animal targets (Odell and Cowan, 1986). Many experiments have been done on clearance of forests in Europe and elsewhere. Stone axes have been surprisingly effective at clearing woodland; one Danish experiment yielded estimates that a man could clear half an acre of forest in a week. Tree ringing and fire have been shown to be effective tree-felling techniques in West Africa and Mesoamerica. Experiments with agriculture over eight or more years have been conducted in the southern Maya lowlands and in Mesa Verde National Park. The latter experiment lasted seventeen years. Two and one-half acres of heavy red clay soil were cultivated and planted with maize, beans, and other small crops. Good crop yields were obtained in all but two of the seventeen years, when drought killed the young crop. The test revealed how important careful crop rotation is to preserving the land's carrying capacity.

Housing Experiments.   Houses of poles and thatch, logs, or hut clay normally survive in the form of postholes, foundation trenches, or collapsed rubble. Unfortunately, traces of the roof and information on wall and roof heights are usually lacking. But this absence has not deterred experimenters from building replicas of Mississippian houses in Tennessee, using excavated floor plans associated with charred poles, thatching grass, and wall-clay fragments (Nash, 1968). Two types of houses dating to A.D. 1000–1600 were rebuilt. One of these was a "small pole" type with slender poles bent over to form an inverted, basketlike rectangular structure with clay plaster on the exterior. Later houses were given long walls, which supported steep, peaked roofs. In this, as in many other instances, many details of the rafter and roof design are probably lost forever.

Butser Hill, England.   An ambitious long-term experimental archaeology project flourishes at Butser Hill in southern England, where Peter Reynolds reconstructed a communal Iron Age round house dating to about 300 B.C. (Figure 14.9). The house is built of hazel rods and a binding mixture of clay, earth, animal hair, and hay. This is part of a much larger experimental project that is exploring every aspect of Iron Age life. Reynolds and other members of the Butser team have grown prehistoric cereals using Iron Age technology, have kept a selection of livestock that resembles prehistoric breeds, and have even stored grain in subterranean storage pits. The project is concerned not only with how individual aspects of Iron Age subsistence operated but also with how they fitted together. Some fascinating results have come from the Butser experiment. For instance, Reynolds found that wheat yields were far higher than had been expected and that grain could be stored underground for long periods without rotting. The Butser experiment provides valuable information that can be used for calculating prehistoric crop yields and land carrying capacities (P. J. Reynolds, 1979).

Figure 14.9   A reconstructed Iron Age village nestles in the heart of the English countryside, complete with small fields.

Overton Down. One of the longest experiments in archaeological interpretation is that of the Overton Down earthwork in England's chalk country, scene of some of the classic prehistoric excavations of the twentieth century. In 1960 the British Association for the Advancement of Science built the Overton experiment as a 128-year-long observation (Jewell and Dimbleby, 1966). The earthwork and its associated ditch were built on chalk subsoil, with profiles approximating those of prehistoric monuments. Archaeological materials, including textiles, leather, wood, animal and human bones, and pottery, were buried within and on the earthwork. The Overton Down earthwork was built partly with modern picks, shovels, and hatchets and partly with red deer antlers and ox shoulder blades in an attempt to establish relative work rates for different technologies. The difference was about 1.3:1.0 in favor of modern tools, mostly because modern shovels were more efficient. Overton Down was then abandoned, but small and very precise excavations of the ditch and bank are taking place at intervals of 2, 4, 8, 16, 32, 64, and 128 years. The digs are used to check the decay and attrition of the earthwork and the silting of the ditch over a lengthening period. The project is yielding priceless information of great use for interpreting archaeological sites of a similar type on chalk soils (for an assessment, see Ashbee and Jewell, 1998).

Such types of controlled, long-term experiments will give archaeologists the objective data they need to understand the static archaeological record as studied in the dynamic present. They will help us evaluate our ideas about the past and to answer the question of questions: not "What happened?" but "Why?"

Summary

Ethnographic analogy helps in ascribing meaning to the prehistoric past. Analogy itself is a form of reasoning that assumes that if objects have some similar attributes, they will share other similarities as well. It involves using a known, identifiable phenomenon to identify unknown ones of a broadly similar type. Most simple analogies are based on technology, style, and function of artifacts, as they are defined archaeologically. Such analogies, however, based as they are on people's beliefs, can be unreliable.

Direct historical analogies and comparisons made with the aid of texts are common, but meaningful analogies for American and Paleolithic sites are much harder to achieve. One approach has been to devise test implications, using several analogies. This technique is based on the functional approach assuming that cultures are not made up of random traits but are integrated in various ways. Thus, analogies are made between recent and prehistoric societies with closely similar general characteristics.

Middle-range research is carried out on living societies, using ethnoarchaeology, experimental archaeology, and historical documents. It is designed to create a body of middle-range theory, objective theoretical devices for forging a link between the dynamic living systems of today and the static archaeological record of the past.

Ethnoarchaeology is ethnographic archaeology with a strongly materialist bias. Archaeologists engage in ethnoarchaeology as part of middle-range research in attempts to make meaningful interpretations of artifact patterns in the archaeological record.

Experimental archaeology seeks to replicate prehistoric technology and lifeways under carefully controlled conditions. As such, it is a form of archaeological analogy. Experiments have been conducted on every aspect of prehistoric culture, from lithics to housing. Archaeology by experiment provides insights into the methods and techniques used by prehistoric cultures.

Key Terms

ethnoarchaeology   experimental archaeology   middle-range theory

Guide to Further Reading

BINFORD, LEWIS R. 1978. *Nunamiut Ethnoarchaeology.* Orlando, FL: Academic Press. A descriptive monograph about ethnoarchaeology among caribou hunters. A must for the serious student.

———. 2001. *In Pursuit of the Past.* Rev. ed. New York: Thames and Hudson. Includes an account of living archaeology and middle-range theory for a more general audience. Strongly recommended for beginners.

COLES, JOHN M. 1979. *Archaeology by Experiment.* London: Heinemann. An introduction to experimental archaeology with numerous examples, mainly from the Old World.

DAVID, NICHOLAS, and CAROL KRAMER, eds. 2001. *Ethnoarchaeology in Action.* Cambridge: Cambridge University Press. An important collection of essays covering new ethnoarchaeological research worldwide.

HODDER, IAN, ed. 1982. *Symbols in Action.* Cambridge: Cambridge University Press. Ethnoarchaeological studies in tropical Africa that are used to support a structural and symbolic approach to archaeology.

YELLEN, JOHN E. 1977. *Archaeological Approaches to the Present: Models for Predicting the Past.* Orlando, FL: Academic Press. Ethnoarchaeology among the San of the Kalahari Desert. A technical work with broad implications.

CHAPTER 15

Settlement Archaeology

Exemplary area excavations expose structures built on the once-busy Roman town site of Silchester, England.

"I am my own aborigine," Irish archaeologist Seamus Caulfield once commented. We were standing on the forbidding limestone cliffs of County Mayo in northwestern Ireland, gazing at the rolling bogland of Céide Fields. Caulfield grew up in nearby Belderigg, a hamlet of small houses surrounded by ancient field walls built and rebuilt over thousands of years. As a small boy, he went barefoot for six months of the year, feeling underfoot the texture of narrow pathways, marshlands, and small fields. Years later, Seamus Caulfield still has a tactile relationship with his home community and with the farmland that once sustained it, the kind of close relationship with environment and landscape once enjoyed by preindustrial societies all over the globe. He calls these familiar farmlands his "landscape of memory." Thanks to archaeology, Caulfield has traced his ancestry back on this land to a long-forgotten Stone Age field system built before 3000 B.C.

Caulfield inherited a passion for archaeology from his schoolteacher father, who had discovered stone walls deep under the peat that mantles the local landscape. In 1983, he began to map the buried stone walls at nearby Céide Fields. First, he tried using aerial photographs to identify the field systems, but the peat covered everything. Then he turned to the low-tech tools of his youth, a 6-foot-long (2-m-long) iron T-bar and a special spade used for cutting peat sods. Caulfield and his students laid out lines across the hills and ran transects of probes at 1-foot (0.3-m) intervals across the bogland. The peat was much shallower where the buried stone walls lay. Soon, hundreds of bamboo poles marked walls and fields.

Season after season, Caulfield returned to Céide Fields until he had mapped more than 4 square miles (103 sq. km) of intact farming landscape, undisturbed since 2400 B.C. (Figure 15.1). With the help of geologists and palynologists, Caulfield showed that the warmer and wetter climate after the Ice Age brought pine forests to the area. Tree rings tell us that the forest suddenly vanished in 2800 B.C., opening up

Figure 15.1   Céide Fields, Ireland, with the Visitors Center in the background.

grassland ideal for cattle grazing. For nearly five hundred years, small groups of farmers separated their pastures with low stone walls, dividing the land into a patchwork of lines, rectangles, and squares. Each family lived in a small thatched round house set within a stone enclosure amidst a mosaic of constantly changing fields modified over successive generations.

After five centuries, the damp climate defeated the farmers. Wet bog, with its mosses, heathers, and moor grass, spread inexorably across the hills. The grasslands vanished, the cattle herders retreated inland, and the boundary walls disappeared under peat. County Mayo was a peaceful part of Ireland. No Roman armies or social catastrophes disrupted life at Céide Fields, ensuring a high level of cultural continuity in this corner of Ireland. Seamus Caulfield's family has lived at Belderigg for generations. Thanks to his research, he feels he can safely claim himself as an "aborigine," a distant descendant of the local farmers of some two hundred generations ago.

The Céide Fields project is a classic example of settlement archaeology, the topic of this chapter—the ways in which archaeologists study households, communities, and ancient cultural landscapes. So far we have examined the ways in which archaeologists study artifacts and prehistoric subsistence and the various technologies that people developed to adapt to their environments. We also discussed some methods used to reconstruct the prehistoric environment itself. In this chapter, we examine some of the ways in which archaeologists have studied changing settlement patterns in prehistoric times.

Discovery

Catherwood and Stephens at Copán, Honduras, 1839

In 1839, New York traveler-turned-lawyer John Lloyd Stephens and Scottish artist Frederick Catherwood journeyed deep into the Central American rain forest, following rumors of vanished civilizations and great ruins masked by primordial jungle. They came first to the tiny village of Copán, in present-day Honduras, where "around them lay the dark outlines of ruins shrouded by the brooding forest. . . . The only sound that disturbed the quiet of this buried city was the noise of monkeys moving around among the tops of the trees" (Stephens, 1841:48). You can still imagine the powerful effect Copán had on Catherwood and Stephens over 150 years ago.

While Catherwood drew the intricate hieroglyphs he had found on stone columns still standing among the ruins, Stephens tried to buy the ancient city of Copán for $50, so he could transport it block by block to New York City. The deal fell through when he found he could not float the antiquities down the nearby Copán River.

Stephens and Catherwood subsequently visited many other famous Maya cities, among them Palenque, Uxmal, and Chichén Itzá. They were the first travelers to recognize the Maya as the builders of these great sites. Stephens wrote: "These cities . . . are not the works of peoples who have passed away . . . but of the same great race . . . which still clings around their ruins" (p. 222). All subsequent research into the Maya civilization is based on the work of these two tough pioneers.

Settlement Archaeology and Settlement Patterns

Settlement archaeology is the study of changing human settlement patterns as part of the analysis of adaptive interactions between people and their external environment, both natural and cultural (Chang, 1968). It requires a combination of a well-developed research design, common sense, archaeological survey, careful excavation, and, often, innovative remote-sensing methods (Chapters 8 and 9). **Settlement patterns,** the layout and distribution of human settlements on the landscape, are the result of relationships between people who decided, on the basis of practical, cultural, social, political, and economic considerations, to place their houses, settlements, and religious structures in certain ways. Thus, settlement archaeology offers the archaeologist a chance to examine not only relationships within different communities but also trading networks, resource exploitation, social organization, and cultural trends.

Human settlements are not randomly distributed across the landscape. If you find certain kinds of settlements near water sources, trade routes, food resources, or easily defended areas, you can reasonably assume that there were sound, practical reasons behind the site distributions. Within the villages themselves, a complex variety of cultural, social, and even personal factors dictated the layout of houses in relation to one another. For instance, the Chumash Indians of southern California lived on the islands and shores of the Santa Barbara Channel, where ocean upwelling nourished one of the richest inshore fisheries on the earth. Seven hundred years ago, this rich, if unpredictable bounty of marine resources allowed Chumash hunter-gatherers to live in densely populated, permanent settlements with as many as a thousand inhabitants. The most important of these villages clustered at sheltered spots on the coast that had good canoe landings, kelp fisheries close offshore, and sea mammal rookeries within easy reach—all important considerations in terms of Chumash subsistence.

At another level, an entire village or city may reflect a society's worldview. The ancient Mesoamericans placed great emphasis on lavish public ceremonies set in the heart of large ceremonial centers. Fifteen hundred years ago, great lowland Maya cities such as Copán and Tikal were replicas in stone and stucco of the layered Mesoamerican spiritual world of the heavens, the living world, and the underworld (Figure 15.2). Their pyramids were sacred mountains; the doorways of the temples atop them were the sacred openings by which the ruler, as intermediary with the spiritual world, traveled to the Otherworld up and down the *Wacah Chan,* the symbolic World Tree that connected the layers of the Maya universe (for Aztec Tenochtitlán, see Figure 15.3).

The relationship between an individual and the landscape can be as complex as that of an entire society. A Central African farmer works a patchwork of small gardens, some intensely cultivated, others lying fallow as the soil regenerated after years of use. The casual observer might see very little, but to the farmer there are the subtle signs of regenerating soil, grasses to be eaten by his cattle in the weeks ahead, and flowering

Figure 15.2   Temple 1 at Tikal, Guatemala, which dates to about A.D. 700, is a replica in stone and stucco of a sacred mountain.

Figure 15.3   The central precincts of the Aztec capital, Tenochtitlán, with the temple of the sun god Huitzilopochtli and the rain god Tlaloc at left—the axis of the Aztec universe.

Source: American Museum of Natural History.

nut trees that come into harvest at the end of the wet season: the landscape a quilt of gardens, plants, and animals protected by his ancestors, who are the spiritual guardians of the land.

Settlement archaeology is about these many layers of dynamic relationships, some of which are nearly impossible to discern without the careful use of analogy with living societies (Chapter 14). For instance, we know from modern analogies in Africa and New Guinea that village layout may be determined by the need to protect one's herds against animal predators or war parties. Other settlements may be strung out at regular intervals along an important trade artery, such as a river. Even the positioning of individual houses is dictated by a complex variety of social, economic, and even personal factors that can defy explanation.

The determinants of settlement patterns operate at different levels, each formed by factors that differ in quality and degree from the ones that shape other levels (Trigger, 1968b).

1. *Buildings and Activity Areas.* Houses, buildings, and activity areas are minimal units of archaeological settlement analysis.
2. *Communities.* The arrangement of houses and activity areas into a single group constitutes a community. The term *community* is defined as a maximal group of persons who normally reside in face-to-face association.
3. *Distribution of Communities.* The density and distribution of communities, whatever their size, are determined to a considerable extent by the natural resources in the environment and by the nutritional requirements, technological level, and sociopolitical complexity of the population, as well as by social and religious constraints.

The ultimate objective of the exercise is to study ancient settlement systems as an aspect of the whole picture of an ancient society. In this connection, "off-site" features, such as field systems, are also of great importance in providing insight into the full range of past human activity.

Households

Households are homes, dwellings or residences where people lived. Meticulous excavation can reveal the activities of individual households, provided the house has remained isolated from surrounding household activities and undisturbed by more recent occupations or natural processes. Archaeologically, households may be represented by structural remains, as well as artifacts and features left by the households' residents. These materials may include clearly delineated activity areas, areas where a specific activity, such as stone tool making, craft activities, or food processing took place (Kent, 1984). Remains of houses, disintegrating walls, and the distribution of hearths, stone grinders, and other artifacts abandoned when the owners left can be used to reconstruct the activities of individual households.

Archaeological sites, whether small hunting camps, humble farming villages, or vast cities, are archives of human interaction. A **household unit** is defined by the artifact patterns that reflect activities that take place around a house; they are assumed to belong to one household. People lived and died in these places. They grew up, got married, had children, and quarreled with neighbors. These daily interactions, between men and women, rich and poor, traders and their customers, slaves and masters, come down to us in the form of distinctive artifact patterning. The anonymous testimony of artifacts from individual houses, neighborhoods, palaces, and temples reveals the full, and often unsuspected, diversity of ancient human communities.

At times, archaeological preservation may provide unique insight into household life. For example, 1,700 years ago, the Romans controlled the Mediterranean world and its lucrative trade routes through a network of cities and ports from Spain to Egypt. On July 21, A.D. 365, an early-morning earthquake ripped through a small Roman port at Kourion in southwestern Cyprus. Three shock waves flattened the town. The quake caused huge tsunamis that rolled ashore in the eastern Mediterranean. Archaeologist David Soren recovered a treasure trove of information about the households in Kourion by excavating the individual buildings and plotting the artifacts of daily life preserved in the collapsed dwellings (Soren and James, 1988). He recovered the skeletal remains of a family still abed. The husband died vainly trying to shield his young wife and infant from a rain of beams and limestone blocks (Figure 15.4). In a nearby courtyard, Soren's excavators found a stable where a young girl died trying to calm a restless mule, whose skeleton lay by a stone trough.

Fortunately for the archaeologist, individuals within different societies tend to use similar construction methods and build their houses in similar ways, so researchers can use the variations in house designs and artifact patterning between houses as evidence for different subsistence practices, social status, wealth, and manufacturing activities. Like a shipwreck on the seabed, a well-excavated ancient house can be a time capsule of a single moment, which an expert can read just like a book.

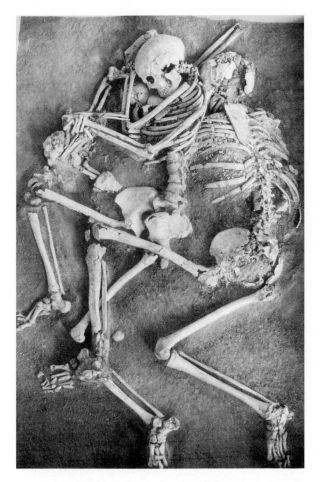

Figure 15.4   Earthquake victims at Kourion. A family died while sleeping, the child clasped in the mother's arms.

Excavating a Household

When a house is excavated, the objective is to try to define the entire household unit (Figure 15.5), comprised not only of the dwelling itself but also any surrounding storage pits, graves, and **activity areas** indicating food preparation and other tasks associated with a household. Kourion is a dramatic find, and individual households were preserved by the very cataclysm that destroyed them. More often, the archaeologist finds more subtle patterning of household activities—indeed, in the majority of cases identifying even faint traces of timber and hide shelters or evidence of ancient mud walls may be impossible. Households require careful, large area excavations so that all traces of the household and any surrounding features can be identified. Archaeologists plot the exact position of each artifact, bone, and feature where they lie in the hope of finding evidence of stone tool making, cooking, or domestic crafts preserved within the boundaries of long-vanished dwellings. Household archaeology is a classic application of the law of association, described in Chapter 6.

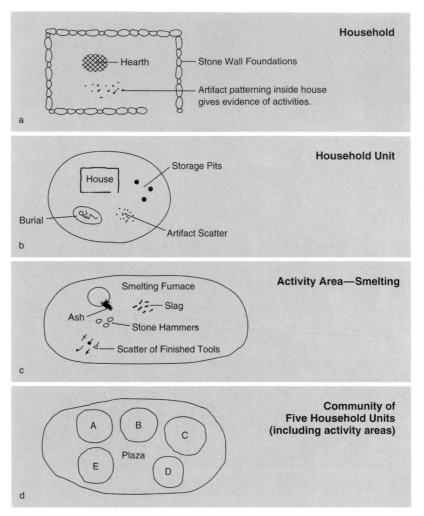

Figure 15.5   Various spatial units used by archaeologists in studying human settlement: (a) household; (b) household unit; (c) activity area; (d) community.

The distinctive patterning of artifacts in houses, storage pits, and other areas form **activity sets,** groups of artifacts associated with specific activities, such as wire-making tools and copper rods indicating the manufacture of fine copper wire ornaments. Sometimes, evidence of past activities can be determined while excavation is still in progress—stone tool manufacture surviving as a scatter of waste flakes and cores, or the butchering of a rabbit by a cluster of broken bones. More often, however, computer analysis is the best source of information, allowing researchers to call up the position of every potsherd of a certain style or all ox forelimb bones. It is then that they can discern unexpected associations, subtle signposts to long-forgotten domestic activities or even of children playing. This type of excavation is invaluable when studying male and female roles or the cultural diversity of a household revealed by distinctive artifacts. Short of a burial or a house belonging to a known historical individual, this is about as close as one can get in archaeology to discerning individuals, as opposed to households.

Households at Cerén, San Salvador

Activity sets sometimes provide startlingly complete stories of the past, especially at sites where preservation conditions are exceptional. One August evening in the sixth century A.D., a sudden rumble shook a quiet Maya village at Cerén in El Salvador (see also Chapter 4). An underground fissure less than a mile away erupted without warning. A fast-moving cloud of ash darkened the twilight sky. The villagers fled for their lives, leaving everything behind. In minutes, their houses lay under a thick layer of volcanic debris. Fifteen hundred years later, archaeologist Payson Sheets (1992) used subsurface radar to locate several buried houses deep under the ash (Chapter 8). He then excavated the dwellings. Plotting every artifact, even individual wall fragments, seeds, and pieces of thatch, he discovered households where the people fled the cascading ash at the end of the evening meal.

One household lived in a complex of four buildings: a kitchen, a workshop, a storehouse, and a residence, where the residents socialized, ate, and slept (see Figure 4.9). The residence had a front porch open on three sides. The main room covered 43 square feet (4 sq. m), with storage pots against the back wall. One pot contained a spindle whorl for making cotton thread. A large adobe bench on the east side of the room served as a sleeping place. During the day, people rolled up their mats and stored them among the rafters. Even the sharp-edged obsidian knife blades, stored high in the roof for safety, still lay among the thatch.

A walkway linked the dwelling to a nearby storehouse, passing by a food-grinding area where a metate (grinding stone) still stood on forked sticks about 20 inches (50 cm) above the ground. The household owned a well-tended garden along the side of the storehouse, with carefully spaced rows of three species of medicinal herbs standing about 3 feet (1 m) apart, each plant standing in a small mound of soil. Just to the south, an ash-covered field contained ridges of young maize plants about 8 to 15 inches (20 to 38 cm) high, typical corn growth for August in this environment.

Early Mesoamerican Houses

The study of individual households gives us an intimate look at daily life. By comparing households, researchers can gain a broader impression of how people interacted with one another. In studying early Mesoamerican houses, Kent Flannery and his colleagues distinguished carefully among the households themselves; the household unit of associated features, such as storage pits and graves; and the various activity areas sometimes associated with them (Flannery and Marcus, 1983; Winter, 1976).

Between 1350 and 850 B.C., the one-room, thatched wattle-and-daub house became the most common dwelling type in Early Formative Mesoamerican villages. In the Valley of Oaxaca in Mexico, Early Formative houses were generally rectangular. The floors were sand-covered and dug out from the subsoil, and the thatched roof was supported by pine posts. The puddled clay walls were smoothed and sometimes white-washed (Flannery, 1976; Flannery and Marcus, 1983).

Many of the houses had been swept clean before abandonment, but several contained accumulations of debris that included not only potsherds and bone tools but food remains as well. Marcus Winter broke down the houses' contents into at least five possible activities, including sewing and basketry (needles), cooking and food consumption (pots and food remains), and cutting and scraping (stone tools). He plotted the individual house contents (Figure 15.6) in an attempt to distinguish the craft activities of the family that had occupied each dwelling. The Oaxacan study offered some potential for identifying division of labor within a household and arti-facts used by children rather than adults. (For discussion of this topic, see Gero and Conkey, 1991; Scott, 1994; Vogt, 1967; Wilk, 1991.)

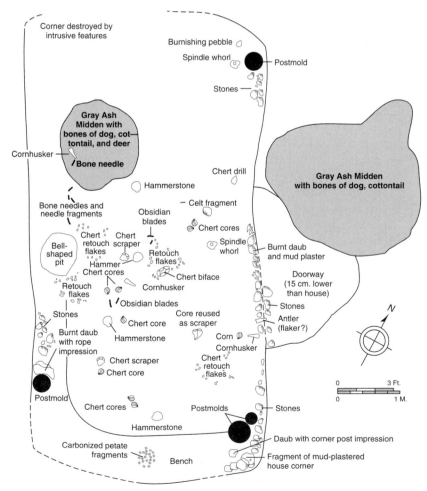

Figure 15.6   Plan of a house at Tierras Largas, Valley of Oaxaca, Mexico, from around 900 B.C., with selected artifacts plotted on the floor.

Communities

Communities are the arrangement of houses and activity areas within a single settlement: a group of individuals and households who normally reside in face-to-face association. Communities cover the vast spectrum of human settlements, from tiny hunter-gatherer camps to enormous cities. Expanded versions of the same survey and excavation methods used to investigate individual households operate at the community level, but a researcher's concerns range far wider than individual household activities and the layout of the settlement itself. Both environmental conditions and subsistence constraints limit the size and permanence of human settlements (Figure 15.7). Most hunter-gatherer societies, such as the !Kung of southern Africa's Kalahari Desert or the Hadza of Tanzania, East Africa, are constantly on the move, so their camps are short-lived, sometimes occupied for little more than a few days. In contrast, the farmers of Çatalhöyük, a Turkish farming settlement of 6000 B.C., lived in the same crowded village of mud houses separated by narrow alleys for many centuries, because they were anchored to their nearby fields (Mellaart, 1967) (see Figure 3.6).

Communities are never static entities. Peoples' children grow up, marry, and start new households nearby. Houses burn down or collapse, so new dwellings are

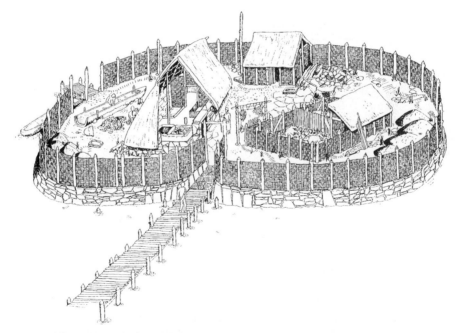

Figure 15.7   Environment and community: an adaptation to cool, damp conditions. An artist's reconstruction of a Neolithic house and associated structures from a small settlement at Loch Olabhat, Hebrides, Scotland. A wooden causeway leads through a narrow entrance. The house is at left, cut away to show the hearth inside. The artist has conveyed the excavators' uncertainty about the function of the structure to the right with masterly ambiguity.

Doing Archaeology

Winter Houses at Keatley Creek, British Columbia

When archaeologist Brian Hayden (1996) excavated a series of large Native American winter houses at Keatley Creek near the Fraser River in British Columbia, he unearthed over 115 house depressions, excavated partially into the ground, some over 66 feet (20 m) across. The dwellings were dug up to 6 feet (2 m) into the subsoil, then roofed with timber, bark, grass, or mats. Access was usually by ladder through the smoke hole. The site lies on a dry terrace above the Fraser River in a semiarid environment. Mountains rise behind the site. There are a number of important salmon-harvesting sites nearby, which were among the most productive in the region in early historic times. Many surrounding groups came to the area to trade for dried salmon, which probably gave Keatley Creek unusual importance as a settlement.

Most of the house pits excavated by Hayden and his colleagues date to between 3500 B.C. and A.D. 950. The workers excavated each house pit carefully, recording not only basic dimensions but also the sizes of hearths and storage pits and the depth of fire-reddening beneath each hearth. Using fine screens, they acquired as much accurate information on the positions of individual artifacts and food

remains as possible. In addition, they sampled house-floor deposits for their soil chemistry and used flotation to recover small plant remains, tiny artifacts, and bone fragments. They combined these data with sourcing studies of toolmaking materials (Chapter 11) and studied ways of distinguishing floor surfaces from the remains of collapsed thatched roofs.

The analysis of all these data revealed some interesting social differences. One large pithouse had a series of hearths forming a circle about 6 feet (2 m) from the pit wall, as if a series of domestic groups had resided in the same dwelling. Each hearth had its own fire-cracked rocks and stone tools used for domestic activities. The distributions of stone artifact fragments and waste by-products revealed that messier tasks such as animal butchery and spear making had taken place in the center of the dwelling, where there was more space and headroom. Activities such as projectile-point manufacture and sewing had occurred in the domestic areas, which were more comfortable.

The layout of hearths in the same house revealed another interesting pattern. The deeper, more fire-reddened hearths were in

built in their place. As often happened with Iroquois villages in the American Northeast, a settlement would outgrow its fortifications and then erect an extended palisade to protect new houses. The study of an ancient community is a study of constant interactions between individuals, households, and members of the settlement.

In small communities, family and kin ties were of overwhelming importance, affecting the layout of houses, household compounds, and groups of dwellings. By mapping and analyzing artifact patterns and house inventories, excavators can sometimes find traces of different residential clusters within a single community. Kent Flannery and a University of Michigan research team (1976) used such data plots to find at least four residential wards (barrios) within the rapidly growing village of San

the western area of the dwelling, and the smaller and more superficially reddened ones were to the east. By the same token, the larger storage pits were also to the west. Hayden believes that these patterns reflect not separate activity areas but socioeconomic variations between wealthier, more powerful people living by the larger hearths and pits and poorer families located elsewhere.

The Keatley Creek excavations revealed possible evidence for social organization, but other lines of evidence were needed to confirm the hypothesis. In fact, other excavations on Northwest Coast houses and ethnographic accounts from living groups support Hayden's theory, for they reveal large dwellings where the richer and more powerful families occupied one-half of the house.

Ethnographic accounts report that the most important fishing sites in the region were owned by members of individual households, perhaps passed down from one generation to the next. Ken Berry's analysis of the salmon bones from Keatley Creek revealed that poorer families consumed mostly "pink salmon," readily identified by the two-year growth rings in their backbones. Pink salmon are the easiest to catch, but they are the smallest and have the lowest fat content. In contrast, the inhabitants of the larger dwellings ate not only pink salmon but also chinook and sockeye, larger forms that could be caught in quantity only from rocks projecting far into the water or from specially constructed platforms. The fact that such salmon bones are found only in larger houses strongly confirms ethnographic accounts that such sites were owned by only a few families or kin groups. Salmon provided over 70 percent of the protein in the local diet. Dried fish was traded widely in historic times and, presumably, earlier; it was a trade controlled by elite families, who retained others, both commoners and slaves, to do the monotonous fishing and processing work.

Finally, archaeologist Ed Bakewell studied the sources of the toolmaking chert found in the large house pits. Each such dwelling had its own distinctive source, or a constellation of sources that it drew on, as if they had formed separate economic entities, each exploiting its own stone sources and hunting grounds in the mountains. Furthermore, analysis of the stone tools in the middens along the rims of the house pits revealed remarkably little change over the long duration of the site, as if the same corporate groups had exercised control over local fishing rights and their own territories for more than a thousand years. Hayden claims that this is the longest-lived example of such economic and social stability known anywhere.

José Mogote, which flourished in Mexico's Valley of Oaxaca after 1350 B.C. A trash-filled erosion gully separated each cluster of square thatched houses from its neighbors.

The Keatley Creek excavations described in the Doing Archaeology box are a good example of the ability of fine-grained excavation to reveal long-term social and economic relationships. However, the use of artifact distributions to infer human activities is challenging.

Archaeologists frequently use analogies with modern populations and theoretical models to help them conceptualize life in past settlements. Gerald Oetelaar (1993) studied site structure at the Bridges site, a late Mississippian settlement in southern Illinois occupied between A.D. 1100 and 1300. To better understand activities within the settlement, he developed a research model that subdivides small settlements into four major activity zones: a communal front region for public activities; family front and back regions for domestic tasks, entertainment, and messy tasks; and a communal back region (Figure 15.8). These diverse activities generate different debris, the model providing an analytical framework for inferring the organization and use of space at the site. Oetelaar argues that the model shows long-term stability at the settlement, the large communal areas depicting a degree of collaboration among different families, perhaps at planting and harvest seasons. Models like this allow researchers to study the interactions among households within the confines of a single site and may also enable the identification of specific activities at individual settlements within a larger settlement pattern.

Ethnoarchaeology at Wiae, Ghana

Ethnoarchaeology, the ethnographic study of material culture with particular relevance to the interpretation of archaeological remains, also helps archaeologists to model the types of variables that impact the arrangement and distribution of settlements. Examinations of modern communities reveal a diversity of sociocultural, economic, and political variables that dictate how people arrange their communities.

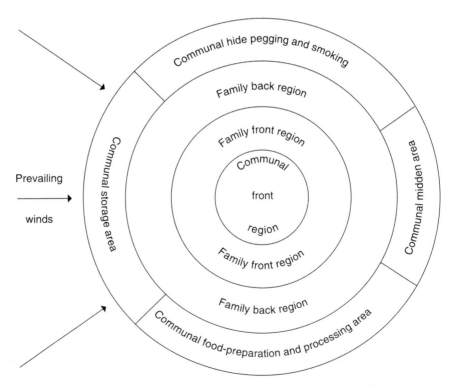

Figure 15.8a   Site structure. A hypothetical model showing a possible arrangement of work spaces in a small settlement.

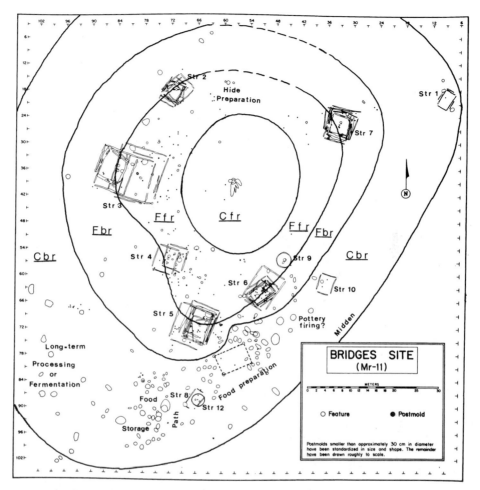

Figure 15.8b   Site structure. A plan of the Bridges site, showing activity zones plotted over archaeological finds (Cfr = communal front region, and so on).

Source: Gerald A. Oetelaar, additions to original plan by Thomas Gatlin, Center for Archaeological Excavations. Copyright © 1993, Board of Trustees, Southern Illinois University. Reprinted by permission.

These are of particular help in interpreting archaeological sites associated with the ethnographically observed population. As well, they also provide general insight into the types of factors that may impact the arrangement of communities.

The potential of ethnoarchaeological research is illustrated by the work conducted over the past twenty years by E. Kofi Agorsah on sites relating to the Nchumuru people of Wiae, in the northern Volta Basin of Ghana (Agorsah, 1983, 1985, 2003). Agorsah was interested in examining the sociocultural factors that come into play in the arrangement of Nchumuru settlements. He was fortunate in having a very rich material record to study. The site of Old Wiae burned, and the people moved to New

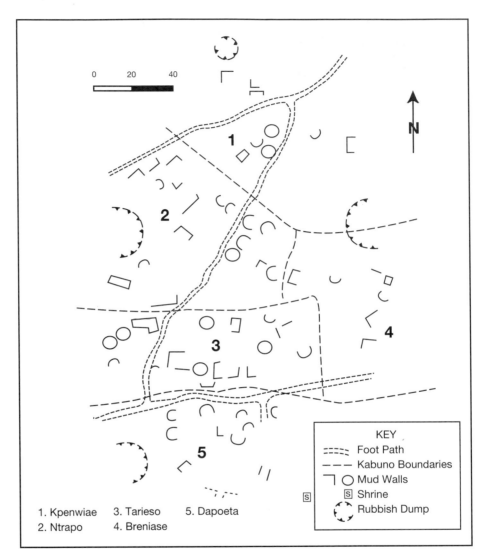

Figure 15.9 Map showing clan (*kabuno*) areas of Old Wiae. Ethnoarchaeological studies such as these provide clues to material aspects of social organization that may be present in archaeological sites.

Source: Reprinted from *Journal of Anthropological Archaeology* 7: 231–47, Figure 2, page 239. Copyright © 1988, with permission from Elsevier.

Wiae, which is still occupied. Agorsah was thus able to compare archaeological data from Old Wiae with ethnographic observations at the new town (Figure 15.9).

Agorsah found that spatial arrangements within the communities were dictated by a number of local rules, particularly family organization and clan membership. Archaeologically, the ethnographic observations were born out in discrete clustering of houses within settlements reflecting the different Nchumuru clan groups. Ancestral shrines associated with each clan were located near the houses of clan heads. Individual household units incorporated houses with at least two rooms, a courtyard, kitchen, and backyard. Typically, these areas served a diversity of functions, including food processing and preparation, sleeping, and storage, but some differences could be identified. For example, older women's rooms were marked by a raised platform bed and smaller platforms along the walls for holding pots. The only areas that had a clearly specialized function were those that held household shrines.

Agorsah's observations of the Wiae settlements are very useful in examining archaeological data from Nchumuru archaeological sites, as well as those of neighboring ethnic groups that share similar sociocultural practices. At a more general level, however, such observations help archaeologists think about the types of factors that might be reflected in archaeological data, allowing them to evaluate cultural processes in past societies (for a Native American example of this type of interpretation see the box on Broken K Pueblo in Chapter 3, pp. 66–67).

Estimating Community Size

Implicit in the preceding discussions is variation in settlement size. Community population estimates are important because they can give insights into resource exploitation, past sociopolitical organization, and social dynamics. What, for example, was the maximum size that early Mesoamerican hamlets and villages could reach before further growth was impossible? Typically, societies that were not organized into large states tended to live in small villages, which frequently split off from one another as further growth at the mother settlement was cut off. This process is straightforward enough, and in early Mesoamerica many villages split off in just this manner. But others, such as the Olmec settlement at San Lorenzo, were able to grow larger and still remain viable settlements. Why was this growth possible?

How does one estimate community populations? In historically documented settings, written records, or even census data, may provide fairly accurate population estimates, as in sixteenth-century Algonquian villages (Figure 15.10). Using analogy, such information can sometimes be applied to archaeological settings—the size, number, and layout of the known settlement used to evaluate the relative size of excavated communities. In most cases, however, written records are not available or of uncertain value. Many variables might contribute to erroneous census data, and historic population densities and household sizes do not necessarily correspond to those of prehistoric times.

For the most part, researchers must turn to archaeological data to evaluate population. The most reliable estimates of population are obtained when a fairly accurate assessment of the number of households at any one moment in a community's history can be determined. René Millon's guesses about Teotihuacán's population, for example, are based on such house counts (Millon, 1981). Using samples of early Mesoamerican villages, Joyce Marcus (1976) also showed that perhaps 90 percent were small hamlets with one to ten or twelve households and up to sixty people. But some villages were much larger than this average.

The relative areas occupied by a settlement provides some indication of population and some researchers have attempted to estimate population sizes with

The towne of Pomeiock and true forme of their howses, couered
and enclosed some wth matts, and some wth barcks of trees. All compassed
abowt wth smale poles stock thick together in stedd of a wall.

Figure 15.10 Example of a community. Algonquian village in North Carolina, sketched by John White in 1585. (Copyright The British Museum)

mathematical formulas that allocate so much living space to each individual and each family. But population density within settlements varies. Consequently, the relationship between settlement size and population is not constant. Theoretical models can provide important insight into the relative size of settlements and relative population growth within a region, but intangible variables, ranging from ideosyncratic behavior to social restrictions and cultural norms, make it difficult to develop a standard (see De Roche, 1983).

Estimates of the rates at which people accumulate refuse middens or densities of ceramic sherds over long periods have also been used to calculate population size, but these approaches have the same limitations as the others mentioned (de Barros, 1988; Zubrow, 1976). For these reasons, archaeological assessments of population are guarded, with a clear statement of the criteria used in reaching a conclusion.

Studying Large Communities

The behaviors and interactions of people living in large communities such as cities raise special challenges. Whereas subsistence needs and environmental realities often affect the siting of smaller communities, more complex factors, such as religious authority, sociopolitical organization, and status differences, come into play with

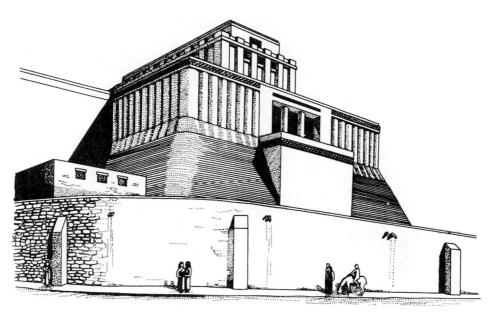

Figure 15.11   Reconstruction of the temple at Eridu, Iraq, showing the platform
supporting the shrine, c. 3000 B.C.

ancient cities. For example, the city of Eridu in southern Iraq was the largest human
settlement on the earth in 4000 B.C. Eridu lay close to the Euphrates River, with easy
access to the wider world of the Persian Gulf. Approximately five thousand people
clustered in the crowded precincts of the city, perhaps, at first, little more than an ag-
glomeration of villages of close kin or specialist artisans living close together for mutual protection and economic interest. They lived in the shadow of the great mud-
brick ziggurat temple-mound of the god Enlil, a veritable artificial mountain that
reached toward the wide heavens above (Postgate, 1993) (Figure 15.11). Eridu's temple was the highest point in the flat countryside for many miles around, a symbol of a
very sacred place favored by the gods. Compelling political and religious factors
helped determine the site of Eridu, the chosen city of Enlil. As were many other ancient cities, this oldest of human cities was a symbolic center of the universe, the holi-
est place on the earth.

Teotihuacán, Mexico

We tend to think of ancient cities in terms of their signature public structures—
palaces, pyramids, and magnificent temples. But archaeology allows us to look far beyond the lavish façade and huge plazas into a humbler world. The city of Teotihuacán,
at the edge of the Basin of Mexico, was a cluster of villages in 250 B.C. Over the next
two centuries, the villages became a city of an estimated 40,000 people (Millon, 1973,
1981). Five hundred years later, between 100,000 and 200,000 nobles, artisans, and
common folk dwelt within its precincts, which covered 7 square miles (18 sq. km)

Figure 15.12   The Pyramid of the Sun at Teotihuacán, Mexico. The Street of the Dead runs in front of the Pyramid.

(Figure 15.12). Teotihuacán had become rich on obsidian trade, and it was a place of sacred pilgrimage ruled by powerful lords. In its heyday, the city dwarfed medieval London, with its few tens of thousands of citizens, and was one of the largest human settlements in the world. Then, in about A.D. 750, Teotihuacán abruptly collapsed, for reasons that are still not understood. The Aztecs still revered its sacred pyramids eight centuries later. They believed that Teotihuacán was the place where their world began.

As we saw in Chapter 8, archaeologists René Millon, Bruce Dewitt, and George Cowgill undertook the ambitious task of mapping the entire city of Teotihuacán in the 1960s. They showed that, unlike most ancient cities, Teotihuacán had not grown haphazardly. Mapping revealed that the city's architects had worked to a layout devised early in the city's development and had adhered to it for centuries. For its entire existence, Teotihuacán was a model in clay, stone, and stucco of an all-pervasive spiritual world. This brilliant conception was a symbolic landscape of artificial mountains (pyramids) and foothills separated by open spaces.

The archaeologists found that the city had been built in four quadrants, according to the master plan that had been established by the original architects. The famous Street of the Dead bisects the city on a north-south axis, bordered on its east side by the 200-foot-high (61-m-high) Pyramid of the Sun, built in five stages over a natural cavern discovered during excavations in 1971. This cave was the most sacred place in the city, a gateway to the Otherworld. The pyramid itself marked the passage of the sun from east to west and the rising of the Pleiades constellation on the day of the

Figure 15.13   Looking down the Street of the Dead at Teotihuacán, Mexico.

equinox. An east-west avenue crosses the Street of the Dead near its southern end, dividing the city into segments coinciding with the four quadrants of the Mesoamerican spiritual world. This basic cruciform layout was established very early, when the great Street of the Dead (Figure 15.13) was laid out (Cowgill and others, 1984).

Thanks to the mapping project, we know that teeming neighborhoods of single-story, flat-roofed, rectangular apartment compounds complete with courtyards and passageways lay beyond the ceremonial precincts. Teotihuacán's population may have reached a peak of more than 150,000 people in A.D. 600. More than two thousand compounds contained thousands of standardized, one-story apartments sharing courtyards and temples with their neighbors. The oldest part of the city lies in the northern quadrant, where most of the city's craftspeople lived. It contains many more structures than the southern quadrants, where exceptionally fertile soils, ideal for irrigation agriculture, are located.

Teotihuacán was a vast urban community made up of hundreds of smaller communities. The city was organized into neighborhoods, or barrios, groups of apartment compounds separated from one another. Some of these compounds contained large concentrations of obsidian flakes or potters' artifacts and were identified as specialist precincts or groups of workshops. Narrow alleyways and streets about 12 feet (3.6 m) wide separated each compound from its neighbors. Each compound housed between 20 and 100 people, perhaps members of the same kin group. Artifact patterning indicate that some compounds sheltered skilled artisans, families of obsidian and shell ornament makers, weavers, and potters.

The Teotihuacán market sold commodities and exotic luxuries from all over the Mesoamerican highlands and lowlands. The Teotihuacános valued their foreign trade so highly that they allowed foreigners to settle among them in special barrios occupied over many centuries. Immigrants from the Veracruz region of the lowlands lived in a neighborhood on the city's eastern side, identified from the remains of distinctive circular adobe houses with thatched roofs identical to those of the inhabitants' Gulf Coast homeland. These people, easily identified by their orange-, brown-, and cream-painted pots, probably traded in exotic tropical luxuries such as brightly colored bird feathers. Another neighborhood on the western side housed Zapotec traders from the Valley of Oaxaca, 250 miles (402 km) south of Teotihuacán. Potsherds from their segregated compounds allow us to identify their presence in the crowded city.

What was life like inside Teotihuacán's anonymous apartment compounds? Mexican archaeologist Linda Manzanilla has investigated one such barrio close to the northwestern edge of Teotihuacán, searching for traces of different activities within the complex. The stucco floors in the apartments and courtyards had been swept clean, so Manzanilla and her colleagues used chemical analyses of the floor deposits to search for human activities. She developed a mosaic of different chemical readings, such as high phosphate readings where garbage had rotted and dense concentrations of carbonate from lime (used in the preparation of both tortillas and stucco) that indicated cooking or building activity. Manzanilla's chemical plans of the compound are accurate enough to pinpoint the locations of cooking fires and eating places, where the inhabitants consumed deer, rabbits, and turkeys. She was able to identify three nuclear families totaling about thirty people who lived in three separate apartments within this community inside a much larger community. Each apartment had specific areas for sleeping, eating, religious activities, and funeral rites.

A major objective of the Teotihuacán research is to understand the diverse internal workings of this remarkable city as an ongoing organization throughout its long history. This result can be achieved only by comprehensive surveys that rely heavily on samples of artifact patterns and analyses of house contents and entire neighborhoods conducted all over this enormous site (Cowgill and others, 1984). Archaeological work at Teotihuacán has revealed the human interactions within and between its tight-knit barrios and the wider universe of the city itself. Today, Teotihuacán is an archaeological skeleton. However, thanks to the mapping project and later researches, we can easily imagine the city in its heyday 1,500 years ago, the brightly painted ceremonial precincts lapped by thousands of flat apartment roofs and the city surrounded by a green patchwork of irrigation canals and cornfields (Berrin and Pasztory, 1993).

Studying Distributions of Communities

The explanation of evolving settlement patterns takes us to a broader area of research, the layout of communities against the entire background of their natural and cultural environments (Hietala, 1984). The **distribution of communities,** the density and spatial patterning of communities across the landscape, depends on many factors.

Some are environmental, such as the availability of game, wild plant foods, or good grazing grass; but some settlement patterns are influenced by economic, social, religious, and technological constraints. Settlement patterns across a landscape evolve in response to three broad variables: shifts in population density, environment, and sociopolitical phenomena.

Population

Of the variables that affect site distribution, population is the hardest to study (Hassan, 1981). Nevertheless, changing population distributions are of great importance, for there is a clear cause-and-effect relationship between population, carrying capacity, agricultural productivity, and sociocultural organization. Global population growth was likely not a major factor in human history until after the Ice Age, which ended about 15,000 years ago. Until that time, naturally occurring plant and animal resources provided sufficient food for hunter-gatherer populations. If the size of a community grew beyond the resources locally available, people simply expanded into new areas. As population increased, some theorize, people turned to new fishing or hunting methods and, ultimately, agriculture.

Growing population densities following the Ice Age were probably a factor in the development of agriculture in southwestern Asia in about 10,000 B.C. and in the appearance of the first cities and civilizations about six thousand years later. In the case of farming, much drier conditions, diminished supplies of wild plant foods, and many more mouths to feed turned many hunter-gatherer groups in the Jordan Valley and modern-day Syria into sedentary farmers within a few centuries. Farmers faced the challenge by developing large-scale irrigation systems capable of producing several crops a year and feeding many more people.

Population, then, is a critical variable in settlement archaeology. Even indicators of general trends are of great interest, for they enable one to monitor large-scale processes such as major changes in subsistence strategies, sociopolitical change, and the rise or fall of entire civilizations. Unfortunately, as seen in the discussion of settlement size, estimating population densities is challenging, despite attempts to develop censuses from house counts and refuse accumulation (see the Doing Archaeology box).

Carrying Capacity and Site-Catchment Analysis

Cultural adaptation to any environment can be understood only in the context of the ancient environment and the resources available therein and the technology of the culture being studied. Once these data are on hand, the archaeologist can proceed to establish which subsistence and economic options the people chose, given the available resources and their technological ability to exploit them.

It is easy enough to make an inventory of the natural resources in any area, but it is not sufficient merely to list them; for it is the ways in which they can be exploited—the seasons of availability of vegetable foods, the migration patterns of game, the months when salmon runs take place—and not just the resources themselves that are significant. These variables, to say nothing of agricultural soils, rainfall

Doing Archaeology

Studying the Maya Collapse at Copán, Honduras

The collapse of Classic Maya civilization in the southern lowlands of Mesoamerica during the ninth century A.D. is one of the great controversies of archaeology. For generations, scholars have argued vehemently over this sudden collapse. Was the decline caused by social unrest, warfare, or ecological collapse? Or did the Maya nobility place too many demands on their farmer subjects? The debate continues, marked by a lack of reliable scientific data from the field, except for a remarkable study of changing settlement patterns and population distributions at the city of Copán in Honduras (Fash, 1991; Freter, 1994).

Copán was one of the greatest Maya cities, founded in a fertile valley before the fifth century A.D. On December 11, A.D. 426, a Maya lord named Kinich Yax K'uk Mo' ("Sun-Eyed Green Quetzal Macaw") founded a dynasty that ruled for four centuries. Copán soon became a major kingdom of the Maya world, with a spectacular urban core that covered 36 acres (14.6 ha) (see Figure 9.13 and Chapter 8). Between 550 and 700, the Copán state expanded dramatically, with most of the population concentrated in the urban core and immediately around it. By 800, between 20,000 and 25,000 people lived in the general Copán Valley area. Then, in 822, the royal dynasty ended and the kingdom collapsed.

What accounts for Copán's decline? Archaeologists David Webster, William Sanders, and many colleagues, working on a long-term investigation of the city, decided to look at the collapse by studying changing settlement patterns and shifting population densities around the abandoned city (Sanders and others, 1979). They developed a large-scale settlement survey modeled after the famous Basin of Mexico survey of some years earlier to examine more than 52 square miles (135 sq. km) around the urban core. Using aerial photographs and systematic field surveys, the research team recorded more than 1,425 archaeological sites containing more than 4,500 structures. Team members mapped and surface-collected each location. Two hundred fifty-two sites were test-pitted to obtain artifact and dating samples so they could be placed within the general chronological framework for the valley.

As the data flowed into the laboratory, the researchers developed a classification of site patterns, and distributions of raw materials, determine the critical element of a settlement pattern: the carrying capacity of the land.

Carrying capacity is the number and density of people that any tract of land can support. It is a flexible statistic that can be affected by factors other than those of the available resources in an area. People can alter the carrying capacity of their land by taking up agriculture or by cultivating a new crop that needs deeper plowing and thus exhausts the land faster. Conversely, the introduction of fertilizer can enable people to settle permanently in one village because their lands are kept fertile artificially. Ancient carrying capacities are difficult to establish, except with carefully controlled data. Recent research has concentrated on systems models and computer simulations of the variables that affect carrying capacity.

types using size and other criteria, classifying them in a hierarchy from simple to complex as a way of developing a portrait of shifting landscape use over many centuries. At the same time, they obtained 2,300 dates, using volcanic glass fragments that could be dated using the obsidian hydration method (Chapter 7). The survey yielded a bird's-eye view of dramatic population changes as human settlement expanded and contracted over the valley landscape.

The earlier sites found in the survey documented rapid population growth, especially in the city itself and nearby. There was only a small, scattered rural population. Between 700 and 800, the Copán Valley reached its greatest sociopolitical complexity, with a rapid population increase to between 20,000 and 25,000 people. These figures, calculated from site size, suggest that the local population was doubling every 80 to 100 years, with about 80 percent of the people living within the urban core and immediate periphery. Rural settlement expanded outward along the valley floor but was still relatively scattered. Now people were farming foothill areas, as the population density of the urban core reached over 8,000 people per 0.3 sq. mile (1 sq. km), with the periphery housing about 500 people per 0.3 sq. mile (1 sq. km). Some 82 percent of the population lived in relatively humble dwellings, an indication of the pyramid-like nature of Copán society.

After A.D. 850, the survey showed dramatic shifts. The urban core and periphery zones lost about half their population, while the rural population increased by almost 20 percent. Small regional settlements replaced the scattered villages of earlier times, a response to cumulative deforestation, overexploitation of even marginal agricultural land, and uncontrolled soil erosion near the capital. By 1150, the Copán Valley population had fallen to between 2,000 and 5,000 people.

The Copán research does not explain why the city collapsed, but it does chronicle the dramatic impact of rapidly growing populations on ecologically fragile landscapes. The evidence hints that environmental degradation was a major factor in the Maya collapse. Maya writings tell us that Maya lords considered themselves the intermediaries between the living and supernatural worlds. However, when the inexorable forces of environmental decline took hold, their authority evaporated and a centuries-old spiritual relationship between farmers and an elaborate cosmic world vanished into near-oblivion.

One approach is **site-catchment analysis,** which is based on the assumption that every human settlement has a catchment area around it. This is a zone of domestic and wild resources within easy walking distance of the settlement. The fundamental assumption is simple: the farther the resources in an area are from a site, the less likely they are to be exploited (Bailey, 1981; Roper, 1979). Two key concepts are important: site-exploitation territory and site-catchment analysis.

Site-exploitation territory is the potential area from which food resources may be obtained. Its boundaries are defined by "least-cost" principles, by the maximum radii of the distances that people are willing to cover on foot. Much depends on the nature of the resources and how they are exploited. For example, in two hours' walking time a person can cover about 6 miles (10 km)—a reasonable distance to travel for some purposes. But a much smaller radius of half a mile (1 km) is useful when analyzing farming economies where land is exploited intensively, for it is the most economical use of labor to cultivate land close to the village. The boundaries of such radii are based on assumptions about normal human behavior and on examination of the economic potential of resources lying within them. Thus site-exploitation territory is little more than a statement of what was potentially available to the site inhabitants.

The **economic catchment area** of a site is quite different from the site-exploitation territory. It is the actual area from which the food resources consumed by the inhabitants are obtained. Such areas vary in size and shape according to the resources exploited, the site function, and the lifeway of its inhabitants. Clearly, the accuracy with which the economic catchment area can be defined will depend on the precision with which one can identify food remains in the site itself.

Site-catchment analysis involves examining both the economic catchment area and the site-exploitation territory as a way of assessing the relationship between what was potentially available in the environment and what was actually exploited. Determining ancient site catchments may be very difficult, as the modern environment may be quite different from that in the past. Analysis using the Geographic Information System (GIS) offers great potential for the study of site catchments; for it allows the archaeologist to overlay such features as topography, hill slopes, soil distributions, and the like, onto site catchments and site-distribution territories. When combined with indications of social and cultural patterns, these data may provide dramatic insight into the past.

Case Studies of Settlement Distribution

For years, the study of community distributions depended on large-scale archaeological surveys that combined aerial photographs with months of systematic foot survey on the ground. William Sanders and a large research team from Pennsylvania State University surveyed the entire Valley of Mexico, center of the Aztec civilization, in the 1970s. They compiled distribution maps of every known archaeological site and plotted them against comprehensive environmental data, with dramatic results. Sanders showed how the population of the basin ebbed and flowed over many centuries, with the rise and fall of the great city of Teotihuacán in the first millennium A.D. (Sanders and others, 1979).

The most dramatic changes came when the growing Aztec capital, Tenochtitlán, achieved overwhelming dominance. Although Sanders's population estimates were only highly informed guesses, the data show a dramatic rise over several centuries. By the end of the fifteenth century A.D., the imperial capital housed at least 200,000 people, living in dense residential areas now buried under the concrete jungle of modern Mexico City. The concentration of sites nearby was such that Sanders estimated that at least 400,000 city and country dwellers occupied a 230-square-mile (370-sq.-km) zone of foothills, plains, and lake bed areas near the capital. He calculated that about 1 million people lived within the confines of the Basin of Mexico at the time.

Site

The Creation of the Aztec World at Teotihuacán, Mexico

A remarkable Franciscan friar, Fray Bernardino de Sahagun (c. 1499–1590), arrived in New Spain (Mexico) less than ten years after the Spanish Conquest of the Aztec empire. He devoted his life to recording Aztec history and culture before it died out with the deaths of his elderly informants. All of them had learned their history in schools where the students learned by oral recitation. Sahagun learned that the Aztecs believed they lived in a finite world. Theirs was the fifth of five successive worlds; it was destined to perish as a result of catastrophic earthquakes. His informants recited the story of the creation of the Aztec world, known as the Fifth Sun, high on the pyramids of Teotihuacán. They told how the gods had assembled atop the Pyramid of the Sun when all was darkness after the destruction of the Fourth Sun. They "took counsel among themselves therein Teotihuacán. . . . Who will carry the burden? Who will take it upon himself to be the sun, to bring the dawn?" (A. Anderson and Dibble, 1955:4)

Two gods presented themselves as volunteers. They fasted for four days and nights, just as Aztec rulers did in later centuries when they visited Teotihuacán. Then they dressed in the correct ceremonial regalia and cast themselves into a great fire as the other gods watched. The god Nanautzin jumped eagerly into the flames. His partner Tecuziztecatl hesitated. So Nanautzin leapt out of the fire as the Sun and smote Tecuziztecatl in the face with a rabbit. Tecuziztecatl became the Moon, with the imprint of the rabbit causing the dark shadows on its surface. Then the wind god Ehecatl "arose and exerted himself fiercely and violently as he blew. At once he could move him [the Sun] who thereupon went his way. . . . When the Sun came to enter the place where he set, then once more the Moon moved" (A. Anderson and Dibble, 1955:5).

Thus was born the world of the Fifth Sun, kept in motion, the Aztecs believed, by the constant offerings of blood from human hearts sacrificed on the altar of the Sun God.

Tenochtitlán stood at the center of an organized landscape, created by ambitious rulers who thought nothing of creating nearly 25,000 acres (10,000 ha) of highly productive swamp gardens in the southern part of the basin alone. The city was a magnet to outlying populations, and its very presence skewed the entire settlement pattern of the basin. So many people lived there that the Aztecs farmed every local environment in the region to ensure that there was enough food to go around. Over less than two centuries, the settlement pattern changed from a patchwork of small states and communities to a highly centralized agricultural landscape capable of meeting the basic food needs of a large population (see the Site box and Figure 15.3).

Few settlement patterns show such dramatic changes as those in the Basin of Mexico. Sanders was a pioneer in combining environmental and archaeological data in settlement archaeology, but his project was unsophisticated by the standards of some of today's projects, which use high technology to integrate field surveys with a wide variety of spatial data.

The Geographic Information System at Roman Wroxeter, England

Studies of settlement distributions have proven particularly useful in examining past sociocultural organization and change (see also Chapter 16). Virconium Cornoviorum, the Roman town at present-day Wroxeter, near Shrewsbury in west-central England, was the fourth largest urban center in Roman Britain. Wroxeter started as a legionary camp in A.D. 60, then became a town thirty years later, flourishing until the fifth or sixth century. Most Roman towns lie under modern cities such as London or York. Fortunately for archaeologists, much of Wroxeter is in open country. For more than a century, generations of excavators investigated the major public buildings and commercial zone of the town. They used aerial photographs and surface collections of potsherds and other artifacts to plot the general outlines of the settlement and to develop a detailed chronology of its buildings.

But these approaches could not answer fundamental questions about the history of a once-strategic military gateway into neighboring and unconquered Wales. Many Roman forts and camps lie close to the town. What impact did these army encampments have on the rural population? What were the consequences of the Roman conquest on local Iron Age farmers?

To answer these questions, Vincent Gaffney and an international team of researchers have combined the powerful technology of the Geographic Information System with aerial photographs and ground surveys. The archaeologists could draw on a massive archive of aerial photographs of the surrounding countryside, taken under every kind of weather condition imaginable over more than half a century. They located over forty farming enclosures and the remains of a once-extensive field system. The researchers "warped" digital images of the aerial photographs onto Britain's national map grid, turning the images into GIS maps so accurate a fieldworker can measure and interpret such features as the Roman street grid at Wroxeter itself with margins of error as small as 3 feet (1 m) (Figure 15.14).

The Wroxeter project is unusual in that the archaeologists working on the ground have the ability to manipulate all available archaeological data on the screen before they go into the field. The fieldworkers rely heavily on volunteers, who are recording the Roman town's topography by taking measurements every 33 feet (10 m). A magnetometer survey combined with ground-penetrating radar has revealed hitherto unknown buildings on the edge of the town. For generations, experts on Roman Britain had called Wroxeter a carefully planned "garden city," with parks and open spaces. The GIS and remote sensing have revealed a less well organized community with uncontrolled expansion at its margins as it drew people from the surrounding countryside.

At Wroxeter, archaeologists are exploring a dynamic, ever-changing settlement pattern on the World Wide Web (the address is provided in the Guide to Further Reading). Within a few years, Wroxeter's archaeologists will be able to answer questions about changing patterns of supply and demand. By assuming that the town was the economic hub of the surrounding area, they will be able to show how mass-produced pottery from remote sites flowed through the region along an existing infrastructure of roads, tracks, and rivers accessible through the GIS database. But a final word of caution: the archaeological data in GIS databases are selected by the researcher

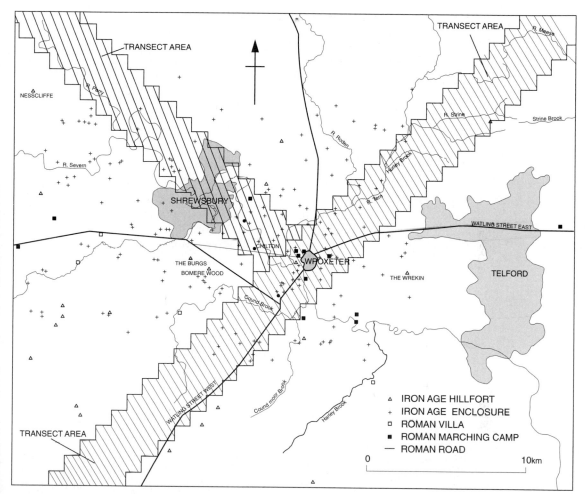

Figure 15.14 Geographic Information System research in the Wroxeter region. These data, derived from many sources, including generations of aerial photographs, provided the background data for the survey of Roman Wroxeter's hinterland. The map shows the Roman city and outlying sites and the three transects walked by archaeologists on the ground. Wroxeter is unique among Roman towns in Britain in not being buried under a modern city. Thus, it is unusually important for settlement studies.

Source: Reprinted by permission of Vincent Gaffney, Department of Archaeology, Birmingham University, England.

and are subject to subjective judgment. Subsequently, GIS interpretations are limited by the data input.

West Africa in the Era of the Atlantic Trade

The Atlantic slave trade, which peaked in the late eighteenth century, engulfed vast portions of West and Central Africa. Between the sixteenth and mid-nineteenth centuries, some 12 million to 15 million enslaved peoples were transported across the Atlantic to provide labor for the burgeoning plantations of the Americas. Although the horror of the slave trade has been widely written about in contemporary accounts and modern studies, evaluation of the consequences and impacts of the slave trade on African societies has been limited by the lack of written records for the majority of the regions where slaves were obtained. Most of the sources that do exist were written by European visitors to the coast who had no familiarity with the vast African hinterland. African oral traditions are also lacking for many areas, or they provide only limited information relevant to the period of the slave trade.

Although written records may be lacking, archaeological evidence of changes in settlement organization, location, and distribution, as well as artifact inventories dating to periods associated with the rise of the Atlantic trade, can be used to infer related social, cultural, and political changes (DeCorse, 2001a). While many parts of Africa remain poorly known archaeologically, relevant information is accumulating. It indicates that the era of the Atlantic trade was a time of tremendous transformation in West Africa. The changes that took place in African societies varied, as did their responses.

The appearance of fortified settlements or the relocation of towns from fertile valleys to rocky, inaccessible—but easily defended—hilltops in some regions provides clues to the need for defense against raids for slaves. Such is the case in many parts of Sierra Leone, Liberia, Ghana, Togo, and Cameroon, where settlements surrounded by ditches, palisades, and impenetrable thickets of thornbushes protect many eighteenth- and nineteenth-century settlements. In the western Adamaoua mountain range of Cameroon, where over one hundred settlements have been mapped, large villages with terraced fields are located beyond a line of fortified camps (Holl, 2001). The camps, surrounded by circular ditches and earthen embankments, were likely defense against slave raiding by neighboring ethnic groups, particularly the Fulani. In other areas, as in coastal Ghana, a pattern of smaller, dispersed settlements, gives way to larger communities, which may have provided more security.

These changes in settlement patterns are indicative of changes in sociopolitical organization. A case in point is the Fulani, who were nomadic pastoralists living in small transitory settlements in the fifteenth century. By the eighteenth and nineteenth centuries they were settled in towns with ruling nobility. The emerging Fulani states expanded into neighboring non-Islamic areas and thus caused dramatic expansion of Islam and Fulani cultural identity.

The Atlantic trade is not necessarily the sole explanation for all of the transformations that occurred in West Africa over the past five centuries, but the fact that the timing of some of the archaeological patterns observed correspond to historically known trade patterns and socioeconomic developments suggests an important link.

The Archaeology of Landscape

Views of the archaeological record of human communities have become increasingly holistic in perspective. Archaeologists have come to think about the "archaeology of landscape" as opposed to settlement distributions. Some mention of this new avenue of archaeological inquiry is important at this juncture because it ties in with two major topics in Chapters 16 and 17: human interactions and the archaeology of the intangible.

The word **landscape** defies easy definition, but everyone agrees that landscapes are created by humans. A landscape is like a piece of marble, which changes in response to the sculptor's hands. In archaeological terms, the landscape around Maya Copán or Stone Age Avebury in southern England has changed ever since humans first settled in both areas. Both landscapes have changed radically within the past century, quite apart from preceding centuries and millennia of different uses. Our challenge is to reconstruct the landscape as its various users saw it, what Seamus Caulfield called his "landscape of memory." As archaeologist Stephanie Whittlesey remarked: "Landscapes are the spatial and material manifestation of the relations between humans and their environment" (1998:27). (See also Crumley and Marquardt, 1987.)

Archaeologists study landscapes in many ways: with ecologically based systems approaches, with technology-laden methods that involve GIS and satellite data, and, at the other extreme, in almost literary fashion, describing such phenomena as eighteenth-century gardens or French markets (Figure 15.15) (Crumley, 1987). A new generation of settlement research is turning to landscape geography as a means of studying actual ancient landscapes, where symbolic relationships to the environment as well as ecology play important roles. The term **landscape signature** describes what archaeologists study in this context: "the material imprints left on the earth's surface by particular constellations of human groups" (Crumley and Marquardt, 1987:4).

Figure 15.15
Archaeology of landscape. The reconstruction of William Paca's eighteenth-century garden in Annapolis, Maryland, which reflected landscape perspectives of his day. The outlines of the garden were established by archaeological investigations; the terraces and plantings are conjectural.

Many archaeologists engaged in landscape research think in terms of three dimensions of organizing landscape (Zedeño and others, 1997): (1) physical characteristics and properties; (2) historical transformations over time; and (3) people's physical and symbolic relationships with their environments.

Landscape analysis is a form of historical ecology, where changing landscapes over long time periods serve as cultural records. Landscapes are symbols of cultural stability that preserve enduring meanings over time. As such, they are as much a cultural record as an individual site and an artifact, and, when considered as a way in which people organize their relationship with the social world, a potentially vital source of information on ideology and cultural intangibles (Chapter 17). Much of this research is informed by ethnographic and historical records. The team of archaeologists who carried out a large-scale CRM survey of the Lower Verde Valley in Arizona were charged with the task of studying changing land-use patterns over long periods of time (Whittlesey and others, 1998). To do this, they recorded contemporary and historical landscapes of both Europeans and Native Americans and then worked from there into the remoter past with a theoretical structure based on landscape theory.

Such research is still new in archaeology, but it is thriving as archaeologists become more aware of the close relationships between indigenous peoples and their land. Robert McPherson eloquently described this relationship among the Navajo:

> The earth is not just a series of dramatically poised topographic features that incite the wonder of man or beckon for exploitation, but is rather a living, breathing entity in an inanimate universe. The land with its water, plants, and animals is a spiritual creation put into motion by the gods in their wisdom. These elements are here to help, teach and protect through an integrated system of beliefs that spell out man's relationship to man, nature, and the supernatural. To ignore these teachings is to ignore the purpose of life, the meaning of existence. (1992:11)

When archaeologists study ancient settlements and their now long-vanished landscapes, they would do well to remember those words.

Summary

Settlement archaeology, the study of changing human settlement patterns, is part of the analysis of adaptive interactions between people and their natural and cultural environments.

Settlement patterns are the layout and distribution of human settlements on the landscape. They are determined by many factors, among them the environment, sociocultural practices, and technology, as well as practical considerations, population growth, and social organization.

Bruce Trigger defines three levels of settlement: buildings and activity areas; the arrangement of structures within individual communities; and the distribution of communities across the landscape. The patterns involved in these levels result from factors that differ in quality and degree from the other levels.

Single structures can be studied from the perspective of form and material or from a functional viewpoint. Social and political institutions also affect the design of individual houses.

A community is a maximal group of people that normally resides in face-to-face associations. The layout of communities is much affected by political and social considerations. The archaeologist looks for clusters of settlement attributes that may indicate a grouping of social units.

Site-catchment analysis is a method used to inventory resources within range of prehistoric sites. It is a study of the relationships between technology and available natural resources.

Population estimates of individual communities are very difficult to obtain, even from comprehensive archaeological data; there simply are too many variables that affect the archaeological record.

Population estimates for prehistoric sites have been made using subjective guesswork, mathematical formulas, and sophisticated estimates of the carrying capacity of the land. Such estimates are rarely precise.

Landscape is a cultural construct, and the archaeology of landscape is an attempt, using scientific data, to look at the intangibles that defined the relationship between people and their ever-changing landscapes.

Key Terms

activity area
activity set
carrying capacity
community
distribution of communities

economic catchment area
household unit
landscape
landscape signature
settlement archaeology

settlement pattern
site-catchment analysis
site-exploitation territory

Guide to Further Reading

BUTZER, KARL W. 1982. *Archaeology as Human Ecology.* Cambridge: Cambridge University Press. An authoritative description of basic environmental and spatial concepts in archaeology. Strongly recommended as a starting point.

FLANNERY, KENT V., ed. 1976. *The Early Mesoamerican Village.* Orlando, FL: Academic Press. A modern classic, a study by a team of Michigan archaeologists of settlement patterns in the Valley of Oaxaca. Enlivened by some hypothetical but highly entertaining debates between fictitious archaeologists of different theoretical viewpoints.

HIETALA, H., ed. 1984. *Intersite Spatial Analysis in Archaeology.* Cambridge: Cambridge University Press. Essays on relationships between sites in the archaeological record.

SANDERS, WILLIAM T., JEFFREY R. PARSONS, and ROBERT S. SANTLEY. 1979. *The Basin of Mexico: Ecological Processes in the Evolution of a Civilization.* 2 vols. Orlando, FL: Academic Press. A settlement-ecological study that gives an admirable impression of the state-of-the-art research in this field.

WHITTLESEY, STEPHANIE, and others, eds. 1998. *Vanishing River: Landscapes and Lives of the Lower Verde Valley.* Tucson, AZ: SRI Press. A state-of-the-art, large-scale CRM project concerned with, among other things, changes in land use over time. Highly technical, but clearly written.
Wroxeter web page:
http://www.english-heritage.org.uk/wroxet.htm

CHAPTER 16

Interactions

People of the Past

A youthful boxing match painted on the wall of a house
at Akrotiri, Santorini Island, Greece, c. 1700 B.C.

Egyptian pharaoh, Maya lord, Pueblo farmer, Ice Age forager—all are equal in the face of death and modern archaeological and medical science. Human skeletons, frozen corpses, and mummies are the medical records of the past, one of the few ways we can study actual individuals from ancient societies. Some famous individuals from the past are known to us by name. The Egyptian king Rameses II's mummy reveals his height (5 feet 8 inches [1.4 m]) and that he suffered from arthritis, dental abscesses, and poor circulation (Figure 16.1). Maya Lord Pacal lay in a magnificent stone sarcophagus adorned with his genealogy under the Temple of the Inscriptions at Palenque, Mexico (Chapter 17). The glyphs on the sarcophagus lid reveal the dates of his reign (A.D. 615 to 683). Most individuals from the past survive as nameless corpses or skeletons, members of long-forgotten communities far from royal courts and magnificent temples. For all their anonymity, their bodies yield priceless information about their lives.

This chapter turns from settlements and landscapes to the actual people of the past and their interactions—as men and women, as small groups within diverse societies, as communities trading with one another.

An Individual: Ötzi the Ice Man

Only rarely do archaeologists have the chance to study a well-preserved individual from the remote past. When they do, the full array of modern medical sciences comes into play.

In September 1991, German mountaineers Helmut and Erika Simon made their way around a narrow gully at 10,530 feet (3,210 m) near Hauslabjoch in the Italian Alps (Barfield, 1994; Spindler, 1994). Erika suddenly spotted a brown object projecting from the ice and glacial meltwater in the bottom of the gully. At first she thought it was merely a doll, but she soon identified the skull, back, and shoulders of

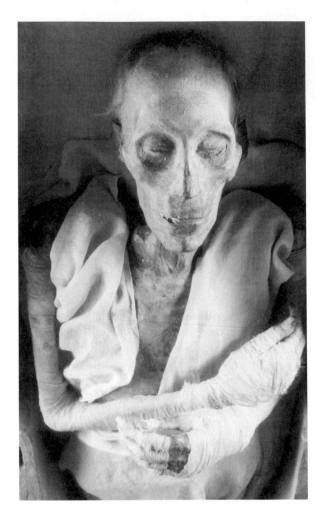

Figure 16.1   The mummy of Egyptian pharaoh Rameses II (1279–1212 B.C.).

a man with his face lying in water. She had stumbled across a casualty of a 5,000-year-old mountain accident.

The first police on the scene also assumed that the man was a climbing victim. A unique archaeological find became corpse number 91/619 on the local coroner's dissection table. Within days, the authorities realized the body was very old and called in archaeologist Konrad Spindler of the University of Innsbruck, Austria. Local archaeologists organized a dig at the site, which was already under 2 feet (0.6 m) of snow. They used a steam blower and a hair dryer to recover parts of a grass cloak, leaves, tufts of grass, and wood fragments. By the end of the excavation, they had established that the man, now nicknamed "Ötzi the Ice Man," had deposited his ax, bow, and backpack on a sheltered ledge. He had lain down on his left side, his head on a boulder, perhaps taking shelter from rapidly deteriorating weather in the small gully. His relaxed limbs suggest that the exhausted man had gone to sleep and frozen to death a few hours later. For 5,000 years, Ötzi's body lay in the gully, which protected his corpse as a glacier flowed overhead.

The Innsbruck University research team called on the latest archaeological and medical science to conserve and study the forty-seven-year-old man. Within a few weeks, five AMS radiocarbon dates dated Ötzi's body to between 3350 and 3150 B.C. Biological anthropologists estimated his height as about 5 feet 2 inches (1.6 m) and took DNA samples, which showed that his genetic makeup was similar to that of late Europeans. Ötzi's stomach was empty, so he was probably weak and hungry at the time of his death. He also suffered from parasites. Smoke inhaled while living in small dwellings with open hearths had blackened his lungs as much as those of a modern-day smoker. Ötzi had endured prolonged malnutrition in his ninth, fifteenth, and six-teenth years. His hands and fingernails were scarred from constant manual labor. He had groups of tattoos—mostly parallel vertical lines—on his lower back, left calf, and right ankle.

On his last day alive, Ötzi wore a leather belt that held up a loin cloth. Sus-penders led from the belt to a pair of fur leggings. He wore an outer coat of alternat-ing stripes of black and brown animal skin and an outer cape of twisted grass, just like those worn in the Alps a century ago. Ötzi's bearskin cap fastened below his chin with a snap. On his feet he wore bearskin and deerskin shoes filled with grass held in place by a string "sock" (Figure 16.2; see also Figure 4.7).

Ötzi was a self-sufficient man on the move. He carried a leather backpack on a wooden frame, a flint dagger, a copper-bladed ax with a wooden handle, and a yew

Figure 16.2 The Ice Man soon after discovery.

longbow and skin quiver filled with fourteen arrows. His equipment included dry fungus and iron pyrite, for lighting fires, and spare arrowheads.

Today, Ötzi lives in a special freezer that replicates glacial conditions. Scientists are still puzzling over the reason why he was so high in the mountains. A few wheat seeds lodged in his fur garments tell us he had recently been in a farming village. Some wild seeds came from a valley south of the Alps, as if he had climbed from the Italian side. Until recently, scientists thought that he had died a peaceful death, perhaps caught out while taking shelter in bad weather. But they have since discovered that he was in a fight before his death. An arrowhead is buried deep in his left shoulder, and there is a dagger wound on one of his hands as he parried a close quarters attack (Gostner and Vigl, 2002). DNA analyses show that he fought with at least four people. Perhaps he killed some of them and escaped their clutches. The injured Ice Man may have fled into the mountains, then succumbed to his wounds.

Ötzi the Ice Man is the earliest European to survive as an identifiable individual, one of the few people of the past to come down to us so well preserved that we know almost more about him than he knew himself—his injuries, his diseases, his parasites. This remarkable discovery comes as somewhat of a jolt, because we come face to face with a once-living person who laughed and cried, worked, played, loved, hated, and interacted with others. Recent advances in molecular biology are adding dimensions to our knowledge of the remote past (see the Doing Archaeology box).

Groups: Ancient Social Organization

Humans interact with one another as individuals and as groups—family, household, community, and so on. They also live in societies with varying degrees of social organization that radically affect their lifeways. Reconstructing ancient social organization is of vital importance to archaeologists. Research into prehistoric social organization is concerned with two basic questions: the size or scale of the society and how it was organized.

Stages of Social Organization

Questions of social scale are important, for they enable the archaeologist to examine not only the complexity of individual societies but also the ways in which they interact with others. Archaeologists look at social organization in prehistory with the aid of general conceptual schemes drawn up by anthropologists. Such schemes are particularly important when examining human cultural evolution. Anthropologist Elman Service, in his classic *Primitive Social Organization* (1971), defined several broad levels of sociocultural evolution that have provided a general framework for tracing the evolution of human social organization from the first simple family structures of the earliest hunter-gatherers to the highly complex state-organized societies of the early civilizations.

All theories of cultural evolution are based on the premise that human societies have changed over long periods of time and that the general trend throughout the past has been toward a greater complexity of human culture and social institutions. Service

Doing Archaeology

DNA and Archaeology

Ever since the identification of the ABO blood system in the early twentieth century, genetics has had a profound effect on the study of human evolutionary history (Sims-Williams, 1998). Modern molecular biological techniques have made it possible to detect and analyze new polymorphic genes (genes present in slightly different forms in different people) that might have medical or anthropological interest. All humans carry in their genes the record of their history. In recent years, studies of mitochondrial DNA (mtDNA) present outside the cell nuclei in small structures called mitochondria have attracted particular attention. Mitochondrial DNA is inherited through the female line and is passed from mothers to offspring virtually unaltered except for rare changes caused by mutation. Large-scale studies of human mtDNA in present-day populations from all parts of the world have shown that there is relatively little mtDNA variation throughout the globe, suggesting that there was a relatively recent branching-out of human populations. The African mtDNAs were the most variable, having had more time to accumulate genetic changes, consistent with the theory that the African human lineages are the oldest ones.

Molecular biologists Rebecca Cann, Mark Stoneking, and Alan Wilson proposed that all modern humanity is descended from a single anatomically modern human population that lived in tropical Africa about 200,000 years ago (R. Cann and others, 1995). This hypothesis has been widely criticized and refined, but it seems increasingly likely that *Homo sapiens sapiens* (ourselves) evolved in Africa, then spread into other parts of the Old World and eventually to the Americas. Mitochondrial DNA research on American populations links them to Siberian ancestors, as one might expect.

The first ancient DNA sequences were reported by Swedish scientist Svaante Pääbo, who extracted and characterized DNA from the skin of a Predynastic Egyptian of about 4000 B.C. in 1985. Since then, DNA has been extracted from bones, teeth, and plant remains using a new technique called polymerase chain reaction (PCR). Pääbo used this technique on a human brain of 3000 B.C. from a hunter-gatherer site at Windover, Florida, and identified an mtDNA strain not previously observed in North America. In recent years, scientists have succeeded in extracting DNA from a Neanderthal bone over 50,000 years old and have shown that these Archaic Europeans were genetically distinct from the modern humans who succeeded them. Mitochondrial DNA analysis of ancient human skeletons from Easter Island in the Pacific has also shown that the ultimate origins of the Easter Islanders lie in Polynesia, for this remote landmass had been colonized from the Society Islands (the Tahiti region) by A.D. 500.

Molecular biology is playing an increasingly important role in the study of ancient human populations and population movements.

divided human societies into bands, tribes, chiefdoms, and states, a classification that has won wide acceptance but is much criticized for its arbitrary rigidity. Because this is a complex and controversial issue, many archaeologists prefer a broader grouping, into which Service's categories fall.

Pre-state societies are societies on a small scale, based on the community, band, or village. They vary widely in their degree of political integration and can be divided into three categories:

1. **Bands** are autonomous and self-sufficient groups that usually consist of only a few families. They are egalitarian, with leadership coming from the experience and personal qualities of particular individuals rather than from political power.
2. **Tribes** are egalitarian, as are bands, but tribes have a greater level of social and cultural complexity. They have developed kin-based mechanisms to accommodate more sedentary living, to redistribute food, and to organize some communal services. Some more complex hunter-gatherer societies, including the Pacific Northwest groups, can be classified as tribal; most were associated with village farming. In egalitarian societies, public opinion plays a major role in decision making.
3. **Chiefdoms** are societies headed by individuals with unusual ritual, political, or entrepreneurial skills and are often hard to distinguish from tribes. Society is still kin-based, but it is more hierarchical, with power concentrated in the hands of powerful kin leaders. Chiefdoms tend to have higher population densities than tribes and to display signs of social ranking, reflected in more elaborate material possessions. The degree of elaboration varies greatly and depends on many factors, including the distribution of population over the landscape. Tahitian chiefs presided over powerful, constantly quarreling chiefdoms, frequently waging ferocious wars against their neighbors. The elaborate Mississippian chiefdoms of the American Midwest and South flourished during the early second millennium A.D. and maintained extensive trade networks and ritual contacts over long distances.

The term *chiefdom* is highly controversial and varies greatly in its definition (Earle, 1991; Yoffee, 1993). Current thinking considers it basically a political unit in which local autonomy at the village or band level has given way to a form of authority in which a paramount chief controls a number of settlements. Chiefdoms organize regional populations, and their form of social stratification and social inequality is less than that of early states, to which they are an alternative trajectory of social development.

State-organized societies operate on a large scale, with centralized social and political organization, class stratification, and intensive agriculture. They have complex political structures, many permanent government institutions, and firm notions of social status (Fagan and Scarre, 2003).

A state-organized society is governed by a full-fledged ruling class whose privileges and powers are supported by a hierarchical secular and religious bureaucracy, at least a rudimentary system of justice, and a system of ranked classes of nobility, warriors, traders, priests, bureaucrats, peasants, and perhaps slaves. The ruler enjoys great wealth and is often regarded as semidivine. Egyptian pharaohs were divine monarchs with absolute powers. Ownership of land and administration of state religion were vested in their hands. The pharaohs ruled by centuries of legal precedent, through an elaborate hierarchy of bureaucrats, among whom the principal officials represented practically hereditary dynasties (Kemp, 1989). Many state societies, such as those of the Maya and the Inca, were organized along rigid lines, with strict classes of nobles, craftsmen, and others. Only the most extraordinary act of military skill or religious devotion would allow a few lucky people entry into the highest classes of society (R. F. Townsend, 1992). All the people knew exactly where they stood in society, even slaves.

State-organized societies were the foundation of the early civilizations of southwestern Asia, China, and the Americas; indeed, they were precursors of the Classical civilizations of Greece and Rome.

Social Ranking

Social inequality has been a feature of human life since the first appearance of farming some 10,000 years ago, and it had been institutionalized in civilization before 3000 B.C. **Social ranking** (social distinctions between individuals, communities, and other units of society) exists in several forms. One form consists of social distinctions between individuals (often reflected in graves), including relationships between individuals, communities, and the wider society, as discerned from the study of architecture, settlement patterns, and distributions of luxury goods such as gold ornaments (Chapter 11). Another form lies in social diversity (ethnicity), social inequality reflected in the relationships between groups within society.

A variety of approaches provide insights into social ranking. Clearly, material evidence for great wealth, such as hoards of buried gold ornaments or fine drinking vessels, suggests some form of ranking that concentrated wealth in a few hands. So do elaborate palaces and public buildings, such as the Mycenaean palaces in Greece or the Sumerian temples in Mesopotamia. As were great Maya ceremonial centers such as Tikal and Palenque in Mesoamerica, many such structures were built as important symbolic statements of political, social, and religious power. Tikal, for example, is a symbolic model of the Maya spiritual world, complete with sacred mountains, trees, and caves (Figure 15.2). Perhaps the most elaborate example of such a structure is the Khmer temple at Angkor Wat, Cambodia, a stunning depiction of the Buddhist world built at enormous expense at the behest of divine kings over a forty-year period about A.D. 1400 (Figure 16.3).

Many such monuments—for example, the Temple of the Sun God Amun at Karnak, Egypt—were adorned with paintings and statues of great leaders (in this case, pharaohs), often in the presence of the gods. Accompanying hieroglyphs and small details of royal costume provide constant, symbolic reminders of royal power and divinely given authority.

Evidence of social ranking can sometimes be inferred from buildings and community layout. Teotihuacán shows every sign of having been an elaborately planned city, with special precincts for markets and craftspeople and the houses of the leading priests and nobles near the Street of the Dead, which bisected the city (Figure 15.12). In such instances, it is easy enough to identify the houses belonging to each class in the society, both by their architecture and by the distinctive artifacts found in them (Figure 16.4).

The Archaeology of Death

Human burials are the most important source of information about prehistoric social organization and ranking (J. A. Brown, 1971). The actual disposal of the corpse is really a minimal part of the sequence of mortuary practice in a society. Funerary rites are a ritual of passage and are usually reflected not only in the position of the body in

Figure 16.3   Angkor Wat, Cambodia, a symbolic depiction of the Buddhist cosmos. One approaches Angkor through an entrance gallery with a tower by a paved causeway that is 500 feet (150 m) long and is flanked with balustrades adorned with multiheaded snakes.

Figure 16.4   Mohenjodaro, a Harappan city of the second millennium B.C. The widest streets were only about 30 feet (9 m) wide, lined by drab houses for commoners, which presented blind brick façades to the street.

Figure 16.5   The Pyramids of Giza, Egypt.

the grave but also in the ornaments and grave furniture that accompany it. The contents of a grave, whether spectacular or extremely simple, are useful barometers of social ranking. The Egyptian pharaoh Khufu expended vast resources on building his pyramid and mortuary temple at Giza (Figure 16.5). Thousands of laborers moved more than 2.3 million limestone blocks weighing between 1.5 and 2.5 tons to build his pyramid alone during his twenty-three-year reign.

The Egyptian pyramids were built by a highly centralized state over a period of little more than a century, at great expense of labor, food, and materials. Then, suddenly, these same resources were diverted to other works and to the provinces, as if there had been major changes in the nature of Egyptian society and government (Lerner, 1997). Archaeologists are still trying to puzzle out the social and political implications of this shift.

Sometimes the differing status of burials may indicate that a society was rigidly ranked. When Leonard Woolley excavated the Early Dynastic royal burials of Ur-of-the-Chaldees in Mesopotamia, he found a great cemetery containing 1,850 graves (Woolley, 1943). Sixteen of them stood out by virtue of their remarkable grave furniture. The royal tombs were sunk into the earlier levels of the mound, and a sepulcher consisting of several rooms was erected in the middle of a huge pit. The royal corpses were decked out in a cascade of gold and semiprecious stone ornaments; gold and silver ornaments were placed next to the biers; and several attendants had been slaughtered to accompany the dead. Once the royal sepulcher was closed, the entire court filed into the grave pit, drank poison, and lay down to die in correct order of protocol (Figure 16.6). Woolley was able to identify the different rankings of the courtiers from their ornaments. In contrast to all this luxury, the average person was buried in a matting roll or a humble coffin.

In burials like this, pharaohs' graves, and even in burials of Iron Age chieftains in Europe, the ranking of society is obvious. But what can we learn about less

Figure 16.6   Hypothetical reconstruction of the Ur funeral, by Leonard Woolley. (© Copyright The British Museum)

affluent societies, in which differences in rank and social status are often more muted? It is very important for archaeologists to be able to recognize such inequalities, for the degree of social ranking is often a measure of the size and complexity of a society. Very often, too, rank appears when centuries-old ties of kin and family are being replaced by rulers who preside over much more elaborate social systems. Brown (1981) pointed out that such variables as age, sex, personal ability, personality, and even circumstances of death can affect the way in which one is buried. The evidence for ranking comes not only from grave furniture and insignia of rank deposited with the deceased but also from the positions of graves in a settlement or cemetery and even from symbolic distinctions that are hard to find in the archaeological record (O'Shea, 1984) (see the Discovery box). In general, however, the greater and more secure a ruler's authority becomes, the more effort and wealth are expended on burial. This lavishness may also extend to immediate relatives and friends (R. Chapman and others, 1981).

The Mississippian ceremonial center at Moundville, Alabama, was in its heyday in the thirteenth and fourteenth centuries A.D. More than twenty mounds topped by temples and elite residences lay inside a wooden palisade covering 370 acres (150 ha) on the banks of the Black Warrior River. More than 3,000 burials have been excavated at Moundville. Archaeologist Chris Peebles (1987) combined a pottery seriation of vessels found with a sample of the burials with a cluster analysis of more than 2,000 graves as a means of grouping them by social rank. Peebles found that the highest-ranking people were buried in or near the earthen mounds with elaborate

Discovery

The Nubian Kings of Kerma, Sudan

Harvard University's George Reisner (1867–1942) learned his archaeology with the famed British Egyptologist Flinders Petrie before World War I. As did his mentor, he believed in the importance of even the smallest artifacts. He was one of the first archaeologists to excavate in ancient Egyptian Nubia, now part of the Sudan. In 1913, he excavated a series of royal burial mounds at Kerma, the capital of a once-powerful African state in the early second millennium B.C.

The kings lived in considerable state and went to their deaths in great splendor. Reisner described royal burial mounds with large numbers of small chambers that contained many sacrificial victims. Using the stains on the room floors, Reisner estimated that at least four hundred people had been killed alongside one dead ruler, all of them, including members of his immediate family, on the same day. Reisner theorized that the victims had entered the small chambers, had lain down in a position of rest, and had then been buried alive. Many of the bodies lay in attitudes that communicated fear, resignation, and the kinds of convulsions resulting from death by slow suffocation. The adults lay mainly in restful positions, but some young females had crawled under beds and other furniture, there to perish slowly in stagnant air pockets. Some of the dead had held their head in their hands or put it between their thighs. Some clasped one another. Reisner argued that the act of sacrifice was a gesture of loyalty, of comfort and continuity that assured the continuation of a royal life in eternity.

Reisner (1923) wrote a vivid account of the ululation and chanting as the funeral procession wended its way to the mound (Figure 16.7). The royal corpse was laid in its chamber, the fine grave offerings laid out in order as the ruler's wives and attendants took their places in the chambers, "perhaps still with shrill cries or speaking only such words as the selection of their places required." Then, at a signal, the waiting crowd cast baskets of sand into the open chambers and onto the still, but still-living, victims on the floors. As the sand rose in the mound, there was a "rustle of fear" that passed through the dying as hundreds of baskets masked them from view. The crowd now feasted on the hundreds of cattle slaughtered in honor of the dead ruler, butchering the beasts and cooking the meat to the west of the tumulus and placing the skulls in a great crescent on the south side of the mound. Reisner's imaginative reconstruction was based on acute observation and careful excavations.

grave furniture, including copper artifacts. A second group had fewer grave goods and were not buried in mounds, and the lowest-ranking people were buried at the edge of the site with almost no grave furniture (Peebles, 1987). Peebles also developed a social hierarchy for Moundville that was headed by seven burials, all of them males (Figure 16.8).

Studying ancient social organization will never be easy in the absence of written or oral records, but the archaeology of death provides a fruitful avenue of inquiry.

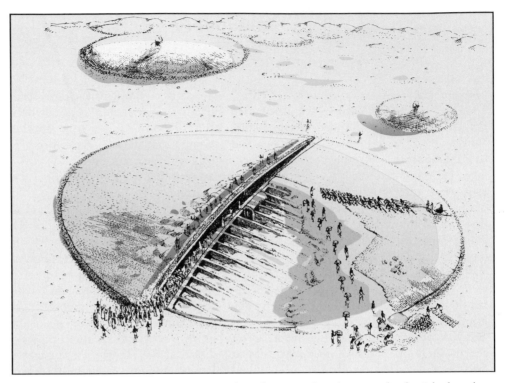

Figure 16.7   A royal tomb at Kerma. People rush to complete the mound as burial takes place.

Gender: Men and Women

Archaeologists have long studied people and households, but only recently have they turned their attention to the complex issue of gender and gender relations, a promising avenue of new research (Scott, 1994). Over the past few decades, the social sciences and the study of history have been transformed by feminist scholarship, but archaeology has lagged behind—although such thought has figured in interpretations of such topics as the origins of the sexual division of labor and changing gender relations. Archaeologists are now framing gender-related questions, taking advantage of an emerging body of feminist theory in other disciplines (Conkey and Gero, 1997; Gero and Conkey, 1991; Nelson, 1997).

Gender is not the same as sex, which refers to the biological male or female. Gender is socially and culturally constructed, so it is a vital part of human social relations and a central issue in the study of ancient human societies.

The expression of gender varies, and has always varied, from society to society and through time. Some archaeologists, such as Margaret Conkey and Joan Gero (1997), write of "engendering archaeology," an attempt to reclaim men and women from the past in nonsexist ways. This goes much farther than merely demonstrating that pots were made by women and stone projectile points by men or trying to identify women's activities in the archaeological record. The **archaeology of gender** deals

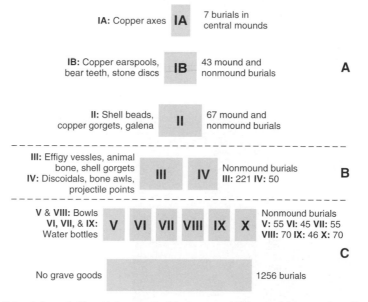

IA: Copper axes | IA | 7 burials in central mounds

IB: Copper earspools, bear teeth, stone discs | IB | 43 mound and nonmound burials — **A**

II: Shell beads, copper gorgets, galena | II | 67 mound and nonmound burials

III: Effigy vessles, animal bone, shell gorgets
IV: Discoidals, bone awls, projectile points | III | IV | Nonmound burials III: 221 IV: 50 — **B**

V & VIII: Bowls
VI, VII, & IX: Water bottles | V | VI | VII | VIII | IX | X | Nonmound burials V: 55 VI: 45 VII: 55 VIII: 70 IX: 46 X: 70 — **C**

No grave goods | 1256 burials

Figure 16.8 Moundville, Alabama. Peebles's pyramidlike social hierarchy of Moundville burials based on the analysis of more than two thousand graves. Artifacts listed against individual skeletons are grave goods found with them.

with the ideology of gender, with roles and gender relations—the ways in which gender intersects with all aspects of human social life. How were roles and social relationships constructed? What contributions did men and women make to ancient societies? An **engendered archaeology** uses a wide diversity of archaeological methods and approaches to find how out gender "worked" in ancient societies, to unravel its cultural meanings.

Grinding Grain at Abu Hureyra, Syria

Farmers' bones reveal telling secrets about male and female roles. The Abu Hureyra farming village in Syria is the earliest known agricultural settlement in the world (Moore, 2000). In about 10,000 B.C., the inhabitants switched from hunting and foraging to growing cereal crops. A thousand years later, they founded a close-knit community of rectangular, one-story mud-brick houses separated by narrow alleyways and courtyards set in the midst of their fields. For hours on end, the Abu Hureyra women would labor on their knees, grinding grain for the evening meal, as the monotonous scraping sound of grinding corn echoed through the settlement. Thanks to some exciting detective work by biological anthropologist Theya Molleson (1989), we can be certain that women rather than men ground grain.

Molleson is an expert on human anatomy and pathological conditions in bones caused by stress and disease. She studied the many skeletons found under the Abu Hureyra houses and found that the people were remarkably healthy, except for bone deformities caused by arduous and repetitive tasks. Then she noticed that some adolescents had enlarged portions on their neck vertebrae, the result of carrying heavy loads. She also identified many knee bones with bone extensions on their articular surfaces, the result of repeated kneeling for long periods of time. Many people also had stressed lower back vertebrae, enlarged toe joints, and gross arthritic conditions of the big toe (Figure 16.9).

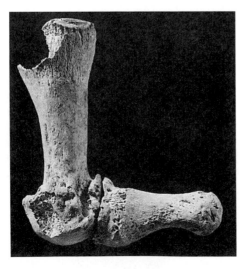

Figure 16.9   A woman's deformed toe bones from Abu Hureyra, Syria.

Molleson was puzzled by these deformities, until one of her colleagues visited Egypt and noticed that kneeling supplicants on the walls of ancient temples always had their toes curled forward. The only activity at Abu Hureyra that could produce the same effect was kneeling in front of the stone grinding querns found set into the house floors. Intrigued, Molleson now reconstructed the grinding process. The grinder put grain on the quern and gripped the grinding stone with both hands. He or she then knelt with the toes bent, pushing the stone forward, arms turning inward as the stone reached the end of the quern. At the end of the stroke, the upper body was almost parallel to the floor. Repeated every day, such back-and-fro movement would cause backbone damage identical to that on the skeletons, would place bending stress on the knee and hip joints, and would eventually cause arthritic conditions in the toes—all conditions found in the Abu Hureyra bones.

Next, Molleson asked who had done the grinding. She measured the first metatarsal bone of the foot. The larger male bones showed little wear, whereas the shorter women's metatarsals displayed signs of heavy wear. Molleson is virtually certain that women and girls suffered repetitive-stress injuries because they shouldered the laborious task of preparing food. This meticulous research is one of the few instances in which we have clear archaeological evidence for the division of labor between men and women in the past.

Engendered Research

To engender the past means to focus not only on major material achievements such as metallurgy or potmaking, or on ancient environments, but also on interpersonal relations and the social dynamics of everyday activity. These are the activities that take up most of people's daily lives—hunting, gardening, preparing meals, building houses, and so on. But gender also has an effect on trade, craft specialization, state formation, religion, and ritual—to mention only a few major human activities.

Gender research in archaeology is concerned not just with women but also with people as individuals and with their contributions to society, as the following examples show.

Maya Figurines, Honduras

Art styles and representations were one powerful way in which struggles for political power were worked out in many ancient societies. Rosemary Joyce (1993) uncovered a pair of cached Maya figurines in the central platform of a small residential group at the Terminal Classic Maya site of Cerro Palenque, Honduras. The two finely made figurines had been buried upright in small pits east and west of an exotic stone slab. The eastern figurine was a male wearing a bird-feather costume and a helmet and carrying a conch shell trumpet. The western figure was a woman in an ankle-length skirt. Her breasts were bare, her left hand was raised, and she balanced a necked, handled jar on her head. Joyce believes that the pair represent a duality of interdependent household members, a symbolic placement on either side of a family shrine. She studied other figurines in Classic Maya and lower Central American societies, especially those buried under house floors, identifying a "significant thematic dichotomy associated with gender," the women often represented as mothers and those responsible for providing food.

In monumental architecture, too, ritual is enacted through the shared actions of men and women, but the unique gestures of each imply different roles. Gender imagery in such art and in painted ceramic vessels associates women with the transformation of raw material (clay, textiles) into finished artifacts, with the labor of grinding grain and preparing food. Classic Maya public art showed elite men and women collaborating in ritual activities. However, in highly stratified Maya society, ceramic images challenged any assumptions that the elite exercised completely centralized control; their depictions of men and women reminded everyone that extended households could be economically independent of such control. Joyce's researches unfolded in an area outside the Maya heartland, where the integrity of the household was not a political issue. Thus, Joyce argues, the status of women, as shown in her Cerro Palenque figurines, was more stable than in a more stratified society where the traditional values of the family and women's roles as food producers were downplayed in the face of powerful ritual messages.

Aztec Weaving, Mexico

"The good middle-aged woman [is] a skilled weaver, a weaver of designs, an artisan, a good cook, a preparer of good food." Thus did Franciscan friar Bernardino de Sahagun's Aztec informants describe a noblewoman's role in Mexican civilization before the Spanish Conquest (Figure 16.10). But this description is grossly misleading and simplistic, for it ignores the links between weaving, cooking, and child rearing (to mention only a few of women's tasks) and the wider society in which the women lived (Brumfiel, 1991). For instance, the population of the Valley of Mexico rose tenfold during the four centuries before the conquest, a striking testimony to the success of the Aztec household economy. Women wove textiles and the capes that were the badges of social status in Aztec society. Their woven products were vital to the enormous tribute system on which Aztec civilization depended. Cotton mantles even served as a form of currency.

Cloth was a primary way of organizing the ebb and flow of goods and services that sustained the state. Elizabeth Brumfiel uses archaeological evidence to refine this general picture. She shows that the women living in the Aztec capital, Tenochtitlán, turned away from weaving to cultivation of swamp gardens and the salting of fish, while weaving to satisfy tribute needs was still the dominant activity at a distance from the city. Here the burden of tribute production fell on female heads. In the city, men and women often labored away from home on food production and other activities, a shift also reflected in a change from wet foods such as stews to tortillas and other dried foods that were easily carried to a work site elsewhere.

Brumfiel shows that the Aztec household and the roles of women were much more varied than those attributed to them by Sahagun's informants. Furthermore, the skills of cooking and weaving were important political tools, ways of maintaining social and political control. Thus, she argues, the idealization of these skills in both Aztec folklore and schooling developed because women were makers of both valuable goods and

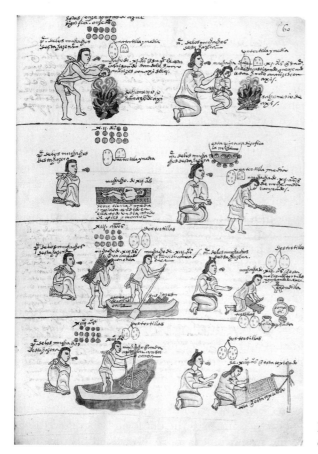

Figure 16.10   An Aztec woman teaches her daughter how to weave.

of people. It was they who ensured the continuity of Aztec kin groups. The simplistic view of Aztec life of Sahagun's informants reflected contemporary ideology but masked the dynamic and highly adaptive role that women played in this remarkable civilization.

Sausa Gender Relations, Peru

The engendering of archaeology is an exciting development, one that will transform our interpretations of human prehistory beyond recognition in coming years. At present, however, gender studies are still in their infancy and are based, for the most part, on extrapolations from ethnoarchaeological and ethnological data. This kind of direct historical approach can be useful. For example, it can be argued that it was women, with their detailed knowledge of botany derived from thousands of years of plant foraging, who first deliberately cultivated native seeds such as sunflowers and sumpweed in eastern North America at least three thousand years ago (Watson and Kennedy, 1991).

In one study, Christine Hastorf (1992) used food remains to study changing gender relations in pre-Hispanic Sausa society in the Andes. The Sausa are maize and potato farmers who live in highland Peru's northern Mantaro Valley. Before the Inca took control in about A.D. 1460, the Sausa lived in local population groups of several thousand people. Their conquerors, anxious to increase maize production, dispersed them into small village settlements. Hastorf was interested in the changing social dynamics resulting from the Inca conquest. How did women's social position change as a result of the new conditions? She approached this fundamental question not by marshaling subjective evidence but by using two different approaches: the distribution of food remains in excavated settlements compared with those in modern house compounds and dietary evidence obtained by stable isotope analyses of male and female skeletons from ancient Sausa villages.

Hastorf, an expert on native plants, believes that modern studies of Sausa houses show a relationship between the distribution of plant remains in dwellings and compounds and the behavior of men and women in those households. In modern Andean households, women are responsible for food preparation and storage. Moreover, in households with male heads, she found the most diverse plant forms in kitchen areas and fewer crop seeds elsewhere in the compound where other activities took place. In contrast, a household with a female head had concentrations of crop seeds not only in the kitchen area but also on the patio, as if there were different constraints acting on preparation and food consumption.

Next, Hastorf plotted the distribution of crop seeds in pre-Hispanic compounds. The pre-Inca structures date from a time when maize was less common and of great sacred value. The inhabitants of every dwelling used and consumed a wide range of plant foods, including potatoes and many legumes. Maize occurred mostly in patio areas. It was here, Hastorf argues, that such communal activities as making beer, a commodity that was a vital part of ritual, social, and political meetings, took place. A later, Inca-period compound yielded fewer potatoes and much more maize. Here the processing of corn was more concentrated, with little burning of corn, as if more of it were consumed as beer. Hastorf wonders if the dense and restricted distribution of maize in the later compound might reflect more intensified processing of corn by women. They were now living under Inca policies that sought a constant rise in maize production, regular taxation in the form of labor and produce, and, therefore, more restricted, intensified roles for women in support of male activities.

Hastorf now turned her attention to male and female skeletons found in the compounds. She studied the stable isotopes in bone collagen extracted from Sausa skeletons. She found that pre-Inca diets were the same for men and women, mainly consisting of quinoa and tubers, with some maize. These similar values suggest that beer was shared between men and women. Then the Inca entered Sausa society. The twenty-one skeletons (twelve males, nine females) from these centuries reveal a higher consumption of maize, but half the male diets were much richer in maize than were those of the women. Hastorf believes that this difference reflects changed social conditions under Inca rule. The women were processing much more maize into beer, which was consumed not by everyone but by a relatively small proportion of the males in the community. Furthermore, most men were eating more meat than were women.

The dietary differences reflect a changed political climate in which the Sausa, once small groups, were now incorporated into a larger political sphere that depended on men becoming involved in far more gatherings, rituals, and obligatory tasks, when beer was consumed. The women worked harder, but their position outside the home was more restricted under the Inca regime. The Inca state depended on the obligatory

Doing Archaeology

Engendered Research at Opovo, Yugoslavia

A small farming village lies in now-drained marshlands north of the Danube River at Opovo in what was once Yugoslavia. A late Neolithic hamlet of rectangular, thatched houses of the Vinca culture flourished in this far-from-favorable agricultural environment between 4400 and 4000 B.C. Traditional interpretations of the site stated that all the dwellings had been destroyed by fire at the end of the occupation. But Ruth Tringham and her Yugoslav colleagues have changed the focus of their investigations from a communitywide study to research into individual dwellings and their fate. They have discovered that the houses had been, almost certainly, burnt down individually at the end of what Tringham calls "the household cycle" (Tringham, 1994). Instead of merely investigating the foundations of the dwellings under the collapsed fire debris, they dissected the rubble and discovered that each fire was confined to an individual house. The entire research project was oriented toward individual households, the resources within them, and the gender relationships therein.

Tringham originally used a processualist approach in excavating Opovo, but her feminist interpretations assume that every aspect of material culture was endowed with some kind of significance for the original occupants. She makes them social actors with individual biographies, genders, and personalities. Each of these actors viewed the place she studied

differently, with perspectives colored by age, gender, power, and life history. So her challenge was to present these multiple perceptions at different scales. She did so by studying the houses as having life histories in order to write a biography of individual places.

Under more traditional interpretations, Tringham would have explained the founding of Opovo as part of a process of dispersal of settlement aimed at maintaining kin-based domestic groups as units of social and economic organization. This tiny hamlet of no more than ten households had only a marginal part to play in this larger process. In her feminist interpretation, she argues that the founding of this village in a marginal farming area where hunting red deer had always been important had major implications for the division of labor within the community. Each household had had a different history of social relations with its neighbors, with kin in other communities. Thus, to write the history of Opovo is to write an intertwined biography of individual households and their members, using an interplay between different levels of archaeological analysis, everything from entire regions to individual lives. Tringham approaches this task by using data collected using a processualist approach, then combining these data and her field notes on the excavation of an individual house with what she calls "plausible scenarios" developed from the data.

mit'a tax, a service tax levied on male household heads. The most common *mit'a* tasks were agriculture and military service, performed by men, who were fed "meat and maize and cornbeer." *Mit'a* tasks separated men and women physically, politically, and symbolically. Archaeological evidence, gathered from two sources, tends to confirm this conclusion, documents the changes in women's position in Sausa society, and makes men and women visible in the archaeological record (for another example, from Europe, see the Doing Archaeology box).

Tringham's Opovo research uses narratives and visual imagery to introduce the "actors," some of the men and women who lived in this particular house over several generations. As the scenario unfolds, they interact with one other, as individuals, as young and old, as men and women, as they move within and without a dwelling that was burned, its well then filled with still-warm rubble. This is archaeology conducted not at a macroscale, as most processual investigations are, but at a microlevel, where the archaeologist interprets domestic social acts within single dwellings, where individuals were actors. This research, and much other feminist archaeology, is a logical extension of sound approaches that have reconstructed general trends, structures, and patterns of the archaeological record. The archaeologist acts as an active mediator of the remote past in a new generation of researches, which promise to be controversial, provocative, and fascinating.

The engendering of archaeology is long overdue and will affect not only basic research but also the ways in which we write about the past. As the Hastorf example shows, the research that studies gender will be a marriage of new approaches, often involving what Tringham (1994) calls "interpretative dialectical interplay between material remains, comparative historical or ethnographic observation, and imagined actors" with high-tech science and well-established methods of archaeological research. This approach will give us the potential to go far beyond the material, to probe the subjective and the gender-driven, even, as Hastorf shows, the ways in which women (and men, for that matter) adapt to changing circumstances. This kind of meticulous, incredibly detailed research, with its concern for the changing dynamics of ancient society, offers great promise for the future.

Ethnicity and Inequality

For the most part, archaeologists have focused their attention on two broad topics. Culture historians have described long-lasting cultural traditions in many parts of the world, and culture ecologists and advocates of processual archaeology have studied the ever-changing relationships between human societies and their natural environments. There has also been a major preoccupation with "origins"—the first Americans, the first farmers, the origins of civilization, and so on (Hodder, 1999). In recent years, however, an increasing number of scholars have used archaeology's unique perspective to study ethnic diversity and what is sometimes called the **archaeology of inequality:** the ways in which people have exercised economic and social power over others (McGuire and Paynter, 1991).

This focus is a reaction against approaches that minimize the importance of social power and assume that ancient societies enjoyed a high degree of cultural uniformity. In fact, many archaeological studies have shown that culture change can occur very rapidly, at times at a speed that is well within the limits of human memory, as it does in our society (Sanders and others, 1979). Nor should one minimize the importance of social power in the appearance of early states, such as those of the Maya or Aztecs (R. F. Townsend, 1992). Despite a few studies that are now focusing on the importance of social ranking and the political power of kings and nobles, almost no archaeologists have studied the phenomenon of resistance to overwhelming social and political power and the archaeology of ethnic minorities (Jones, 1997).

Ideologies of Domination

Elites have used many tactics to exercise power over others, everything from gentle persuasion to divine kingship, precedent, economic monopolies, and naked force. Perhaps most important of all are the **ideologies of domination.** The ancient Maya lords built great ceremonial centers with towering pyramids and vast plazas that were symbolic models of the sacred landscape, of the Maya universe. Their pyramids were sacred mountains, the sites of sacred openings that were the threshold to the spiritual world of the ancestors. It was here that the ruler went into a shamanistic trance, communicating with the gods and ancestors in lavish public ceremonies. Everything validated the complex relationship between the living and the dead and between the ruler and the commoner, displayed in lavish, pointed metaphors that confirmed the divine power of the supreme lords (Schele and Friedel, 1990) (see also Chapter 17).

Mark Leone and his colleagues of the Historical Annapolis Foundation have studied the theories of power that lay behind the planning of two major colonial settlements: Annapolis and nearby St. Mary's City in Maryland (Leone and Hurry, 1998). They argue that baroque principles of urban design were used at both locations. St. Mary's City was once thought to have been a haphazard settlement, when, in fact, archaeology has shown that the principal, brick-built buildings, like the Jesuit chapel, prison, and state house, were placed at nodes of the street system. The baroque system used lines of sight to direct people's eyes to points of reference in space that represented monarchy and social hierarchy. Maryland society was new, with a hierarchy of businessmen and officials who used such principles of urban planning to foster their social status.

Likewise, in Annapolis, in 1696–1710, Governor Francis Nicholson redesigned the original Anne Arundel Town, a settlement of some 200 people, with a master plan of two circles, with streets radiating from them, and a large square, all placed on a series of hills and ridges. The present-day state house and circle are still the focus of Annapolis. Archaeological excavations, GIS, and AutoCad plots have shown that the circle was, in fact, egg-shaped, an artifice necessary to integrate sloped hillsides and hilltops into an overall design. At the same time, Nicholson used diverging sides for the radiating streets so as to give someone approaching the state house the optical illusion that it was larger and closer, adding to the impression of power. This baroque town planning may be connected to the landscape architecture of terraced gardens used by prominent Annapolis residents in later decades (Figure 15.15).

Artifacts, Social Inequality, and Resistance

Political and social power are extremely heterogeneous phenomena that are exercised in many forms. From the archaeologist's point of view, it is fascinating that one can use material objects such as pottery to study how people negotiated their social positions and resisted the submergence of their own culture (Beaudry and others, 1991; Orser, 2004). Artifacts offer a unique way of examining the history of the many communities that kept no written records but expressed their diverse feelings and cultures through the specific artifacts and commodities that they purchased and used.

Fascinating studies of people's resistance to the submerging of their culture are coming from the American South, where the earliest Africans to reach North America brought their own notions of religion, ritual, and supernatural power to their new homes. "The Guinea negroes had sometimes a small inclosure for their god house," wrote one Florida plantation owner in 1839 (L. Ferguson, 1992:65). They even maintained small shrines in their living quarters. Historical records rarely refer to such shrines, but archaeologists have found blue beads and other charms at many slave sites in the North American Southeast. At the Garrison and Kingsmill plantations in Maryland and Virginia, engraved pewter spoons bear motifs remarkably similar to those executed by African Americans living in Suriname in South America at the same date. Bakongo-style marks like those made in Central Africa have come from bowls found in other southern sites (L. Ferguson, 1992; Kelso, 1984). Everything points to people who arrived in North America with cultural values and a worldview radically different from those of their masters.

Slave plantations were part of complex networks that linked planters to other planters, planters to slaves, and slaves to slaves on other plantations. It is significant that slaves within these harsh, oppressive, and racist environments were able to maintain important elements of their own culture. Despite such conditions, African Americans maintained their own beliefs and culture, which they melded over the generations with new ideas and material innovations from their new environment. They believed that their culture, their way of living—everything from cuisine to belief systems—was the best way. African spiritual beliefs in all their variety were highly flexible and were often responses to outside influences, whether political, religious, or economic. Thus, existing spiritual beliefs adapted readily to the new American environment, adopting new artifacts or modifying existing ones over the generations. For example, archaeologists working at Thomas Jefferson's Monticello estate have recovered crystals, pierced coins, and other ritual artifacts from Mulberry Row, where his slaves resided.

Since 1990, Mark Leone and the Archaeology in Annapolis project have excavated seven major sites where African Americans lived, dating from the eighteenth to twentieth centuries (Leone, Fry, and Ruppel, 2001). They have found caches of artifacts placed under chimney bases or hearths, in the northeast corners of rooms, and around doorways. These are ritual bundles of pins, nails, perforated discs like buttons, coins or shells, rings, potsherds, pebbles, glass fragments and crystals. Using historical literature and ethnographic research from West Africa, the researchers were able to decipher some of the meanings and associations of the caches, which were sometimes arranged on X-shaped axes—*cosmograms,* or circles of life. Autobiographies of former slaves, collected during the Great Depression, produced firsthand accounts of religious practices. The caches included protective charms and artifacts used in what has been called a "sacred pharmacopia." They are believed to be part of a religious practice known as Hoodoo, sometimes called *conjure.* Hoodoo acts on the principle that spirits exist, and that they exist to be used—to cure disease, to keep violent masters at bay, to draw out malevolent spirits, and protect. The spirit was in the ritual bundle and one had to behave as the bundle directed. The artifacts in the bundle provided a means to enter and exit a user's body. Hoodoo was a powerful way to resist against a hostile world.

Traditional practitioners operated in a hostile environment, so they were careful to disguise their activities. At the Levi Jordan cotton and sugar plantation in southern Texas, archaeologists Kenneth Brown and Doreen Cooper excavated a cabin occupied by an African American healer-magician. The cabin yielded animal bones, iron spikes, and other artifacts that were part of the paraphernalia of a traditional West African healer. But the same simple artifacts had other uses, too, so much so that an outside observer would not suspect that their owner was engaged in traditional medicine (K. Brown, 1995). To the African American workers on the plantation, the same objects had an entirely different symbolic meaning that was not revealed to outsiders. For this reason, none of the healer's tools-in-trade bore any telltale symbolic decoration that might reveal their true purposes.

African archaeologists and historians have pointed out that the sheer diversity of West African cultures makes it foolhardy to make direct comparisons between African American and African artifacts. But the survival of African beliefs and culture in African American society is well documented as a general phenomenon and has persisted into recent times. All these finds suggest that African Americans maintained their own distinctive culture in the face of repressive slavery. They were disenfranchised from white people in their own villages and slave quarters, to the point that their masters and mistresses may well have been more like parts of their environment than key players in their social lives (Orser, 2004). In South Carolina and Georgia, slaves even spoke a distinctive African American language. Children growing up in this culture used material objects such as earthen bowls that were made by members of this culture and heard stories of magic and religious chants that were important ways of establishing African American identity, maintaining ideological power, and molding values. Although many slaves may not have resisted their inferior, white-bestowed social status on a day-to-day basis, most did ignore European American culture in favor of their own and rejected an ideology that rationalized their enslavement.

Historical archaeologist Leland Ferguson (1992) has documented this resistance in South Carolina, where, in 1740, blacks outnumbered whites by almost 2 to 1, and one-half of that majority was African-born. Here, as elsewhere along the South Atlantic coast, African women arrived with a knowledge of potmaking that they used to fashion domestic wares in their new homes. Their distinctive unglazed earthenware products are found in slave quarters, on plantations, and in cities (Figure 16.11). Once considered Native American pots that had been traded to slaves, these wares were actually the products of complex demographic and cultural forces that resulted from interactions between blacks and whites and between both of those groups and Native Americans. Ferguson undertook a study of this "Colono Ware" from the Southeast, focusing on complete vessels recovered from all manner of locations, including slave quarters, free Native American villages, plantations, and missions. He found that what he calls the "container environment" of South Carolina consisted of wood, basketry, and earthenware manufactures broadly similar to those of the slaves' African homeland. Not only that, but the bowls and other vessels mirrored basic

Figure 16.11   Colono Ware.

eating habits in Africa, for they were used for preparing and serving carbohydrate por-
ridges with a vegetable or meat relish on the side.

Ferguson believes that African American eating habits were quite similar to those
of the peoples of West Africa and were radically different from those of the European
Americans around them. Colono Ware is remarkably similar over a large area, made by
people living in an ethnic environment where reciprocal relationships with one another
were of vital importance and where there were strong ties to ancestral African culture.
It was, Ferguson says, an unconscious resistance to slavery and the plantation system.
The development of southern culture, he concludes, was a long process of quasipoliti-
cal negotiation. It is exciting that one can use archaeology to look at the early stages of
this complex process of negotiation from both sides (see also Leone and Fry, 1999).

Another fascinating chronicle of ethnic resistance comes from an archaeological
investigation of the route taken by a small group of Northern Cheyenne when they
broke out of Fort Robinson, Nebraska, on January 9, 1879. They fought a running
battle with the garrison, across the White River, up some bluffs, and into open country, where it took the military eleven days to capture them (McDonald and others,
1991). This much is beyond controversy, but the route that the Cheyenne took out of
the river valley is disputed. According to military accounts, the escaping party moved
up an exposed sandstone ridge to reach the bluffs. This exposed route was illogical, indeed foolhardy, for there was a full moon. Cheyenne oral traditions insist on another
route to the bluffs through a well-protected drainage that would have offered excellent
cover from pursuing riflemen.

Archaeologists from the University of South Dakota Archaeology Laboratory investigated the escape routes with the collaboration of local Cheyenne representatives.
They used random shovel testing and metal detectors to search for spent bullets in
three areas: two drainages and the exposed ridge mentioned in military accounts. The
survey recovered no bullets from the exposed ridge but did find them in the drainages,
thereby confirming the oral account of the Cheyenne Outbreak. This may seem like a
footnote to modern history, but it is important to remember that the Outbreak has

Site

War Casualties at Thebes, Egypt

Few tales of ordinary people are as vivid as that told by a remarkable discovery made by Egyptologist Herbert Winlock (1942) in a sepulcher close to the tomb of the Middle Kingdom pharaoh Mentuhotep (2061–2010 B.C.) at Thebes in 1911. Sixty soldiers killed in battle were stacked in the tomb. They were dressed in linen shrouds, and their dried-out bodies were so well preserved that they began to decay when removed from the tomb. Winlock used biological and archaeological data to reconstruct their last battle. All the soldiers were young men in the prime of life, each with a thick mop of hair bobbed off square at the nape of the neck. All had perished in an attack on a fort, for their wounds had come from arrows shot from above or from crushing blows from stones thrown down from a fortification. Pictures from the time show attackers sheltering under thin shields as they attempt to breach the defenses under a rain of missiles.

In this case, the fire was too fierce, so the men ran out of range. Some of them were overtaken by a shower of arrows. At least one was hit in the back with an arrow that came out on the other side of his chest. He pitched forward. The slender reed shaft broke off as he fell and bled to death. The defenders now sallied forth and mercilessly clubbed at least a dozen wounded men to death with heavy blows. Then, waiting vultures and ravens descended on the corpses and worried away the flesh with their beaks. A second attack was successful, for the torn bodies were recovered and buried with honor in a special tomb next to their pharaoh.

We do not know where the attack took place, but it was somewhere in Egypt, for the arrows that killed the attackers were of Egyptian design. Few discoveries make such a powerful statement about the lives of the anonymous players of the past.

become a classic story of the American West from the white perspective, immortalized by John Ford's movie *Cheyenne Autumn.* This film tells the story from the victors' perspective and is a form of moral tale of the Old West. Now oral tradition and archaeology have shattered part of the myth, telling the story from the Native American perspective in circumstances in which science has helped fashion a mosaic of the recent past that is the historical truth rather than myth.

Some of the most compelling studies of ethnic minorities' resistance to social domination come from the United States, from historical sites where written records amplify the archaeological record in important ways. As so often happens, methods developed on historical sites will ultimately be applied to prehistoric situations. What, for example, was the position of Oaxacan merchants living at Teotihuacán, Mexico, in A.D. 600 (Paddock, 1983)? Were they treated differently from citizens of the city? Does their material culture reflect carefully orchestrated responses to the dominant culture around them? What was the lifeway of slaves and workers in Egypt? (see the Site box) How did their relationships with their noble masters change through, say, the New Kingdom (Kemp, 1989)? Current examples of ethnic minorities' resistance may help us find some answers to these kinds of questions.

Archaeology, with its rich potential for studying the mundane and the trivial, the minutest details of daily life, is an unrivaled tool for the dispassionate study of social inequality and ethnicity. It also studies broader interactions between people and groups through artifacts passed along exchange and trade routes.

Exchange and Trade

Our lives, like those of the ancients, are a constant process of interaction and negotiation: between friends, family members, households and communities, communities and their neighbors, and entire societies. The study of such interactions in the past involves sophisticated research into trade and exchange, the mechanisms by which people and cultures bought and sold, gave or bartered goods and commodities with one another (Brumfiel and Earle, 1987; Earle and Ericson, 1977; Ericson and Earle, 1982; Sabloff and Lamberg-Karlovsky, 1975).

Many Americans drive Japanese cars. French teenagers like the taste of hamburgers. Pacific Islanders crave Mexican-made television sets. We live in an international world, where economic ties link nations many thousands of miles apart. Over the past two thousand years, and especially during the European Age of Discovery after A.D. 1500, human societies throughout the world have become part of a vast web of economic interconnectedness (Wolf, 1984). But the ultimate roots of our modern-day global economic system date back more than five thousand years, to the dramatic growth of long-distance trade that preceded the appearance of the world's first civilizations in Egypt and Mesopotamia.

Exchange systems were part of human life long before the Sumerians and ancient Egyptians. Shells from the Black Sea appear in late Ice Age hunting encampments deep in Ukraine from at least 18,000 years ago. The Paleo-Indians of the Great Plains exchanged fine-grained toolmaking stone over long distances as early as 10,000 B.C. Few human societies are completely self-sufficient, for they depend on others for resources outside their own territories. And, as the need for raw materials or for prestigious ornaments increased, so did the tentacles of exchange and trade between neighbors near and far. This trade often had powerful political or symbolic overtones, conducted under the guise of formal gift-giving or as part of complex exchange rituals.

Exchange and trade have been defined as the "mutually appropriative movement of goods between hands" (Renfrew, 1975). People make trade connections and set up the exchange systems that handle trade goods when they need to acquire goods and services that are not available to them within their own site-catchment area. The movement of goods need not be over any great distance, and it can operate internally, within a society, or externally, across cultural boundaries—within interaction spheres. Both exchange and trade always involve two elements: the goods and commodities being exchanged and the people doing the exchanging. Thus any form of trading activity implies both procurement and handling of tools and raw materials and some form of social system that provides the people-to-people relationships within which the trade flourishes. Not only raw materials and finished objects but also ideas and information passed along trade routes.

Conventionally, exchange and trade are recognized in the archaeological record by the discovery of objects exotic to the material culture or economy of the host society. For instance, glass was never manufactured in sub-Saharan Africa, yet imported glass beads are widespread in archaeological sites of the first millennium A.D. (Connah, 2001). Until recently, such objects were recognized almost entirely on the basis of style and design—the appearance of distinctive pottery forms far from their known points of origin, and so on. Sometimes exotics such as gold, amber, turquoise, or marine shells, commodities whose general area of origin is known, provide evidence of long-distance exchanges. Between five thousand and two thousand years ago, Late Archaic and Woodland peoples in the North American Southeast used native copper from outcrops near Lake Superior and conch shells from the Gulf Coast, both commodities of known origin (Baugh and Ericson, 1994).

In the early days of archaeology, such exotica were deemed sufficient to identify trade, as well as what were loosely called "influences" or even "invasions." The assumptions made about the nature of human interactions were very limited and never precise (Torrence, 1986). Today, however, studies of prehistoric exchange are far more sophisticated, owing to two major developments (Sabloff and Lamberg-Karlovsky, 1975). The first is a new focus throughout archaeology on cultural process and on regional studies. The second is the development of a wide range of scientific techniques that are capable of describing the composition of certain types of raw material and even of identifying their sources with great precision.

Types of Exchange and Trade

Exchange can be internal, within a society, or external, with other groups. Internal distribution of artifacts and commodities is commonplace even in the least complex societies.

Gift Exchange.   Much internal exchange is **gift exchange,** or gift-giving. Perhaps the most famous example is that of the *kula* ring of Melanesia in the southwestern Pacific. An elaborate network of gift exchanges passes shell necklaces in one direction, arm shells in the other. They are passed as ceremonial gifts from one individual to another, in gift partnerships that endure for decades. These gift exchanges enjoy great prestige, yet serve as a framework for the regular exchange of foodstuffs and other more day-to-day commodities. With all gift exchange, much depends on the types of commodities being exchanged. In the case of the *kula* ring, precious seashell ornaments pass between individuals of high status; foodstuffs are a more common form of transaction involving many individuals and families. And, of course, not only objects but also information can be exchanged, and the exchange of information may lead to technological innovation or social change.

Gift-giving is a common medium of exchange and trade in societies that are relatively self-supporting. The exchange of gifts is designed primarily to reinforce a social relationship between both individuals and groups. The gifts serve as gestures that place obligations on both parties. This form of exchange is common in New Guinea and the Pacific and was widespread in Africa during the past two thousand years, as well as in the ancient Americas. Gift-giving and bartering formed a basic trading mechanism for millennia, a simple means of exchanging basic commodities. But this sporadic interaction between individuals and communities reduced people's self-sufficiency and eventually made them part of a larger society whose members were no longer so self-sufficient and who depended on one another for basic commodities and for social purposes.

Reciprocity.   **Reciprocity** is the mutual exchange of goods between two individuals or groups; it is at the heart of much gift-giving and barter trade. It can happen year after year at the same place, which can be as humble as someone's house. Such central places become the focus of gift-giving and trade. When a village becomes involved in both the production of trade goods and their exchange with other communities, it will probably become an even more important center, a place to which people will travel to trade.

Redistribution.   **Redistribution,** the distribution of goods or commodities received by an individual through a community or group, of trade goods throughout a culture, requires some form of organization to ensure that it is equitable. A redistributive mechanism may be controlled by a chief, a religious leader, or some form of management organization. Such an organization might control production of copper ornaments, or it might simply handle distribution and delivery of trade objects. Considerable social organization is needed for the collection, storage, and redistribution of grain and other commodities. The chief, whose position is perhaps reinforced by religious power, has a serious responsibility to his community that can extend over several villages, as his lines of redistribution stretch out through people of lesser rank to the individual villager. A chief will negotiate exchanges with other chiefs, substituting the regulatory elements of reciprocal trading for a redistributive economy in which less trading in exotic materials is carried out by individual households.

Prehistoric exchange was an important variable that developed in conjunction with sociopolitical organization. In many areas, external trade proceeded from simple reciprocal exchange to the more complex redistribution of goods under a redistributor. In other words, trading is closely tied to growing social and political complexity, although it does not necessarily imply the special production of exotic artifacts specifically for exchange.

Markets.   The term **market** covers both places and particular styles of trading. The administration and organization encourage people to set aside one place for trading and to establish relatively stable prices for staple commodities. This stability does not mean regulated prices, but some regulation is needed in a network of markets in which commodities from an area of abundant supplies are sold to one with strong demand for the same materials. The mechanisms of the exchange relationship, particularly, require some regulation.

Markets are normally associated with more complex societies. No literate civilization ever developed without strong central places where trading activities were regulated and monopolies developed over both sources of materials and trade routes themselves. Successful market trading required predictable supplies of basic commodities and adequate policing of trade routes. For example, most early Mesopotamian and Egyptian trade was riverine, where policing was relatively easy. When the great caravan routes opened, political and military issues—tribute, control of trade routes, and tolls—became paramount. The caravan, predating the great empires, was a form of organized trading that kept to carefully defined routes set up and maintained by state authorities. The travelers moved along these set routes, looking neither left nor right, bent only on delivering and exchanging imports and exports. These caravans were a far cry from the huge economic complex that accompanied Alexander the Great's army across Asia or the Grand Mogul's annual summer progress from the heat in Delhi to the mountains, which moved a half-million people, including the entire Delhi bazaar (Polyani, 1975).

Sourcing

Studying long-distance trade involves far more sophisticated inquiry than merely plotting the distributions of distinctive artifacts hundreds of miles away from their place of manufacture. Fortunately, modern scientific technology allows us to trace the sources of many important trade materials, an approach known as **sourcing.**

By far the most significant of these materials is obsidian, volcanic glass that is ideal for fabricating stone tools, ornaments, and, in Mesoamerica, highly polished mirrors (Figure 16.12). The first studies focused on the Mediterranean and southwestern Asia, where obsidian was a major trade commodity for many thousands of years.

In Mesoamerica, many scholars have attempted to trace the trade routes over which obsidian traveled from highlands to lowlands. The use of source data enables researchers to conceive of exchange on a regional basis, an approach used with success at Copán and combined with obsidian hydration dating to trace changes in obsidian trade networks over many centuries (Freter, 1993, 1994). Nowadays, the ultimate research goal is to identify the exchange mechanisms that distributed the obsidian within each exchange zone. Thus the data requirements have changed. No longer is it sufficient to know the approximate source of a raw material or an artifact. Sources

Figure 16.12   Obsidian mirror from Mesoamerica. (Neg. 312721—Obsidian mirror. Courtesy Dept. of Library Services, American Museum of Natural History.)

must be pinpointed accurately, and distributions of traded goods or commodities must be quantified precisely. Such data provide the groundwork for studies of trade. However, it remains to translate these distributions and the source data into characterizations of human behavior (see the Doing Archaeology box).

Most obsidian studies have concentrated on the use of the rock and the amount of it traded from settlement to settlement. Future studies will have to monitor exchange by taking analogies from ethnohistorical and historical studies of quarrying and trade and by developing new ways of inferring behavior from the archaeological record. Chipped stone is useful in this regard, for one can reconstruct the reduction strategies used to produce traded raw material and finished artifacts and thereby gain insights into efficiency of production and other such facets of human behavior. This approach has worked well with Paleo-Indian sites in North America, for such groups exchanged fine toolmaking stone over enormous areas or traveled long distances to obtain supplies. Ancient quarries, such as those in Greece, Mesoamerica, and Australia, are potentially valuable sources of information on the exchange of exotic materials.

Archaeologist Robin Torrence (1986) studied Aegean obsidian trade, finding that the exchange was noncommercial and noncompetitive: the prehistoric stoneworkers visited quarries and prepared material for exchange with minimal concern for economical use of the raw material. On the island of Melos, for example, the visitors simply quarried what they wanted and left. There is no evidence of specialized production. During early farming times, obsidian mining may have been a seasonal occupation, but during the Bronze Age it became a specialized occupation requiring special voyages to Melos and other quarries. The reason for the shift is unknown. Perhaps it was connected to a rising demand that outstripped the yield from seasonal visits.

Sourcing studies are sometimes called **characterization studies,** as they involve petrology and other approaches for identifying the characteristic properties of the distinctive raw materials used to fashion, say, stone axes. One should stress the word *distinctive,* for the essence of these methods is that one be able to identify the specific source with great accuracy. For example, obsidian from Lipari Island off Sicily, traded over a wide area of the central Mediterranean, has highly specific characteristics that show that it came from Lipari and nowhere else. These are but a few examples of obsidian sourcing, which is now a major specialty in archaeology. Over fifty obsidian sources are known from ancient California alone.

Isotopic chemistry has been highly effective in studying metal sources. For example, the isotopic composition of lead depends on the geological age of the ore source. Lead mines were few and far between in antiquity. Provided their location is known, it is possible to study lead sources in bronze artifacts, and also those of silver, for the latter is extracted from lead ores. This technique has been used to distinguish between Classical Greek silver coins made from mainland ore and those manufactured with metal from the Aegean island of Siphnos and other locations.

A Unique Portrait of Ancient Trade: The Uluburun Ship

Merely studying the distribution of artifacts gives one a grossly inadequate picture of ancient trade, for such factors as the logistics of transportation, as well as local political and economic conditions, affected every aspect of trade and exchange. Few

| Doing Archaeology |

Obsidian Sourcing

Scientists studied the sources of toolmaking stone long before the advent of spectrographic analysis, relying both on petrology and on distinctive rocks, such as the butter-colored and easily recognized Grand Pressigny flint, widely used in France by Stone Age farmers. High-tech analytical methods have revolutionized sourcing since the 1960s, when British archaeologist Colin Renfrew and others used spectrographic analysis to identify no fewer than twelve early farming villages that had obtained obsidian from the Ciftlik area of central Turkey (R. Cann and others, 1995) (Figure 16.13). This pioneer study showed that 80 percent of the chipped stone in villages within 186 miles (300 km) of Ciftlik was obsidian. Outside this "supply zone," the percentages of obsidian dropped away sharply with distance, to 5 percent in a Syrian village and 0.1 percent in the Jordan Valley. If these calculations were correct, each village was passing about half its imported obsidian farther down the line. Renfrew and his colleagues identified no fewer than nine obsidian "interaction zones" between Sardinia and Mesopotamia, each of them linked to well-defined sources of supply, each yielding obsidian with its own distinctive trace elements identifiable spectrographically.

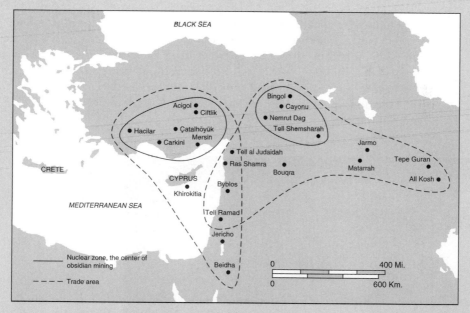

Figure 16.13   Obsidian trade in the eastern Mediterranean region. Sourcing studies reveal that early farming communities in Cyprus, Anatolia, and the Levant obtained their obsidian from two sources in central Anatolia. Meanwhile, villages such as Jarmo in the Zagros Mountains and Ali Kosh far to the southeast relied on sources in Armenia. Settlements like Çatalhöyük in Anatolia were so close to obsidian sources that they probably collected their own supplies. More than 80 percent of their stone artifacts are made of the material, whereas obsidian tools are much rarer down the line, the farther one travels from the source.

archaeological finds rival the extraordinary cargo found aboard a Bronze Age ship wrecked off the rugged Uluburun cliffs in southern Turkey. Shipwrecks offer unique opportunities to study ancient trade, for each ship on the seabed is a sealed capsule, holding a record of trading conditions at the time. George Bass and Cemal Pulak's excavation of the Uluburun ship has yielded a mine of information on the commercial world of the eastern Mediterranean in the fourteenth century B.C. (Bass and others, 1989; see the summary in Fagan, 1995). The heavily laden ship was sailing westward from the eastern Mediterranean when it was shattered on the jagged rocks of Uluburun in about 1316 B.C. (a date determined from tree rings in firewood found in the wreck). It sank in 151 feet (48 m) of water. Bass and Pulak plotted the exact position of every timber and every item of the ship's equipment and cargo as they lifted artifacts from the seabed. They recovered a unique portrait of eastern Mediterranean trade more than three thousand years ago.

The Uluburun ship was laden with six tons of copper ingots, probably mined in Cyprus, and with tin ingots and artifacts (see Figure 1.11). The tin may have come from southern Turkey. Canaanite jars from Palestine or Syria held olives, glass beads, and resin from the terebinth tree, used in religious rituals. The ship's hold contained Baltic amber that probably reached the Mediterranean overland, ebonylike wood from Africa, elephant and hippopotamus ivory, and ostrich eggshells from North Africa or Syria. Egyptian, Levantine, and Mycenaean daggers, swords, spearheads, and woodworking tools were aboard, as were sets of weights, some fashioned in animal forms. There were costly glass ingots, Mesopotamian cylinder seals, a Mycenaean seal stone, even a gold cup and parts of a tortoiseshell lute. The ship carried Egyptian scarabs, dozens of fishing weights, fishhooks, and twenty-three stone anchors, vital when anchoring in windy coves. Even the thorny burnet shrub used to pack the cargo was preserved. One unique find: a diptych, a wooden cover for a wax tablet used to record commercial transactions (Figure 16.14).

Figure 16.14   Diptych from the Uluburun shipwreck.

By using find distributions from land sites and a variety of sourcing techniques, Bass and Pulak have reconstructed the anonymous skipper's last journey. They believe he started his voyage on the Levant coast, sailed north up the coast, crossed to Cyprus, then coasted along the southern Turkish shore. The ship called at ports large and small on its way west, along a well-traveled route that took advantage of changing seasonal winds, to Crete, some Aegean islands, and perhaps to the Greek mainland. The skipper had traversed this route many times, but on this occasion his luck ran out and he lost his ship, the cargo, and perhaps his life on Uluburun's pitiless rocks. From the archaeological perspective, the Uluburun shipwreck is a godsend, for it allows researchers to fill in many details of an elaborate trade network that linked the eastern Mediterranean with Egypt, the Aegean, and Greece more than 3,300 years ago. Bass and Pulak suspect that the Uluburun ship may have been carrying an unusually valuable cargo, but the owners remain a mystery.

The Uluburun ship carried what was an exceptionally rich cargo, perhaps for some monarch. This dramatic find illuminates the remarkable, and often unsuspected, degree of interconnection between even quite distant peoples in ancient times. Thanks to modern science, we can trace its fatal voyage and its cargo with considerable accuracy.

Summary

A new generation of archaeological research is turning away from impersonal cultural processes toward the study of people and small groups. Such research marries modern archaeological data recovery methods with new interpretative approaches that consider the archaeologist an "active mediator" of the archaeological record of the past.

Discoveries of actual individuals from the past, such as the Iceman in the European Alps, allow us to make detailed studies of the health, diet, and activities of single people.

Social ranking is difficult to study from archaeological evidence. It can be studied in the archaeological record by using burials and associated grave furniture, as at Ur in Mesopotamia, and by using structures or artifact patterns.

The archaeology of gender is assuming increasing importance as a means of identifying changing male/female roles in the past and of studying individuals in prehistory. These researches involve detailed studies of grave furniture, studies of female pathology, which reflect such activities as constant grain grinding, and extrapolations of material data into hypothetical scenarios of changing gender relations.

Ethnicity and social inequality have been studied by archaeologists working with African American and other sites in North America. Such researches involve identifying distinctive artifacts that reflect African religious beliefs and material signs of silent resistance to the dominant culture.

Trade and exchange were important means of human interaction from the earliest times. Much early trade probably took the form of gift exchanges and the bartering of food and other commodities between neighboring settlements. Trade is normally recognized in the archaeological record by the discovery of exotic objects far from their places of origin. Prehistoric trade networks are studied by examining the distributions of such objects and the sources of raw materials used to make artifacts. One example is the Uluburun shipwreck off southern Turkey, which revealed the complexity of eastern Mediterranean trading in the fourteenth century B.C.

Key Terms

archaeology of gender
archaeology of inequality
band
characterization studies
chiefdom
engendered archaeology

exchange system
gift exchange
ideologies of domination
market
pre-state societies
reciprocity

redistribution
social ranking
sourcing
state-organized societies
tribe

Guide to Further Reading

EARLE, TIMOTHY K., and JONATHAN E. ERICSON, eds. 1977. *Exchange Systems in Prehistory.* Orlando, FL: Academic Press. Articles dealing with method and theory in the study of prehistoric trade. For the more advanced reader.

FERGUSON, LELAND. 1992. *Uncommon Ground.* Washington, DC: Smithsonian Institution Press. An exemplary study of African American culture in the archaeological record.

GERO, J. M., and M. W. CONKEY, eds. 1991. *Engendering Archaeology: Women and Prehistory.* Oxford: Blackwell. An influential series of essays on gender in archaeology.

McINTOSH, SUSAN KEECH, ed. 1999 *Beyond Chiefdoms: Pathways to Complexity in Africa.* New York: Cambridge University Press. A superb collection of essays that deals with many facets of chiefdoms. Chapter 1 is especially useful.

NELSON, SARAH M. 1997. *Gender in Archaeology.* Walnut Creek, CA: AltaMira Press. A critical analysis of gender research for beginner and advanced reader alike. Strongly recommended.

ORSER, CHARLES E. 2004. *Historical Archaeology.* 2d ed. Upper Saddle River, NJ: Prentice Hall. A basic text on historical archaeology, with numerous examples of studies of social conditions and social inequality with archaeological data.

SABLOFF, JEREMY A., and C. C. LAMBERG-KARLOVSKY, eds. 1975. *Early Civilization and Trade.* Albuquerque: University of New Mexico Press. Conference papers that cover a wide range of problems in the study of prehistoric trade. Strong on theory and actual case studies.

SPINDLER, KONRAD. 1994. *The Man in the Ice.* London: Weidenfeld and Nicholson. A popular account of the Ice Man discovery.

CHAPTER 17

Archaeology
of the Intangible

A Maya noblewoman dressed like a queen in rich textiles wearing a bloodletting crown.

Whenever I (BMF) visit the great city of Teotihuacán in Mexico, I am haunted by the past. I look down from the summit of the Pyramid of the Sun at the tiny human figures dwarfed by the massive artificial mountain and wonder at the scale of a city built by thousands of people working in the service of divine lords and powerful gods. I stand in the plaza at the foot of the pyramid and sense the overwhelming weight of power and supernatural might the builders wished to convey. Teotihuacán is a powerful statement, but so much is lost. The pyramid was once the setting for dazzling spectacles, a stage where masked lords appeared in trance, where brilliantly colored dancers performed, where chants and incense rose into the evening sky. The colors have long faded. No banners fly over temples; the stories told by narrators and priests have vanished on the wind. Teotihuacán is now an empty stage, devoid of the transparent things through which the cosmos once came to life. All that is left are the material remains of the spiritual and the sacred—mirrors of the intangible (Figure 15.12). This chapter describes how archaeologists wrestle with the toughest problem of all: reconstructing the intangible religious beliefs, ideologies, and social relationships of the past.

A Framework of Common Belief

We are *Homo sapiens sapiens,* capable of subtlety, of passing on knowledge and ideas through the medium of language. We have consciousness and self-awareness and are capable of foresight. We can express ourselves and show emotions. Mitochondrial DNA researches trace the roots of modern humans back to tropical Africa between 100,000 and 200,000 years ago. Archaeology tells us *Homo sapiens sapiens* had settled in western Asia by 90,000 years ago, and in western Europe, replacing earlier Neanderthal populations, by 35,000 years before the present. Sometime during this ancient diaspora, we anatomically modern people developed a unique capacity for symbolic and spiritual thought, for defining the boundaries of existence, and for conceptualizing the relationship between the individual, the group, and the cosmos. We do not know when these capabilities first developed, but late Ice Age cave art tells us that humans had melded the living and spiritual worlds by at least 30,000 years ago (Bahn and Vertut, 1988).

Religious beliefs have often linked large areas of the world into gigantic spheres of a common **cosmology** (a view of the world and the universe) and ritual practices, even if the many peoples unified under a common religious banner enjoy widely disparate governmental, societal, and economic institutions. The geographic distribution of Christianity and Islam makes one realize the importance of religion as an integrative force. Thousands of ancient societies were linked by common beliefs and cosmologies, which are reflected in the archaeological record by common artistic traditions, temple and ceremonial-center architecture, wall paintings, and even trade in cult objects. For example, in the American Midwest the Hopewell religious cult, with its preoccupation with ceremonial burial, spread far beyond its Ohio heartland (Fagan, 2005). And in southern Africa, the ceremonial centers at Mapungubwe and Great Zimbabwe are associated with the rainmaking beliefs and ancestor cults of the Shona peoples (Connah, 2001).

By 10,000 years ago, when the first farming societies appeared in western Asia, the various cosmologies began to share several common elements, which are often reflected in archaeological evidence (Fagan, 1998). First, the world of living humans formed part of a multilayered cosmos, sometimes comprising primordial waters, with the heavens and an underworld. Gods, goddesses, spirit beings, and ancestors inhabited the supernatural layers of the cosmos. This universe often began as a dark sea of primordial waters, or, as the book of Genesis puts it, a world "without form."

Second, a vertical axis, often a symbolic tree, or support for the bowl of heaven, linked the various cosmic layers. Mircea Eliade (1954), one of the great religious historians of the twentieth century, stressed the importance of this *axis mundi* (axis of the world), which joined the living and spiritual worlds at a mythic center, a sacred place—either a natural feature such as a cave or a mountain or a human-made structure such as a pyramid.

Such sacred places, and the mythic landscapes associated with them, played a vital role in all societies. Eliade (1954) called them "instruments of orthogenetic transformation," settings for the rituals that ensured the continuity of cultural traditions, a place where the word of the gods rang out in familiar chants passed from one generation to the next. Sacred mountains such as the Hindu Mount Meru, the Greeks' Olympus, or the Lakota Indians' Black Hills often served as the cosmic axis. The Egyptian pharaohs erected pyramids as sacred mountains linking the domain of the sun to the realm of the earth (see Figure 16.5). Maya lords built great ceremonial centers as symbolic representations of their world of sacred mountains, caves, trees, and lakes (see Figure 15.2). To demolish a sacred place was to destroy the essence of human existence itself. In 1521, Spanish conquistador Hernán Cortés razed the Aztec capital Tenochtitlán in the Valley of Mexico, knowing its temples and plazas replicated a cherished and all-encompassing supernatural world (see Figure 15.3).

Third, the material and spiritual worlds formed a continuum, with no boundary between them. An "external" landscape on the earth was also an "internal" landscape of the mind, or "landscape of memory," where colors, jagged peaks, streams, groves of trees, cardinal directions, and other phenomena had spiritual associations and their places in local mythology. Usually, ancestors, those who had gone before, were the intermediaries between the living and the supernatural worlds. They looked after the welfare of the living and were guardians of the land (see the box).

Fourth, individuals with unusual supernatural powers, either **shamans** or spirit mediums, had the ability to pass effortlessly in an altered state of consciousness between the material and spiritual realms, to fly free in the supernatural world through ritual and performance (L. Sullivan, 1989). Such men and women "of power" had direct and personal links to the supernatural world. Shamans moved easily into the spiritual world. There they "dreamt," going through visionary experiences in which they saw dots, lines, spirit animals, and even gods and ancestors. From their dream journeys, they acquired the wisdom to keep their world in balance with the sacred and the power to influence events in the natural world. They were healers; they brought rain; they became sorcerers who could bring disease or cause factional strife or even war. The shaman was a spiritual actor who functioned as an intermediary to the ancestors and the spiritual world.

Last, human life was governed by the cycles of the seasons, by seasons of planting, growth, and harvest, identified by movements of the heavenly bodies. Notions of fertility, procreation, life, and death lay at the core of such a cyclical human existence. Myth and ritual played an important part in defining this world order. They allowed the material and spiritual worlds to pass one into the other as a single constellation of belief. Through poetry, music, dance, and evocative surroundings, a deep sense of a sacred order emerged.

The intangible assumed many forms, but these commonalities, observed by anthropologists and religious historians in many human societies throughout the world, provide a viable framework for scientific investigation of ancient sacred places, the settings for mythic performance. The stone circles at Avebury and Stonehenge in Britain, the courts of the Palace of Knossos on Crete, and Maya pyramids—all tell us much of long-vanished religious beliefs.

Cognitive Archaeology

About a generation ago, a small group of archaeologists challenged their colleagues to move beyond artifacts and food remains. They asked: Why should we interpret the past in terms of purely ecological, technological, and other material factors? Some of the best minds in archaeology are grappling with a scientific methodology for studying human consciousness, especially religion and belief.

From an archaeological perspective, the term **cognitive archaeology** covers the whole spectrum of human behavior, especially religion and belief, but also the development and expression of human consciousness. Since the very early days of archaeology, researchers have been concerned with ancient religion, belief, and expression, the subject matter of cognitive archaeology, sometimes called the archaeology of mind. How can we define cognitive archaeology? Is it possible to study human cognition from the material remains of the archaeological record, even if we cannot afford to ignore it? As discussed in Chapter 3, a cognitive-processual approach draws on both old and new models and methods to try and assess ancient belief systems.

Discovery

The Sepulcher of the Maya Lord Pacal, Palenque, Mexico

Palenque is a Maya city, famous both for its architecture and for a long dynasty of talented lords, starting with Chan-Bahlum (Snake-Jaguar), who ascended to the throne on March 11, A.D. 431. The dynasty flourished for just under four hundred years, achieving the height of its power under the rule of Pacal (Shield) and his son in the seventh century. Pacal ruled for sixty-three years and turned Palenque into a major political force in the Maya lowlands. When he died, he was buried in an underground sepulcher beneath a pyramid and the celebrated Temple of the Inscriptions, built over fifteen years.

In 1949, Mexican archaeologist Alberto Ruz, convinced that a royal tomb lay beneath the pyramid, lifted a flagstone in the floor of the temple and cleared a rubble-filled stairway leading into the heart of the artificial mountain (Ruz, 1953). Five months of backbreaking work over two seasons cleared a stairway with forty-five steps, then a sharp U-turn, which led to another short twenty-one-step stairway and a corridor at the same level as the foot of the pyramid. After removing a stone and lime obstruction, Ruz came to a triangular doorway slab, guarded by six young sacrificial victims. He moved the stone enough to slip into an enormous rock-cut crypt with a procession of priests in stucco around the walls. A huge stone slab bearing intricate hieroglyphs filled the floor of the chamber (Figure 17.1).

To lift the 5-ton stone, Ruz's workers felled a hardwood tree, lowered four sections of the trunk down the stairway, then levered up the sarcophagus lid with car jacks and the timbers. Inside the sepulcher lay a tall man wearing jade and mother-of-pearl ornaments. He wore a jade mosaic mask with eyes of shell, each iris of obsidian. At the time of the excavation, no one could read Maya glyphs, so the identity of the ruler remained unknown. We now know it was Pacal. His carved sarcophagus lid commemorates his divine ancestry.

Figure 17.1 Drawing of the sarcophagus lid of Pacal the Great's tomb, Palenque, A.D. 683. The dead lord falls through huge fleshless jaws into the Underworld. Above him grows the World Tree, with the bird-monster Wuqub 'Kaqix sitting on top of it. A band of celestial bodies and ancestral figures surrounds the scene.

Cognitive archaeology covers all of the human past, but it can be divided into two broad areas of concern. One involves the study of the cognitive facilities of early hominids and Archaic humans, the relationships between toolmaking and cognitive abilities, the origins of language, and the social contexts of early human behavior (Donald, 1991; Gibson and Ingold, 1993). The other covers the past 40,000 years and the cognitive aspects of modern human culture.

One of the aims of recent research in cognitive archaeology has been to make mainstream archaeology more holistic. For example, Kent Flannery and Joyce Marcus (1993) have attempted to understand ancient Zapotec subsistence behavior in Mexico's Valley of Oaxaca by taking into account early Spanish descriptions of local Native American cosmology. Flannery and Marcus consider cognitive archaeology to be "the study of all those aspects of ancient culture that are the product of the ancient mind." This includes cosmology, religion, ideology, iconography, and all forms of human intellectual and symbolic behavior.

In the Valley of Oaxaca, many village farming communities functioned without any apparent ranking between 1400 and 1150 B.C. Between 1150 and 850 B.C., the first artistic depictions of supernatural lineage ancestors appear; some represent the earth; others, the sky, in the form of lightning or a fire serpent. Some form of hereditary social ranking seems to accompany the new art (Flannery and Marcus, 1993). Then the Zapotec state came into being, with a powerful elite ruling from Monte Alban. A tiny minority became associated with depictions of sky and lightning, while earth and earthquake symbols faded into obscurity. It was as if those who rose to prominence were associated with lightning's descendants, in an ideological shift in which hereditary social inequality was condoned for the first time (Flannery and Marcus, 1996).

All cultures have a theory of the universe in which they live. Their cosmology, like that of Western civilization constitutes a theory of the origin of the universe, defines space and time, and can provide a structure for religion and ideology. Many cultures, among them ancient Greek and Maya, envisage a cosmos inhabited by supernatural beings, another link to religious beliefs. Although cosmology can have a strong influence on both settlement and subsistence, as, for example, in cases where certain aspects of the environment, such as pristine forest, may be held sacred, it is difficult if not impossible to reconstruct cosmology from animal and plant remains alone.

Religious beliefs provide ethics and values, often within the framework of a quest for the values of an ideal life. A well-defined worldview links cosmology and religion, the latter providing the rituals and practices that help the worshiper attain the ideal. Clearly, ethics and values can have a powerful effect on human behavior, even on such pragmatic areas of life as obtaining food and trading. Religion can be a powerful catalyst for social and political change, as was the case, for example, when Buddhist merchants brought their religion to southeastern Asia and changed the course of history by providing the spiritual inspiration for a series of brilliant kingdoms, such as those of the Khmer (Wheatley, 1975).

Any archaeologist concerned with the appearance of ranked, as opposed to egalitarian, societies is studying fundamental changes in ideology, simply because egalitarian societies tend to have leveling mechanisms that prevent one individual or group from attaining superior rank. Again, these changes can only be documented through judicious use of historical analogies and artifacts.

Cognitive archaeology is no shortcut, but an approach to cosmology, religion, ideology, and iconography based on rigorous analysis and data from many sources. It is a theoretical perspective that offers enormous promise for the future, but it falls far short of reconstructing entire ideologies from the orientation of a building or a single carving.

Renfrew (1993a) considered the challenge for cognitive archaeology to be establishing a coherent methodology. This methodology may emerge from the convergence of such diverse fields as cognitive psychology, artificial intelligence, computer simulation, and cognitive archaeology itself. But this convergence, and the potential intellectual leap forward that might result, will not depend on rigorous research methods. Thus, it can be used only when the body of supporting data is rich (L. Sullivan, 1989). Otherwise, it becomes "little more than speculation, a kind of bungee jump into the Land of Fantasy" (Flannery and Marcus, 1993:110).

In practical terms, and for obvious reasons, cognitive archaeology is usually most effective when historical records are available to amplify the archaeological record, as they are when working with archaeological evidence and Maya inscriptions (Schele and Friedel, 1990). Flannery and Marcus (1993) believe that one approach to reconstructing ancient religions is to construct models from ethnohistoric sources, then to isolate temples, artifacts, art styles, and other cultural elements that can be identified archaeologically. These features are studied in their cultural context, and the observed archaeological remains are compared with the model from ethnohistoric documents.

Iconography—the "analysis of the way ancient peoples represented religious, political, ideological, or cosmological objects or concepts in their art" (Flannery and Marcus, 1993)—offers a fertile avenue for cognitive archaeology. Again, ethnohistory and history provide vital background for the interpretation of the archaeological record, for without such information one is engaged in little more than guesswork. Such studies, based very often on intuition and "aesthetic sense," reflect the author's personality more than reality.

Cognitive archaeology reaches a high degree of refinement when document-aided, as is the case with the Aztec civilization of Mexico or the Inca of the Andes. But earlier societies—for instance, the first farming societies of southwestern Asia, with their female figures and plastered human skulls—offer greater challenges. It is all too easy to call each female figure a "fertility figurine" and to talk of ancient mother goddesses, when there is, in fact, no scientific basis for such conclusions.

Ethnographic Analogy and Rock Art

The late Ice Age rock paintings of southwestern France and northern Spain are justly famous for their brilliant depictions of long-extinct game animals, painted between 15,000 and 30,000 years ago (Bahn and Vertut, 1988). For generations, scholars have grappled with the meaning of the paintings, for they realized long ago that they were

Doing Archaeology

Copying South African Rock Paintings

All research into the meaning of rock art starts with accurate copies. Scientists have striven for a high degree of accuracy ever since the early twentieth century, when color photography was unknown. The French priest and archaeologist Abbé Henri Breuil was a gifted artist, whose copies of late Ice Age paintings at such sites as Altamira in northern Spain are justly famous (Bahn and Vertut, 1988). He spent weeks lying on his back tracing paintings onto translucent rice paper by flickering acetylene lantern light. He taped the paper to the rock or had an assistant, who was roundly cursed if he fidgeted, hold it there. Many times, he made a sketch, then finished it later. Breuil had inadequate lighting and materials but achieved miracles of improvisation (see Figure 2.6 for an example of Breuil's work). Today's rock art copyist has an arsenal of superior materials and photographic methods at his or her disposal. Artists set up sheets in front of a wall to avoid direct contact with the painting, then trace, checking their drawings with photographs and measurements. Color photography allows accurate recording without affecting the images, but today's researchers use both color and black-and-white film, various light sources, and a wide array of filters to enhance different colors (see Figure 1.5). Infrared film or light makes red ochers transparent, so the observer can see other pigments under red figures.

Ultraviolet light sources cause calcite and living organisms on cave walls to fluoresce, thereby allowing assessment of damage caused by wall growths. The sophisticated recording processes of today go hand in hand with AMS radiocarbon dating using tiny flecks of charcoal and other paints.

As in Europe, scholars in southern Africa have experimented with various methods for copying rock art. In the 1890s, the Abbé Breuil was the first archaeologist to make color reproductions of South African rock art, using butcher paper. Another early scholar, Walter Battiss, painted in watercolors. The beginnings of a revolution in San rock art studies came with the development of affordable color photography in the 1950s. A South African rock art expert, Alex Willcox, photographed thousands of paintings, especially in the Drakensberg Mountains, where some of the finest cave paintings in Africa are to be found. Willcox was somewhat of a romantic. Captivated by the beauty and variety of the paintings, he waxed lyrical about the leisurely, prosperous life of the ancient San. He wrote (1956) of expert artists who took great joy in their depictions of animals and people. This, he said, was art for art's sake. In reality, the paintings were an invaluable source of information about ancient San life and hunting practices (Figure 17.2).

far more than merely art for art's sake. In an era when AMS radiocarbon dating allows researchers to date individual paintings, and chemical analyses are deciphering the composition of the ancient paints, we can reasonably hope that we can achieve a greater understanding of the meaning of the art in the future. This greater comprehension will result, in part, from some remarkable research in southern Africa (see the Doing Archaeology box).

Figure 17.2   San rock art from South Africa. Shamans execute a trance dance. Their elongated bodies convey the sense of being stretched out that is felt by people in an altered state of consciousness. Dots along the spine of the central figure depict what the present-day San describe as a "boiling" sensation as supernatural power rises up the spine and "explodes" in the head. The power is derived from certain animals, such as the eland depicted to the right.

Source: David Lewis-Williams, Rock Art Research Centre, Department of Archaeology, University of the Witwatersrand, Johannesburg, South Africa. Reprinted by permission.

Patricia Vinnecombe (1976) also worked in the Drakensberg region and compiled a remarkable statistical record with drawings and color photography. A 1970s scholar, Harold Pager, photographed the paintings in black and white, measured the drawings, and then returned to the site to color in the photographs. Another photographer, Neil Lee, used color film, shooting the art from an overall perspective, then moving closer and closer to take detailed close-up photographs. This approach allowed him to study the painter's technique, the draftsmanship, the types of brushes used, and the different paint types.

Today's sophisticated theories about San rock art are based on a growing database of carefully recorded paintings. To accumulate such a database is an urgent priority, for many paintings are vanishing rapidly through natural causes, excess tourism, or vandalism.

The rock art painted by Stone Age artists in southern Africa are justly famous, but they are very different from those of late Ice Age Europe. Whereas most rock paintings and engravings in Europe depict animals, human hands, and numerous signs, the art in southern Africa commemorates not only animals but also scenes of the hunt, women gathering, people in camp, and elaborate ceremonies (see Figure 13.13). Until recently, we had no idea of the meaning of these paintings, until archaeologist

David Lewis-Williams (1981) came across the long-forgotten research notebooks of a German linguist named Wilhelm Bleek. Bleek made a lifetime's study of African languages. In 1870, he discovered there were twenty-eight San convicts working on the breakwaters of Cape Town harbor, arranged for them to be released into his supervision, and used them as informants. Bleek and his sister-in-law Lucy Lloyd recorded an enormous body of San mythology and folklore over nearly twenty years. Their work lay neglected in the University of Cape Town Library until Lewis-Williams discovered them in the 1970s.

The Bleek archive contains numerous accounts of rainmaking and other rituals recounted by men who had practiced the rituals themselves. Bleek himself was familiar with a few rock paintings. His informants were able to explain scenes of men charming a mythic rainmaking animal with sweet-smelling grasses.

Lewis-Williams realized the paintings were the result of thought patterns that reflected shared beliefs and behavior over large areas where paintings were to be found. He talked to living !Kung in the Kalahari Desert and showed them pictures of paintings. His informants were able to identify antelope of different sexes and groupings of them painted at different times of year. Lewis-Williams became particularly interested in the eland, a large, fat antelope that is so slow on its feet that a hunter can run it down on foot. A single eland can feed a small band for days, so they assumed great importance in environments where food supplies could be irregular. Bleek's informants had recited myths that associated the scent of recently killed eland with honey.

Lewis-Williams has examined hundreds of eland paintings in the Drakensberg Mountains and elsewhere, including scenes of eland staggering in their death throes as dancers cavort around the animal. White dots depict the sweat dripping from a dancer who is "dying" in trance. Lewis-Williams believes that these dancers were acquiring the potency released by the death of the eland, a process shown by the antelope heads, feet, and hair on the dancers. He realized that painting after painting linked society with the supernatural, the medium responsible for this linking being a shaman, who induced a trance by intense concentration, prolonged rhythmic dancing, and hyperventilation. Today, the !Kung still dance next to the carcass of a freshly killed eland as a shaman enters trance.

By combining careful observations from ethnographic data with archaeological observations, Lewis-Williams believes he can "read" some of the rock paintings as meaningful scenes. Dance, miming, and sounds made the dead eland "appear" real before the participants. As the shaman dances, he hallucinates and "sees" the eland standing in the darkness beyond the glow of the fire. As the dance continues, the dancers become as one with the eland spirit and the transfiguration is complete. Afterward, the shaman-artists remembered their trance experiences and painted what they had hallucinated on the walls of rock shelters. The visions of the unconscious are painted, then transferred to the world of the conscious. Lewis-Williams points out that many of the hallucinogenic experiences of Stone Age artists were very similar to those induced in modern times by LSD, peyote, or other hallucinogens (Lewis-Williams, 1995; for a contrary view, see Solomon, 1997).

The Lewis-Williams research shows that paintings were far more than art; they were objects of significance in and of themselves—images with potent ingredients of ocher and eland blood. In many paintings, a figure or an animal enters or leaves a crack in the wall, climbs an uneven rock surface, or emerges from the shelter wall. These paintings may reflect a belief that an underground world takes a shaman to the spiritual world. An informant showed Lewis-Williams how San once danced in the painted rock shelter to which she took him. They raised their hands during the dance and turned to the paintings to identify their potency. Thus, the paintings began to affect the flow of mental images that entered the dancers' minds as they moved, clapped, and sang. The people may have visited the same locations again and again; frequent visits would account for the jumble of paintings at some presumably potent locations.

The symbolic meaning of at least some southern African art is well documented, but we certainly cannot use the San experience and ethnography to interpret late Ice Age paintings in Europe. There are, however, some general similarities: the placement of animal images in dark caves, the presence of occasional human-animal figures, and a combination of naturalistic and geometric images that carry an undertone of altered consciousness (Lewis-Williams, 2002). And one scene in the Grotte de Chauvet in southeastern France depicts a man in a bison skin as part of an animal frieze; he is facing the entrance of the chamber as if awaiting his audience (Chauvet and others, 1996). Native American rock art, such as that of the Chumash of southern California, has strong and well-documented shamanistic overtones.

The Archaeology of Death

The Maya lord Pacal ruled over the city of Palenque and its surrounding domains from A.D. 615 for no less than sixty-seven years. He turned Palenque into a major political force in the Maya lowlands by political marriages, diplomatic offensives, trade, and conquest (Schele and Friedel, 1990). Pacal erected the Temple of the Inscriptions as his burial place, one of the masterpieces of Maya architecture. The builders dug a large burial chamber with an immense sarcophagus below ground, then erected the temple pyramid atop it. A secret internal stairway led to the sanctuary of the temple on the summit of the sacred mountain. Mexican archaeologist Alberto Ruz probed under the temple floor, cleared the stairway of rubble, and found Pacal under a richly carved sarcophagus lid that depicted his sacred genealogy. The great ruler wore a magnificent jade mask; his hair was adorned with jade tubes; elaborate ornaments masked his body; and all the grave furniture reflected his status as a powerful personage with supernatural powers.

The symbolism of death and burial is an important source of information on ancient religious beliefs as well as social ranking, most notably in the regalia and artifacts deposited with the deceased. For Egyptian pharaohs, the actual disposal of the corpse was really a minimal part of the sequence of mortuary practice in a society. Funerary rites were a ritual of passage and were usually reflected not only in the position of the body in the grave but also in the ornaments and grave furniture that accompanied it (Clayton, 1994; Reeves, 1990). For instance, the Egyptian pharaoh Khufu expended vast resources on building his pyramid and mortuary temple at Giza in 2550 B.C. (Lerner, 1997) (see Figure 16.5). The royal tomb was looted within a few centuries, but the pyramid shape endures, a powerful statement of Egyptian kingship. Egyptian pharaohs were considered to be the living embodiment of the Sun God Ra and joined him in the skies at their death. The pyramids were symbolic sun rays, like the sun bursting through clouds overhead, a type of ladder to heaven for their owner.

Some Native American groups, notably the Hopewell people of eastern North America, buried magnificent ceremonial artifacts with prominent individuals. Such artifacts as soapstone pipes, copper sheet portraits, and masks reflected not only the status of the owners but also their clan affiliation and importance as shamans or priests (see Figure 11.12) (Fagan, 2005).

Artifacts: The Importance of Context

In 1953, British archaeologist Kathleen Kenyon unearthed a cache of human skulls covered with plaster in a pit under a house floor at Jericho in the Jordan Valley. Each head was a naturalistic, individual portrait, with nose, mouth, and ears modeled with remarkable delicacy onto the skull (Figure 17.3).

Apparently, they were portraits of ancestors. The cowrie-shell eyes of the others glare unblinkingly at the beholder, giving an impression of inner wisdom. We will never know what ritual surrounded these ancestor portraits, but their context, buried under a hut floor, speaks volumes about the close relationship between living households and their ancestors. Plastered human skulls, like other art objects and tools

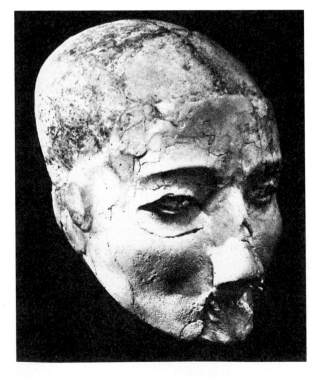

Figure 17.3   Plastered human skull from Jericho, Jordan, thought to be a portrait of an ancestor, c. 9000 B.C.

of all kinds, can give us insights into ancient beliefs. Very often, their contexts within sites are as important as the objects themselves.

Clay figurines are commonplace in eastern Mediterranean site. Some may depict goddesses. Others may be little more than trade tokens or children's toys. Often their religious associations are controversial (Ucko, 1968).

Despite the figurine controversy, the occurrence of distinctive artifacts and ritual buildings in a site or a society may be significant. In Mexico's Valley of Oaxaca, public buildings appear between 1400 and 1150 B.C., many of them oriented 8 degrees west of north and built on adobe and earth platforms (Flannery, 1976). Rare conch-shell trumpets and turtle-shell drums traded from the coastal lowlands were apparently used in public ceremonies in such buildings. Clay figurines of dancers wearing costumes and masks that make them look like fantastic creatures and animals, as well as pottery masks, are also signs of communal ritual (Figure 17.4). The ritual of self-mutilation by bloodletting was widespread in early Mesoamerica. The Spanish described how the Aztec nobles would gash themselves with knives or with fish and stingray spines as acts of penance before the gods, imposed by religion. A few stingray spines have come from early Oaxacan villages, probably traded into the far interior for the specific use of community leaders. Flannery suggests that bloodletting fish spines were kept and used at home and that they were also used in public buildings. The ritual artifacts in the Oaxacan villages enabled Flannery and his colleagues to identify three levels of religious ceremony: personal bloodletting; dances run by kin groups, which

Figure 17.4 Ritual scene composed of four clay figurines from San José Mogote in the Valley of Oaxaca, Mexico. They may represent the burial of a high-status individual with three retainers.

| Doing Archaeology |

The Shrine at Phylakopi, Melos, Greece

The small Mycenaean town of Phylakopi on the island of Melos in the Aegean Sea was home to an estimated 1,400 to 2,100 people between 1390 and 1090 B.C. The settlement was a maze of small stone houses, narrow alleyways, and courtyards, excavated by Colin Renfrew using a 33-foot (10-m) grid that allowed him to record architectural changes and stratigraphy with great precision. This excavation method, combined with meticulous studies of the Mycenaean pottery, provided very precise contexts for the finds and enabled Renfrew to identify an important shrine in the town (Renfrew, 1985).

He first suspected a shrine when he recovered broken animal and human figurines in his trenches. Slow-moving excavation over the floors of the putative shrine rooms revealed stone platforms and exotic objects such as seal stones. But the evidence for religious activity was modest at best—until the excavators uncovered a side chamber and a wall niche in the westernmost shrine room. This contained a pedestaled vase, the fragments of an ox-like figure, other figurines, and a remarkable female figurine, which stood upright in the room. "The Lady of Phylakopi," as Renfrew named her, had a conical stem painted like a long skirt, a bulbous body with

small breasts, a painted brown chin, staring eyes, and eyebrows and hair outlined in brown (Figure 17.5). Another complete female figurine stood to one side.

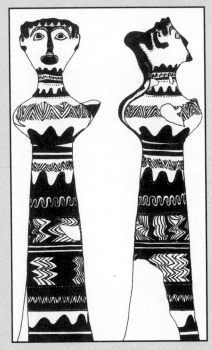

Figure 17.5   "The Lady of Phylakopi," Melos, Greece. (One-third full size.)

cut across household lines; and public rituals in ceremonial buildings, involving a region wider than one village (see the Doing Archaeology box).

Artifacts and Art Styles

Ideology is a product of society and politics. It is a body of doctrine, myth, and symbolism associated with a social movement, an institution, class, or group of individuals, often with reference to some political or cultural plan, along with the strategies for putting the doctrine into operation.

The figurines could have come from a storeroom, so Renfrew studied the design of the chambers. He found that the builders had laid them out in such a way that the symmetrically placed platforms were the focus of attention. The objects displayed on them would have caught attention at once. Furthermore, the "shrines" yielded conch-shell trumpets, identical to those blown by priestesses on seals from Crete. Perforated tortoiseshell fragments were the remains of lyre bodies. The fine pottery found inside the two shrines was of much better quality than that from elsewhere on the site (Figure 17.6).

The precise contexts of these finds allowed Renfrew to conclude that he had found the town shrine, which is duplicated, at least superficially, at other sites on Crete and the Greek mainland.

Figure 17.6   Reconstruction by Alex Daykin of the West Shrine at Phylakopi.

Writing is power, especially in societies where only a tiny proportion of the population is literate. For most people, knowledge of all kinds—hunting expertise, farming know-how, weaving skills, and religious beliefs—passed from one generation to the next by word of mouth, through chants, rituals, and many other means. Art and architecture are powerful ways of propagating religious beliefs and ideologies, especially in highly centralized societies where the entire fabric of society depends on social conformity.

Strong ideologies drove all preindustrial civilizations. The Egyptian pharaohs were seen as living personifications of the Sun God Ra. Maya lords had divine ancestry and unique abilities to intercede with the supernatural world. The supreme Inca

Figure 17.7 Olmec figure with snarling lips.
(© Copyright The British Museum)

ruler epitomized the sun. The ideologies that reinforced these beliefs surrounded everyone; they were depicted with familiar motifs on textiles and pottery, on temple walls, and in carvings. Artifacts and buildings were often expressions of widely held religious beliefs.

Such ideologies come down to us in highly attenuated form. We see them in the snarling faces on Olmec portrait heads, axes, and altars from lowland Mesoamerica, where lords and jaguars had close associations, and where human shamans transformed themselves in trance into fierce beasts (Figure 17.7). We see them on the fine copper portraits of rulers and animals crafted by Hopewell artisans and buried with prominent individuals over two thousand years ago. Mississippian art motifs preserved on shell ornaments, pots, and other artifacts reflect religious beliefs that have survived, in modified form, into historic times. Decoding such messages is extremely difficult, especially when there are no ethnographic or historical accounts to guide the researcher.

The Moche state on the north coast of Peru enjoyed a flamboyant ideology and set of religious beliefs that are known to us only from the magnificent burials of the lords of Sipán (see Figure 1.4) and from detailed studies of sculpted and painted clay vessels crafted by Moche artisans (Alva and Donnan, 1993). Archaeologist Christopher Donnan has attempted to decode the iconography behind the pottery but has succeeded in only the most general terms (Donnan and McClelland, 1979). For example, he has identified a complex ceremony involving human sacrifice that was performed before warrior-priests wearing regalia precisely the same as that worn by the lords of Sipán (Alva and Donnan, 1993). The Sipán regalia reflect an ancient Andean duality between sun and moon, day and night, but to go into more detail without written sources is well-nigh impossible. Fortunately, some other exceptional studies of native South American religions, ancient and modern, give insights into such institutions as shamanism and ancestor worship in earlier times (L. Sullivan, 1989).

Research like Donnan's requires exceptional rigor, for it is all too easy to rely on intuition and aesthetic sense rather than demanding analysis. Another scholar, Olga Linares, has studied the ideology behind high-status cemeteries in central Panama. Using sixteenth-century Spanish eyewitness accounts of local Panamanian chiefdoms engaged in constant warfare and raiding and detailed information on local animal species, Linares (1977) studied graves and the flamboyant polychrome vessels found in them. They were open pots designed to be viewed from above, where mourners could see the animal motifs painted on them. Sometimes, apparently, the pots were so valuable that they were exhumed from one grave and put in another.

Ethnohistorical accounts mention that the highly competitive chiefs vied constantly for leadership and prestige, painting and tattooing their bodies with badges of rank and bravery. Each group of warriors wore distinctive symbols that associated them with their leader. They went to their graves with helmets, weapons, other military paraphernalia, and painted pottery. Linares noticed that the art styles rarely depicted plants, but rather many animal species, motifs that commemorated qualities of aggression and bravery. Crocodiles, large felines, sharks, stingrays, scorpions, and even poisonous snakes were the animals that were dangerous and, therefore, symbols of bravery. They often appeared on clay vessels, and sometimes parts of their bodies, such as sharks' teeth and stingray spines, were buried with the dead. In contrast, prey species and animals with soft parts like, say, monkeys, were largely ignored by the artists. Thus, the Panamanian chiefdoms used carefully selected animals to communicate the qualities most admired in chiefs and warriors.

Most of what we know about ancient religion comes from literate societies, where documents and inscriptions amplify the archaeological record in dramatic ways. We know a great deal about Mesopotamian and ancient Egyptian religion, but the most dramatic advances of recent years have come with the decipherment of Maya glyphs. For example, Linda Schele and David Friedel (1990, 1993) have studied Maya images and hieroglyphs and have used changes in them to trace changes in the meaning of symbols associated with political power. For example, they theorize that the religious symbolism of the late Preclassic two thousand years ago was based on the passage of Venus as morning and evening star with the rising and setting of the sun. The people of any Maya community could identify and verify their cosmos simply by observing the sky.

As time went on, Maya cosmology was expanded and elaborated. The names of late Preclassic rulers were not recorded publicly. Perhaps such permanent verification on public monuments had not yet been deemed necessary. Classic rulers followed a quite different strategy. They legitimized their rule through genealogies, public ceremonies, and monuments; much Classic Maya art was erected as part of this process of legitimizing rulers, who claimed identity with gods in the Maya cosmos. Schele and

Friedel believe that the metaphor of the twin ancestors—Venus and the sun—provided a potent image for lateral blood ties between lineages, communities, and everyone who believed in the same myths. Just as twins are of the same womb and blood, so all Maya are of common ancestry and blood.

Research on Maya glyphs and archaeological sites shows that archaeologists should never think of religion and ritual in isolation but rather as integral to social organization, economic life, and political systems. The ideas and beliefs, the core of all religions, are reflected in many aspects of human life, especially in art and architecture. Every society has its own model of how the world is put together, its own ultimate beliefs. These sacred propositions are interpreted for the faithful through a body of theology and rituals associated with it. Many rituals are more or less standardized religious acts, often repeated at regular times of the year—harvests, plantings, and other key times (Eliade, 1954). Others are performed when needed: marriages, funerals, and the like. Some societies, such as those of the ancient Egyptians and the Maya, made regular calendars to time religious events and astronomical cycles. These regular ceremonies performed important functions not only in integrating society but also in such activities as redistributing food, controlling population through infanticide, and dispersing surplus male cattle in the form of ritually accumulated wealth (see the Doing Archaeology box).

Religious experiences are predominantly emotional, often supernatural and awe-inspiring. Each aspect of religion—sacred propositions, ritual, experience—supports the others. A religion will operate through sanctified attitudes, values, and messages, an ethic that adds a sacred blessing, derived from the ultimate sacred propositions of the society, to elicit predictable responses from the people. Such predictability, sparked by directives from some central religious authority, ensures orderly operation of society. In time, as in Mesopotamia, that authority can become secular as well. The institutions and individuals associated with these messages can become sanctified, for they are associated with the sacred propositions that lie at the heart of the society's beliefs. As societies became more complex, so did the need for a stable framework to administer the needs of the many increasingly specialized subgroups that made up society as a whole. And architecture and sacred places played a central role in this ideological framework.

Sacred Places

Notre Dame de Chartres cathedral, France, built in a mere quarter-century in about A.D. 1195, is the sixth church built on the same site, a masterpiece where the infinite becomes a miracle in stone and glass (Figure 17.8). The cathedral is all windows, the great rose window of the western front symbolizing the Virgin Mary. Stained glass windows were a major element in Gothic architecture, ethereal settings among soaring beams and graceful arches. At Chartres, they became a form of new language, bringing together ancient principles of Christianity, many of them derived from even older cosmic beliefs. The rose was a powerful symbol that evoked soul, eternity, wheel, sun, and the cosmos. It was sacred to the Egyptian goddess Isis, to Greek Aphrodite, and to

Doing Archaeology

The Maya World through Glyphs

The decipherment of Maya glyphs was a magnificent scientific triumph, which resulted from inspired teamwork between epigraphers living in many countries (Coe, 1993). The process of decipherment continues to this day, to the point that we now have a rudimentary understanding of the intricate cosmology and religious beliefs of the ancient Maya, even if many details remain controversial. The glyphs give us a new understanding of the complex, multilayered Maya world. Great cities such as Copán, Palenque, and Tikal depicted the geography of the sacred world. Maya glyphs tell us that the world was alive and imbued with a sacredness that was concentrated at sacred points such as caves and mountains. The gods had created these spots when they created the cosmos. Living people built cities and communities within the matrix of the sacred landscape, which merged with divinely created patterns in caves and at the summits of humanly raised pyramids. At the same time, the world of human beings was connected to the Otherworld along the axis of a World Tree, which ran through the center of existence. This axis moved constantly but could be materialized through powerful rituals at any point in the natural and human-made landscapes.

Glyphs tell us how Maya lords went into hallucinogenic trances atop pyramid-mountains. They gashed their penises with stingray spines, a bloodletting ritual that brought the World Tree into existence through the middle of the temple atop the pyramid. The temple doorway became a sacred entrance to the Otherworld. Here, the ruler would mediate between the people and the gods and ancestors. Clouds of incense rose high above the temple as the ritual unfolded. This was the Vision Serpent, whose twisting coils symbolized the path of communication that linked the living and supernatural worlds.

Maya artists depicted the cosmos on special tripod plates designed to catch the blood that helped open the door to the Otherworld. A great bearded serpent with gaping jaws emitted the pure, life-bearing waters of the earth. Below, the dark waters of the Underworld flowed, with the World Tree emerging from the head of the Eveningstar god as he rose from primordial black waters.

A new generation of Maya research is combining glyphs with archaeology in efforts to decipher royal genealogies, to identify the builders of temples and pyramids, and to untangle the complex political history of a flamboyant, volatile civilization.

Venus, as a symbol of human love transcending passion. The major rose windows at Chartres depict the Virgin and Child (north), martyrs who spread the Word and the New Testament (south), and the wounded Christ at the center of the Last Judgment (west). All use the same vocabulary of color, form, geometry, and symbol. The gemlike transmutation of the light shining through the windows creates transcendental effects that could heal and revivify worshipers crowded in the nave. The pictures in the windows communicate the message of God for the illiterate who come to pray.

As did ancient Egyptian artists, the medieval artisans followed a standard vocabulary of forms as far as the disposition of figures and backgrounds were concerned.

Figure 17.8   Notre Dame de Chartres Cathedral, France.

They made use of unique geometrical compositions to structure the motifs of the windows, often with close ties to astrological and cosmological images and zodiacal symbolism. Chartres' windows were an integral part of a setting that brought heaven to earth and joined the secular and spiritual, as did the Aztec great temple at Tenochtitlán, Mexico, the Egyptian pyramids, and the Maya centers.

Chartres served the same purpose as much older sacred places. The cathedral was a magnet. The permanent population of medieval Chartres may have been no more than 1,500 people. The cathedral regularly attracted 10,000 worshipers, an offering to God as powerful as the human sacrifices of the Aztecs and the propitiating killing of children for Minoan deities. The cathedral provided a way of connecting the divine to the living world, for all things emanated from the Kingdom of God. Requiring enormous expenditures of human labor and sometimes extreme deprivation, Gothic cathedrals were expensive outpourings of love for the Deity as well as metaphorical sacrifices in stone and material goods offered in the expectation of divine favors in return. Chartres was the setting for dazzling spectacles. Sung masses and mystery plays depicting the life of Jesus or episodes in the lives of saints brought on intense emotional reactions among the faithful. The great cathedral bells tolled at times of joy, at moments of mourning. They sounded warnings and rang out in exultation and in crisis. Great preachers attracted huge crowds. Baptisms, marriages, funerals and prayers for the dead, ordinations and excommunications, victory celebrations and public meetings: the cathedral was the focus of human life.

As did Mesoamerican Indians, medieval Christians worried about the fertility of the land, the continuity of life itself. Every Easter Eve, a New Light was kindled, celebrating the Resurrection and the year's start. A thousand tapers were lit and carried from town to village, village to household, as life renewed. Autumn harvest festivals saw churches decorated with the fruits of the soil, commemorating the bounty of the soil, reminiscent of the Green Corn ceremonies of eastern North American groups. Seven centuries ago, the medieval cathedral was the Bible of the poor, an image of the cross and of the body of Christ, a corner of God's kingdom.

Sacred places were among ancient humanity's greatest achievements, mirrors of their spiritual world. Great Maya cities such as Copán (see Figure 9.13) and Tikal (see Figure 15.2) were vast replicas of the spiritual world wrought in stone and stucco, with sacred mountains (pyramids), carved stelae (trees), and reservoirs (lakes). They were oriented with the heavenly bodies and were settings for elaborate ceremonies when powerful lords would appear before their subjects in trance. Angkor Wat in Cambodia is one of the masterpieces of the ancient world. Khmer King Suryavarman II erected Angkor Wat as an observatory, shrine, and mausoleum in the early twelfth century A.D. (see Figure 16.3). The temple honors Vishnu, ruler of the western quarter of the compass. The five multitiered towers of the temple depict Mount Meru, home of the gods and center of the universe. Celestial maidens twist and cavort in endless dances on Angkor's walls, depicting the pleasures of paradise. More than a dozen Khmer princes built their shrines near this sacred place.

The great temple or ceremonial center was the focus of human life, the sanctified terrain where scheduled rituals guaranteed the seasonal renewal of cyclic time and where the splendor, potency, and wealth of rulers symbolized the well-being of the whole community. Such centers ensured the continuity of cultural traditions; the religious and moral models of society were laid down in sacred canons recited in temples in reassuring chants passed from generation to generation.

Such sacred places lay in the heart of much wider cultural landscapes, defined by generations of experience with supernatural qualities. They were the focus of much wider worlds, which is why settlement archaeology plays such an important role in the study of ancient religions. For instance, the celebrated stone circles at Avebury in southern Britain formed part of a much larger sacred landscape, defined not only by natural landmarks but also by burial mounds, sacred avenues delineated by stone uprights, and structures where the bodies of the dead were exposed before burial in communal tombs (see Figure 8.1). In recent years, teams of archaeologists have been gradually reconstructing this long-vanished, fragmentary landscape with survey and excavation that reveal its gradual evolution over many centuries (Whittle, 1993; Whittle and others, 1993).

Cahokia, Illinois

The great Mississippian center Cahokia lies on the Mississippi floodplain near St. Louis in the heart of a pocket of extremely fertile bottomland known as the American Bottom. At the height of its powers, between A.D. 1050 and 1250, Cahokia covered an area of more than 5 square miles (13 sq. km), about the size of the ancient city of

Figure 17.9   Artist's reconstruction of the central plaza of Cahokia, Illinois, as it would have appeared at its peak, c. A.D. 1150.

Teotihuacán in the Valley of Mexico (Milner, 1998). Several thousand people lived in pole-and-thatch houses covering about 2,000 acres (800 ha), clustered on either side of a central east-west ridge. More than 100 earthen mounds of various sizes, shapes, and functions dot the Cahokia landscape, most grouped around open plazas. The largest, Monk's Mound, dominates the site and the surrounding landscape. Monk's Mound rises in four terraces to a height of 100 feet (31 m) and covers 16 acres (6.4 ha), slightly larger an area than Egypt's Great Pyramid of 13 acres (5.3 ha) (Figure 17.9). Fortunately for science, the ancient cosmology and religious beliefs behind Cahokia can be pieced together, at least partially, from a combination of archaeology in the American Bottom and ethnohistory derived from historic southeastern Indian groups (Emerson, 1997; Pauketat and Emerson, 1997).

The layout of Cahokia reflects a traditional Southeastern cosmos with four opposed sides, as seen in the layout of their platform mounds, great mounds, and imposing plazas. By A.D. 1050, the rectangular plaza surrounded by mounds reenacted the ancient quadripartite pattern of the cosmos, seen in much earlier settlements along the Mississippi. Four-sided Mississippian platform mounds may portray the cosmos as "earth-islands," just as modern-day Muskogean Indians thought of the world as flat-topped and four-sided. Archaeologist John Douglas uses ethnographic and archaeological data to argue that the four-sided cosmos had a primary axis that ran northwest to southeast, with an opposite axis dividing the world into four diamond-shaped quarters (Pauketat and Emerson, 1997). Cahokia is oriented along a slightly different north-south axis, but it certainly perpetuates the notion of spiritual links between opposites and a cosmos divided into quarters. Researchers believe the orientation reflects observations of the sun rather than the moon, as if Cahokia's rulers used the sun to schedule the annual rituals that commemorated the cycles of the agricultural year (Aveni, 1993).

Cosmology in historic Southeastern Indian societies revolved around dualities. In the case of Cahokia, these may have included the Upper and Lower Worlds and a powerful and pervasive fertility cult linked to commoners and the elite. These dualities were carried through to the smallest ritual centers. Changing settlement layouts imply that, at first, local communities and kin groups controlled fertility rituals in dispersed households divided into symbolic quarters, with ceremonial structures facing a central square. Later, centers display more formal layouts, with central plazas, elaborate sacred buildings, and storage and ritual pits filled with offerings made during fertility and world-renewal ceremonies. By this time, experts believe, power was passing from local kin leaders to a powerful elite based at Cahokia, a shift reflected in increasingly elaborate ceremonial architecture, residences for local leaders at local centers, and special mortuary complexes. Their carefully laid out centers brought two central ritual themes together: the spiritual realm of fertility and life and the validation of living rulers, who were intermediaries with the supernatural realm. Cahokia and other Mississippian centers reflect an ancient cosmology in a symbolic language intelligible to noble and commoner alike.

Astroarchaeology and Stonehenge

Astroarchaeology is the study of ancient astronomical observances (Aveni, 1993). The movements of the sun and moon and other heavenly bodies played an important role in many ancient societies, among them ancient Egyptian civilization, the Maya, and many Andean cultures. Astroarchaeology is an important source of information about ancient religious beliefs and cosmologies.

Astroarchaeology is a far cry from the crazy theories of cultists who claim Egypt's Pyramids of Giza were a giant, highly sophisticated astronomical observatory run with computers. (Correspondence from such "theorists" lands in a file in BMF's office named "Pyramidiots.") Modern research into ancient astronomy uses computer software to examine the sky over the Maya homeland on specific years and makes highly accurate observations of astronomical alignments at Stonehenge, Hopewell monuments in Ohio, and other sites known to have astronomical associations.

More nonsense has been written about the stone circles at Stonehenge, England, than about almost any other archaeological site in the world (Chippindale, 1994) (see Figure 2.2). After more than three centuries of sporadic research, scientists are still deeply divided about the significance of this extraordinary monument, the prehistoric equivalent of a Norman cathedral, used and modified from about 2950 to 1600 B.C. Was it the center of some long-forgotten religious cult, or was it an observatory, a sophisticated place of dialogue with the sun and stars? (Cleal and others, 1995).

In the 1960s, Boston astronomer Gerald Hawkins (1965) used an IBM mainframe computer to plot the positions of 165 key points: stones, stone holes, earthworks, and other fixed points. He found "total sun [and moon] correlation" with a network of thirteen solar and eleven lunar alignments, all of them based on features of early, rather than later, Stonehenge, where the alignments were less precise. Hawkins called Stonehenge a "Neolithic computer" used for predicting lunar eclipses. From the archaeologists' point of view, the fatal flaw in Hawkins's reasoning was his assumption that any alignments he saw, as a twentieth-century astronomer, were also known to the original builders. Hawkins was familiar with abstruse astronomical data. How could one assume Stone Age or Bronze Age farmers had the same expertise, especially since they had to cope with the cloudy and unpredictable sighting conditions of the British heavens? Hawkins's astronomy was little more than an anecdotal way of explaining Stonehenge. A decade later, retired engineering professor Alexander Thom announced that Stonehenge's stone circles were a "central backsight for observing heavenly bodies," used with no less than eight "foresights," mostly earthworks identified on the visible horizon. Unfortunately, Thom failed to reconcile the archaeological and astronomical evidence. Nearly all his "foresight" earthworks are of later date than the stone circles of the "backsight" (Thom, 1971).

Was Stonehenge an observatory? One cannot speak of it in the same breath as sophisticated Maya observatories or of the builders as astronomers on a par with Babylonian priests. We have known since the seventeenth century that Stonehenge was aligned on the axis of the midsummer sun. But the stone circles were never an elaborate device for predicting eclipses or measuring the sky. Rather, Stonehenge reflects a distinctive idea of time, which revolved around the cyclical movements of sun, moon, and stars across the heavens, as indicators of the passing seasons (Aveni, 1993).

The farmers who built the later Stonehenge lived in a demanding environment where the passage of the seasons governed their lives. Every year, the eternal cycles of planting, growth, and harvest, of symbolic life and death, repeated themselves in endless successions of good and bad harvests, of drought and excess rainfall, of famine and plenty (Fagan, 1998). The people placed great store in death rituals, in reverence of the ancestors, the guardians of the land. They devoted enormous resources to the great stone circles in the midst of their sacred landscape, where their priests and shamans used the stone uprights and simple stone alignments to observe the passage of the seasons. At midsummer sunrise and, perhaps, on the shortest day of the year, about December 21, the priests stood at the open side of the horseshoes to observe sunrise or sunset. In winter, the setting of the winter sun at the solstice signaled the beginning of lengthening days and the certainty that the cycle of the seasons would begin anew.

We have great difficulty envisaging Stonehenge in its heyday, sitting as it does in the midst of a late-twentieth-century landscape. Our only impressions can come from our physical perceptions of what it was like to move around both outside and inside the monument. These perceptions must be fundamentally similar to those of the ancients, for the stone uprights still tower overhead and restrict the view, as they did 4,500 years ago. With the exercise of ritual power, setting is everything. Stonehenge was such a setting.

The lesson of Stonehenge lies in the continuities of farming life, rather than changes. Chieftains lived and died, achieved great power and supernatural authority, and, in time, became ancestors. As villages prospered and more people crowded the densely farmed landscape, always at the center of this busy world lay a set of ancient values and beliefs epitomized by the weathered stone circles of Stonehenge. The seasons came and went, and so did human life itself, while Stonehenge remained an idea of time, a place where relationships between the living, the dead, and the supernatural were commemorated in stone.

Southwestern Astronomy and Chaco Canyon

Agriculture and religion intersected the lives of the ancient Pueblo Indians of the Southwest, living as they did in a region of unpredictable rainfall, where the timing of harvest and planting was everything. The Pueblo world was one of close interdependence between farming and religious observance and between isolated communities, large and small. The major ceremonies of the summer and winter solstices brought people together in implicit recognition of this interdependence (Lekson, 1999).

The Pueblo tied their world to the horizon and the heavens by making a calendar out of the environment around them. The Hopi, for example, oriented themselves to the points on the horizon that mark the places of sunrise and sunset at the summer and winter solstices (Zeilik, 1985). The Pueblo anchored time, and their ritual cycles, to these events, especially to the winter solstice, when the sun is at its southernmost point. They believed that if the sun did not turn round, then it would fall off into the underworld. Some groups observed a period of "staying still," to keep the sun in its winter house. Winter solstice ceremonies guided the sun in the correct direction. The sun priests set the days for these ceremonies, as well as the lesser celebrations in the annual calendar, starting their prayers and observations about twenty-eight days before the winter solstice and twenty-nine days before the summer. They used a chosen spot in the village for their work, tracking the sun's seasonal position with the aid of horizon markers, which showed up clearly at sunrise. Sometimes, they employed windows in buildings to manipulate light and shadow.

Sun watching required much more than observation of solstices and other events. The sun priest had to make anticipatory observations over three weeks before an event such as a solstice celebration to allow for preparations to be made. He also required lengthy training, so he could predict events during times of bad weather. This is why he had to know the position of sunrise relative to horizon markers several weeks before the event. At the solstice, the sun stands still on the horizon for four days, making the observation of the actual solstice day impossible beforehand. So the sun priest had to make his observations at a time when the sun was still moving perceptibly every day, in human-eye terms, about 10 minutes of arc (arcmins) a day. He could predict the day of the solstice by making the observation and then keeping a tally of days on a notched stick. This approach solved the problem of cloud cover and bad weather. By using any clear day well ahead of time, the observer could use his notched stick to calculate the correct day even if the sky was overcast.

Predictions of the summer solstice based on this method are remarkably accurate, almost invariably to within a day and a half. Such accuracy was essential. A major disaster would occur if the ceremonies took place and the sun had already turned or was still moving toward its turning point, as if it were about to fall off the earth. Accurate predictions reinforced priestly power, strengthened bonds within the community, and validated the worldview.

Ecological time served the Pueblo well. They lived a well-regulated life attuned to the solstices and to the realities of their arid environment. The yearly cycle repeated itself endlessly. As one year ended, another began, measured in the passage of moons and days.

Fortunately for science, pre-Columbian astronomers used buildings, pictographs, and other human-manufactured objects for their observations, enabling us to trace Pueblo astronomy back to the Ancestral Pueblo (formerly called the Anasazi, "the ancient ones") whose primordial roots extend back as far as 2,500 years ago.

The best archaeological evidence for Pueblo astronomy comes from Hovenweep Pueblo in Colorado, erected by Ancestral Pueblo people related to nearby Mesa Verde communities between the late twelfth and mid-thirteenth centuries. The pueblo includes round, square, or D-shaped towers. At least one, Hovenweep Castle, has special sun-sighting ports aligned with the summer and winter solstices. Nearby, Holly House contains petroglyph panels with symbols that may represent the sun and other heavenly bodies (Cordell, 1997).

The first farmers of the Southwest dwelt in small communities of pit houses. By A.D. 900, Southwestern farming populations rose considerably. Many Ancestral Pueblo communities moved into large, well-constructed towns, epitomized by the great pueblos of Chaco Canyon (Vivian, 1990). For two and a half centuries the Chaco Canyon pueblos flourished, during a time of constant climatic change. By 1050, the Chaco Phenomenon (an archaeological term) was in full swing. The Phenomenon expanded from its canyon homeland to encompass an area of more than 24,900 square miles (65,000 sq. m) of the surrounding San Juan Basin and adjacent uplands. Roads and visual communication systems linked outlying communities with the canyon. Great pueblos such as semicircular Pueblo Bonito housed hundreds of people (Figure 17.10). The population of Chaco Canyon rose from a few hundred to at least 5,500 inhabitants, with many more people visiting for major ceremonies and trading activities.

Figure 17.10   Pueblo Bonito in Chaco Canyon, New Mexico.

During the 1970s and 1980s, aerial photographs and side-scan radar placed Chaco at the center of a vast ancient landscape (Cordell, 1997). A web of over 400 miles (650 km) of unpaved ancient roadways links Chaco with more than thirty outlying settlements. The Ancestral Pueblo had no carts or draft animals, but they built shallow trackways up to 40 feet (12 m) wide, cut a few inches into the underlying soil or demarcated by low banks or stone walls. Each highway runs straight for long distances, some as far as 60 miles (95 km), each linked to a major pueblo at the canyon itself. The people approached the canyon along straight walkways, descending to the pueblos down stone-cut steps in the cliffs.

The Chacoan "roads" are a mystery. Were they used for travel or transportation of vital commodities? For years, archaeologists have argued for some form of integrating Chacoan cultural system that would have unified a large area of the Southwest a thousand years ago (see the summary in Fagan, 2005). One authority, archaeologist James Judge, believes that the San Juan Basin's harsh and unpredictable climate, with its frequent droughts, caused isolated pueblos to form loosely structured alliances for exchanging food and other vital commodities. Chaco lay at the hub of the exchange system and also served as the ritual center for major rainmaking ceremonies and festivals. The canyon's Great Houses were the homes of privileged families who were able to predict the movements of heavenly bodies and controlled ritual activity.

In Judge's scenario, the roads were pilgrimage and trading walkways (see the summary of arguments in Vivian, 1997). However, archaeologist John Roney of the Bureau of Land Management points out that there are no signs of domestic rubbish or encampments along the roads. On the ground, he has followed many of the fuzzy lines on air photographs, verifying more than sixty road segments, many of them short and without specific destination. Roney is certain that major north and south tracks radiated from Chaco, but he is cautious about joining segments into long lines uniting distant places on the map. He is sure of a mere 155 miles (250 km) of roads, and believes that the Chacoans constructed the walkways as monuments, as a ritual gesture, not to be used.

Do roads have to lead to a destination, as we Westerners always believe? The answer to the Chaco road mystery may lie not in the archaeological record but in Pueblo Indian cosmology. The so-called Great North Road is a case in point. Several roadways from Pueblo Bonito and Chetro Ketl ascend Chaco's north wall to converge on Pueblo Alto. From there, the road travels 13 degrees east of north for about 2 miles (3 km) before heading due north for nearly 30 miles (50 km) across open country to Kutz Canyon, where it vanishes. North is the primary direction in the mythology of modern-day Keresan-speaking Pueblo peoples, who may have ancestry among Chaco communities. North led to the place of origin, the place where the spirits of the dead went. Chaco's Great North Road may have been an umbilical cord to the underworld, a conduit of spiritual power. Another Pueblo concept, that of the Middle Place, was the point where the four cardinal directions converged. Pueblo Bonito, with its cardinal layout, may have been the Middle Place.

The Great Houses and trackways of Chaco Canyon may have formed a sacred landscape, a symbolic stage where the Ancestral Pueblo acted out their beliefs and commemorated the passage of seasons. Fortunately, new scientific technologies such

Discovery

The 'Ain Ghazal Figurines, Jordan

Studying ancient religious beliefs using only material remains is one of the hardest challenges for an archaeologist. Fortunately, an occasional remarkable discovery yields compelling evidence for the intangible. The village of 'Ain Ghazal in Jordan was a flourishing community of cereal farmers and goatherds before 7500 B.C. The site was discovered during road work on the edge of modern-day Amman. The excavations yielded well-planned dwellings and even the toe bones of goats with scarring caused by the tethering ropes used in their pens.

The most remarkable 'Ain Ghazal discovery came in 1974, when archaeologists Gary Rollefson and Alan Simmons discovered a cache of badly fractured, plaster human figures in an early farming settlement. The figures date to about 7000 B.C. They look like department store mannequins with square, stylized torsos supporting lifelike shoulders and long necks with heads that bear calm,

expressive faces. The incised eyes, inlaid with bitumen, stare into space in an almost eerie fashion (Figure 17.11). Some figures had two heads, as if they memorialized a husband and wife or dual deities.

No one knows exactly what the figures were used for, but there is good reason to believe that they were revered ancestor figures in farming societies with close ties to the land, which was farmed by the same families for many generations. Rollefson and Simmons believe that the figures may once have worn garments, perhaps cloaks or ceremonial gowns that covered their torsos and nonexistent arms. Headdresses or long scarves may have adorned their heads.

Whether ancestors, gods, or just prominent individuals, the 'Ain Ghazal figures once commemorated powerful but intangible beliefs that have long vanished into oblivion. They offer a good example of the challenge facing archaeologists studying ancient human beliefs.

Figure 17.11 'Ain Ghazal figurines.

as the Geographic Information System (GIS) are combining multispectrum imagery, color infrared photographs, and 1930s half-tone images. By enhancing different light, heat, and vegetational conditions, fieldworkers can go into the field with information on hitherto invisible features, locating themselves on the ground with the satellite-driven global positioning system (GPS), which can fix their position within a few feet. A new generation of survey work will establish the true extent of Chacoan roads and place them in a precise topographical context.

It is hard for us to reconstruct the intangible religious beliefs of the remote past, separated as we are from them by many centuries. Just how hard can be imagined by listening to modern-day storytellers as they recite well-known tales to an audience that has heard them again and again but never tires of the story and its morals. I have heard Pueblo Indian storytellers recite from memory, face to face with their audiences, often for as long as an hour at time, holding their listeners spellbound with tales that bind living people to the world of the sun and the moon, of animals and plants like humans. The plots twist and turn, with heroes and terrifying hazards, tests of skill and wisdom. Almost invariably, the tale involves deeply felt religious beliefs and the spiritual world. Only a fraction of these tales survive, lovingly transcribed, edited, and translated as a permanent record of a vanishing world. Many tell of the sun, whose powers of warmth and light sustained life itself. One Hopi tale recounts how a young man was conceived by the Sun and journeyed to visit his father. After many adventures, including a journey across the heavens, he returned happy: "I saw for myself how he attends to our needs every single day of our lives. Therefore we must live out our lives in a good manner, and he will never forsake us" (Swann, 1994:678).

Fortunately, a new generation of archaeological research is beginning to study the fascinating and complex world of the ancient intangible (see the Discovery box).

Summary

Archaeologists study the religious beliefs of ancient societies by using material remains and information from a variety of sources. Many ancient religions shared common features: a multilayered cosmos, a cyclical existence, important locations that were axes of the world, and a concern with ancestors and shamanism.

Cognitive archaeology studies both the cognitive abilities of early hominids and Archaic humans and the cognitive aspects of modern human behavior. It is an approach to cosmology, religion, ideology, and iconography based on rigorous analysis and data from many sources.

Ethnographic analogy plays an important role in studying ancient rock art, thanks to anthropological research among the San of southern Africa a century ago. Richly adorned burials can provide information on religious beliefs as well as social ranking, but the major source of such information comes from art and artifacts. The context of artifacts in time and space is of vital importance, because it can often reveal more information than the objects themselves. Rigorous studies of art styles, such as that of the Moche of Peru or the Maya, can yield valuable information on ancient ideologies, especially if combined with ethnographic or written records.

Artifacts and art styles offer valuable insights into ancient religious beliefs through their use of standardized themes. Sacred places such as Cahokia, Illinois, medieval cathedrals, or Maya cities were vital catalysts for religious beliefs, for they were the settings for rituals of validation and other ceremonies.

Settlement archaeology plays an important role in studying such locations in the context of their wider landscape. So does astroarchaeology, the study of ancient astronomy, notably successful in the American Southwest, at Stonehenge, England, and with the Maya civilization.

Key Terms

astroarchaeology

cognitive archaeology

cosmology

iconography

ideology

shaman

Guide to Further Reading

AVENI, ANTHONY. 1993. *Ancient Astronomy.* Washington, DC: Smithsonian Books. An excellent summary of what we know about the astronomy of the ancients; for the wider audience.

CHIPPINDALE, CHRISTOPHER. 1994. *Stonehenge Complete.* 2d ed. London: Thames and Hudson. The best source on Stonehenge for the general reader.

FAGAN, BRIAN. 1998. From *Black Land to Fifth Sun.* Reading, MA: Perseus Books. A survey of the archaeology of mind for the general reader that consists mainly of case studies.

LEWIS-WILLIAMS, J. DAVID. 2002. *The Mind in the Cave.* London and New York: Thames and Hudson. A general survey of prehistoric rock art, with discussion of shamanistic theories.

LINARES, OLGA. 1977. *Ecology and the Arts in Ancient Panama: On the Development of Social Rank and Symbolism in the Central Provinces.* Washington, DC: Dumbarton Oaks. The definitive monograph on her research.

PAUKETAT, TIMOTHY R., and THOMAS E. EMERSON, eds. 1997. *Cahokia: Domination and Ideology in the Mississippian World.* Lincoln: University of Nebraska Press. A technical series of essays on Mississippian religious beliefs and archaeology.

SCHELE, LINDA, and DAVID FRIEDEL. 1990. *A Forest of Kings.* New York: William Morrow. A popular account of Maya civilization that is a mine of information on religion, iconography, and social ranking. Controversial, engrossing, and readable.

———. 1993. *Maya Cosmos.* New York: William Morrow. A companion to the preceding reference that explores the Maya heavens.

SULLIVAN, LAWRENCE. 1989. *Icanchu's Drum.* New York: Free Press. Sullivan's study of ancient and modern Latin American indigenous religions is a remarkable monograph that should be read by every archaeologist.

PART VII

Cultural Resource Management

> *These great towns and temples and buildings rising from the water, all made of stone, seemed like an enchanted vision. . . . Indeed some of our soldiers asked whether it was not all a dream. . . . I stood looking at it, and thought no land like it would ever be discovered in the whole world. . . . But today all that I then saw is overthrown and destroyed; nothing is left standing.*
>
> Bernal Díaz del Castillo on Aztec Tenochtitlán,
> *The Conquest of New Spain*, A.D. *1519*

We have almost completed our journey through the complexities of contemporary archaeology, a journey that should leave you with some insights into the processes of archaeological research. Our discussion of contemporary archaeology would be incomplete, however, without considering cultural resource management and public archaeology, two of the most pressing and complex aspects of the discipline. A major crisis confronts archaeologists: destruction of finite resources. Chapter 18 is devoted entirely to the management of the past and the public archaeology associated with it; both deserve more extended discussion in their own right.

CHAPTER 18

Managing the Past
and Public Archaeology

CRM excavation in the center median of Interstate 10, Tucson, Arizona.

As we saw in Chapter 1, archaeology in North America has turned from a purely academic discipline into a profession as much concerned with conservation and management of the finite resources of the past as it is with the pursuit of knowledge for knowledge's sake (Green and Doershuk, 1998).

American archaeologists have always been concerned about the destruction of the archaeological record, but this concern has deepened since the 1960s with rapid population growth, accelerated road construction and urban development, and the intensification of strip mining and industrial-scale deep plowing (Fowler, 1982). The looting of sites for salable antiquities further threatens to the material record of the past. In many areas the situation has reached crisis proportions. It has, for example, been estimated that less than 5 percent of the pre-1850s archaeological record of Los Angeles County remains undisturbed. Charles McGimsey (1972) estimated that at least 25 percent of the sites that existed in Arkansas in 1750 were destroyed by agricultural and other land use, to say nothing of looters, between 1962 and 1972.

In North America, the management and stewardship of precious archaeological resources is now the primary way in which archaeologists go about their business. This chapter is principally concerned with cultural resource management in the United States, where most of our readership resides. But cultural resource management and cultural heritage are of worldwide concern.

Cultural Resources and Antiquities Legislation

Cultural resources are the human-made and natural features associated with human activity. They are the unique and nonrenewable sites, structures, and artifacts that make up the material record of the human past. **Cultural resource management (CRM)** is the application of management skills to preserve important parts of our cultural heritage, both historic and prehistoric, for the benefit of the public today and in the future (Figure 18.1).

Figure 18.1   The Great Serpent Mound, Hopewell, Adams County, Ohio, an early example of archaeological conservation. This remarkable monument, a depiction of a serpent devouring a burial mound, was saved by the efforts of Harvard archaeologist Frederick Putnam and a group of Boston women in 1886. In recent years, the mound was again saved from development through the concerted efforts of local archaeologists. (Courtesy, National Museum of the American Indian, Smithsonian Institution. [N21598] Photo by Major Dache M. Reeves.)

The first formal legal efforts to preserve America's past began with the passage of the Antiquities Act of 1906, which was primarily aimed at controlling a lucrative trade in painted pueblo pots from the Southwest. Unfortunately, this act only extended protection to archaeological sites on land owned or controlled by the United States government; archaeological resources located on nongovernment lands continued to be looted. There matters remained until the 1940s, when widespread archaeological surveys in areas threatened by federal dam projects yielded a mass of information on site distributions and key cultural sequences before the sites where they occurred vanished forever under man-made lakes (Fowler, 1986).

Since World War II, the accelerating destruction of archaeological sites throughout North America has resulted in a jigsaw pattern of legislation that serves as a framework for cultural resource management. CRM has emerged as a sophisticated phenomenon, its practice surrounded by an elaborate framework of laws, regulations, and statutes, not only at the federal and state levels but also at the county, city, and Native American tribal levels (see the Doing Archaeology box) (Cleere, 1989; Hardesty and Little, 2000; Hutt and others, 1993; Neumann and Sanford, 2001; G. S. Smith and Ehrenhard, 1991). Such local laws have become essential to deal with both looting and an explosion of destructive urban development, as well as with additional concerns such as public education and the repatriation of Native American skeletal remains. CRM archaeology is now an enormous enterprise, ranging in scope from multi-million-dollar projects to small-scale operations involving no more than a small urban plot or a simple survey of a few acres of farmland.

Cultural resource legislation is not the only protective tool available to archaeologists. Other laws may be invoked to protect archaeological sites, particularly in cases where the sites are on private lands. In some instances, private groups have also played central roles in the protection of resources. The Archaeological Conservancy is a bright hope, a privately funded membership organization formed in the early 1980s to purchase threatened archaeological sites and manage them as permanent archaeological preserves on hundred-year management plans. The sites this organization has purchased include the Hopewell Mound group in Ohio; Savage Cave in Kentucky, a site with human occupation from Paleo-Indian to Mississippian times; and San Marcos Pueblo in New Mexico, a 200-room pueblo near Santa Fe. (You can join by writing to the Archaeological Conservancy at 5301 Central Ave NE, Suite 1218, Albuquerque, NM 87108.)

Although local situations vary, it is federal CRM legislation that provides the principal means of protecting the nation's cultural resources. The most important federal legislation, including the Reservoir Salvage Act, Historical Preservation Act, National Environmental Policy Act, Executive Order 11593, Archaeological Resources Protection Act, Abandoned Shipwreck Act, and Native American Grave Protection and Repatriation Act, are discussed in the Doing Archaeology box.

The result of all this legislation has been a dramatic explosion in the amount of archaeological effort, much of it contracted by government agencies, as well as by private companies undertaking development work. Whereas fifty years ago most archaeologists in the United States were employed by universities or museums, the majority now work in a variety of federal and state departments and private companies concerned with cultural resource management (DeCorse and DiSanto, 1999; Zeder, 1997). The money expended on the salvage and mitigation of archaeological sites has resulted in some of the largest excavations in recent history and in some the most innovative approaches to remote sensing and scientific applications.

What Is Protected?

Most Americans likely assume that the nation's historic sites and archaeological resources are well protected and safe for archaeologists to study and future generations to enjoy. However, the actual protection that cultural resources are afforded differs from state to state and from site to site. The legal compliance process on a project is, at best, an attempt to see that cultural resources threatened by the project are properly managed—recorded, evaluated, protected, or, if necessary, salvaged.

The legal basis for the protection of archaeological sites continues to be modified, but there are many gaps. While the United States has better CRM legislation

Doing Archaeology

Some Cultural Resource Management Legislation in the United States, 1960 Onward

This is a summary of some of the key features of federal legislation, which built on the Historic Sites Act of 1935. This baseline act gave the National Park Service a broad mandate to identify, protect, and preserve cultural properties (T. F. King, 1998). Numerous state, local, and Native American tribal laws amplify and complicate this already complex legislative picture.

Reservoir Salvage Act of 1960

This act authorized archaeologists to dig and salvage sites that were in danger of destruction as a result of federally owned and funded dam projects. The act led to a number of large surveys and mitigation projects.

Historic Preservation Act of 1966 (amended in 1976 and 1980)

This act set up a national framework for historic preservation, requiring the federal government to establish a nationwide system for identifying, protecting, and rehabilitating what are commonly called "historic places." The act called for the establishment of the National Register of Historic Places (a "historic place" could include prehistoric and historic archaeological sites) and required federal agencies to protect Register properties when development projects were planned.

National Environmental Policy Act (NEPA) of 1969

NEPA went far beyond protection and laid down a comprehensive policy for government land-use planning and resource management. It requires federal agencies to weigh environmental, historical, and cultural values whenever federally owned land is modified or private land is modified with federal funds. NEPA ordered all federal agencies to take the lead in historic preservation and to locate properties that might qualify for the National Register. They were also to develop programs to contribute to the protection of important historic properties on nonfederal lands.

Executive Order 11593 (1972)

Executive Order 11593 and NEPA developed requirements that made it essential for archaeologists to prepare and maintain extremely comprehensive information on archaeological resources on state, federal, and privately owned land. This information would enable them to assess, at short notice, the potential effects of development on these resources. In addition, the states had developed historic preservation programs of their own, as required by the Historic Preservation Act of 1966.

Archaeological Resources Protection Act (ARPA) of 1979

ARPA gave more stringent protection to archaeological sites over one hundred years old on federal land. People removing archaeological materials from federal lands without a permit are committing a felony and can be fined up to $10,000 and sentenced to a year in prison. The penalties rise sharply when more valuable finds are involved. This legislation is aimed at commercial vandals; it does not forbid individuals from removing arrowheads "located on the surface of the ground." Unfortunately, it gives no protection to archaeological resources on privately owned land. Amendments to ARPA in recent years have tightened the definition of what constitutes an "archaeological resource" and have legislated far more severe penalties for violations of the original law.

Abandoned Shipwrecks Act of 1988

This act extends protection to shipwrecks and defined ownership of abandoned vessels in state and federal waters more clearly. It is an important weapon in the fight against unauthorized looting of shipwrecks, looting that all too often masquerades as "underwater archaeology" (Figure 18.2).

Native American Grave Protection and Repatriation Act of 1990

NAGPRA requires all museums and institutions receiving federal funds to inventory their holdings of Native American human remains, funerary objects, sacred objects, and what are called "objects of cultural patrimony" in the collections they control. They must establish, as best they can, whether their individual holdings have cultural affiliations, or, in the case of skeletons, lineal descendants in living Native American groups. If relationships are established, the institutions are required to notify the relevant Native American organization about the existence of the materials and offer to repatriate them. NAGPRA also protects all Native American graves and other cultural objects found within archaeological sites on federal and tribal land. This requirement encourages the in situ preservation of archaeological sites, or at least those parts of them that contain graves. It also requires anyone carrying out archaeological investigation on federal and tribal lands to consult with affiliated or potentially affiliated Native Americans concerning the treatment and disposition of any finds, whether made during formal investigations or by accident.

Figure 18.2   Underwater archaeologists battle constantly against unauthorized looting of ancient shipwrecks, which enjoy only limited protection against disturbance.

than some countries do, it lags behind some others in protecting cultural resources. The Archaeological Resources Protection Act of 1979, which gives federal resource managers and prosecutors access to stringent criminal and civil penalties, was passed relatively recently. Until that time the United States had no laws forbidding the export of antiquities. Penalties for looting have slowed the destruction of sites on public lands (G. S. Smith and Ehrenhard, 1991). The Abandoned Shipwrecks Act of 1988 has finally extended a degree of protection to shipwrecks in U.S. waters, though not before incalculable damage was done by professional treasure hunters and amateur divers. Even now, certain types of development still threaten these resources.

The ethics of archaeology demand that as many sites as possible be preserved. Ideally, sites are not threatened by development and are excavated on the basis of scientific considerations and with clear research designs. However, in reality many other variables—project budgets, mitigation costs, public interest, and project design alternatives, to mention only a few—come into play when sites are threatened by imminent destruction.

Then there is the problem of "secondary impacts," when unexpected spin-offs of the main project destroy unprotected resources outside the main project area. Don Fowler (1982) cited the classic example of the monstrous, and later canceled, MX missile project in the Great Basin, which would have affected archaeological resources in no fewer than twenty-three valleys in the region. Although the project would have primarily affected sites in the lowlands, the archaeologists pointed out that most of the sites lay in the foothills and uplands nearby. These sites would have been affected disastrously by secondary activities such as seismic testing, survey work, and the sheer numbers of construction workers and military personnel brought into the area during the MX project. Whether effective ways of mitigating these secondary impacts would have been possible is questionable. Few, if any, agencies consider such impacts, but they are often critical to archaeologists.

In general, archaeological sites on government lands, including national and state parks, forests, reservoirs, and military bases, are well protected. These areas are required by law to have management plans in place, and an active effort is made to document and protect their archaeological resources. Government archaeologists oversee development and contract private archaeologists to conduct work (see the Doing Archaeology box on Fort Drum, pp. 494–495). Some of the nation's best documented and protected archaeological sites, albeit somewhat inaccessible to the public, are located on military reservations. A case in point is the China Lake Naval Air Weapons Station in southern California, site of the Coso Petroglyphs National Historic Site, which includes some of the nation's most spectacular rock art (Whitley, 1998b). The sites are open to the public only through special arrangements on a limited basis.

The largest gap in cultural resource protection in the United States is on private lands. Despite the comprehensive appearance of antiquities legislation, for the most part it remains focused on government lands and development projects requiring government funding and permits. In many countries, antiquities are considered the property of the state regardless of where they are found. In contrast, the law in the United States is ambiguous because the Fifth Amendment to the U.S. Constitution forbids the seizure of private property for public use without just compensation. Private property is almost sacrosanct, and over the years, archaeological resources on private land have come to be thought of as part of that land and, therefore, the private property of the owner. The power of eminent domain, zoning, easements, tax incentives, and even laws concerning burials are tools that may be used to protect cultural resources on private land. Yet these tools were designed to meet other needs and are irregularly and inadequately applied to CRM concerns.

Although many owners take the preservation of archaeological resources on their land very seriously, others do not. Unrecorded sites may be unknowingly plowed over, while others are destroyed by landowners who regard sites as sources of income. As legal and official pressures on looters and pothunters increase, prices in the auction room and on the illegal market go up. More and more sites on private and public land are being mined secretly for profit. Among the pieces most in demand are the beautifully painted Mimbres ceramics from the valley of that name in New Mexico (see Figure 13.14). Almost all major Mimbres sites, including those on federal and state land, have been ravaged in recent years, many with backhoes. The pace of damage is accelerating.

It is in the West that the most extensive damage has been done, for the stunning basketry and pottery of Southwest Native Americans have attracted collectors and dealers for more than a century. One Anasazi basket alone went for $152,000 in a London auction room some years ago, while a Mississippian stone ax was sold in New Orleans for $150,000. Even relatively prosaic vessels may be worth several hundred dollars, so there is a flourishing commercial, but underground, trade, which is probably a network of well-connected operators. Their work may not lead to fabulous profits, but it does yield enough to keep the enterprise alive. The situation is eerily like that of the drug trade. A crackdown in the field leads to higher prices; in the case of American Indian artifacts, there are plenty of wealthy private collectors at home and overseas who care nothing about ethics. Native Americans have long fought against such activities, which they regard as sacrilege, theft of their native patrimony, and common greed. Today, archaeologists and Native Americans are developing a sometimes uneasy alliance against a common enemy—the looter.

Managing the Past

Cultural resource management, and the archaeological research that goes with it, are but one component of a much larger enterprise: the consequences of human activity on the entire landscape (see Chapter 8; Adovasio and Carlisle, 1988). In this context, decisions concerning the finite archaeological record are part of the greater concern for the fragile ecology of North America and human impact on the environment (Fowler, 1986). Indeed, the National Environmental Protection Act (NEPA) provided the legal framework for **environmental impact statements,** the studies required for all major federal and state projects that can affect human life on earth. CRM work often takes place within this context.

Doing Archaeology

The GE Mound Case, Indiana

There have been some successful prosecutions under the Archaeological Resources Protection Act of 1979. The 2,000-year-old GE (General Electric) Mound is a Middle Woodland Hopewell mound at the Mt. Vernon site in southern Indiana (Munson and others, 1995). Artifacts from the mound came to light in 1988, during road-building operations for an adjacent construction project monitored by a professional archaeologist. Subsequently, looters entered General Electric's property, digging and removing artifacts from the mound without the company's permission. Following anonymous tips, authorities established with scientific test excavation that looting had taken place. While GE installed fences and motion detectors on-site, the U.S. Department of Justice became involved when the chief of the Miami Nation of Indiana expressed concern that the looted artifacts might be sold in other states. One Indiana man was soon arrested and agreed to cooperate with authorities. Subsequently, many of the artifacts were recovered.

A two-and-a-half-year investigation led to the conviction of five men for ARPA violations. The ringleader, Arthur Gerber, a commercial photographer from Tell City, Indiana, pleaded guilty to three counts of purchase and transport of unlawfully removed artifacts from the GE Mound, of illegal transport, and of unlawful commercial sale. He plea-bargained a fine of $5,000, a sentence of twelve months in prison on each count, and three years of supervised release during which he could not purchase, barter, or excavate archaeological resources or attend artifact shows. Two vehicles used in the looting were confiscated, and Gerber agreed to return all GE Mound artifacts in his possession. Four associates were convicted of lesser offenses.

The recovered artifacts included copper axes, breastplates and other artifacts, more than two thousand bifaces, freshwater pearls, fragments of wooden and leather objects, and cloth. In court, Gerber and his supporting witnesses claimed they were doing "recovery archaeology," when, in fact, they were using shovels and picks to unearth very delicate, exceptionally well-preserved artifacts. The judge told the defendant he was "stealing history" and that he had been doing so for twenty-five years. Gerber's attorneys appealed the case as far as the U.S. Supreme Court, but the appeal was denied.

Once the case was closed, the artifacts were reburied, following intense controversy, which revealed widely differing perspectives on reburial and archaeological research practices among archaeologists. The GE Mound case unfolded against a background of shifts in public opinion toward protecting local sites against looters. But many collectors raised the issue of individual rights on private land, lobbying for changes in federal and state legislation. To some members of Indiana's Native American Council, the reburied artifacts were a symbol to establish political power and personal prestige while promoting Native American beliefs in heritage rights and spiritual journeys (for discussion, see Munson and others, 1995).

The process of identifying, assessing, and managing archaeological resources is often discussed in terms of three phases that reflect increasing levels archaeological fieldwork and research (Hardesty and Little, 2000; Neumann and Sanford, 2001). The objective of each phase is to evaluate the cultural resources present on the basis of the research undertaken and to make recommendations concerning the management of the resources and the need for additional archaeological fieldwork.

Phase 1.   This provides the preliminary identification and assessment of cultural resources within a project area. It may also be referred to as a reconnaissance survey or a cultural resource inventory. An overview of cultural resources within the project area is compiled, ideally including environmental background, the known culture history of the area, a review of previous research, and a description of relevant historical and ethnographic information. The survey area is clearly laid out on maps, and landowners within the study area are contacted concerning the project.

Phase 1 archaeological fieldwork is aimed at identifying the distribution, horizontal extent, and cultural affiliations of the archaeological resources present. This is done though surface survey and limited subsurface testing, such as STPs. Using this information, the authors assess the research potential of the area, that is, the potential presence of undisturbed archaeological deposits, and make management recommendations. If the assessment indicates that the area has been highly disturbed by previous construction, or if no evidence of cultural materials is found, the Phase 1 report may recommend that no further work be undertaken, and development work begins. Alternatively, the preliminary study may suggest the possibility that significant resources may be present and Phase 2 research is recommended.

Phase 2.   The focus of Phase 2 research is on determining the significance of the archaeological resources present and their potential for listing in the National Register of Historic Places. Fieldwork involves the examination or reexamination of sites identified by previous research or during the Phase 1 work. It may include clearly specified surface collection, limited test excavations, deep trenching to identify buried deposits, and the stripping of disturbed surface deposits to reveal buried features. The specific objective is to determine the presence of stratigraphically intact archaeological deposits and to assess the potential significance of the site in terms of its contribution to the understanding of an important person or event, or the culture represented. The completed Phase 2 report discusses the cultural resources identified with regard to the relevant CRM legislation and makes recommendations concerning the need for additional research to determine their eligibility for the National Register of Historic Places.

Phase 3.   This is the final and most intensive stage of cultural resource management work undertaken. The proposal for Phase 3 work spells out a management plan for cultural resources eligible for listing in the National Register of Historic Places that will be affected or destroyed by the planned development. It establishes suitable mitigation measures for the protection of the archaeological sites that minimize the impact of development or for excavation to salvage data from sites that will be inevitably destroyed. **Mitigation** may include changing the design of a building so that it avoids archaeological resources, or the total excavation of sites, or portions of sites, that cannot be preserved with the aim of recovering as much information as possible. The final report on Phase 3 work, submitted to the appropriate government agency or contracting firm, describes and synthesizes the data recovered, providing a record of the archaeological resources studies.

The **compliance process** (often called the Section 106 process after the clause of that number in the National Historic Preservation Act of 1966) can be complex, involving the archaeologist in both recommending management strategies and conducting delicate negotiations with several government agencies at once. To be effective, a management plan should be regarded as a constantly evolving document, maintained and changed as archaeologists continue to manage and monitor the area. For example, Phase 3 excavation may reveal the presence of archaeological resources that were not identified in previous work, and consequently a new mitigation plan providing for additional research must be developed.

The same process involves both federal and state agencies in other management duties as well. They have the responsibility for protecting sites against vandalism, a major problem in some areas. The value of each individual resource must also be assessed, either on the basis of its scientific value established within the context of a research design, or because it merits preservation in situ. Agencies must also consider how a site can be utilized for the public good. This responsibility means interpreting it for the public, who may either visit the location, as they do at, say, Chaco Canyon, or learn about it through books, television programs, and popular articles.

Management versus Research

Cultural resource management for the most part involves gathering and assessing archaeological data from very specific areas dictated by development concerns, such as the site of an oil-drilling pad or the locations of pylons along a power line corridor. Often the areas covered may be small and encompass no cultural material or only portions of sites, but larger scale projects can sometimes embrace entire regions or river drainages. The very nature of CRM work means a heavy emphasis on survey and limited excavation, on basically descriptive investigations aimed at satisfying compliance requirements. The identification and preservation of the archaeological record have sometimes been seen as the first and only priority of CRM (Lipe, 1970). This is a relatively theory-free and descriptive approach in which management decisions about land use are based on a catalog of sites within an area. Until recently, most contracting agencies thought of archaeology as a discipline able to conduct piecemeal research. Sites or areas were selected by such criteria as imminence of destruction or availability of salvage funds. Agencies assumed that the results from each small project would somehow eventually become part of a grand, final synthesis.

Although such requirements may satisfy cultural resource management guidelines, scholarly needs often most emphatically are not (T. F. King, 1983). The descriptive recording of archaeological sites, devoid of any synthesis, appeared to be at odds with the more anthropological archaeology that came into fashion in the 1960s and 1970s, with its emphasis on explicit research designs and explanatory objectives (see Chapter 3). Many academic archaeologists thought of the descriptive, salvage archaeology that characterized CRM as entirely inconsistent with the problem-oriented nature of research. As a result, there was a dangerous and often unthinking tendency to segment archaeology into two broad camps: academic researchers taking on specific problems on one side, and the contract archaeologists involved with salvage, management, and compliance on the other.

This insidious distinction is, of course, a gross simplification that fails to recognize the importance of CRM archaeology. CRM archaeology, especially when conducted on a large scale, offers unique opportunities for answering basic questions about the past. The challenge is to grasp these opportunities and to exploit them to the fullest (Figure 18.3). Any notion that academic archaeology is somewhat superior to CRM research at its best is arrogant nonsense. North American archaeology is CRM.

Today, there is constant feedback between emerging archaeological theory and methodology and the realities of contract work. Many cultural resource management projects are redefining the way North American archaeologists go about their work, in part because of sound research designs and also because they are often funded at a far higher level than even the most ambitious academic projects—not only for survey and

Figure 18.3 CRM excavation goes on year-round. Excavations at the Howorth-Nelson site in southwestern Pennsylvania were carried on through the cold winter months under a heated inflatable shelter.

excavation but for analysis and, sometimes, for publication as well (Adovasio and Carlisle, 1988; Whittlesey and others, 1998). A problem-oriented approach regards CRM as part of contemporary archaeology with all its sophisticated theoretical apparatus for studying and evaluating the past.

Some CRM projects have involved massive archaeological operations and the expenditure of millions of dollars in survey and excavation. The Texas-California pipeline, the Dolores Project in Colorado, the Lower Verde Valley project in Arizona (Whittlesey and others, 1998), and the Black Mesa project in the Southwest (Gumerman, 1984) have all yielded important methodological contributions and, sometimes, major theoretical perceptions. CRM work on historic period sites has also involved some large-scale meticulous excavations that have greatly enhanced our understanding of the past (Joseph, 2002; Wheaton, 1990).

Some of the most successful of these projects have been conducted by large private companies that specialize in environmental impact work or by CRM archaeologists with close ties to academic institutions. For instance, researchers at the Institute of Archaeology and Anthropology at the University of South Carolina have developed a strong partnership with the university that allows them to carry out major CRM projects in an academic setting. With their excellent technical resources and large project budgets, they are able to conduct detailed research and fine-grained field and laboratory investigations that are beyond the budgetary scope of all but a few purely academic research projects.

As a long-term project, archaeologists are pulling together enormous quantities of raw settlement data and other culture-historical information into detailed syntheses of the southeastern United States. Such efforts maximize the value of local CRM projects and bring the vast amounts of data they accumulate into a meaningful summary of great intellectual value (D. G. Anderson and Sassaman, 1996; Sassaman and Anderson, 1996). The potential of this type of work is dramatically illustrated by Stanley South's examination of artifact patterning and cultural process at Brunswick Town, North Carolina and other sites, which had a major impact on the method and theory in historical archaeology (South, 1977).

CRM archaeology is the only viable way to identify and document rapidly vanishing archaeological resources in North America, the very kinds of data required to fulfill one of archaeology's major objectives—the explanation of cultural processes. This is not only a matter of economic realities but also one of perceiving the opportunity to make major intellectual advances in archaeology while still meeting the requirements of individual contracts.

CRM Research Strategies

With CRM the dominant force in archaeological fieldwork in North America, the problem of ensuring quality research is of major concern. For all the debate about conflicting approaches, and, to be frank, a good deal of dubious research, CRM has brought extensive methodological benefits to basic research, among them a much greater emphasis on prehistoric settlement patterns, sampling procedures, computer applications, and, above all, remote sensing. The major methodological contributions come in three areas: geomorphology, safety, and technology (Green and Doershuk, 1998).

Geomorphology.   CRM projects have combined geomorphological expertise with four-dimensional views of landscapes (time being the fourth dimension) to better understand the development of ancient landscapes and for locating and evaluating deeply buried sites. For example, the Upper Mississippi Valley has experienced much sustained CRM work that combines studies of landscape change with paleoecology and buried site archaeology. The result: maps of Late Wisconsin and Holocene landforms for a 300-mile (500-km) stretch of the valley. This is a superb basis for accurate assessment of cultural resource potential (Bettis and others, 1996; for other references, see Green and Doershuk, 1998). A similar approach has been used by researchers with the Cultural Resource program at Fort Drum, New York (see the Doing Archaeology box). In the past, much of the military base had been covered by Glacial Lake Iroquois, which gradually receded over the past 10,000 years. Mapping of fossil beaches has allowed archaeologists to model prehistoric occupation from Paleo-Indian times, through the Archaic and Woodland periods.

Safety.   Archaeologists face special safety issues and CRM researchers have taken the lead in introducing high safety standards to the field, which has brought archaeology more in line with guidelines in other fields such as construction, engineering, and drilling. Occupational Safety and Health Administration (OSHA) regulations and various local laws may be relevant to archaeological fieldwork. For example, with the need to determine the presence of archaeological resources in areas with thick soil deposits, and an increasing number of geomorphological studies, comes deeper trenching. Excavation units extending more than 4–5 ft. (1.2–1.5 m) deep must be shored up to ensure the safety of workers. In some instances, archaeologists have to evaluate sites that may be polluted by toxic waste, and fieldworkers have to wear protective clothing.

Technology.   CRM archaeologists lead their colleagues in applications of high-technology remote-sensing devices, computer-based data collection, and data management systems. Because of the often pressing need to quickly identify and excavate sites, CRM projects often employ ground-penetrating radar, magnetometers, and resistivity surveys to locate sites and features without time-consuming excavation. Problems of data storage and the dissemination of information, faced by all archaeologists, are made especially pressing by the volume of CRM work. CRM archaeologists have led the way in the innovative use of computer databases and data management programs to address these concerns (see the discussion on management challenges). Geographic Information Systems (GIS) have also played a leading role in many CRM projects, as does the technology of site protection (Green and Doershuk, 1998).

To these innovations may be added a diversity of other developments that have largely emerged within the context of CRM research. Some truly remarkable investigations combine these and other innovations under often severe all-weather

Doing Archaeology

CRM at Fort Drum, New York

Federal government lands, including national parks, national forests, reservoirs, and military bases, encompass some of the nation's best documented and protected archaeological sites. Management plans that provide for the identification, evaluation, and protection of cultural resources in these areas are mandated by the Historic Preservation Act of 1966. Like all archaeologists concerned with cultural resource management, researchers working in these locales often walk a tightrope, balancing between the protection and management of archaeological resources, on one hand, and the practical concerns of modern life, on the other.

Management efforts at Fort Drum in central New York state illustrate the comprehensive efforts needed to effectively manage cultural resources and how careful planning and innovative research strategies can facilitate this process. Initially established in 1908, today Fort Drum is home to the Tenth Mountain Division and covers 10,000 acres, just northeast of Watertown, New York. Military training can have serious impacts on cultural resources, and the base encompasses a diversity of prehistoric and historic archaeological sites. To ensure that cultural resources are not damaged, the Fort Drum Cultural Resources program follows an Integrated Resources Management Plan (ICRMP), which changes as cultural resources are identified and the base's needs evolve (Figure 18.4).

The first challenge to effective management is identifying sites before they are impacted. Thus far, six abandoned villages, more than 360 Historic Period farms, and over 200 prehistoric sites have been identified. While some of the historic sites could be located using maps and documentary sources, many had to be identified through archaeological survey, test excavations, and nonintrusive subsurface detection methods, such as ground-penetrating radar, electrical resistivity, and magnetometer surveys. Sensitivity modeling is used to target areas for survey that are likely to contain archaeological resources. Drawing on geomorphological studies, archaeologists were able to trace the boundaries of Glacial Lake Iroquois, which has receded over the past 10,000 years. By tracing ancient shorelines, researchers were able to predict areas that were likely locations for early settlements.

Special attention is paid to areas that are likely to be impacted by base activities. To mitigate damage to sites, a variety of options are employed. In some cases, areas that contain or potentially contain cultural resources are placed off-limits. In other cases, historic foundations or sites are "hardened": covered with filter fabric and buried with layers of sand and gravel. When this is done, sites are strong enough to withstand tank traffic. Another protective measure involves the revegetation of areas with indigenous plant species to prevent erosion. In these cases, vehicle traffic and digging may be prohibited, but low-impact pedestrian traffic is allowed. In areas of high use, the excavation and salvage of archaeological material may be the only option. For example, barracks construction

Figure 18.4 Archaeology at Fort Drum, New York, involved close collaboration with the U.S. Army.

required the partial excavation of Fort Drum prehistoric site number 1093, a Middle Woodland village. More recently, Phase III work had to be undertaken at the site of the nineteenth-century LeRaysville Sawmill that was going to be totally destroyed by the construction of a new dam.

The Fort Drum Cultural Resources program includes a very proactive approach to public archaeology and Native American concerns. The staff presents information about archaeological discoveries in a variety of forums, such as publications, posters, and scientific papers, that bring information to other archaeologists and the interested public. Following Department of Defense policy, archaeologists working at Fort Drum consult with Native American tribes with cultural interest in the area. This includes agreement over the procedures to be followed when Native American skeletal remains are inadvertently discovered.

Work at Fort Drum illustrates the far-ranging concerns and methodologies that must be employed in the management of cultural resources. The researchers are fortunate in that the vast area they are concerned with is under the purview of a single authority and governed by a uniform policy. They also benefit from excellent technical and equipment support. Sadly, many cultural resources do not receive such treatment.

Note: The authors acknowledge with gratitude the assistance of Dr. Laurie Rush with the research for this box.

conditions. For example, a CRM project on a Civil War–era foundry in New York State was undertaken under heated domes, with heaters operating twenty-four hours a day. The research combined computerized GIS remote-sensing techniques with computer transit mapping, image analysis, and three-dimensional photogrammetry. The field conservation and curation facility processed as many as five thousand artifacts a week, each being washed, X-rayed, computer inventoried, decontaminated where appropriate, and conserved. All this activity was carried out under OSHA and EPA hazardous materials procedures and precautions, then combined with documentary evidence to provide a story of intelligence operations that were carried out under President Lincoln's direct authority (Grossman, 1994).

Management Challenges

Although CRM has transformed American archaeology—for the most part, for the better—it has also brought its own set of problems. While these difficulties to a large extent are problems faced by all archaeologists, some are particularly challenging because of the sheer volume of CRM work undertaken.

Some of the most pressing problems concern the quality of the archaeological research. Although federal legislation spells out guidelines, their implementation varies in different states and community settings. State Historic Preservation Offices (SHPOs), the state institutions mandated by the Historic Preservation Act to oversee CRM work, are often understaffed, and many find it difficult to keep up with oversight. The amount of activity is so great that the only long-term solution to the crisis of quality lies in the increasing integration of the goals and research techniques of scientific archaeology, on the one hand, and the realities and demands of cultural management and contract archaeology, on the other.

Attempts have been made at self-regulation. Most professional societies that archaeologists belong to now have both statements on ethics and guidelines for archaeological research. Organizations such as the Register of Professional Archaeologists (**www.rpanet.org**) and the American Cultural Resources Association (**www.acra-crm .org**) have stringent guidelines for research, as well as for the archaeologists' responsibilities to the public, clients, and fellow archaeologists. If adhered to, these would ensure uniformly high standards of behavior and research. Unfortunately, the value of the guidelines is only as good as the organizations' memberships, which are entirely voluntary. Rather like the Better Business Bureau, enforcement of ethics is difficult and censure limited. Regrettably, some archaeologists have, in fact, seen membership in organizations like the RPA as a substitute for graduate training in archaeology that would help make CRM into a less descriptive, more analytical discipline.

Site Records

Some of the other basic problems are in some respects easily remedied, but the solutions lie in financial and resource investments that are too often lacking. In particular, the accessibility of CRM data for planning, the curation of archaeological materials, and the dissemination and recording of information are growing concerns.

The recording of archaeological data is especially important, as the study of community and archaeological site distributions is integral to effective cultural resource management. Only when sites are identified and the information is provided to development planners can sites be protected or salvage work undertaken. The collection and organization of these data can, however, be challenging. Information on archaeological sites within a region is often obtained from a variety of sources that may vary tremendously in terms of detail and quality and be scattered in a diversity of different reports, archives, and publications. For example, information on academic projects and archaeological work by amateurs may not be located in the same repositories as CRM reports.

Fortunately, computerized databases and electronic media such as CD-ROMs hold great potential for the future. In order to address management concerns in central New York, Douglas Armstrong, LouAnn Wurst, and Elizabeth Kellar created a unified regional archaeological site file (Armstrong et al., 2000). The Syracuse University Intermodal Systems Transportation Enhancement Act (ISTEA) Project was sponsored by the New York State Office of Parks, Recreation and Historic Preservation, which saw the task as a necessary prerequisite for effective regional planning. A central part of the research was the development of a GIS program that allowed information on archaeological and historic resources from a wide variety of sources to be incorporated and overlaid on maps of the study area. The result was a comprehensive tool for development planning.

The information collected by Armstrong and his colleagues included Native American and historic sites identified by academic research projects, cultural resource management studies, and work by amateur archaeologists, as well as National Register Historic Properties, local landmarks, Historic Markers, Native American trails, and historic data (Figure 18.5). GIS allows the distribution of cultural resources to be sorted and graphically displayed by source, time period, cultural association, or activity area represented, providing an immediate assessment of cultural resources within a particular area.

The Syracuse University ISTEA Project was primarily intended to address cultural resource management concerns—to protect archaeological and historical sites from destruction. But the data obtained can be used to address a diversity of research issues. One of the things revealed by the project was the gaps in coverage, in terms of time periods, areas, and types of sites recorded. For example, the study revealed that historic period domestic sites in both town and rural areas were virtually overlooked in archaeological surveys (Wurst et al., 2000). This type of information is useful to archaeologists, as well as planners, in evaluating the importance of sites.

At the national level, there is the National Archaeological Data Base, an online system that contains almost 15,000 records of archaeological reports. Any archaeologist with a telephone line or an electronic mail system can now access the database, which also provides comprehensive site distribution from many states and background environmental information through the Geographic Resources Analysis Support System (GRASS), the GIS system used by the National Park Service. This resource is really a database of databases; it allows managers to acquire information on everything from county-level site data to progress on reburial and repatriation of burials. The National Archaeological Data Base is managed by the Center for Advanced Spatial Technology at the University of Arkansas, Fayetteville. This powerful resource is an invaluable tool for North American archaeologists of all specialties and is mirrored by others being developed in other countries, notably Denmark (see Chapter 15).

Curation

Then there is the issue of what is called **curation,** the management, storage and conservation of artifacts and other data recovered in the course of archaeological activities. Archaeology has always been an area of intensive research. Once artifacts from a site have been excavated and analyzed, what happens to them? Archaeological surface collections and excavations can easily amass hundreds of thousands of artifacts, many

(a)

Figure 18.5   The Syracuse ISTEA Project involves a unified regional archaeological site file for central New York. Information on archaeological and historic resources from a wide variety of sources is included and overlaid on maps of the study area. The result is a comprehensive tool for development planning. GIS allows the distribution of cultural resources to be sorted and graphically displayed by source, time period, cultural association, or activity area represented, providing an immediate assessment of cultural resources within a particular area.

    a.   Iroquois longhouse at the Howlet Hill Site, New York.
    b.   An STP survey: Onondaga County, New York.
    c.   Historic photo of the Wesleyan Methodist Church, Syracuse, New York.
    d.   Historic Marker at the Harriet Tubman House, Auburn, New York.
    e.   Inset map showing the area involved.

(b)

(c)

(d)

(e)

Figure 18.5   (*cont.*)

of which require conservation if they are to be preserved. While in the past artifacts were sometimes discarded after analysis, keeping the collections for future study or additional analysis is clearly desirable: Material from previous studies may be reexamined as part of new projects, and new methods of analysis may yield information undreamed of by the original excavators.

Many archaeological organizations and institutions have established guidelines for the curation of materials. The National Park Service, for example, has issued regulations for the curation of federal collections, as required under amendments to existing legislation. Unfortunately, curation is expensive, and the costs of providing permanent conservation and storage are prohibitive. Many museums and other designated repositories are grappling with seemingly insurmountable mountains of archaeological finds that pour in from CRM projects. Aside from the space they occupy, the finds must be labeled, cataloged, and placed in plastic bags or boxes that will neither disintegrate nor damage poorly preserved materials. The conservation—cleaning, stabilizing, and preserving—of deteriorating artifacts is a huge problem with some artifacts such as ancient baskets or metal objects that will disintegrate unless properly treated.

Curation is an easily surmountable problem—given time and resources. Archaeologists and museum technicians know what needs to be done, but realization is another issue. Efforts to inventory and curate collections have led to improved guidelines and new facilities. However, there is simply not enough space to house many collections, and there are not enough funds to pay the real costs of curation. Consequently, curation will likely be an issue of continuing concern.

Publication and Dissemination

Proliferating contract archaeology and CRM work have caused an explosion not only of raw data but also of publications and reports on completed projects. The essence of publishing archaeological data is, of course, to make them available to as wide an audience of archaeologists as can make use of them. This distribution is achieved through books and national and international journals, and regional periodicals such as the *Plains Anthropologist* or the *New Hampshire Archeologist.* Many of these are widely distributed, peer-reviewed publications, where the submitted contributions are read, evaluated, and edited prior to publication. Ideally, this type of process would be used for all CRM reports and the results of important projects published.

However, reports on many smaller projects are often purely descriptive and incorporate limited synthesis of data outside of the narrow scope of the project. Although some such reports are potentially useful, many more are sterile, rote descriptions that add little to our understanding of the past and are solely designed to meet CRM legislation. Even reports on important studies do not receive the degree of external, editorial peer review found in academic journals. This is one reason that archaeologists such as Ian Hodder (1999) have insisted on the vital importance of a marriage between theory and excavation, which is not merely a sterile recording process (see also Green and Doershuk, 1998).

Another problem lies with the availability of CRM reports. Even many excellent CRM reports are either restricted-circulation documents deeply buried in the files of government agencies or private companies or, at best, photocopied publications that have a severely limited circulation—the so-called "gray literature." One authority estimated that there were about 200,000 gray literature reports in existence in the early 1990s, with an additional 10,000 to 20,000 reports accruing annually (McManamon, 1994). The number has proliferated since then. Sometimes within months they are forgotten, even destroyed, and the vital data in them are as good as lost to science. The problem of failure to publish CRM data in more widely accessible forums is enormous. Ironically, now that awareness about destruction of the archaeological record is greater than ever, the results of much of this anxiety are being buried, almost as effectively as if they had been destroyed, in inaccessible publications.

Public Involvement and Public Archaeology

One of the most important benefits of CRM has been the increasing input from the public into archaeological research. This is important because it is ultimately the greater public who should benefit from CRM research and it is the public who ultimately funds the research undertaken.

Although expenditures on contract archaeology may no longer be at the levels of the late 1970s, arguments rage about the worth of even a tenth of such expenditure. Though one can argue that knowledge in itself is valuable and is worth spending money on, one must show something for the money beyond an abundance of technical and often inaccessible reports. CRM legislation identifies sites and provides a basis for management decisions about cultural resources, but do these designations mesh with public perceptions? Archaeologists may wax lyrical about the scientific significance of a small hunting site or a nineteenth-century farmstead, but the public is often much more interested in visually striking sites with humanistic significance.

A great deal of the effectiveness in protecting archaeological sites depends on public attitudes toward the past. Cultural and adventure tourism are of growing importance, and many sites are also significant expressions of national identity. Diminutive Fort Necessity in Pennsylvania would likely have received far less attention from archaeologists and tourists alike had it not been hastily constructed in 1754 by a young lieutenant colonel named George Washington (Harrington, 1977). Gettysburg has a supreme place in our national heritage, as does Mesa Verde. Both are visited by tens of thousands of people each year.

The basic question is easily stated: Is the public benefiting in practical ways from the expenditure of enormous funds on archaeology? Many people think of archaeology as a luxury and wonder how much taxpayer money is spent on cultural resource management. They are ambivalent about protecting the past, let alone spending money on it. Yet thousands of other interested citizens have joined amateur archaeological societies in many parts of the country. In response to both of these opinions, archaeologists have increasingly tried to share the importance of cultural resource management with the wide public.

Education and Archaeology

In recent years, to draw public attention to cultural resource management concerns, considerable effort has gone into informing the public about archaeology, to the point that many archaeologists now talk of **public archaeology,** a form of archaeology open and accessible to the public through television, state-sponsored "archaeology weeks," special museum displays and activities, and the Internet (McManamon, 1994). Many archaeological societies and museums have workshops and activities aimed at school-children and the wider public. This new outward-looking perspective is vital to the future conservation and preservation of the world's archaeological heritage.

But there is still a long way to go. Although such agencies as the Bureau of Land Management are now expending significant resources on public education, most CRM work has had little effect on public involvement in archaeology. A few projects provide excellent examples of how to reach a wider audience. In areas such as historic Alexandria, Virginia, and Annapolis, Maryland, archaeologists have worked closely with historians and the local communities to provide walking tours, lectures, and other educational programs that share archaeological discoveries and management concerns with visitors (Potter, 1994).

Native American Concerns

In an important development, more and more research designs in American archaeology are taking account of Native American attitudes toward the proposed work. Most archaeological research in the Americas has involved the excavation of Native American sites, though the majority of the researchers have been of non-Native ancestry. The long-held presumption has been that the knowledge obtained from scientific archaeological research is of benefit to all, including indigenous peoples. CRM concerns about the protection and management of archaeological sites would also seem to place Native Americans and archaeologists on the same side. Despite these presumed common interests, Native American views about what sites should be preserved, how archaeological research should be conducted, and the ways in which archaeological remains should be treated are often dramatically different from those of archaeologists (see Mihesuah, 2000; Wesler, 2001).

Particularly serious areas of conflict have surrounded ritual areas and objects and burials. While archaeologists see such items as important clues to past religious beliefs, social organization, and health, many Native groups view their excavation as sacrilegious and disrespectful of their cultural heritage. Such was the case when local Native Americans insisted that the Chimney Rock Mesa skeletons in Colorado, disturbed by vandals, be reburied. Archaeologists wanted to conserve and study the human remains, but they were overruled by the federal land manager on legal grounds.

Most archaeologists have thought of themselves as objective observers of the past or as favorably inclined toward Native Americans. But, as Bruce Trigger pointed out (1985, 1986), many archaeologists have been influenced by popular stereotypes of indigenous peoples. Only recently have they become aware of the social significance of their studies. They have also come to realize that archaeology can no longer be undertaken independently of society. Ethics statements by professional organizations now include statements concerning the rights of indigenous peoples and the need to consider Native American concerns in archaeological research.

The inclusion of Native American rights in cultural resource management decisions is mandated by a number of federal laws. The American Indian Religious Freedom Act of 1978 guarantees access to sacred sites, requires federal agencies to adjust management policies to reflect its provisions, and recognizes the existence of sacred sites.

This legislation and the Native American Grave Protection and Repatriation Act of 1990 (discussed below) have profoundly affected U.S. archaeology, for it often involves consulting with tribal and religious leaders if religious sites are to be disturbed. It has given Native Americans considerable say in the conduct of CRM on public lands, and they have reacted strongly to development projects on sacred, privately owned lands as well. Some groups, such as the Hopi, Navajo, and Zuni of the Southwest, are now working closely with archaeologists, using their own archaeological units (see the discussion below; see also Anyon and Ferguson, 1995; Carmean, 2003).

Repatriation

By far the most serious area of disagreement between Native Americans and archaeologists revolves around the treatment of skeletal remains. Often encountered in excavations, they are the focus of a great deal of study by both archaeologists and physical anthropologists. Many Indian communities are incensed by the excavation of prehistoric burials and have pushed for laws forbidding such activity and compelling reburial or repatriation of excavated skeletons. Their activist policies, and a growing public awareness of the complex issues involved, led to passage of the Native American Grave Protection and Repatriation Act of 1990 (Mihesuah, 2000; Powell and others, 1993; Thomas, 2000).

The 1990 act establishes two main requirements. First, all federal agencies and museums receiving federal funds are required to inventory their holdings of Native American human remains and associated funerary objects. They must also develop written summaries for funerary objects not found in graves, sacred objects, and what are called "objects of cultural patrimony" that are in the collections they control. This inventorying process, which will take years to complete, also requires that agencies and museums establish, as best they can, whether their individual holdings have any cultural affiliation, or, in the case of skeletons, lineal descendants in living Native American groups. If they do establish a relationship, then they are required to notify the relevant Native American organization about the existence of the materials and offer to repatriate them. Even if they have no cultural affiliation with museum holdings, or disagree with the museum's identifications, a group can still request **repatriation.**

The second requirement protects all Native American graves and other cultural objects found within archaeological sites on federal and tribal lands. This requirement encourages the in situ preservation of archaeological sites, or at least those parts of them that contain graves. It also requires anyone carrying out archaeological investigation on federal and tribal lands to consult with affiliated or potentially affiliated Native Americans concerning the treatment and disposition of any finds, whether made during formal investigations or by accident. The Repatriation Act also stipulates that illegal trafficking in human remains or cultural objects may result in criminal penalties, authorizes the Secretary of the Interior to set up a grant program to assist museums and Native American tribes in complying with the law, and authorizes the development of regulations to administer the provisions of the act in consultation with a national review committee.

The Native American Grave Protection and Repatriation Act mandates a level of consultation and concern for Native American rights that is far greater than had previously been the norm in the United States. The signing of the act came after years of controversy that pitted, and still pits, Native Americans against scientists. The archaeologists and anthropologists point out that revolutionary new research techniques are beginning to yield a mine of information about prehistoric North Americans. To rebury the database for such research deprives science, and future generations of Americans, of a vital resource, they argue. Others, including some archaeologists, respond that this is an ethical and moral issue, and that such considerations outweigh any potential scientific gains. Many museums, universities, and other institutions have adopted repatriation policies, and the Society for American Archaeology and other professional organizations have drafted ethical statements on the problem—not that these efforts have dampened emotions on either side of the issue.

There will be no quick resolution of the repatriation issue, however promptly and sensitively archaeologists and their institutions respond to Native American concerns and comply with the provisions of the 1990 act. Many of the issues are inchoate, of great moral importance and sensitivity, and address basic questions about the morality of all archaeological research. Only one thing is certain; no archaeologist in North America, and probably elsewhere, will be able to excavate a prehistoric or historic burial without the most careful and sensitive preparation. This involves working closely with native peoples in ways that archaeologists have not imagined until recently. Nothing but good can come of this.

The repatriation issue has international overtones, for indigenous groups outside North America, notably the Australian Aborigines, have striven for strict control of burial excavations. Increasingly, archaeologists and native peoples are working together to hammer out long-term agreements, or at least statements of principle, to cover repatriation and burial excavation. On the international front, the executive committee of the World Archaeological Congress has adopted an accord that calls on archaeologists to be sensitive to the concerns of indigenous peoples. Named the Vermillion Accord after the town of Vermillion, South Dakota, where it was drafted, the statement calls for respect both for the dead and for the wishes of their descendants, as well as for the scientific research value of human remains. It establishes the principle that agreement on the disposition of human remains be established on the basis of mutual respect between the legitimate concerns for the correct burial of ancestors and the concerns of science and education.

Working Together: The Hopi Example

The Hopi tribe's Cultural Preservation Office has used existing historic preservation legislation as a way of ensuring input on management decisions about archaeological sites on their reservations and in adjacent areas. Their tribe-funded organization includes a tribal archaeologist, project archaeologists, a transcriber, and Hopi research specialists. Its mandate is to preserve the "spiritual and cultural essence of the Hopi, encompassing . . . archaeology, ethnology, recovery of stolen sacred artifacts, farming, and the preservation of the Hopi language" (T. J. Ferguson and others, 1995). The Cultural Preservation Office is developing appropriate ways for villages, clans, and religious societies to participate in ongoing research activities. Since clan histories are ritual knowledge, rarely shared with members of other clans, let alone with non-Indians, involvement of Hopi elders, the guardians of sacred knowledge, is vital.

The Cultural Preservation Office works closely with an advisory group of representatives from each Hopi community, from clans, priesthoods, and religious societies—people who possess vital information for the management of cultural resources. The consultation process is time-consuming but essential to overcome the suspicions many Hopi have of archaeologists and other Western scientists. The Hopi have stated that their participation in the compliance process does not mean that they endorse a specific project or development. They will never condone the destruction of a site, but they will recommend mitigation through scientific study, on the grounds that a written report of an ancient site is better than no record at all, so that the memory is not lost forever.

The Hopi definition of a site worth preserving is far more wide-reaching than found in federal and state legislation. In legal terms, they, and other Native American groups, define every ancestral archaeological site as a traditional cultural property to be protected and left alone. The same term, *traditional cultural property,* is applied to shrines, sacred sites, springs, quarries, and prehistoric landforms with place names commemorating prehistoric or historic events—some of which bear no visible traces of human activity. Thus, archaeological sites play a central role in the transmission and retention of Hopi culture.

In practical terms, this broad definition, which many archaeologists now accept, raises interesting problems. For example, the Hopi want sites registered in the state archaeological databases, but they want to keep the locations of certain cultural properties secret. Both the archaeologists and the Hopi are working to develop accurate ways of defining sites while respecting these concerns.

Many Native Americans are interested in preserving sites, but they are not interested in archaeology as such. The Hopi, however, are interested in archaeology, in how archaeologists collect data, and in how the data are analyzed. Some elders want to compare archaeological findings with their own system of knowledge. T. J. Ferguson and his colleagues (1995) pointed out that agreement between archaeological and traditional data is often explained in the context of Hopi ritual knowledge. For instance, Hopi prophecies of a time when even the ash left by the ancestors will be used to prove their claims have been connected to the flotation methods used to dissect ancient hearths.

Hopi standards of what constitutes legitimate research are evolving, as all parties become more familiar with one another and as archaeology itself evolves. At the same time, tribal members may feel a new need to acquire information about their past, because they do not want to lose their identity as Hopi (T. J. Ferguson and others, 1995; for another example, see Ravensloot, 1993).

Collaboration between indigenous peoples and archaeologists involves far more than management and mitigation. It involves profound respect and sensitivity toward the values and expectations of others in the interests of the long-term public good.

Cultural Resource Management in Global Perspective

Our discussion has dealt primarily with cultural resource management in the United States, but the preservation of the past and the protection of cultural resources are of worldwide concern (see Cleere, 1989; Isar, 1986; Layton, 1989; Prott and O'Keefe, 1984; Schmidt and McIntosh, 1996). The threat of unchecked development and the looting of archaeological sites for antiquities are worries that plague other countries as well.

Many archaeological sites and cultural resources face eminent destruction as national governments try to balance the need for development with concern about their pasts. The problem is especially pressing in developing countries. The independence of many former colonies in the 1950s and 1960s resulted in substantial investment and economic aid, and the emergence of development as a dominant theme (Cleere, 1989). Yet the interrelated consequences of increasing construction, urbanization, and resource exploitation became a source of worry. While development brought needed improvements, it also created further threat to the archaeological past. The consequences of economic development have often included widespread devastation of large tracts of hitherto undisturbed natural and historical landscapes.

In an increasingly interconnected, multicultural world, affluent, adventure tourism is often viewed as a desirable source of foreign income. Archaeological sites have emerged as major money earners in the United States, Europe, Asia, South America, and Mesoamerica (for example, see Bruner, 1996; Ekechukwu, 1990; Isar, 1986; Layton, 1989). But this source of wealth has also increased both the threat of development and the intentional looting of archaeological sites for salable antiquities. This aspect of economic development has drawn the international community's attention to the preservation and marketing of archaeological resources. The development pressures of the 1960s, followed by the environmental movement in the 1970s, led many countries to pass legislation replacing the outdated, ineffectual statutes of a less stressful pre–World War II era (Cleere, 1989).

It was these new laws that gave birth to cultural resource management (Hutt et al., 1993:15; Messenger, 1989; Schmidt and McIntosh, 1996). The establishment of the United Nations Environmental Program (UNEP) in 1972 provided funding to mitigate the impact of development. In 1988, UNESCO launched the "World Decade for Cultural Development" (Serageldin and Taboroff, 1994). It stressed the need to recognize the cultural dimension of development. Individual nations have taken varied steps toward improved management practices (for examples of legislation and implementation, see Arinze, 1990; McIntosh, 1994; Schmidt, 1996b). This concern of the international community is a result of the awareness that the archaeological heritage is a major, vulnerable, and nonrenewable resource.

Unfortunately, concern has arisen because heritage legislation in most countries permits the private ownership of archaeological resources, which makes it challenging to safeguard them from development. In developing countries, the problem is made worse by the lack of trained personnel and inadequate funding to identify and evaluate antiquities and effectively manage cultural heritage. The plight of Africa's past, highlighted in a number of publications, illustrates the severity of the situation in many world areas (Kankpeyeng and DeCorse, in press; Schmidt and McIntosh, 1996; Seragelden and Taboroff, 1994). Attention has focused on the looting of archaeological sites for the antiquities trade, issues of cultural patrimony, historic preservation, and archaeological resource management—major concerns worldwide. Governments have far to go to safeguard the record of the past.

All archaeologists are managers of a finite resource that is banked in various ways—in the ground, within the pages of a report, or by finds and records in a museum storeroom. We have two alternatives for the future: either collect and interpret information about our cultural resources in a useful manner as an activity that contributes to the public good, or take the easy way out and abandon the archaeological record to extinction.

Summary

Cultural resource management (CRM) involves the development of overall strategies for conservation priorities and management of a finite resource, the archaeological record.

The 1960s saw the development of the concept of cultural resource management. In the United States, new federal legislation, notably the National Historic Preservation Act of 1966, the National Environmental Policy Act of 1969, and the Archaeological Resources Protection Act of 1979, laid down regulations for land use and resource policies and also defined archaeological resources as any artifact more than a century old.

Federal legislation, in combination with many state, local, and tribal laws, provides the legal means of protecting the country's archaeological heritage. Some of the best protected archaeological sites in the United States are in national and state parks, forests, reservoirs, and military reservations, where management plans require the identification and protection of archaeological resources. The biggest gaps in the protection of archaeological resources in the United States are on private lands.

The primary concern of CRM archaeology has been the identification, description, and protection of archaeological resources. Many CRM projects are small scale and the reports descriptive. However, larger-scale projects often provide opportunities for major archaeological excavations and surveys that have important bearing on the development of archaeological method and theory. CRM is having an increasingly important impact on the future direction of American archaeology, on account of both its large budgets and its unique opportunities for large-scale field and laboratory research.

The sheer volume of CRM research has led to problems. In some cases inadequate oversight has allowed inadequate archaeological research to be accepted. The recording of sites, the curation and storage of artifacts, and the publication and dissemination of important discoveries are also issues that need to be addressed.

One of the most important benefits of CRM has been the increasing input from the public into archaeological research. This is important because it is ultimately the greater public who should benefit from CRM research and it is the public who ultimately funds the research undertaken. To inform the public about archaeology, many archaeologists now talk of public archaeology, a form of archaeology open and accessible to the public through television, state-sponsored "archaeology weeks," special museum displays and activities, and the Internet.

Native American concerns figure increasingly strongly in North American archaeology. Native American groups have demanded that many Indian skeletons in public and private collections be returned to them, a movement that culminated in the passing of the Native American Grave Protection and Repatriation Act of 1990. This legislation protects Native American graves on federal and tribal lands, requires museums and government agencies to inventory their holdings, and provides for the repatriation of remains with direct affiliations with living groups. Archaeologists are working more closely with Native American communities when excavating sites where burials are likely to be found.

CRM and the destruction of archaeological resources are of global concern. The threat of unchecked development and the looting of archaeological sites for antiquities are worries that plague other countries as well. The problem is especially pressing in developing countries, where the consequences of economic development have often included widespread devastation of large tracts of hitherto undisturbed natural and historical landscapes. All archaeologists are managers of a finite resource that requires immediate attention.

Key Terms

compliance process
cultural resource management
  (CRM)
cultural resources

curation
environmental impact
  statements
mitigation

public archaeology
repatriation

Guide to Further Reading

The literature on cultural resource management has proliferated enormously in the past ten years. No one can master the entire spectrum of the literature, but here are some key references that help you navigate through a maze of articles, edited volumes, and reports.

CLEERE, HENRY, ed. 1989. *Archaeological Heritage Management in the Modern World.* London: Unwin Hyman. A series of essays on CRM in different countries under radically different governments. A fascinating comparative exercise.

FOWLER, DON D. 1982. "Cultural Resources Management." *Advances in Archaeological Method and Theory* 5: 1–50. A superb essay on the basic issues of CRM in the early 1980s. Still to the point, and recommended for its clear exposition and comprehensive references.

GREEN, WILLIAM, and JOHN F. DOERSHUK. 1998. "Cultural Resource Management and American Archaeology." *Journal of Archaeological Research* 6(2): 121–167. A masterly synthesis of the state of CRM in the late 1990s. This is the best starting point for exploring the subject. The bibliography is comprehensive and superb.

HARDESTY, DONALD L., and BARBARA J. LITTLE. 2000. *Assessing Site Significance.* Walnut Creek, CA: AltaMira Press. An up-to-date and readable discussion of the methods and criteria archaeologists use to assess the importance of archaeological sites.

KING, THOMAS F. 1998. *Cultural Resource Laws and Practice: An Introductory Guide.* Walnut Creek, CA: AltaMira Press.

————. 2003. *Places That Count: Traditional Cultural Properties in Cultural Resource Management.* Walnut Creek, CA: AltaMira Press. Two essential guides to current legislation and practice that should be on every CRM archaeologist's bookshelf.

NEUMANN, THOMAS W., and ROBERT M. SANFORD. 2001. *Cultural Resource Archaeology.* Walnut Creek, CA: AltaMira Press. A widely used basic textbook on CRM for beginners.

WHITTLESEY, STEPHANIE M., and others, eds. 1998. *Vanishing River: Landscapes and Lives of the Lower Verde Valley.* Tucson, AZ: SRI Press. An exemplary synthesis based on large-scale CRM research.

PART VIII

Careers and Resources

We are Ahabs pursuing our great white whale. We will never catch him. . . . It is our limitations of thought, of understandings, of imagination we test as we quarter these strange waters. And then we think we see a darkening in the deeper water, a sudden surge, the roll of a fluke—and then the heart-lifting glimpse of the great white shape, its whiteness throwing back its own particular light, there on the glimmering horizon.
Historian Inga Clendinnen on the challenges of the ancient intangible,
The Aztecs: An Interpretation (1991)

This chapter is about archaeology—as a career and a hobby, as an avocation and part of all of our lives. In short, it's about archaeology and you.

CHAPTER 19

Becoming an Archaeologist

Archaeologists work on a stone-strewn hillside at the reputed site of
Camelot, King Arthur's palace at Cadbury, southwestern England.

I (BMF) became an archaeologist by sheer accident, having entered Cambridge University in England without any idea of potential careers. I was admitted on condition that I studied anything except Greek and Latin, for which I had no aptitude whatsoever! So, I took a list of potential subjects and chose archaeology and anthropology on a whim, with no intention of making either a career. My first lecturer was a Stone Age archaeologist named Miles Burkitt, who was famous for his classroom stories. He had studied late Ice Age rock art under the legendary French archaeologist Henri Breuil before 1910. His enthusiastic reminiscences triggered my interest in the past. By chance, while still an undergraduate, I met another famous archaeologist, the African prehistorian Desmond Clark, and ended up working in a museum in Central Africa after I graduated. I have been an archaeologist ever since, a career choice I have never regretted.

This chapter is a brief essay on becoming (or not becoming) an archaeologist (for general career discussion, see Omohundro, 2001; Salzman and Rice, 2004).

Archaeology as a Profession

Archaeology still has an aura of romance and spectacular discovery about it, which probably accounts for why many of you took the course that assigned this book in the first place. You learn pretty fast that modern-day archaeology, while often fascinating and sometimes conducted in remote lands, is a highly technical discipline in which spectacular discoveries are few and far between. True, exciting finds occasionally hit the headlines, such as the Moche lords of Sipán or the Uluburun shipwreck, but the fact remains that most archaeologists labor far from the public eye, often on unspectacular and sometimes downright monotonous sites or obscure problems. An Indiana Jones–like personality is certainly not a qualification for archaeology; indeed, it has never been. Indiana Jones himself is complete fiction, a character built up from a group of well-known pioneer archaeologists of the early twentieth century whose discoveries and adventures were indeed larger than life. Today's archaeologist is about as far from Professor Jones as you can get and probably works a long way from the halls of academe.

What, then, are the qualities that make a good archaeologist in these days of highly specialized research and wide diversity of career options? Qualities of character

511

Doing Archaeology

Personal Qualities Needed by an Archaeologist

Anyone wanting to become an archaeologist needs far more than academic credentials. Here are some essentials:

- *Enthusiasm,* indeed a passion for archaeology and for the past, the touchstone for anyone who enters this field. Archaeology thrives on enthusiasm, for the best archaeologists are those with the kind of fire in their bellies that enables them to raise money, overcome major practical obstacles, and carry out their work. Personal charisma breeds good archaeological leaders, provided they have the patience for the small details as well.
- *Infinite patience* to carry out fieldwork and other research that can involve slow-moving, repetitive tasks and dealing with sometimes-difficult people.
- *A mind that thrives on detail,* since a great deal of archaeology is minutiae—noticing the small attributes of stone tools and potsherds, analyzing computerized data, studying tiny details of the past for weeks on end. Both excavation and survey, to say nothing of laboratory work, require great patience and a concern for detail.
- *Adaptability,* an ability to put up with long journeys, sometimes uncomfortable fieldwork, and often primitive living conditions. You need to be fit enough to walk long distances and to thrive on improvisation under difficult conditions. Imagine, for example, filing Land Rover wheel bearings out of nails when you are several hundred miles from a service station so you can get home. We know archaeologists who have done that. They had to.

- *Good organizational skills,* since a great deal of archaeology is logistics and organization, of field crews, site archives, even camp kitchens. A good mind for organization is a great asset.
- *Cultural sensitivity* and *good people skills* are essential. Many of archaeology's most successful practitioners invest enormous amounts of time in cultivating people and communicating with Native Americans and other cultural groups. Such skills require great patience and sensitivity, but the personal satisfaction and rewards are immense. This is one reason why a background in anthropology is so important to an archaeologist.
- A *commitment* to ethical archaeology is also necessary. Do not become an archaeologist unless you are prepared to adhere to the ethical standards demanded of such professionals, some of which are spelled out in Chapter 2.
- A *sense of humor* may seem self-evident, but it is vital, for many archaeologists take themselves far too seriously. Have you ever spent a week writing a paper, then had your computer implode before you have backed up your text? Moments like that beset all field research. That's why archaeologists need a sense of humor, because sometimes everything that can go wrong goes wrong—all at once.

The most important considerations are commitment and enthusiasm. They will carry you through almost anything.

are as important as academic qualifications, which we discuss subsequently, for you will never become rich as an archaeologist. This is a profession that has its own unique rewards. Money is not one of them (see the Doing Archaeology box).

Deciding to Become an Archaeologist

Many people become archaeologists almost by chance. The occasional fieldwork experiences they had as an undergraduate were interesting and left them wanting more. This is not like becoming a priest or a nun, or signing up with the military, where a high degree of initial commitment is needed. You can ease your way into the field, and have a great time doing so, up to the point when you apply to graduate school.

Almost everyone we meet who is contemplating a career in archaeology either encountered the subject in high school or became interested as a result of taking an introductory course at a college or university. Many people are lucky enough to have a truly inspiring teacher, one who fires them with enthusiasm for a possible career they have never encountered before. What, then, should you do once your appetite for the past has been whetted?

First, take more courses in archaeology at the upper division level from as broad a cross section of instructors as possible. Begin with an advanced method and theory course. (If that does not turn you off, then you know you are onto something, for such courses are not remarkable for their excitement!) Then take a selection of area courses, so you can find out what general areas of specialty interest you and what do not. Remember, if you apply to graduate school, you will need some specific interest as the potential focus of your degree.

Second, give yourself as thorough and as broad an education in general biological and cultural anthropology as possible, both to focus your interests and to see if living people interest you more than dead ones. If you do go on to become a professional, you will never regret this exposure.

Third, take as many courses as you can in related disciplines, so that you emerge with strongly developed multidisciplinary interests. The most important and fascinating problems in archaeology—for example, the origins of agriculture—can be approached only from a multidisciplinary perspective. Much CRM archaeology is strongly multidisciplinary.

Last, gain significant field and laboratory experience while still an undergraduate. Such experience looks good on graduate applications, especially if it is broadly based. Even more important, it allows you to experience the challenges, discomforts, and realities of field and laboratory work before they become your job (and you should think of graduate school as a job).

If you take the trouble to acquire a broad-based experience of archaeology in your undergraduate years, you will be well equipped for graduate education and its pathways to a professional career.

Gaining Fieldwork Experience

"How do I go on a dig?" We're asked this question dozens of times a year, especially by beginning students. The good news is that there are more opportunities to go into the field as an undergraduate than ever before, provided you are prepared to make the effort to find them. Begin by taking your department's field course, if it offers one, then look further, using personal contacts and departmental bulletin boards as a start (see the Doing Archaeology box).

Career Opportunities in Archaeology

This is not a good time to become an academic archaeologist, for jobs are rare and the competition intense. But it is certainly an excellent time to consider a career in government or the private sector, both of which effectively administer or carry out most archaeology in North America.

Doing Archaeology

Fieldwork Opportunities

Fieldwork opportunities abound, if you take the trouble to look for them. Here are some possibilities:

Volunteering on an excavation or survey sponsored by your own institution. Ask your instructors about possible opportunities. Once they see you are serious, they may be delighted to use you in the field or laboratory.

Volunteering on fieldwork sponsored by a local or national organization, such as a historical society, museum, or government agency. Many of our students have served as interns for the National Park Service and other organizations. The World Wide Web is a useful source of information on such opportunities, as is your department bulletin board, which advertises fieldwork opportunities (see listings at chapter's end).

Attending field school. Many institutions sponsor summer field schools for credit. The most popular and rigorous field schools are in heavy demand and are filled by competitive application, sometimes by graduate students. General field schools are worthwhile because they combine excavation, laboratory analysis, and academic instruction into one intensive experience. And the camaraderie among participants in such digs can be memorable. Very often, attendance at a field school gives you a basic qualification that will help in getting summer work with a

research institute or a private contract firm. The Society for American Archaeology (see Useful Addresses later in the chapter) and the World Wide Web will provide information, as will mailings sent to your department. Choose your field school with care! All are not equal, and you should take advice from your instructors before committing yourself. A word to the wise: Beware of summer field schools that offer you a chance to excavate on archaeological sites in remote lands. Some of them, especially in the eastern Mediterranean, charge high fees and use students as unskilled labor, so you learn little. Check carefully before signing up, and insist on getting names of former students you can contact beforehand.

Participating in professional excavations overseas. The Archaeological Institute of America and the Council for British Archaeology (see Useful Addresses) maintain lists of professional excavations that rely on serious volunteers. Sometimes they provide cheap or even free accommodation if you stay for a while.

Volunteering on CRM excavation. Many of our students get their first fieldwork experience by working as laborers on local CRM projects. Many of them begin as volunteers and are later paid for their work. It is worth checking with any private-sector CRM firms in your area, or consult your instructor, who may have contacts.

Academic Archaeology.   This field is shrinking. A generation ago, almost all archaeologists were faculty members at academic institutions or worked in museums or research institutions. Purely academic archaeology still dominates both undergraduate and graduate training, and there are many people who enter graduate school with the resolute ambition of becoming a "traditional" research scholar. But growth in academic positions is now very slow. Some programs are shrinking (Zeitlin, 1997).

Most archaeology in North America and many parts of Europe is now conducted as CRM projects, much of it mandated by law. This means that more and more (but certainly not all) academic archaeology in American universities is conducted outside the United States, most commonly in Europe, Mesoamerica, and the Andes. There is intense competition for the rare vacant academic jobs in such well-trodden areas as Mesoamerica and even more applicants for the rare academic positions in North American archaeology.

A recent study of U.S. archaeologists found that only about 35 percent worked in academia, and the number is shrinking every year (Zeitlin, 1997). The moral is simple: If you want to become an academic archaeologist, beware of overspecializing or of working in too-crowded fields, and have other qualifications such as CRM or computer skills at your disposal.

Museum jobs are hard to come by, especially purely research positions. A career in museum work is rewarding, and requires specialized training in conservation, exhibits, curation, or some other aspect of collections care in addition to academic training.

Cultural Resource Management and Public Archaeology. These areas offer almost open-ended opportunities to persons seeking a career in managing and saving the archaeological record (Green and Doershuk, 1998). The greatest opportunities in archaeology during this century lie in the public archaeology arena and in the private sector, where the challenges are far more demanding than the traditional academic concerns.

If you are interested in public archaeology or CRM, you have the choice of working either in government or for some form of organization engaged in CRM activity, which can be either a not-for-profit group, perhaps attached to a museum, college, or university or a for-profit company operating entirely in the private sector. The latter come in many forms and sizes, with larger companies offering the best opportunities and career potential, especially for entry-level archaeologists. Most public archaeology activity operates through government, although a few private-sector firms also specialize in this work.

If you choose to work in the public sector, you can find opportunities in many federal government agencies, among them the National Park Service and the Bureau of Land Management. Many archaeologists work for state archaeological surveys and other such organizations. Historical societies, such as that in Ohio, often employ archaeologists.

Academic Qualifications: Graduate School

An undergraduate degree in archaeology qualifies you to work as a gofer on a CRM excavation or an academic dig and little else, except for giving you a better knowledge than most people have of the human past—not something to denigrate as a source of enlightenment and enjoyment in later life. Many people work on CRM projects for a number of years and live in motels; they even have their own informal newsletter!

Any form of permanent position in archaeology requires a minimum of an M.A. (Master of Arts), which will qualify you for many government and private-sector positions. All academic positions at research universities and, increasingly, teaching posts require a Ph.D. (Doctor of Philosophy).

Typically, an M.A. in archaeology requires two years of coursework and some form of data-based paper and, at some institutions, an oral examination. The M.A. may have a specialized slant, such as CRM or historic preservation, but most are general degrees that prepare you to teach at some two- or four-year colleges and universities and open you to many CRM or government opportunities. The advantage of the M.A. degree is that it gives you a broad background in archaeology, which is essential for any professional. It is the qualification of choice for many government and CRM or public archaeology positions.

The Ph.D. is a specialized research degree, which qualifies you as a faculty member to teach at a research university and at many institutions that stress teaching and not research. This is the professional "ticket" for academic archaeologists and is certainly desirable for someone entering government or the private sector, where complex research projects and management decisions are often needed. The typical Ph.D. program requires at least two years of seminar, course, and field training, followed by comprehensive examinations (written and often oral), M.A. papers, then a formal research proposal and a period of intensive fieldwork that, in written form, constitutes the Ph.D. thesis.

The average doctoral program takes about seven years to complete and turns you into a highly specialized professional, with some teaching and research experience. After these seven years, you then have to find a job in a highly competitive marketplace. Yes, it is a daunting prospect to face seven years or more of genteel poverty, but the intellectual and personal rewards are considerable for someone with a true passion for archaeology and academic research. However, be aware that the Ph.D. is a *research* degree, not a qualification for carrying out CRM and other professional activities that often require other skills.

Do not consider applying for a graduate program in archaeology unless you have the following:

- An academic record well above average, with in-depth coverage of archaeology and anthropology. An A-minus grade point average is a minimal requirement for good graduate schools; you also need good GRE scores.
- A strong background in anthropology and a multidisciplinary perspective are essential.
- Some field experience on a dig or survey.
- An ability to write good, clear English and to speak fluently in public (both skills acquired by experience).
- Strong and meaningful support from at least two qualified archaeologists who are able to write letters for you, who know you really well. The old adage about getting to know your professors is so true. A letter written by someone who knows you both as a person and as a student stands out from the crowd.
- A specific research interest, which is spelled out carefully in the statement of intent required on most graduate applications. It is very important that your emerging specialist interests coincide with those of the department of your choice and with the faculty members who work there. For example, it's no use applying to the University of California at Santa Barbara for Ph.D. study in eastern North America. They have no one who teaches it! An obvious point, one would think, but one often ignored.
- A strong passion for archaeology and for teaching as well as research, a realistic expectation as far as the tight job market is concerned, and a moral commitment not to collect artifacts for profit or for personal gain.

A final word to the wise: If you feel your passion and interest in archaeology waning as you progress through your graduate years, do not hesitate to quit. The experience may be traumatic in the short term, but there are many people in archaeology who quietly wish they had never chosen a career with seemingly limited prospects. They may not readily admit it, but they are out there. Do not become one of them!

Thoughts on Not Becoming a Professional Archaeologist

Over many years of teaching archaeology, we've introduced thousands of people to the subject. Only a handful have become professional archaeologists. Most students who pass through our courses go on to an enormous variety of careers—Army Rangers, bureaucrats, international businesspeople, lawyers, politicians, real estate tycoons, teachers, and even chefs and pastry cooks. At least two of our former students are in jail! But every one of them is aware of archaeology and its role in the contemporary world, of the remarkable achievements of our ancient forebears. This is by far the most important teaching that we do, of far greater significance than any amount of professional training we may give graduate students.

Our task as teachers of introductory courses is not to recruit people to the field but to help create what the National Science Foundation calls "an informed citizenry." Many of our students end up with no interest in archaeology whatsoever; they find it boring and irrelevant to their lives (this quite apart from finding us tiresome!). But you can be sure they have heard of the subject and its remarkable achievements and have decided where it fits in their lives. This is, after all, one of the objectives of an undergraduate education.

On the other hand, many people take a single course in archaeology and develop an active interest in the subject that endures through the rest of their lives. If you are one of those individuals, you can stay involved, at least tangentially, with archaeology in many ways.

Archaeology depends on informed amateur archaeologists (often called "avocationals"), who volunteer on excavations, in laboratories, and in museums. Many highly important contributions to archaeology come from amateur archaeologists, often members of local archaeological societies, who participate in digs and keep an eye out for new discoveries in their areas. There is a strong tradition of amateur scholarship in archaeology, especially in Europe, where some avocationals have become world authorities on specialized subjects such as ancient rabbit keeping or specific pottery forms, and they publish regularly in academic journals.

Archaeology could not function without volunteers, whether on Earthwatch-supported excavations or through quiet work behind the scenes cataloging artifacts or running lecture programs. If you have a serious interest in volunteering and pursuing archaeology on a regular basis as an amateur, there are many ways to become involved through local organizations such as colleges, museums, archaeological societies, and chapters of the Archaeological Institute of America. In these days of highly specialized research and professional scholarship, it is easy to say there is no place for amateurs. This arrogant statement is nonsense and misses the point. Amateurs bring an extraordinary range of skills to archaeology. During our careers, we have worked with, among others, an accountant (who straightened out our excavation books), an architect, a professional photographer and artist (who was a godsend in the field), a jeweler (who analyzed gold beads), and an expert on slash-and-burn agriculture (who had a passion for environmental history). Your talents are invaluable, and don't take no for an answer!

Many people develop an interest in the past, which comes to the fore when they travel. Their background in archaeology obtained as an undergraduate enables them to visit famous sites all over the world as an informed observer and to enjoy the achievements of ancient peoples to the fullest. Our files are full of postcards and letters from obscure places, like one mailed from Stonehenge: "Thank you for introducing me to archaeology," it reads. "I enjoyed Stonehenge so much more after taking your course." This postcard makes one's day, for archaeology cannot survive without the involvement and enthusiasm not just of professionals but of everyone interested in the past. We are all stewards of a priceless, and finite, resource that is vanishing before our eyes.

Our Responsibilities to the Past

All of us, whether professional archaeologist, avocational fieldworker, casually interested traveler, or basically uninterested citizen, share a common responsibility for the past (Vitelli, 1997). It is our collective cultural heritage, whether the Parthenon, the pyramids of Giza, Cahokia, or the tomb of Chinese emperor Qin Shihuangdi. This past extends back deep into the Ice Age for more than 2.5 million years—a precious legacy of cultural achievement that is unique to humanity and something that we must cherish and pass on to generations still unborn. We are as much stewards of the past as we are of the oceans, forests, and every part of the natural environment. Archaeology is different in one important respect: Once destroyed, its archives can never be reconstructed. They are gone forever. Professional archaeologists subscribe to strict and explicit ethics in their dealings with the past, but, in the final analysis, preserving the past for the future is the responsibility of us all (see the Doing Archaeology box).

As we have emphasized many times in these pages, the world's archaeological sites are under attack from many sources: industrial development, mining, and agriculture, as well as treasure hunters, collectors, and professional tomb robbers. As long as there is a demand for antiquities among collectors and as long as we maintain our materialistic values about personal possessions, destruction of archaeological sites will continue unabated. Even the necessary legal controls to prevent destruction of archaeological sites are just barely in force in most parts of the world. Yet there is still hope, which stems from the enormous numbers of informed people who have gained an interest in archaeology from university and college courses, or from chance encounters with archaeologists, or from their travels. If sufficient numbers of laypeople can influence public behavior and attitudes toward archaeological sites and the morality of collecting, there is still hope that our descendants will have archaeological sites to study and enjoy (Messenger, 1989).

We are glad we became archaeologists and that our passion for the past remains unabated after many years in the field, laboratory, and classroom. We've met many extraordinary people and have been challenged by complex research problems that have

Doing Archaeology

A Simple Code of Archaeological Ethics for All

Treat all archaeological sites and artifacts as finite resources.

Never dig an archaeological site.

Never collect artifacts for yourself or buy and sell them for personal gain.

Adhere to all federal, state, local, and tribal laws relating to archaeological sites.

Report all accidental archaeological discoveries.

Avoid disturbing any archaeological site, and respect the sanctity of all burial sites (Lynott and Wylie, 2000).

taken our career in unexpected directions. But the moments we cherish most are those occasions when we've stood on an archaeological site or among some deserted earthworks or weathered buildings and the past has suddenly come to life. We're lucky to have experienced this many times: high in the Greek amphitheater at Epidauros, where Euripides' stanzas echoed with perfect acoustics; on cloud-mantled earthworks in Britain, where you could almost hear the cries of Roman legionaries advancing into battle; and on a coastal shell midden in southern California, where one could imagine planked canoes landing on a fine summer evening. These moments come without warning and are deeply emotional, triggered by evocative sunsets, effects of cloud and light, or even by a chance thought, but they are utterly precious. The past is personal to us, however dedicated a scientist we are, or however casually we visit a site. If the archaeological record vanishes, with all its great achievements and moments of brilliant success and long-forgotten tragedy, our successors will never be able to learn from the experience of our forebears or enjoy the powerful and extraordinarily satisfying emotional pull of the past. We owe this legacy to our grandchildren.

Summary

This chapter summarized the essential qualities of someone seeking to become an archaeologist and identified some of the career opportunities.

Career opportunities for professional archaeologists can be found in universities, colleges, museums, government service, and private businesses, both in the United States and abroad.

Most archaeological jobs require at least an M.A. and very often a Ph.D. Do not consider becoming a professional archaeologist unless you have an above-average academic record, some field experience, strong support from your professors, and a moral commitment not to collect artifacts for profit.

Even people who have no intention of becoming professional archaeologists can gain digging experience by attending a field school or by digging overseas. Archaeology can give you insight into the past and the potential for involvement as an informed layperson. It will also enable you to enjoy the major archaeological sites of the world in a unique way and to aid in archaeologists' attempts to preserve the past.

All of us have ethical responsibilities to the past: not to collect artifacts, to report new finds, and to obey federal, state, and tribal laws that protect archaeological sites. Unless we all take our responsibility to the past seriously, the past has no future.

Guide to Further Reading

LYNOTT, MARK J., and ALISON WYLIE. 2000. *Ethics in American Archaeology: Challenges for the 1990s.* Rev. ed. Washington, DC: Society for American Archaeology. Very much a working document, this important volume lays out the fundamentals of archaeological ethics as a basis for discussion in the profession.

MESSENGER, PHYLLIS M., ed. 1989. *The Ethics of Collecting Cultural Property.* Albuquerque: University of New Mexico Press. Invaluable essays on the international trade in antiquities and the ethics behind the controversy.

VITELLI, KAREN, ed. 1997. *Archaeological Ethics.* Walnut Creek, CA: AltaMira Press. A useful anthology of ethical issues in archaeology designed for students.

ZEITLIN, MARILYN. 1997. *The American Archaeologist: A Profile.* Walnut Creek, CA: AltaMira Press. A study of American archaeologists based on the membership of the Society for American Archaeology that gives valuable information on trends, careers, and so forth.

Useful Addresses

Information on archaeological field schools can be obtained from fliers posted on university department bulletin boards and also from the Society for American Archaeology. Here are four addresses from which you can obtain information about archaeological activities and excavations that need volunteers:

Archaeological Institute of America
Box 1901, Kenmore Station
Boston, MA 02215

The Archaeological Institute of America publishes the *Archaeological Fieldwork Opportunities Bulletin.* Members receive *Archaeology Magazine.* The *Fieldwork Bulletin* can be accessed on the Web at **http://www.archaeological.org**

Society for American Archaeology
900 Second Street NE, #12
Washington, DC 20002-3557

The Society for American Archaeology is the professional organization for all American archaeologists and many professionals in other fields.

Society members receive a newsletter, *The Archaeological Record,* and *American Antiquity* or *Latin American Antiquity,* both more technical journals than *Archaeology Magazine.* You can contact the society at **http://www.saa.org**

The Council for British Archaeology
Bowes Morrell House
111 Walmgate
York YO1 2UA, England

Contact the Council for British Archaeology for excavation opportunities overseas. This admirable organization maintains complete details of volunteer excavations in Britain and sometimes in other parts of the world. Go to **http:www.britarch. ac.uk**

American Anthropological Association
2200 Wilson Blvd., Suite 600
Arlington, VA 22201

The American Anthropological Association maintains some information on field schools and fieldwork opportunities. **http://www.aaanet.org**

This glossary is designed to give informal definitions of words and ideas in the text, particularly those that are theoretical; it is not a comprehensive dictionary of archaeology. Jargon is kept to a minimum, but a few technical expressions are inevitable. Terms such as *adaptation* and *mutation,* which are common in contexts other than archaeology, are not listed; a good dictionary will clarify them. The key terms are in boldface type in the text. However, we have also included some commonly used words in the archaeological vocabulary (e.g., *unaerated*) in case you need them; they are not boldface in the text.

absolute (chronometric) chronology: Dating in calendar years before the present; chronometric dating.

accelerator mass spectrometry (AMS) radiocarbon dating: A radiocarbon dating method that uses a mass spectrometer; more accurate than conventional radiocarbon dating.

activity area: A pattern of artifacts in a site indicating that a specific activity, such as stone tool making, took place.

activity set: A set of artifacts that reveals the activities of an individual.

alluvium: Geological deposit laid down by the action of a river or a stream.

analogy: A process of reasoning whereby two entities that share some similarities are assumed to share many others.

analysis: A stage of archaeological research that involves describing and classifying artifactual and nonartifactual data.

annealing: The process of heating and cooling metal to make it less brittle.

anthropology: The study of humanity in the widest possible sense. Anthropology studies humanity from the earliest times to the present; it includes cultural and physical anthropology and archaeology.

antiquarian: Someone interested in the past who collects and digs up antiquities unscientifically, in contrast to the scientific archaeologist.

archaeological context: See context.

archaeological culture: A group of assemblages at several sites representing the surviving remains of an extinct culture.

archaeological record: Artifacts, sites, and other human-manufactured features or results of ancient human behavior and their matrices.

archaeological region: A well-defined geographic area bounded by a conspicuous geographic feature, such as an ocean, a lake, or mountains.

archaeological survey: Systematic attempts to locate, identify, and record the distribution of archaeological sites on the ground and against the natural geographic and environmental background.

archaeological theory: A body of theoretical concepts providing both a framework and a means for archaeologists to look beyond the facts and material objects for explanations of events that took place in prehistory.

archaeological unit: An arbitrary unit of classification set up by archaeologists to separate conveniently one grouping of artifacts in time and space from another.

archaeologist: Someone who studies the past using scientific methods, with the motive of recording and interpreting ancient cultures rather than collecting artifacts for profit or display.

archaeology: A special form of anthropology that studies extinct human societies using the material remains of their behavior. The main objectives of archaeology are to understand and reconstruct culture history, study cultural process, and conserve and manage archaeological sites.

archaeology of gender: The study of gender relations in the past.

archaeology of inequality: The study of social inequality in the past.

archaeology of mind: The study of religious beliefs and other ancient intangibles.

archaeomagnetic dating: Chronometric dating using magnetic alignments from buried features, such as pottery kilns, which can be compared with known fluctuations in the earth's magnetic field to produce a date in years.

Archaic: In the New World, a period when hunter-gatherers were exploiting a broad spectrum of resources and may have been experimenting with agriculture.

area excavation: See horizontal (area) excavation.

artifact: Any object manufactured or modified by human beings.

assemblage: All the artifacts found at a site, including the sum of all subassemblages at the site.

association: The relationship between an artifact and other archaeological finds and a site level, or another artifact, structure, or feature in the site.

Assyriologist: A student of the Assyrian civilization of Iraq.

astroarchaeology: The study of ancient astronomical knowledge.

attribute: A well-defined feature of an artifact that cannot be further subdivided. Archaeologists identify types of attributes, including form, style, and technology, in order to classify and interpret artifacts.

attribute analysis: Analyzing artifacts using many of their features. Normally these attributes are studied statistically to produce clusters of attributes that can be used to identify statistical classes of artifacts.

attritional age profile: The distribution of ages at death of animals in a population that were killed by selective hunting or predation.

auger: A drill, either hand- or power-driven, used to probe subsurface deposits.

Australopithecus: Primate whose fossil remains have been found mainly in eastern and southern Africa. Thought to be closely related to the first human beings, who may indeed have evolved from australopithecines.

band: The simple form of human social organization that flourished for most of prehistory. A band consists of a family or a series of families, normally with twenty to fifty people.

biblical archaeology: The study of the archaeology of the Scriptures.

biosphere: All the earth's living organisms interacting with the physical environment.

blade technology: An advanced stone technology that produces parallel-sided stone flakes, normally removed from a carefully prepared core, often by means of a punch.

bowsing: Technique for detecting buried features by thumping the ground and sensing the differences between compacted and undisturbed earth.

bulbar surface: The surface upon which the bulb of percussion occurs.

bulb of percussion: The conelike effect caused by conchoidal fracture on siliceous rocks.

burin: A blade tool, flaked on one or both ends to form a small chisel or grooving tool.

cambium: A viscid substance under the bark of trees in which the annual growth of wood and bark takes place.

carrying capacity: The number and density of people per square mile that a specified area of land can support, given a particular subsistence level.

catastrophic age profile: Distribution of ages at death of animals in a population that died as a result of natural causes.

central-place theory: A geographic theory applied to archaeology, stating that human settlements will space themselves evenly across a landscape as a function of the availability of natural resources and other factors. Eventually, these will evolve into a hierarchy of settlements of different size that depend on one another.

ceramic analysis: The analysis of clay objects, especially pottery.

ceramic ecology: The interaction of resources, local knowledge, and style that ultimately leads to a finished clay vessel.

ceramics: Objects of fired clay.

characterization study: The study of sources of raw materials used to make artifacts.

Chavín: A distinctive art style that spread widely over the Andean region after 900 B.C. Sometimes referred to as the Chavín Horizon.

chiefdom: A form of social organization, more complex than a tribal society, that has evolved some form of leadership structure and some mechanisms for distributing goods and services throughout the society. The chief who heads such a society and the specialists who work for the chief are supported by the voluntary contributions of the people.

chronological types: Types defined by form that are time markers.

chronometric dating: Dating in years before the present; absolute dating.

civilization: See state-organized society.

clan: A group of people from many lineages who live in one place and have a common line of descent; a kin grouping.

class: A general group of artifacts, such as "hand axes," that can be broken down into specific types, such as "ovates," and so on.

Classic: In Mesoamerica, the period of vigorous civilization characterized by numerous ceremonial centers and small states.

classical archaeology: The study of the classical civilizations of Greece and Rome.

classification: The ordering of archaeological data into groups and classes, using various ordering systems.

cognitive archaeology: The study of human intangibles using archaeological data.

cognitive-processual approach: An approach to archaeology that combines the processual approach with analogy and other methods to reconstruct ancient ideologies and intangibles.

community: In archaeology, the tangible remains of the activities of the maximum number of people who together occupied a settlement at any one period.

complex: In archaeology, a chronological subdivision of different artifact types, such as stone tools or pottery.

compliance process: In CRM, the process of complying with legislative requirements. Sometimes called the Section 106 process after that section of the National Historic Preservation Act of 1966.

component: An association of all the artifacts from one occupation level at a site.

conchoidal fracture: A characteristic fracture pattern that occurs in siliceous rocks, such as obsidian and flint.

condition: An event that forces people to make decisions about how to deal with a new situation.

confirmatory (inferential) statistics: Statistical procedures used to make informed inferences about the characteristics of a population or the relationship between variables on the basis of data collected from a sample of the population.

conservation archaeology: Another name for cultural resource management.

context: The position of an archaeological find in time and space, established by measuring and assessing its associations, matrix, and provenance. The assessment includes study of what has happened to the find since it was buried in the ground.

coprolite: Excrement preserved by desiccation or fossilization.

core: In archaeology, a lump of stone from which human-struck flakes have been removed.

core borer: A hollow tubelike instrument used to collect samples of soils, pollens, and other materials from below the surface.

cosmology (cosmos): A society's view of the universe.

cranial: Of or pertaining to the skull (cranium).

critical archaeology: The study of the meanings behind ancient material culture.

crop mark: Differential growth in crops and vegetational cover that reveals the outlines of archaeological sites from the air.

cross-dating: Dating of sites by means of objects or associated artifacts of known age.

cultural anthropology: The aspects of anthropology focusing on human social life, past and present, and on how cultures adapt to the environment.

cultural ecology: The study of the dynamic interactions between human societies and their environments. Under this approach, culture is the primary adaptive mechanism used by human societies.

cultural evolution: A theory similar to that of biological evolution that argues that human cultures change gradually over time as a result of a number of cultural processes.

cultural materialism: An approach to archaeology that stresses the complex relationships between technology, economy, and environment.

cultural process: A deductive approach to archaeological research that is designed to study the changes and interactions in cultural systems and the processes by which human cultures change throughout time. Processual archaeologists use both descriptive and explanatory models.

cultural resource management (CRM): The conservation and management of archaeological sites and artifacts as a means of protecting the past.

cultural resources: Human-made and natural physical features associated with human activity.

cultural selection: The process that leads to the acceptance of some cultural traits and innovations that make a culture more adaptive to its environment; somewhat akin to natural selection in biological evolution.

cultural system: A perspective on culture that views culture and its environment as a number of linked systems in which change occurs through a series of minor, linked variations in one or more of these systems.

cultural tradition: In archaeology, a distinctive tool kit or technology that lasts a long time, longer than the duration of one culture, at one locality or several localities.

cultural transformations: Changes in the archaeological record resulting from later human behavior, such as digging beneath a rubbish pit into earlier levels.

culture: A set of designs for living that help mold human responses to different situations. Culture is our primary means of adapting to our environment. In archaeology, a culture is an arbitrary unit applied to similar assemblages of artifacts found at several sites, defined in a precise context of time and space.

culture area: An arbitrary geographic or research area in which general cultural homogeneity is found.

culture history: An approach to archaeology that assumes that artifacts can be used to build up a generalized picture of human culture and descriptive models in time and space and that these can be interpreted.

cumulative recording: Excavating and recording a trench in three dimensions, using both horizontal and vertical observations to reconstruct events at the site.

cuneiform: The earliest known script from Mesopotamia, consisting of wedge-shaped markings (from the Latin *cuneus,* "wedge").

curation: Deliberate attempts by prehistoric peoples to preserve key artifacts and structures for posterity. Also used in a modern context to describe the careful management of artifacts and other data recovered in archaeological research.

cylinder hammer technique: Stone-flaking technique using a bone hammer that removes small, flat flakes from a core.

data: The natural materials recognized by the archaeologist as significant evidence, all of which are collected and recorded as part of the research.

datum point: A location from which all measurements on a site are made. The datum point is tied into local survey maps.

debitage: Waste by-products resulting from the manufacture of stone tools.

deduction: A process of reasoning that involves testing generalizations by generating hypotheses and trying them out with data. Deductive research is cumulative and involves constant refining of hypotheses. Contrasts with inductive approaches, which proceed from specific observations to general conclusions.

deductive-nomological approach: A way of explaining observable phenomena by means of formal scientific methods, testing hypotheses generated from general laws governing human behavior. Some archaeologists believe that this is the appropriate way to explain cultural processes.

deductive reasoning: The formulation of specific implications from a generalized hypothesis.

demography: The study of population.

dendrochronology: Tree-ring chronology.

deposited assemblage: The carcasses or portions of carcasses that come to rest in a site.

descriptive statistics: Techniques that provide a means for organizing and quantifying archaeological data in a manner that facilitates objective comparison while preserving the inherent structure of the data.

descriptive types: Types based on the physical or external properties of an artifact.

diet: What is eaten by humans (or animals).

diffusion: The spread of a culture trait from one area to another by means of contact among people.

direct historical approach: The archaeological technique of working backward in time from historic sites of known age into earlier times.

distal: Describing the end of a bone farthest from the skeleton's center line; opposite of proximal.

distribution of communities: The density and spatial patterning of communities across the landscape, as determined by economic, environmental, social and religious, subsistence, and technological constraints.

ecofact: Archaeological finds that are of cultural significance but were not manufactured by humans, such as bones and vegetal remains. Not a commonly used term.

ecological approach: An approach to archaeology that studies the relationship between ancient societies and their changing environments.

economic catchment area: The area from which the food resources consumed by the inhabitants of a site are obtained.

ecosystem: An environmental system maintained by the regulation of trophic levels (vertical food chains) and by patterns of energy flow.

ecotone: A transition zone between habitats.

Egyptologist: A student of the cultures of ancient Egypt.

electronic spin resonance (ESR) dating: A dating technique that measures radiation-induced defects or the density of trapped electrons within a bone or shell sample without the need to heat them.

engendered archaeology: An approach to archaeology that uses a wide diversity of archaeological methods and approaches to find out how gender functioned in ancient societies, to unravel its cultural meanings.

environmental determinism: In archaeology, a school of thought that considers climatic and environmental change as the primary causes of culture change.

environmental impact statement: A document that spells out the impact of modern development on the archaeological record in a specific area.

epigrapher: One who studies inscriptions.

epiphysis: The articular end of a long bone, which fuses at adulthood.

ethnoarchaeology: Living archaeology, a form of ethnography that deals mainly with material remains. Archaeologists carry out living archaeology to document the relationships between human behavior and the patterns of artifacts and food remains in the archaeological record.

ethnography: A descriptive study, normally an in-depth examination of a culture.

ethnohistory: Study of the past using non-Western, indigenous historical records and especially oral traditions.

ethnology: A cross-cultural study of aspects of various cultures, usually based on theory.

eustatic: Referring to a process of adjustments in sea levels and the earth's crust resulting from expansion and contraction of Pleistocene ice sheets.

evolutionary approach: An explanatory framework for the past that accounts for structure and change in the archaeological record.

excavation: The digging of archaeological sites, removing the matrix and observing the provenance and context of the finds therein, and recording them three-dimensionally.

exchange system: A system for exchanging goods and services between individuals and communities.

exogamy: A rule requiring marriage outside a social or cultural unit (endogamy means the opposite).

experimental archaeology: The use of carefully controlled modern experiments to provide data to aid in the interpretation of the archaeological record.

exploratory data analysis (EDA): Quantitative methods specifically designed to aid in detecting patterns and deviations in sets of data by relying heavily on visual displays of data rather than on summary statistics and statistical significance tests.

extrasomatic: Outside the body.

faience: Glazed terra-cotta.

feature: An artifact such as a storage pit or a posthole that cannot be removed from a site; normally, it is only recorded, not removed.

feces: Excrement.

feedback: A concept in archaeological applications of systems theory reflecting the continually changing relationship between cultural variables and their environment.

fire setting: Quarrying stone by using fire to shatter the outcrops of rock.

fission-track dating: Observing accumulations of radioactivity in glass and volcanic rocks to produce absolute dates.

flake tools: Stone tools made of flakes removed from cores.

flotation: In archaeology, recovering plant remains by using water to separate seeds from their surrounding deposit.

focus: Approximately equivalent to a phase.

form: The physical characteristics—size and shape or composition—of any archaeological find. Form is an essential part of attribute analysis.

formal attributes: Such features as the shape of the artifact, its measurable dimensions, and its components.

form analysis: Analysis of artifacts based on the assumption that the shape of a pot or other tool directly reflects its function.

formation processes: Human-caused or natural processes by which an archaeological site is modified during or after occupation and abandonment.

Formative: In Mesoamerica, the period when more complex societies and settlement patterns were coming into being; these led to the complex states of later times (contemporary with the rise of agriculture).

frequency seriation: A seriation method that employs percentages of artifacts and their features to develop cultural sequences.

functional approach: An approach to anthropology and archaeology that argues that human societies can only be understood by looking at the network of complex relationships that form their underlying structure.

functionalism: The notion that a social institution within a society has a function in fulfilling all the needs of a social organism.

functional types: Types based on cultural use or function rather than on outward form or chronological position.

general systems theory: The notion that any organism or organization can be studied as a system broken down into many interacting subsystems or parts; sometimes called cybernetics.

geoarchaeology: Archaeological research using the methods and concepts of the earth sciences.

geochronology: Geological dating.

Geographic Information System (GIS): A system for mapping archaeological and other data in digitized form, thereby allowing it to be manipulated for research purposes.

gift exchange: An exchange system that operates on the basis of gift-giving relationships sustained between individuals or groups.

glaze: A form of pottery slip with additives that cause the coating to vitrify in the kiln.

ground-penetrating radar (GPR): Radar used by archaeologists to locate subsurface features.

habitat: An area in the biome where different communities and populations flourish, each with specific locales.

half-life: The time required for one-half of a radioactive isotope to decay into a stable element. Used as a basis for radiocarbon and other dating methods.

heuristic: Serving to find out; a means of discovery.

hieroglyphs: Ancient writing featuring pictographic or ideographic symbols; used in Egypt, Mesoamerica, and elsewhere.

historical archaeology: The study of archaeological sites in conjunction with historical records. Sometimes called historic sites archaeology.

historical particularism The use of anthropological data to plot culture areas.

historiography: The process of studying history.

history: The study of the past through written records.

Holocene Epoch: The geological epoch since the Ice Age (from the Greek *holos,* "recent").

hominid: A member of the family Hominidae, represented today by one species, *Homo sapiens sapiens.*

__Homo erectus:__ Human beings who evolved from Lower Pleistocene hominids. They possessed larger brains and made more elaborate stone tools than their predecessors and settled in much more extreme environments, as far apart as western Europe, Asia, and tropical Africa.

horizon: A widely distributed set of culture traits and artifact assemblages whose distribution and chronology allow researchers to assume that they spread rapidly. Often, horizons are formed of artifacts that were associated with widespread, distinctive religious beliefs.

horizontal (area) excavation: Excavation of a large horizontal area, designed to uncover large areas of a site, especially houses and settlement layouts.

household unit: An arbitrary archaeological unit defining artifact patterns reflecting the activities that take place around a house and assumed to belong to one household.

iconography: The study of ancient beliefs through symbols.

ideology: The knowledge or beliefs developed by human societies as part of their cultural adaptation.

ideology of domination: A set of beliefs used to propagate any form of social inequality.

inductive reasoning: Reasoning by which one proceeds from specific observations to general conclusions.

industrial archaeology: The study of sites of the Industrial Revolution and later.

industry: All the particular artifacts (bone, stone, wood) found at a site that were made at the same time by the same population.

inevitable variation: The notion that cultures change in small cumulative increments over time. The reasons for these changes are little understood.

inferential statistics: See confirmatory (inferential) statistics.

inorganic materials: Objects that are not part of the animal or plant kingdom, including objects of stone, clay, and metal.

intensive survey: Archaeological survey that seeks to locate every site in an area.

interpretation: The stage in research at which the results of archaeological analyses are synthesized and we attempt to explain their meaning.

invention: Some kind of innovation, material or otherwise, produced by a person or group at one place at a single moment in time.

isostatic: Referring to a process that causes the earth's crust to compensate for the additional weight of glacial ice during glacial episodes.

kiln: An oven used for baking clay vessels and other ceramic objects at a high temperature.

kinship: In anthropology, relationships between people that are based on real or imagined descent or, sometimes, on marriage. Kinship ties impose mutual obligations on all members of a kin group; these ties were at the core of most prehistoric societies.

knapper: One who manufactures stone artifacts.

landscape: A perception of an environment created by humans.

landscape signature: The imprint of human activity on a natural landscape.

leaching: Water seeping through the soil and removing the soluble materials from it.

Levallois technique: Stoneworking technique that involves preparing a bun-shaped core from which one preshaped flake is removed.

life assemblage: A community of live animals in their natural environment.

lineage: A kinship that traces descent through either the male or the female members.

linguistics: The study of language, which sometimes helps determine past events, such as the origins of Indo-Europeans.

lithic: Of or pertaining to stone.

lithic analysis: The study of stone tool technology, including replication of said technologies.

loess: Windblown glacial soil.

lost-wax technique: A method of bronze-working that employs a wax model of the object. The mold is assembled with wax in place of the artifact. The wax is then melted and replaced with molten bronze. The technique was much used by the Shang bronze workers of China.

magnetometer survey: A survey done with a subsurface detection device that measures minor variations in the earth's magnetic field and locates archaeological features before excavation.

market: A place set aside specifically for trading.

material culture: Technology and artifacts.

matriarchal: Characterized by family authority resting with the woman's family.

matrilineal: Characterized by descent reckoned through the female line only.

matrilocal: Characterized by married couples' living with or near the wife's mother.

matrix: The surrounding deposit in which archaeological finds are situated.

Mesoamerica: The area of Central America where state-organized societies (civilizations) developed.

Mesolithic: A dated term sometimes applied by Old World archaeologists to the period of transition between the Paleolithic and Neolithic eras. No precise economic or technological definition has been formulated.

mica: A mineral that occurs in a glittering, scaly form; widely prized for ornament.

midden: A deposit of occupation debris, rubbish, or other by-products of human activity.

middle-range theory: A way of seeking accurate means for identifying and measuring specified properties of past cultural systems.

Midwestern Taxonomic Method: A hierarchical approach to classifying artifacts and human culture developed in the American Midwest during the 1930s.

migration: The movement of an entire population from one area to another.

minimum number of individuals (MNI): A count of the number of individuals necessary to account for all the identifiable bones.

mitigation: In archaeology, measures taken to minimize destruction on archaeological sites.

model: A theoretical reconstruction of a set of phenomena, devised to explain them. Archaeological models can be descriptive or explanatory.

multilinear cultural evolution: A theory of cultural evolution that sees each human culture as evolving in its own way through adaptation to its particular environment. Sometimes divided into four broad stages of evolving social organization (band, tribe, chiefdom, and state-organized society).

natural transformations: Changes in the archaeological record resulting from natural phenomena that occur after the artifacts are deposited in the ground.

natural type: An archaeological type coinciding with an actual category recognized by the original toolmaker.

negative feedback: A response to a system that lessens the chance of change.

Neolithic: A dated Old World term referring to the period of the Stone Age when people were cultivating without metals.

niche: The physical space occupied by an organism, its functional role in the community, and how it is constrained by other species and external forces.

nomology: The study of general laws.

noncultural processes: Site formation processes that result from natural processes rather than human actions.

nondestructive archaeology: See nonintrusive archaeology.

nonintrusive archaeology: Archaeological research that studies the past but does not involve disturbance of artifacts, sites, or their context.

normative view of culture: A view of human culture arguing that one can identify the abstract rules regulating a particular culture; a commonly used basis for studying archaeological cultures over time.

number of identified specimens (NISP): A count of the number of bones or bone fragments from each species in a bone sample.

nutrition: The ability of a diet to maintain a body in its environment.

object clustering: An approach to typology based on clusters of human artifacts that are seen as specific classificatory types.

obsidian: Volcanic glass.

obsidian hydration dating: A dating method that measures the thickness of the hydration layer in obsidian artifacts. The hydration layer is caused by absorption of water on exposed surfaces of the rock.

off-site areas: Areas with low artifact densities that were important to ancient groups, such as field systems.

Oldowan: A cultural complex that flourished in eastern Africa about 2.5 to 2.0 million years ago, characterized by simple stone technology. Associated with the earliest toolmaking hominids.

opal phytoliths: Minute particles of silica from plant cells created from hydrated silica dissolved in groundwater that is absorbed through a plant's roots and carried through its vascular system.

open system: In archaeology, a cultural system that interchanges both energy and information with its environment.

operational taxonomic units (OTUs): Units based on similarities between all possible pairs of objects, using similarity coefficients.

oral tradition: Historical traditions, often genealogies, passed down from generation to generation by word of mouth.

ordering: In archaeology, the arranging of artifacts in logical classes and in chronological order.

organic materials: Materials such as bone, wood, horn, or hide that were once living organisms.

ossification: The fusion of a limb bone with its articular end. Implies calcification of soft tissue into bonelike material.

osteologist: One who studies bones.

paleoanthropology: The study of the earliest human beings.

paleobotanist: One who studies ancient botany.

paleoecology: The modern study of past ecology.

Paleolithic: The Old Stone Age.

paleontology: The study of fossil (or ancient) animal bones.

palynology: The analysis of ancient vegetational change through the use of fossil pollen grains.

patination: Natural weathering on the surface of rocks and artifacts.

patrilineal: Characterized by descent reckoned through the male line only.

patrilocal: Characterized by married couples' living with or near the husband's father.

pedology: The scientific study of soil.

periglacial: Surrounding a glacial area.

period: An archaeological unit defining a major stretch of prehistoric time; it contains several phases and pertains to a wide area.

permafrost: Permanently frozen subsoil.

petrological analysis: Examination of thin sections of stone artifacts to determine the provenance of the rock used to make them.

petrology: The study of rocks; in archaeology, analysis of trace elements and other characteristics of rocks used to make such artifacts as ax blades that were traded over long distances.

phase: An archaeological unit defined by characteristic groupings of cultural traits that can be identified precisely in time and space. A phase lasts for a relatively short time and is found at one or more sites in a locality or region. Its culture traits are clear enough to distinguish it from other phases.

physical anthropology: Biological anthropology, which includes the study of fossil human beings, genetics, primates, and blood groups.

planimetric maps: Maps used to record details of archaeological sites; they contain no topographic information.

Pleistocene Epoch: The last major geological epoch before recent times (the Holocene Epoch), extending from about 2 million years ago until about 11,500 years ago. It is sometimes called the Great Ice Age.

pollen analysis: See palynology.

population: In sampling methods, the sum of sampling units selected within a data universe.

positive feedback: A system's response to external stimuli that leads to further change and reinforces it.

Postclassic: A stage in Mesoamerican prehistory during which militarism arose, such as that of the Aztec.

postprocessual archaeology: Theoretical approaches that search for the meaning of the archaeological record, for the ideology and structure of ancient societies. A reaction to processual archaeology.

potassium-argon dating: An absolute dating technique based on the decay rate of potassium-40, which becomes argon-40.

potsherd: A fragment of a clay vessel.

Preclassic: See Formative.

prehistorian: One who studies prehistoric archaeology.

prehistoric archaeology: The study of prehistoric times.

prehistory: The millennia of human history preceding written records.

pressure flaking: A stoneworking technique in which thin flakes are removed from a core or an artifact by applying hand or chest pressure.

pre-state society: An egalitarian society without stratified social classes or centralized government.

primary context: An undisturbed association, matrix, and provenance.

probability sampling: Archaeological sampling based on formal statistical criteria. This method enables researchers to use probability statistics in analyzing data.

process: In archaeology, the culture change that takes place as a result of interactions between a cultural system's elements and the system's environment.

processual archaeology: An approach to archaeology that studies the processes of culture change, usually through a systems, environmental approach.

provenance: The position of an archaeological find in time and space, recorded three-dimensionally.

proximal: Describing the end of a bone nearest to the skeleton's center line; opposite of distal.

public archaeology: A form of archaeology open and accessible to the public through a variety of media.

pulse radar: Use of a pulse induction meter that applies pulses of magnetic field to the soil; this method can be used to find graves, metals, and pottery.

Quaternary: Geological period since the beginning of the Pleistocene Epoch up to recent times (the Holocene Epoch). The exact date of its commencement is uncertain, but it was more than 2 million years ago.

radiocarbon dating: An absolute dating method based on measuring the decay rate of the carbon isotope carbon-14 to stable nitrogen. The resulting dates are calibrated with tree-ring chronologies to convert radiocarbon ages into dates in calendar years.

random sampling: Sampling based on a totally random selection of sample units to be investigated.

reciprocity: In archaeology, the exchange of goods between two parties.

reconnaissance survey: Archaeological survey carried out on a preliminary basis, often using sampling methods.

redistribution: The dispersing of trade goods from a central place throughout a society, a complex process that was a critical part of the evolution of civilization.

reduction sequence: The sequence of actions involved in the manufacture of an artifact by means of reductive technology.

reductive (subtractive) technology: Stone-working technique in which stone is acquired, then shaped by removing flakes until the desired form is achieved.

refitting: The reassembling of stone debitage and cores to reconstruct ancient lithic technologies.

relative chronology: A time scale developed by the law of superposition or artifact ordering.

remote sensing: Reconnaissance and site survey methods using such devices as aerial photography to detect subsurface features and sites.

research design: A carefully formulated and systematic plan for executing archaeological research.

resistivity survey: The measurement of differences in electrical conductivity in soils, used to detect buried features such as walls and ditches.

sample assemblage: The bone sample that is collected by zooarchaeologists and analyzed in the laboratory.

sample unit: An arbitrary or nonarbitrary unit of the data universe, used for sampling archaeological data.

scanner imagery: A method of recording sites from the air using infrared radiation that is beyond the practical spectral response of photographic film. Useful for tracing prehistoric agricultural systems that have disturbed the topsoil over wide areas.

science: A way of acquiring knowledge and understanding about the parts of the natural world that can be observed and measured; a disciplined and highly ordered search for knowledge carried out systematically.

scientific method: A method of inquiry that is based on the formal testing of hypotheses, cumulative research, and replicable experiments.

seasonality: Seasonal occupation.

secondary context: A context of an archaeological find that has been disturbed by subsequent human activity or natural phenomena.

selective excavation: Archaeological excavation of parts of a site using sampling methods or carefully placed trenches that do not uncover the entire site.

seriation: Methods used to place artifacts in chronological order; artifacts closely similar in form or style are placed close to one another.

settlement archaeology: The study of changing ancient settlement patterns against their environment.

settlement pattern: Distribution of human settlement on the landscape and within archaeological communities.

shadow site: Archaeological site identified from the air, where oblique light can show up reduced topography of sites invisible on the ground.

shaman: An individual with unusual supernatural powers and the ability to communicate with the spiritual world.

shovel unit: A small cutting made with a shovel to test the limits of a site and to collect artifact samples.

site: Any place where objects, features, or ecofacts manufactured or modified by human beings are found. A site can range from a living site to a quarry site, and it can be defined in functional and other ways.

site assessment: The assessment of the significance of a site by survey and other nonintrusive means.

site-catchment analysis: Inventorying natural resources within a given distance of a site.

site-exploitation territory: The potential area from which food resources may be obtained.

site-formation processes: Cultural and noncultural phenomena that act on the formation of the archaeological record.

site survey: The collection of surface data and evaluation of each site's archaeological significance.

slip: A fine, wet finish applied to the surface of a clay vessel before it is fired and decorated.

social anthropology: The study of human society and social organization.

social ranking: Social distinctions between individuals, communities, and other units of society.

sociocultural: Combining social and cultural factors.

soil mark: A distinctive mark that turns up in plowed fields when subsurface features show up on aerial photographs.

sondage: See test pit.

sourcing: See characterization study.

spatial context: The relationships between the positions of different objects in archaeological deposits.

spectrographic analysis: Chemical analysis that involves passing the light from a number of trace elements through a prism or diffraction grating that spreads out the wavelengths in a spectrum. It enables researchers to separate the emissions and identify different trace elements. A useful approach for studying metal objects and obsidian artifacts.

stable carbon isotope analysis: A method of identifying types of plant foods from the isotopic analysis of ancient bone and hair. By using the ratio between two stable carbon isotopes—carbon-12 and carbon-13—in animal tissue, researchers can evaluate ancient diets.

stage: A technological subdivision of prehistoric time that has little chronological meaning but denotes the level of technological achievement of societies within it, such as the Stone Age.

state-organized society: A socially stratified society with strongly centralized government, social complexity, and, often, writing.

statistical typologies: Artifact classifications developed by statistical grouping of artifact atributes.

stela (or stele): A column or stone slab, often with an inscribed or sculptured surface; plural, stelae.

stewardship: In archaeology, the conservation and management of the archaeological record for future generations.

stratified sampling: A probabilistic sampling technique used to cluster and isolate sample units, when regular spacing is inappropriate for cultural reasons.

stratigraphy: Observation of the superimposed layers in an archaeological site.

stratum: A single deposited or cultural level.

structural approach (structural archaeology): A theoretical approach to archaeology based on the assumption that codes and rules produce observed systems of relations in human culture.

structure: A feature intended for household or group activity, such as a house or a temple.

stylistic analysis: Artifact analysis that emphasizes style and decoration.

stylistic attributes: Attributes based on stylistic features such as color and decoration.

stylistic types: Types based on stylistic distinctions.

subarea: The subdivision of an archaeological area, normally defined by geographic or cultural considerations.

subassemblage: An association of artifacts denoting a particular form of activity practiced by a group of people.

superposition: The relationship between two objects, structures, or layers in the vertical plane.

surface survey: The collecting of archaeological finds from sites with the objective of gathering representative samples of artifacts from the surface. Surface surveys also establish the types of activity on the site, locate major structures, and gather information on the most densely occupied areas of the site that could be most productive for total or sample excavation.

synthesis: The assembling and analyzing of data preparatory to interpretation.

systematics: In archaeology, procedures for creating sets of archaeological units derived from a logical system for a particular purpose.

systematic sampling: A refinement of random sampling in which one unit is chosen, then others at regular intervals from the first; useful for studying artifact patterns.

systems-ecological approach: An approach to archaeology that is based on a systems approach to culture change and to the complex relationships between human cultural systems and their ecological systems.

taphonomy: The study of the processes by which animal bones and other fossil remains are transformed after deposition.

taxonomy: An ordered set of operations that results in the subdividing of objects into ordered classifications.

technological analysis: The study of technological methods used to make an artifact.

technological attributes: Attributes based on technological features of an object, such as the materials used.

tectonic: Referring to the earth's crust; a tectonic movement is an earthquake.

tell: An Arabic word for small hill or mound; used to refer to archaeological sites of this type in southwestern Asia.

temper: Coarse material such as sand or shell added to fine pot clay to make it bond during firing.

tempering: A process for hardening iron blades that involves heating and rapid cooling.

test pit: An excavation unit used to sample or probe a site before large-scale excavation or to check surface surveys.

theory: The overall framework for archaeological research.

thermoluminescence (TL) dating: A chronometric dating method that measures the amount of light energy released by a baked clay object when heated rapidly. Gives an indication of the time elapsed since the object was last heated.

thermoremnent magnetism: The alignment of magnetic particles fixed by heating.

Three-Age System: A technological subdivision of the prehistoric past developed in 1806 for Old World prehistory.

topographic maps: Maps that can be used to relate archaeological sites to basic features of the natural landscape.

total excavation: Complete excavation of an archaeological site. Normally confined to small sites, such as burial mounds or campsites and avoided where possible.

trace elements: Minute amounts of chemical elements found in rocks that emit characteristic wavelengths of light when heated to incandescence. Trace-element analysis is used to study the sources of obsidian and other materials traded over long distances.

tradition: A persistent technological or cultural pattern identified by characteristic artifact forms. These persistent forms outlast a single phase and can occur over a wide area.

transformational processes: Processes that change an abandoned prehistoric settlement into an archaeological site through the passage of time. These processes can be initiated by natural phenomena or by human activity.

tribe: A group of bands unified by sodalities and governed by a council of representatives from the bands, kin groups, or sodalities within it.

trypanosomiasis: Sleeping sickness.

tsetse: A fly that carries trypanosomiasis. Belts of tsetse-fly country in Africa prevent inhabitants from raising cattle.

tuff: Solidified volcanic ash.

type: In archaeology, a grouping of artifacts created for comparison with other groups. This grouping may or may not coincide with the tool types as they would have been intended by the original manufacturers.

type fossil: A tool characteristic of a particular "archaeological era," a dated concept borrowed from geology.

typology: The classification of types.

unaerated: Not exposed to the open air.

underwater archaeology: The study of archaeological sites and shipwrecks beneath the surface of the water.

uniformitarianism: The doctrine that the earth was formed by the same natural geological processes that are operating today.

unilinear cultural evolution: A late-nineteenth-century evolutionary theory envisaging all human societies as evolving, or being capable of evolving, along one track of cultural evolution, from simple hunting and gathering to literate civilization.

unit: In archaeology, an artificial grouping used for describing artifacts.

uranium series dating: A dating method that measures the steady decay of uranium into various daughter elements inside any formation made up of calcium carbonates, such as limestone or cave stalactites.

use-wear analysis: Microscopic analysis of artifacts to detect signs of wear through use on their working edges.

vertical excavation: Excavation undertaken to establish a chronological sequence, normally covering a limited area.

votive: Intended as an offering as a result of a vow.

zooarchaeology: The study of animal remains in archaeology.

BIBLIOGRAPHY

This bibliography is not intended as a comprehensive reference guide to method and theory in archaeology. Rather, it is a compilation of some sources used to compile this book and a cross section of important methodological and theoretical research. Readers interested in probing more deeply into the literature should consult the Guide to Further Reading at the end of each chapter. In order to keep the bibliography within manageable limits, we have tended to cite general works, on the assumption that readers will use the references in them to delve more deeply into the literature.

ADAMS, R. E. W., and others. 1981. "Radar Mapping, Archaeology, and Ancient Maya Land Use." *Science* 213 (4515): 1457–1462.

ADAMS, W. Y., and E. W. ADAMS. 1991. *Archaeological Typology and Practical Reality*. Cambridge: Cambridge University Press.

ADKINS, L., and R. ADKINS. 1989. *Archaeological Illustration*. Cambridge: Cambridge University Press.

ADOVASIO, J. M. 1979. *Basketry Technology: A Guide to Identification and Analysis*. Hawthorne, NY: Aldine.

ADOVASIO, J. M., and R. C. CARLISLE. 1988. "Some Thoughts on Cultural Resource Management Archaeology in the United States." *Antiquity* 62: 72–87.

AGORSAH, E. K. 1983. "Social Behavior and Spatial Context." *African Studies Monographs* 4: 119–128.

———. 1985. "Archaeological Implications of Traditional House Construction among the Nchumuru of Northern Ghana." *Current Anthropology* 26(1): 103–115.

———. 2003. *Ethnoarchaeological Analysis of Human Functional Dynamics in the Volga Basin in Ghana: Before and After the Akosombo Dam*. New York: Mellen Studies in Archaeology.

AHLSTROM, R. V. N., and others. 1991. "Evaluating Tree-Ring Interpretations at Walpi Pueblo, Arizona." *American Antiquity* 56 (4): 628–644.

AIKENS, C. M. 1970. *Hogup Cave*. University of Utah Anthropological Papers No. 93.

AITKEN, M. J. 1984. *Thermoluminescence Dating*. London: Academic Press.

———. 1990. *Science-Based Dating in Archaeology*. New York: Longmans.

AKAZAWA, T., and C. M. AIKENS. 1986. *Prehistoric Hunter-Gatherers in Japan*. Tokyo: University Museum Bulletin 27.

ALLEY, R. 2000. *The Two Mile Time Machine*. Princeton, NJ: Princeton University Press.

ALVA, W., and C. DONNAN. 1993. *Royal Tombs of Sipán*. Los Angeles: Fowler Museum of Cultural History, University of California.

ANAWALT, P. 1981. *Indian Clothing before Cortés*. Norman: University of Oklahoma Press.

ANDERSON, A. O., and C. DIBBLE. 1955. *The Florentine Codex*. Salt Lake City: University of Utah Press.

ANDERSON, D. G., and K. E. SASSAMAN, eds. 1996. *The Paleoindian and Early Archaic Southeast*. Tuscaloosa: University of Alabama Press.

ANTON, F. 1988. *Ancient Peruvian Textiles*. London: Thames and Hudson.

ANYON, R., and T. J. FERGUSON. 1995. "Cultural Resources Management at the Pueblo of Zuni, New Mexico, U.S.A." *Antiquity* 69: 913–930.

ARINZE, E. N. 1990. "Establishing National Registers of Historic Cultural Property in Africa: The Nigerian Case." *Cultural Resource Management* 172–178.

ARMSTRONG, D. V., L. WURST, and E. J. KELLAR. 2000. *Archaeological Sites and Preservation Planning in Central New York: A Unified Site File and GIS Database for NYSDOT Region 3*. Albany: New York State Preservation Office.

ARNOLD, B. 1992. "The Past as Propaganda." *Archaeology* 45 (4): 30–37.

ARNOLD, D. E. 1985. *Ceramic Theory and Cultural Process.* Cambridge: Cambridge University Press.

ARNOLD, J., ed. 2001. *Origins of a Pacific Coast Chiefdom.* Salt Lake City: University of Utah Press.

ARNOLD, P. J. 1991. *Domestic Ceramic Production and Spatial Organization.* Cambridge: Cambridge University Press.

ARRIAZA, B. 1995. "Chile's Chinchorro Mummies." *National Geographic* 103 (3): 68–88.

ASHBEE, P., and P. JEWELL. 1998. "The Experimental Earthworks Revisited." *Antiquity* 72: 485–504.

AVENI, A. 1993. *Ancient Astronomy.* Washington, DC: Smithsonian Books.

AVERY, G., and L. G. UNDERHILL. 1986. "Seasonal Exploitation of Seabirds by Late Holocene Coastal Foragers." *Journal of Archaeological Science* 13: 339–360.

BAHN, P. 1992. *Easter Island, Earth Island.* New York: Thames and Hudson.

———, ed. 1996. *The Cambridge Illustrated History of Archaeology.* Cambridge: Cambridge University Press.

BAHN, P., and J. VERTUT. 1988. *Images of the Ice Age.* New York: Viking Penguin.

BAILEY, G. N., ed. 1981. *Hunter-Gatherer Economy in Prehistory.* Cambridge: Cambridge University Press.

BAILLIE, M. G. L. 1982. *Tree-Ring Dating and Archaeology.* Chicago: University of Chicago Press.

BARFIELD, L. 1994. "The Iceman Reviewed." *Antiquity* 68 (258): 10–26.

BARKER, P. 1995. *Techniques of Archaeological Excavation.* New York: Humanities Press.

BARNES, G. 1999. *China, Korea, and Japan.* New York: Thames and Hudson.

BASS, G. F. 1966. *Archaeology Underwater.* London: Thames and Hudson.

———. 1970. *A History of Seafaring from Underwater Archaeology.* London: Thames and Hudson.

———, ed. 1988. *Ships and Shipwrecks of the Americas.* London: Thames and Hudson.

BASS, G. F., and others. 1989. "The Bronze Age Shipwreck at Ulu Burun: 1986 Campaign." *International Journal of Nautical Archaeology* 93: 1–29.

BAUGH, T. G., and J. E. ERICSON, eds. 1994. *Prehistoric Exchange Systems in North America.* New York: Plenum Press.

BEATTIE, O., and J. GEIGER. 1986. *Frozen in Time: The Fate of the Franklin Expedition.* London: Bloomsbury.

BEAUDRY, M., and others. 1991. "Artifacts and Active Voices: Material Culture as Social Discourse." In R. McGuire and R. Paynter, eds., *The Archaeology of Inequality.* Oxford: Blackwell.

BERNAL, M. 1987. *The Afroasiatic Roots of Classical Civilization.* New Brunswick, NJ: Rutgers University Press.

BERRIN, K., and E. PASZTORY. 1993. *Teotihuacán: Art from the City of the Gods.* New York: Thames and Hudson.

BETTIS III, E. A., and others. 1996. *Landform Sediment Assemblage (LSA) Units in the Upper Mississippi River Valley.* Technical Report 95-1004-11b. Springfield: Quaternary Studies Program, Illinois State Museum.

BIERS, W. R., and P. E. McGOVERN, eds. 1990. *Organic Contents of Ancient Vessels: Materials Analysis and Archaeological Investigation.* Philadelphia: MASCA, University Museum.

BINFORD, L. R. 1962. "Archaeology as Anthropology." *American Antiquity* 28: 217–225.

———. 1964. "A Consideration of Archaeological Research Design." *American Antiquity* 29: 425–441.

———. 1968. "Archaeological Perspectives." In S. R. Binford and L. R. Binford, eds., *New Perspectives in Archaeology,* pp. 5–32. Hawthorne, NY: Aldine.

———. 1972. *An Archaeological Perspective.* New York: Seminar Press.

———, ed. 1977. *For Theory Building in Archaeology.* Orlando, FL: Academic Press.

———. 1978. *Nunamiut Ethnoarchaeology.* Orlando, FL: Academic Press.

———. 1980. "Willow Smoke and Dog's Tails: Hunter-Gatherer Settlement Systems and Archaeological Site Formation." *American Antiquity* 45: 4–20.

———. 1981a. "Behavioral Archaeology and the Pompeii Premise." *Journal of Anthropological Research* 37: 195–208.

———. 1981b. *Bones: Ancient Men and Modern Myths.* Orlando, FL: Academic Press.

———. 1983. *Working at Archaeology.* Orlando, FL: Academic Press.

———. 1987. "Data, Relativism, and Archaeological Science." *Man* 22: 391–404.

———. 2001. *In Pursuit of the Past.* Rev. ed. Berkeley: University of California Press.

BINFORD, S. R., and L. R. BINFORD, eds. 1968. *New Perspectives in Archaeology.* Hawthorne, NY: Aldine.

BINTCLIFF, J. 1991. "Post-Modernism, Rhetoric, and Scholasticism at TAG: The Current State of British Archaeological Theory." *Antiquity* 65(247): 274–278.

———. 1993. "Why Indiana Jones Is Smarter Than the Postprocessualists." *Norwegian Archaeological Review* 26: 91–100.

———, ed. 2004. *A Companion to Archaeology.* Oxford: Blackwell.

BISSON, M. S. 1977. "Prehistoric Copper Mining in North West Zambia." *Archaeology* 29: 242–247.

BLITZER, H. 1990. "NAIKA: Storage-Jar Production and Trade in the Traditional Aegean." *Hesperia* 59: 675–711.

BORDAZ, J. 1970. *Tools of the Old and New Stone Age.* Garden City, NY: Natural History Press.

BORDES, F. 1968. *The Old Stone Age.* New York: McGraw-Hill.

BRADLEY, R., and M. EDMONDS. 1993. *Interpreting the Axe Trade.* Cambridge: Cambridge University Press.

BRAIDWOOD, R. J., and L. S. BRAIDWOOD, eds. 1983. *Prehistoric Archaeology along the Zagros Flanks.* Chicago: Oriental Institute.

BRAIN, C. K. 1981. *The Hunters or the Hunted: An Introduction to African Cave Taphonomy.* Chicago: University of Chicago Press.

BRAY, T. L., and T. W. KILLION, eds. 1994. *Reckoning with the Dead: The Larsen Bay Repatriation and the Smithsonian Institution.* Washington, DC: Smithsonian Institution Press.

BROSCHIER, J., and others. 1992. "Shepherds and Sediments: Geoethnoarchaeology of Pastoral Sites." *Journal of Anthropological Archaeology* 11(1): 47–102.

BROWN, J. A., ed. 1971. *Approaches to the Social Dimensions of Mortuary Practices.* Memoirs of the Society for American Archaeology, vol. 25.

———. 1981. "The Search for Rank in Prehistoric Burials." In R. Chapman, I. Kinnes, and K. Randsborg, eds., *The Archaeology of Death,* pp. 25–38. Cambridge: Cambridge University Press.

———. 1982. "On the Structure of Artifact Typologies." In R. A. Whallon and J. A. Brown, eds., *Essays on Archaeological Typology,* pp. 176–190. Evanston, IL: Center for American Archaeology.

BROWN, J. A., and S. STRUEVER. 1973. "The Organization of Archaeological Research: An Illinois Example." In C. L. Redman, ed., *Method and Theory in Current Archaeology,* pp. 261–280. New York: Wiley Interscience.

BROWN, K. L. 1995. "Material Culture and Community Structure: The Slave and the Tenant Community at Levi Jordan's Plantation, 1848–1892." In J. Larry Hudson, *Working Toward Freedom: Slave Society and Domestic Economy in the American South,* pp. 95–118. Rochester, NY: University of Rochester Press.

BRUMFIEL, E. O. 1991. "Weaving and Cooking: Women's Production in Aztec Mexico." In J. M. Gero and M. W. Conkey, eds., *Engendering Archaeology: Women and Prehistory,* pp. 224–253. Oxford: Blackwell.

BRUMFIEL, E. O., and T. K. EARLE, eds. 1987. *Specialization, Exchange, and Complex Societies.* Cambridge: Cambridge University Press.

BRUNER, E. M. 1996. "Tourism in Ghana: The Representation of Slavery and the Return of the Black Diaspora." *American Anthropologist* 98(2): 290–304.

BRYANT, V. M. 1974. "Prehistoric Diet in Southwest Texas: The Coprolite Evidence." *American Antiquity* 39: 407–420.

BUIKSTRA, J. 1984. "The Lower Illinois River Region: A Prehistoric Context for the Study of Ancient Diet and Health." In M. N. Cohen and G. J. Armelagos, eds., *Paleopathology at the Origins of Agriculture,* pp. 217–236. Orlando, FL: Academic Press.

BUTZER, K. W. 1974. *Environment and Archaeology.* 3d ed. Hawthorne, NY: Aldine.

———. 1982. *Archaeology as Human Ecology.* Cambridge: Cambridge University Press.

BYERS, D. S., ed. 1967. *The Prehistory of the Tehuacán Valley.* Austin: University of Texas Press.

CAHEN, D., and L. H. KEELEY. 1980. "Not Less Than Two, Not More Than Three." *World Archaeology* 12: 166–180.

CAMERON, E. M., and S. A. TOMKA, eds. 1993. *Abandonment of Settlements and Regions: Ethnoarchaeological and Archaeological Approaches.* Cambridge: Cambridge University Press.

CANN, J. R., and A. C. RENFREW. 1964. "The Characterization of Obsidian and Its Application to the Mediterranean Region." *Proceedings of the Prehistoric Society* 30: 111–133.

CANN, R. L., and others. 1995. "Mitochondrial DNA and Human Evolution: One Lucky Mother." In M. H. Nitecki and V. Nitecki, eds., *Origins of Anatomically Modern Humans,* pp. 135–148. New York: Plenum Press.

CARMEAN, K. 2003. *Spider Woman Walks This Land: Traditional Cultural Properties and the Navajo Nation.* Walnut Creek, CA: AltaMira Press.

CARR, C. 1982. *Handbook on Soil Resistivity.* Evanston, IL: Center for American Archaeology Press.

CARTER, H., and others. 1923–1933. *The Tomb of Tutankhamun.* London: Cassell.

CARTER, R. J. 1998. "Reassessment of Seasonality at the Early Mesolithic Site of Star Carr." *Journal of Archaeological Science* 25(9): 831–856.

CARVER, M. 1998. *Sutton Hoo: Burial Place of Kings?* Philadelphia: University of Pennsylvania Press.

CASTEEL, R. W. 1976. *Fish Remains in Archaeology and Paleoenvironmental Studies.* Orlando, FL: Academic Press.

CERAM, C. W. 1953. *Gods, Graves, and Scholars.* New York: Knopf.

CHANG, K. C., ed. 1968. *Settlement Archaeology.* Palo Alto, CA: National Press.

———. 1984. *The Archaeology of Ancient China.* 3d ed. New Haven, CT: Yale University Press.

CHAPMAN, J., and H. HAMEROW, eds. 1997. *Migrations and Invasions in Archaeological Explanation.* Oxford: British Archaeological Reports.

CHAPMAN, R., I. KINNES, and K. RANDSBORG, eds. 1981. *The Archaeology of Death.* Cambridge: Cambridge University Press.

CHASE-DUNN, C., and T. H. HALL, eds. 1991. *Core/Periphery Relations in Precapitalist Worlds.* San Francisco: Westview Press.

CHAUVET, J. M., and others. 1996. *Dawn of Art: The Chauvet Cave.* New York: Abrams.

Childe, V. G. 1925. *The Danube in Prehistory.* London: Routledge and Kegan Paul.

———. 1942. *What Happened in History.* Baltimore: Pelican.

———. 1956. *Piecing Together the Past.* London: Routledge and Kegan Paul.

———. 1958. "Retrospect." *Antiquity* 32: 69–74.

CHIPPENDALE, C. 1994. *Stonehenge Complete.* 2d ed. London: Thames and Hudson.

CHISHOLM, B. S., and others. 1983. "Marine and Terrestrial Protein in Prehistoric Diets on the British Columbia Coast." *Current Anthropology* 24: 396–398.

CHITTICK, H. N. 1974. *Kilwa.* Nairobi: British Institute in Eastern Africa.

CHUBB, M. 1954. *Nefertiti Lived Here.* New York: HarperCollins.

CLARK, A. 1997. *Seeing beneath the Soil.* London: Batsford.

CLARK, J. D. 1959. *The Prehistory of Southern Africa.* Baltimore: Pelican.

CLARK, J. G. D. 1952. *Prehistoric Europe: The Economic Basis.* Palo Alto, CA: Stanford University Press.

———. 1954. *Star Carr.* Cambridge: Cambridge University Press.

CLARKE, D. L. 1968. *Analytical Archaeology.* London: Methuen.

CLAYTON, P. 1994. *Chronicle of the Pharaohs.* London: Thames and Hudson.

CLEAL, R. M. J., and others. 1995. *Stonehenge in Its Landscape: Twentieth Century Excavations.* London: English Heritage.

CLEERE, H., ed. 1989. *Archaeological Heritage Management in the Modern World.* London: Unwin Hyman.

CLENDINNEN, I. 1991. *The Aztecs: An Interpretation.* Cambridge: Cambridge University Press.

CLUTTON-BROCK, J. 1981. *Domesticated Animals from Early Times.* Austin: University of Texas Press.

———. 1989. *The Walking Larder.* London: Unwin Hyman.

COE, M. D. 1993. *Breaking the Maya Code.* London and New York: Thames and Hudson.

———. 2002. *The Maya.* 7th ed. New York: Thames and Hudson.

COLES, B., and J. M. COLES. 1986. *Sweet Track to Glastonbury.* New York: Thames and Hudson.

———. 1989. *People of the Wetlands.* New York: Guild Publishing.

COLES, J. M. 1979. *Archaeology by Experiment.* London: Heinemann.

COLLEY, S. M. 1990. "The Analysis and Interpretation of Archaeological Fish Remains." *Archaeological Method and Theory* 2: 39–46.

COLLIS, J. 1997. *European Iron Age.* London: Routledge.

CONKEY, M. W., and J. GERO. 1997. "Programme to Practice: Gender and Feminism in Archaeology." *Annual Review of Anthropology* 26: 411–437.

CONKEY, M. W., and C. HASTORF, eds. 1990. *The Uses of Style in Archaeology.* Cambridge: Cambridge University Press.

CONKEY, M. W., and R. TRINGHAM. 1996. "Archaeology and the Goddess: Exploring the Contours of Feminist Archaeology." In A. Stewart and D. Stanton, eds., *Feminism in the Academy: Rethinking the Disciplines,* pp. 27–43. Ann Arbor: University of Michigan Press.

CONNAH, G. 2001. *African Civilizations.* 2d ed. Cambridge: Cambridge University Press.

CONYERS, L. B., and D. GOODMAN. 1997. *Ground-Penetrating Radar: An Introduction for Archaeologists.* Walnut Creek, CA: Altamira Press.

COOK, D. C. 1984. "Subsistence and Health in the Central Illinois Valley: Osteological Evidence." In M. N. Cohen and G. J. Armelagos, eds., *Paleopathology at the Origins of Agriculture,* pp. 237–270. Orlando, FL: Academic Press.

CORDELL, L. 1997. *Prehistory of the Southwest.* 2d ed. Orlando, FL: Academic Press.

COTTERELL, B., and J. KAMMINGA. 1989. *Mechanics of Pre-Industrial Technology.* Cambridge: Cambridge University Press.

COURTY, M. A., and others, eds. 1993. *Soils and Micromorphology in Archaeology.* Cambridge: Cambridge University Press.

COWGILL, G. L. 1982. "Clusters of Objects and Associations between Variables: Two Approaches to Archaeological Classification." In R. A. Whallon and J. A. Brown, eds., *Essays in Archaeological Typology,* pp. 30–55. Evanston, IL: Center for American Archaeology.

COWGILL, G. L., and others. 1984. "Spatial Analysis of Teotihuacán: A Mesoamerican Metropolis." In H. Hietala, ed., *Intrasite Spatial Analysis in Archaeology,* pp. 154–195. Cambridge: Cambridge University Press.

CRABTREE, D. E. 1972. *An Introduction to Flintworking.* Pocatello: Idaho State Museum.

CRABTREE, R. M. 1963. "Archaeological Investigations at Batiquitos Lagoon, San Diego County." *California Archaeological Survey Annual Report,* 319–462.

CRADDOCK, P. T. 1995. *Early Metal Mining and Production.* Washington, DC: Smithsonian Institution Press.

CRONYN, J. M. 1990. *The Elements of Archaeological Conservation*. London: Routledge.

CRUMLEY, C. 1987. "Periodic Markets in Contemporary Southern Burgundy." In C. L. Crumley and W. H. Marquardt, eds., *Regional Dynamics: Burgundian Landscapes in Historical Perspective,* pp. 335–360. San Diego, CA: Academic Press.

———. 1994. *Historical Ecology: Cultural Knowledge and Changing Landscapes*. Sante Fe, NM: SAR Press.

CRUMLEY, C., and W. H. MARQUARDT, eds. 1987. *Regional Dynamics: Burgundian Landscapes in Historical Perspective*. San Diego, CA: Academic Press.

CUNLIFFE, B., ed. 1997. *Prehistoric Europe: An Illustrated History*. Oxford: Oxford University Press.

DALRYMPLE, G. B., and M. A. LAMPHERE. 1970. *Potassium-Argon Dating*. New York: W. H. Freeman.

DANCEY, W. S. 1981. *Archaeological Field Methods: An Introduction*. Minneapolis, MN: Burgess.

DANIEL, G. 1962. *The Idea of Prehistory*. London: Watts.

———. 1981. *A Short History of Archaeology*. New York: Thames and Hudson.

DÄNIKEN, E., VON. 1970. *Chariots of the Gods?* New York: Bantam.

———. 1998. *Arrival of the Gods*. Geneva, Switzerland: Huasmas.

DARWIN, C. 1859. *On the Origin of Species*. London: John Murray.

DAVID, N., and C. KRAMER, eds. 2001. *Ethnoarchaeology in Action*. Cambridge: Cambridge University Press.

DAVID, N., and others. 1991. "Ethnicity and Material Culture in North Cameroon." *Canadian Journal of Archaeology* 15: 171–177.

———. 1999. *Keyword Bibliography of ethnoarchaeology and related topics.* **http://www.acs.calgary.ca/~ndavid**

DAVIS, M. 2001. *Late Victorian Holocausts*. New York: Verso.

DAVIS, S. J. M. 1987. *The Archaeology of Animals*. London: Batsford.

DEACON, H. 1979. "Excavations at Boomplaas Cave—A Sequence through the Upper Pleistocene and Holocene in South Africa." *World Archaeology* 10: 241–257.

DEACON, H. J., and J. DEACON. 1999. *Human Beginnings in South Africa*. Walnut Creek, CA: AltaMira Press.

DEAGAN, K. 1983. *Spanish Saint Augustine: The Archaeology of a Colonial Creole Community*. Orlando, FL: Academic Press.

———. 1995. *Fort Mose: Colonial America's Black Fortress of Freedom*. Gainesville: University of Florida Press.

DEAN, J. S. 1970. "Aspects of Tsegi Phase Soil Organization." In W. A. Longacre, ed., *Reconstructing Prehistoric Pueblo Societies*. Albuquerque: University of New Mexico Press.

———. 1988. "A Model of Anasazi Behavioral Adaptation." In G. Gumerman, ed., *The Anasazi in a Changing Environment,* pp. 25–44. Cambridge: Cambridge University Press.

DEAN, J. S., and G. S. FUNKHAUSER. 1994. "Dendroclimatic Reconstructions for the Southern Colorado Plateau." In W. J. Waugh, ed., *Climatic Change in the Four Corners and Adjacent Regions,* pp. 85–104. Grand Junction, CO: Mesa State College.

DE BARROS, P. L. 1988. "Societal Repercussions of the Rise of Large-Scale Traditional Iron Production: A West African Example." *African Archaeological Review* 6: 91–113.

———. 2001. "The Effect of the Slave Trade on Bassar Ironworking Society, Togo." In C. R. DeCorse, ed., *West Africa during the Atlantic Slave Trade,* pp. 59–80. New York: Leicester University Press.

DECORSE, C., ed. 2001a. *West Africa during the Atlantic Slave Trade: Archaeological Perspectives*. New York: Leicester University Press.

———. 2001b. *An Archaeology of Elmina: Africans and Europeans on the Gold Coast, 1400–1900*. Washington, DC: Smithsonian Institution Press.

DECORSE, C. R., and B. DISANTO. 1999. "Historical Archaeology in America: Results of the 1998 SHA Membership Survey." Unpublished report, Society for Historical Archaeology.

DEETZ, J. 1967. *Invitation to Archaeology.* Garden City, NY: Natural History Press.

———. 1977. *In Small Things Forgotten.* Garden City, NY: Anchor/Doubleday.

———. 1983. "Scientific Humanism and Humanist Science." *Geoscience and Man* 23: 27–34.

DEITH, M. R. 1983. "Molluscan Calendars." *Journal of Archaeological Science* 10: 423–440.

DELORIA, V., JR. 1995. *Red Earth, White Lies.* New York: Scribner's.

DE NIRO, M. J. 1987. "Stable Isotopy and Archaeology." *American Scientist* 75: 182–191.

DE ROCHE, C. D. 1983. "Population Estimates from Settlement Area and Number of Residences." *Journal of Field Archaeology* 10: 187–192.

DETHLEFSEN, E., and J. DEETZ. 1966. "Death's Heads, Cherubs, and Willow Trees: Experimental Archaeology in Colonial Cemeteries." *American Antiquity* 31: 502–510.

DIGBY, B. 1926. *The Mammoth and Mammoth-Hunting in North-East Siberia.* London: Macmillan.

DILLEHAY, T. D. 2000. *First Settlement of America.* New York: Basic Books.

DIMBLEBY, G. W. 1985. *The Palynology of Archaeological Sites.* London: Academic Press.

DONALD, M. 1991. *Origins of the Modern Human Mind.* Cambridge, MA: Harvard University Press.

DONGOKSE, K., M. ALDENDERFER, and K. DOEHNER, eds. 2000. *Working Together: Native Americans and Archaeologists.* Washington, DC: Society for American Archaeology.

DONNAN, C., and D. MCCLELLAND. 1979. *The Burial Theme in Moche Iconography.* Washington, DC: Dumbarton Oaks.

DORAN, J. E. 1987. "Formal Methods and Archaeology." *Journal of Field Archaeology* 18: 21–37.

DORRELL, P. 1994. *Photography in Archaeology and Conservation.* Cambridge: Cambridge University Press.

DRENNAN, R. 1996. *Statistics for Archaeologists.* New York: Plenum.

DUMOND, D. E. 1987. *The Eskimos and Aleuts.* 2d ed. London: Thames and Hudson.

DUNNELL, R. C. 1970. "The Seriation Method and Its Evaluation." *American Antiquity* 35: 305–319.

———. 1971. *Systematics in Prehistory.* New York: Free Press.

———. 1978. "Style and Function: A Fundamental Dichotomy." *American Antiquity* 43: 192–202.

———. 1980. "Evolutionary Theory and Archaeology." *Advances in Archaeological Method and Theory* 3: 38–99.

———. 1982. "Science, Social Science, and Common Sense: The Agonizing Dilemma of Modern Archaeology." *Journal of Anthropological Research* 38: 1–25.

———. 1986. "Methodological Issues in Americanist Artifact Classification." *Advances in Archaeological Method and Theory* 9: 149–208.

DUNNELL, R. C., and W. S. DANCEY. 1983. "The Siteless Survey: A Regional Scale Data Collection." *Advances in Archaeological Method and Theory* 6: 267–288.

EARLE, T. K. 1997. *How Chiefs Come to Power: The Political Economy in Prehistory.* Stanford, CA: Stanford University Press.

———, ed. 1991. *Chiefdoms: Power, Economy, and Ideology.* Cambridge: Cambridge University Press.

EARLE, T. K., and J. E. ERICSON, eds. 1977. *Exchange Systems in Prehistory.* Orlando, FL: Academic Press.

EARLE, T. K., and R. W. PREUCEL. 1987. "Processual Archaeology and the Radical Critique." *Current Anthropology* 28: 501–538.

EKECHUKWU, L. C. 1990. "Encouraging National Development through the Promotion of Tourism: The Place of Archaeology." *Cultural Resource Management* 20: 120–125.

ELIADE, M. 1954. *The Myth of the Eternal Return.* New York: Pantheon.

ELPHICK, R. 1977. *Kraal and Castle.* New Haven, CT: Yale University Press.

EMERSON, T. 1997. *Cahokia and the Ideology of Power.* Tuscaloosa: University of Alabama Press.

ERICKSON, C. L. 1992. "Applied Archaeology and Development: Archaeology's Potential Contribution to the Future." *Journal of the Steward Anthropological Society* 20(1, 2): 1–16.

ERICSON, J. E., and T. K. EARLE, eds. 1982. *Contexts of Prehistoric Exchange.* Orlando, FL: Academic Press.

ERICSON, J. E., and B. A. PURDY, eds. 1984. *Prehistoric Quarries and Lithic Production.* Cambridge: Cambridge University Press.

EVANS, J. 1943. *Time and Chance.* London: Longmans.

EZZO, J. A. 1993. "Dietary Change and Variability at Grasshopper Pueblo, Arizona." *Journal of Anthropological Archaeology* 11: 219–289.

FAGAN, B. M. 1985. *The Adventure of Archaeology.* Washington, DC: National Geographic Society.

———. 1991. *The Journey from Eden.* London: Thames and Hudson.

———. 1995. *Time Detectives.* New York: Simon & Schuster.

———. 1998. *From Black Land to Fifth Sun.* Reading, MA: Perseus.

———. 1999. *Floods, Famines, and Emperors: El Niño and the Fate of Civilizations.* New York: Basic Books.

———. 2001. *Grahame Clark: An Intellectual Biography of an Archaeologist.* Boulder, CO: Westview Press.

———. 2003. *People of the Earth.* 11th ed. Upper Saddle River, NJ: Prentice Hall.

———. 2004. *The Long Summer: How Climate Changed Civilization.* New York: Basic Books.

———. 2005. *Ancient North America.* 4th ed. London: Thames and Hudson.

———. 2005. *A Brief History of Archaeology: Classical Times to the Twenty-first Century.* Upper Saddle River, NJ: Prentice Hall.

FAGAN, B. M., D. PHILLIPSON, and S. G. H. DANIELS. 1969. *Iron Age Cultures in Zambia.* Vol. 2, *Dambwa, Ingombe Ilede, and the Tonga.* London: Chatto and Windus.

FAGAN, B. M., and C. SCARRE. 2003. *Ancient Civilizations.* 2d ed. Upper Saddle River, NJ: Prentice Hall.

FAGAN, B. M., and F. VAN NOTEN. 1971. *The Hunter-Gatherers of Gwisho.* Tervuren, Belgium: Musée Royal de l'Afrique Centrale.

FASH, W. L. 1991. *Scribes, Warriors and Kings.* New York: Thames and Hudson.

FEDER, K. L. 2001. *Frauds, Myths, and Mysteries.* 4th ed. New York: McGraw-Hill.

FEDICK, S., ed. 1996. *The Managed Mosaic.* Salt Lake City: University of Utah Press.

FERGUSON, L. 1992. *Uncommon Ground.* Washington, DC: Smithsonian Institution Press.

FERGUSON, T. J., and others. 1995. "Working Together: Hopi Oral History and Archaeology." *SAA Bulletin* 13(2, 3): 12–15, 10–13.

FINNEY, B. 1994. *A Voyage of Rediscovery: A Cultural Odyssey through Polynesia.* Berkeley: University of California Press.

FISH, S. K., and S. A. KOWALEWSKI, eds. 1990. *The Archaeology of Regions: A Case for Full-Coverage Survey.* Washington, DC: Smithsonian Institution Press.

FLANNERY, K. V. 1968. "Archaeological Systems Theory and Early Mesoamerica." In B. J. Meggers, ed., *Anthropological Archaeology in the Americas,* pp. 67–87. Washington, DC: Anthropological Society of Washington.

———. 1973. "The Origins of Agriculture." *Biennial Review of Anthropology* 12: 271–310.

———, ed. 1976. *The Early Mesoamerican Village.* Orlando, FL: Academic Press.

———. 1982. "The Golden Marshalltown: A Parable for the Archaeology of the 1980s." *American Anthropologist* 84: 265–278.

FLANNERY, K. V., and J. MARCUS, eds. 1983. *The Cloud People.* Orlando, FL: Academic Press.

———. 1993. "Cognitive Archaeology." *Cambridge Archaeological Journal* 3(2): 260–267.

———. 1996. *Zapotec Civilization.* London and New York: Thames and Hudson.

FLEISCHER, R. L. 1975. "Advances in Fission Track Dating." *World Archaeology* 7: 136–150.

FLENNIKEN, J. J. 1984. "The Past, Present, and Future of Flintknapping: An Anthropological Perspective." *Annual Review of Anthropology* 13: 187–203.

FOWLER, D. D. 1982. "Cultural Resources Management." *Advances in Archaeological Method and Theory* 5: 1–50.

———. 1986. "Conserving American Archaeological Resources." In D. Meltzer, D. D. Fowler, and J. A. Sabloff, eds., *American Archaeology Past and Future,* pp. 135–162. Washington, DC: Smithsonian Institution Press.

———. 1987. "Uses of the Past: Archaeology in the Service of the State." *American Antiquity* 52: 229–248.

FOX, C. 1932. *The Personality of Britain.* Cambridge: Cambridge University Press.

FRETER, A. C. 1993. "Obsidian-Hydration Dating: Its Past, Present, and Future Application in Mesoamerica." *Ancient Mesoamerica* 4: 285–303.

———. 1994. "The Classic Maya Collapse at Copán, Honduras: An Analysis of Maya Rural Settlement." In G. M. Schwartz and S. E. Falconer, eds., *Archaeological Views from the Countryside,* pp. 160–176. Washington, DC: Smithsonian Institution Press.

FRIEDEL, D. A., and J. A. SABLOFF. 1984. *Cozumel: Late Maya Settlement Patterns.* Orlando, FL: Academic Press.

FRISON, G. 1978. *Prehistoric Hunters of the High Plains.* Orlando, FL: Academic Press.

GAFFNEY, V., and Z. STANCIC. 1991. *GIS Approaches to Regional Analysis: A Case Study of the Island of Hvar.* Ljubljana, Yugoslavia: Znanstveni institut Filozofske fakultete.

GALINAT, W. 1985. "Domestication and Diffusion of Maize." In R. I. Ford, ed., *Prehistoric Food Production in North America,* pp. 245–278. Ann Arbor: University of Michigan Museum of Anthropology.

GAMBLE, C. 1999. *The Palaeolithic Settlement of Europe.* Cambridge: Cambridge University Press.

GAMBLE, C., and W. A. BOISMIER, eds. 1991. *Ethnoarchaeological Approaches to Mobile Campsites: Hunter-Gatherer and Pastoralist Case Studies.* Ann Arbor, MI: International Monographs in Prehistory.

GANN, D. 1994. "Pompeii Forum Project Under Way." *CSA Newsletter* 7(3): 6–10.

GARLAKE, P. 1973. *Great Zimbabwe.* London: Thames and Hudson.

GERO, J. M. 1996. "Archaeological Practice and Engendered Encounters with Field Data." In R. Wright, ed., *Gender and Archaeology,* pp. 251–280. Philadelphia: University of Pennsylvania Press.

GERO, J. M., and M. W. CONKEY, eds. 1991. *Engendering Archaeology: Women and Prehistory.* Oxford: Blackwell.

GEYH, M. A., and H. SCHLEICHER. 1990. *Absolute Age Determinations: Physical and Chemical Dating Methods and Their Application.* Translated by R. Clark Newcomb. New York: Springer-Verlag.

GIBBON, G. 1984. *Anthropological Archaeology.* New York: Columbia University Press.

GIBSON, K. R., and T. INGOLD, eds. 1993. *Tools, Language, and Cognition in Human Evolution.* Cambridge: Cambridge University Press.

GILBERT, R. I., and others, eds. 1985. *Analysis of Prehistoric Diet.* Orlando, FL: Academic Press.

GLANTZ, M. 2001. *Currents of Change.* 2d ed. New York: Cambridge University Press.

GLOB, P. V. 1969. *The Bog People.* London: Faber and Faber.

GOSTNER, P., and E. VIGL. 2002. "Insight: Report of Radiological-Forensic Findings on the Ice Man." *Journal of Archaeological Science* 29: 323–326.

GOUDIE, A. 1992. *Environmental Change.* 2d ed. Oxford: Oxford University Press.

GOULD, R. A. 1980. *Living Archaeology.* Cambridge: Cambridge University Press.

———. 2000. *Archaeology and the Social History of Ships.* Cambridge: Cambridge University Press.

GOWLETT, J. A. J. 1987. "The Archaeology of Radiocarbon Accelerator Dating." *Journal of World Prehistory* 1: 127–170.

GRÄSLUND, B. 1981. "The Background to C. J. Thomsen's Three Age System." In G. Daniel, ed., *Towards a History of Archaeology,* pp. 45–50. London: Thames and Hudson.

GRAYSON, D. K. 1981. "A Critical View of the Use of Archaeological Vertebrates in Paleoenvironmental Reconstruction." *Journal of Ethnobiology* 1: 28–38.

———. 1983. *The Establishment of Human Antiquity.* Orlando, FL: Academic Press.

———. 1984. *Quantitative Zooarchaeology.* Orlando, FL: Academic Press.

GREEN, W., and J. F. DOERSHUK. 1998. "Cultural Resource Management and American Archaeology." *Journal of Archaeological Research* 6(2): 121–167.

GROSSMAN, J. W. 1994. "High-Caliber Discovery." *Federal Archaeology* 7(2): 38–43.

GRYGIEL, R., and P. BOGUCKI. 1997. "Early Farms of North-Central Europe: 1989–1994 Excavations at Oslonki, Poland." *Journal of Field Archaeology* 24(2): 161–178.

GUIDON, N., and G. DELIBRIAS. 1986. "Carbon 14 Dates Point to Man in the Americas 32,000 Years Ago," *Nature* 321: 769–771.

GUMERMAN, G. J. 1984. *A View from Black Mesa: The Changing Face of Archaeology.* Tucson: University of Arizona Press.

HALL, E. S., et al., eds. 1990. *The Utqiavik Excavations.* Barrow, AK: North Slope Borough Council on Iñupiat History.

HAMMERSLEY, M. 1992. *What's Wrong with Ethnography: Methodological Explorations.* London: Routledge.

HANCOCK, G. 1995. *Fingerprints of the Gods.* New York: Crown.

HARDESTY, D. L., and B. J. LITTLE. 2000. *Assessing Site Significance.* Walnut Creek, CA: AltaMira Press.

HARP, E., JR. 1978. *Photography for Archaeologists.* Orlando, FL: Academic Press.

HARRINGTON, J. C. 1977. *New Light on Washington's Fort Necessity: A Report on the Explorations at Fort Necessity National Battlefield Site.* Richmond, VA: Eastern National Park and Monument Association.

HARRIS, E. C. 1989. *Principles of Archaeological Stratigraphy.* 2d ed. Orlando, FL: Academic Press.

HARRIS, E. C., and others. 1993. *Practices of Archaeological Stratigraphy.* London: Academic Press.

HARRIS, M. 1968. *The Rise of Anthropological Theory.* New York: W. W. Crowell.

———. 1979. *Cultural Materialism: The Struggle for a Science of Culture.* New York: Random House.

———. 1999. *Theories of Culture in Post-Modern Times.* Walnut Creek, CA: AltaMira Press.

HARRIS, R. L. 1995. *The World of the Bible.* London and New York: Thames and Hudson.

HASSAN, F. 1981. *Demographic Archaeology.* Orlando, FL: Academic Press.

HASTORF, C. 1992. *Agriculture and the Onset of Inequality before the Inka.* Cambridge: Cambridge University Press.

HAUG, G., and others. 2003. "Climate and the Collapse of Maya Civilization." *Science* 299: 1731–1735.

HAWKES, J. G. 1983. *The Diversity of Crop Plants.* Cambridge, MA: Harvard University Press.

HAWKINS, G. 1965. *Stonehenge Decoded.* Boston: Boston University Press.

HAYDEN, B., ed. 1979. *Lithic Wear Analysis.* Orlando, FL: Academic Press.

———, ed. 1987. *Lithic Studies among the Contemporary Highland Maya.* Tucson: University of Arizona Press.

———. 1996. *The Pithouses of Keatley Creek.* New York: Harcourt.

HAYS-GILPIN, K., and D. S. WHITLEY, eds. 1998. *Reader in Gender Archaeology.* New York: Routledge.

HEGMON, M. 2003. "Setting Theoretical Egos Aside: Issues and Theory in North American Archaeology." *American Antiquity* 68(2): 213–244.

HEMPEL, C. G. 1966. *Philosophy of Natural Science.* Englewood Cliffs, NJ: Prentice Hall.

HESTER, T. R., H. J. SHAFER, and K. L. FEDER. 1997. *Field Methods in Archaeology.* 7th ed. New York: McGraw-Hill.

HEYERDAHL, T. 1950. *The Kon-Tiki Expedition.* New York: Random House.

HIETALA, H., ed. 1984. *Intersite Spatial Analysis in Archaeology.* Cambridge: Cambridge University Press.

HIGHAM, C. 1996. "The Princess of Khok Phanom Di, Thailand." In B. M. Fagan, ed., *Eyewitness to Discovery,* pp. 280–287. New York: Oxford University Press.

HILL, J. N. 1968. "Broken K Pueblo: Patterns of Form and Function." In L. and S. Binford, eds., *New Perspectives in Archaeology,* pp. 103–142. Chicago: Aldine.

HILLMAN, G. C. 1989. "Late Palaeolithic Plant Foods from Wadi Kubbaniya in Upper Egypt: Dietary Diversity, Infant Weaning, and Seasonality in the Riverine Environment." In D. R. Harris and G. C. Hillman, eds., *Foraging and Farming,* pp. 207–239. London: Unwin Hyman.

HILLMAN, G. C., S. M. COLLEDGE, and D. R. HARRIS. 1989. "Plant-Food Economy during the Epipalaeolithic Period at Tell Abu Hureyra, Syria: Dietary Diversity, Seasonality, and Modes of Exploitation." In D. R. Harris and G. C. Hillman, eds., *Foraging and Farming,* pp. 240–268. London: Unwin Hyman.

HILLMAN, G. C., and M. S. DAVIS. 1990. "Measured Domestication Rates in Wild Wheats and Barley under Primitive Cultivation and Their Archaeological Implications." *Journal of World Prehistory* 4(2): 157–222.

HINDE, R. 1987. *Individuals, Relationships, and Culture.* Cambridge: Cambridge University Press.

HODDER, I., ed. 1982a. *Symbolic and Structural Archaeology.* Cambridge: Cambridge University Press.

———, ed. 1982b. *Symbols in Action.* Cambridge: Cambridge University Press.

———. 1984. *The Present Past.* New York: Pica.

———. 1986. *Reading the Past.* Cambridge: Cambridge University Press.

———. 1995. *Theory and Practice in Archaeology.* Cambridge: Cambridge University Press.

———. 1999. *The Archaeological Process: An Introduction.* Oxford: Blackwell.

HODDER, I., and C. EVANS. 1999. *Excavations at Haddenham.* Cambridge: English Heritage and Macdonald Institute.

HOLL, A. 2001. "500 Years in the Cameroons: Making Sense of the Archaeological Record." In C. R. DeCorse, ed., *West Africa during the Atlantic Slave Trade,* pp. 152–178. New York: Leicester University Press.

HORNE, P. D. 1985. "A Review of the Evidence of Human Endoplasm in the Pre-Columbian New World through the Study of Coprolites." *Journal of Field Archaeology* 12: 299–310.

HOSLER, D. 1995. *The Sounds and Colors of Power.* Cambridge, MA: MIT Press.

HOWARD, H. 1929. "The Avifauna of Emeryville Shellmound." *University of California Publications in Zoology* 23: 378–383.

HUDSON, J., ed. 1993. *From Bones to Behavior: Ethnoarchaeological and Experimental Contributions to the Interpretation of Faunal Remains.* Carbondale: Center for Archaeological Investigations, Southern Illinois University.

HUTT, S., and others. 1993. *Archaeological Resource Protection.* Washington, DC: National Trust for Historic Preservation.

HUTTON, J. 1784. *Theory of the Earth.* London: John Williams.

HUTTON, R. 1997. "The Neolithic Great Goddess." *Antiquity* 271: 91–99.

HUXLEY, T. 1863. *Man's Place in Nature.* London: Macmillan.

INGERSOLL, D., J. E. YELLEN, and W. MACDONALD, eds. 1977. *Experimental Archaeology.* New York: Columbia University Press.

ISAAC, G. L., and B. ISAAC. 1989. *The Archaeology of Human Origins.* Cambridge: Cambridge University Press.

ISAR, Y. R. 1986. *The Challenge to Our Cultural Heritage: Why Preserve the Past.* Washington, DC: Smithsonian Institution/UNESCO.

JETT, S., and P. B. MOYLE. 1986. "The Exotic Origins of Fishes Depicted in Prehistoric Mimbres

Pottery from New Mexico." *American Antiquity* 51: 688–720.

JEWELL, P. A., and G. W. DIMBLEBY. 1966. "The Experimental Earthwork at Overton Down, Wiltshire, England." *Proceedings of the Prehistoric Society* 32: 313–342.

JOHNSON, L. 1968. *Item Seriation as an Aid for Elementary Scale and Cluster Analysis.* Eugene: University of Oregon.

JOHNSON, M. 1993. "Notes toward an Archaeology of Capitalism." In C. Tilley, ed., *Interpreting Archaeology,* pp. 110–116. Oxford: Berg.

JONES, S. 1997. *The Archaeology of Ethnicity.* New York: Routledge.

JOSEPH, J. W. 2002. *An African-American Presence: Archaeological Investigations at the 1818 Hickman Log Cabin and the Cook's House at Pond Spring Plantation.* Stone Mountain, GA: New South Associates Technical Report No. 997.

JOUKOWSKY, M. 1981. *Complete Manual of Field Archaeology.* Englewood Cliffs, NJ: Prentice Hall.

JOYCE, R. 1993. "Women's Work: Images of Production and Reproduction in Pre-Hispanic Southern Central America." *Current Anthropology* 34(3): 255–274.

KACZOR, M. J., and J. WEYMOUTH. 1981. "Magnetic Prospecting: Results of the 1980 Field Season at the Toltec Site, 3LN42." *Proceedings of the Southeast Archaeological Conference* 24: 118–123.

KANKPEYENG, B. W., and C. R. DeCORSE. In press. "Ghana's Vanishing Past: Development Antiquities and the Destruction of the Archaeological Record." *African Archaeological Review.*

KAY, M. 1996. "Microwear Analysis of Some Clovis and Experimental Stone Tools." In G. H. Odell, ed., *Stone Tools: Theoretical Insights into Human Prehistory,* pp. 315–344. New York: Plenum.

———. 2000. "Use-Wear Analysis." In N. H. Lopinot, J. H. Ray, and M. D. Connor, eds., *The 1999 Excavations at the Big Eddy Site (23CE4260),* pp. 177–220. Springfield: Center for Archaeological Research. Southwest Missouri State University.

KEELEY, L. H. 1980. *Experimental Determination of Stone Tool Uses.* Chicago: University of Chicago Press.

KEENE, D. 1985. *Survey of Medieval Winchester.* Oxford: Clarendon Press.

KELLEY, J. H., and M. P. HANAN. 1988. *Archaeology and the Methodology of Science.* Albuquerque: University of New Mexico Press.

KELSO, W. M. 1984. *Kingsmill Plantation.* Orlando, FL: Academic Press.

KEMP, B. 1989. *Ancient Egypt: Anatomy of a Civilization.* London: Routledge and Kegan Paul.

KENT, S. 1984. *Analyzing Activity Areas: An Ethnoarchaeological Study of the Use of Space.* Albuquerque: University of New Mexico Press.

KIDDER, A. V. 1924. *An Introduction to the Study of Southwestern Archaeology.* New Haven, CT: Yale University Press.

KILLINGLEY, J. S. 1981. "Seasonality of Mollusk Collecting Determined from O-18 Profiles of Midden Shells." *American Antiquity* 46: 152–158.

KING, C., T. BLACKBURN, and E. CHANDONET. 1968. "The Archaeological Inventory of Three Sites on the Century Ranch, Western Los Angeles County, California." *California Archaeological Survey Annual Report* 10: 12–161.

KING, M. E. 1978. "Analytical Methods and Prehistoric Textiles." *American Antiquity* 43: 89–96.

KING, T. F. 1983. "Professional Responsibility in Public Archaeology." *Annual Review of Anthropology* 12: 143–164.

———. 1998. *Cultural Resource Laws and Practice: An Introductory Guide.* Walnut Creek, CA: AltaMira Press.

———. 2003. *Places That Count: Traditional Cultural Properties in Cultural Resource Management.* Walnut Creek, CA: AltaMira Press.

KIRCH, P. V., and M. SAHLINS. 1992. *Anahulu: The Anthropology of History in the Kingdom of Hawaii.* Chicago: University of Chicago Press.

KIRK, R. 1974. *Hunters of the Whale.* New York: William Morrow.

KLEIN, R. G. 1977. "Environment and Subsistence of Prehistoric Man in the Southern Cape Province, South Africa." *World Archaeology* 5: 249–284.

KLEIN, R. G., and K. CRUZ-URIBE. 1983. "The Computation of Ungulate Age (Mortality) Profiles from Dental Crown Heights." *Paleobiology* 9: 70–78.

———. 1984. *The Analysis of Animal Bones from Archaeological Sites.* Chicago: University of Chicago Press.

KLUCKHOHN, C. 1940. "The Conceptual Structure in Middle American Studies." In A. M. Tozzer, ed., *The Maya and Their Neighbors.* Norwalk, CT: Appleton and Lang.

KNIGHT, V. J., and V. P. STEPONAITIS, eds. 1998. *Archaeology of the Moundville Chiefdom.* Washington, DC: Smithsonian Institution Press.

KNUDSON, R. 1986. "Contemporary Cultural Resource Management." In D. J. Meltzer, D. D. Fowler, and J. A. Sabloff, eds., *American Archaeology Past and Future,* pp. 395–413. Washington, DC: Smithsonian Institution Press.

KOHL, P. L., and C. FAWCETT, eds. 1995. *Nationalism, Politics, and the Practice of Archaeology.* Cambridge: Cambridge University Press.

KRAMER, C. 1985. "Ceramic Ethnoarchaeology." *Annual Review of Anthropology* 14: 77–102.

———. 1997. *Pottery in Rajasthan.* Washington, DC: Smithsonian Institution Press.

KROEBER, A. L., and C. KLUCKHOHN. 1952. *Culture: A Critical Review of Concepts and Definitions.* Cambridge, MA: Harvard University, Peabody Museum of American Archaeology and Ethnology.

KROEBER, T. 1965. *Ishi in Two Worlds.* Berkeley: University of California Press.

KUNIHOLM, I. 2001. "Dendrochronology and Other Applications of Tree-Ring Studies in Archaeology." In D. R. Brothwell and A. M. Pollard, eds., *Handbook of Archaeological Sciences,* pp. 35–47. Chichester, England: John Wiley.

KURTÉN, B. 1968. *Pleistocene Mammals in Europe.* Hawthorne, NY: Aldine.

KVAMME, K. L. 1989. "Geographical Information Systems in Regional Archaeological Research and Data Management." *Archaeological Method and Theory* 1: 110–131.

LARSEN, C. S. 1987. "Bioarchaeological Interpretations of Subsistence Economy and Behavior from Human Skeletal Remains." *Advances in Archaeological Method and Theory* 10: 27–56.

———. 1997. *Bioarchaeology: Interpreting Behavior from the Human Skeleton.* Cambridge: Cambridge University Press.

LAVILLE, H., and others. 1980. *Rockshelters of the Perigord.* New York: Academic Press.

LAYARD, A. H. 1849. *Nineveh and Its Remains.* London: John Murray.

LAYTON, R. 1989. *Who Needs the Past?* London: Unwin Hyman.

———, ed. 1994. *Conflict in the Archaeology of Living Traditions.* London: Unwin Hyman.

———. 1998. *An Introduction to Anthropological Theory.* Cambridge: Cambridge University Press.

LEAKEY, L. S. B. 1951. *Olduvai Gorge, 1931–1951.* Cambridge: Cambridge University Press.

———. 1971. *Olduvai Gorge.* Vol. 1. Cambridge: Cambridge University Press.

LEAKEY, M. D. 1973. *Olduvai Gorge.* Vol. 3. Cambridge: Cambridge University Press.

LEAKEY, M. D., and J. HARRIS. 1990. *Laetoli: A Pliocene Site in Northern Tanzania.* Oxford: Oxford University Press.

LEE, R. B. 1979. *The !Kung San.* Cambridge: Cambridge University Press.

LEGGE, A. J., and P. A. ROWLEY-CONWY. 1987. "Gazelle Killing in Stone Age Syria." *Scientific American* 257: 76–83.

———. 1988. *Star Carr Revisited.* London: Birkbeck College.

LEKSON, S. 1999. *The Chaco Meridian.* Walnut Creek, CA: AltaMira Press.

LEONE, M. P. 1982. "Childe's Offspring." In I. Hodder, ed., *Structural Archaeology,* pp. 179–184. Cambridge: Cambridge University Press.

———. 1984. "Interpreting Ideology in Historical Archaeology: The William Paca Garden in Annapolis, Maryland." In D. Miller and C. Tilley, eds., *Ideology, Power, and Prehistory*, pp. 25–35. Cambridge: Cambridge University Press.

LEONE, M. P., and G. FRY. 1999. "Conjuring in the Big Kitchen: An Interpretation of African American Belief Systems Based on the Uses of Archaeology and Folklore." *Journal of American Folklore* 112(445): 372–403.

LEONE, M. P., G. FRY, and T. RUPPEL. 2001. "Spirit Management among Americans of African Descent." In C. Orser, ed., *Race and the Archaeology of Identity*, pp. 143–147. Salt Lake City, UT: University of Utah Press.

LEONE, M. P., and S. D. HURRY. 1998. "Seeing: The Power of Town Planning in the Chesapeake." *Journal of the Society for Historical Archaeology* 32(4): 34–62.

LEONE, M. P., and others. 1987. "Toward a Critical Archaeology." *Current Anthropology* 28: 283–302.

LERNER, M. 1997. *The Complete Pyramids.* London: Thames and Hudson.

LEUTE, J. 1987. *Archaeometry.* Weinheim, West Germany: VCH.

LÉVI-STRAUSS, C. 1966. *The Savage Mind.* Chicago: University of Chicago Press.

LEWARCH, D. E., and M. J. O'BRIEN. 1981. "The Expanding Role of Surface Assemblages in Archaeological Research." *Advances in Archaeological Method and Theory* 4: 297–343.

LEWIN, R. 1998. *Principles of Human Evolution: A Core Textbook.* Cambridge, MA: Blackwell.

LEWIS-WILLIAMS, D. 2002. *The Mind in the Cave.* London and New York: Thames and Hudson.

LEWIS-WILLIAMS, J. D. 1981. *Believing and Seeing: Symbolic Meanings in Southern San Rock Paintings.* Orlando, FL: Academic Press.

———. 1995. "Modelling the Production and Consumption of Prehistoric Rock Art." *South African Archaeological Bulletin* 50(162): 143–154.

———. 2002. *The Mind in the Cave.* London and New York: Thames and Hudson.

LIBBY, W. F. 1955. *Radiocarbon Dating.* Chicago: University of Chicago Press.

LIGHTFOOT, K. G., and R. M. CERRATO. 1988. "Prehistoric Shellfish Exploitation in Coastal New York." *Journal of Field Archaeology* 15: 141–149.

LINARES, O. F. 1977. *Ecology and the Arts in Ancient Panama: On the Development of Social Rank and Symbolism in the Central Provinces.* Washington, DC: Dumbarton Oaks.

LIPE, W. D. 1970. "A Conservation Model for American Archaeology." *Kiva* 3: 213–243.

LITTLE, B. 1994. "'She Was . . . an Example to Her Sex': Possibilities for a Feminist Historical Archaeology." In P. Shackel and B. Little, eds., *Historical Archaeology of the Chesapeake*, pp. 123–131. Washington, DC: Smithsonian Institution Press.

LLOYD, S. 1963. *Mounds of the Near East.* Hawthorne, NY: Aldine.

LONGACRE, W. 1991. *Ceramic Ethnoarchaeology.* Tucson: University of Arizona Press.

LONGACRE, W. A., and J. M. SKIBO, eds. 1994. *Kalinga Ethnoarchaeology: Expanding Archaeological Method and Theory.* Washington, DC: Smithsonian Institution Press.

LOWE, J. J., and M. J. C. WALKER. 1997. *Reconstructing Quaternary Environments.* 2d ed. Upper Saddle River, NJ: Prentice Hall.

LYMAN, R. L. 1994. *Vertebrate Taphonomy.* Cambridge: Cambridge University Press.

LYMAN, R. L., M. O'BRIEN, and R. DUNNELL. 1996. *The Rise and Fall of Culture History.* New York: Plenum Press.

LYMAN, R. L., and others. 2003. *W. C. McKern and the Midwestern Taxonomic Method.* Tuscaloosa, AL: University of Alabama Press.

LYNOTT, M. J., and A. WYLIE. 2000. *Ethics in American Archaeology.* 2d ed. Washington, DC: Society for American Archaeology.

MACNEISH, R. S., ed. 1970. *The Prehistory of the Tehuacán Valley.* Vol. 3. Austin: University of Texas Press.

MACQUILTY, W. 1965. *Abu Simbel.* London: Macmillan.

MADSEN, D. P., and J. F. O'CONNELL, eds. 1982. *Man and Environment in the Great Basin.* Washington, DC: Society for American Archaeology.

MALLORY, J. P., and V. H. MAIR. 1999. *Mystery Mummies of Ancient China.* London: Thames and Hudson.

MARCUS, J. 1976. "The Size of the Early Mesoamerican Village." In K. V. Flannery, ed., *The Early Mesoamerican Village,* pp. 79–88. Orlando, FL: Academic Press.

MARCUS, M. 1994. "Dressed to Kill: Women and Pins in Early Iran." *Oxford Art Journal* 17(2): 3–15.

MAREAN, C. W., and others. 1992. "Captive Hyena Bone Choice and Destruction, the Schlepp Effect and Olduvai Archaeofaunas." *Journal of Archaeological Science* 19: 101–121.

MARQUARDT, W. H. 1978. "Advances in Archaeological Seriation." *Advances in Archaeological Method and Theory* 1: 28–64.

MARTIN, P. S., and F. T. PLOG. 1973. *The Archaeology of Arizona.* Garden City, NY: Doubleday.

MATSON, R. G. 1981. "Prehistoric Subsistence Patterns in the Fraser Delta: The Evidence from the Glenrose Cannery Site." *BC Studies* 48: 64–85.

McBRYDE, I., ed. 1985. *Who Owns the Past?* Melbourne, Australia: Oxford University Press.

McDONALD, J. D., and others. 1991. "The Northern Cheyenne Outbreak of 1879: Using Oral History and Archaeology as Tools of Resistance." In R. McGuire and R. Paynter, eds., *The Archaeology of Inequality,* pp. 64–78. Oxford: Blackwell.

McGIMSEY, C. 1972. *Public Archaeology.* New York: Seminar Press.

McGUIRE, R. H. 1992. *A Marxist Archaeology.* San Diego, CA: Academic Press.

McGUIRE, R. H., and R. PAYNTER, eds. 1991. *The Archaeology of Inequality.* Oxford: Blackwell.

McINTOSH, S. K. 1994. "Archaeological Heritage Management and Site Inventory Systems in Africa: The Role of Development." In I. Serageldin and J. Taboroff, eds., *Culture and Development in Africa, Environmentally Sustainable Development Proceedings Series No. 1,* pp. 387–409. Washington, DC: International Bank for Reconstruction and Development.

———, ed. 1999. *Beyond Chiefdoms: Pathways to Complexity in Africa.* New York: Cambridge University Press.

McKERN, W. C. 1939. "The Midwestern Taxonomic System as an Aid to Archaeological Culture Study." *American Antiquity* 4: 301–313.

McMANAMON, F. P. 1984. "Discovering Sites Unseen." *Advances in Archaeological Method and Theory* 7: 223–292.

———. 1992. "Presenting Archaeology to the Public in the USA." In P. Stone and B. Molyneaux, eds., *The Presented Past: Heritage, Museums, and Education,* pp. 61–81. London: Routledge.

McPHERSON, R. S. 1992. *Sacred Land, Sacred View: Navajo Perceptions of the Four Quarters Region.* Provo, UT: Brigham Young University.

MEEHAN, B. 1982. *Shell Bed to Shell Midden.* Canberra: Australian Institute of Aboriginal Studies.

MELLAART, J. 1967. *Çatal Höyük.* London: Thames and Hudson.

MELLARS, P., and P. DARK. 1999. *Star Carr in Context.* Cambridge: McDonald Institute Monographs and the Vale of Pickering Research Trust.

MELTZER, D. J. 1983. "The Antiquity of Man and the Development of American Archaeology." *Advances in Archaeological Method and Theory* 6: 1–51.

———. 2003. "Peopling of North America." In A. Gillespie, S. C. Porter, and B. Atwater, eds., *The Quaternary Period in the United States.* New York: Elsevier Science.

MELTZER, D. J., D. D. FOWLER, and J. A. SABLOFF, eds. 1986. *American Archaeology Past and Future.* Washington, DC: Smithsonian Institution Press.

MELTZER, D. J., and T. DILLEHAY, eds. 1991. *The First Americans: Search and Research.* Boca Raton, FL: CRC Press.

MELTZER, D. J., and others. 1994. "On a Pleistocene Human Occupation at Pedra Furada, Brazil." *Antiquity* 68(261): 695–714.

MESSENGER, P. M., ed. 1989. *The Ethics of Collecting Cultural Property: Whose Property?* Albuquerque: University of New Mexico Press.

MEYER, K. 1992. *The Plundered Past.* 2d ed. Baltimore: Pelican.

MIHESUAH, D. A., ed. 2000. *Repatriation Reader: Who Owns American Indian Remains?* Lincoln: University of Nebraska Press.

MILANICH, J. T., and S. MILBRATH, eds. 1989. *First Encounters.* Gainesville: University of Florida Press.

MILLER, D. 1997. *Material Cultures.* London: University College London Press.

MILLON, R. 1973. *The Teotihuacán Map: Urbanization of Teotihuacán, Mexico.* Vol. 1. Austin: University of Texas Press.

———. 1981. "Teotihuacán: City, State, and Civilization." In J. A. Sabloff, ed., *Supplement to the Handbook of Middle American Indians,* pp. 198–243. Austin: University of Texas Press.

MILNER, G. R. 1998. *The Cahokia Chiefdom.* Washington, DC: Smithsonian Institution Press.

MITHEN, S. 1989. "Evolutionary Theory and Postprocessual Archaeology." *Antiquity* 63: 483–494.

———. 1996. *Prehistory of the Mind.* London: Thames and Hudson.

MOLLESON, T. 1989. "Seed Preparation in the Neolithic: The Osteological Evidence." *Antiquity* 63(239): 356–362.

MOMMSEN, H., and others. 1992. "Provenance Determination of Mycenaean Sherds Found in Tell el Amarna by Neutron Activation Analysis." *Journal of Archaeological Science* 19: 295–302.

MONKS, G. C. 1981. "Seasonality Studies." *Advances in Archaeological Method and Theory* 4: 177–240.

MOORE, A. M. T. 1985. "Neolithic Societies in the Near East." *Advances in World Prehistory* 4: 1–69.

———. 2000. *Village on the Euphrates.* New York: Oxford University Press.

MORGAN, L. H. 1877. *Ancient Society.* Fort Worth, TX: Holt, Rinehart & Winston.

MORLOT, A. 1861. "General Views on Archaeology." *Annual Report of the Smithsonian Institution for 1860,* pp. 284–293. Washington, DC.

MOSELEY, M. 2000. *The Inca and Their Ancestors.* 2d ed. New York: Thames and Hudson.

MUELLER, J. A., ed. 1974. *Sampling in Archaeology.* Tucson: University of Arizona Press.

MUENSTERBERGER, W. 1994. *Collecting, an Unruly Passion: Psychological Perspectives.* Princeton, NJ: Princeton University Press.

MUHLY, J. D., and T. A. WERTIME, eds. 1980. *The Coming of the Age of Iron.* New Haven, CT: Yale University Press.

MUNSON, C. A., M. M. JONES, and R. E. FRY. 1995. "The GE Mound Case: An ARPA Case Study." *American Antiquity* 60(1): 313–359.

NASH, C. H. 1968. *Residence Mounds: An Intermediate Middle Mississippian Settlement Pattern.* Memphis, TN: Memphis State University Anthropological Research Center.

NELSON, S. M. 1997. *Gender in Archaeology.* Walnut Creek, CA: AltaMira Press.

NEUMANN, T. W., and R. M. SANFORD. 2001. *Cultural Resource Archaeology.* Walnut Creek, CA: AltaMira Press.

NOËL HUME, I. 1982. *Martin's Hundred.* New York: Knopf.

———. 1983. *Historical Archaeology: A Comprehensive Guide.* Rev. ed. New York: Knopf.

NORBACH, L. C., ed. 1997. *Early Iron Production: Archaeology, Technology, and Experimentation.* Lejre, Denmark: Historical-Archaeological Experimental Center.

O'CONNELL, J. F. O., and others. 1992. "Patterns in the Distribution, Site Structure and Assemblage Composition of Hadza Kill-Butchering Sites." *Journal of Archaeological Science* 19: 319–345.

O'CONNOR, T. 2000. *The Archaeology of Animal Bones.* College Station: Texas A&M University Press.

ODELL, G. H., ed. 1996. *Stone Tools: Theoretical Insights into Human Prehistory.* New York: Plenum Press.

ODELL, G. H., and F. COWAN. 1986. "Experiments with Spears and Arrows on Animal Targets." *Journal of Field Archaeology* 13: 195–212.

OETELAAR, G. A. 1993. "Identifying Site Structure in the Archaeological Record: An Illinois Mississippian Example." *American Antiquity* 58(4): 662–687.

OLIN, J. S., and A. D. FRANKLIN, eds. 1982. *Archaeological Ceramics.* Washington, DC: Smithsonian Institution Press.

OMOHUNDRO, J. 2001. *Careers in Anthropology.* New York: McGraw-Hill.

ORSER, C. E. 1996. *A Historical Archaeology of the Modern World.* New York: Plenum Press.

———. 2004. *Historical Archaeology.* 2d ed. Upper Saddle River, NJ: Prentice Hall.

ORTON, C. 2000. *Sampling in Archaeology.* Cambridge: Cambridge University Press.

ORTON, C., P. TYERS, and A. VINCE. 1993. *Pottery in Archaeology.* Cambridge: Cambridge University Press.

O'SHEA, J. M. 1984. *Mortuary Variability: An Archaeological Investigation.* Orlando, FL: Academic Press.

PADDOCK, J. 1983. "The Oaxaca Barrio at Teotihuacán." In K. Flannery and J. Marcus, eds., *The Cloud People,* pp. 170–175. Orlando, FL: Academic Press.

PALMER, M., and P. NEAVERSON. 1998. *Industrial Archaeology: Principles and Practice.* London and New York: Routledge.

PARMALEE, P., and W. E. KLIPPEL. 1974. "Freshwater Mollusca as a Prehistoric Food Resource." *American Antiquity* 39: 421–434.

PAUKETAT, T. R., and T. E. EMERSON, eds. 1997. *Cahokia: Domination and Ideology in the Mississippian World.* Lincoln: University of Nebraska Press.

PAUL, A., and S. A. TURPIN. 1986. "The Ecstatic Shaman Theme of Paracas Textiles." *Archaeology* 39(5): 20–27.

PEARSALL, D. 1989. *Paleoethnobotany: A Handbook of Procedures.* Orlando, FL: Academic Press.

PEARSALL, D., and D. R. PIPERNO. 1990. "Antiquity of Maize Cultivation in Ecuador: Summary and Reevaluation of the Evidence." *American Antiquity* 55: 324–337.

PEEBLES, C. S. 1987. "Moundville from 1000–1500 A.D." In R. D. Drennan and C. A. Uribe, eds., *Chiefdoms in the Americas,* pp. 21–41. Lanham, MD: University Press of the Americas.

PETERSEN, J. B., and others. 1984. "Netting Technology and the Antiquity of Fish Exploitation in Eastern North America." *Midcontinental Journal of Archaeology* 9: 199–226.

PETRIE, F. 1889. "Sequences in Prehistoric Remains." *Journal of the Royal Anthropological Institute* 29: 295–301.

PETTIT, J. R., and others. 1999. "Climate and Atmospheric History of the Past 420,000 Years from the Vostok Ice Core, Antarctica." *Nature* 399: 429–436.

PHILLIPS, P. 1988. "Traceology (Microwear) Studies in the USSR." *World Archaeology* 19: 111–125.

PIGGOTT, S. 1985. *Ancient Europe.* Hawthorne, NY: Aldine.

PIPERNO, D. R. 1988. *Phytolith Analysis: An Archaeological and Geological Perspective.* Orlando, FL: Academic Press.

PIPERNO, D. R., and I. HOLT. 1998. "The Presence of Starch Grains on Prehistoric Stone Tools from the Humid Neotropics." *Journal of Archaeological Science* 75: 765–776.

PLOG, S. 1983. "Analysis of Style in Artifacts." *Annual Review of Anthropology* 12: 125–142.

POLYANI, K. 1975. "Traders and Trade." In J. A. Sabloff and C. C. Lamberg-Karlovsky, eds., *Early Civilization and Trade,* pp. 133–154. Albuquerque: University of New Mexico Press.

POPE, S. T. 1923. *Hunting with the Bow and Arrow.* San Francisco: James H. Barry.

POSTGATE, N. 1993. *Early Mesopotamia: Economy and Society at the Dawn of History.* London: Routledge.

POTTER, P. B., JR. 1994. *Public Archaeology in Annapolis.* Washington, DC: Smithsonian Institution Press.

POWELL, S., and others. 1993. "Ethics and Ownership of the Past: The Reburial and Repatriation

Controversy." *Archaeological Method and Theory* 5: 14–55.

PRICE, D., and G. FEINMAN. 2004. *Images of the Past.* 4th ed. New York: McGraw-Hill.

PROTT, L., and P. J. O'KEEFE. 1984. *Law and the Cultural Heritage.* Abingdon, England: Professional Books.

PRYOR, F. 1991. *Flag Fen.* London: Batsford and English Heritage.

PURDY, B., ed. 1988. *Wet Site Archaeology.* Caldwell, NJ: Telford Press.

RADCLIFFE-BROWN, E. E. 1931. *The Nuer.* Oxford: Clarendon Press.

RAPOPORT, A. 1968. "Foreword." In W. Buckley, ed., *Modern Systems Research for the Behavioral Sciences.* Hawthorne, NY: Aldine.

RATHJE, W. H., and C. MURPHY. 1992. *The Archaeology of Garbage.* New York: HarperCollins.

RAVENSLOOT, J. C. 1993. "The Road to Common Ground." *Federal Archaeology* 7(3): 36–40.

REDDY, S. N. 1997. "If the Threshing Floor Could Talk: Integration of Agriculture and Pastoralism during the Late Harappan in Gujerat, India." *Journal of Anthropological Archaeology* 16: 162–189.

REDMAN, C. L. 1978. *The Rise of Civilization.* New York: W. H. Freeman.

REEVES, N. 1990. *The Complete Tutankhamun.* London: Thames and Hudson.

REINHARD, J. 1996. "Peru's Ice Maiden." *National Geographic,* pp. 64–80.

———. 1999. "More Inca Mummies from the Andes." *National Geographic,* pp. 94–101.

REINHARD, K. J., and V. M. BRYANT. 1992. "Coprolite Analysis: A Biological Perspective on Archaeology." *Archaeological Method and Theory* 4: 245–288.

REISNER, G. 1923. *Excavations at Kerma.* Cambridge, MA: Peabody Museum.

REITZ, E. J., and E. S. WING. 1999. *Zooarchaeology.* Cambridge: Cambridge University Press.

RENFREW, A. C. 1975. *The Emergence of Civilization.* London: Methuen.

———. 1985. *The Archaeology of Cult: The Sanctuary at Phylakopi.* London: British School of Archaeology at Athens and Thames and Hudson.

———. 1987. *The Archaeology of Language.* London: Cape.

———. 1993a. "Cognitive Archaeology: Some Thoughts on the Archaeology of Thought." *Cambridge Archaeological Journal* 3(2): 248–250.

———. 1993b. "What Is Cognitive Archaeology?" *Cambridge Archaeological Journal* 3(2): 247–270.

———. 1994. "Toward a Cognitive Archaeology." In C. Renfrew and E. Zubrow, eds., *The Ancient Mind,* pp. 1–23. Cambridge: Cambridge University Press.

RENFREW, A. C., and P. BAHN. 2004. *Archaeology: Theories, Methods, and Practice.* 4th ed. New York: Thames and Hudson.

RENFREW, A. C., J. E. DIXON, and J. R. CANN. 1966. "Obsidian and Early Cultural Contact in the Near East." *Proceedings of the Prehistoric Society* 32: 1–29.

REYNOLDS, B. 1967. *The Material Culture of the Gwembe Tonga.* Manchester, England: Manchester University Press.

REYNOLDS, P. J. 1979. *Iron Age Farm.* London: British Museum.

RICE, P. M. 1987. *Pottery Analysis: A Sourcebook.* Chicago: University of Chicago Press.

RILEY, C. L. 1971. *Man across the Sea.* Austin: University of Texas Press.

RILEY, D. N. 1987. *Air Photography and Archaeology.* London: Duckworth.

ROBERTS, N. 1999. *The Holocene: An Environmental History.* 2d ed. Oxford: Blackwell.

ROBINSON, A. 1995. *The Story of Writing.* London and New York: Thames and Hudson.

ROPER, D. C. 1979. "The Method and Theory of Site Catchment Analysis: A Review." *Advances in Archaeological Method and Theory* 2: 120–142.

ROSKAMS, S. 2001. *Excavation.* Cambridge: Cambridge University Press.

ROUSE, I. 1972. *Introduction to Prehistory: A Systematic Approach.* New York: McGraw-Hill.

RUZ, A. 1953. "An Astonishing Discovery." *Illustrated London News,* August 29, 1953.

RYAN, W., and W. PITMAN. 1998. *Noah's Flood: New Scientific Discoveries about the Event That Changed History.* New York: Simon & Schuster.

SABLOFF, J. A. 1975. *Excavations at Seibal: Ceramics.* Cambridge, MA: Harvard University, Peabody Museum of American Archaeology and Ethnology.

SABLOFF, J. A., and C. C. LAMBERG-KARLOVSKY, eds. 1975. *Early Civilization and Trade.* Albuquerque: University of New Mexico Press.

SABO, G., and others, eds. 1990. *Archaeological Investigations at 3MR80-Area D in the Rush Development Area, Buffalo National River, Arkansas.* Vol. 1. Santa Fe, NM: Southwest Cultural Resources Center, Professional Paper 38.

SACKETT, J. 1966. "Quantitative Analysis of Upper Paleolithic Stone Tools." *American Anthropologist* 68: 356–394.

———. 1977. "The Meaning of Style in Archaeology." *American Antiquity* 43: 369–382.

———. 1981. "From de Mortillet to Bordes: A Century of French Upper Palaeolithic Research." In G. Daniel, ed., *Towards a History of Archaeology,* pp. 85–99. London: Thames and Hudson.

SALMON, M. 1987. *The Philosophy of Archaeology.* Orlando, FL: Academic Press.

SALZMAN, P. C., and P. C. RICE. 2004. *Thinking Anthropologically: A Practical Guide for Students.* Upper Saddle River, NJ: Prentice Hall.

SANDERS, W. T., J. R. PARSONS, and R. S. SANTLEY. 1979. *The Basin of Mexico: Ecological Processes in the Evolution of a Civilization.* 2 vols. Orlando, FL: Academic Press.

SANDERS, W. T., and D. WEBSTER. 1978. "Unilinealism, Multilinealism, and the Evolution of Complex Societies." In C. L. Redman and others, eds., *Social Archaeology,* pp. 249–302. Orlando, FL: Academic Press.

SASSAMAN, K. E., and D. G. ANDERSON, eds. 1996. *Archaeology of the Mid-Holocene Southeast.* Gainesville: University of Florida Press.

SCARRE, C., ed. 1988. *Past Worlds: The Times Atlas of Archaeology.* London: Times Books.

SCHELE, L., and D. FRIEDEL. 1990. *A Forest of Kings.* New York: William Morrow.

———. 1993. *Maya Cosmos.* New York: William Morrow.

SCHELE, L., and M. E. MILLER. 1992. *The Blood of Kings: Dynasty and Ritual in Maya Art.* 2d ed. New York: Thames and Hudson.

SCHIFFER, M. B. 1987. *Site Formation Processes of the Archaeological Record.* Tucson: University of New Mexico Press.

SCHIFFER, M. B., and J. H. HOUSE. 1976. *The Cache River Archaeological Project.* Fayetteville: Arkansas Archaeological Survey.

SCHLIEMANN, H. 1875. *Troy and Its Remains.* London: John Murray.

SCHMIDT, P., ed. 1996a. *The Culture and Technology of African Iron Production.* Gainesville: University of Florida Press.

———. 1996b. "The Human Right to a Cultural Heritage." In P. R. Schmidt and R. J. McIntosh, eds., *Plundering Africa's Past,* pp. 18–28. Bloomingon: Indiana University Press.

SCHMIDT, P. R., and R. J. MCINTOSH, eds. 1996 *Plundering Africa's Past.* Bloomington: Indiana University Press.

SCHMIDT, P., and T. C. PATTERSON, eds. 1995. *Making Alternative Histories: The Practice of Archaeology and History in Non-Western Settings.* Santa Fe, NM: School of American Research.

SCOLLAR, I., and others. 1990. *Archaeological Prospecting and Remote Sensing.* Cambridge: Cambridge University Press.

SCOTT, E. M., ed. 1994. *Those of Little Note: Gender, Race, and Class in Historical Archaeology.* Tucson: University of Arizona Press.

SCUDDER, T. 1962. *The Ecology of the Gwembe Tonga.* Manchester, England: Manchester University Press.

SERAGELDIN, I., and J. TABOROFF, eds. 1994. *Culture and Development in Africa, Environmentally Sustainable Development Proceedings Series No. 1.* Washington, DC: International Bank for Reconstruction and Development.

SERVICE, E. 1971. *Primitive Social Organization.* New York: Random House.

SEVER, T., and J. WISEMAN. 1985. *Remote Sensing and Archaeology: Potential for the Future.* Picayune, MS: NASA Earth Sciences Laboratory.

SHACKLETON, N. J., and N. D. OPDYKE. 1973. "Oxygen Isotope and Paleomagnetic Stratigraphy of Equatorial Pacific Ocean Core V28–238." *Quaternary Research* 3: 38–55.

SHACKLEY, M. L. 1985. *Environmental Archaeology.* London: Batsford.

SHANKS, M., and R. MCGUIRE. 1996. "The Craft of Archaeology." *American Antiquity* 61: 75–88.

SHANKS, M., and C. TILLEY. 1987a. *Reconstructing Archaeology: Theory and Practice.* Cambridge: Cambridge University Press.

———. 1987b. *Social Theory and Archaeology.* Albuquerque: University of New Mexico Press.

SHARER, R. J., and W. ASHMORE. 2002. *Archaeology: Discovering the Past.* 3d ed. New York: McGraw-Hill.

SHEETS, P. D. 1992. *The Cerén Site.* New York: Harcourt Brace Jovanovich.

SHEETS, P. D., and G. R. MUTO. 1972. "Pressure Blades and Total Cutting Edge." *Science* 175: 632–634.

SHENNAN, S. 1988. *Quantifying Archaeology.* Orlando, FL: Academic Press.

SHEPARD, A. O. 1971. *Ceramics for the Archaeologist.* 2d ed. Washington, DC: Smithsonian Institution.

SHIPMAN, P. 1981. *Life History of a Fossil: An Introduction to Taphonomy and Paleoecology.* Cambridge, MA: Harvard University Press.

SHREEVE, J. 1992. "The Dating Game." *Discover* 13(6): 76–83.

SIMON, M. 1997. *The Archaeology of Human Bones.* New York: Routledge.

SIMS-WILLIAMS, P. 1998. "Genetics, Linguistics, and Prehistory." *Antiquity* 72: 505–527.

SKIBO, J. M., and others, eds. 1995. *Expanding Archaeology.* Salt Lake City: University of Utah Press.

SMITH, B. D. 1992. *Rivers of Change: Essays on Early Agriculture in Eastern North America.* Washington, DC: Smithsonian Institution Press.

———. 1999. *The Emergence of Agriculture.* New York: Scientific American Library.

SMITH, G. E. 1911. *The Ancient Egyptians.* London: Macmillan.

SMITH, G. S., and J. E. EHRENHARD, eds. 1991. *Protecting the Past.* Boca Raton, FL: CRC Press.

SMITH, M. 1996. *The Aztecs.* New York: Oxford University Press.

SNODGRASS, A. M. 1987. *An Archaeology of Greece: The Present State and Future Scope of a Discipline.* Berkeley: University of California Press.

SOFFER, O. 1985. *The Upper Paleolithic of the Central Russian Plain.* Orlando, FL: Academic Press.

SOLOMON, A. 1997. "The Myth of Ritual Origins? Ethnography, Mythology and Interpretation of San Rock Art." *South African Archaeological Bulletin* 52: 3–13.

SOREN, D., and J. JAMES. 1988. *Kourion: The Search for a Lost Roman City.* Garden City, NY: Anchor/Doubleday.

SOUTH, S. 1977. *Research Strategies in Historical Archaeology.* Orlando, FL: Academic Press.

SPAULDING, A. C. 1953. "Statistical Techniques for the Study of Artifact Types." *American Antiquity* 18: 305–313.

———. 1960. "Statistical Description and Comparison of Artifact Assemblages." In R. F. Heizer and S. F. Cook, eds., *Quantitative Methods in Archaeology,* pp. 60–92. New York: Viking Penguin.

———. 1973. "Archaeology in the Active Voice: The New Anthropology." In C. L. Redman, ed., *Research and Theory in Current Archaeology,* pp. 337–354. New York: Wiley Interscience.

SPENCER, H. 1855. *Social Statistics.* London: Macmillan.

SPETH, J. D. 1983. *Bison Kills and Bone Counts: Decision Making by Ancient Hunters.* Chicago: University of Chicago Press.

SPINDLER, K. 1994. *The Man in the Ice.* London: Weidenfeld and Nicholson.

STEFFY, R. 1994. *Wooden Shipbuilding and the Interpretation of Shipwrecks.* College Station: Texas A & M University Press.

STEIN, J. K. 1987. "Deposits for Archaeologists." *Advances in Archaeological Method and Theory* 11: 337–398.

———, ed. 1992. *Deciphering a Shell Midden.* Orlando, FL: Academic Press.

STEPHENS, J. L. 1841. *Incidents of Travel in Central America, Chiapas, and Yucatán.* New York: Harper & Row.

STEWARD, J. 1938. *Basin-Plateau Aboriginal Sociopolitical Groups.* Washington, DC: Smithsonian Institution.

———. 1955. *A Theory of Culture Change.* Urbana: University of Illinois Press.

STIMMELL, C., and others. 1982. "Indian Pottery from the Mississippi Valley: Coping with Bad Raw Materials." In J. S. Olin and A. D. Franklin, eds., *Archaeological Ceramics,* pp. 219–228. Washington, DC: Smithsonian Institution Press.

STIRLAND, A. 1987. *Human Bones in Archaeology.* Aylesbury, England: Shire Press.

STRONG, W. D. 1935. *An Introduction to Nebraska Archaeology.* Washington, DC: Smithsonian Institution.

STRUEVER, S. 1971. "Comments on Archaeological Data Requirements and Research Strategy." *American Antiquity* 36: 10.

STRUEVER, S., and F. A. HOLTON. 1979. *Koster.* Garden City, NY: Anchor/Doubleday.

STUIVER, M., and others. 1998. "Radiocarbon Calibration Issue." *Radiocarbon* 40(3).

SULLIVAN, A. P., and K. C. ROZEN. 1985. "Debitage Analysis and Archaeological Interpretation." *American Antiquity* 50: 755–779.

SULLIVAN, L. 1989. *Icanchu's Drum.* New York: Free Press.

SWANN, B., ed. 1994. *Coming to Light.* New York: W. W. Norton.

SWANSON, E., ed. 1975. *Lithic Technology: Making and Using Stone Tools.* Hawthorne, NY: Aldine.

SWISHER, C., and others. 1994. "Age of the Earliest Known Hominids in Java, Indonesia." *Science* 263: 1118–1121.

TALALAY, L. E. 1987. "Rethinking the Function of Clay Figurine Legs from Neolithic Greece: An Argument by Analogy." *American Journal of Archaeology* 91: 161–169.

TAYLOR, R. E., and M. J. AITKEN, eds. 1998. *Chronometric Dating in Archaeology.* New York: Plenum Press.

TAYLOR, R. E., A. LONG, and R. S. KRA, eds. 1992. *Radiocarbon Dating after Four Decades: An Interdisciplinary Perspective.* New York: Springer Verlag.

TAYLOR, W. W. 1948. *A Study of Archaeology.* Menasha, WI: American Anthropological Association.

THOM, A. 1971. *Megalithic Lunar Laboratories.* Oxford: Clarendon Press.

THOMAS, D. H. 1983a. *The Archaeology of Monitor Valley.* Vols. 1 and 2. New York: Anthropological Papers of the American Museum of Natural History.

———. 1983b. "On Steward's Models of Shoshonean Sociopolitical Organization: A Great Bias in the Basin." In E. Tooker, ed., *The Development of Political Organization in Native North America,* pp. 56–68. Washington, DC: American Ethnological Society.

———. 1986. "Contemporary Hunter-Gatherer Archaeology in America." In D. J. Meltzer, D. D. Fowler, and J. A. Sabloff, eds., *American Archaeology Past and Future,* pp. 237–276. Washington, DC: Smithsonian Institution Press.

———. 2000. *Skull Wars: Kennewick Man, Archaeology, and the Battle for Native American Identity.* New York: Basic Books.

———. 2003. *Archaeology: Down to Earth.* 3d ed. New York: Harcourt Brace.

THOMPSON, L. 1986. "A 1500-Year Tropical Ice Core Record of Climate: Potential Relations to Man in the Andes." *Science* 234: 361–364.

THOMPSON, L., and others. 1984. "El Niño-Southern Oscillation and Events Recorded in the Stratigraphy of the Tropical Quelccaya Ice Cap." *Science* 226: 50–53.

THOMPSON, R. H. 1956. "The Subjective Element in Archaeological Inference." *Southwestern Journal of Anthropology* 12: 327–332.

TOBIAS, P. V. 1971. *Olduvai Gorge.* Vol. 2. Cambridge: Cambridge University Press.

TOPHAM, J., and D. MCCORMICK. 2000. "Focus: A Dendrochronological Investigation of Stringed Instruments of the Cremonese School (1666–1757) Including the "Messiah" Violin Attributed to Antonio Stradivari." *Journal of Archaeological Science* 27: 183–192.

TORRENCE, R. 1986. *Production and Exchange of Stone Tools.* Cambridge: Cambridge University Press.

TOTH, N., and K. D. SCHICK. 1993. *Making Silent Stones Speak: Human Evolution and the Dawn of Technology.* New York: Simon & Schuster.

TOWNSEND, R. F. 1992. *The Aztecs.* New York: Thames and Hudson.

TOWNSEND, W. H. 1969. "Stone and Steel Tool Use in a New Guinea Society." *Ethnology* 8: 199–205.

TRAILL, D. A. 1995. *Schliemann of Troy: Treasure and Deceit.* New York: St. Martin's Press.

TRIGGER, B. G. 1968a. *Beyond History: The Methods of Prehistory.* Fort Worth, TX: Holt, Rinehart & Winston.

———. 1968b. "The Determination of Settlement Patterns." In K. C. Chang, ed., *Settlement Archaeology,* pp. 53–78. Palo Alto, CA: National Press.

———. 1980. *Gordon Childe: Revolutions in Archaeology.* London: Thames and Hudson.

———. 1984. "Alternative Archaeologies: Nationalist, Colonialist, Imperialist." *Man* 19: 355–370.

———. 1985. "The Past as Power: Anthropology and the American Indian." In I. McBryde, ed., *Who Owns the Past?* pp. 11–40. Melbourne, Australia: Oxford University Press.

———. 1986. "Prehistoric Archaeology and American Society." In D. J. Meltzer, D. D. Fowler, and J. A. Sabloff, eds., *American Archaeology Past and Future,* pp. 187–216. Washington, DC: Smithsonian Institution Press.

———. 1989. *A History of Archaeological Interpretation.* Cambridge: Cambridge University Press.

———. 1991. "Distinguished Lecture in Archaeology: Constraint and Freedom." *American Anthropologist* 93(3): 551–569.

———. 1995. "Expanding Middle-Range Theory." *Antiquity* 69(264): 449–458.

TRINGHAM, R. 1994. "Engendered Places in Prehistory." *Gender, Place, and Culture: A Journal of Feminist Geography* 1(2): 169–204.

TSCHAUNER, H. 1996. "Middle-Range Theory, Behavioural Archaeology, and Post-Empiricist Philosophy of Science in Archaeology." *Journal of Archaeological Method and Theory* 3: 1–30.

TURNER, B. L., and P. D. HARRISON. 1983. *Pulltrouser Swamp: Ancient Maya Habitat, Agriculture, and Settlement in Northern Belize.* Austin: University of Texas Press.

TUROSS, N., and others. 1994. "Subsistence in the Florida Archaic: The Stable-Isotope and Archaeobotanical Evidence from the Windover Site." *American Antiquity* 59(2): 288–303.

TYLECOTE, R. F. 1992. *A History of Metallurgy.* London: Institute of Materials.

TYLOR, E. B. 1871. *Primitive Culture.* London: John Murray.

———. 1878. "Anthropology." *Encyclopaedia Britannica* 1: 334–335.

UCKO, P. J. 1968. *Anthropomorphic Figurines.* London: Andrew Szmidla.

———, ed. 1995. *Theory in Archaeology: A World Perspective.* London and New York: Routledge.

VAN ANDEL, T. 1997. "Middle and Upper Palaeolithic Environments and Carbon 14 Beyond 10000 BP." *Antiquity* 72(278): 26–33.

VAN RIPER, A. B. 1993. *Men among the Mammoths: Victorian Science and the Discovery of Human Prehistory.* Chicago: University of Chicago Press.

VAUGHAN, P. 1985. *Use-Wear Analysis of Flaked Stone Tools.* Tucson: University of Arizona Press.

VILLA, P., and J. COURTIN. 1983. "The Interpretation of Stratified Sites: A View from Underground." *Journal of Archaeological Science* 10: 267–281.

VINNECOMBE, P. 1960. "A Fishing Scene from the Tsoelike River, Southwestern Basutoland." *South African Archaeological Bulletin* 15: 15–19.

————. 1976. *People of the Eland.* Pietermaritzburg, South Africa: Natal University Press.

VITELLI, K. D., ed. 1997. *Archaeological Ethics.* Walnut Creek, CA: AltaMira Press.

VIVIAN, G. 1990. *The Chacoan Prehistory of the San Juan Basin.* Orlando, FL: Academic Press.

————. 1997. "Chacoan Roads: Morphology" and "Chaco Roads: Function." *The Kiva* 63(1): 7–34, 35–67.

VOGT, E. Z. 1967. *A Maya Community in the Highlands of Chiapas.* Cambridge, MA: Belknap Press.

WALLERSTEIN, I. 1974. *The Modern World-System: Capitalist Agriculture and the Origins of the European World-Economy in the Sixteenth Century.* New York: Academic Press.

————. 1979. *The Capitalist World-Economy.* New York: Cambridge University Press.

————. 1980. *The Modern World-System: II. Mercantilism and the Consolidation of the European World-Economy, 1600–1750.* New York: Academic Press.

WASELKOV, G. 1987. "Shellfish Gathering and Shell Midden Archaeology." *Advances in Archaeological Method and Theory* 10: 112–167.

WATERS, M. R. 1993. *The Principles of Geoarchaeology: A North American Perspective.* Tucson: University of Arizona Press.

WATKINS, J. E. 2003. "Beyond the Margin: American Indians, First Nations, and Archaeology in North America. *American Antiquity* 68(2): 273–288.

WATSON, P. J., S. A. LE BLANC, and C. L. REDMAN. 1984. *Archaeological Explanation: The Scientific Method in Archaeology.* 2d ed. New York: Columbia University Press.

WATSON, P. J., and M. C. KENNEDY. 1991. "The Development of Horticulture in the Eastern Woodlands." In J. M. Gero and M. W. Conkey, eds., *Engendering Archaeology,* pp. 255–276. Oxford: Blackwell.

WAUCHOPE, R. 1972. *Lost Tribes and Sunken Continents.* Chicago: University of Chicago Press.

WEEKS, K. R. 1998. *The Lost Tomb.* New York: William Morrow.

WENDORF, F., and others. 1968. *The Prehistory of Nubia.* Dallas, TX: Southern Methodist University Press.

————. 1980. *Loaves and Fishes: The Prehistory of Wadi Kubbaniya.* Dallas, TX: Southern Methodist University Press.

WESLER, K. W. 2001. *Excavations at Wickliffe Mounds.* Tuscaloosa: University of Alabama Press.

WEYMOUTH, J. W. 1986. "Geophysical Methods of Archaeological Site Survey." *Advances in Archaeological Method and Theory* 10: 311–396.

WHALLON, R. A., and J. A. BROWN, eds. 1982. *Essays on Archaeological Typology.* Evanston, IL: Center for American Archaeology.

WHEAT, J. B. 1972. *The Olsen-Chubbock Site: A Paleo-Indian Bison Kill.* Washington, DC: Smithsonian Institution and the Society for American Archaeology.

WHEATLEY, D., and M. GILLINGS. 2002. *Spatial Technology and Archaeology: Archaeological Applications of GIS.* New York: Taylor and Francis.

WHEATLEY, P. 1975. "Satyantra in Suvarnadvipa: From Reciprocity to Redistribution in Ancient Southeast Asia." In J. A. Sabloff and C. C. Lamberg-Karlovsky, eds., *Early Civilization and Trade,* pp. 227–265. Albuquerque: University of New Mexico Press.

WHEATON, T. R. 1990. *James City North Carolina: Archaeological and Historical Study of an African-American Urban Village.* Stone Mountain, GA: New South Associates, Technical Report No. 6.

WHEELER, A., and A. K. G. JONES. 1989. *Fishes.* Cambridge: Cambridge University Press.

WHEELER, R. E. M. 1943. *Maiden Castle.* London: Society of Antiquaries.

————. 1954. *Archaeology from the Earth.* Oxford: Clarendon Press.

WHITE, J. P., and J. O'CONNELL. 1982. *A Prehistory of Australia, New Guinea, and Sahul.* Orlando, FL: Academic Press.

WHITE, L. 1949. *The Evolution of Culture.* New York: McGraw-Hill.

WHITE, R. 1986. *Dark Caves, Bright Images.* New York: American Museum of Natural History.

WHITE, T. D. 1999. *Human Osteology.* New York: Academic Press.

WHITLEY, D. S., ed. 1998a. *Reader in Archaeological Theory: Post-Processual and Cognitive Approaches.* New York: Routledge.

WHITLEY, D. S. 1998b. *Following the Shaman's Path: Walking Guide to the Little Petroglyph Canyon, Coso Range, California.* Ridgecrest, CA: Maturango Museum Publication 13.

WHITTLE, A. 1993. "The Neolithic of the Avebury Area: Sequence, Environment, Settlement, and Monuments." *Oxford Journal of Archaeology* 12(1): 29–53.

WHITTLE, A., and others. 1993. "A Neolithic Downland Monument in Its Environment: Excavations at the Easton Down Long Barrow, Bishops Canning, North Wiltshire." *Proceedings of the Prehistoric Society* 59: 197–239.

WHITTLESEY, S. M. 1998. "Archaeological Landscapes: A Methodological and Theoretical Discussion." In S. M. Whittlesey and others, eds., *Vanishing River: Landscapes and Lives of the Lower Verde Valley,* pp. 17–28. Tucson, AZ: SRI Press.

WHITTLESEY, S. M., and others, eds. 1998. *Vanishing River: Landscapes and Lives of the Lower Verde Valley.* Tucson, AZ: SRI Press.

WILK, R. R. 1991. *Household Ecology: Economic Change and Domestic Life among the Kekchi Maya in Belize.* Tucson: University of Arizona Press.

WILLCOX, ALEX L. 1956. *Rock Paintings of the Drakensberg.* London: Max Parrish.

WILLEY, G. R. 1953. *Prehistoric Settlement Patterns in the Virú Valley, Peru.* Washington, DC: Smithsonian Institution, Bureau of American Ethnology.

———. 1966. *An Introduction to American Archaeology.* Vol. 1, *North America.* Englewood Cliffs, NJ: Prentice Hall.

———. 1971. *An Introduction to American Archaeology.* Vol. 2, *Middle and South America.* Englewood Cliffs, NJ: Prentice Hall.

WILLEY, G. R., and P. PHILLIPS. 1958. *Method and Theory in American Archaeology.* Chicago: University of Chicago Press.

WILLEY, G. R., and J. A. SABLOFF. 1993. *A History of American Archaeology.* 3d ed. New York: W. H. Freeman.

WINLOCK, H. E. 1942. *Excavations at Deir el Bahri, 1911–1931.* New York: Metropolitan Museum of Art.

WINTER, M. C. 1976. "The Archaeological Household Cluster in the Valley of Oaxaca." In K. V. Flannery, ed., *The Early Mesoamerican Village,* pp. 25–30. Orlando, FL: Academic Press.

WINTLE, A. G. 1996. "Archaeologically-Relevant Dating Techniques for the Next Century." *Journal of Archaeological Science* 23: 123–138.

WOLF, E. 1984. *Europe and the People without History.* Berkeley: University of California Press.

WOLFMAN, D. 1984. "Geomagnetic Dating Methods in Archaeology." *Advances in Archaeological Method and Theory* 7: 363–458.

WOOD, W. R., and D. L. JOHNSON. 1978. "A Survey of the Disturbance Processes in Archaeological Site Formation." *Advances in Archaeological Method and Theory* 1: 112–146.

WOOLLEY, C. L. 1929. *Ur of the Chaldees.* London: Ernest Benn.

———. 1943. *Ur Excavations.* Vol. 2, *The Royal Cemetery.* Philadelphia: University of Pennsylvania Museum.

———. 1954. *Excavations at Ur.* New York: Barnes and Noble.

WORSAAE, J. J. A. 1843. *Danmarks Oldtid.* Copenhagen.

WRIGHT, T. 1852. "Wanderings of an Antiquary: Part VII." *Gentleman's Magazine* (October): 569.

WURST, L., D. V. ARMSTRONG, and E. KELLAR. 2000. "Between Fact and Fantasy: Assessing Our Knowledge of Domestic Sites." In J. P. Hart and C. L. Fisher, eds., *Nineteenth- and Early Twentieth-Century Domestic Site Archaeology in New York State,* pp. 17–27. Albany: New York State Museum Bulletin 495.

WYLIE, A. 1985. "The Reaction against Analogy." *Advances in Archaeological Method and Theory* 8: 63–111.

———. 1988. *The New Archaeology: Tensions in Theory and Practice.* Orlando, FL: Academic Press.

YELLEN, J. E. 1977. *Archaeological Approaches to the Present: Models for Predicting the Past.* Orlando, FL: Academic Press.

YENTSCH, A. 1994. *A Chesapeake Family and Their Slaves.* Cambridge: Cambridge University Press.

YOFFEE, N. 1993. "Too Many Chiefs? (or, Safe Texts for the '90s)." In N. Yoffee and A. Sherratt, eds., *Archaeological Theory: Who Sets the Agenda?,* pp. 60–78. Cambridge: Cambridge University Press.

YOFFEE, N., and A. SHERRATT, eds. 1993. *Archaeological Theory: Who Sets the Agenda?* Cambridge: Cambridge University Press.

ZEDEÑO, M. N. 1994. *Sourcing Prehistoric Ceramics at Chodistaas Pueblo, Arizona.* Tucson: University of Arizona Press.

ZEDEÑO, M. N., and others. 1997. *Landmark and Landscape: A Contextual Approach to the Management of American Indian Resources.* Tucson: Bureau of Applied Research in Anthropology, University of Arizona.

ZEDER, M. A. 1997. *The American Archaeologist: A Profile.* Walnut Creek, CA: AltaMira Press.

ZEDER, M., and B. HESSE. 2000. "The Initial Domestication of Goats (*Capra hircus*) in the Zagros Mountains 10,000 Years Ago." *Science* 287: 2254–2257.

———, et al., eds. 2002. *Documenting Domestication: New Genetic and Archaeological Paradigms.* Washington, DC: Smithsonian Institution Press.

ZEILIK, M. 1985. "The Ethnoastronomy of the Historic Pueblos, I: Calendrical Sun Watching." *Astroarchaeology* 8: 1–24.

ZEITLIN, M. 1997. *The American Archaeologist: A Profile.* Walnut Creek, CA: AltaMira Press.

ZUBROW, E. 1976. *Demographic Anthropology: Quantitative Approaches.* Albuquerque: University of New Mexico Press.

Neg./Transparency no. 4936(7). Photo by D. Finnin/C. Chesek. Courtesy Dept. of Library Services, American Museum of Natural History: frontispiece; Yannis Behrakis/Reuters/Corbis/Bettmann: iii; Brian M. Fagan: xxxiii (top); Steve Sartori/Syracuse University/Christopher R. DeCorse: xxxiii (bottom).

Chapter 1. Corbis/Bettmann: 4; Victoria & Albert Museum, Seright Collection. Photograph: Photographic Survey, Courtauld Institute of Art: 6; Susan Einstein/UCLA Fowler Museum of Cultural History: 7; The Ancient Art & Architecture Collection Ltd.: 9; Florida Museum of Natural History, University of Florida: 10; Photo by Kenny Barkely, courtesy of David Pollack, The Kentucky Heritage Council, Cheryl Munson, Indiana University and Kentucky Archaeological Survey: 15; Hester A. Davis, "Is There a Future for the Past?" *Archaeology* 24:4. Copyright © 1971 Archaeological Institute of America: 16 (top); Plenge/Robert Harding World Imagery: 16 (bottom); Yannis Behrakis/Reuters/Corbis/Bettmann: 22; Colonial Williamsburg Foundation: 23; Courtesy of the Institute of Nautical Archaeology, Texas A&M University/Photo by Don A. Frey: 24.

Chapter 2. Louis Delaporte "Voyage Au Cambodge" 1880: 32; Copyright Werner Forman/Art Resource, NY: 34; Adam Woolfitt/Robert Harding World Imagery: 35 (top); Courtesy of the Library of Congress: 35 (bottom); Courtesy of the Royal Anthropological Institute. Redrawn from "The Swanscombe Skull: A Survey of Research on Pleistocene Site" (*Journal of the Royal Anthropological Institute,* 20, fig. 23.6): 36; Corbis/Bettmann: 38; J. Oster/Musee de l'Homme, Phototheque: 43.

Chapter 3. John Reader/Science Photo Library/Photo Researchers, Inc.: 55; The Ohio Historical Society: 60; Marija Gimbutas, "The Civilization of the Goddess" (San Francisco: Harper, 1991); from *Catal Huyuk: A Neolithic Town in Anatolia* by James Mellaart (Thames and Hudson, 1967): 73.

Chapter 4. Sheridan/The Ancient Art & Architecture Collection Ltd.: 77; University of Pennsylvania Museum, Philadelphia (Neg. #S8-139326): 85; Professor John Coles: 87; © Silkeborg Museum, Denmark: 88; Ruth Kirk with Richard D. Daugherty, *Hunters of the Whale,* 1974, New York: William Morrow & Company/HarperCollins Publishers, Inc.: 89; Utah Museum of Natural History, University of Utah: 90; Wieslav Smetek/Stern/Black Star: 92; Stephen Alvarez/NGS Image Collection: 93; From Payson D. Sheets, "The Ceren Site," Harcourt Brace Jovanovich: 95.

Chapter 5. George Holton/Photo Researchers, Inc.: 98.

Chapter 6. Corbis/Bettmann: 112; Biblioteca Nazionale Centrale Firenze B.R.232. c.70r: 116; Richard Lee/Anthro-Photo File: 119; © Society of Antiquaries of London: 124.

Chapter 7. C. Bowman/Robert Harding World Imagery: 133; Gordon Gahan/NGS Image Collection: 150 (top); Georg Gerster/Photo Researchers, Inc.: 153.

Chapter 8. Museum of Fine Art, Boston. Francis Bartlett donation © 1985: 167; Robert Harding World Imagery: 169; AP/Wide World Photos: 171; Gavin Heller/Robert Harding World Imagery: 172; Robert Harding World Imagery: 173; Joe Ben Wheat/University of Colorado Museum–Boulder: 174; Carnegie Institution of Washington: 178; Dr. Vincent Gaffney, University of Birmingham, England: 179; Copyright reserved Cambridge University Collection of Air Photographs: 183; Jet Propulsion Laboratory/NASA Headquarters: 185; Fondazione Lerici Prospezione Archeologiche–Rome: 197 (left and right); Professor Payson Sheets, Department of Anthropology, University of Colorado, Boulder: 198.

Chapter 9. Historic Royal Palaces Enterprises Ltd: 201; The Danebury Trust: 207; Photo by Del Baston and courtesy of the Center for American Archeology: 208; © The Society of Antiquaries of London: 211 (top); Courtesy Quirigua Project, University of Pennsylvania Museum: 211 (bottom); Courtesy William D. Finlayson, This Land Archaeology, Inc.: 212; Historic St. Augustine Preservation Board: 213; Illinois Transportation Archaeological Research Program (ITARP) and Illinois Department of Transportation (IDOT), University of Illinois: 215; Professor Norman Hammond: 218; Hillel Burger/Peabody Museum, Harvard University: 225; Hilary John Deacon: 227; A. L. Smith/Peabody Museum, Harvard University: 229; © The Society of Antiquaries of London: 231 (top); Copyright © H. T. Bunn, University of Wisconsin: 231 (bottom); Mr. Francis Wilfred Shawcross: 231; Harappa.com: 233 (bottom).

Chapter 10. Embassy of Pakistan: 237; Courtesy of the Phoebe Hearst Museum of Anthropology and the Regents of the University of California: 242; From *Invitation to Archaeology* by James Deetz. Illustrated by Eric Engstrom. © 1967 by James Deetz. Used by permission of Doubleday, a division of Random

House, Inc.: 243; Institute of Human Origins, Arizona State University, Tempe, Arizona: 251.

Chapter 11. Photo by Tyler Dingee. Courtesy of the Museum of New Mexico, Neg. No. 44191: 271; Michael S. Bisson: 281; Chang, K.C. *The Archaeology of Ancient China,* 3rd Edition (1977), page 277. Yale University Press. From Shih Chang-ju, Bulletin of the Institute of History and Philology, Academia Sinjca, Nanking, Lichuang, and Taiei, 26, 1955, pp. 113, 117: 282 (right); Courtesy of the University of Alaska Museum, Archaeology Department. Used with permission: 284; Courtesy of the Library of Congress: 285.

Chapter 12. San Heritage Centre/Rock Art Research Centre/ University of the Witwatersrand, Johannesburg: 290; Tortoll/ The Ancient Art & Architecture Collection Ltd.: 292; Marilyn Bridges/Corbis/Bettmann: 317.

Chapter 13. Robert Frerck/Odyssey Productions, Inc.: 319; Eugene Gordon: 321; Andrew Moore/RIT. © Abu Hureyra Excavation: 347; Photograph by Fred Stimson. "Private Collection": 351 (bottom); Vaughn M. Bryant: 355.

Chapter 14. National Museum of Anthropology, Mexico City/Werner Forman Archive/Art Resource, NY: 357; David L. Brill/Brill Atlanta: 359; Smithsonian Institution, National Anthropological Archives, photo T-13,301: 361; James F. O'Connell, University of Utah: 367; Bryan Hayden, Department of Archaeology, Simon Fraser University: 369; Photograph by Lewis R. Binford. From: *A History of American Archaeology* by Willey and Sabloff. Copyright © 1988 by W. H. Freeman and Company. Used with permission: 372 (top and bottom); "Ishi hunting with a bow." Courtesy of Phoebe Apperson Hearst Museum of Anthropology and the Regents of the University of California: 375; Butzer Ancient Farm: 377.

Chapter 15. Amanda Clarke: 380; Consulate General of Ireland: 382; The Ancient Art & Architecture Collection Ltd.: 384; Neg./Transparency no. 326597. Courtesy Dept. of Library Services, American Museum of Natural History: 385; Martha Cooper/NGS Image Collection: 387; Boltin Picture Library: 400; Leslie Newhart: 401; Brian M. Fagan: 411.

Chapter 16. R. Sheridan/The Ancient Art & Architecture Collection Ltd.: 414; O. Louis Mazzatenta/NGS Image Collection: 416; Corbis Sygma: 417; Ewing Galloway, Inc.: 421; Embassy of Pakistan: 422; Robert Frerck/Odyssey Productions, Inc.: 423; Gordan Gahan/National Geographic Image Collection: 427 (top); Theya Molleson, Natural History Museum of London: 428; Brian M. Fagan: 431; South Carolina Institute of Archaeology and Anthropology, University of South Carolina, Columbia: 438; Courtesy of the Institute of Nautical Archaeology, Texas A&M University/Photo by Don A. Frey: 446.

Chapter 17. Rollout photograph © Justin Kerr 1980: 449; Drawing by Linda Schele. Thames and Hudson, London: 453; David Lewis-Williams, Rock Art Research Institute: 457; Archaeological Museum: 460; Figure from "Contextual Analysis of Ritual Paraphernalia from Formative Oaxaca" [excavator J. W. Rick] by Kent Flannery in *The Early Mesoamerican Village,* copyright © 1976, Academic Press. Reproduced by permission of publisher: 461; Reproduced with permission of the British School at Athens: 462; Reproduced with permission of the British School at Athens: 463; Andrew Ward/Life File/Getty Images, Inc.–Photodisc: 468; Cahokia Mounds State Historic Site, painting by Lloyd K. Townsend: 470; Muench Photography, Inc.: 474; Photograph from The Arthur Sackler Gallery, Washington, D.C. and reproduced with the permission of the Jordan Department of Antiquities: 476.

Chapter 18. © Copyright: all rights reserved. Adriel Heisey Photography: 480; © Joe Oliver/Odyssey/Chicago: 485; Dr. J. M. Adovasio/Mercyhurst Archaeological Institute: 491; Dr. Laurie Rush/Fort Drum Archaeology, Courtesy U.S. Army: 495; James A. Tuck: 498; Doug Armstrong/Christopher R. DeCorse: 499 (top left and bottom left); Christopher R. DeCorse: 499 (top right).

Chapter 19. British Tourist Authority: 510.

Note: Page numbers for figures are followed by *f.*

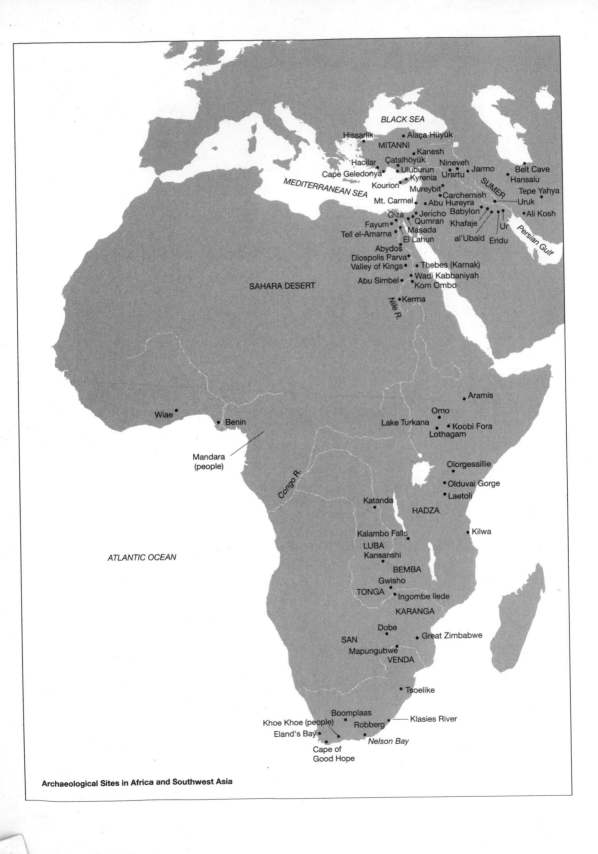

Archaeological Sites in Africa and Southwest Asia